Steps to Writing an Argument

The cover of this book makes a visual argument about genetically modified food. Use these steps to develop your own arguments about food or other topics in the book.

Step 1 Find a Topic

Read your assignment and determine what type of argument is called for (see pages 25–26).

Find a topic that interests you by reading, talking, and exploring (see pages 23–24).

Step 2 Make a Claim and Support It with Good Reasons

Make a claim designed to change readers' views or persuade them to take action.

List your main points and think about the order of those points.

Step 3 Think About What's at Stake

What exactly is the problem or issue, what causes it, and who is most affected?

Has anyone tried to do anything about it? If so, why haven't they succeeded?

Step 4 Analyze Your Potential Readers

Who are your readers?

How familiar will they be with what you are arguing?

Which claims are they most likely to accept and which will they disagree with?

Step 5 Write a Draft

Introduction

Set out the issue or problem, and give some background if necessary.

Argue for the seriousness of the issue or problem.

Give your thesis in one sentence.

Body

Present and interpret your evidence and its significance.

Keep your focus narrow and make your structure clear to your readers.

Take a few minutes to think about other views on your issue or problem.

Conclusion

Leave your readers with something interesting and provocative.

Issue a call to action—if your readers agree with you, they will want to take action.

Step 6 Revise, Edit, Proofread

For detailed instructions, see Chapter 5.

For a checklist to use to evaluate your draft, see pages 61–62.

Good Reasons

with Contemporary Arguments

HIGH SCHOOL EDITION

Lester Faigley

University of Texas at Austin

Jack Selzer

The Pennsylvania State University

Josephine Pirrone

The Pennsylvania State University

PEARSON

Boston   Columbus   Indianapolis   New York   San Francisco   Upper Saddle River
Amsterdam   Cape Town   Dubai   London   Madrid   Milan   Munich   Paris   Montreal   Toronto
Delhi   Mexico City   São Paulo   Sydney   Hong Kong   Seoul   Singapore   Taipei   Tokyo

In memory of our teacher and friend, James L. Kinneavy (1920–1999)

Senior Acquisitions Editor: Brad Potthoff
Director of Development: Mary Ellen Curley
Development Editor: Anne Stameshkin
Senior Marketing Manager: Sandra McGuire
Senior Supplements Editor: Donna Campion
Executive Digital Producer: Stefanie Snajder
Digital Project Manager: Janell Lantana
Digital Editor: Sara Gordus
Production/Project Manager: Eric Jorgensen
Product Manager: Alicia Orlando
Project Coordination, Text Design, and Electronic Page Makeup: PreMediaGlobal
Cover Designer/Design Manager: John Callahan
Cover Art: Kasza/Shutterstock
Senior Manufacturing Buyer: Dennis Para
Printer/Binder: LSC Communications, Inc.
Cover Printer: LSC Communications, Inc.

For permission to use copyrighted material, grateful acknowledgment is made to the copyright holders on pp. 615–616, which are hereby made part of this copyright page.

Library of Congress Cataloging-in-Publication Data

Faigley, Lester, 1947-
  Good reasons with contemporary arguments : high school edition / Lester Faigley,
Jack Selzer, Josephine Pirrone. — [5th ed.]
    p. cm.
  Includes bibliographical references and index.
  ISBN 978-0-13-275111-7
  1. English language—Rhetoric.   2. Persuasion (Rhetoric)   3. Report writing.
I. Selzer, Jack.   II. Pirrone, Josephine.   III. Title.
  PE1431.F35 2012b
  808'.042—dc23

        2012029227

www.PearsonSchool.com/Advanced

ISBN 10: 0-132-75111-9
ISBN 13: 978-0-132-75111-7

7 2019

Detailed Contents

Analyzing Arguments   83

Writing Arguments   125

PART 4 Researching Arguments 239

Contemporary Arguments 307

PART 5

Preface

Nothing students learn in high school or college will prove to be more important to them than the ability to write an effective argument.

Students are aware that life at school and beyond is itself filled with arguments. There are hot-button public issues that engage our communities—standardized testing, for example, or making a school more environmentally sustainable. Meanwhile, in the classroom and in extracurricular programs, you and your academic peers present arguments on current controversies such as climate change and economic policy as well as on scholarly topics such as the workings of evolution, the cultural achievements of ancient Egypt, or the means of determining the material composition of the planet Mercury.

In high school, in college, and beyond, students will particularly need to communicate their ideas and point of view effectively. Their grades and then their livelihood and engagement in the community will depend on it. Sometimes as citizens they will be moved to register views on the local school system or local downtown development; or as members of a neighborhood group or a civic organization, they will be suggesting ways of making a positive difference. And certainly in the workplace they will often be making arguments to propose ideas.

Good Reasons gives students a set of rules of thumb that can be used in the high school classroom, in college, and after in order to mount effective arguments. For a number of years we have studied arguments, taught both high school and college students how to argue, and listened to others talk and write about the art of persuasion. What we have found is that while there is no simple recipe for effective arguments, there are strategies and tactics that writers can rely on in almost any situation to ensure that their ideas are considered seriously.

Key Features

- **Aligned to Common Core State and AP Language & Composition Standards** to support teacher and student success in meeting the cornerstone of the writing objectives, argument.

- **Annotated sample student papers** provide working models students can use to help revise and develop their own work on every type of argument covered in *Good Reasons with Contemporary Arguments*.

- **Professional readings**, in thematically arranged chapters. Annotations or apparatus spark discussion and help students recognize and apply features of effective argument writing in their own papers. **Issue in Focus** sections provide casebooks on more specific issues within larger topics, offering opportunities for practicing synthesis and analyzing and developing arguments in more depth.

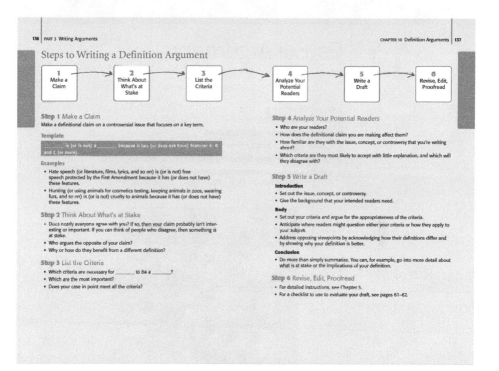

- **"Steps to Writing" guides** provide a concise, visual overview of the process for drafting, developing, and revising each type of argument covered in *Good Reasons,* helping students to review and apply the concepts and strategies presented in each chapter.

- Students will find **learning objectives** in the **Quick Take preview** at the beginning of each chapter, reflecting the content that appears in that chapter. MyWritingLab extends the instruction with additional resources, practice, and assessments aligned to the core content.

- An entire chapter leads students through the process of **synthesizing source materials** into an effective argument.

- **Mini-arguments**, including many visual and multimodal examples, represent every type of argument with an accessible, contemporary example to help students recognize and grasp how different kinds of arguments work today.

11 | Causal Arguments

In this chapter, you will learn that

1. Causal arguments take three basic forms (see page 150)
2. Causes can be identified using four methods (see page 151)
3. Effective causal arguments go beyond the obvious causes to explore complex relationships (see page 153)

Each year, we hear that American students are falling behind their international peers. Different groups argue that the solution lies in investing more in funding for additional teacher training, or smaller classrooms, or more technology in the classroom. Yet America invests billions more in education than some nations whose students surpass American students in achievement rankings. Still others have suggested that America's problem lies in a wide-scale cultural shift that has created an American student who is less motivated than those of the past. How can America's schools become world leaders again?

Resources for Teachers and Students

Teacher's Manual

The **Teacher's Manual** (978-0-13-275130-8) that accompanies this text was written by Josephine Pirrone, a former high school English teacher who is now at The Pennsylvania State University, and is designed to be useful for new and experienced teachers alike. The Teacher's Manual briefly discusses the ins and outs of teaching the material in each chapter. Also provided are in-class exercises, homework assignments, discussion questions for each reading selection, model paper assignments and syllabi, and strategies for integrating the resources in MyWritingLab into your course. Teaching argumentation and composition becomes a process that has genuine—and often surprising—rewards.

Test Bank

The Test Bank is available online only through the **Instructor Resource Center (IRC)**. With over 200 test questions, this resource gives teachers an opportunity to assess student understanding and mastery of the concepts and offers students additional practice with questions they are likely to encounter on an exam.

To obtain Instructor Resource Center access, please go to www.PearsonSchool .com/Access_Request and select Instructor Resource Center. You will be required to complete a brief, one-time registration subject to verification of educator status. Upon verification, access information and instructions will be sent to you via email. Once logged into the IRC, enter your textbook ISBN (9780132751117) in the **Search our Catalog** box to locate your resources.

An Interactive Pearson eText in MyWritingLab

An e-book version of *Good Reasons with Contemporary Arguments* is available in MyWritingLab. This dynamic, online version of the text is integrated throughout MyWritingLab to create an enriched, interactive learning experience for students.

MyWritingLab is a personalized learning environment that helps students to master the core writing skills they need for course success. This eminently flexible program empowers student writers and teachers by integrating a composing space and assessment tools with multimedia tutorials, services (such as online tutoring) and exercises for writing, grammar, and research. Students can use MyWritingLab on their own, benefiting from self-paced diagnostics and a personal study plan that recommends the instruction and practice each student needs to improve his or her writing skills. Teachers can recommend it to students for self-study, set up courses to track student progress, or leverage the power of administrative features to be more effective and save time. The assignment builder and commenting tools, developed specifically for use in writing courses, bring teachers closer to their student writers, make managing assignments and evaluating papers more efficient, and put powerful assessment within reach. Students receive feedback within the context of their own writing, which encourages critical thinking and revision and helps them to develop skills based on their individual needs.

Teacher and student access to MyWritingLab with eText is provided upon textbook adoption.

For FREE Teacher Preview Access: Register at www.PearsonSchool.com/ Access_Request. Using Option #2, Teacher Preview Access, select Language Arts, select Faigley, Good Reasons, MyWritingLab with eText. After following the registration prompts you will receive a confirmation email with login and access information.

For Adoption Access

Register at www.PearsonSchool.com/Access_Request. Using Option #3, Access for Textbook Adopters, select Language Arts, select Faigley, Good Reasons, MyWritingLab with eText. After following registration prompts you will receive a confirmation eMail with login and access information for teacher and students within 48 hours. Accounts are good for one year from date of activation. Each year thereafter (in or around May), for the life of the adoption, the registered teacher will receive a new set of teacher and student access codes via email for the following school year. Teachers are responsible for distributing access codes to their students each year. Teachers may chose to "copy" their course from year to year or to create a new course each year. In the event of a personnel change in the school, the new teacher responsible for this course and textbook can follow the above instructions to receive their own access and register their email to receive the annual renewal registration for the balance of the adoption cycle. For more information about MyWritingLab visit: www.PearsonSchool.com/MyEnglishLabs

100% Digital Solutions

Good Reasons with Contemporary Arguments is also available as a stand-alone eText within MyWritingLab (9780133125061). If you are interested in 100% digital delivery of this program, please contact your Account Executive for more information or to place an order.

Acknowledgments

We are much indebted to the work of many outstanding scholars of argument and to our colleagues who teach argument at Texas and at Penn State and in high schools. We are also grateful to the many students we've taught in our own classes, who have given us opportunities to test these materials in class and who have taught us a great deal about the nature of argument. Special thanks go the students whose work is included in this edition.

We have greatly benefited from working with Brad Potthoff, senior editor, and Anne Stameshkin, development editor, who contributed so much to both the vision and the details of this High School edition of *Good Reasons*. Special thanks go to our co-author Josephine Pirrone for an outstanding revision of the Instructor's Manual, and to Laura Newcomer for her fine assistance in locating selections for readings. Lindsay Bethoney at PreMediaGlobal and Jacqueline Martin and Eric Jorgensen at Pearson did splendid work in preparing our book for publication. We were quite fortunate to have Elsa van Bergen as our copyeditor, who has no peer in our experience. Finally, we thank our families, who make it all possible.

Lester Faigley
Jack Selzer
Josephine Pirrone

Reading and Discovering Arguments

1

1 | Making an Effective Argument

QUICK TAKE

In this chapter, you will learn that

1. Arguments in academic writing are different from arguments in casual conversation (see below)
2. People who argue responsibly give evidence for their claims and cite their sources (see page 6)
3. Written arguments are like turns in an ongoing conversation (see page 7)
4. Your readers will take you seriously if you convince them that you are concerned, well informed, fair, and ethical (see page 10)

MadV's *The Message* consists of a series of extremely short videos from YouTube members of words written on hands like this one.

What Exactly Is an Argument?

One of the best-known celebrities on YouTube is an anonymous video director who wears a Guy Fawkes mask and uses the name MadV. In November 2006 he posted a short video in which he held up his hand with the words "One World" written on his palm and invited viewers to take a stand by uploading a video to YouTube. They responded by the thousands, writing short messages written on their palms. MadV then compiled many of the responses in a 4-minute video titled *The Message* and posted it on YouTube.

MadV's project has been praised as a celebration of the values of the YouTube community. The common theme that we all should try to love and better understand other people is one that few oppose. Yet the video also raises the question of how any of the goals might be achieved. One hand reads "Stop Bigotry." We see a great deal of hatred in written responses to many YouTube videos. Slogans like "Open Mind," "Be Colorblind," "Love Is Stronger," "No more racism," and "Yup One World" seem inadequate for the scope of the problem.

Like the ink-on-hand messages, bumper stickers usually consist of unilateral statements ("Be Green," "Save the Whales," or "Share the Road") but provide no supporting evidence or reasons for why anyone should do what they say. People committed to a particular cause or belief often assume that their reasons are self-evident, and that everyone thinks the same way. These writers know they can count on certain words and phrases to produce predictable responses.

In education, in public life, and in professional careers, however, written arguments cannot be reduced to signs or slogans. Writers of effective arguments do not assume that everyone thinks the same way or holds the same beliefs. They attempt to change people's minds by convincing them of the validity of new ideas or the superiority of a particular course of action. Writers of such arguments not only offer evidence and reasons to support their position but also examine the assumptions on which an argument is based, address opposing arguments, and anticipate their readers' objections.

Extended written arguments make more demands on their readers than most other kinds of writing. Like bumper stickers, these arguments often appeal to our emotions. But they typically do much more.

- They expand our knowledge with the depth of their analysis.
- They lead us through a complex set of claims by providing networks of logical relationships and appropriate evidence.
- They build on what has been written previously by providing trails of sources.

Finally, they cause us to reflect on what we read, in a process that we will shortly describe as critical reading.

Finding | Good Reasons

Who's Using Up Earth's Resources?

ECOLOGICAL DEBTOR AND CREDITOR COUNTRIES, 1961 and 2005

Eco-debt: Footprint relative to biocapacity ■ more than 150% greater ■ 100-150% greater ■ 50-100% greater ▒ 0-50%greater
Eco-credit: Biocapacity relative to footprint ▒ 0-50%greater ■ 50-100% greater ■ 100-150% greater ■ more than 150% greater   ▒ Insufficient data

1961
(2005 country
boundaries)

2005

In the *Living Planet Report* for 2008, the World Wildlife Fund compared the ecological footprints from 1961 and 2005 for each country on Earth. The ecological footprint of a country is determined by its population, the amount of food, timber, and other resources consumed by its average citizen, the area required to produce food, fishing grounds, and the area required to absorb CO_2 emissions minus the amount absorbed by oceans.

Countries fall into four categories: ecological debtor nations (which consume more resources than they can produce), ecological creditor nations (which produce more than they consume), and two categories of ecologically balanced nations, where production and consumption are relatively balanced. In this map you can see that the United States, Mexico, Western Europe, China, India, Pakistan, Japan, and the nations of the Middle East have become ecological debtors with footprints more than 50 percent of their biocapacity—what they are able to produce. Nations such as Canada, Russia, Australia, New Zealand, and most nations in South America are ecological creditors, with footprints less than 50 percent of their biocapacity. In its entirety, the *Living Planet Report* makes the argument that nations should live in balance with what their land, rivers, lakes, and seas can support.

Write about it

1. What might be some of the causes of the differences among the ecological footprints of nations?

2. What is likely to happen in the future when some nations have enough resources (such as clean water and food) and others lack them?

3. Does the map succeed as an argument on its own? Does it contain any of the features of written arguments listed on pages 5–6?

4. The information presented in the *Living Planet Report* implies that citizens of ecological debtor nations need to dramatically reduce consumption of goods and services. What additional information would you need in order to support or refute this proposition?

Writing Academic Arguments

The requirements of effective writing vary considerably from course to course. A lab report for a biology course looks quite different from a paper in your English class, just as a classroom observation in a sociology course differs from a case study report in an accounting class.

Nevertheless, much of the writing you will do in school consists of making successful arguments. Some common expectations about effective arguments extend across disciplines. For example, you could be assigned to write a proposal for a downtown light-rail system in a number of different classes—economics, government, or business. The emphasis of such a proposal would change depending on the course. In all cases, however, the proposal would require a complex argument in which you describe the problem that the light-rail system would improve, make a specific proposal that addresses the problem, explain the benefits of the system, estimate the cost, identify funding sources, assess alternatives to your plan, and anticipate possible opposition. It's a lot to think about.

Setting out a specific proposal or claim supported by reasons and evidence is at the heart of most academic writing, no matter what the course. Some expectations of arguments (such as including a thesis statement) may be familiar to you, but others (such as the emphasis on finding alternative ways of thinking about a subject and finding facts that might run counter to your conclusions) may be unfamiliar.

WRITTEN ARGUMENTS . . .	WRITERS ARE EXPECTED TO . . .
State explicit claims	Make a claim that isn't obvious. The main claim is often called a **thesis.** (see pages 53–54)
Support claims with reasons	Express reasons in a **because clause** after the claim (We should do something *because* _____). (see pages 25–26)
Base reasons on evidence	Provide evidence for reasons in the form of facts, statistics, testimony from reliable sources, and direct observations. (see pages 37–38)
Consider opposing positions	Help readers understand why there are disagreements about issues by accurately representing differing views. (see pages 29–31)
Analyze with insight	Provide in-depth analysis of what they read and view. (see Chapters 7 and 8)

(*continued*)

WRITTEN ARGUMENTS...	WRITERS ARE EXPECTED TO...
Investigate complexity	Explore the complexity of a subject by asking "Have you thought about this?" or "What if you discard the usual way of thinking about a subject and take the opposite point of view?" (see pages 34–36)
Organize information clearly	Make the main ideas evident to readers and to indicate which parts are subordinate to others. (see pages 57–58)
Signal relationships of parts	Indicate logical relationships clearly so that readers can follow an argument without getting lost. (see page 64)
Document sources carefully	Provide the sources of information so that readers can consult the same sources the writer used. (see Chapter 20)

How can you argue responsibly?

In Washington, D.C., cars with diplomatic license plates are often parked illegally. Their drivers know they will not be towed or ticketed. People who abuse the diplomatic privilege are announcing, "I'm not playing by the rules."

When you begin an argument by saying "in my opinion," you are making a similar announcement. First, the phrase is redundant. A reader assumes that if you make a claim in writing, you believe that claim. More important, a claim is rarely *only* your opinion. Most beliefs and assumptions are shared by many people. If a claim truly is only your opinion, it can be easily dismissed. If your position is likely to be held by at least a few other people, however, then a responsible reader must consider your position seriously. You argue responsibly when you set out the reasons for making a claim and offer facts to support those reasons. You argue responsibly when you allow readers to examine your evidence by documenting the sources you have consulted. Finally, you argue responsibly when you acknowledge that other people may have positions different from yours.

How can you argue respectfully?

Our culture is competitive, and our goal often is to win. Professional athletes, top trial lawyers, or candidates for president of the United States either win big or lose. But most of us live in a world in which our opponents don't go away when the game is over.

Most of us have to deal with people who disagree with us at times but continue to work and live in our communities. The idea of winning in such situations can only be temporary. Soon enough, we will need the support of those who were on the other side of the most recent issue. You can probably think of times when a friendly argument resulted in a better understanding of all peoples' views. And probably you can think of a time when an argument created hard feelings that lasted for years.

Usually, listeners and readers are more willing to consider your argument seriously if you cast yourself as a respectful partner rather than as a competitor. Put forth your arguments in the spirit of mutual support and negotiation—in the interest of finding the *best* way, not "my way." How can you be the person that your reader will want to join rather than resist? Here are a few suggestions for both your written arguments and for discussing controversial issues.

- **Try to think of yourself as engaged not so much in winning over your audience as in courting your audience's cooperation.** Argue vigorously, but not so vigorously that opposing views are vanquished or silenced. Remember that your goal is to invite a response that creates a dialogue and continuing partnership.

- **Show that you understand and genuinely respect your listener's or reader's position even if you think the position is ultimately wrong.** Remember to argue against opponents' positions, not against the opponents themselves. Arguing respectfully often means representing an opponent's position in terms that he or she would accept. Look for ground that you already share with your opponent, and search for even more. See yourself as a mediator. Consider that neither you nor the other person has arrived at a best solution. Then carry on in the hope that dialogue will lead to an even better course of action than the one you now recommend. Expect and assume the best of your listener or reader, and deliver your best.

- **Cultivate a sense of humor and a distinctive voice.** Many textbooks about argument emphasize using a reasonable voice. But a reasonable voice doesn't have to be a dull one. Humor is a legitimate tool of argument. Although playing an issue strictly for laughs risks not being taken seriously, nothing creates a sense of goodwill quite as much as tasteful humor. A sense of humor can be especially welcome when the stakes are high, sides have been chosen, and tempers are flaring.

Arguments as Turns in a Conversation

Consider your argument as just one move in a larger process that might end up helping you. Most times, we argue because we think we have something to offer. In the process of researching what has been said and written on a particular issue, however, often your own view is expanded and you find an opportunity to add your voice to the ongoing conversation.

A Case Study: The Microcredit Debate

Two women financed by microcredit sell scarves in Quito, Ecuador.

World Bank researchers reported in 2009 that 1.4 billion people—over 20 percent of the 6.7 billion people on earth—live below the extreme poverty line of $1.25 a day, with 6 million children starving to death every year. One cause of continuing extreme poverty is the inability of poor people to borrow money because they have no cash income or assets. Banks have seldom made loans to very poor people, who have had to turn to moneylenders that charge high interest rates sometimes exceeding 100 percent a month.

In 1976, Muhammad Yunus observed that poor women in Bangladesh who made bamboo furniture could not profit from their labor because they had to borrow money at high interest rates to buy bamboo. Yunus loaned $27 to forty-two women out of his pocket. They repaid him at an interest rate of two cents per loan. The success of the experiment eventually led to Yunus securing a loan from the government to create a bank to make loans to poor people. The Grameen Bank (Village Bank) became a model for other microfinancing projects in Bangladesh, serving 7 million people, 94 percent of whom are women. For his work with the Grameen initiative, Yunus received the Nobel Peace Prize in 2006.

Microcredit now has many supporters, including Hollywood stars like Natalie Portman and Michael Douglas, companies like Benetton and Sam's Club, and former

President Bill Clinton. But the success in Bangladesh has not been replicated in many other poor countries. Many critics point to the shortcomings of microcredit. This debate can be better understood if you consider the different points of view on microcredit to be different voices in a conversation.

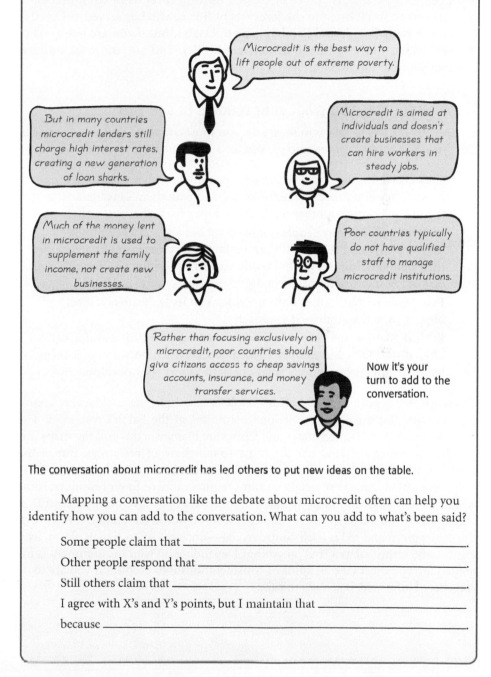

Microcredit is the best way to lift people out of extreme poverty.

But in many countries microcredit lenders still charge high interest rates, creating a new generation of loan sharks.

Microcredit is aimed at individuals and doesn't create businesses that can hire workers in steady jobs.

Much of the money lent in microcredit is used to supplement the family income, not create new businesses.

Poor countries typically do not have qualified staff to manage microcredit institutions.

Rather than focusing exclusively on microcredit, poor countries should give citizens access to cheap savings accounts, insurance, and money transfer services.

Now it's your turn to add to the conversation.

The conversation about microcredit has led others to put new ideas on the table.

Mapping a conversation like the debate about microcredit often can help you identify how you can add to the conversation. What can you add to what's been said?

Some people claim that _____.

Other people respond that _____.

Still others claim that _____.

I agree with X's and Y's points, but I maintain that _____

because _____.

Think About Your Credibility

A few writers begin with instant credibility because of what they have accomplished. If you're a tennis player, likely you will pay attention to advice from Serena Williams. If you're interested in future trends in computers and entertainment, you'll listen to the forecasts of Ji Lee, who has served as Creative Director at both Google and Facebook, or Bill Gates. But if you are like most of the rest of us, you don't have instant credibility, and so you must build it through your communication itself.

Think about how you want your readers to see you

To get your readers to take you seriously, you must convince them that they can trust you. You need to get them to see you as

> **Concerned.** Readers want you to be committed to what you are writing about. They also expect you to be concerned with them as readers. After all, if you don't care about them, why should they read what you write?
>
> **Well informed.** Many people ramble on about any subject without knowing anything about it. If they are family members, you have to suffer their opinions, but it is not enjoyable. Academic writing requires that you do your homework on a subject.
>
> **Fair.** Many writers look at only one side of an issue. Readers respect objectivity and an unbiased approach.
>
> **Ethical.** Many writers use only the facts that support their positions and often distort facts and sources. Critical readers often notice what is being left out. Don't try to conceal what doesn't support your position.

The maps that appear on page 4 of this book, for example, make a visual reference to countries that use a disproportionate amount of the Earth's resources. The maps imply that the United States and China are blameworthy, and the maps imply that all nations should use the same rough share of resources. But in the United States and in many other parts of the world, the issue is highly controversial: some would argue that certain cultures require more or fewer resources; some would contend that the map "penalizes" countries that have been successful in raising living standards for their people; and some would contend that the use of the colors green and red is itself controversial—since red often signals alarm, who wants to be identified as a "red" anything? Depending on who the argument is intended for, you must take all kinds of considerations into account if you are to be considered informed, fair, and ethical.

Build your credibility

Know what's at stake. What you are writing about should matter to your readers. If its importance is not evident, it's your job to explain why your readers should consider it important.

LESS EFFECTIVE:
We should be concerned about two-thirds of Central and South America's 110 brightly colored harlequin frog species becoming extinct in the last twenty years. (*The loss of any species is unfortunate, but the writer gives us no other reason for concern.*)

MORE EFFECTIVE:
The rapid decline of amphibians worldwide due to global warming may be the advance warning of the loss of cold-weather species such as polar bears, penguins, and reindeer.

Have your readers in mind. If you are writing about a specialized subject that your readers don't know much about, take the time to explain key concepts.

LESS EFFECTIVE:
Reduction in the value of a debt security, especially a bond, results from a rise in interest rates. Conversely, a decline in interest rates results in an increase in the value of a debt security, especially bonds. (*The basic idea is here, but it is not expressed clearly, especially if the reader is not familiar with investing.*)

MORE EFFECTIVE:
Bond prices move inversely to interest rates. When interest rates go up, bond prices go down, and when interest rates go down, bond prices go up.

Think about alternative solutions and points of view. Readers appreciate a writer's ability to see a subject from multiple perspectives.

LESS EFFECTIVE:
We will reduce greenhouse gas and global warming only if we greatly increase wind-generated electricity. (*Wind power is an alternative energy source, but it is expensive and many people don't want windmills in scenic areas. The writer also doesn't mention using energy more efficiently.*)

MORE EFFECTIVE:
If the world is serious about limiting carbon emissions to reduce global warming, then along with increasing efficient energy use, all non-carbon-emitting energy sources must be considered, including nuclear power. Nuclear power now produces about 20 percent of U.S. electricity with no emissions—the equivalent of taking 58 million passenger cars off the road.

Be honest. Readers also appreciate writers who admit what they aren't sure about. Leaving readers with unanswered questions can lead them to think further about your subject.

LESS EFFECTIVE:

The decline in violent crime during the 1990s was due to putting more people in jail with longer sentences.

MORE EFFECTIVE:

Exactly what caused the decline in violent crime during the 1990s remains uncertain. Politicians point to longer sentences for criminals, but the decrease in the population most likely to commit crimes—the 16-to-35 age group—may have been a contributing factor.

Write well. Nothing impresses readers more than graceful, fluent writing that is clear, direct, and forceful. Even if readers don't agree with you in the end, they still will appreciate your writing ability.

LESS EFFECTIVE:

Nobody can live today without taking some risks, even very rich people. After all, we don't know what we're breathing in the air. A lot of food has chemicals and hormones in it. There's a big hole in the ozone, so more people will get skin cancer. And people are spending more and more time online.
(The impact of the point is lost with unfocused writing.)

MORE EFFECTIVE:

We live in a world of risks beyond our control to the extent that it difficult to think of anything that is risk free down to the most basic human acts—eating in an era of genetically altered food, walking outside in an ozone-depleted atmosphere, drinking water and breathing air laden with chemicals whose effects we do not understand.

PEARSON
mywritinglab

For additional writing resources that will help you master the objectives of this chapter, go to www.mywritinglab.com.

2 | Reading Arguments

QUICK TAKE

In this chapter, you will learn that

1. Controversies that are represented in the media as having two sides often involve many nuanced positions (see below)
2. Reading an argument critically involves asking questions before you start reading and rereading it several times (see page 14)
3. Mapping an argument is a good way to understand its structure (see page 17)

Explore Controversies

People in general agree on broad goals for their society: clean water, abundant healthy food, efficient transportation, good schools, full employment, affordable health care, safe cities and neighborhoods, and peace with others near and far. People in general, however, often disagree on how to define and achieve these goals. Controversies surround major issues and causes.

Often controversies are portrayed in the media as pro and con or even take on political labels. But if you read and listen carefully to what people have to say about a particular issue, you usually find a range of different positions on the issue, and you often discover nuances and complexities in the reasons people offer for their positions.

Find controversies

Online subject directories can help you identify the differing views on a large, general topic. Try the subject index of your library's online catalog. You'll likely find subtopics listed under large topics. Also, your library's Web site may have a link to the *Opposing Viewpoints* database.

One of the best Web subject directories for finding arguments is Yahoo's *Society and Culture* directory. This directory provides subtopics for major issues and provides links to the Web sites of organizations interested in particular issues.

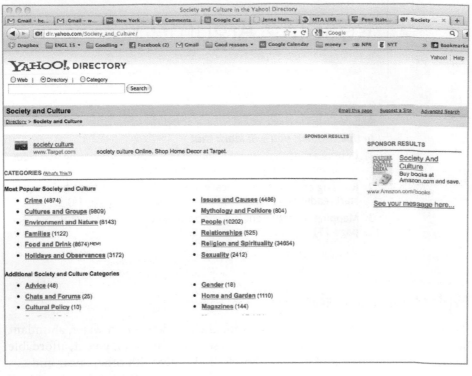

Yahoo! *Society and Culture* directory <dir.yahoo.com/Society_and_Culture/>

Read Critically

After you survey the landscape of a particular issue, turn to careful reading of individual arguments, one at a time.

Before you begin reading, ask these questions

- ■ Where did the argument first appear? Was it published in a book, newspaper, magazine, or electronic source? Many items in library databases and on the Web were published somewhere else first.
- ■ Who wrote this argument? What do you know about the author?
- ■ What does the title suggest that the argument might be about?

Read the argument once without making notes to gain a sense of the content

- ■ When you finish, write one sentence that sums up the argument.

Finding Good Reasons

Has The Internet Made Everyone Writers?

Video blogs, known as vlogs, became a popular genre on YouTube.

Before the Internet was invented, readers had to make some effort to respond to writers by writing to them directly, sending a letter to the editor, or even scribbling or spray-painting a response. The Internet has changed the interaction between writers and readers by allowing readers to respond easily to writers and, in turn, turning readers into writers. Look, for example, at Amazon.com. An incredible amount of writing surrounds any best-selling book—often an author's Web site and blog, newspaper reviews, and over a hundred readers' reviews. Or read a political, sports, culture, fashion, or parenting blog and the comments by readers of those blogs. Think about how the Internet has changed the relationship between readers and writers.

To find a blog that interests you, use a blog search engine such as *Bloglines* (www.bloglines.com), *Google Blog Search* (blogsearch.google.com), *IceRocket* (blogs.icerocket.com), or *Technorati* (www.technorati.com).

Write about it

1. Using a blog search engine or an online newspaper, find a blog by an author, politician, or news columnist. Answer as many of the questions for critical reading on page 16 as you can.
2. Write a summary of the blog entry.
3. What kinds of reasons do blog writers give for their responses to what they read?
4. Write a brief response to the opinion presented in the blog, affirming the writer's opinion or offering a different view on the subject.

Read the argument a second and third time and make notes

- Go back through the text and underline the author's thesis.
- Does your sentence and the author's thesis match? If not, look at the text again and either adjust your sentence or check if you underlined the correct sentence.
- How is the argument organized? How are the major points arranged?
- What reasons or evidence does the writer offer in support of the thesis?
- How does the writer conclude the argument? Does the conclusion follow from the evidence presented?
- Who is the intended audience? What does the writer assume the readers know and believe?
- Do you detect a bias in the writer's position?
- Where do the writer's facts come from? Does the writer give the sources? Are the sources reliable?
- Does the writer acknowledge other views and unfavorable evidence? Does the writer deal fairly with the views of others?
- If there are images or graphics, are they well integrated and clearly labeled?

Annotate what you read

- **Mark major points and key concepts.** Sometimes major points are indicated by headings, but often you will need to locate them.
- **Connect with your experience.** Think about your own experiences and how they match up or don't match up with what you are reading.
- **Connect passages.** Notice how ideas connect to each other. Draw lines and arrows. If an idea connects to something from a few pages earlier, write a note in the margin with the page number.
- **Ask questions.** Note anything that puzzles you, including words you don't know and need to look up.

Map a controversy

Read broadly about an issue and identify three or more sources that offer different points of view on that issue. The sources may approach the issue from different angles or raise different questions instead of simply stating differing positions on the issue. Draw a map that represents the different views. The map on the next page shows some of the different positions on sustainable agriculture.

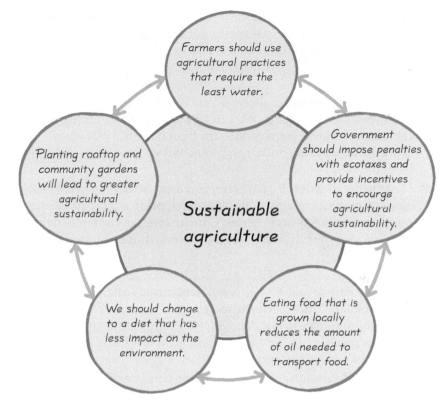

Map of different issues about sustainable agriculture

Recognize Fallacies

Recognizing where good reasons go off track is one of the most important aspects of critical reading. What passes as political discourse is often filled with claims that lack evidence or substitute emotions for evidence. Such faulty reasoning often contains one or more **logical fallacies**. For example, politicians know that the public is outraged when the price of gasoline goes up, and they try to score political points by accusing oil companies of price gouging. It sounds good to angry voters—and it may well be true—but unless the politician defines what *price gouging* means and provides evidence that oil companies are guilty, the argument has no more validity than children calling each other bad names on the playground.

Following are some of the more common fallacies.

Fallacies of logic

- **Begging the question** *Politicians are inherently dishonest because no honest person would run for public office.* The fallacy of begging the question occurs when the claim is restated and passed off as evidence.

■ **Either-or** *Either we eliminate the regulation of businesses or else profits will suffer.* The either-or fallacy suggests that there are only two choices in a complex situation. Rarely, if ever, is this the case.

■ **False analogies** *Japan quit fighting in 1945 when we dropped nuclear bombs on Hiroshima and Nagasaki. We should use nuclear weapons against other countries.* Analogies always depend on the degree of resemblance of one situation to another. In this case, the analogy fails to recognize that circumstances today are very different from those in 1945. Many countries now possess nuclear weapons, and we know their use could harm the entire world.

■ **Hasty generalization** *We have been in a drought for three years; that's a sure sign of climate change.* A hasty generalization is a broad claim made on the basis of a few occurrences. Climate cycles occur regularly over spans of a few years. Climate trends, however, must be observed over centuries.

■ **Non sequitur** *A university that can raise a billion dollars from alumni should not have to raise tuition.* A non sequitur (a Latin term meaning "it does not follow") ties together two unrelated ideas. In this case, the argument fails to recognize that the money for capital campaigns is often donated for special purposes such as buildings and athletic facilities and is not part of a university's general revenue.

■ **Oversimplification** *No one would run stop signs if we had a mandatory death penalty for doing it.* This claim may be true, but the argument would be unacceptable to most citizens. More complex, if less definitive, solutions are called for.

■ *Post hoc* **fallacy** *The stock market goes down when the AFC wins the Super Bowl in even years.* The *post hoc* fallacy (from the Latin *post hoc, ergo propter hoc,* which means "after this, therefore because of this") assumes that events that follow in time have a causal relationship.

■ **Rationalization** *I could have finished my paper on time if my printer had been working.* People frequently come up with excuses and weak explanations for their own and others' behavior. These excuses often avoid actual causes.

■ **Slippery slope** *If we allow offshore drilling for oil, the commercial fishing industry will be completely depleted.* The slippery slope fallacy maintains that one thing inevitably will cause something else to happen.

Fallacies of emotion and language

■ **Bandwagon appeals** *It doesn't matter if I copy a paper off the Web because everyone else does.* This argument suggests that everyone is doing it, so why shouldn't you? But on close examination, it may be that everyone really isn't doing it—and in any case, it may not be the right thing to do.

- **Name-calling** *Every candidate running for office in this election is either a left-wing radical or a right-wing ideologue.* Name-calling is frequent in politics and among competing groups. People level accusations using names such as tax-and-spend liberal, racist, fascist, ultra-conservative extremist. Unless these terms are carefully defined, they are meaningless.
- **Polarization** *Feminists are all man haters.* Like name-calling, polarization exaggerates positions and groups by representing them as extreme and divisive.
- **Straw man** *Environmentalists won't be satisfied until not a single human being is allowed to enter a national park.* A straw man argument is a diversionary tactic that sets up another's position in a way that can be easily rejected. In fact, only a small percentage of environmentalists would make an argument even close to this one.

Note fallacies while you read

Marta Ramos noted a fallacy in James McWilliams's argument against locavorism. You can read her rebuttal argument on pages 216–219.

Consider fruit and vegetable production in New York. The Empire State is naturally equipped to grow a wide variety of fruits, including pears, cherries, strawberries, and some peaches. But none of these compare to its ability to grow apples and grapes, which dominate production (accounting for 94 percent of all fruit grown).

At current levels of fruit production, apples are the only crop that could currently feed New Yorkers at a level that meets the U.S. Recommended Dietary Allowances. Every other fruit that the state produces is not being harvested at a level to provide all New Yorkers with an adequate supply. Other fruits such as bananas and oranges are not produced at all because conditions are unfavorable for growing them.

What does this situation mean in terms of feeding the state with the state's own produce?

In a nutshell, <u>it means citizens would have to give up tropical fruits altogether</u>; rarely indulge in a pear, peach, or basket of strawberries; and gorge on grapes and apples—most of them in processed form (either as juice, in a can, or as concentrate).

McWilliams makes a straw man argument. Locavores prioritize locally produced food but don't argue that it's only what people should eat.

James E. McWilliams. *Just Food: Where Locavores Get It Wrong and How We Can Truly Eat Responsibly.* New York: Little, Brown, 2009.

Map and Summarize Arguments

When you finish annotating a reading, you might want to map it.

Draw a map

Marta Ramos drew a map of James McWilliams's argument.

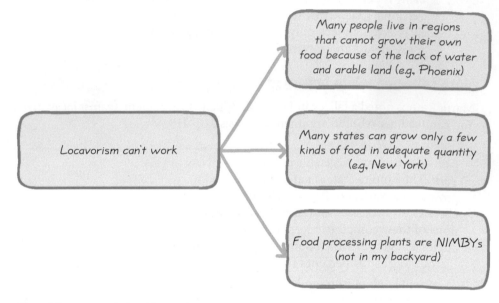

Map of the argument about locavorism.

Write a summary

A summary should be a concise but thorough representation of the source.

- Begin your summary with the writer's name, the title of the argument, and the main point.
- Then report the key ideas. Represent the author's argument in condensed form as accurately as you can, quoting exact words for key points (see pages 277–278 for how to quote and integrate an author's words into your summary).
- Your aim is to give your readers an understanding of what the author is arguing for. Withhold judgment even if you think the author is dead wrong. Do not insert your opinions and comments. Stick to what the author is saying and what position the author is advocating.
- Usually summaries are no longer than 150 words. If your summary is longer than 150 words, delete excess words without eliminating key ideas.

McWilliams, James. *Just Food: Where Locavores Get It Wrong and How We Can Truly Eat Responsibly*. New York: Little, Brown, 2009.

Summary

In his argument about locavorism, James McWilliams argues that locavorism—the development of local food-supply systems—is an impractical goal. He offers three reasons why locavorism is not achievable. First, many people live in regions where they cannot grow their own food because of lack of water and arable land (for example, Phoenix). Second, many states can grow only a few kinds of food in adequate quantity (for example, New York), thus restricting food choices and limiting consumption to processed fruits and vegetables for much of the year. Third, many people will not like food-processing plants near their homes.

PEARSON
mywritinglab

For additional writing resources that will help you master the objectives of this chapter, go to www.mywritinglab.com.

3 | Finding Arguments

QUICK TAKE

In this chapter, you will learn that

1. Everyday conversations with friends can be rich sources of ideas for written arguments (see page 23)
2. Writing assignments often contain key words that you can use to determine the type of argument you need to write (see page 25)
3. Reading widely about a topic will help you become familiar with the points of view already being debated on an issue (see page 31)
4. Reasons need to be supported with convincing evidence (see page 37)

The slogans printed on T-shirts often express the views of the persons who wear them, but the slogans usually cannot be considered arguments because they lack supporting reasons. Nevertheless, you can often supply reasons that are implied by a slogan. Think of reasons supporting the claim that bicycles make a community better.

Find Arguments in Everyday Conversations

Let's look at an example of a conversation. When the pain in his abdomen didn't go away, Jeff knew he had torn something while carrying his friend's heavy speakers up a flight of stairs when they moved into their college dorm room. He went to the student health center and called his friend Maria when he returned home.

JEFF: I have good news and bad news. The pain is a minor hernia that can be repaired with day surgery. The bad news is that the fee we pay for the health center doesn't cover hospital visits. We should have health coverage.

MARIA: Jeff, you didn't buy the extra insurance. Why should you get it for nothing?

JEFF: Because health coverage is a right.

MARIA: No it's not. Everyone doesn't have health insurance.

JEFF: Well, in some other countries like Canada, Germany, and Britain, they do.

MARIA: Yes, and people who live in those countries pay a bundle in taxes for the government-provided insurance.

JEFF: It's not fair in this country because some people have health insurance and others don't.

MARIA: Jeff, face the facts. You could have bought the extra insurance. Instead you chose to buy a new car.

JEFF: It would be better if the university provided health insurance because students could graduate in four years. I'm going to have to get a second job and drop out for a semester to pay for the surgery.

MARIA: Neat idea, but who's going to pay to insure every student?

JEFF: OK, all students should be required to pay for health insurance as part of their general fee. Most students are healthy, and it wouldn't cost that much more.

In this discussion, Jeff starts out by making a **claim** that students should have health coverage. Maria immediately asks him why students should not have to pay for health insurance. She wants a **reason** to accept his claim.

Distinguishing arguments from other kinds of persuasion

Scholars who study argument maintain that an argument must have a claim and one or more reasons to support that claim. Something less might be persuasive, but it isn't an argument.

A bumper sticker that says NO TOLL ROADS is a claim, but it is not an argument because the statement lacks a reason. Many reasons support an argument against building toll roads.

- We don't need new roads but should build light-rail instead.
- We should raise the gas tax to pay for new roads.
- We should use gas tax revenue only for roads rather than using it for other purposes.

When a claim has a reason attached, then it becomes an argument.

The basics of arguments

A reason is typically offered in a **because clause**, a statement that begins with the word *because* and that provides a supporting reason for the claim. Jeff's first attempt is to argue that students should have health insurance *because* health insurance is a right.

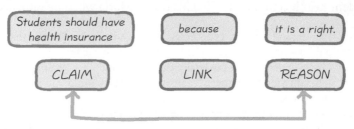

The word *because* signals a link between the reason and the claim. Every argument that is more than a shouting match or a simple assertion has to have one or more reasons. Just having a reason for a claim, however, doesn't mean that the audience will be convinced. When Jeff tells Maria that students have a right to health insurance, Maria replies that students don't have that right. Maria will accept Jeff's claim only if she accepts that his reason supports his claim. Maria challenges Jeff's links and keeps asking "So what?" For her, Jeff's reasons are not good reasons.

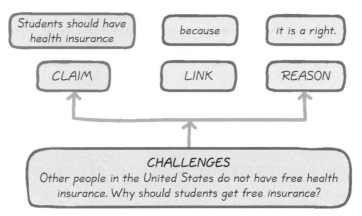

By the end of this short discussion, Jeff has begun to build an argument. He has had to come up with another claim to support his main claim: All students should be required to pay for health insurance as part of their general fee. If he is to convince Maria, he will probably have to provide a series of claims that she will accept as linked to his primary claim. He will also need to find evidence to support these claims.

Benjamin Franklin observed, "So convenient a thing it is to be a rational creature, since it enables us to find or make a reason for every thing one has a mind to do." It is not hard to think of reasons. What *is* difficult is to convince your audience that your reasons are good reasons. In a conversation, you get immediate feedback that tells you whether your listener agrees or disagrees. When you are writing, you usually don't have someone you can question immediately. Consequently, you have to (1) be more specific about what you are claiming, (2) connect with the values you hold in common with your readers, and (3) anticipate what questions and objections your readers might have, if you are going to convince someone who doesn't agree with you or know what you know already.

When you write an argument, imagine a reader like Maria who is going to listen carefully to what you have to say but who is not going to agree with you automatically. Readers like Maria will expect the following.

- A **claim** that is interesting and makes them want to find out more about what you have to say
- At least one **good reason** that makes your claim worth taking seriously
- Some **evidence** that the good reason or reasons are valid
- Some acknowledgment of the **opposing views** and **limitations** of the claim

The remainder of this chapter will guide you through the process of finding a topic, making a claim, finding good reasons and evidence, and anticipating objections to your claim.

Find a Topic

When your instructor gives you a writing assignment, look closely at what you are asked to do. Assignments typically contain a great deal of information, and you have to sort through that information. First, circle all the instructions about the length, the due date, the format, the grading criteria, and anything else about the production and conventions of the assignment. This information is important to you, but it doesn't tell you what the paper is supposed to be about.

Read your assignment carefully

Often your assignment will contain key words such as *analyze, define, evaluate*, or *propose* that will assist you in determining what direction to take. *Analyze* can mean several things. Your instructor might want you to analyze a piece of writing (see Chapter 7), an image (see Chapter 8), or the causes of something (see Chapter 11). *Define* usually means writing a **definition argument**, in which you argue for a definition based on the criteria you set out (see Chapter 10). *Evaluate* indicates an **evaluation argument**, in which you argue that something is good, bad, the best, or the worst in its class according to criteria that you set out (see Chapter 12). An assignment that contains the instructions *Write about an issue using your personal experience* indicates a **narrative argument** (see Chapter 13), while one that says *Take a position in regard to a reading* might lead you to write a **rebuttal argument** (see Chapter 14). *Propose* means that you should identify a particular problem and explain why your solution is the best one in a **proposal argument** (see Chapter 15).

What is not arguable

- **Statements of fact.** Most facts can be verified by doing research. But even simple facts can sometimes be argued. For example, Mount Everest is usually acknowledged to be the highest mountain in the world at 29,028 feet above sea level. But if the total height of a mountain from base to summit is the measure, then the volcano Mauna Loa in Hawaii is the highest mountain in the world. Although the top of Mauna Loa is 13,667 feet above sea level, the summit is 31,784 above the ocean floor. Thus the "fact" that Mount Everest is the highest mountain on the earth depends on a definition of *highest*. You could argue for this definition.

- **Claims of personal taste.** Your favorite food and your favorite color are examples of personal taste. If you hate fresh tomatoes, no one can convince you that you actually like them. But many claims of personal taste turn out to be value judgments using arguable criteria. For example, if you think that *Alien* is the best science-fiction movie ever made, you can argue that claim using evaluative criteria that other people can consider as good reasons (see Chapter 12). Indeed, you might not even like science fiction and still argue that *Alien* is the best science-fiction movie ever.

- **Statements of belief or faith.** If someone accepts a claim as a matter of religious belief, then for that person, the claim is true and cannot be refuted. Of course, people still make arguments about the existence of God and which religion reflects the will of God. Whenever an audience will not consider an idea, it's possible but very difficult to construct an argument. Many people claim to have evidence that UFOs exist, but most people refuse to acknowledge that evidence as even being possibly factual.

If you remain unclear about the purpose of the assignment after reading it carefully, talk with your instructor.

Thinking about what interests you

Your assignment may specify the topic you are to write about. If your assignment gives you a wide range of options and you don't know what to write about, look first at the materials for your course: the readings, your lecture notes, and discussion boards. Think about what subjects came up in class discussion.

If you need to look outside class for a topic, think about what interests you. Subjects we argue about often find us. There are enough of them in daily life. We're late for work or class because the traffic is heavy or the bus doesn't run on time. We can't find a place to park when we get to school or work. We have to negotiate through various bureaucracies for almost anything we do—making an

Finding Good Reasons

Are Traffic Enforcement Cameras Invading Your Privacy?

Cameras that photograph the license plates and drivers of vehicles who run red lights, speed, or ride illegally in high-occupancy-vehicle (HOV) and bus lanes are currently in use in many U.S. cities and states. Cameras aimed at catching speeders, already common in Europe, are beginning to be installed in U.S. cities as well. Traffic cameras have become money machines for some communities, but they also have provoked intense public opposition and even vandalism—people have spray painted and shot cameras in attempts to disable them.

Write about it

1. How do you feel about using cameras to catch red-light runners? Speeders? Illegal drivers in HOV and bus lanes? People who don't pay parking tickets? Make a list of as many possible topics as you can think of about the use of cameras to scan license plates.

2. Select one of the possible topics. Write it at the top of a sheet of paper, and then write nonstop for five minutes. Don't worry about correctness. If you get stuck, write the same sentence again.

3. When you finish, read what you have written and circle key ideas.

4. Put each key idea on a sticky note. If you think of other ideas, write them on separate sticky notes. Then look at your sticky notes. Put a star on the central idea. Put the ideas that are related next to each other. You now have the beginning of an idea map.

5. Working from the map you created, write a short position paper arguing for your views about the use of cameras to enforce traffic laws.

appointment to see a doctor, getting a course added or dropped, or correcting a mistake on a bill. Most of the time we grumble and let it go at that. But sometimes we stick with a subject. Neighborhood groups in cities and towns have been especially effective in getting something done by writing about it—for example, stopping a new road from being built, getting better police and fire protection, and getting a vacant lot turned into a park.

Listing and analyzing issues

A good way to get started is to list possible issues to write about. Make a list of questions that can be answered "YES, because . . ." or "NO, because . . ." Think about issues that affect your school, your community, the nation, and the world. Which issues interest you? About which issues could you make a contribution to the larger discussion?

School

- Should varsity athletes be excused from taking phys ed classes?
- Would an "open campus" policy allowing upperclassmen to leave school grounds for lunch be practical?
- Should the School Board invest in computers for every classroom or pay for renovations to older classrooms?
- Would the benefits of starting the school day one hour later outweigh the drawbacks?
- Should students be required to wear uniforms?
- Should the school charge students a fee for participation in extra curricular activities?

Community

- Should people who ride bicycles and motorcycles be required to wear helmets?
- Should high schools be allowed to search students for drugs at any time?
- Should bilingual education programs be eliminated?
- Should bike lanes be built throughout your community to encourage more people to ride bicycles?
- Should more tax dollars be shifted from building highways to funding public transportation?

Nation/World

- Should driving while talking on a cell phone be banned?
- Should capital punishment be abolished?
- Should the Internet be censored?
- Should the government be allowed to monitor all phone calls and all e-mail to combat terrorism?
- Should handguns be outlawed?
- Should beef and poultry be free of growth hormones?
- Should people who are terminally ill be allowed to end their lives?
- Should the United States punish nations with poor human rights records?

Narrowing a list

1. Put a check beside the issues that look most interesting to write about or the ones that mean the most to you.
2. Put a question mark beside the issues that you don't know very much about. If you choose one of these issues, you will probably have to do in-depth research—by talking to people, by using the Internet, or by going to the library.
3. Select the two or three issues that look most promising. For each issue, make another list:
   - Who is most interested in this issue?
   - Whom or what does this issue affect?
   - What are the pros and cons of this issue? Make two columns. At the top of the left one, write "YES, because." At the top of the right one, write "NO, because."
   - What has been written about this issue? How can you find out what has been written?

Explore Your Topic

When you identify a potential topic, make a quick exploration of that topic, much as you would walk through a house or an apartment you are thinking about renting for a quick look. One way of exploring is to visualize the topic by making a map.

If you live in a state on the coast that has a high potential for wind energy, you might argue that your state should provide financial incentives for generating more electricity from the wind. Perhaps it seems like a no-brainer to you because wind power consumes no fuel and causes no air pollution. The only energy required is for the manufacture and transportation of the wind turbines and transmission lines. But your state and other coastal states have not exploited potential wind energy for three reasons:

1. **Aesthetics.** Some people think wind turbines are ugly.
2. **Hazard to wildlife.** A few poorly located wind turbines have killed birds and bats.
3. **Cost.** Wind power costs differ, but wind energy is generally more expensive than electricity produced by burning coal.

To convince other people that your proposal is a good one, you will have to answer these objections.

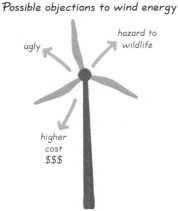

Possible objections to wind energy

ugly

hazard to wildlife

higher cost $$$

The first two objections are relatively easy to address. Locating wind farms 10 kilometers offshore keeps them out of sight of land and away from most migrating birds and all bats. The third objection, higher cost, is more difficult. One strategy is to argue that the overall costs of wind energy and energy produced by burning coal are comparable if environmental costs are included. You can analyze the advantages and disadvantages of each by drawing maps.

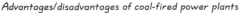

Advantages/disadvantages of coal-fired power plants

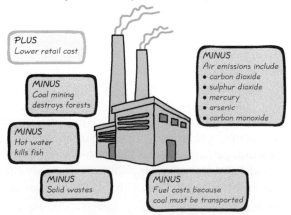

PLUS
Lower retail cost

MINUS
Coal mining destroys forests

MINUS
Hot water kills fish

MINUS
Solid wastes

MINUS
Air emissions include
• carbon dioxide
• sulphur dioxide
• mercury
• arsenic
• carbon monoxide

MINUS
Fuel costs because coal must be transported

Advantages/disadvantages of wind energy

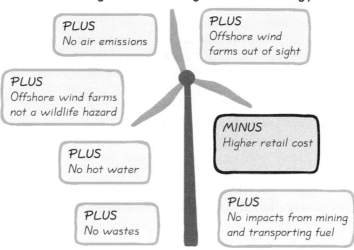

These maps can help you organize an argument for providing financial incentives for wind energy.

Read About Your Topic

Much academic writing draws on and responds to sources—books, articles, reports, and other material written by other people. Every significant issue discussed in today's world has an extensive history of discussion involving many people and various points of view. Before you formulate a claim about a significant issue, you need to become familiar with the conversation that's already happening by reading widely about it.

One of the most controversial and talked-about subjects in recent years is the outsourcing of white-collar and manufacturing jobs to low-wage nations. Since 2000 an estimated 400,000 to 500,000 American jobs each year have gone to cheap overseas labor markets. The Internet has made this migration of jobs possible, allowing companies to outsource not only low-skilled jobs but highly skilled jobs in fields such as software development, data storage, and even examining X-rays and MRI scans.

You may have read about this or another complex and controversial topic in one of your courses. Just as in a conversation with several people who hold different views, you may agree with some people, disagree with some, and with others agree with some of their ideas up to a point but then disagree.

Fox Business Network news anchor Lou Dobbs has been sharply critical of outsourcing. In *Exporting America: Why Corporate Greed Is Shipping American Jobs Overseas* (2006), Dobbs blames large corporations for putting profits ahead of the good of the nation. He accuses both Republicans and Democrats of ignoring the effects of a massive trade deficit and the largest national debt in American history, which Dobbs claims will eventually destroy the American way of life.

Thomas Friedman, columnist for the *New York Times*, takes a different viewpoint on outsourcing in *The World Is Flat: A Brief History of the Twenty-first Century* (2006). By *flat*, Friedman means that the nations of the world are connected like never before through the Internet and the lowering of trade barriers, putting every nation in direct competition with all the others. Friedman believes that outsourcing is not only unstoppable, but also desirable. He argues that Americans need to adapt to the new reality and rethink our system of education, or else we will be left hopelessly behind. (A version of Friedman's argument appears in Chapter 24.)

If you decide to write an argument about the issue of outsourcing, you might use either Dobbs's or Friedman's book as your starting point in making a claim. You could begin by taking on the role of **skeptic,** disagreeing with the author; the role of **contributor,** agreeing with the author and adding another point; or the role of the **analyst,** finding some points to agree with while disagreeing with others.

The skeptic: Disagreeing with a source

It's easy to disagree by simply saying an idea is dumb, but readers expect you to be persuasive about why you disagree and to offer reasons to support your views.

X claims that _____, but this view is mistaken because _____.

Example claim: Arguing against outsourcing resulting from free trade policies

Thomas Friedman claims that the world is "flat," giving a sense of a level playing field for all, but it is absurd to think that the millions of starving children in the world have opportunities similar to those in affluent countries who pay $100 for basketball shoes made by the starving children.

Example claim: Arguing in favor of outsourcing resulting from free trade policies

Lou Dobbs is a patriotic American who recognizes the suffering of manufacturing workers in industries like steel and automobiles, but he fails to point out that the major cause of the loss of manufacturing jobs in the United States and China alike is increased productivity—the 40 hours of labor necessary to produce a car just a few years ago has now been reduced to 15.

The contributor: Agreeing with a source with an additional point

Sources should not make your argument for you. With sources that support your position, indicate exactly how they fit into your argument with an additional point.

I agree with _____ and will make the additional point that
_____.

Example claim: Arguing against outsourcing resulting from free trade policies

Lou Dobbs's outcry against the outsourcing of American jobs also has a related argument: We are dependent not only on foreign oil, but also on foreign clothing, foreign electronics, foreign tools, foreign toys, foreign cars and trucks—indeed, just about everything—which is quickly eroding the world leadership of the United States.

Example claim: Arguing in favor of outsourcing resulting from free trade policies

Thomas Friedman's claim that the Internet enables everyone to become an entrepreneur is demonstrated by thousands of Americans, including my aunt, who could retire early because she developed an income stream by buying jeans and children's clothes at garage sales and selling them to people around the world on eBay.

The analyst: Agreeing and disagreeing simultaneously with a source

Incorporating sources is not a matter of simply agreeing or disagreeing with them. Often you will agree with a source up to a point, but you will come to a different conclusion. Or you may agree with the conclusions, but not agree with the reasons put forth.

I agree with _____ up to a point, but I disagree with the conclusion _____ because _____.

Example claim: Qualifying the argument against outsourcing resulting from free-trade policies

Lou Dobbs accurately blames our government for giving multinational corporations tax breaks for exporting jobs rather than regulating the loss of millions of jobs, but the real problem lies in the enormous appetite of Americans for inexpensive consumer products like HD televisions that is supported by borrowing money from overseas to the point that our dollar has plummeted in value.

> **Example claim: Qualifying the argument in favor of outsourcing resulting from free-trade policies**
>
> Thomas Friedman's central claim that the world is being "flattened" by globalization and there is not much we can do to stop it is essentially correct, but he neglects the social costs of globalization around the world, where the banner of free trade has been the justification for devastating the environment, destroying workers' rights and the rights of indigenous peoples, and ignoring laws passed by representative governments.

Find Good Reasons

Get in the habit of asking these questions every time you are asked to write an argument.

Can you argue by definition?

Probably the most powerful kind of good reason is an argument from definition. You can think of a definition as a simple statement: _____ _is a_ _____. You use these statements all the time. When you need a course to fulfill your social-science requirement, you look at the list of courses that are defined as social-science courses. You find out that the anthropology class you want to take is one of them. It's just as important when _____ _is not a_ _____. Suppose you are taking Latin, which is a language course taught by the language department, yet it doesn't count for the language requirement. The reason it doesn't count is because Latin is not defined as a modern language. So if you want to keep studying Latin you have to enroll in French or Spanish also.

Many definitions are not nearly as clear-cut as the language requirement. If you want to argue that figure skaters are athletes, you will need to define what an athlete is. You start thinking. An athlete competes in an activity, but that definition alone is too broad, since many competitions do not require physical activity. Thus, an athlete must participate in a competitive physical activity and must train for it. But that definition is still not quite narrow enough, because soldiers also train for competitive physical activity. You decide to add that the activity must be a sport and that it must require special competence and precision. Your _because_ clause turns out as follows: _Figure skaters are athletes because true athletes train for and compete in physical sporting competitions that require special competence and precision._

If you can get your audience to accept your definitions, you've gone a long way toward convincing them of the validity of your claim. That is why the most controversial issues in our culture—affirmative action, women's rights, privacy rights, gun control, global warming, foreign aid, universal health care, the death penalty—are argued from definition. Is providing assistance to citizens of other countries the responsibility of the United States government? Is privacy one of the rights guaranteed in the Constitution? Is the death penalty just or cruel and inhuman? You can see from these examples that definitions often rely on deeply held beliefs.

Because people have strong beliefs about controversial issues, they often don't care about the practical consequences. Arguing that it is much cheaper to execute prisoners who have been convicted of first-degree murder than to keep them in prison for life does not convince those who believe that it is morally wrong to kill. (See Chapter 10.)

Can you argue from value?

A special kind of argument from definition, one that often implies consequences, is the argument from value. You can support your claim with a "because clause" (or several of them) that includes a sense of evaluation. Arguments from value follow from claims like _____ *is a good* _____, *or* _____ *is not a good* _____.

Evaluation arguments usually proceed from the presentation of certain criteria. These criteria come from the definitions of good and bad, of poor and not so poor, that prevail in a given case. A great burger fulfills certain criteria; so does an outstanding movie, an excellent class, or the best laptop in your price range. Sometimes the criteria are straightforward, as in the burger example. A great burger has to have tasty meat—tender and without gristle, fresh, never frozen—a fresh bun that is the right size, and your favorite condiments.

But if you are buying a laptop computer and want to play the latest games along with your school tasks, you need to do some homework. For realistic graphics the best laptop will have a fast chip, preferably a dual core system. It will be equipped with a wireless modem, so you have access to the Internet at wireless hot spots. The battery life should last several hours, the hard drive should be large enough for your needs, the construction should be sturdy, and the warranty should cover the computer for at least three years. The keys for evaluation arguments are finding the appropriate criteria and convincing your readers that those criteria are the right criteria (see Chapter 12).

Can you argue from consequence?

Another powerful source of good reasons comes from considering the possible consequences of your position: Can you sketch out the good things that will follow from your position? Can you establish that certain bad things will be avoided if your position is adopted? If so, you will have other good reasons to use.

Causal arguments take the basic form of _____ *causes* _____ (*or* _____ *does not cause* _____). Very often, causal arguments are more complicated, taking the form _____ *causes* _____ *which, in turn, causes* _____ and so on. In one famous example, environmentalist Rachel Carson in *Silent Spring* makes powerful arguments from consequence. Rachel Carson's primary claim is that *DDT should not be sprayed on a massive scale because it will poison animals and people.* The key to her argument is the causal chain that explains how animals and people are poisoned. Carson describes how nothing exists alone in nature. When a potato field is sprayed with DDT, some of that poison is absorbed by the skin of the potatoes and some washes into the groundwater, where it contaminates drinking water. Other poisonous residue is absorbed into streams, where it is ingested by insect larvae, which in turn are eaten by fish. Fish are eaten by other fish, which are then eaten by waterfowl and people. At each stage, the poisons become more concentrated. (See Chapter 11 for additional examples of causal arguments.)

Proposal arguments are future-oriented arguments from consequence. In a proposal argument, you cannot stop with naming good reasons; you also have to show that these consequences would follow from the idea or course of action that you are arguing. For example, if you are proposing designated lanes for bicycles on the streets of your city, you must argue that they will encourage more people to ride bicycles to work and school, reducing air pollution and traffic congestion for everyone. (See Chapter 15.)

Can you counter objections to your position?

Another good way to find convincing good reasons is to think about possible objections to your position. If you can imagine how your audience might counter or respond to your argument, you will probably include in your argument precisely the points that will address your readers' particular needs and objections. If you are successful, your readers will be convinced that you are right. You've no doubt had the experience of mentally saying to a writer in the course of your reading, "Yeah, but what about this other idea?"—only to have the writer address precisely this objection.

You can impress your readers if you've thought about why anyone would oppose your position and exactly how that opposition would be expressed. If you are writing a proposal argument for a computer literacy requirement for all high school graduates, you might think about why anyone would object, since computers are critical for our jobs and lives. What will the practical objections be? What about philosophical ones? Why hasn't such a requirement been put in place already? By asking such questions in your own arguments, you are likely to develop robust because clauses.

Sometimes, writers pose rhetorical questions. You might say, "But won't paying for computers for all students make my taxes go up?" Stating objections explicitly can be effective if you make the objections as those of a reasonable person with an alternative point of view. But if the objections you state are ridiculous ones, then you risk being accused of setting up a **straw man**—that is, making the position opposing your own so simplistic that no one would likely identify with it. (See Chapter 14.)

Find Evidence to Support Good Reasons

Good reasons are essential ingredients of good arguments, but they don't do the job alone. You must support or verify good reasons with evidence. Evidence consists of hard data, examples, personal experiences, episodes, or tabulations of episodes (known as statistics) that are seen as relevant to the good reasons you are putting forward. Thus, a writer of arguments puts forward not only claims and good reasons but also evidence that those good reasons are true.

How much supporting evidence should you supply? How much evidence is enough? As is usual in the case of rhetoric, the best answer is, "It depends." If a reader is likely to find one of your good reasons hard to believe, then you should be aggressive in offering support. You should present detailed evidence in a patient and painstaking way. As one presenting an argument you have a responsibility not just to *state* a case but to *make* a case with evidence. Arguments that are unsuccessful tend to fail not because of a shortage of good reasons; more often, they fail because the reader doesn't agree that there is enough evidence to support the good reason that is being presented.

If your good reason isn't especially controversial, you probably should not belabor it. Think of your own experiences as a reader. How often do you recall saying to yourself, as you read a passage or listened to a speaker, "OK! OK! I get the point! Don't keep piling up all of this evidence for me because I don't want it or need it." However, such a reaction is rare, isn't it? By contrast, how often do you recall muttering under your breath, "How can you say that? What evidence do you have to back it up?" When in doubt, err on the side of offering too much evidence. It's an error that is seldom made and not often criticized.

When a writer doesn't provide satisfactory evidence to support a because clause, readers might feel that there has been a failure in the reasoning process. In fact, in your previous English courses, you may have learned about various fallacies associated with faulty arguments (pages 17–19).

Strictly speaking, there is nothing false about these so-called logical fallacies. The fallacies most often refer to failures in providing evidence; when you don't provide enough good evidence to convince your audience, you might be accused of committing a fallacy in reasoning. You will usually avoid such accusations if the evidence that you cite is both *relevant* and *sufficient*.

Relevance refers to the appropriateness of the evidence to the case at hand. Some kinds of evidence are seen as more relevant than others for particular audiences. On the one hand, in science and industry, personal testimony is seen as having limited relevance, while experimental procedures and controlled observations have far more credibility. Compare someone who defends the use of a particular piece of computer software because "it worked for me" with someone who defends it because "according to a journal article published last month, 84 percent of the users of the software were satisfied or very satisfied with it." On the other hand, in writing to the general public on controversial issues such as gun control, personal experience is often considered more relevant than other kinds of data.

Sufficiency refers to the amount of evidence cited. Sometimes a single piece of evidence or a single instance will carry the day if it is especially compelling in some way—if it represents the situation well or makes a point that isn't particularly controversial. More often, people expect more than one piece of evidence if they are to be convinced of something. Convincing readers that they should approve a statewide computer literacy requirement for all high school graduates will require much more evidence than the story of a single graduate who succeeded with her computer skills. You will likely need statistical evidence for such a broad proposal.

If you anticipate that your audience might not accept your evidence, face the situation squarely. First, think carefully about the argument you are presenting. If you cannot cite adequate evidence for your assertions, perhaps those assertions must be modified or qualified in some way. If you remain convinced of your assertions, then think about doing more research to come up with additional evidence.

PEARSON
mywritinglab

For additional writing resources that will help you master the objectives of this chapter, go to www.mywritinglab.com.

4 | Synthesis: Incorporating Arguments from Multiple Sources

QUICK TAKE

In this chapter, you will learn that

1. Using evidence from several sources strengthens your position (see below)
2. It is important to carefully choose what evidence to use to support your argument (see page 41)
3. You need to integrate data and explain its significance as you develop your discussion (see pages 44–45)

Health care professionals draw on multiple sources of evidence to diagnose and treat illnesses. What are some other professions that regularly rely on gathering and assessing *sufficient, relevant* evidence?

How Much Is Enough?

In the previous chapters, you learned how to get started with a good argument: explore a subject, do some reading, establish your own position, support your position with **good reasons**, and support those good reasons with evidence. In this chapter we explain how to synthesize the information you gather, especially from your reading, in a way that helps you to find good reasons and good evidence.

Let's begin with **evidence**. How much evidence do you need to convince people? That will depend on the given case, of course; there is no formula to determine exactly how many outside sources you need to consult in order to locate the data— quotations, statistics, endorsements—that will help make your case. But as a general rule we can say that it is unlikely that you will find a sufficient amount of evidence to support your argument by referring to only one or two sources. The trick is to have **sufficient** evidence that is **relevant** to your discussion to convince your readers of the strength of your argument (see pp. *249–252*). But gathering information is just the beginning. It isn't effective to just set out a long list of quotes or numbers. You need to integrate information and ideas from several sources into a coherent discussion of your topic. In other words, you need to be able to **synthesize**.

Entering the Conversation

It's good practice to place yourself firmly within the existing discourse about your subject. Use what you learn as you explore your topic to explain the context for your argument; provide the background information your readers need in order to recognize your contribution to the discussion. Carefully consider your audience: How much do they already know about the subject? Do they already have strong opinions about it? Or are they curious but uncommitted to a position?

If, for example, you decide to examine the use of animals in research to improved cosmetics, you would discover through your reading that the practice has a long history—and has long been the focus of heated debate. Animal experimentation is considered by some to be an essential tool for the development of safe new cosmetics, but others believe that the benefits are outweighed by ethical considerations. Making yourself aware of how the controversy has been playing out over the years will give your argument authority and allow you to provide needed context. You can get background information from Web resources such as *procon.org, yahoo, CQ Report,* or *Opposing Viewpoints.*

State Your Position

It isn't always necessary to make an explicit statement of your thesis or your intent. But it is imperative that you are clear about your position. Your readers want to know what you believe, and they want to know who you agree with and whose ideas you are challenging. Whether you choose to clearly broadcast or to subtly imply your stance, your reader should not be left wondering what you finally stand for.

Choose Appropriate Evidence

If you do a thorough job as you explore your topic, you should have more than enough data to work with. All of the research you do will inform your discussion, but when you write, you don't need to reference every source you consulted. Be discriminating as you decide which sources work best to bolster your argument.

For example, suppose you are proposing that the use of animals in cosmetic research should be absolutely forbidden. There are many people who already agree with this position, but their opinions may be based on different reasons. Some argue that the practice is inherently cruel, and that we should not engage in behaviors that are harmful to other living beings. Others take the stance that animals should be granted full rights and protections under the law. In that case, animals could not be forced to participate in research trials unless they have given their informed consent (an agreement to willingly participate in a research project, having a clear understanding of potential risks). Still others feel that the science of animal experimentation is unreliable and inconclusive—that extrapolating the results to humans doesn't always work. Which of these reasons lines up most closely with your views? Which are most likely to resonate with your audience? Would it be more effective to focus on one line of argument or to address several reasons for your position?

A cautionary note: Don't pick and choose your evidence or present it in a way that misrepresents the intent of the person you are citing. If you find an eloquent statement that seems to bolster your position only if the statement is taken out of context, you do yourself, your source, and your readers a disservice by using the quotation.

Establish credibility

When you demonstrate that your discussion builds on the work of others you enhance your credibility—your **ethos**, so to speak. Your credibility relies on the reliability of the sources you cite.

It may be true that all of your peers think that using animals for cosmetic research is wrong. But a small group of young adults, or even a large group of facebook friends, doesn't constitute an expert source. Your argument will carry more weight if you refer instead to an organization like the Johns Hopkins University Center for Alternatives to Animal Testing (CAAT). Johns Hopkins University is highly respected, with a long history of excellence in medical research and treatment. Noting CAAT's goal to "promote humane science by supporting the creation, development, validation, and use of alternatives to animals in research" lends its authority to your writing.

Use compelling evidence

Legislation was proposed to prevent the use of animals in cosmetic and medical research as early as 1966. That interesting and important bit of information would be useful if your goal is to present an historical perspective on the issue. Otherwise, that legal dispute is so far out of date as to be almost irrelevant. You should always use current, valid, and reliable outside sources that address the central points in your discussion. What ideas do you want to convey? What did you find in your research to reinforce those concepts?

Most people believe that hurting animals is unacceptable. That isn't enough, though, to assume your readers will automatically join you in your fight for an outright ban on animal experimentation in the cosmetics industry. To convince people to take action against the practice, you might document the number of animals used in clinical trials, describe the conditions of research laboratories, and detail the costs of this kind of experimentation.

Balance your approach

A well-shaped argument includes good reasons that appeal to both logic and emotion. A combination of statistics, expert testimony, accounts of historical events, and results of scientific inquiry present an argument grounded in reason and supported by concrete evidence. Anecdotes, descriptions, images, and allusions to literary texts tend to tap into emotions. Your topic, purpose, and audience will determine the appropriate balance of **logos** and **pathos**. Always ask yourself what kinds of evidence are most likely to sway your audience to agree with your interpretation or proposal. Remember, there is a big difference between *stating* your case and *making* your case.

Acknowledge opposing views

As you look for data that supports your position, you will encounter alternative views about the best course of action or the most reasonable solution for the issue at hand. Don't be dismissive of your opponents or assume that their motives are immoral. Those who support the use of animals in cosmetic research are concerned about safety in humans, and they too are often concerned about the ethical treatment of animals. Making sweeping generalizations that discount any possibility of a different but also otherwise valid perspective may in fact weaken your position. Treating with respect those who disagree with you is another way to build your own ethos. It is nice to be able to occupy the high moral ground, but if you take that ground by depicting others as immoral, it may compromise your effectiveness. In general, treat those who disagree with you as misinformed rather than immoral.

The amount of "page space" you devote to specifying opposing positions will—as always—be determined by your audience and purpose. Be respectful of your adversaries, present their beliefs accurately, and cite your source!

Select an organizational pattern

Settle on an organizational scheme for your discussion. The most common methods to organize an argument and integrate proof from a variety of sources are to use a **sequential** or an **alternating** pattern.

If you choose to present your points sequentially, first list all of your main points. Then in the second part of your paper, explain each more fully, providing supporting evidence. Or you could present your ideas by alternating each point with the appropriate explanation and evidence. The outlines below include the same points. Which pattern do you think presents the argument in a more convincing manner?

SEQUENTIAL	ALTERNATING
Point A It would be immoral to experiment on human beings as research subjects for new proposed cosmetics.	**Point A** It would be immoral to experiment on human beings as research subjects for new proposed cosmetics.
Point B Regulations about the treatment of animal subjects ensure they are treated humanely.	**Counterpoint A** It is immoral to exploit animals solely to benefit people.
Point C Research using animals has led to numerous medical advances.	**Point B** Regulations about the treatment of animal subjects ensure they are treated humanely.
Counterpoint A It is immoral to exploit animals solely to benefit people.	**Counterpoint B** Existing regulations offer some guidelines.
Counterpoint B Existing regulations offer some guidelines.	**Point C** Medical research using animals has led to numerous medical advances.
Counterpoint C Once alternative methods become widely accepted in the scientific community, studies that don't rely on animal experimentation will become equally productive.	**Counterpoint C** Once alternative methods become widely accepted in the scientific community, studies that don't rely on animal experimentation will become equally productive.

Don't forget that each point needs to be developed by adding appropriate evidence and explanations.

Synthesize the Evidence

Avoid the temptation to simply string together quote after statistic after anecdote without any explanation of how each piece of evidence fits together to craft your argument. The impulse to showcase all of your research is understandable, but an unfiltered inventory of facts and figures will not serve your purpose.

Central to your discussion should be your position, interpretation, or refutation. Everything you cite should be in the service of your argument. Even if you are writing a critical review or a rhetorical analysis, focus on the best reasons and evidence and incorporate those examples smoothly into your assessment. Note how these principles are in play in the sample essay at the end of this chapter and in the essay on "Tribe Fever" that appears on page 38.

Identify the source

Name the speaker you are quoting and include information that indicates the person's expertise about the subject.

For example:

> Pat Thomas is the health editor of the British magazine *The Economist*. In explaining the persistence of animal experimentation, he points out the "long standing difficulty in trying to get research which contradicts the current enthusiasm for animal testing published in major medical journals."
>
> In explaining the persistence of animal experimentation, Pat Thomas (the health editor of the British magazine *The Economist*) points out that the "long standing difficulty in trying to get research which contradicts the current enthusiasm for animal testing published in major medical journals."

Signal your attitude

Phrases like "he wrote" and "she said" give your reader rudimentary information about the source, but using more specific signal phrases indicates how each idea fits into your discussion. It also makes for more lively—and therefore more interesting—writing. Choose verbs and modifiers that reflect your attitude.

Note the contrast in tone that is created by using different signal phrases to attribute the same information:

> Economics professor Jane Smith exaggerates when she claims, "Unless there are more jobs created in the next five years, young adults will never gain the economic independence they deserve."

As highly acclaimed economist Dr. Jane Smith thoughtfully observes, "Unless there are more jobs created in the next five years, young adults will never gain the economic independence they deserve."

See page 280 for a list of signal phrases.

Explain the connection

Most of us have had the frustrating experience of being in a conversation that turns into an argument. When we are firmly convinced of our own opinions, it seems to be the only way to think about the issue. Your reasons seem self-evident, but your friends probably feel the same way about their contrasting positions. Insisting that you're right and they are wrong won't ease the impasse. You need to clearly explain the basis of your beliefs.

For example, you may want to convince your readers to buy clothing made only in America. According to the United States Department of Labor, there were almost 214,000 fewer people working in the clothing industry in 2011 than there were in 2001. That is a staggering statistic, but what's the "so what?" The issue here is the loss of jobs in the manufacturing sector. You could use this demographic statistic to make an emotional appeal to your readers and suggest that if we "buy American," fewer people will lose their jobs.

Cite the source

No matter how thorough your research, how compelling your evidence, or how clear your explanation, you will undermine all of the good work you have done if you don't cite your sources. Demonstrate that you are drawing on the work of reputable people, working from reliable data sources, and recognizing the range of positions about your subject. Give credit where credit is due. If you don't, you will be guilty of plagiarism, a sure way to destroy your ethos and cut the discussion short (see Chapter 20). If you do, you will be supporting your points with credible and convincing evidence.

Incorporating evidence in a rhetorical analysis

You may not need to refer to outside sources when you write a rhetorical analysis of a single text—a poem, a novel, or an article in a journal or magazine. In this case, you need to find specific evidence *in* the piece to support your argument. The process of finding and synthesizing evidence in a rhtetorical analysis is similar to the process that we outlined earlier:

- **Read, re-read, and read once again.** Make note of significant, puzzling, or especially beautiful passages.
- **Draft a working thesis.** Remember that as you write, your thesis may evolve to become more precise and nuanced.

- **Outline or map your main points.** Focus your discussion: narrow in on only one or two key elements of the text.
- **Choose compelling evidence.** A detailed summary isn't necessary, but if your readers are unfamiliar with the work you are analyzing, give enough information for them to understand what you are writing about. Focus on the details that get to the crux of your argument. Show that your interpretation is correct by citing the information that led you to that conclusion.
- **Acknowledge opposing views.** This is especially important if you are arguing against a conventional interpretation.
- **Explain the connection** between your thesis and the passages you quote. The word *essay* comes from the old French *essai*, an attempt or a trial. Think of writing as an attempt to understand a text and then to clearly explain that understanding. Help your readers follow your train of thought by leading them through your analysis. Place your evidence strategically to act as guideposts along the path.

Finding | Good Reasons

What Is The Value Of A College Education?

If paying for college is an investment, what are some of the potential returns—the kind that cannot be quantified? How might experiences like this one enhance and inform students' futures?

Many Americans believe that the path to a successful future begins with a college degree. The end goal for most college students is to get a good job. In the past three decades, the percentage of 18 to 24-year-olds enrolled in college has steadily increased, from 24 percent in 1973 to a record high of almost 40 percent in 2008. At the same time that more and more people are attending college, costs are skyrocketing. Because of rising costs in the face of a shrinking job market, the value of a traditional postsecondary education is being questioned.

Tuition is viewed as a financial investment; the payoff is expected in the opportunity to earn a large salary. But the increasing costs of tuition have led some to question whether the benefits of earning a 4-year degree outweigh the investment in time and money.

On the other hand, higher education has value beyond the financial trade-off. Or does it? Some believe that the true value of a university education is personal growth and an understanding of the information and ideas on which our culture rests. Yet another view is that people need to be educated in order to participate fully and effectively in civil society. (For a selection of arguments about the value of a college degree, see pages 385–388.)

Write about it

1. Do some research to find out why people choose to attend or not to attend college. You might want to conduct some field research—for example, administer an informal survey or interview several people you know. What explanations do they cite for their decision?

2. What evidence can you find that justifies or disputes the value of a college degree? Is there evidence that supports the benefits of any of the abstract reasons to spend four (or more) years in school after graduating from high school?

3. Integrate evidence from several different sources to build an argument about whether a college degree warrants the requisite investment of time and money.

Sample Student Synthesis Essay

Sometimes your instructor will give you a specific topic to write about and require that you consult a specific number of resources and specific types of resources. Here's an example taken from a college rhetoric course:

Assignment

For many years, the Republican and the Democratic parties have dominated the political process in the United States. But occasionally candidates from outside the two major parties have been important players and helped shape the political landscape. Locate at least six texts produced in different media (news reports, analyses, and commentaries in print and electronic formats; political cartoons; letters to the editor; filmed debates; blogs; signs, posters, and buttons) about third-party campaigns.

Then write an essay evaluating the impact of third-party candidates on national elections. Synthesize at least three sources for support. Make note of all the sources you used in your research in a Works Consulted (rather than a Works Cited) list.

(As you read the essay that came out of that assignment, note that Pat Lane-Smith synthesized information and ideas from a variety of sources: a PBS Web site, a political cartoon, an op-ed column, letters to the editor in the online version of a national newspaper, and an article posted on an online newspaper that focuses on political issues. The cartoon by Stantist that Lane-Smith refers to appears on page 46.)

Lane-Smith 1

Pat Lane-Smith
Professor Jackson
RHET 201
10 January 2012

The Power of Three

"Let me warn you, in the most solemn manner, against the baneful effects of the spirit of party." Our first president, George Washington, famously expressed his concern that the formation of political parties would have lasting negative effects on the governance of the newly formed country (Timeline).

Lane-Smith 2

Washington was not able to stop the establishment or the influence of powerful political alliances. For better or for worse, for most of our history, two parties have held sway over the political process. There have always been other, smaller parties, but their influence has varied greatly. But especially in turbulent times, third-party candidates have had a lasting impact on national political debates and made their mark on legislative agendas. We are living in one of those times.

(By opening his essay with an historical quote and ending his introductory paragraph with a reference to the current political situation, Lane-Smith indicates that the discussion about third-party candidates has been going on for more than 200 years. He uses this tactic to enter the conversation and to state his position.)

In the early twenty-first century, the Democratic and Republican parties have staked out dramatically divergent positions on issues from foreign aid to school vouchers to funding for public broadcasting. Political cartoonist Scott Stantist illustrated the resulting impasse by depicting a debate between candidates from each party. The entirety of the discussion is one sentence: "I'm not him!" The frustration of many American citizens is represented by the discouraged expression on the face of Uncle Sam, caught between the symbolic donkey and elephant (*US News*).

As opposition positions have become more entrenched, a significant portion of the electorate has become more disillusioned. They are "wishing that we had more options today than our two-party system is putting forward." In fact, there have been calls for the creation of a "viable, centrist, third presidential ticket" (Friedman).

(Lane-Smith describes an image that conveys the emotion behind the desire expressed by the columnist.)

Thomas Friedman is a well-known editorialist for the *New York Times*. Other, less-known writers echo his call:

> A centrist third party could prosper in today's political environment and end the stalemate in Washington. There is a large body of moderate Republicans, disaffected Democrats and dissatisfied independents looking for the kind of political home that this party could provide. Unhappiness with the political options now available to Americans will sooner or later translate into a groundswell for alternatives. (Levine)

Freidman and Levine articulate what appears to be a common sentiment. But not everyone agrees with the solution they present. Another *Times* reader joins the discussion to point out his belief that "Any efforts to form a third party would likely result in splintering into multiple, smaller parties, each with its own agenda" (Loughlin).

(*Lane-Smith chooses credible sources: PBS*, US News & World Report, *and the* New York Times.)

Lane-Smith 3

The level of frustration with the two-party system expressed by Freid-man and Levine has propelled third-party candidates into the national spotlight before. Ralph Nader didn't win the election, but his bid for president in 2000 affected the outcome of that race. His primary message was that politicians in both parties were dishonest (Zelizer).

(*In this paragraph, Lane-Smith synthesizes ideas taken from three sources.*)

Freidman uses his column to endorse an innovative approach taken by a group called Americans:Elect. On their Web site, the group describes themselves as "a nonpartisan nonprofit whose only mission is to let the American people directly nominate *their* choice for president." Americans:Elect has developed a creative alternative to the system of choosing a candidate through a series of primary elections and a national convention. Whether they are successful or not, it is likely that the fact that they are making use of the Internet to hold a "secure, on-line convention" may influence future campaigns (*Americans: Elect 2012*). In 1992, Ross Perot used television appearances as a central method of his campaign for president. As a result, his message reached a huge audience. The issues he addressed became central to the debate and his use of broadcast media, new at the time, is now commonplace (Zelizer).

(*Lane-Smith introduces the organization by citing the reference made in the op-ed piece, then uses a quote from the Web site for clarification.*)

Julian Zelizer is a history professor at Princeton University. In an article in *Politico* he thoughtfully concludes that "Third-party candidates still matter. . . . Third parties don't win in contemporary U.S. politics, but they can make a difference and they certainly can tell us a great deal about some of the underlying dynamics shaping the electorate and the political process." Without a doubt, third parties have had an important and invaluable impact on American politics.

(*Naming the speaker as a professor at a prestigious university and using the signal phrase "thoughtfully concludes," Lane-Smith aligns himself with a respected authority.*)

Works Consulted

Americans: Elect 2012. Americans Elect. 2011. Web. 8 Jan. 2012.

Donvan, John, David Brooks, Arianna Huffington, Zev Chafets, and P. J. O'Rourke. "Intelligence Squared Debate: Two-Party Political System." Video recording. 11 Mar. 2011. *Bloomberg*. 2012. Web. 5 Jan. 2012.

Friedman, Thomas L. "Make Way for the Radical Center." *New York Times Sunday Review*. New York Times. 23 July 2011. Web. 8 January 2012.

(*This assignment specified the use of a Works Consulted list, so Lane-Smith included a recorded debate he used in his research although he did not cite it in his essay.*)

Levine, Robert A. "Sunday Dialogue: Will a Third Party Help? The Letter." *New York Times Sunday Review.* New York Times. 23 Dec. 2011. Web. 8 Jan. 2012.

Loughlin, Kevin R. "Sunday Dialogue: Will a Third Party Help? Readers React." *New York Times Sunday Review.* New York Times. 28 Dec. 2011. Web. 8 Jan. 2012.

Stantis, Scott. "The Great Debate 2010." Cartoon. *2010 Election Campaign Cartoons. US News & World Report.* US News & World Report, 2012. 7 Jan. 2012.

"A Timeline of Third Party Events." *The Story of Third Party Candidates in America.* PBS.org. n.d. Web. 5 Jan. 2011.

Zelizer, Julian E. "Third-party Candidates Still Matter." *Politico.* Politico LLC. 13 Oct. 2011. Web. 7 Jan. 2012.

PEARSON
mywritinglab

For additional writing resources that will help you master the objectives of this chapter, go to www.mywritinglab.com.

5 | Drafting and Revising Arguments

QUICK TAKE

In this chapter, you will learn that

1. Focusing and evaluating your thesis is critical to writing a successful argument (see below)
2. Keeping your readers in mind will help you write your argument (see page 56)
3. Writing an engaging title and introduction will draw your readers into your argument (see page 59)
4. Evaluating your draft using specific strategies will help you identify your goals for revision (see pages 59–60)

People frequently revise things that they own. What objects have you revised?

State and Evaluate Your Thesis

Once you have identified a topic and have a good sense of how to develop it, the next critical step is to write a **working thesis**. Your **thesis** states your main claim. Much writing that you will do in academic settings and later in your career will require an explicit thesis, usually placed near the beginning.

Focusing your thesis

The thesis can make or break your paper. If the thesis is too broad, you cannot do justice to the argument. Who wouldn't wish for fewer traffic accidents, better medical care, more effective schools, or a cleaner environment? Simple solutions for these complex problems are unlikely.

Stating something that is obvious to everyone isn't an arguable thesis. Don't settle for easy answers. When a topic is too broad, a predictable thesis often results. Narrow your focus and concentrate on the areas where you have the most questions. Those are likely the areas where your readers will have the most questions too.

The opposite problem is less common: a thesis that is too narrow. If your thesis simply states a commonly known fact, then it is too narrow. For example, the growth rate of the population in the United States has doubled since 1970 because of increased immigration. The U.S. Census Bureau provides reasonably accurate statistical information, so this claim is not arguable. But the policies that allow increased immigration and the effects of a larger population—more crowding and higher costs of health care, education, and transportation—are arguable.

> **Not arguable:** The population of the United States grew faster in the 1990s than in any previous decade because Congress increased the rate of legal immigration and the government stopped enforcing most laws against illegal immigration in the interior of the country.

> **Arguable:** Allowing a high rate of immigration helps the United States deal with the problems of an increasingly aging society and helps provide funding for millions of Social Security recipients.

> **Arguable:** The increase in the number of visas to foreign workers in technology industries is the major cause of unemployment in those industries.

Evaluating your thesis

Once you have a working thesis, ask these questions.

- Is it arguable?
- Is it specific?
- Is it manageable given your length and time requirements?
- Is it interesting to your intended readers?

Example 1
Sample thesis

> We should take action to resolve the serious traffic problem in our city.

Is it arguable? The thesis is arguable, but it lacks a focus.

Is it specific? The thesis is too broad.

Is it manageable? Transportation is a complex issue. New highways and rail systems are expensive and take many years to build. Furthermore, citizens don't want new roads running through their neighborhoods.

Is it interesting? The topic has the potential to be interesting if the writer can propose a specific solution to a problem that everyone in the city recognizes.

When a thesis is too broad, it needs to be revised to address a specific aspect of an issue. Make the big topic smaller.

Revised thesis

> The existing freight railway that runs through the center of the city should be converted to a passenger railway because this is the cheapest and quickest way to decrease traffic congestion downtown.

Example 2
Sample thesis

> Over 60 percent of Americans play computer games on a regular basis.

Is it arguable? The thesis states a commonly acknowledged fact. It is not arguable.

Is it specific? The thesis is too narrow.

Is it manageable? A known fact is stated in the thesis, so there is little to research. Several surveys report this finding.

Is it interesting? The popularity of video games is well established. Nearly everyone is aware of the trend.

There's nothing original or interesting about stating that Americans love computer games. Think about what is controversial. One debatable topic is how computer games affect children.

Revised thesis

> Computer games are valuable because they improve children's visual attention skills, literacy skills, and computer literacy skills.

Finding Good Reasons

Should Driving While Talking Be Banned?

In a movement to improve driving safety, California, Connecticut, the District of Columbia, New Jersey, New York, Oregon, Utah, and Washington have passed laws banning the use of handheld cell phones while driving except for emergency workers and people making 911 calls. Several other states have banned cell phones while driving for drivers aged 18 and younger.

Proponents of the ban point to a National Highway Traffic Safety Administration study, reporting that approximately 25 to 30 percent of motor vehicle crashes—about 1.2 million accidents each year—are caused by driver distraction. Opponents of the ban argue that anything that distracts the driver—eating potato chips, talking with passengers, spilled coffee—can cause an accident. The answer, they say, is driver education.

Write about it

1. Write a thesis arguing in support of a ban on cell phones while driving, against a ban, or in support of a more limited position such as banning cell-phone use for drivers 18 and under.

2. Think about the audience that would likely oppose your position. For example, if you support a ban on talking while driving, think about the likely responses of high school students, salespeople who spend much of their workdays driving from place to place, and workers who receive assignments by phone. What good reasons would convince readers who hold an opposing view?

3. What reasons would people who oppose your position likely offer in response? What counterarguments could you give to answer these objections?

4. Write a draft that clearly sets out your position. Focus on the two to four supporting arguments you think are most likely to convince those who disagree with you.

5. Work with a classmate; make suggestions to improve each other's papers.

Think About Your Readers

Thinking about your readers doesn't mean telling them what they might want to hear. Instead, imagine yourself in a dialogue with your readers. What questions will they likely have? How might you address any potential objections?

Understanding what your readers know—and do not know

Your readers' knowledge of your subject is critical to the success of your argument. If they are not familiar with the necessary background information, they probably won't understand your argument fully. If you know that your readers will be unfamiliar with your subject, you have to supply background information before attempting to convince them of your position. A good tactic is to tie your new information to what your readers already know. Comparisons and analogies can be very helpful in linking old and new information.

Understanding your readers' attitudes toward you

To get your readers to take you seriously, you must convince them that they can trust you. You need to get them to see you as

- **Concerned:** Readers want you to be committed to your subject. They also expect you to be concerned about them. After all, if you don't care about them, why should they read what you write?
- **Well informed:** Many people ramble on about any subject without knowing anything about it. Academic writing requires that you do your homework on a subject.
- **Fair:** Many writers look at only one side of an issue. Readers respect objectivity and an unbiased approach.
- **Ethical:** Many writers use only the facts that support their positions and often distort facts and sources. Critical readers often notice what is being left out. Don't try to conceal what doesn't support your position.

Understanding your readers' attitudes toward your subject

People have prior attitudes about controversial issues. You must take these attitudes into consideration as you write or speak. Imagine, for instance, that you are preparing an argument for a guest editorial in your school newspaper. You are advocating that your state government should provide parents with choices between public and private schools. You plan to argue that the tax dollars that now automatically go to public schools should go to private schools if parents so choose. You have evidence that the sophomore-to-senior dropout rate in private schools is less than half the rate in public schools. Furthermore, students from private schools attend college at nearly twice the rate of public-school graduates. You intend to argue that one of the reasons private schools are more successful is that they spend more money on instruction and less on administration. And you believe that school choice speaks to the American desire for personal freedom.

Not everyone will agree with your position. How might the faculty feel about this issue? How about the administrators, the staff, other students, and interested community members who read the student newspaper? What are their attitudes toward public funding of private schools? How are you going to deal with the objection that many students in private schools do better in school because they come from more affluent families?

Even when you write about a much less controversial subject, you must think carefully about your audience's attitudes toward what you have to say or to write. Sometimes your audience may share your attitudes; other times, your audience may be neutral. At still other times, your audience will have attitudes that differ sharply from your own. Anticipate these various attitudes and act accordingly. If these attitudes are different from yours, you will have to work hard to counter them without insulting your audience.

Organize Your Argument

Asking a series of questions can generate a list of good reasons, but even if you have plenty, you still have to decide which ones to use and in what order to present them. Thinking about your readers' knowledge, attitudes, and values will help you to decide which reasons to present to your audience.

Writing plans often take the form of outlines, either formal outlines or working outlines. A **formal outline** typically begins with the thesis statement, which anchors the entire outline.

Managing the Risks of Nanotechnology While Reaping the Rewards

THESIS: The revolutionary potential of nanotechnology has arrived in an explosion of consumer products, yet our federal government has yet to recognize the potential risks or to fund research to reduce those risks.

I. Nanotechnology now is in many consumer products.
  A. The promise of nanotechnology to revolutionize medicine, energy production, and communication is years in the future, but consumer products are here now.
  B. Nanotechnology is now in clothing, food, sports equipment, medicines, electronics, and cars.

      C.   Experts predict that 15 percent of manufactured products worldwide will contain nanotechnology in 2014.

      D.   The question that hasn't been asked: Is nanotechnology safe?

II. Americans have little awareness of nanotechnology.

      A.   Companies have stopped mentioning and advertising nanotechnology.

      B.   Companies and the insurance industry paid $250 billion in asbestos claims in the United States alone.

      C.   Companies fear exposure to lawsuits if nanotechnology is found to be toxic.

A **working outline** is a sketch of how you will arrange the major sections.

Managing the Risks of Nanotechnology While Reaping the Rewards

SECTION 1: Begin by defining nanotechnology—manipulating particles between 1 and 100 nanometers (nanometer is a billionth of a meter). Describe the rapid spread of nanotechnology in consumer products including clothing, food, sports equipment, medicines, electronics, and cars. State projection of 15 percent of global manufactured goods containing nanotechnology in 2014.

SECTION 2: Most Americans know nothing about nanotechnology. Companies have stopped advertising that their products contain nanotechnology because of fear of potential lawsuits. Asbestos, once thought safe, now is known to be toxic and has cost companies $250 billion in lawsuits in the United States alone.

SECTION 3: Relatively little research has been done on the safety of nanotechnology. No testing is required for new products because the materials are common, but materials behave differently at nano-scale (example—aluminum normally inert but combustible at nano-scale).

SECTION 4: Nanoparticles are highly mobile and can cross the blood-brain barrier and through the placenta. They are toxic in brains of fish and may collect in lungs.

SECTION 5: Urge that the federal government develop a master plan for identifying and reducing potential risks of nanotechnology and provide sufficient funding to carry out the plan.

Write an Engaging Title and Introduction

Many writers don't think much about titles, but they are very important. A good title makes the reader want to see what you have to say. Be as specific as you can in your title, and if possible, suggest your stance.

Get off to a fast start in your introduction. Convince your reader to keep reading. Cut to the chase. Think about how you can get your readers interested. Consider using one of the following.

- State your thesis concisely.
- Provide a hard-hitting fact.
- Ask a question.
- Give a vivid description of a problem.
- Discuss a contradiction or paradox.
- Describe a scenario.

Managing the Risks of Nanotechnology While Reaping the Rewards

The revolutionary potential of nanotechnology for medicine, energy production, and communication is now at the research and development stage, but the future has arrived in consumer products. Nanotechnology has given us products we hardly could have imagined just a few years ago: socks that never stink; pants that repel water yet keep you cool; eyeglasses that won't scratch; "smart" foods that add nutrition and reduce cholesterol; DVDs that are incredibly lifelike; bandages that speed healing; tennis balls that last longer; golf balls that fly straighter; pharmaceuticals that selectively deliver drugs; various digital devices like palm pilots, digital cameras, and cell phones that have longer battery lives and more vivid displays; and cars that are lighter, stronger, and more fuel efficient. These miracle products are now possible because scientists have learned how to manipulate nano-scale particles from 1 to 100 nanometers (a nanometer is a billionth of a meter; a human hair is about 100,000 nanometers in width). Experts estimate that 15 percent of all consumer products will contain nanotechnology by 2014. In the rush to create new consumer products, however, one question has not been asked: Is nanotechnology safe for those who use the products and the workers who are exposed to nanoparticles daily?

Write a Strong Conclusion

Restating your thesis usually isn't the best way to finish a paper. Conclusions that offer only a summary bore readers. The worst endings say something like "in my paper I've said this." Effective conclusions are interesting and provocative, leaving readers with something to think about. Give your readers something to take away besides a straight summary. Try one of these approaches.

- Issue a call to action.
- Discuss the implications.
- Make recommendations.
- Project into the future.
- Tell an anecdote that illustrates a key point.

> The potential risks of nanotechnology are reasonably well known. Among the more obvious research questions are the following:
>
> - How hazardous are nanoparticles for workers who have daily exposure?
> - What happens to nanoparticles when they are poured down the drain and eventually enter streams, lakes, and oceans?
> - How readily do nanoparticles penetrate the skin?
> - What happens when nanoparticles enter the brain?
> - What effect do airborne nanoparticles have on the lungs?
>
> Nanotechnology promises untold benefits beyond consumer goods in the fields of medicine, energy production, and communication, but these benefits can be realized only if nanotechnology is safe. The federal National Nanotechnology Initiative spent over $1.7 billion in 2009 on nanotechnology science and engineering research, but it budgeted only $74 million on environmental, health, and safety research in 2009. The federal government needs to create a master plan for risk research and to increase spending at least tenfold to ensure sufficient funding to carry out the plan.

When you finish your conclusion, read your introduction again. The main claim in your conclusion should be closely related to the main subject, question, or claim in your introduction. If they do not match, revise the subject, question, or claim in the introduction to match the conclusion. Your thinking evolves and develops as you write, and often your introduction needs some adjusting if you wrote it first.

Evaluate Your Draft

To review and evaluate your draft, pretend you are someone who is either uninformed about your subject or informed but likely to disagree with you. If possible, think of an actual person and imagine yourself as that person.

Read your draft aloud all the way through. When you read aloud, you often hear clunky phrases and catch errors, but just put checks in the margins so you can return to them later. You don't want to get bogged down with the little stuff. What you are after in this stage is an overall sense of how well you accomplished what you set out to do.

Use the questions in the box on the next two pages to evaluate your draft. Note any places where you might make improvements. When you finish, make a list of your goals for the revision. You may have to write another draft before you move to the next stage.

Checklist for evaluating your draft

Does your paper or project meet the assignment?

- Look again at your assignment, especially at key words such as *define, analyze causes, evaluate,* and *propose.* Does your paper or project do what the assignment requires? If not, how can you change it?

- Look again at the assignment for specific guidelines including length, format, and amount of research. Does your work meet these guidelines?

Can you better focus your thesis and your supporting reasons?

- You may have started out with a large topic and ended up writing about one aspect of it. Can you make your thesis even more precise?

- Can you find the exact location where you link each reason to your thesis?

Are your main points adequately developed?

- Can you explain your reasons in more detail?

- Can you add evidence to better support your main points?

- Do you provide enough background on your topic?

Is your organization effective?

- Is the order of your main points clear? (You may want to make a quick outline of your draft if you have not done so already.)

- Are there any abrupt shifts or gaps?
- Are there sections or paragraphs that should be rearranged?

Are your key terms adequately defined?

- What are your key terms?
- Can you define these terms more precisely?

Do you consider other points of view?

- Where do you acknowledge views besides your own? If you don't acknowledge other views, where can you add them?
- How can you make your discussion of opposing views more acceptable to readers who hold those views?

Do you represent yourself effectively?

- Forget for the moment that you wrote what you are reading. What is your impression of the writer?
- Is the tone of the writing appropriate for the subject?
- Are the sentences clear and properly emphatic?
- Did you choose words that convey the right connotations?

Can you improve your title and introduction?

- Can you make your title more specific and indicate your stance?
- Can you think of a way to start faster and to get your readers interested in what you have to say?

Can you improve your conclusion?

- Can you think of an example that sums up your position?
- Can you discuss an implication of your argument that will make your readers think more about the subject?
- If you are writing a proposal, can you end with a call for action?

Can you improve your visual presentation?

- Is the type style easy to read and consistent?
- Would headings and subheadings help to mark the major sections of your argument?
- If you have statistical data, do you use charts?
- Would illustrations, maps, or other graphics help to explain your main points?

Respond to the Writing of Others

Your instructor may ask you to respond to the drafts of your classmates. Responding to other people's writing requires the same careful attention you give to your own draft. To write a helpful response, you should go through the draft more than once.

First reading

Read at your normal rate the first time through without stopping. When you finish you should have a clear sense of what the writer is trying to accomplish. Try writing the following:

- **Main idea and purpose:** Write a sentence that summarizes what you think is the writer's main idea in the draft.
- **Purpose:** Write a sentence that states what you think the writer is trying to accomplish in the draft.

Second reading

In your second reading, you should be most concerned with the content, organization, and completeness of the draft. Make notes in pencil as you read.

- **Introduction:** Does the writer's first paragraph effectively introduce the topic and engage your interest?
- **Thesis:** What exactly is the writer's thesis? Is it clear? Note in the margin where you think the thesis is located.
- **Focus:** Does the writer maintain focus on the thesis? Note any places where the writer seems to wander off to another topic.
- **Organization:** Are the sections and paragraphs arranged effectively? Do any paragraphs seem to be out of place? Can you suggest a better order for the paragraphs?
- **Completeness:** Are there sections or paragraphs that lack key information or adequate development? Where do you want to know more?
- **Conclusion:** Does the last paragraph wrap up the discussion in a way that leaves the reader satisfied? Is it thought-provoking and memorable? (See Chapter 21.)
- **Sources:** Are outside sources cited accurately? Are quotations used correctly and worked into the fabric of the draft? (See Chapter 4.)

Third reading

In your third reading, turn your attention to matters of audience, style, and tone.

- **Audience:** Who are the writer's intended readers? What does the writer assume the audience knows and believes?

- **Style:** Does the writer have sentences that are accurate and that empha-size things? Can you suggest sentences that could be eliminated or combined? (See Chapter 6.)
- **Tone:** Is the tone appropriate for the writer's purpose and audience? Is the tone consistent throughout the draft? Are there places where another word or phrase might work better?

When you have finished the third reading, write a short paragraph on each bul-leted item above. Refer to specific paragraphs in the draft by number. Then end by answering these two questions:

- What does the writer do especially well in the draft?
- What one or two things would most improve the draft in a revision?

Edit and Proofread Carefully

When you finish revising, you are ready for one final careful reading with the goals of improving your style and eliminating errors.

Edit for style

- **Check connections between sentences and paragraphs.** Notice how your sentences flow within each paragraph and from paragraph to para-graph. If you need to signal the relationship from one sentence or para-graph to the next, use a transitional word or phrase (e.g., *in addition, moreover, similarly, however, nevertheless*).
- **Check your sentences.** Often you will pick up problems with individ-ual sentences by reading aloud. If you notice that a sentence doesn't sound right, think about how you might rephrase it. If a sentence seems too long, consider breaking it into two or more sentences. If you notice a string of short sentences that sound choppy, consider combining them. See Chapter 6 for information on how to revise sentences for emphasis, clarity, and grace.
- **Eliminate wordiness.** Look for wordy expressions such as *because of the fact that* and *at this point in time*, which can easily be shortened to *because* and *now*. Reduce unnecessary repetition such as *attractive in appearance* or *visible to the eye* to *attractive* and *visible*. Remove unnecessary words like *very, really,* and *totally*. See how many words you can remove without losing the meaning. Choose words with the right concreteness, the right level of formality, and the right connotation. (See Chapter 6.)
- **Use active verbs.** Make your style more lively by replacing forms of *be* (*is, are, was, were*) or verbs ending in *–ing* with active verbs. Sentences that be-gin with *There is (are)* and *It is* can often be rewritten with active verbs.

Proofread carefully

In your final pass through your text, eliminate as many errors as you can. To become an effective proofreader, you have to learn to slow down. Some writers find that moving from word to word with a pencil slows them down enough to find errors. Others read backwards to force them to concentrate on each word.

- **Know what your spelling checker can and can't do.** Spelling checkers are the greatest invention since peanut butter. They turn up many typos and misspellings that are hard to catch. But spelling checkers do not catch wrong words (*to much* for *too much*), missing endings (*three dog*), and other similar errors.

- **Check for grammar and punctuation.** Nothing hurts your credibility more than leaving errors in what you write. Many college and

As you revise papers, you can schedule one-on one meetings with your teacher or with a classmate whose input you trust. Most colleges have writing centers where students can work with trained peer tutors to develop and focus ideas and to otherwise improve their writing projects.

job applications get tossed in the reject pile because of a single, glaring error. Readers probably shouldn't make such harsh judgments when they find errors, but often they do. Keep a grammar handbook bookmarked on or beside your computer, and use it when you are uncertain about what is correct.

For additional writing resources that will help you master the objectives of this chapter, go to www.mywritinglab.com.

6 | Arguing with Style

QUICK TAKE

In this chapter, you will learn that

1. You can emphasize different things in a sentence by constructing sentences in different ways (see below)
2. You can use punctuation to reveal meaning and emphasis (see pages 73–75)
3. You can add figures of speech to your prose to give it force and class (see pages 75–78)
4. You can choose words on the basis of their level of generality, their level of formality, and their connotations (see pages 79–80)

In everyday life, how do we use style and presentation to both serve and enhance our larger purposes?

Reading and Writing with Style

A key premise of this book is that reading and writing are mutually supportive. Getting better at one usually makes you better at the other. And so it is
with studies of style. Learning how to make good decisions about sentences
and words will give your writing more force and clarity and power, and it will
also make you a more sensitive and appreciative reader of what others write.
Style in writing is a complicated matter, and this chapter cannot do anything
close to full justice to the subject. But what we *can* do in this chapter is to give
you a few key principles to depend on and to build on as your education
continues.

In particular, we cover some basic principles governing effective sentences, we give key principles about punctuation and figures of speech that
will lend clarity and grace to your prose, and we offer some guidelines about
word choice that will help make your prose sparkle. The aim is to make you a
better crafter of your own prose and a more sensitive critic of the writing of
others.

Giving Sentences Their Proper Emphasis

When you are speaking, it's easy enough to give emphasis to what's important. In
general, you can just raise your speaking voice (or even shout! with hand gestures
to match!) to give weight to what you most want people to attend to, or you can
use a lower or neutral tone of voice (and use no physical gestures) to signal that
something isn't quite so important. If people do not appreciate what you care
about in oral communication, you can see that by watching their reaction—and
then repeat yourself, if necessary, for emphasis.

But how do you show emphasis in written prose? How can you make
certain that your reader will know what you want to stand out? Here are
five tips.

1. Put more important information in important clauses (known as "independent clauses") and put less important things in less important clauses
   (known as "dependent clauses") and in phrases.
2. Use the first and last positions in a sentence for important things, and put
   less important things in the middle of the sentence.
3. Use unusual sentence patterns to highlight what is important.
4. Repeat important words within the sentence.
5. Punctuate for emphasis as well as clarity.

Five Style Principles

Principle 1: If something is important, put it into an independent clause; if it's not so important, put it into a dependent clause (or make it a modifier)

Consider the following two pairs of sentences.

Pair #1
- When Hall of Fame catcher Johnny Bench was still in high school, he learned a foolproof way to hit curve balls.
- Hall of Fame catcher Johnny Bench was still in high school when he learned a foolproof way to hit curve balls.

Pair #2
- Although Yellowstone Park was once praised by Theodore Roosevelt for its great natural beauty, it is now the site of many tacky souvenir stands.
- Yellowstone Park was once praised by Theodore Roosevelt for its great natural beauty, although it is now the site of many tacky tourist stands.

The two sentences in each pair are very similar, but can you sense a subtle difference between them? In the first pair, one sentence emphasizes that Johnny Bench learned a foolproof way to hit curve balls (and deemphasizes that he was in high school when he did it), while the other emphasizes that he was in high school when he learned to hit curves. In the second pair, one sentence emphasizes what Yellowstone Park is like now, while the other emphasizes what it once was. That is because the sentences feature different items in their independent clauses. An independent clause, you will recall, is one that has a subject and verb and that can stand as a complete sentence—such as "Yellowstone Park was once praised by Theodore Roosevelt for its great natural beauty." A dependent clause has a subject and verb but cannot stand on its own—such as "Although Yellowstone Park was once praised by Theodore Roosevelt for its great natural beauty."

With practice you can learn to manipulate sentences to make one or another item part of the independent clause. *The trick is to start by putting your best information into the independent clause(s); then drape other information onto that independent clause.* For example, here are four sentences that contain roughly the same information but that also emphasize different material by putting different things in independent and dependent clauses:

- While Mark Twain sold boatloads of books in his lifetime, he repeatedly squandered his fortune by investing in ill-advised printing contraptions.
- Mark Twain sold boatloads of books in his lifetime, although he repeatedly squandered his fortune by investing in ill-advised printing contraptions.

- Mark Twain invested in ill-advised printing contraptions, so that while he sold boatloads of books in his lifetime, he repeatedly squandered his fortune.
- Mark Twain sold boatloads of books during his lifetime, but he repeatedly squandered his fortune by investing in ill-advised printing contraptions.

Note too that sometimes you can combine two sentences in order to deemphasize one of them. Ask yourself these questions: "Does this sentence really deserve to be a full sentence, or should it only be part of a sentence? Is it important enough to get that kind of status? Should I combine it with another sentence to create a more appropriate sense of emphasis?" Take, for example, the following paragraph.

Our road trips to Florida were long ones, but they never seemed too long. That's because we always had so much fun. The first leg of our trip was always given over to "Broadway." My two brothers and I would create and then perform three or four skits for my parents. For example, we once put on "The Courtship of Our Parents" as we imagined it, plus "A Trip to the Principal's Office" and then a musical called "Blue Christmas." My parents would judge the skits, and the best performer would get an extra dip of ice cream at our lunch stop. After lunch we moved to stage two. We called it "Professional Wrestling." It allowed us to blow off steam after lunch and usually led into a nap. Then we started getting close to South of the Border. South of the Border is a pit stop and a tourist trap located about halfway between New York and our Florida destination. We stopped there on every trip for two or three hours. My brothers and I would go on all the rides and sample the attractions, while our parents would rest. (They needed the rest, believe me.) We would always make sure to eat one of the foot-long hot dogs that South of the Border was famous for. And who can forget South of the Border cotton candy? South of the Border was always a great treat for us. Not only was it a lot of fun, but it marked the halfway point to grandma's house. When the day was over, we would stay at a motel a couple of hours south of South of the Border. After a good night's sleep, we'd be off again.

Should any of the sentences in this paragraph be combined to reflect proper emphasis? If so, how can the combining take place in order to make the best use of the independent clause? You can experiment with many versions of this paragraph in order to make different things stand out (or recede) in importance.

Principle 2: If something is important, try to put it into the first or last position in the sentence.

It's not always easy to change what goes into an independent clause. Fortunately there is another way to emphasize things in a sentence: pay attention to what falls into the first and last position. After all, readers typically remember best what comes first and last (whether it's what comes first and last in an argument, in a paragraph, or in a sentence). Compare these two sentences:

- *Tootsie*, starring Dustin Hoffman, is one of the five best movie comedies of all time.
- One of the five best movie comedies of all time is *Tootsie*, starring Dustin Hoffman.

These sentences are very similar in content and they have the same independent clause, but you will probably agree that Dustin Hoffman comes off as more prominent in the second sentence. He appears at the very end of sentence 2 (that is, in an emphatic spot), whereas in the first sentence he gets buried in the middle.

With practice, you can learn to make small changes in your sentences to ensure that the most appropriate material comes first or last. Pay special attention to what comes at the very end of sentences so that your sentences don't end on a dull anticlimactic note. Compare, for instance, these two sentences.

- The sixth-largest city in the United States in 1850 was Cincinnati, located on the banks of the Ohio River.
- The sixth-largest city in the United States in 1850, located on the banks of the Ohio River, was Cincinnati.

Principle 3: If something is important, signal it by putting it into an unusual spot in the sentence.

"Something there is that doesn't love a wall," wrote Robert Frost in his famous poem "Mending Wall." He could have written, "There is just something that doesn't love a wall," and in fact that would have been the typical way for that sentence to unfold. But by taking "Something" out of its expected position in the sentence and placing it first, Frost drew attention to the word—an attention that is completely warranted because the rest of the poem meditates on exactly what it is that makes people want to put up walls.

Sentences in English have an expected word order: subjects are followed by verbs and verbs by direct objects; adjectives normally precede the words they modify. There is nothing unusual, therefore, about a sentence such as this one:

- Police quickly learned, during the Prohibition era, to avoid organized, armed, and dangerous thugs like Al Capone.

But what about other versions of the sentence? Notice how the following versions emphasize different words by putting them into unusual positions.

- During the Prohibition Era, the police quickly learned to avoid organized, armed, and dangerous thugs like Al Capone.

- During the Prohibition Era, the police learned, quickly, to avoid organized, armed, and dangerous thugs like Al Capone.
- During the Prohibition Era, the police quickly learned to avoid thugs like Al Capone—organized, armed, and dangerous.

Principle 4: If something is important, think about repeating it within the sentence.

Abraham Lincoln was aware of this principle when in his Gettysburg Address he wrote that "We here highly resolve . . . that government of the people, by the people, and for the people shall not perish from the earth." Repeating a key term (*people* in Lincoln's case) always creates emphasis, and you can do it by using what is called a "resumptive modifier"—a modifier that allows a sentence to start up a second time, as it were. The following five versions of roughly equivalent sentences will illustrate this usage:

- Malcolm X famously embraced the Nation of Islam, but in his stirring speeches he frequently cited the Christian Bible.
- Malcolm X famously embraced the Nation of Islam—embraced it with unwavering commitment—but in his stirring speeches he frequently cited the Christian Bible.
- Malcolm X famously embraced the Nation of Islam—the Nation of Islam that he first encountered in prison—but in his stirring speeches he frequently cited the Christian Bible.
- Malcolm X famously embraced the Nation of Islam, but in his stirring speeches—stirring in their eloquence and rhetorical exuberance—he frequently cited the Christian Bible.
- Malcolm X embraced the Nation of Islam, but in his speeches he frequently cited the Christian Bible, the Christian Bible that his father loved.

Experiment with your sentence structures so that you too can repeat key words within a sentence in order to give those words special emphasis.

Principle 5: If something is important (or unimportant), use punctuation marks—dashes and parentheses and even colons—to signal that importance (or lack of importance)

Let's return to a sentence that we discussed under Principle 3: "During the Prohibition Era, the police quickly learned to avoid thugs like Al Capone—organized, armed, and dangerous." The words *organized, armed, and dangerous* stand out because they are at the end of the sentence, because they are in an unusual spot after the noun that they modify—and because they follow a dash, not a comma.

Don't forget that punctuation marks can be used to emphasize or deemphasize. Dashes in particular are meant to tell the reader "Pay special attention!" while parentheses signal to the reader that something unimportant is coming (so unimportant, perhaps, that we often pay little attention to what comes in parentheses).

Once again, compare several versions of a sentence so that you can see the principle in action:

- Charles Darwin, who dropped out of college for a time, who transferred to another university before his senior year, and who, for lack of anything better to do, drifted aboard *The Beagle* right after graduation, is an inspiration to many contemporary twenty-somethings.

- Charles Darwin—who dropped out of college for a time, who transferred to another university before his senior year, and who, for lack of anything better to do, drifted aboard *The Beagle* right after graduation—is an inspiration to many contemporary twenty-somethings.

- Charles Darwin (who dropped out of college for a time, who transferred to another university before his senior year, and who, for lack of anything better to do, drifted aboard *The Beagle* right after graduation), is an inspiration to many contemporary twenty-somethings.

- Charles Darwin, who dropped out of college for a time, who transferred to another university before his senior year—and who (for lack of anything better to do) drifted aboard *The Beagle* right after graduation— is an inspiration to many contemporary twenty-somethings.

- Charles Darwin, who dropped out of college for a time, who transferred to another university before his senior year (and who, for lack of anything better to do, drifted aboard *The Beagle* right after graduation), is an inspiration—that's right, an inspiration!—to many contemporary twenty-somethings.

In all these cases, commas and dashes and parentheses come in pairs. If you separate a subject from its verb with an interrupter, you will normally want to help the reader by signaling where the interruptions begin and end with a pair of commas, a pair of dashes, or a pair of parentheses. The dashes will emphasize what is enclosed in the interrupter; the parentheses will deemphasize the interruption, and the commas will be neutral.

Additionally, the colon can be used for emphasis. Many people assume that a colon is used only to introduce a list: a series of nouns ("truth, justice, and The American Way"), a series of adjectives ("good, bad, and ugly"), or even a series of phrases or clauses ("of the people, by the people, for the people"). But as a matter of fact, colons when correctly used fulfill two functions: they come at the end (or before—but not within) an independent clause; and they signal the movement from general to specific or specific to general. Sometimes what is specific can be a list of items, but it can also be a single item.

- CORRECT: Martin Luther King, Jr. led four particularly noteworthy civil rights campaigns: the Montgomery bus boycott, the Birmingham demonstrations of 1963, the March on Washington, and the march from Selma to Montgomery in 1965.
- INCORRECT: Four particularly important civil rights campaigns: the Montgomery bus boycott, the Birmingham demonstrations of 1963, the March on Washington, and the march from Selma to Montgomery in 1965, were led by Martin Luther King, Jr.
- CORRECT: *The Godfather*, *Some Like It Hot*, and *Toy Story 3*: these are the three movies I would take with me if I had to spend my life on a deserted island.
- INCORRECT: There are three movies: *The Godfather*, *Some Like It Hot*, and *Toy Story 3*—that I would take with me if I had to spend my life on a deserted island.

And note what happens—emphasis!—when a colon is used to point to an important item (or series of items) that come at the end of a sentence. Here are some examples.

- There's one thing that drives me crazy about him: procrastination.
- There's one thing that drives me crazy about him: his tendency to procrastinate before Christmas.
- There's one thing that drives me crazy about him: every year, no matter what, he procrastinates about buying Christmas gifts.

In the first sentence, a single emphasized noun follows the colon. In the second case, it's an emphatic phrase. It the third, it's a complete independent clause that gets the emphasis. And in all three cases, it is not a series of items that is introduced by the colon, but one single item. Again, the colon marks the movement from general to specific, whether it's a series of several specifics or just one.

A Few Additional Comments on Punctuation

A good grammar handbook will cover myriad uses of the comma, as well as many other forms of punctuation; there is no way to cover everything about the comma in one short chapter. For now, here are a few additional hints about punctuation, some hints designed to generate clarity, emphasis, and grace in your writing.

Use commas within independent clauses to signal key items

Another useful function of commas is using them to alert readers to the key items within independent clauses. Although you should avoid interrupting the subject and verb and direct object with punctuation, you should use marks of punctuation—usually commas, but sometimes dashes or parentheses—to signal whenever there are interrupting items between the subject, verb, and object. Also use marks of punctuation to signal when the subject and verb and object (the independent clause, in other words) begin and end.

Example 1:

> Because Florence houses Michelangelo's most famous sculpture, David, travelers sometimes forget the city's remarkable food, notably its magnificent cheeses and grilled meats.

Example 2:

> Visitors to Florence, thrilled by their viewing of Michelangelo's most famous sculpture, David, sometimes forget the city's remarkable food.

In Example #1, no marks of punctuation interrupt the independent clause ("travelers sometimes forget the city's remarkable food"), but the introductory dependent clause ("Because . . . ") and the final phrase in the sentence (beginning with "notably") are set off from the independent clause by means of commas.

In Example #2, commas mark where the main clause is interrupted: there's a comma after the subject ("Visitors to Florence") and before the verb phrase ("sometimes forget"). You could also substitute a pair of parentheses or dashes.

Use semicolons to separate independent clauses, and for clarity

The semicolon is most commonly used to separate two independent clauses; in a sentence like this one, for example, a semicolon is used instead of a comma plus a coordinating conjunction like *and* or *but*. Remember that the semicolon is typically equivalent to a period; don't use a semicolon unless you could substitute a period for it.

Additionally, semicolons can add clarity to sentences by separating items in a series containing internal commas within the items. For instance:

- Bob Dylan arrived in New York determined to be a folk singer; however, he quickly and repeatedly adapted to new musical forms.
- Bob Dylan arrived in New York determined to be a folk singer, after the example of his hero Woody Guthrie; but before the next decade had passed, a decade that produced electric guitars, he had adapted to new musical forms.
- When Bob Dylan arrived in New York in 1961, the leading recording artists were Chubby Checker, Henry Mancini, and Judy Garland.

■ When Bob Dylan arrived in New York in 1961, the leading recording artists were Chubby Checker, whose series of "Twist" songs would make him wealthy; Judy Garland, whose comeback album *Judy Garland at Carnegie Hall* won a Grammy Award; and, amazingly enough, Henry Mancini, whose "Moon River" was derided as "make-out music" by everyone under 25.

Consult a handbook

There are also many special uses for colons, semicolons, and commas—in citations, for example; and titles, dates, numbers, and so forth. Get a handbook and consult it to guide you through those special uses. No one can remember all the special rules, but everyone can look them up as a way to signal their professionalism.

Use Simple Figures of Speech for a Touch of Class

Emphasizing the proper elements of a sentence is an important key to sentence effectiveness. But would you also like to lend a touch of class and elegance to your prose? In most situations, clarity and emphasis are all that is needed, but sometimes you will want to lend special eloquence to something you are writing. When you want to make something resonate in a special way, what can you do? In ancient times, rhetoricians concocted a number of techniques for giving memorable sparkle to written prose. They called those techniques *tropes* (when they involved a word or two) and *schemes* (when they involved more than a few words). You can Google "schemes" and "tropes" to get a full list of these many techniques. Here we recommend a few particularly effective ones that you can easily incorporate into your prose: metaphors, hyperbole (exaggeration) and litotes (understatement), isocolon (or parallelism), and deliberate fragments and rhetorical questions.

Metaphors

You probably already use metaphors, sometimes unconsciously, but you probably do not use them very frequently. It takes some practice, but with a little thought you can usually come up with a **metaphor** that works—an implied comparison that illuminates and adds emotional punch. "I have a dream," proclaimed Martin Luther King, Jr., at the March on Washington, as he compared our nation's imagined future to a metaphorically beautiful dream. (King was especially good at developing powerful metaphors.) Let us "bind up the nation's wounds," implored Abraham Lincoln, as he compared the body politic to a metaphorical body. But even everyday essays use metaphors for effect, as you can see in the paragraph by E. B. White that is reproduced on page 81.

Hyperbole and litotes: exaggeration and understatement

If it's raining hard outside, you might say to a friend, "We must have had a foot of rain in the past twenty-four hours." A **hyperbole**, or exaggeration, like this is common in oral discourse.

Or you might say, "We've been having a little dampness outside." A **litotes**, or understatement, is another way of making the same point about terrible weather.

You can do the same thing on occasion in your written prose. Hyperbole and litotes can give a sense of voice and texture to your written prose. Especially consider using these tactics in titles, in topic sentences, or in conclusions to paragraphs and segments to add bite to your arguments and to permit you to connect with your readers in a personal way.

One memorable use of litotes was employed by Martin Luther King, Jr. in his 1963 "Letter from Birmingham Jail." King's critics, eight local clergymen, had condemned the demonstrations that he was sponsoring in Birmingham as "untimely." They exhorted him to wait for a better moment, to delay the demonstrations until the newly elected city council had time to settle in. In response to this criticism, King launched a lengthy paragraph defending his actions and condemning segregation. "Perhaps it is easy for those who have never felt the stinging darts of segregation to say 'Wait,'" he wrote—and then he unfurled an amazing sentence of over three hundred words (with items in a series separated by semicolons) that summarized the poverty, humiliation, and abuse that the demonstrators had been putting up with for years. After that came his understated concluding sentence: "I hope, sirs, you can understand our legitimate and unavoidable impatience."

Parallelism

Dr. King, like all good stylists, was also adept at using parallel structure (**isocolon**) to help his readers through difficult sentences and to make his statements more memorable. You have no doubt experienced sentences like these from his "I Have a Dream" speech of August 28, 1963:

- "Now is the time to rise from **the desolate valley of segregation** to **the sunlit path of racial justice**."
- "Nineteen sixty-three is **not an end but a beginning**."
- "We will not be satisfied until **justice rolls down like the waters** and **righteousness like a mighty stream**."
- "I have a dream that my four little children will one day live in a nation where they will be judged not **by the color of their skin** but **by the content of their character**."
- "With this faith we will be able to hew out of the mountain of despair a stone of hope. With this faith we will be able to transform the jangling discords of our nation into a beautiful symphony of brotherhood. With this faith we will be able to work together, to pray together, to struggle together, to go to jail together, to stand up for freedom together, knowing that we will be free one day."

You do not have to be as masterful a stylist as King to create parallel structures in your prose. All you need is some practice.

The rhetorical question

Did you ever begin a paragraph with a question? In oral discourse, questions are common, but they are surprisingly infrequent in written prose. Consider using a rhetorical question in the first position in a paragraph, as a kind of topic sentence. "How do I love thee?" wrote Elizabeth Barrett Browning in the famous love poem addressed to her even more famous husband Robert Browning:

> How do I love thee? Let me count the ways.
> I love thee to the depth and breadth and height
> My soul can reach, when feeling out of sight
> For the ends of being and ideal grace.
> I love thee to the level of every day's
> Most quiet need, by sun and candle-light.
> I love thee freely, as men strive for right.
> I love thee purely, as they turn from praise.
> I love thee with the passion put to use
> In my old griefs, and with my childhood's faith.
> I love thee with a love I seemed to lose
> With my lost saints. I love thee with the breath,
> Smiles, tears, of all my life; and, if God choose,
> I shall but love thee better after death.

Browning structures her poem as a set of answers to an introductory question that organizes her sonnet. As a result, the poem is easy to read, easy to follow. (Note also how Browning effectively repeats her most important word—*love*—and how she effectively uses a semicolon to lend balance to her final sentence. She also uses an isocolon for special effect in the couplet "I love thee freely, as men strive for right. / I love thee purely, as they turn from praise.")

Introductory questions serve prose as well as poetry, and you will find skilled writers using questions to state succinct topics that the rest of paragraphs and segments will address. Rhetorical questions create intimacy with an audience; they indicate that the author has the reader's needs in mind; they personalize prose. And sometimes a rhetorical question at the end of a paragraph or section or even an entire essay can be effective. You've seen that many times, haven't you?

But limit your use of rhetorical questions; used too frequently, they lose their effect, become predictable, and can suggest a patronizing tone, as if the writer is addressing a child.

The deliberate fragment

Another stylistic choice—to make sparingly—is using fragments. Fragments are incomplete sentences that lack a subject, verb, or both—deliberately. Especially in informal and nonacademic writing situations, deliberate

Finding Good Reasons

Can You Distinguish One Style From Another?

Understanding style means being able to make effective choices about the sentences and words you choose in your own prose. But it also means understanding the choices that others make. The following two passages express the same information, but they express it in different ways.

These two images depict the same scene, but with very different styles. How are these styles different? What audience and situation is appropriate for each?

Many plants that are pollinated by insects and animals—examples would be anything pollinated by ants or by the proverbial birds and bees—develop their flowers in three distinct stages. First, there is an initial phase; during this period the plant produces a small but increasing number of flowers each day. Next comes a short peak phase during which most of the flowers are produced. Last comes a final phase when the plant produces a small and decreasing number of flowers each day. Recently many evolutionary biologists, including Dr. Daniel Janzen of the University of Pennsylvania, have been concentrating their efforts on studying the effects of this mass flowering pattern: on how pollinators like bees and ants are attracted to plants and how and why they move from plant to plant. These scientists are showing that many kinds of floral visitors (for example, the ants) prefer to eat plants that produce large numbers of flowers per day. That is presumably because these individual plants are highly conspicuous and because it takes less effort for the pollinators to do their work since the plants are so close together.

Did you ever wonder why the birds and bees seem to be attracted to some flowering plants and not to others? A great many plants, ecologists know, which are pollinated by insects and animals (not by the wind), develop their flowers in three phases. First, a plant such as a catalpa tree will produce a small but increasing number of flowers each day. Next comes a brief peak phase during which the catalpa and its friends produce most of their flowers. Finally, flowering plants will produce a small and decreasing number of flowers per day. In recent years many ecologists have been studying the effects of this mass-flowering pattern on pollinators, questioning how certain flowering patterns attract and influence their behaviors. So far the scientists have established that many species of floral visitors are drawn to eat plants that produce lots of flowers each day, presumably because those plants are easy to spot and produce very satisfying meals. Think of those plants as the McDonald's of the plant world.

Write about it

1. Compare and contrast the sentences and words in the two passages.
2. What audience and situation would be suitable for the first passage? For the second passage?
3. Suppose this information was being presented not in writing but orally. What changes would you recommend for an oral delivery, and how would the passages go?

fragments can be used for emphasis or emotional impact. Examine these two sentences.

- Napoleon, who started to lose his hair at 23, tried several kinds of "cures" for baldness: chicken dung, olive oil, vinegar, even snake venom.
- Napoleon, who started to lose his hair at 23, tried several kinds of "cures" for baldness: chicken dung, olive oil, vinegar. Even snake venom.

The picture of mighty Napoleon as vain enough to worry about hair loss makes us smile, and we smile even more when the last item in the series—snake venom—gets punctuated as if it were its own sentence. It makes Napoleon's narcissism even more dramatic and comic.

Deliberate fragments are usually considered inappropriate in academic writing because its relative formality is incompatible with the tone created by deliberate fragments. And in any writing situation, if you overuse fragments, they lose their special effect.

Choosing Words: Abstract and Concrete, Formal and Informal, Denotation and Connotation

Linguists are fond of saying that there are no exact synonyms in a language like English. True, many words have close equivalents, and we call them synonyms. But they actually have differences based on their relative abstractness, relative formality, and their emotional connotations. When you choose words, think about those three matters.

Abstract and concrete

Words in English can be arrayed in a hierarchy based on relative abstraction. Consider this particular hierarchy:

person
man
athlete
football player
professional football player
professional quarterback
New England Patriots quarterback
Tom Brady

As you move down this list, the words gain in concreteness and lose abstraction. In a given sentence, any one of these words might make sense. Compare "The quarterback at our school will never be a professional quarterback" and "The quarterback at our school will never be a Tom Brady." As a general rule, topic sentences typically require more general language, and supporting sentences work best when they are specific.

Formal and informal

Sometimes you wear formal clothing; sometimes you wear sports clothes; and sometimes you wear jeans and a T-shirt. And so it is with writing: sometimes you will want to choose formal words; sometimes you will find less formal words appropriate; and sometimes you'll pick colloquialism. Compare the following sentences and you will immediately see what we mean.

- Whenever our physics teacher announces an impending examination, it is an invitation to study assiduously.
- When our physics teacher announces a test, it motivates me to study all weekend.
- When the math teach drops an exam on us, it pays to hit the books.

No wonder Abraham Lincoln at Gettysburg said "Fourscore and seven years ago, our fathers brought forth on this continent a new nation" and not "Eighty-seven years ago the founders made the U.S. of A."

Denotation and connotation

As you write, note that many words carry ***connotations***, emotional associations that go beyond dictionary definitions; other words are relatively neutral. To put it another way, two words might denote the same thing—that is, they point to the same activity or concept or proper noun—but have very different meanings depending on the emotional values attached to the words. Suppose, for example, that after a championship victory, fans might gather to celebrate; they take over some streets, block traffic, and things begin to get out of hand. Some minor damage ensues, a few people are injured and some are arrested when they refuse police commands to leave, and people litter the area with debris. Most people would term what happened a "riot," especially if there are injuries and extensive mayhem; but some of the celebrators would call it a "disturbance" because they would wish to minimize the significance of the damage. "Riot" and "disturbance": the two have very different connotations. And what would be the connotation if the event were called "a wild party"?

Summing Up

Becoming a stylist—and becoming a wise observer of style—takes practice and attention. It is really a lifetime process of attending to nuances in sentences, words, and punctuation marks. This chapter is only a start, something to build on. In the end, developing an effective style is about generating a variety of possibilities and choosing from among them. Don't settle on your first version of a sentence; play with it and generate several versions. Concoct alternatives and listen to the differences. Then pick the version that is most suitable to your aim and audience. And have fun doing it.

The following is excerpted from E. B. White's 1939 essay "Education." Note White's use of figurative language, particularly his use of metaphor and hyperbole. In addition, note White's use of specific diction that is often highly connotative. How do those figures of speech and word choices reinforce White's purpose? (White's essay is printed in full on pages 195–197.)

Note how the school bus is compared with "death," a death that is punctual and as hungry as a wild animal.

hyperbole

What are the connotations of words such as "old sweater," "cold curb," "suck in," "worked on," "athletic instructor," and so forth?

Note the hyperboles "sallied forth" and "scholar"

Note this second metaphor for the bus: it is like an impersonal train that treats people like baggage.

hyperbole

His days were rich in formal experience. Wearing overalls and an old sweater (the accepted uniform of the private seminary), he sallied forth at morn accompanied by a nurse or a parent and walked (or was pulled) two blocks to a corner where the school bus made a flag stop. This flashy vehicle was as punctual as death: seeing us waiting at the cold curb, it would sweep to a halt, open its mouth, suck the boy in, and spring away with an angry growl. It was a good deal like a train picking up a bag of mail. At school the scholar was worked on for six or seven hours by half a dozen teachers and a nurse, and was revived on orange juice in mid-morning. In a cinder court he played games supervised by an athletic instructor, and in a cafeteria he ate lunch worked out by a dietitian. He soon learned to read with gratifying facility and discernment and to make Indian weapons of a semi-deadly nature.

Analyzing Arguments

PART

2

7 | Analyzing a Written Argument

In this chapter, you will learn that

1. A rhetorical analysis aims to understand how people attempt to persuade through language and other actions (see below)

2. A rhetorical analysis examines how a text is structured, including choices of language, subject matter, organization, and appeals to the audience (see pages 85–89)

3. A rhetorical analysis considers the broader context, including how a particular text takes part in a larger conversation going on at the time (see pages 89–93)

What Is Rhetorical Analysis?

To many people, the term *rhetoric* suggests speech or writing that is highly ornamental or deceptive or manipulative. You might hear someone say, "That politician is just using a bunch of rhetoric" or "The rhetoric of that advertisement is very deceiving." But *rhetoric* is also used these days in a positive or neutral sense to describe human communication; for instance, "*Silent Spring* is one of the most influential pieces of environmental rhetoric ever written." When we study rhetoric, we usually associate it with effective communication, following Aristotle's classic definition of rhetoric as "the art of finding in any given case the available means of persuasion."

Rhetoric is not just a means of *producing* effective communication. It is also a way of *understanding* communication. The two aspects mutually support one another: becoming a better writer makes you a better interpreter, and becoming a better interpreter makes you a better writer.

Rhetorical analysis is the effort to understand how people attempt to influence others through language and more broadly through every kind of symbolic action—not only speeches, articles, and books, but also architecture, movies, television shows, memorials, Web sites, advertisements, photos and other images, dance, and popular songs. It might be helpful to think of rhetorical analysis as a kind of critical reading. Critical reading—rhetorical analysis, that is—involves studying carefully any kind of persuasive action in order to understand it better and to appreciate the tactics that it uses.

Build a Rhetorical Analysis

Rhetorical analysis examines how an idea is shaped and presented to an audience in a particular form for a specific purpose. There are many approaches to rhetorical analysis and no one "correct" way to do it. Generally, though, approaches to rhetorical analysis can be placed between two broad extremes—not mutually exclusive categories but extremes at the ends of a continuum.

At one end of the continuum are analyses that concentrate more on **texts** than on contexts. They typically use rhetorical concepts and terminologies to analyze the features of texts. Let's call this approach **textual analysis**. At the other extreme are approaches that emphasize **context** over text. These focus on reconstructing the cultural environment, or context, that existed when a particular rhetorical event took place. That reconstruction provides clues about the persuasive tactics and appeals. Those who undertake **contextual analysis** regard particular rhetorical acts as parts of larger communicative chains, or "conversations."

Now let's examine these two approaches in detail.

Analyze the Rhetorical Features: Textual Analysis

Just as expert teachers in every field of endeavor—from baseball to biology—devise vocabularies to facilitate specialized study, rhetoricians too have developed a set of key concepts to describe rhetorical activities. A fundamental concept in rhetoric is audience. But there are many others. Classical rhetoricians in the tradition of Aristotle, Quintilian, and Cicero developed a range of terms around what they called the canons of rhetoric in order to describe some of the actions of communicators: *inventio* (invention—the finding or creation of information for persuasive acts, and the planning of strategies), *dispostio* (arrangement), *elocutio* (style), *memoria* (the recollection of rhetorical resources that one might call upon, as well as the memorization of what has been invented and arranged), and *pronuntiatio* (delivery). These five canons generally describe the actions of any persuader, from preliminary planning to final delivery.

Over the years, as written discourse gained in prestige against oral discourse, four canons (excepting *memoria*) led to the development of concepts and terms useful for rhetorical analysis. Terms like *ethos, pathos,* and *logos,* all associated with invention, account for features of texts related to the trustworthiness and credibility of the writer or speaker (**ethos**), for the persuasive good reasons in an argument that derive from a community's mostly deeply held values (**pathos**), and for the good reasons that emerge from intellectual reasoning (**logos**). Fundamental to the classical approach to rhetoric is the concept of *decorum,* or "appropriateness": Everything within a persuasive act can be understood as reflecting a central rhetorical goal that governs consistent choices according to occasion and audience.

The statue of Castor stands at the entrance of the Piazza del Campidoglio in Rome. A textual analysis focuses on the statue itself. The size and realism of the statue makes it a masterpiece of classical Roman sculpture.

An example will make textual rhetorical analysis clearer. Let's look at the "Statement on the Articles of Impeachment" by Barbara Jordan at the end of this chapter, and at the student rhetorical analysis that follows it (pp. 100–108). In this chapter we use the fundamental concepts of rhetoric to better understand the presentation by Barbara Jordan.

Jordan's purpose and argument

What is the purpose of Jordan's speech? She presented it over thirty-five years ago, but it remains compellingly readable because it concerns a perennial (and very contemporary) American issue: the limits of presidential power. In this case, Jordan argues in favor of bringing articles of impeachment against President Richard Nixon. She feels that the drastic step of impeachment is called for because President Nixon had violated the Constitution. Essentially Jordan's argument comes down to this: Nixon, like any abuser of the Constitution, should be removed from office because he has been guilty of causing "the dimunition, the subversion, the destruction, of the Constitution" (para. 3 of Jordan's speech). The Founders of the nation established clear grounds for impeachment, and Nixon trespassed on those grounds by covering up crimes and by stonewalling efforts to investigate misdeeds. He "committed offenses, and planned and directed and acquiesced in a course of conduct which the Constitution will not tolerate" (para. 20). Jordan's

A contextual analysis focuses on the surroundings and history of the statue. According to legend, Castor (left of staircase) and his twin brother Pollux (right of staircase), the mythical sons of Leda, assisted Romans in an early battle. Romans built a large temple in the Forum to honor them. The statues were discovered in the sixteenth century and in 1583 were brought to stand at the top of the Cordonata, a staircase designed by Michelangelo as part of a renovation of the Piazza del Campidoglio commissioned by Pope Paul III Farnese in 1536.

speech amounts to a definition of impeachment in general, based on the Constitution, which then calls for President Nixon's impeachment in particular.

Jordan's use of logos, pathos, and ethos

Logos

Jordan constructs her case in favor of impeachment through a carefully reasoned process. She begins by presenting a patient account of the meaning of impeachment as it appears in the Constitution, on which her "faith is whole; it is complete; it is total" (para. 3). The Constitution defines impeachment not as conviction but as a kind of indictment of a president for misconduct; once a president is impeached, a trial then follows, conducted by the House of Representatives and judged by the Senate. Only after conviction by two-thirds of the senators, after a fair trial, could the president be removed. (You might remember that President Clinton was impeached while in office, but the Senate found him not guilty.) The Constitution offers grounds for impeachment only on very general terms: Article III, section 4, explains that presidents can be removed from office for treason, bribery, or other high crimes and misdemeanors.

Do Nixon's actions qualify as impeachable? Jordan must refer to the statements that the Founders made during the ratification process for the Constitution to lay out exactly what might be considered an impeachable high crime. After a lengthy explanation of what qualifies as impeachable—"the misconduct of public men" only in "occasional and extraordinary cases," and only "if the President be connected in any suspicious manner with any person and there [are] grounds to believe he will shelter him," and only if there are "great misdemeanors" and not simple "maladministration"—she then applies the definition to Nixon's actions. Carefully and systematically she offers the evidence. She ties "misconduct," the cover-up of crimes, and the sanctioning of other misdeeds to Nixon: "the President had knowledge that these funds were being paid" (para. 15); he consorted with a range of suspicious characters and "knew about the break-in of the psychiatrist's office" (para. 16); and he "engaged in a series of public statements and actions designed to thwart the lawful investigation of government prosecutors" (para. 17). The conclusion follows rationally and inevitably. The president must be impeached.

Pathos

The logical appeals in Jordan's speech are reinforced by her emotional appeals. Her repeated references to the Constitution have a strong emotional appeal. Because Americans have a deep respect for the Constitution, any attempt to undermine it must be resisted firmly and forcefully.

Perhaps the speech's most powerful emotional moment comes in the second paragraph. By bringing up the famous "We the people" opening of the Constitution early in the speech, Jordan rouses passions and brings listeners to her side. She calls attention to how she as an African American woman was originally left out of the Constitution because it defined citizens only as white males. The appeal to fair play certainly rouses emotions in her listeners; it gains considerable sympathy for Jordan.

You can probably note many other points in the speech that carry an emotional dimension. Jordan concludes her speech by rightly saying that "it is reason, and not passion, which must guide our deliberations, guide our debate, and guide our decision." But she also brings considerable pathos to bear on her argument. Jordan appeals to the whole person.

Ethos

Why do we take Jordan's word about the legal precedents and evidence that she cites? It is because she establishes her *ethos*, or trustworthiness, early in the essay and sustains it throughout. Jordan's scholarship establishes her credibility as a lawyer and as a citizen. Jordan comes through as a thorough professional, as an educated lawyer who has studied constitutional law and has done her homework, and as a deeply concerned citizen. Consequently, we can trust her word and trust her judgment. Particularly effective is her citation of the historical record on impeachment. She has sifted the records to draw from the most respected of the framers of the Constitution—notably James Madison—and from authorities later in our national history. She buttresses her trustworthiness in other ways too:

- She quotes widely, if unobtrusively: by using precise quotations, she adds a trustworthy scholarly dimension to her presentation.
- She touches lightly on her own status as an African American woman to lend firsthand authority to what she has to say.
- She demonstrates a knowledge of history and constitutional law.
- She connects herself to America generally by linking herself to traditional American values such as freedom, ethnic pride, fair play, and tolerance.

Jordan knew that Nixon's supporters were depending on being able to make the case against Nixon into a partisan matter, Democrats vs. Republicans. So in her speech Jordan goes to great length to avoid being placed in a partisan camp and to be regarded as fair-minded. Overall, she comes off as hard-working, honest, educated and patriotic. And definitely credible.

Jordan's arrangement

We have already said some things about the arrangement of Jordan's speech. We especially noted how the overall structure follows the pattern of most definition arguments: Jordan offers her definition of impeachment and then in the final third of the talk applies that definition to the case of Richard Nixon. Note how she begins with an introductory comment about her personal situation; the tone of the first few sentences is light-hearted as she offers gentle humor to "Mr. Chairman." And then she turns to a personal anecdote about her being left out of the Constitution "by mistake." In many ways, then, Jordan organizes very conventionally— she has a clear beginning, middle, and end.

And yet in other ways the arrangement is not so conventional. Rather than sticking with a light tone, Jordan turns deadly serious in paragraph 3. In the manner of a lawyer stating a legal case, a lawyer offering a final argument after evidence has been heard, she announces that her presentation will be based solely on constitutional law, and she then follows with point after point of a formal legal brief in favor of impeachment. Note that Jordan does not announce her conclusion early; just as if she were addressing a jury, she postpones her thesis ("If the impeachment provision in the Constitution will not reach the offenses charged here, then perhaps that 18th-century Constitution should be abandoned to a 20th-century paper shredder": para. 19) until the very end. Had she begun with such an explicit statement of her thesis, had she begun by stating her conclusion early, her speech might have been dismissed as a partisan speech and not a legal case.

Jordan's style

What about Jordan's style? How is it appropriate to her purposes? Would you describe it as "lawyerly" or not?

In one sense, Jordan speaks very much as a lawyer would speak to other lawyers. Her fourth paragraph, for example, consists solely of legal language—so legal that it is difficult for a layperson to understand where these quotations come from and what they mean. And further quotations from law cases show up as the speech continues. It is as if Jordan is addressing lawyers because she repeatedly uses legal terminology: "proceed forthwith"; "obfuscation"; "the powers relating to impeachment are an essential check in the hands of the body of the legislature against and upon the encroachments of the executive"; "the framers confided in the Congress the power, if need be, to remove the President"; "a narrowly channeled exception to the separation-of-powers maxim"; and so on.

And yet in another sense, Jordan is speaking in an accessible way to a larger audience of all Americans. Rather than sustaining the legal language, she speaks in simple sentences and simple cadences from beginning to the very end—from "Today I am an inquisitor. . . . My faith in the Constitution is whole; it is complete; it is total" to "That's the question. We know that. We know the question. . . . It is reason, not passion, which must guide our deliberations, guide our debate, and guide our decision." Whenever legal jargon threatens to take over, Jordan returns to everyday language accessible to all: "The Constitution doesn't say that"; "they [the framers] did not make the accusers and the judgers the same person"; "we are trying to be big because the task before us is a big one"; "we know the nature of impeachment. We've been talking of it awhile now." In sum, Jordan's style is in keeping with her ethos. Because she wishes to come off as both a concerned citizen and a legal expert, she chooses a style that is one part newspaper reporting—simple, straightforward, unadorned (in one spot she even misspeaks, substituting "attended" for "intended")—and one part legal brief, technical and jargony, full of convolutions and qualifications.

There is more to say about the rhetorical choices that Jordan made in crafting her "Statement on the Articles of Impeachment," but this analysis is enough to illustrate our main point. Textual rhetorical analysis employs rhetorical terminology—in this case, terms borrowed from the rhetorical tradition such as ethos, pathos, logos, arrangement, style, and tone—as a way of helping us to understand how a writer makes choices to achieve certain effects. And textual analysis cooperates with contextual analysis.

Analyze the Rhetorical Context

Communication as conversation

Notice that in the previous discussion, the fact that Barbara Jordan's "Statement on the Articles of Impeachment" was originally delivered before the House Judiciary Committee did not matter much. Nor did it matter when the speech was published

(July 24, 1974), who gave it, who exactly heard the speech, what their reaction was, or what other people were saying at the time. Textual analysis can proceed as if the item under consideration "speaks for all time," as if it is a museum piece unaffected by time and space. There's nothing wrong with museums, of course; they permit people to observe and appreciate objects in an important way. But museums often fail to reproduce an artwork's original context and cultural meaning. In that sense, museums can diminish understanding as much as they contribute to it. Contextual rhetorical analysis is an attempt to understand communications through the lens of their environments, examining the rough-and-tumble, real-world setting or scene out of which any communication emerges. Contextual analysis thus complements textual analysis; the two work together.

Contextual analysis, like textual analysis, may be conducted in any number of ways. But contextual rhetorical analysis always proceeds from a description of the **rhetorical situation** that motivated the event in question. It demands an appreciation of the social circumstances that call rhetorical events into being and that orchestrate the course of those events. It regards communications as anything but self-contained.

- Every communication is a response to other communications and to other social practices.
- Communications, and social practices more generally, reflect the attitudes and values of the living communities that sustain them.
- Analysts seek evidence of how those other communications and social practices are reflected in texts.

Rhetorical analysis from a contextualist perspective understands individual pieces as parts of ongoing conversations.

The challenge is to reconstruct the conversation surrounding a specific piece of writing or speaking. Sometimes it is easy to do so. For example, sometimes there are obvious references to the context in the very words of an argument. Or sometimes you may have appropriate background information on the topic, as well as a feel for what is behind what people are writing or saying about it. People who have strong feelings these days about the environment, stem cell research, college sports, or any number of other current issues are well informed about the arguments that are converging around those topics.

But other times it takes some research to reconstruct the conversations and social practices related to a particular issue. If the issue is current, you need to study how the debate is conducted in current blogs, magazines, newspapers, talk shows, movies and TV shows, Web sites, and so forth. If the issue is from an earlier time, you must do archival research into historical collections of newspapers, magazines, books, letters, and other documentary sources in order to develop a feel for the rhetorical situation that generated the argument under analysis. Archival research usually involves libraries, special research collections, or film and television archives where it is possible to learn quite a bit about context.

Let's return now to a discussion of Jordan's "Statement" on pages 100–103. With a bit of research it is possible to reconstruct some of the "conversations" that Jordan is participating in, and the result will be an enhanced understanding of her speech as well as an appreciation for how you might do a contextual rhetorical analysis yourself.

Jordan's life and works

You can begin by learning more about Jordan herself because ethos is not simply a textual presence; ethos also can be something that a writer or speaker brings to a performance. The headnote to the speech on page 100 provides some facts about her (e.g., that she was African American, that she went to law school, that she was elected to the U.S. House of Representatives at the age of just 36; that she came to prominence during the Watergate hearings). The speech itself suggests a few additional details: that protecting the Constitution was a special passion of hers, and that she had a reputation for doing her homework. You can learn more about Jordan by using the Internet and your library's Web site. Jordan's credibility, her ethos, is established not just by the decisions she made within her speech but also by her prior reputation.

Perhaps the most relevant information concerning Jordan that is available online is about her early political career. Jordan was a relative unknown when she gave her speech; even her colleagues in Congress did not know her well. She had recently been elected to Congress as a young woman in part because of the support of Lyndon Johnson, a fellow Texan who preceded Richard Nixon as president. Johnson then advocated for her placement on the House Judiciary Committee, chaired by Democrat Peter Rodino of New Jersey; this was a highly prized, prestigious appointment that rarely goes to a freshman congressperson. Thus Jordan came to her speech with a reputation as being beholden to Johnson and the Democratic party. Her challenge therefore was to avoid the appearance of partisanship—as we will show below, that explains many of her rhetorical choices. Then again, few Americans outside Washington and Texas knew of her reputation. She essentially delivered her speech to the nation and to her congressional colleagues as a relative unknown. (Incidentally, Jordan continued to serve in Congress until 1978, when she stepped down voluntarily, for health reasons.)

The context of the speech

In one sense, the audience of Jordan's speech consisted of the other 34 members of the House Judiciary Committee, gathered together to decide whether or not to recommend impeachment. And yet Jordan was not at all speaking to a closed committee meeting. Her speech was very public.

The Senate Watergate hearings had been televised the summer before Jordan's speech, from May through July of 1973. Millions of Americans had become accustomed to watching sensational testimony presented by a host of witnesses.

The hearings produced charges that President Nixon may well have authorized break-ins at Democratic campaign headquarters in Washington during the 1972 election season, that he and members of his leadership team covered up their sponsorship of the break-ins, and that the White House was involved in all sorts of other dirty tricks and improprieties.

Americans remained deeply divided about these accusations until it was discovered that Nixon had himself collected possible hard evidence. He had taped many conversations in the Oval Office, tapes that could support or refute the charges against the president. But for the next year, Nixon engaged in a protracted legal battle to keep the tapes from being disclosed, on the grounds that they were private conversations protected under "executive privilege." During that time Nixon's vice president, Spiro Agnew, was forced to resign, and a number of his advisers were indicted and convicted on charges of obstructing justice. Partial and edited transcripts of the tapes were produced sporadically by the president, under pressure, but those produced only further rancor, particularly when 18 minutes of a key conversation were mysteriously erased.

These events created a continuing national uproar and sustained headlines that fueled discussion. The House Judiciary Committee opened hearings into whether the president should be impeached beginning on May 9 of 1974. Those closed meetings moved slowly, deliberately, and inconclusively through the entire summer. On July 24, 1974, the courts ruled that Nixon had to turn all his remaining tapes over. That same day, knowing that hard evidence was now at hand, the House Judiciary Committee immediately went into session to vote whether to impeach Nixon. In keeping with the Senate Watergate hearings, these sessions were open and televised to the nation. Each member of the committee was given 15 minutes to make an opening statement that would be carried on television to the nation. Barbara Jordan was therefore speaking not just to congressional colleagues but to millions of citizens who had never heard of her but who were very interested in what she would have to say.

Jordan was scheduled to speak at 9 p.m.—prime time. The nation was ready to listen to her argument, and she was ready to deliver: she would call for impeachment, and she would do so in a way that was absolutely principled and nonpartisan.

The larger conversation

We could offer much more contextualizing background here. We could cite a host of articles, books, news reports, and TV broadcasts in order to establish the nature of the conversation about impeachment that was raging in the nation from the summer of 1973 until President Nixon finally resigned on August 8, 1974. Such an account would establish a rather simple point: the country was bitterly divided on three related issues.

The first was a question of partisanship. His fellow Republicans naturally gave the benefit of the doubt to President Nixon, and that benefit was quite considerable, given that Nixon had won the 1972 election over George McGovern in a

landslide. By contrast, Democrats controlled the Senate and the House of Representatives, and they were aggressive in pursuing a case against the president
because they stood to gain politically. (Indeed, Jimmy Carter would win the
presidency in the 1976 election largely because he stood as an honest antidote to
the scandal of Watergate.) But partisanship was not supposed to be an issue in
an impeachment. When Andrew Johnson was impeached by the House during
1867–1868 (and narrowly acquitted by the Senate), it was apparent that his impeachment was politically motivated. In subsequent years, it therefore was understood that impeachment should never be partisan, should never be
politically motivated but based on "treason, bribery, or high crimes and misdemeanors." In the weeks leading up to July 24, supporters of President Nixon, led
by his lawyer James D. St. Clair, constantly charged that his adversaries were motivated by purely political purposes. Representative David Dennis of Indiana
spoke explicitly of "a political lynching," Representative Charles Sandman of
New Jersey and other Republicans had emphasized partisanship earlier in the
day during their own 15-minute presentations, and millions of average citizens
also suspected that opponents of Nixon wanted to remove him simply to gain
political power. On a practical level, since Nixon could be convicted in the Senate only by a two-thirds majority, it was essential that some Republicans come
to support conviction. A purely partisan vote—Democratic vs. Republicans—
could not succeed.

Barbara Jordan's task was therefore formidable. She had to take the majority,
Democratic position—without seeming to take it *because* she was a Democrat. And
she had to do so even though she was indeed a committed Democrat, recently installed in part through the intercession of Lyndon Johnson and embodying her
Democratic credentials because of her black skin. (Nixon had swept the Southern
states in the 1972 election in part because he appealed directly to white voters
there.) If you scan issues of *Newsweek*, *Time*, the *Washington Post*, or the *New York
Times* from the summer of 1974, you will see how frequently the Republicans were
claiming that President Nixon was the victim of a "partisan vendetta." It was the
strategy of his defense team to do so. By contrast, Democrats needed to get at least
a half-dozen Republican members of the House Judiciary Committee to support
impeachment if the actual impeachment were to succeed in the Senate.

Jordan consequently adopted a number of tactics to establish her nonparti-
sanship. She begins by identifying herself as a youthful, junior member of the committee, not a Democratic member, and quickly follows by claiming particular and
fervent allegiance to the Constitution, not to any political party. Speaking as a cus-
todian of "the public trust," she quotes the Constitution, its framers, and respected
authorities such as Alexander Hamilton, Woodrow Wilson, James Madison—
several of them southerners—and avoids names with a partisan identification. And
she consistently and frequently uses the pronoun *we* to refer to the entire committee, Republicans and Democrats alike. In all these ways Jordan sought to address
the nation on nonpartisan grounds. (And she must have succeeded: over the next
three days, when the House Judiciary Committee voted in favor of three articles of

impeachment—obstruction of justice, abuse of presidential power, and contempt of Congress—six of the seventeen Republican committee members voted in favor of the first, six in favor of the second, and two supported the third article. Only ten of the seventeen Republicans opposed all three articles.)

The second concern in the nation on July 24, 1974, was about hard evidence. The president's former lawyer, John Dean, had accused Nixon of obstructing justice and conspiring to give hush money to Watergate burglars; Watergate gangster Charles Colson at his sentencing hearing had recently claimed that the president obstructed justice; and many other charges had been raised. But supporting evidence was seen as circumstantial; it all appeared to be the president's word against the word of others. The conversation swirling around Barbara Jordan, therefore, was very much concerned with hard evidence, or a so-called "murder weapon" or "smoking gun." Supporters of the president, including Representatives Trent Lott and Charles Wiggins on the Judiciary Committee, constantly claimed that while the charges against Nixon were serious, they were not corroborated by irrefutable evidence. (This claim was ultimately addressed by the tapes that Nixon had collected: earlier on the very day that Jordan spoke, the Supreme Court in an 8–0 vote demanded that Nixon turn over 64 tapes to investigators, and those tapes provided the damning evidence that finally brought Nixon to resign two weeks later. The Supreme Court decision is alluded to in the first sentence of paragraph 13, when Jordan mentions the "new evidence that would be forthcoming" because of what happened "today.")

In her speech, Jordan addresses the evidence question explicitly, beginning in paragraph 11: "we were told that the evidence which purports to support the allegations . . . is thin . . . [and] insufficient." The paragraphs that follow rehearse hard evidence already established—evidence about the break-ins and other crimes committed by Howard Hunt as well as payments to Hunt; evidence about the payment of hush money (para. 15); evidence cited in paragraphs 16 and 17, including that "the President has made public announcements and assertions bearing on the Watergate case which . . . he knew to be false." The emphasis on evidence in Jordan's speech definitely derives from the conversations that she was enmeshed in during July 1974.

The third national concern that Jordan addressed in her speech had to do with a legal issue, one that as a lawyer Jordan was especially qualified to address: Were the actions of President Nixon serious enough to be "impeachable offenses"? As the evidence of presidential wrongdoing piled up, many Americans could see that Nixon had committed all sorts of transgressions. But were they serious enough to justify impeachment? Everyone agreed that if the president had committed a felony, he should be removed; but what about lesser offenses—how high did a crime have to reach in order to be a "high crime," and what "misdemeanors" justified impeachment? As we have already shown in our textual analysis, Jordan in paragraph 6 defines the circumstances of impeachment by quoting the framers of the Constitution directly, and in paragraph 7 concedes that a president should not be removed for incompetence (i.e., "maladministration"). The following paragraphs indicate that public officials should not be removed for "petty reasons" but only for "the grossest offenses." By agreeing that a president should be removed only for very serious offenses, and by establishing that there was indeed hard evidence of the president's guilt in serious offenses, Jordan in just 10 or 12 minutes summed up for the nation the case for impeachment. And as we have seen, she did it in a language that was convincing both to her congressional colleagues and to the millions of citizens watching at home.

Barbara Jordan's specific contribution to the conversation about impeachment in 1974 could be extended for a long time—indefinitely, in fact. There is no need to belabor the point, however; our purpose has been simply to illustrate that contextual analysis of a piece of rhetoric can enrich our understanding of it.

Write a Rhetorical Analysis

Effective rhetorical analysis, as we have seen, can be textual or contextual in nature. But we should emphasize again that these two approaches to rhetorical analysis are not mutually exclusive. Indeed, many if not most analysts operate between these two extremes; they consider the details of the text, but they also attend to the particulars of context. Textual analysis and contextual analysis inevitably complement each other. Getting at what is at stake in Barbara Jordan's speech on impeachment or any other sophisticated argument takes patience and intelligence. Rhetorical analysis, as a way of understanding how people argue, is both enlightening and challenging.

Try to use elements of both kinds of analysis whenever you want to understand a rhetorical event more fully. Rhetoric is "inside" texts, but it is also "outside" them: specific rhetorical performances are an irreducible mixture of text and context, and so interpretation and analysis of those performances must account for both text and context. Remember, however, the limitations of your analysis. Realize that your analysis will always be somewhat partial and incomplete, ready to be deepened, corrected, modified, and extended by the insights of others. Rhetorical analysis can itself be part of an unending conversation—a way of learning and teaching within a community.

Finding Good Reasons

"How Can We Understand the Formulation and Development of Public Policy?"

Barbara Jordan speaks during the Watergate hearings.

When Barbara Jordan made her "Statement on the Articles of Impeachment," she spoke in her capacity as a respected member of Congress. She was positioned to influence her primary audience, the House Judiciary Committee. That body was about to make one of the most significant decisions ever made by the United States legislature. She had an opportunity to influence that decision through her reasoned and thoughtful recommendation. Few of us will find ourselves in the situation where we can have such a direct impact on policy decisions. But as a citizen one has the right—some would say the responsibility—to participate in the conversation. And in order to participate, citizens also have a responsibility to understand contributions to the conversation—a responsibility to engage in rhetorical analysis.

The op-ed pages of newspapers and magazines provide a forum for individual citizens to express their opinions about any number of issues: Should schools eliminate Latin language programs to cut costs? Should a new athletic field be built in a local park? Should the United States become involved in political conflicts in other countries? Those op-edd contributions can engage you in the act of rhetorical analysis.

Write about it

1. Make a list of the issues being discussed in the local or national media right now. Then find an op-ed article in a print or online newspaper or magazine about a topic you are interested in.

2. What do you know about the context of the discussion? Why do people hold their views on various sides of the issue? Is the author of the item you are analyzing an expert in the field or a respected analyst? You may need to do some research in order to fully understand the larger public discussion.

3. Using the discussion of Jordan's speech and the guidelines on page 98–99, write an analysis of the text you have chosen. Given its context, how effective and adequate is the writer's argument? What choices has the writer made in order to support his or her points?

Steps to Writing a Rhetorical Analysis

Step 1 Select an Argument to Analyze

Find an argument to analyze—a speech or sermon, an op-ed in a newspaper, an ad in a magazine designed for a particular audience, or a commentary on a talk show.

Examples

- Editorial pages of newspapers (but not letters to the editor unless you can find a long and detailed letter)
- Opinion features in magazines such as *Time, Newsweek*, and *U.S. News & World Report*
- Magazines that take political positions such as *National Review, Mother Jones, New Republic, Nation*, and *Slate*
- Web sites of activist organizations (but not blog or newsgroup postings unless they are long and detailed)

Step 2 Analyze the Context

Who is the author?

Through research in the library or on the Web, learn all you can about the author.
- How does the argument you are analyzing repeat arguments previously made by the author?
- What motivated the author to write? What is the author's purpose for writing this argument?

Who is the audience?

Through research, learn all you can about the publication and the audience.
- Who is the anticipated audience?
- How do the occasion and forum for writing affect the argument?

What is the larger conversation?

Through research, find out what else was being said about the subject of your selection. Track down any references made in the text you are examining.
- When did the argument appear?
- What other concurrent pieces within the "cultural conversation" (e.g., TV shows, other articles, speeches, Web sites) does the item you are analyzing respond to or "answer"?
- Think of the author of the item you are analyzing as facing a "challenge": what difficulties does the author have to overcome in order to persuade his or her audience?

Step 3 Analyze the Text

Summarize the argument
- What is the main claim?
- What reasons are given in support of the claim?

- How is the argument organized? What are the components, and why are they presented in that order?

What is the medium and genre?

- What is the medium? A newspaper? a scholarly journal? a Web site?
- What is the genre? An editorial? an essay? a speech? an advertisement? What expectations does the audience have about this genre?

What appeals are used?

- Analyze the ethos. How does the writer represent himself or herself? Does the writer have any credentials as an authority on the topic? How does the writer establish reliability and trust—or fail to do so?
- Analyze the logos. Where do you find facts and evidence in the argument? What kinds of facts and evidence does the writer present? Direct observation? statistics? interviews? surveys? quotations from authorities?
- Analyze the pathos. Does the writer attempt to invoke an emotional response? Where do you find appeals to important shared values?

How would you characterize the style?

- Is the style formal, informal, satirical, or something else?
- Are any metaphors or other rhetorical figures used?

Step 4 Write a Draft

Introduction

- Describe briefly the argument you are analyzing, including where it was published, how long it is, and who wrote it.
- If the argument is about an issue unfamiliar to your readers, supply the necessary background.

Body

- Analyze the context, following Step 2.
- Analyze the text, following Step 3.

Conclusion

- Do more than simply summarize what you have said. You might, for example, end with an example that typifies the argument.
- You don't have to end by either agreeing or disagreeing with the writer. Your task in this assignment is to analyze the strategies the writer uses.

Step 5 Revise, Edit, Proofread

For detailed instructions, see Chapter 5.
For a checklist to evaluate your draft, see pages 61–62.

Barbara Jordan

Statement on the Articles of Impeachment

Barbara Jordan (1936–1996) grew up in Houston and received a law degree from Boston University in 1959. Working on John F. Kennedy's 1960 presidential campaign stirred an interest in politics, and in 1966 Jordon became the first African American woman elected to the Texas State Senate. In 1972 she was elected to the United States House of Representatives and thus became the first African American woman from the South ever to serve in Congress. Jordan was appointed to the House Judiciary Committee. Soon she was in the national spotlight when that committee considered articles of impeachment against President Richard Nixon, who had illegally covered up a burglary of Democratic Party headquarters during the 1972 election. When Nixon's criminal acts reached the Judiciary Committee, Jordan's opening speech on July 24, 1974, set the tone for the debate and established her reputation as a moral beacon for the nation. Nixon resigned as president on August 9, 1974, when it was evident that he would be impeached

T hank you, Mr. Chairman.
   Mr. Chairman, I join my colleague Mr. Rangel in thanking you for giving the junior members of this committee the glorious opportunity of sharing the pain of this inquiry. Mr. Chairman, you are a strong man and it has not been easy, but we have tried as best we can to give you as much assistance as possible.

2   Earlier today, we heard the beginning of the Preamble to the Constitution of the United States: "We, the people." It's a very eloquent beginning. But when that document was completed on the seventeenth of September in 1787, I was not included in that "We, the people." I felt somehow for many years that George Washington and Alexander Hamilton just left me out by mistake. But through the process of amendment, interpretation, and court decision, I have finally been included in "We, the people."

3   Today I am an inquisitor. Any hyperbole would not be fictional and would not overstate the solemnness that I feel right now. My faith in the Constitution is whole; it is complete; it is total. And I am not going to sit here and be an idle spectator to the diminution, the subversion, the destruction, of the Constitution.

4   "Who can so properly be the inquisitors for the nation as the representatives of the nation themselves?" "The subjects of its jurisdiction are those offenses which proceed from the misconduct of public men." And that's what we're talking about. In other words, [the jurisdiction comes] from the abuse or violation of some public trust.

5   It is wrong, I suggest, it is a misreading of the Constitution for any member here to assert that for a member to vote for an article of impeachment means that that member must be convinced that the President should be removed from office. The Constitution doesn't say that. The powers relating to impeachment are an essential check in the hands of the body of the legislature against and upon the encroachments of the executive. [By creating] the division between the two branches of the legislature, the House and the Senate, assigning to the one the right to accuse and to the other the right to judge, the framers of this Constitution were very astute. They did not make the accusers and the judgers the same person.

6   We know the nature of impeachment. We've been talking about it awhile now. It is chiefly designed for the President and his high ministers to somehow be called into account. It is designed to "bridle" the executive if he engages in excesses. "It is designed as a method of national inquest into the conduct of public men." The framers confided in the Congress the power, if need be, to remove the President in order to strike a delicate balance between a President swollen with power and grown tyrannical, and preservation of the independence of the executive.

7   The nature of impeachment: [it is] a narrowly channeled exception to the separation-of-powers maxim. The Federal Convention of 1787 said that. It limited impeachment to high crimes and misdemeanors and discounted and opposed the term *maladministration*. "It is to be used only for great misdemeanors," so it was said in the North Carolina ratification convention. And in the Virginia ratification convention: "We do not trust our liberty to a particular branch. We need one branch to check the other."

8   "No one need be afraid"—the North Carolina ratification convention—"No one need be afraid that officers who commit oppression will pass with immunity." "Prosecutions of impeachments will seldom fail to agitate the passions of the whole community," said Hamilton in the Federalist Papers, number 65. "We divide into parties more or less friendly or inimical to the accused." I do not mean political parties in that sense.

9   The drawing of political lines goes to the motivation behind impeachment; but impeachment must proceed within the confines of the constitutional term "high crime[s] and misdemeanors." Of the impeachment process, it was Woodrow Wilson who said that "Nothing short of the grossest offenses against the plain law of the land will suffice to give them speed and effectiveness. Indignation so great as to overgrow party interest may secure a conviction; but nothing else can."

10   Common sense would be revolted if we engaged upon this process for petty reasons. Congress has a lot to do: Appropriations, Tax Reform, Health Insurance, Campaign Finance Reform, Housing, Environmental Protection, Energy Sufficiency, Mass Transportation. Pettiness cannot be allowed to stand in the face of such overwhelming problems. So today we are not being petty. We are trying to be big, because the task we have before us is a big one.

11   This morning, in a discussion of the evidence, we were told that the evidence which purports to support the allegations of misuse of the CIA by the President is thin.

We're told that that evidence is insufficient. What that recital of the evidence this morning did not include is what the President did know on June the 23rd, 1972.

12   The President did know that it was Republican money, that it was money from the Committee for the Re-Election of the President, which was found in the possession of one of the burglars arrested on June the 17th. What the President did know on the 23rd of June was the prior activities of E. Howard Hunt, which included his participation in the break-in of Daniel Ellsberg's psychiatrist, which included Howard Hunt's participation in the Dita Beard ITT affair, which included Howard Hunt's fabrication of cables designed to discredit the Kennedy Administration.

13   We were further cautioned today that perhaps these proceedings ought to be delayed because certainly there would be new evidence forthcoming from the President of the United States. There has not even been an obfuscated indication that this committee would receive any additional materials from the President. The committee subpoena is outstanding, and if the President wants to supply that material, the committee sits here. The fact is that only yesterday, the American people waited with great anxiety for eight hours, not knowing whether their President would obey an order of the Supreme Court of the United States.

14   At this point, I would like to juxtapose a few of the impeachment criteria with some of the actions the President has engaged in. Impeachment criteria: James Madison, from the Virginia ratification convention: "If the President be connected in any suspicious manner with any person and there be grounds to believe that he will shelter him, he may be impeached."

15   We have heard time and time again that the evidence reflects the payment to the defendants of money. The President had knowledge that these funds were being paid and these were funds collected for the 1972 presidential campaign. We know that the President met with Mr. Henry Petersen 27 times to discuss matters related to Watergate, and immediately thereafter met with the very persons who were implicated in the information Mr. Petersen was receiving. The words are: "If the President is connected in any suspicious manner with any person and there be grounds to believe that he will shelter that person, he may be impeached."

16   Justice Story: "Impeachment is intended for occasional and extraordinary cases where a superior power acting for the whole people is put into operation to protect their rights and rescue their liberties from violations." We know about the Huston plan. We know about the break-in of the psychiatrist's office. We know that there was absolute complete direction on September 3rd when the President indicated that a surreptitious entry had been made in Dr. Fielding's office, after having met with Mr. Ehrlichman and Mr. Young. "Protect their rights." "Rescue their liberties from violation."

17   The Carolina ratification convention impeachment criteria: those are impeachable "who behave amiss or betray their public trust." Beginning shortly after the Watergate break-in and continuing to the present time, the President has engaged in a series of public statements and actions designed to thwart the lawful investigation by government prosecutors. Moreover, the President has made public announcements and assertions bearing on the Watergate case, which the evidence will show he knew to be false. These assertions, false assertions, impeachable, those who misbehave. Those who "behave amiss or betray the public trust."

18   James Madison again at the Constitutional Convention: "A President is impeachable if he attempts to subvert the Constitution." The Constitution charges the President
with the task of taking care that the laws be faithfully executed, and yet the President
has counseled his aides to commit perjury, willfully disregard the secrecy of grand jury
proceedings, conceal surreptitious entry, attempt to compromise a federal judge, while
publicly displaying his cooperation with the processes of criminal justice. "A President
is impeachable if he attempts to subvert the Constitution."

19   If the impeachment provision in the Constitution of the United States will not
reach the offenses charged here, then perhaps that 18th-century Constitution should
be abandoned to a 20th-century paper shredder.

20   Has the President committed offenses, and planned, and directed, and acquiesced in a course of conduct which the Constitution will not tolerate? That's the question. We know that. We know the question. We should now forthwith proceed to answer
the question. It is reason, and not passion, which must guide our deliberations, guide
our debate, and guide our decision.

21   I yield back the balance of my time, Mr. Chairman.

Sample Student Rhetorical Analysis

T. Jonathan Jackson

Dr. Netaji

English 1102

11 October 2012

An Argument of Reason and Passion: Barbara Jordan's

"Statement on the Articles of Impeachment"

Barbara Jordan's July 24, 1974 speech before the U.S. House Judiciary Committee helped convince the House of Representatives, and the American public, that President Richard Nixon should be impeached. Nixon was under investigation for his role in the cover-up of the Watergate scandal. He knew about the burglary of Democratic Party headquarters, but denied having any knowledge of it and illegally shielded those responsible. Jordan used her speech to argue that the president should be impeached because his actions threatened the Constitution and the people of the United States; however, Jordan never explicitly states this position in her speech. Instead, she establishes her credibility and then uses logic to set out the evidence against the president. •———

> Jonathan Jackson provides background information in the first paragraph and his thesis at the end.

In one sense, the audience of Jordan's speech consisted of the other 34 members of the House Judiciary Committee, gathered together to decide whether or not to recommend impeachment. And yet Jordan was not speaking just to a committee meeting; her speech was very public.

The Senate Watergate hearings had been televised during the months before her speech, and millions of Americans watched sensational testimony by a host of witnesses. The Senate hearings produced charges that Nixon authorized break-ins at Democratic campaign headquarters in Washington during the 1972 election and that the White House was involved in many political dirty tricks and improprieties.

But the accusations remained only accusations—and Americans remained deeply divided about them—until it was discovered that Nixon had himself collected possible hard evidence: he had taped many conversations in the Oval Office, tapes that could support or refute the charges against the president. Nixon engaged in a protracted legal battle to keep the tapes from being disclosed, on the grounds that they were private

Jackson 2

conversations protected under "executive privilege," and he released only partial and edited transcripts. Finally on July 24, 1974, the courts ruled that Nixon had to turn all his remaining tapes over. That same day, knowing that hard evidence was now at hand, the House Judiciary Committee immediately went into session to vote whether to impeach Nixon. Each member of the committee was given fifteen minutes for an opening statement.

Nixon was a Republican and Jordan, like the majority of the committee, was a Democrat. Jordan had to convince her audience she was not biased against the president simply because of her party affiliation. Jordan was also new to Congress, relatively unknown outside of Texas, and a low-ranking member of the committee. Consequently, she had to establish her ethos to the committee as well as to the television audience. She had to present herself as fair, knowledgeable, and intellectually mature.

At the heart of Jordan's argument is her faith in the Constitution. She begins her speech from a personal perspective, pointing out that the Constitution is not perfect because it originally excluded African Americans like her. But now that the Constitution recognizes her as a citizen, Jordan says, her faith in it "is whole; it is complete; it is total." She even implies that, as a citizen, she has a moral duty to protect the Constitution, saying, "I am not going to sit here and be an idle spectator to the diminution, the subversion, the destruction of the Constitution." Jordan's emotional connection to the Constitution shows the audience that she is motivated by a love of her country, not by party loyalty. She establishes herself as someone fighting to defend and protect American values.

Jordan describes the Constitution as the accepted authority on the laws related to impeachment. She shows the audience how the Constitution gives her the authority to act as an "inquisitor," or judge. She depicts the Constitution and the American people as potential victims, and the president as the potential criminal. She warns of the need to remove "a President swollen with power and grown tyrannical."

The appeals to pathos and ethos in the opening of the speech establish Jordan's motivations and credibility, allowing her to next lay out her logical arguments. Jordan proceeds to explain how the Constitution

Jackson observes that Jordan had a formidable assignment in establishing her ethos in a short speech.

Jackson analyzes how Jordan's fervent allegiance to the Constitution made her appear unbiased.

Jackson 2

defines impeachment, and she fleshes out this brief definition with evidence from several state Constitutional Conventions. She also quotes Supreme Court Justice Joseph Story. Using evidence from the North Carolina and Virginia Constitutional Conventions, Jordan shows that impeachment was intended only for "great misdemeanors," and that the branches of government were intended to act as a check upon one another.

Next Jordan uses quotations from James Madison, Justice Story, and others to define impeachable offenses. For each offense, Jordan provides an example of an act that President Nixon was known to have committed, and she shows how his actions meet the definition of impeachable offenses. She compares Nixon's meetings with Watergate suspects to Madison's statement that "if the President is connected in any suspicious manner with any person and there be grounds to believe that he will shelter that person, he may be impeached." She pairs Justice Story's statement that impeachment should "protect [citizens'] rights and rescue their liberties from violation" with Nixon's knowledge of the burglary of a private psychiatrist's office. She links Nixon's attempts to bribe a judge and thwart grand jury proceedings with Madison's statement that "a President is impeachable if he attempts to subvert the Constitution."

> Jordan uses quotations from respected figures in American history to apply to Nixon's misdeeds.

> Jordan had to confront a legal issue: Were the actions of President Nixon serious enough to justify impeachment?

Throughout this section, Jordan repeats the historical quotes before and after her descriptions of the president's acts. This repetition makes the connections stronger and more memorable for the audience. Jordan also contrasts the formal, high-toned language of the Founders and the Constitution with descriptions that make President Nixon's actions sound sordid and petty: He knew about money "found in the possession of one of the burglars arrested on June the 17th," about "the break-in of Daniel Ellsberg's psychiatrist," about "the fabrication of cables designed to discredit the Kennedy Administration." Words like "burglars," "arrested," "break-in," and "fabrication" sound like evidence in a criminal trial. These words are not the kind of language Americans want to hear describing the actions of their president.

Jordan then adds another emotional appeal, implying that the Constitution is literally under attack. "If the impeachment provisions will not reach the offenses charged here," she says, "then perhaps that 18th-century Constitution should be abandoned to a 20th-century paper

Jackson 3

Jackson notes that the metaphor of the paper shredder adds emotional force.

shredder." This dramatic image encourages the audience to imagine President Nixon shredding the Constitution just as he had destroyed other evidence implicating him in the Watergate scandal. It implies that if the president is not stopped, he will commit further abuses of power. Jordan also makes the American people responsible for this possible outcome, saying that "we" may as well shred the Constitution if it cannot be used to impeach Nixon. This emotional appeal has the effect of shaming those who say they cannot or should not vote for impeachment.

In his conclusion Jackson points out how Jordan shifts the focus to her audience in her conclusion.

Jordan concludes her speech not by calling for impeachment, but by calling for an answer to the question, "Has the President committed offenses, and planned, and directed, and acquiesced in a course of conduct which the Constitution will not tolerate?" It almost seems like Jordan is being humble and trying not to judge by not stating her position outright. However, the reverse is true: Jordan doesn't state her position because she doesn't need to. The evidence she presented led Congress and the American public inescapably to one conclusion: President Nixon had committed impeachable offenses. Just two week later, Nixon resigned from office. Jordan had made her point.

Jackson 4

Works Cited

Jordan, Barbara. "Statement on the Articles of Impeachment." *American Rhetoric: Top 100 Speeches*. American Rhetoric, 25 July 1974. Web. 25 Sept. 2010.

8 | Analyzing Visual and Multimedia Arguments

QUICK TAKE

In this chapter, you will learn that

1. Visual arguments have similarities and differences with verbal arguments (see below)

2. Photos and videos used as evidence in visual arguments need to be evaluated critically (see pages 112–114)

3. Visual arguments can be analyzed using strategies similar to those used to analyze a written argument (see pages 114–115)

4. An effective visual analysis takes into account the context of the image as well as its visual elements and any surrounding text (see pages 116–119)

What Is a Visual Argument?

We live in a world flooded with images. They pull on us, compete for our attention, push us to do things. But how often do we think about how they work?

Can there be an argument without words?

Arguments in written language are visual in one sense: we use our eyes to read the words on the page. But without words, can there be a visual argument? Certainly some visual symbols take on conventional meanings. Signs in airports or other public places, for example, are designed to communicate with speakers of many languages.

Some visual symbols even make explicit claims. A one-way street sign says that drivers should travel only in the one direction. But are such signs arguments? In Chapter 3 we point out that scholars of argument do not believe that everything *is* an argument. Most scholars define an argument as a claim supported by one or more reasons. A one-way sign has a claim: all drivers should go in the same direction. But is there a reason? We all know an unstated reason the sign carries: drivers who go the wrong way violate the law and risk a substantial fine (plus they risk a head-on collision with other drivers).

Visual arguments require viewer participation

The *Deepwater Horizon* oil spill (also known as the BP oil spill) was the largest off-shore oil spill in the history of the United States. Caused by an explosion on April 20, 2010, the spill dumped millions of gallons of oil every day for months in spite of efforts to contain it. People around the world were reminded of the spill when they turned on their televisions and saw video of the oil gushing from the well, and nearly everyone was outraged.

People interpreted the oil flowing from the pipe quite differently, inferring multiple *because* clauses. Citizens were angry for different reasons.

The *Deepwater Horizon* oil spill was a disaster because

- eleven workers were killed and seventeen were injured.
- enormous harm was done to Gulf wetlands, birds, fish, turtles, marine mammals, and other animals.
- the tourism industry suffered another major blow just five years after Hurricane Katrina.
- the fishing and shrimping industries suffered huge losses.
- President Obama declared a moratorium on deep-water drilling, threatening the loss of jobs.
- BP and its partners were negligent in drilling the well.
- the spill was an unfortunate act of God like Hurricane Katrina.

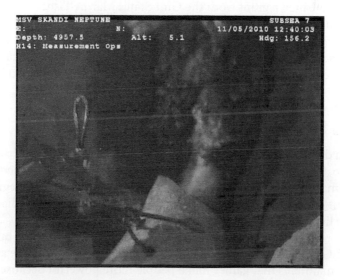

The main oil leak from the *Deepwater Horizon* wellhead. © BP p.l.c.

What argument is presented by this logo, which represents fish producers in the Gulf Coast areas affected by the BP oil spill of 2010?

Differing interpretations of visual arguments extended beyond the spill it-self. At the Taste of Chicago festival, one booth sported a banner reading "OUR LOBSTER AND SHRIMP ARE NOT FROM THE GULF COAST." A news producer in Chicago took a now infamous photograph (which you can easily locate online) of that booth and sent it to a friend in New Orleans, who sent it to a food writer, who posted it on Twitter. The mayor of New Orleans called the banner "disgraceful." Talk shows in both Chicago and New Orleans ranted about the photo, and one comment was perhaps telling about the source of the rage: a menu disclaimer would have been acceptable, but a prominent visual argument, even in text form, was hitting below the belt.

Soon thereafter, a grant from the Gulf States Marine Fisheries Commission helped the gulf's fisheries recover by funding a vital public relations and marketing campaign to educate the public and help them feel comfortable buying and eating seafood from the region. This clean logo, together with its slogan, sends an inviting message that focuses on the delicious taste of the gulf's seafood.

What Is a Multimedia Argument?

Multimedia describes the use of multiple content forms including text, voice and music audio, video, still images, animation, and interactivity. Multimedia goes far back in human history (texts and images were combined at the beginnings of writing), but digital technologies and the Web have made multimedia the fabric of our daily lives. But what exactly are multimedia arguments?

For example, games provide intense multimedia experiences, but are they arguments? Game designers such as Jane McGonigal believe they are arguments. McGonigal maintains that games make people more powerful because they connect them into larger wholes.

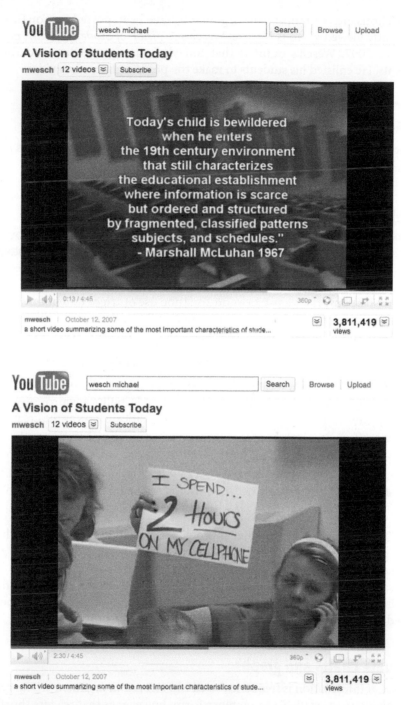

Images from Michael Wesch's *A Vision of Students Today.*

Thousands of multimedia arguments have been posted on YouTube. One frequently viewed video is Michael Wesch's *A Vision of Students Today*, posted in October 2007. Wesch's point is that today's education is ill-suited for most students. He enlisted his students to make the point with text and video.

Analyze Visual Evidence

Videos without narration, images, and graphics seldom make arguments on their own, but they are frequently used to support arguments.

Evaluate photographs and videos as evidence

Almost from the beginnings of photography, negatives were manipulated but realistic results required a high skill level. In the digital era anyone can alter photographs. Perhaps there's nothing wrong with using Photoshop to add absent relatives to family photographs or remove ex-boyfriends and ex-girlfriends. But where do you draw the line? Not only do many videos on YouTube use outright deception, but newsmagazines and networks have also been found guilty of these practices.

Ask questions about what you view.

- Who created the image or video? What bias might the creator have?
- Who published the image or video? What bias might the publisher have?
- Who is the intended audience? For example, political videos often assume that the viewers hold the same political views as the creators.
- What is being shown, and what is not being shown? For example, a video ad promoting tourism for the Gulf of Mexico will look very different from a video showing sources of pollution.
- Who is being represented, and who is not being represented? Who gets left out is as important as who gets included.

The ease of cropping digital photographs reveals an important truth about photography: a photograph represents reality from a particular viewpoint. A high-resolution picture of a crowd can be divided into many smaller images so that each says something different about the event. The act of pointing the camera in one direction and not in another shapes how photographic evidence will be interpreted. (See the examples on page 113.)

Evaluate charts and graphs

Statistical information is frequently used as evidence in arguments. The problem with giving many statistics in sentence form, however, is that readers shortly lose track of the numbers. Charts and graphs present statistics visually, allowing readers to take in trends and relationships at a glance.

A photographer's choices about who and what to photograph shapes how we see an event.

However, charts and graphs can also be misleading. For example, a chart that compares the amounts of calories in competing brands of cereal might list one with 70 calories and another with 80 calories. If the chart begins at zero, the difference looks small. But if the chart starts at 60, the brand with 80 calories appears to have twice the calories of the brand with 70. Furthermore, the chart is worthless if the data is inaccurate or comes from an unreliable source. Creators of charts and graphs have an ethical obligation to present data as fairly and accurately as possible and to provide the sources of the data.

Evaluate informational graphics

Informational graphics more sophisticated than standard pie and bar charts have become a popular means of conveying information. Many are interactive, allowing viewers of a Web site to select the information they want displayed. These information graphics are a form of narrative argument, and the stories they tell have a rhetorical purpose. (See the examples on page 115.)

Ask these questions when you are analyzing charts and graphs

- Is the type of chart appropriate for the information presented?

 Bar and column charts make comparisons in particular categories. If two or more charts are compared, the scales should be consistent.

 Line graphs plot variables on a vertical and a horizontal axis. They are useful for showing proportional trends over time.

 Pie charts show the proportion of parts in terms of the whole. Segments must add up to 100 percent of the whole.

- Does the chart have a clear purpose?
- Does the title indicate the purpose?
- What do the units represent (dollars, people, voters, percentages, and so on)?
- What is the source of the data?
- Is there any distortion of information?

Build a Visual Analysis

It's one thing to construct a visual argument yourself; it's another thing to analyze visual arguments that are made by someone else. Fortunately, analyzing arguments made up of images and graphics is largely a matter of following the same strategies for rhetorical analysis that are outlined in Chapter 7—except that you must analyze images instead of (or in addition to) words. To put it another way, when you analyze a visual argument, think about the image itself as well as its relationship to other images (and discourses). The arguments implied by visual images, like the arguments made through text alone, are carried both by the context and by the image.

Analyze context

A critical analysis of a visual image, like the analyses of written arguments that we discuss in the previous chapter, must include a consideration of context. Consider, for example, the advertisement on page 116 for Hofstra University. The context for

The **East Side**

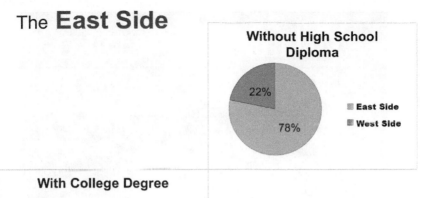

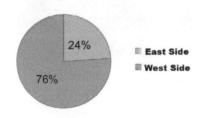

The **East Side**

West Side   East Side

As of April 2012

Charts can make points vividly. In a comparison of the east side and west side of a city, the unequal number of Starbucks locations has a high correlation with the education level of the residents.

What does it take to be the best?

Determination and hard work, at any age, can lead to being the best.
Hofstra University, just 50 years old, is already among the
top ten percent of American colleges and universities in
almost all academic criteria and resources.
Professionally accredited programs in such major areas as business,
engineering, law, psychology and education.
A library with over 1.1 million volumes *on campus*—a collection
larger than that of 95% of American universities.
Record enrollments with students from 31 states and 59 countries—
with a student-faculty ratio of only 17 to 1.
The largest, most sophisticated non-commercial television facility
in the East. A high technology undergraduate teaching
resource with broadcast-quality production capability.
A ranking in *Barron's Guide to the Most Prestigious Colleges*—one of
only 262 colleges and universities chosen from almost 4,000.
At Hofstra, determination, inspiration and hard work are qualities
our faculty demands in itself and instills in our students.
These qualities are what it takes to be the best. In anything.

HOFSTRA UNIVERSITY
WE TEACH SUCCESS.

50th Anniversary
Hempstead, L.I., New York 11550

Ad for Hofstra University, 1989.

the ad is not difficult to uncover through a bit of research. The ad appeared in 1989
and 1990 when Hofstra, located on Long Island 25 miles from New York City, was
celebrating its fiftieth anniversary and hoping to use the occasion to enhance its
esteem. At the time, Hofstra enjoyed a good reputation for its professional programs,
particularly in education and business (which one-third of the 7,500 students were
majoring in). However, it was not as highly regarded in the core science
and humanities disciplines that are often associated with institutional prestige.

In addition, Hofstra was quite well known in the New York metropolitan area—half its students were commuting to school rather than living in dormitories—but it was not attracting many students from outside the region, and its campus life was consequently regarded as mediocre. Its student body was generally well prepared, hardworking, and capable, but its most outstanding applicants were too often choosing other universities.

Feeling that its performance was exceeding its reputation and that it was capable of attracting a more diverse and talented student body, Hofstra developed a national ad campaign designed to change the opinions of prospective students and their parents, as well as the general public. It placed the ads—the ad reproduced here is one of a series—in several magazines and newspapers in order to persuade people that Hofstra was an outstanding university not just in the professions but in all fields, and that the opportunities available to its students were varied and valuable.

Analyze visual and textual elements

Ads make arguments, and the message of the Hofstra ad is something like this: "Hofstra is a prestigious, high-quality institution that brings out the best in students because of its facilities, its academic reputation, its student body, and the strength of its faculty and academic programs." The text of the Hofstra ad expresses that argument specifically: "The best" and "we teach success" are prominently displayed; the size of the print visually reinforces the message; and the fine print supports the main thesis by mentioning Hofstra's facilities (the large library with "a collection [of volumes] larger than that of 95% of American universities," the "television facility . . . with broadcast quality production capability"); its reputation (its ranking in *Barron's Guide to the Most Prestigious Colleges* and its "professionally accredited programs"); and its faculty and students. The ad works by offering good reasons and supporting arguments that are based on logical reasoning and evidence, as well as appeals to our most fervently held values. By placing the ad in prestigious publications, Hofstra enhanced its credibility even further.

In this chapter, however, we are emphasizing visuals in arguments. What kind of argument is made and supported by the image of the young girl with the flute? The photo of the girl is black and white, so that it can be printed easily and inexpensively in newspapers and magazines. But the black and white format also contributes a sense of reality and truthfulness, in the manner of black and white photos or documentary films. (Color images, on the other hand, can imply flashiness or commercialism.) Even in black and white, the image is quite arresting. In the context of an ad for Hofstra, the image is particularly intriguing. The girl is young—does she seem about ten or twelve years of age?—and her readiness for distinguished performance suggests that she is a prodigy, a genius—in other words, the kind of person that Hofstra attracts and sustains. The ad implies that you might encounter her on the Hofstra campus sometime: if she is not a student at Hofstra now, she soon will be. Come to Hofstra, and you too can acquire the traits associated with excellence and success.

The girl is dressed up for some kind of musical performance, and the details of her costume imply that the performance is of a high order: it is not just any costume, but one associated with professional performances of the most rarefied kind, a concert that calls for only the best musicians. The delicacy and refinement of the girl are implied by the posture of her fingers, the highly polished flute that she holds with an upright carriage, and the meticulousness of her tie, shirt, and coat. The girl's expression suggests that she is serious, sober, disciplined, but comfortable—the kind of student (and faculty member) that Hofstra features. (The layout and consistent print style used in the ad reinforce that impression: by offering a balanced and harmonious placement of elements and by sticking to the same type style throughout, the ad stands for the values of balance, harmony, consistency, and order.) The girl is modest and unpretentious in expression, yet she looks directly at the viewer with supreme self-confidence. Her age suggests innocence, yet her face proclaims ambition; her age and the quasi-masculine costume (note that she wears neither a ring nor earrings) give her an innocence that is in keeping with the contemplative life. Come to Hofstra, the image proclaims, and you will meet people who are sober and graceful, self-disciplined and confident, ambitious without being arrogant. The ad is supporting its thesis with good reasons implied by its central image—good reasons that we identified with logos and pathos in the previous chapter.

Speaking of pathos, what do you make of the fact that the girl is Asian? On one hand, the Asian girl's demeanor reinforces cultural stereotypes. Delicate, small, sober, controlled, even humorless, she embodies characteristics that recall other Asian American icons (particularly women), especially icons of success through discipline and hard work. On the other hand, the girl speaks to the Asian community. It is as if she is on the verge of saying, "Come and join me at Hofstra, where you too can reach the highest achievement. And read the copy below me to learn more about what Hofstra has to offer." In this way the girl participates in Hofstra's ambition to attract highly qualified, highly motivated, and high-performing minority students—as well as any other high-performing student, regardless of ethnicity or gender, who values hard work, academic distinction, and the postponement of sensual gratification in return for long-term success.

If she is Asian, the girl is also thoroughly American. She appears not to be an international student but an American of immigrant stock. Her costume, her controlled black hair, and her unmarked face and fingers identify her as achieving the American dream of material success, physical health and well being, and class advancement. If her parents or grandparents came to New York or California as immigrants, they (and she) are now naturalized—100 percent American, completely successful. The social class element to the image is unmistakable: the entire ad speaks of Hofstra's ambition to be among the best, to achieve an elite status. When the ad appeared in 1989, Hofstra was attracting few of the nation's elite students. The girl signals a change. She displays the university's aspiration to become among the nation's elite—those who enjoy material success as well as the leisure, education, and sophistication to appreciate the finest music. That ambition is reinforced by the university's emblem in the lower right-hand corner of the ad. It resembles a coat of arms and is associated with royalty. Hofstra may be a community that is strong in the professions, but it also values the arts.

No doubt there are other aspects of the image that work to articulate and to support the complex argument of the ad. There is more to be said about this ad, and you may disagree with some of the points we have offered. But consider this: By 2009, twenty years after the ad was run, Hofstra's total enrollment had climbed above 12,000, with 7,500 undergraduates. Its admissions were more selective, its student body was more diverse and less regional in character, its graduation rate had improved, its sports teams had achieved national visibility, and its minority student population had grown. Many factors contributed to the university's advancement, but it seems likely that this ad was one of them.

Write a Visual Analysis

Like rhetorical analysis, effective visual analysis takes into account the context of the image as well as its visual elements and any surrounding text. When you analyze a visual image, look carefully at its details and thoroughly consider its context. What visual elements grab your attention first, and how do other details reinforce that impression—what is most important and less important? How do color and style influence impressions? How does the image direct the viewer's eyes and reinforce what is important? What is the relationship between the image and any text that might accompany it? Consider the shapes, colors, and details of the image, as well as how the elements of the image connect with different arguments and audiences.

Consider also what you know or can learn about the context of an image and the design and text that surround it. Try to determine why and when it was created, who created it, where it appeared, and the target audience. Think about how the context of its creation and publication affected its intended audience. What elements have you seen before? Which elements remind you of other visuals?

Sample Student Visual Analysis

A sample student visual analysis appears on page 123. The analysis is in the form of a discussion board posting, which is a frequent assignment in writing courses. Usually they are short essays, no more than 300 words. Sources of any information still need to be cited. The assignment for this post was to find and analyze an example of a visual metaphor.

Steps to Writing a Visual Analysis

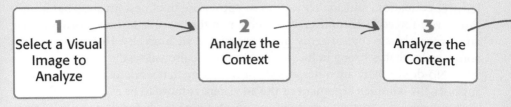

Step 1 Select a Visual Image to Analyze

Find an image to analyze. Remember that not all images convey a point of view; some symbols have only one commonly agreed-upon meaning. So be sure that the subject of your analysis is something that presents an argument.

Examples

- A print advertisement in a popular magazine such as *Time, Newsweek,* or *Sports Illustrated*—or a special interest magazine like *Field and Stream* or *Flex* or *Country Woman* or *Latina*
- A poster for a movie, concert, or political event
- A group of bumper stickers that address the same issue in different ways
- A Web site for a college or university

Step 2 Analyze the Context

Who created or produced the image?
    Through research in the library or on the Web, learn as much as you can about who designed the image.

- If the piece is attributed to an individual, learn as much as you can about his or her work.
- If no individual artist or designer is identified, learn as much as you can about the sponsoring organization, business, or institution.

Who is the audience?
    Through research in the library or on the Web, learn as much as you can about where and for whom the image was first presented.

- Where is the image located? How does its position affect the way the message is conveyed?
- Who is the target audience?
- What is the purpose of the visual argument?

What is the larger conversation?
    Through research in the library or on the Web, learn as much as you can about the subject of your selection.

- When was the image originally published or presented?
- Were there similar objects produced at about the same time that conveyed either complementary or contrasting messages?

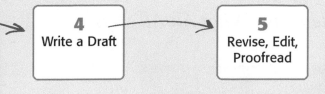

- How was the image received at the time it originally appeared? Was it effective in achieving its purpose? Is there anything controversial about the item depicted?

Step 3 Analyze the Content

Summarize the argument

- What message is conveyed through the visual image?

Consider the elements of design

- What colors, textures, and shapes are most prominent?
- How are the separate parts of the design put together to create one overall impression?
- If text is included, where is it located in relation to the visual elements? How is the text incorporated into the design? Do the words effectively support, reinforce, or extend the message?

Step 4 Write a Draft

Introduction

- Describe the image you are analyzing.
- Supply any background information your readers will need to know.
- State your thesis.

Body

- Analyze the context, following Step 2.
- Analyze the content, following Step 3.

Conclusion

- Explain whether the image was effective in conveying its argument by noting any specific consequences of its presentation or publication.

Step 5 Revise, Edit, Proofread

For detailed instructions, see Chapter 5.
For a checklist to evaluate your draft, see pages 61–62.

How Can You Understand What An Ad Says About Education?

The visual images used by businesses and institutions to promote their products or services change to reflect changes in the social, political, and economic environment. In 2008, Hofstra University's print ads, like the one printed above, looked very different from the one published in 1989 (see page 116). Even at first glance, the contrast is striking.

What does the 2008 ad say (especially when it is compared with the 1989 ad) about changing perspectives regarding the value and purpose of a college education? What do students (and their parents) look for when they choose which university to attend and what field of study to take up? What do colleges want to convey through the visual images that appear in printed media and in the mailboxes of high school students?

Write about it

1. Using the analysis on pages 120–122 as a guide, carefully examine Hofstra University's 2008 ad. Begin by describing your initial impression and the overall composition of the image.

2. Make a point-by-point comparison, noting the contrasts in the images of the young women in each; the size and appearance of the text; the content of the printed information; even the location, size, and style of the fonts used.

3. Write an analysis of the 2008 ad. What is the nature of the appeal made in the ad? Does it present an effective argument for choosing to attend Hofstra rather than another college or university?

Thread: "Use Only What You Need": The Denver Water Conservation Campaign
Author: Chrissy Yao
Posted Date: March 1, 2010 1:12 PM

Partial bus bench from Denver Water's conservation campaign

In 2006, Denver Water, the city's oldest water utility, launched a ten-year water conservation plan based on using water efficiently ("Conservation"). Denver Water teamed up with the Sukle Advertising firm and produced the "Use Only What You Need" campaign to help alleviate the water crisis that the city was enduring (Samuel). The campaign uses billboard advertising, magazine ads, and even stripped-down cars to impart messages of water conservation and efficiency.

Clever visual metaphors are at the heart of the campaign. One example is a park bench with available seating only for one individual. The words "USE ONLY WHAT YOU NEED" are stenciled in on the back of the bench. The bench, which can actually be used for sitting, conveys the idea that if only one person were using the bench, that person would only need a small area to sit on, not the whole thing. The bench makes concrete the concept of water conservation.

The innovative ad campaign that uses objects in addition to traditional advertising has proven successful. The simplicity and minimalist style of the ads made a convincing argument about using resources sparingly. The average water consumption of Denver dropped between 18% and 21% annually from 2006 to 2009.

> Yao describes the ad campaign, which uses the partial bus bench.

> Yao analyzes the visual metaphor.

Works Cited

"Conservation." *Denver Water*. Denver Water, 2010. Web. 23 Feb. 2010.

Samuel, Frederick. "Denver Water." *Ad Goodness*. N.p., 16 Nov. 2006.
    Web. 24 Feb. 2010.

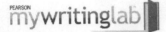

For additional writing resources that will help you master the objectives of this chapter, go to www.mywritinglab.com.

Writing Arguments

PART

3

9 | Putting Good Reasons into Action

QUICK TAKE

In this chapter, you will learn that

1. Most arguments use multiple approaches to achieve a specific purpose (see below)
2. Thinking explicitly about the structure of arguments can help identify different ways to approach your topic (see below)
3. Using different kinds of arguments can help you get started writing about a complex topic (see page 128)

Find a Purpose for Writing an Argument

Imagine that you bought a new car in June and you are taking some of your friends to your favorite lake over the Fourth of July weekend. You have a great time until, as you are heading home, a drunk driver—a repeat offender—swerves into your lane and totals your new car. You and your friends are lucky not to be hurt, but you're outraged because you believe that repeat offenders should be prevented from driving, even if that means putting them in jail. You also remember going to another state that had sobriety checkpoints on holiday weekends. If such a check-point had been in place in your state, you might still be driving your new car. You live in a town that encourages citizens to contribute to the local newspaper, and you think you could get a guest editorial published. The question is, how do you want to write the editorial?

- You could tell your story about how a repeat drunk driver endangered the lives of you and your friends.
- You could define driving while intoxicated (DWI) as a more legally culpable crime.
- You could compare the treatment of drunk drivers in your state with the treatment of drunk drivers in another state.
- You could cite federal government statistics that alcohol-related accidents killed 10,288 people in 2010.
- You could evaluate the present drunk-driving laws as insufficiently just or less than totally successful.

Finding Good Reasons

How Do We Measure Scientific Progress?

As scientists learn more about the physical world, their findings are often put to use to create technological tools intended to improve our lives. Americans are witnessing huge shifts in the fields of medicine, agriculture, transportation, entertainment, energy production, and environmental protection. An array of devices now facilitate communication across time and space, none of which existed thirty years ago. Each has revolutionized the way we interact with each other and with the world. The jury is out, though, about whether or not the changes that accompany these new tools and technologies are uniformly positive.

Do advancements in science and technology always improve our lives? Is *change* always synonymous with *progress*?

Write about it

1. Formulate your own definition of progress (see Chapter 10).

2. Evaluate the effects of adopting new tools and techniques. Have recent innovations improved the quality of life of significant numbers of people? Are there some research findings that would be better left in the lab and out of our lives? Or should all new technologies be brought into the public sphere as soon as possible (see Chapter 12)?

3. If you are concerned about negative consequences of unfettered scientific research and technological innovation, write a proposal to limit public support (see Chapter 15). If, on the other hand, you believe the benefits far outweigh the drawbacks, write a rebuttal argument against efforts to restrict funding (see Chapter 14).

- You could propose taking vehicles away from repeat drunk drivers and forcing them to serve mandatory sentences.
- You could argue that your community should have sobriety checkpoints at times when drunk drivers are likely to be on the road.
- You could do several of the above.

The next few chapters of *Good Reasons* will explain how to take up these various alternatives.

Get Started Writing About Complex Issues

You're not going to have much space in the newspaper, so you decide to argue for sobriety checkpoints. You know that they are controversial. One of your friends who was in the car with you said that the checkpoints are unconstitutional because they involve search without cause. However, after doing some research to find out whether checkpoints are defined as legal or illegal, you learn that on June 14, 1990, the U.S. Supreme Court upheld the constitutionality of using checkpoints as a deterrent and enforcement tool against drunk drivers.

But you still want to know whether most people would agree with your friend that sobriety checkpoints are an invasion of privacy. You find opinion polls and surveys going back to the 1980s that show that 70 to 80 percent of those polled support sobriety checkpoints. You also realize that you can argue by analogy that security checkpoints for alcohol are similar in many ways to airport security checkpoints that protect passengers. You decide you will finish by making an argument from consequence. If people who go to the lake with plans to drink know in advance that there will be checkpoints, they will find a designated driver or some other means of safe transportation, and everyone else will also be a lot safer.

The point of this example is that people very rarely set out to define something in an argument for the sake of definition, to compare for the sake of comparison, or to adopt any of the other ways of structuring an argument. Instead, they have a purpose in mind, and they use the kinds of arguments that are discussed in Chapters 10–15—most often in combination—as means to an end. Most arguments use multiple approaches and multiple sources of good reasons.

^{PEARSON}
mywritinglab

For additional writing resources that will help you master the objectives of this chapter, go to www.mywritinglab.com.

10 | Definition Arguments

QUICK TAKE

In this chapter, you will learn that

1. Definition arguments set out criteria and argue that something meets or doesn't meet those criteria (see page 130)

2. Definitions work by classification and example (see page 131)

3. Because definition arguments are so powerful, they are often at the center of the most important debates in American culture (see page 132)

Graffiti dates back to the ancient Egyptian, Greek, Roman, and Mayan civilizations. Is graffiti vandalism? Or is it art? The debate has gone on for three decades. In the 1980s New York City's subways were covered with graffiti. Many New Yorkers believe that removing graffiti from subway cars was a first step toward the much-celebrated social and economic recovery of the city. For them graffiti was a sign that the subways were not safe. But at the same time, Martha Cooper and Henry Chalfant released a book titled *Subway Art*—a picture book—that celebrated graffiti-covered subways as an art form. Should we appreciate graffiti as the people's art? Or should graffiti be removed as quickly as possible, as a destructive eyesore?

Understand How Definition Arguments Work

Definition arguments set out criteria and then argue that whatever is being defined meets or does not meet those criteria.

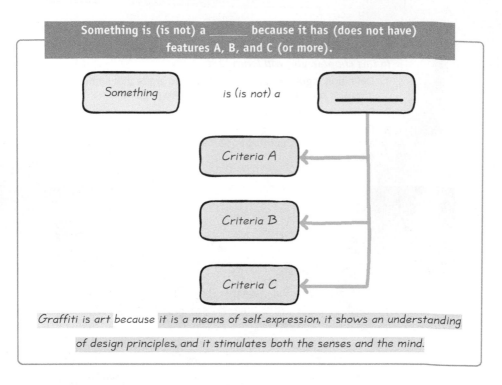

Something is (is not) a _____ because it has (does not have) features A, B, and C (or more).

Something   is (is not) a   _____

Criteria A

Criteria B

Criteria C

Graffiti is art because it is a means of self-expression, it shows an understanding of design principles, and it stimulates both the senses and the mind.

Recognize Kinds of Definitions

Rarely do you get far into an argument without having to define something. Consider the different ways we define what it means to be an adult. Certain rights and responsibilities are conferred on individuals once they officially cross the line from adolescence to adulthood. If there were some clear physical marker, it would be easy to recognize when this happens. But there isn't one definitive biological change that we can observe or measure that can serve this purpose. Instead, we often rely informally on the abstract concept of "maturity." To gain the full rights accorded adults, we must be mature enough to accept full responsibility for our actions.

But there is little agreement about when this happens. For that reason, we need a legal definition as well as an informal one. Each state typically defines "legal adulthood" as arriving at a specific age—states specify when people are "old enough" to marry, drink alcohol, operate motor vehicles, and so forth. And yet there is no real agreement about how old is old enough. The variety in state laws regarding driver's licenses is a good example of the disagreement. It is possible to get a learner's permit if you are 14 years old in Alabama, but not until you are 16 in Kentucky. In Delaware, you can be issued a license with no restrictions when you are 17, but if you live in the District of Columbia, you will pay higher fines for traffic violations until you are 21. And regardless of where you live, you can't rent a car without paying a steep penalty until you're 25.

Every state has established an "age of majority," at which time a person is considered responsible for his actions. But this isn't the same as the "age of reason," when someone is able to distinguish right from wrong. At what age can we make decisions based on a moral code? That depends who you ask. But financial rights and legal responsibilities are interpreted differently, depending on which definition is used.

In any event, you can see that a great deal hangs on questions of definition. And you can see that definitions are of different types. When you make a definition argument, it's important to think about what kind of definition you will use. Descriptions of three types follow.

Formal definitions

Formal definitions typically categorize an item into the next-higher classification and provide criteria that distinguish the item from other items within that classification. Most dictionary definitions are formal definitions. For example, fish are cold-blooded aquatic vertebrates that have jaws, fins, and scales and are distinguished from other cold-blooded aquatic vertebrates (such as sea snakes) by the presence of gills. If you can construct a formal definition with a specific classification and differentiating criteria that your audience will accept, then likely you will have a strong argument. The key is to get your audience to agree to your classification and criteria. Often your argument will amount to revising your audience's view of the classification or criteria (or both). For instance, imagine that you want to change your audience's view of contemporary universities. You might construct a thesis statement something like this: "While most people still think of universities as institutions of higher learning [classification] that prepare people for citizenship and the workplace [differentiating criteria], they are actually nothing more than big businesses" [revised classification]. Or consider the example on page 129: If you want to change the way your audience thinks about graffiti, you might construct a thesis statement like this: "While most people continue to think of graffiti as a kind of delinquency [classification] that is both irritating and ugly [differentiating criteria], in fact graffiti is an art form" [revised classification].

Operational definitions

Many concepts cannot be easily defined by formal definitions. Researchers in the natural and social sciences must construct **operational definitions** that they use for their research. For example, in order to evaluate the financial health of business and government, economists rely on measures or indicators such as gross domestic product, personal income and spending, monthly retail sales, and home ownership. While they generally agree that each of these measures is important, there is significant disagreement about which is the most reliable indicator of economic stability. Theorists don't all use the same members to define "acceptable unemployment" or "sustainable growth." No matter what the number, researchers must argue that the particular definition is one that suits the concept.

Definitions from example

Many human qualities such as honesty, courage, creativity, deceit, and love must be defined by examples that the audience accepts as representative of the concept. Few would not call the firefighters who entered the World Trade Center on September 11, 2001, courageous. Most people would describe someone with a diagnosis of terminal cancer who refuses to feel self-pity as courageous. But what about a student who declines to go to a concert with her friends so she can study for an exam? Her behavior might be admirable, but most people would hesitate to call it courageous. The key to arguing a **definition from example** is that the examples must strike the audience as typical of the concept, even if the situation is unusual.

Build a Definition Argument

Because definition arguments are so powerful, they are found at the center of some of the most important debates in American history. Definition arguments were at the heart of the abolition of slavery, for example, and many of the major arguments of the civil rights movement were based on definitions. Martin Luther King, Jr.'s "Letter from Birmingham Jail" is one eloquent example.

U.S. National Guard troops block off Beale Street in Memphis, Tennessee, as striking sanitation workers wearing placards reading "I *AM* A MAN" pass by on March 29, 1968. Rev. Martin Luther King, Jr. returned to Memphis to lead the march and was assassinated a week later on April 4.

King was jailed in April 1963 for leading a series of peaceful protests in Birmingham, Alabama. While he was being held in solitary confinement, Rev. King wrote a letter to eight white Birmingham clergymen. These religious leaders had issued a statement urging an end to the protests in their city. King argued that it was necessary to act now rather than wait for change. His purpose in writing the argument was to win acceptance for the protests and protestors and to make his audience see that the anti-segregationists were not agitators and rabble-rousers, but citizens acting responsibly to correct a grave injustice. A critical part of King's argument is his definition of "just" and "unjust" laws.

Supporters of segregation in Birmingham had obtained a court order forbidding further protests, and the eight white clergymen urged King and his supporters to obey the courts. Our society generally assumes that laws, and the courts that enforce them, should be obeyed. King, however, argues that there are two categories of laws, and that citizens must treat one category differently from the other. Morally just laws, King argues, should be obeyed, but unjust ones should not. But how are just laws to be distinguished from unjust ones? By distinguishing two different kinds of laws, King creates a rationale for obeying some laws and disobeying others.

His argument rests on the clear moral and legal criteria he uses to define just and unjust laws. Without these criteria, people could simply disobey any law they chose, which is what King's detractors accused him of advocating. King had to show that he was in fact acting on principle, and that he and his supporters wanted to establish justice, not cause chaos. First, King states that a "just law is a man-made code that squares with the moral law of God" and "an unjust law is a code that is out of harmony with the moral law." Second, King notes that "any law that degrades human personality is unjust." Finally, King states that just laws are ones that hold for everyone because they were arrived at through democratic processes, while unjust laws are those that are inflicted on a minority that, because they were not permitted to vote, had no participation in approving them.

The definitions that King offers promote his goals. He maintains in his famous "Letter" that people have a moral responsibility to obey just laws, and, by the same logic, "a moral responsibility to disobey unjust laws." He then completes his definitional argument by showing how segregation laws fit the definition of "unjust" that he has laid out. Once his audience accepts his placement of segregation laws in the "unjust" category, they must also accept that King and his fellow protestors were right to break those laws. He answers his critics effectively through a powerful definition argument.

Note how King's three definitions all fit the structure described at the beginning of this chapter:

Something is (or is not) a ___ because it has (does not have) features A, B, and C.

Building an extended definition argument like King's is a two-step process. First, you have to establish the criteria for the categories you wish to define. In King's letter, consistency with moral law and uplifting of the human spirit are set forth as criteria for a just law. King provides arguments from St. Thomas Aquinas, a religious authority likely to carry significant weight with Birmingham clergymen and others who will read the letter.

Second, you must convince your audience that the particular case in question meets or doesn't meet the criteria. King cannot simply state that segregation laws are unjust; he must provide evidence showing how they fail to meet the criteria for a just law. Specifically, he notes that segregation "gives the segregator a false sense of superiority and the segregated a false sense of inferiority." These false senses of self are a distortion or degradation of the human personality.

Sometimes definition arguments have to argue for the relevance and suitability of the criteria. King, in fact, spent a great deal of his letter laying out and defending his criteria for just and unjust laws. While he addressed his letter to clergymen, he knew that it would find a wider audience. Therefore, he did not rely solely on criteria linked to moral law, or to Thomas Aquinas, or the "law of God." People who were not especially religious might not be convinced by those parts of his argument. So King presents two additional criteria for just laws that he knows will appeal to those who value the democratic process.

When you build a definition argument, often you must put much effort into identifying and explaining your criteria. You must convince your readers that your criteria are the best ones for what you are defining and that they apply to the case you are arguing.

King's extended definition argument

After establishing criteria for two kinds of laws, *just* and *unjust*, King argues that citizens must respond differently to laws that are unjust, by disobeying them. He then shows how the special case of *segregation laws* meets the criteria for unjust laws. If readers accept his argument, they will agree that segregation laws belong in the category of unjust laws, and therefore must be disobeyed.

Criteria for Just Laws	Criteria for Unjust Laws	Segregation Laws
Consistent with moral law	Not consistent with moral law	✓
Uplift human personality	Damage human personality	✓
Must be obeyed by all people	Must be obeyed by some people, but not others	✓
Made by democratically elected representatives	Not made by democratically elected representatives	✓
Appropriate Response to Just Laws: All citizens should obey them.	Appropriate Response to Unjust Laws: All citizens should disobey them.	

Finding Good Reasons

What Is Parody?

The Colbert Report is a parody of shows by cable news pundits. Colbert's tradition of having the audience cheer for him, not his guests, pokes fun at programming driven by personalities, not issues.

Downfall, a German film released in 2004 about Hitler's last days, has been used for hundreds of popular YouTube parodies. Most parodies use the same scene of a defeated Hitler, played by Bruno Ganz, unleashing a furious speech to his staff in German with YouTubers adding English subtitles on topics as varied as the plot of *Avatar*, the upgrade to Windows 7, Apple's iPad, academic grant reviews, and the failure of various sports teams to win big games.

The owner of the rights to the film, Constantin Films, demanded that YouTube take down the parodies in April 2010, and YouTube complied. Critics of the move complained that Constantin Films used YouTube's Content ID filter to determine what is acceptable rather than the fair use provisions of copyright law. They argue that fair-use law allows a film clip, a paragraph from an article, or a short piece of music to be adapted if the purpose is to create commentary or satire.

Write about it

1. Which of the following criteria do you think must be present for a work to be considered a parody? Are there any criteria you might change or add?
   - the work criticizes a previous work
   - the work copies the same structure, details, or style of the previous work
   - the connections to the previous work are clear to the audience
   - the work is humorous
   - the title is a play on the previous work
   - the work is presented in either a print, visual, or musical medium

2. Do the various uses of the *Downfall* clip meet the criteria above? Would you define them as parodies? Why or why not?

3. Write a letter to the owners of Constantin Films either supporting their demand to have the clips removed or asking that they reconsider their position based on your definition of *parody*.

Steps to Writing a Definition Argument

1 Make a Claim → **2** Think About What's at Stake → **3** List the Criteria →

Step 1 Make a Claim

Make a definitional claim on a controversial issue that focuses on a key term.

Template

_____ is (or is not) a _____ because it has (or does not have) features A, B, and C (or more).

Examples

- Hate speech (or literature, films, lyrics, and so on) is (or is not) free speech protected by the First Amendment because it has (or does not have) these features.
- Hunting (or using animals for cosmetics testing, keeping animals in zoos, wearing furs, and so on) is (or is not) cruelty to animals because it has (or does not have) these features.

Step 2 Think About What's at Stake

- Does nearly everyone agree with you? If so, then your claim probably isn't interesting or important. If you can think of people who disagree, then something is at stake.
- Who argues the opposite of your claim?
- Why or how do they benefit from a different definition?

Step 3 List the Criteria

- Which criteria are necessary for _____ to be a _____?
- Which are the most important?
- Does your case in point meet all the criteria?

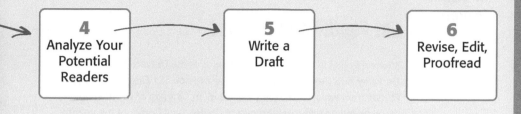

Step 4 Analyze Your Potential Readers

- Who are your readers?
- How does the definitional claim you are making affect them?
- How familiar are they with the issue, concept, or controversy that you're writing about?
- Which criteria are they most likely to accept with little explanation, and which will they disagree with?

Step 5 Write a Draft

Introduction

- Set out the issue, concept, or controversy.
- Give the background that your intended readers need.

Body

- Set out your criteria and argue for the appropriateness of the criteria.
- Anticipate where readers might question either your criteria or how they apply to your subject.
- Address opposing viewpoints by acknowledging how their definitions differ and by showing why your definition is better.

Conclusion

- Do more than simply summarize. You can, for example, go into more detail about what is at stake or the implications of your definition.

Step 6 Revise, Edit, Proofread

- For detailed instructions, see Chapter 5.
- For a checklist to use to evaluate your draft, see pages 61–62.

Michael
Pollan

Eat Food: Food Defined

Michael Pollan is a journalism professor at the University of California,
Berkeley, and the author of *In Defense of Food: An Eater's Manifesto*
(2008), from which this excerpt is taken. *In Defense of Food* received
many prizes and was named one of the ten best books of the year by
the *New York Times* and the *Washington Post*. Pollan is also the author
of *Second Nature* (1991), *A Place of My Own* (1997), *The Botany of Desire: A Plant's Eye View of the World* (2001), *The Omnivore's Dilemma: A
Natural History of Four Meals* (2006), and *Food Rules* (2010). He is also
a contributing writer for the *New York Times Magazine*.

Pollan asks why Americans worry so much about nutrition
and yet seem so unhealthy. The title, *In Defense of Food*, is one of
the many paradoxes that Pollan examines in the book. After all, why
should food need defending if it is plentiful and we eat so much of
it? Pollan argues that the answer lies in how we define food.

Pollan begins by asking why does food need to be defined?

The first time I heard the advice to "just eat food" it was in a
speech by Joan Gussow, and it completely baffled me. Of course
you should eat food—what else is there to eat? But Gussow,
who grows much of her own food on a flood-prone finger of land
jutting into the Hudson River, refuses to dignify most of the
products for sale in the supermarket with that title. "In the thirty-four
years I've been in the field of nutrition," she said in the same
speech, "I have watched real food disappear from large areas of
the supermarket and from much of the rest of the eating world."
Taking food's place on the shelves has been an unending stream
of foodlike substitutes, some seventeen thousand new ones every
year—"products constructed largely around commerce and hope,
supported by frighteningly little actual knowledge." Ordinary food is
still out there, however, still being grown and even occasionally sold
in the supermarket, and this ordinary food is what we should eat.

Pollan claims that everything that pretends to be food really isn't food, thus establishing the need for a definition.

2   But given our current state of confusion and given the thousands of products calling themselves food, this is more easily
said than done. So consider these related rules of thumb. Each
proposes a different sort of map to the contemporary food
landscape, but all should take you to more or less the same place.

Don't eat anything your great grandmother wouldn't recognize as food.

3   Why your great grandmother? Because at this point your
mother and possibly even your grandmother is as confused as
the rest of us; to be safe we need to go back at least a couple generations, to a time before the advent of most modern foods. So
depending on your age (and your grandmother), you may need to

go back to your great- or even great-great grandmother. Some nutritionists recommend going back even further. John Yudkin, a British nutritionist whose early alarms about the dangers of refined carbohydrates were overlooked in the 1960s and 1970s, once advised, "Just don't eat anything your Neolithic ancestors wouldn't have recognized and you'll be OK."

Pollan's first criterion of what is food offers a simple concept.

4   What would shopping this way mean in the supermarket? Well, imagine your great grandmother at your side as you roll down the aisles. You're standing together in front of the dairy case. She picks up a package of Go-Gurt Portable Yogurt tubes—and has no idea what this could possibly be. Is it a food or a toothpaste? And how, exactly, do you introduce it into your body? You could tell her it's just yogurt in a squirtable form, yet if she read the ingredients label she would have every reason to doubt that that was in fact the case. Sure, there's some yogurt in there, but there are also a dozen other things that aren't remotely yogurt like, ingredients she would probably fail to recognize as foods of any kind, including high-fructose corn syrup, modified corn starch, kosher gelatin, carrageenan, tri-calcium phosphate, natural and artificial flavors, vitamins, and so forth. (And there's a whole other list of ingredients for the "berry bubblegum bash" flavoring, containing everything but berries or bubblegum.) How did yogurt, which in your great grandmother's day consisted simply of milk inoculated with a bacterial culture, ever get to be so complicated? Is a product like Go-Gurt Portable Yogurt still a whole food? A food of any kind? Or is it just a food product?

Another way of defining food is to define what isn't food, what Pollan calls "food products."

5   There are in fact hundreds of foodish products in the supermarket that your ancestors simply wouldn't recognize as food: breakfast cereal bars transected by bright white veins representing, but in reality having nothing to do with, milk; "protein waters" and "nondairy creamer"; cheeselike food-stuffs equally innocent of any bovine contribution; cakelike cylinders (with creamlike fillings) called Twinkies that never grow stale. Don't eat anything incapable of rotting is another personal policy you might consider adopting.

6   There are many reasons to avoid eating such complicated food products beyond the various chemical additives and corn and soy derivatives they contain. One of the problems with the products of food science is that, as Joan Gussow has pointed out, they lie to your body; their artificial colors and flavors and synthetic sweeteners and novel fats confound the senses we rely on to assess new foods and prepare our bodies to deal with them. Foods that lie leave us with little choice but to eat by the numbers, consulting labels rather than our senses.

7   It's true that foods have long been processed in order to preserve them, as when we pickle or ferment or smoke, but industrial processing aims to do much more than extend shelf life. Today foods are processed in ways specifically designed to sell us more food by pushing our evolutionary buttons—our inborn preferences

for sweetness and fat and salt. These qualities are difficult to find in nature but cheap and easy for the food scientist to deploy, with the result that processing induces us to consume much more of these ecological rarities than is good for us. "Tastes great, less filling!" could be the motto for most processed foods, which are far more energy dense than most whole foods: They contain much less water, fiber, and micronutrients, and generally much more sugar and fat, making them at the same time, to coin a marketing slogan, "More fattening, less nutritious!"

8   The great grandma rule will help keep many of these products out of your cart. But not all of them. Because thanks to the FDA's willingness, post–1973, to let food makers freely alter the identity of "traditional foods that everyone knows" without having to call them imitations, your great grandmother could easily be fooled into thinking that that loaf of bread or wedge of cheese is in fact a loaf of bread or a wedge of cheese. This is why we need a slightly more detailed personal policy to capture these imitation foods; to wit:

What food is can also be defined by what it isn't, hence a list of criteria for what isn't food.

Avoid food products containing ingredients that are a) unfamiliar set, b) unpronounceable, c) more than five in number, or that include d) high-fructose corn syrup.

9   None of these characteristics, not even the last one, is necessarily harmful in and of itself, but all of them are reliable markers for foods that have been highly processed to the point where they may no longer be what they purport to be. They have crossed over from foods to food products.

10   Consider a loaf of bread, one of the "traditional foods that everyone knows" specifically singled out for protection in the 1938 imitation rule. As your grandmother could tell you, bread is traditionally made using a remarkably small number of familiar ingredients: flour, yeast, water, and a pinch of salt will do it. But industrial bread—even industrial whole-grain bread—has become a far more complicated product of modern food science (not to mention commerce and hope). Here's the complete ingredients list for Sara Lee's Soft & Smooth Whole Grain White Bread. (Wait a minute—isn't "Whole Grain White Bread" a contradiction in terms? Evidently not any more.)

Pollan points out that the language used for food products is as convoluted as the ingredients.

> Enriched bleached flour [wheat flour, malted barley flour, niacin, iron, thiamin mononitrate (vitamin B), riboflavin (vitamin B_2), folic acid], water, whole grains [whole wheat flour, brown rice flour (rice flour, rice bran)], high fructose corn syrup [hello!], whey, wheat gluten, yeast, cellulose. Contains 2% or less of each of the following: honey, calcium sulfate, vegetable oil (soybean and/or cottonseed oils), salt, butter (cream, salt), dough conditioners (may contain one or more of the following: mono- and diglycerides, ethoxylated mono- and diglycerides, ascorbic acid, enzymes, azodicarbonamide),

guar gum, calcium propionate (preservative), distilled vinegar, yeast nutrients (monocalcium phosphate, calcium sulfate, ammonium sulfate), corn starch, natural flavor, beta-carotene (color), vitamin D_3, soy lecithin, soy flour.

11 There are many things you could say about this intricate loaf of "bread," but note first that even if it managed to slip by your great grandmother (because it is a loaf of bread, or at least is called one and strongly resembles one), the product fails every test proposed under rule number two: It's got unfamiliar ingredients (monoglycerides I've heard of before, but ethoxylated monoglycerides?); unpronounceable ingredients (try "azodicarbonamide"); it exceeds the maximum of five ingredients (by roughly thirty-six); and it contains high-fructose corn syrup. Sorry, Sara Lee, but your Soft & Smooth Whole Grain White Bread is not food and if not for the indulgence of the FDA could not even be labeled "bread."

12 Sara Lee's Soft & Smooth Whole Grain White Bread could serve as a monument to the age of nutritionism. It embodies the latest nutritional wisdom from science and government (which in its most recent food pyramid recommends that at least half our consumption of grain come from whole grains) but leavens that wisdom with the commercial recognition that American eaters (and American children in particular) have come to prefer their wheat highly refined—which is to say, cottony soft, snowy white, and exceptionally sweet on the tongue. In its marketing materials, Sara Lee treats this clash of interests as some sort of Gordian knot—it speaks in terms of an ambitious quest to build a "no compromise" loaf—which only the most sophisticated food science could possibly cut.

13 And so it has, with the invention of whole-grain white bread. Because the small percentage of whole grains in the bread would render it that much less sweet than, say, all-white Wonder Bread—which scarcely waits to be chewed before transforming itself into glucose—the food scientists have added high-fructose corn syrup and honey to to make up the difference; to overcome the problematic heft and toothsomeness of a real whole grain bread, they've deployed "dough conditioners," including guar gum and the aforementioned azodicarbonamide, to simulate the texture of supermarket white bread. By incorporating certain varieties of albino wheat, they've managed to maintain that deathly but apparently appealing Wonder Bread pallor.

14 Who would have thought Wonder Bread would ever become an ideal of aesthetic and gustatory perfection to which bakers would actually aspire—Sara Lee's Mona Lisa?

15 Very often food science's efforts to make traditional foods more nutritious make them much more complicated, but not necessarily any better for you. To make dairy products low fat, it's not enough to remove the fat. You then have to go to great lengths to

preserve the body or creamy texture by working in all kinds of food additives. In the case of low-fat or skim milk that usually means adding powdered milk. But powdered milk contains oxidized cholesterol, which scientists believe is much worse for your arteries than ordinary cholesterol, so food makers sometimes compensate by adding antioxidants, further complicating what had been a simple one-ingredient whole food. Also, removing the fat makes it that much harder for your body to absorb the fat-soluble vitamins that are one of the reasons to drink milk in the first place.

16   All this heroic and occasionally counterproductive food science has been undertaken in the name of our health—so that Sara Lee can add to its plastic wrapper the magic words "good source of whole grain" or a food company can ballyhoo the even more magic words "low fat." Which brings us to a related food policy that may at first sound counterintuitive to a health-conscious eater:

Avoid Food Products That Make Health Claims.

17   For a food product to make health claims on its package it must first have a package, so right off the bat it's more likely to be a processed than a whole food. Generally speaking, it is only the big food companies that have the wherewithal to secure FDA-approved health claims for their products and there trumpet them to the world. Recently, however, some of the tonier fruits and nuts have begun boasting about their health-enhancing properties, and there will surely be more as each crop council scrounges together the money to commission its own scientific study. Because all plants contain antioxidants, all these studies are guaranteed to find something on which to base a health-oriented marketing campaign.

18   But for the most part it is the products of food science that make the boldest health claims, and these are often founded on incomplete and often erroneous science—the dubious fruits of nutritionism. Don't forget that trans-fat-rich margarine, one of the first industrial foods to claim it was healthier than the traditional food it replaced, turned out to give people heart attacks. Since that debacle, the FDA, under tremendous pressure from industry, has made it only easier for food companies to make increasingly doubtful health claims, such as the one Frito-Lay now puts on some of its chips—that eating them is somehow good for your heart. If you bother to read the health claims closely (as food marketers make sure consumers seldom do), you will find that there is often considerably less to them than meets the eye.

19   Consider a recent "qualified" health claim approved by the FDA for (don't laugh) corn oil. ("Qualified" is a whole new category of health claim, introduced in 2002 at the behest of industry.) Corn oil, you may recall, is particularly high in the omega-6 fatty acids we're already consuming far too many of.

> Very limited and preliminary scientific evidence suggests that eating about one tablespoon (16 grams) of corn oil daily may reduce the risk of heart disease due to the unsaturated fat content in corn oil.

20   The tablespoon is a particularly rich touch, conjuring images of moms administering medicine, or perhaps cod-liver oil, to their children. But what the FDA gives with one hand, it takes away with the other. Here's the small-print "qualification" of this already notably diffident health claim:

> [The] FDA concludes that there is little scientific evidence supporting this claim.
>
> To achieve this possible benefit, corn oil is to replace a similar amount of saturated fat and not increase the total number of calories you eat in a day.

Close reading of labels undercuts health claims of food products.

21   This little masterpiece of pseudoscientific bureaucratese was extracted from the FDA by the manufacturer of Mazola corn oil. It would appear that "qualified" is an official FDA euphemism for "all but meaningless." Though someone might have let the consumer in on this game: The FDA's own research indicates that consumers have no idea what to make of qualified health claims (how would they?), and its rules allow companies to promote the claims pretty much any way they want—they can use really big type for the claim, for example, and then print the disclaimers in teeny-tiny type. No doubt we can look forward to a qualified health claim for high-fructose corn syrup, a tablespoon of which probably does contribute to your health—as long as it replaces a comparable amount of, say, poison in your diet and doesn't increase the total number of calories you eat in a day.

22   When corn oil and chips and sugary breakfast cereals can all boast being good for your heart, health claims have become hopelessly corrupt. The American Heart Association currently bestows (for a fee) its heart-healthy seal of approval on Lucky Charms, Cocoa Puffs, and Trix cereals, Yoo-hoo lite chocolate drink, and Healthy Choice's Premium Caramel Swirl Ice Cream Sandwich—this at a time when scientists are coming to recognize that dietary sugar probably plays a more important role in heart disease than dietary fat. Meanwhile, the genuinely heart-healthy whole foods in the produce section, lacking the financial and political clout of the packaged goods a few aisles over, are mute. But don't take the silence of the yams as a sign that they have nothing valuable to say about health.

Pollan adds a playful touch by echoing the title of a popular movie to make a point.

Sample Student Definition Argument

Conley 1

Patrice Conley
Ms. Douglas
English
15 Nov. 2010

Flagrant Foul: The NCAA's Definition of Student Athletes as Amateurs

Every year, thousands of student athletes across America sign the National Collegiate Athletic Association's Form 08-3a, the "Student-Athlete" form, waiving their right to receive payment for the use of their name and image (McCann). The form defines student athletes as amateurs, who cannot receive payment for playing their sports. While their schools and coaches may make millions of dollars in salaries and endorsement deals and are the highest-paid public employees in many states, student athletes can never earn a single penny from their college athletic careers.

Make no mistake: college athletics are big business. The most visible college sports—big-time men's football and basketball—generate staggering sums of money. For example, the twelve universities in the Southeastern Conference receive $205 million each year from CBS and ESPN for the right to broadcast its football games (Smith and Ourand). Even more money comes in from video games, clothing, and similar licenses. In 2010, the *New York Times* reported, "the NCAA's licensing deals are estimated at more than $4 billion" per year (Thamel). While the staggering executive pay at big corporations has brought public outrage, coaches' salaries are even more outlandish. Kentucky basketball coach John Calipari is paid over $4 million a year for a basketball program that makes about $35-40 million a year, more than 10% of the entire revenue. Tom Van Riper observes that no corporate CEO commands this large a share of the profits. He notes that if Steve Ballmer, the CEO at Microsoft, had Calipari's deal, Ballmer would make over $6 billion a year.

How can colleges allow advertisers, arena operators, concession owners, athletic gear manufacturers, retailers, game companies, and media moguls, along with coaches and university officials, to make millions and pay the stars of the show nothing? The answer is that colleges define

Patrice Conley sets out the definition she is attempting to rectify: amateurs are athletes who aren't paid.

Conley identifies what's at stake.

Conley disputes the definition that college sports are amateur sports.

The huge salaries paid to college coaches are comparable to those in professional sports.

Conley 2

athletes as amateurs. Not only are student athletes not paid for playing their sport, they cannot receive gifts and are not allowed to endorse products, which may be a violation of their right to free speech. The NCAA, an organization of colleges and schools, forces student athletes to sign away their rights because, it says, it is protecting the students. If student athletes could accept money from anyone, the NCAA argues, they might be exploited, cheated, or even bribed. Taking money out of the equation is supposed to let students focus on academics and preserve the amateur status of college sports.

The definition of amateur arose in the nineteenth century in Britain, when team sports became popular. Middle-class and upper-class students in college had ample time to play their sports while working-class athletes had only a half-day off (no sports were played on Sundays in that era). Teams began to pay top working-class sportsmen for the time they had to take off from work. Middle-class and upper-class sportsmen didn't want to play against the working-class teams, so they made the distinction between amateurs and professionals. The definition of amateur crossed the Atlantic to the United States, where college sports became popular in the 1880s. But it was not long until the hypocrisy of amateurism undermined the ideal. Top football programs like Yale had slush funds to pay athletes, and others used ringers—players who weren't students—and even players from other schools (Zimbalist 7). The Olympic Games maintained the amateur-professional distinction until 1988, but it was long evident that Communist bloc nations were paying athletes to train full-time and Western nations were paying athletes through endorsement contracts. The only Olympic sport that now requires amateur status is boxing. The college sports empire in the United States run by the NCAA is the last bastion of amateurism for sports that draw audiences large enough to be televised.

Colleges might be able to defend the policy of amateurism if they extended this definition to all students. A fair policy is one that treats all students the same. A fair policy doesn't result in some students getting paid for professional work, while other students do not. Consider the

Conley 3

students in the Butler School of Music at the University of Texas at Austin, for example. Many student musicians perform at the professional level. Does the school prevent them from earning money for their musical performances? No. In fact, the school runs a referral service that connects its students with people and businesses who want to hire professional musicians. The university even advises its students on how to negotiate a contract and get paid for their performance ("Welcome").

> Comparisons show that colleges do not apply the definition of amateur consistently.

Likewise, why are student actors and actresses allowed to earn money from their work and images, while student athletes are not? Think about actress Emma Watson, who enrolled at Brown University in Rhode Island. Can you imagine the university officials at Brown telling Watson that she would have to make the next two *Harry Potter* films for free, instead of for the $5 million she has been offered? Can you imagine Brown University telling Watson that all the revenue from Harry Potter merchandise bearing her likeness would have to be paid directly to the university for the rest of her life? They would if Watson were an athlete instead of an actress.

> Do you think this analogy is effective?

In fact, compared to musicians and actors, student athletes have an even greater need to earn money while they are still in college. Athletes' professional careers are likely to be much shorter than musicians' or actors'. College may be the only time some athletes have the opportunity to capitalize on their success. (Indeed, rather than focusing student athletes on their academic careers, the NCAA policy sometimes forces students to leave college early, so they can earn a living before their peak playing years are over.) Student athletes often leave school with permanent injuries and no medical insurance or job prospects, whereas student musicians and actors rarely suffer career-ending injuries on the job.

Student athletes are prevented from profiting from their name and image. The NCAA says this rule preserves their standing as amateurs and protects them from the celebrity and media frenzy surrounding professional sports stars. Search for a "Tim Tebow Jersey" online, and you can buy officially branded Florida Gators shirts, ranging in price from $34.99 to $349.99 (autographed by Tebow). The NCAA, the University of Florida, Nike, and the other parties involved in the production and sale of these products get around the problem of using an amateur's name by

Conley 4

using his team number instead. Tebow's name doesn't appear anywhere on the jerseys—just his number, 15. Yet all these jerseys are identified as "Official Tim Tebow Gators merchandise," and they are certainly bought by fans of Tebow rather than by people who just happen to like the number 15. Nobody is saying how much money these jerseys have made for Nike, or for the NCAA. What we do know for sure is the amount Tim Tebow has made off the jerseys: nothing.

Defenders of the current system argue that student athletes on scholarships are paid with free tuition, free room and board, free books, and tutoring help. The total package can be the equivalent of $120,000 over four years. For those student athletes who are motivated to take advantage of the opportunity, the lifetime benefits can be enormous. Unfortunately, too few student athletes do take advantage of the opportunity. Seldom does a major college football and men's basketball program have graduation rates at or close to overall student body. A study by the University of North Carolina's College Sports Research Institute released in 2010 accuses the NCAA of playing fast and loose with graduation rates by counting part-time students in statistics for the general student body, making graduation rates for athletes look better in a comparison. Student athletes must be full-time students, thus they should be compared to other full-time students. The North Carolina Institute reports that 54.8% of major college (Football Bowl Subdivision) football players at 117 schools graduated within six years, compared to 73.7% of other full-time students. The gap between basketball players was even greater, with 44.6% of athletes graduating compared to 75.7% of the general student body (Zaiger). For the handful of talented athletes who can play in the National Football League or the National Basketball Association, college sports provide training for their future lucrative, although short-lived, profession. But as the NCAA itself points out in its ads, the great majority of student athletes "go pro in something other than sports." For the 55% of college basketball players who fail to graduate, the supposed $120,000 package is an air ball.

The NCAA would be wise to return to the older definition of *amateur*, which comes from Latin through old French, meaning "lover of." It doesn't

The example of Tim Tebow illustrates how the definition of amateur works against college athletes.

Conley gives evidence that undercuts the argument that college athletes are compensated with a college degree.

The clever use of "air ball" reinforces Conley's argument that the NCAA's definition of amateur is outdated and unfair.

Conley 5

necessarily have to have anything to do with money. Whether it's a jazz performer or a dancer or an athlete, an amateur ought to be considered someone in love with an activity—someone who cares deeply about the activity, studies the activity in depth, and practices in order to be highly proficient. NBA players, Olympians, college athletes, high school players, and even bird watchers, star gazers, and open-source programmers: they're all amateurs. If they are lucky enough to be paid, so be it.

Conley concludes with her main claim. She proposes a new definition of amateur, one that would permit salaries and royalties to go to the college athlete.

Conley 6

Works Cited

McCann, Michael. "NCAA Faces Unspecified Damages, Changes in Latest Anti-Trust Case." *SI.com*. Time, Inc., 21 July 2009. Web. 3 Nov. 2010.

National Collegiate Athletic Association. Advertisement. *NCAA.org*. NCAA, 13 Mar. 2007. Web. 3 Nov. 2010.

Smith, Michael, and John Ourand. "ESPN Pays $2.25B for SEC Rights." *SportsBusiness Journal*. Smith and Street, 25 Aug. 2008. Web. 1 Nov. 2010.

Thamel, Pete. "N.C.A.A. Fails to Stop Licensing Lawsuit." *New York Times*. New York Times, 8 Feb. 2010. Web. 1 Nov. 2010.

Van Riper, Thomas. "The Highest-Paid College Basketball Coaches." *Forbes.com*. Forbes, 8 Mar. 2010. Web. 3 Nov. 2010.

"Welcome to the Music Referral Service." *Butler School of Music*. Univ. of Texas at Austin, n.d. Web. 5 Nov. 2010.

Zaiger, Alan Scher. "Study: NCAA Graduation Rate Comparisons Flawed." *ABC News*. ABC News, 20 Apr. 2010. Web. 1 Nov. 2010.

Zimbalist, Andrew. *Unpaid Professionals: Commercialism and Conflict in Big-Time College Sports*. Princeton UP, 2001. Print.

PEARSON
mywritinglab

For additional writing resources that will help you master the objectives of this chapter, go to www.mywritinglab.com.

11 | Causal Arguments

Each year, we hear that American students are falling behind their international peers. Different groups argue that the solution lies in investing more in funding for additional teacher training, or smaller classrooms, or more technology in the classroom. Yet America invests billions more in education than some nations whose students surpass American students in achievement rankings. Still others have suggested that America's problem lies in a wide-scale cultural shift that has created an American student who is less motivated than those of the past. How can America's schools become world leaders again?

Understand How Causal Arguments Work

Causal claims can take three basic forms:

1. One cause leads to one or more effects.

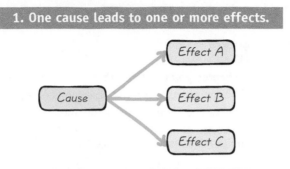

The invention of the telegraph led to the commodities market, the establishment of standard time zones, and news reporting as we know it today.

2. One effect has several causes.

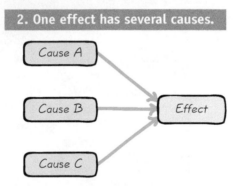

Hurricanes are becoming more financially destructive to the United States because of the greater intensity of recent storms, an increase in the commercial and residential development of coastal areas, and a reluctance to enforce certain construction standards in coastal residential areas.

3. A series of events form a chain, where one event causes another, which then causes a third, and so on.

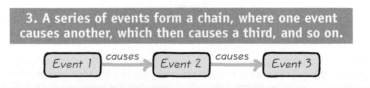

Unusually high numbers of people facing long-term unemployment led to a significant decrease in tax revenue for states and municipalities. This loss of revenue resulted in budget deficits that required forced layoffs of dozens of public sector workers and a decrease in services provided.

Find Causes

The causal claim is at the center of the causal argument. Writing a clear claim about cause and effect can be difficult because if a cause is worth writing about, it is likely to be complex. Obvious cases of cause and effect (staying out in the sun too long without skin protection causes sunburn) usually do not require written arguments because everyone is convinced that the causal relationship exists. Many of the causal claims that most people now accept without question—smoking causes cancer, shifting plates on the Earth's crust cause earthquakes, DDT causes eggshell thinning in bald eagles—were "settled" only after long and complex arguments.

The philosopher John Stuart Mill devised four ways for an investigator to go about finding causes.

- **The Common Factor Method.** Sometimes causes can be identified because two or more similar events share a common factor. The common factor may be the cause. For example, if two people in two different states both develop a rare disease, and both of them recently traveled to Madagascar, they were probably exposed to the illness while there.

- **The Single Difference Method.** Causes can often be identified when two situations or events have different outcomes. If there is a single difference in the two scenarios, that difference may be the cause. At the 1998 Winter Olympics in Nagano, Japan, the speed skating team from the Netherlands introduced a technological innovation to the sport—clap skates, which improve skaters' performance by keeping the skate blade in contact with the ice longer. Racing against the best skaters in the world, the Dutch on their clap skates won eleven of thirty medals, five of which were gold. By the 2002 Winter Olympics, all speed skaters had switched over to the new skates, and the medal count was much more evenly distributed. That year the United States, the Netherlands, and Germany each won three gold medals, and a total of eight medals apiece. Clap skates were the most likely cause of the Netherlands' dominance four years earlier.

- **Concomitant Variation.** Some causes are discovered by observing a shared pattern of variation in a possible cause and possible effect. For example, scientists noticed that peaks in the 11-year sunspot cycle match disruptions in high-frequency radio transmission on earth, leading them to conclude that the solar activity somehow causes the disruptions.

- **Process of Elimination.** Another way to establish causation is to identify all the possible causes of something, and then test them one by one to eliminate those that can't be the cause. When an electrical appliance stops working, electricians often trace the problem this way, by checking switches one at a time to see if current can flow across them. The switch that doesn't show a continuous flow of current is the one that needs replacing.

A frequent error of people looking for cause and effect is to mistake correlation for causation. Just because one event happens after or at the same time as another one, you cannot assume that the first one caused the second. Sometimes it's just a coincidence. For example, you may observe that every time the mail carrier comes to your door, your dog barks at him, and then the mail carrier leaves. You might assume that your dog's barking causes the mail carrier to leave (your dog is probably convinced of this). However, the more likely cause is that the carrier has finished delivering your mail, so he goes on to the next house. Using Mills's methods will help you avoid mistaking correlation for causation in your own causal arguments.

To understand how you might use Mills's methods of identifying causes, suppose you want to research the cause of the increase in legalized lotteries in the United States. You research the history of lotteries in order to look for possible causes. You would discover that lotteries go back to colonial times, but were controversial because they were run by private companies that sometimes failed to pay the winners. Laws against lotteries were passed in 1840, but after the Civil War, the defeated states of the Confederacy needed money to rebuild bridges, buildings, and schools. Southerners ran lotteries and sold tickets throughout the nation. But once again, these lotteries were run by private companies, and some of them simply took people's money without paying out winnings. Eventually, lotteries were banned again.

In 1964, New Hampshire became the first state to authorize a lottery to fund the state's educational system. Soon other states, realizing that their citizens were spending their money on lottery tickets from New Hampshire, established lotteries of their own. During the 1980s, states began approving other forms of state-run gambling such as keno and video poker. By 1993 only Hawaii and Utah had no legalized gambling of any kind.

Knowing this background, you can begin using Mills's methods to look for the causes of lotteries' recent popularity. Using the common factor method, you consider what current lotteries have in common with earlier lotteries. That factor is easy to identify: It's economic. The early colonies and later the states have turned to lotteries again and again as a way of raising money without raising taxes. But, you wonder, why have lotteries spread so quickly since 1964, and raised so little concern? The single difference method shows you the likely reason: Lotteries in the past were run by private companies, and inevitably someone took off with the money instead of paying it out. Today's lotteries are operated by state agencies or contracted under state control. While they are not immune to scandal, they are much more closely monitored than lotteries in the past.

Mills's other methods might also lead you to potential causes. If you find, for example, that lotteries grow in popularity in the aftermath of wars, this concomitant variation might lead you to suspect that the economic damage of war can be one cause of lotteries' popularity. This in turn might suggest inflation caused by the Vietnam War as a possible contributing cause to the rise of state lotteries in the 1960s and 1970s. The process of elimination could also lead you to some probable causes for lotteries' popularity, although for such a complex topic it would be time-consuming. You might begin by making a list of all the reasons you could think of: Perhaps people these days are more economically secure, and don't mind risking a few dollars on lottery tickets? Or maybe people are more desperate now, and lotteries represent one of the few ways they can accumulate wealth? Each of these possibilities would require research into history, economics, and psychology, but this might lead you to some interesting conclusions about the complex forces contributing to today's extensive lottery system.

Build a Causal Argument

Effective causal arguments move beyond the obvious to get at underlying causes. One great causal mystery today is global warming. Scientists generally agree that the average surface temperature on Earth has gone up by 1.3 degrees Fahrenheit or 0.7 degrees Celsius over the last hundred years, and that the amount of carbon dioxide in the atmosphere has increased by 25 percent since 1960. But the causes of those phenomena are disputed. Some people argue that the rise in temperature is caused by natural climate variations, and that the increase in carbon dioxide has little or nothing to do with it. Others argue that the rise in carbon dioxide traps heat in the atmosphere and has increased the earth's temperature. They argue further that the increased carbon dioxide is the result of human activity, especially the burning of fossil fuels and the destruction of tropical forests. The debate over global warming continues because the causation at work is not simple or easy to prove.

There are many events that may be caused by global warming, and they are more dramatically evident in arctic and subarctic regions. The decade from January 2000 to December 2009 is the warmest decade since modern temperature records began in the 1880s. Arctic sea ice shrank by 14 percent—an area the size of Texas—from 2004 to 2005, and Greenland's massive ice sheet has been thinning by more than 3 feet a year.

Many scientists consider these phenomena to be effects of global warming. They argue that a single cause—the rise in the Earth's temperature—has led to many dire effects, and will lead to more. If you wanted to make an argument along these lines, you would need to construct a causal chain:

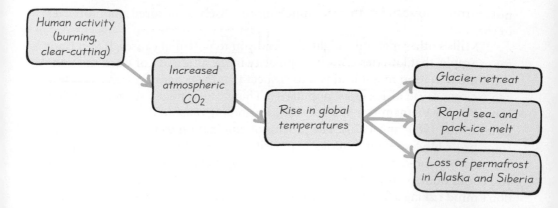

At each step, you would need to show the links between an event and its consequences, and you would need to convince readers that that link is real, not mere coincidence. You might find common factors, single differences, or concomitant variation that supports each causal link. You would also need to use a process of elimination to show that other possible causes are not in fact involved in your causal chain.

Some climate scientists have doubts about all these causal links. While the observable events—the loss of sea ice, glacier retreat, and so on—may be caused by human activity, they may be caused instead by naturally recurring cycles.

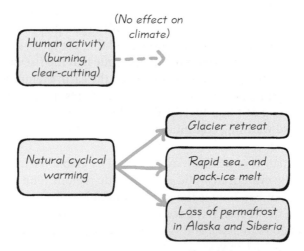

Or, the effects could be caused partly by natural cycles and partly by humans.

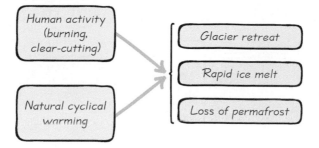

It is difficult to say for certain because much of the detailed data about the great melt in the north goes back only to the early 1990s—not long enough to rule out short-term climate cycles. However, computer models suggest a very low probability that such rapid change could occur naturally. So even if we are in a natural, short-term warming cycle, we still must ask if human activities are contributing to the documented warming, and making it even worse.

Identifying the causes of global warming is important because if we do not know the real causes, we cannot make the necessary changes to stop, reduce, or reverse it. If global warming continues unabated, the economic and human costs will be disastrous. But efforts to stop it are expensive and politically risky. Thus correctly establishing the causes of global warming is a crucial first step in solving the problem.

Glaciers in many parts of the world are melting at rates faster than scientists thought possible just a few years ago. Even major oil companies have acknowledged that global warming is real. Yet the American public has taken little notice of world climate change—perhaps because it's difficult to get excited about the mean temperature rising a few degrees and the sea level rising a few feet. What would get Americans thinking seriously about global warming?

Steps to Writing a Causal Argument

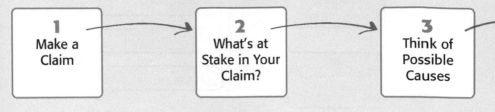

Step 1 Make a Claim

Make a causal claim on a controversial trend, event, or phenomenon.

Template

> SOMETHING does (or does not) cause SOMETHING ELSE.

—or—

> SOMETHING causes SOMETHING ELSE, which, in turn, causes SOMETHING ELSE.

Examples

- One-parent families (or television violence, bad diet, and so on) are (or are not) the cause of emotional and behavioral problems in children.
- Firearms control laws (or right-to-carry-handgun laws) reduce (or increase) violent crimes.
- Putting grade school children into competitive sports teaches them how to succeed in later life (or puts undue emphasis on winning and teaches many who are slower to mature to have a negative self-image).

Step 2 What's at Stake in Your Claim?

- If the cause is obvious to everyone, then it probably isn't worth writing about.

Step 3 Think of Possible Causes

- Which are the immediate causes?
- Which are the background causes?
- Which are the hidden causes?
- Which are the causes that most people have not recognized?

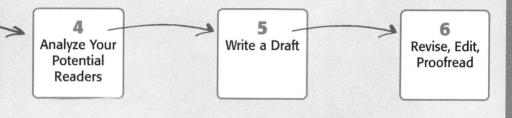

Step 4 Analyze Your Potential Readers

- Who are your readers?
- How familiar will they be with the trend, event, or phenomenon that you're writing about?
- What are they likely to know and not know?
- How likely are they to accept your causal explanation?
- What alternative explanation might they argue for?

Step 5 Write a Draft

Introduction
- Describe the controversial trend, event, or phenomenon.
- Give the background that your intended readers will need.

Body
- Explain the cause or chain of causation of a trend, event, or phenomenon that is unfamiliar to your readers.
- Set out the causes that have been offered and reject them one by one. Then you can present the cause that you think is most important.
- Treat a series of causes one by one, analyzing the importance of each.

Conclusion
- Do more than simply summarize. Consider describing additional effects beyond those that have been noted previously.

Step 6 Revise, Edit, Proofread

- For detailed instructions, see Chapters 4–5.
- For a checklist to use to evaluate your draft, see pages 61–62.

Finding Good Reasons

Why Are Americans Gaining Weight?

Eric Schlosser, author of *Fast Food Nation* (2001), chows down on a grilled cheese sandwich, fries, and a soda. *Fast Food Nation* traces the rise of fast-food restaurants against the background of American culture based on the automobile. Schlosser claims that one of the effects of fast food is the increase in the number of overweight Americans.

There is no doubt that Americans have grown larger. A 2004 survey of Americans published in *JAMA: The Journal of the American Medical Association* found that nearly one-third (32.5 percent) of adults are obese and two-thirds (66.3 percent) are overweight. An especially disturbing aspect of this trend is that children are increasingly obese. The Center for Disease Control and Prevention reports that the percentage of obese children aged 6 to 11 almost quadrupled from 4 percent in 1974 to 15 percent in 2000, and the percentage of obese children aged 12 to 19 increased from 6 percent in 1974 to 15 percent in 2000. (For additional readings about the "obesity epidemic," see the Issue in Focus in Chapter 27.)

Write about it

1. To what extent do you think fast food is the cause of the trend toward excess weight? To what extent do you think lifestyle changes and the content of food are causes? In addition to the amount of fast food Americans consume, consider the following:
   - more sedentary lifestyle with more driving and less walking
   - more time spent watching television, using computers, and playing video games
   - introduction of high-fructose corn syrup in many foods, from ketchup and peanut butter to chocolate milk and yogurt
   - inadequate physical education and reduced outdoor recess periods in schools
   - more food advertising directed at children

2. Which of the issues listed above do you think are the most likely causes of the steady increase in the number of Americans who are overweight? Do some research: can you find evidence to support your thinking?

3. Write 2–3 pages presenting data that establishes (or refutes) a causal link between a specific dietary or behavioral factor and obesity.

Emily Raine

Why Should I Be Nice to You? Coffee Shops and the Politics of Good Service

Emily Raine recently received a master's degree in communication studies at McGill University in Montreal. She writes about graffiti and street art. This article appeared in the online journal *Bad Subjects* in 2005.

In this article, Raine explains why work in a coffee chain is worse than work in other kinds of service jobs. She also outlines the causes for what she sees as a destructive dynamic in the coffee chain culture and provides a possible alternative.

> "There is no more precious commodity than the relationship of trust and confidence a company has with its employees."
>
> — *Starbucks Coffee Company chairman Howard Schultz*

I actually like to serve. I'm not sure if this comes from some innate inclination to mother and fuss over strangers, or if it's because the movement and sociability of service work provides a much-needed antidote to the solitude of academic research, but I've always found something about service industry work satisfying. I've done the gamut of service jobs, from fine dining to cocktail waitressing to hip euro-bistro counter work, and the only job where I've ever felt truly whipped was working as a barista at one of the now-ubiquitous specialty coffee chains, those bastions of jazz and public solitude that have spread through urban landscapes over the last ten years or so. The pay was poor, the shifts long and oddly dispersed, the work boring and monotonous, the managers demanding, and the customers regularly displayed that unique spleen that emerges in even the most pleasant people before they've had the morning's first coffee. I often felt like an aproned Coke machine, such was the effect my sparkling personality had on the clientele. And yet, some combination of service professionalism, fear of termination and an imperative to be "nice" allowed me to suck it up, smile and continue to provide that intangible trait that the industry holds above all else, good service.

Raine establishes a credible, ethical stance in her introduction.

2   Good service in coffee shops doesn't amount to much. Unlike table service, where interaction with customers spans a minimum of half an hour, the average contact with a café customer lasts less than ten seconds. Consider how specialty cafés are laid

Even before identifying the effect that she intends to analyze, Raine identifies the cause—an efficient but impersonal assembly-line approach to service.

3   out: the customer service counter is arranged in a long line that clients move along to "use" the café. The linear coffee bar resembles an assembly line, and indeed, café labor is heavily grounded in the rationalism of Fordist manufacturing principles, which had already been tested for use in hospitality services by fast food chains. Each of the café workers is assigned a specific stage in the service process to perform exclusively, such as taking orders, using the cash registers, or handing clients cups of brewed coffee.

4   The specialization of tasks increases the speed of transactions and limits the duration of any one employee's interaction with the clientele. This means that in a given visit a customer might order from one worker, receive food from the next, then brewed coffee or tea from yet another, then pay a cashier before proceeding down the line of the counter, finishing the trip at the espresso machine which is always situated at its end. Ultimately, each of the café's products is processed and served by a different employee, who repeats the same preparation task for hours and attends to each customer only as they receive that one product.

Raine argues that the assembly-line service model precludes real interaction with customers.

Needless to say, the productive work in cafés is dreary and repetitive. Further, this style of service severely curtails interaction with the clientele, and the very brevity of each transaction precludes much chance for authentic friendliness or conversation—even asking about someone's day would slow the entire operation. The one aspect of service work that can be unpredictable—people—becomes redundant, and interaction with customers is reduced to a fatiguing eight-hour-long smile and the repetition of sentiments that allude to good service, such as injunctions to enjoy their purchases or to have a nice day. Rather than friendly exchanges with customers, barista workers' good service is reduced to a quick rictus in the customer's direction between a great deal of friendly interaction with the espresso machine.

Do you agree with this description of a typical coffee shop?

5   As the hospitality industry really took off in the sixties, good service became one of the trademarks of its advertising claims, a way for brands to distinguish themselves from the rest of the pack. One needn't think too hard to come up with a litany of service slogans that holler the good graces of their personnel—at Starbucks where the baristas make the magic, at Pacific Southwest Airlines where smiles aren't just painted on, or at McDonald's where smiles are free. Employee friendliness emerged as one of the chief distinguishing brand features of personal services, which means that the workers themselves become an aspect of the product for sale.

6   Our notions of good service revolve around a series of platitudes about professionalism—we're at your service, with a smile,

where the customer's always right—each bragging the centrality of the customer to everything "we" do. Such claims imply an easy and equal exchange between two parties: the "we" that gladly serves and the "you" that happily receives. There is, however, always a third party involved in the service exchange, and that's whoever has hired the server, the body that ultimately decides just what the dimensions of good service will be.

This "third party"—management, ownership—is the ultimate cause of the phenomenon under discussion.

7   Like most employees, a service worker sells labor to an employer at a set rate, often minimum wage, and the employer sells the product of that labor, the service itself, at market values. In many hospitality services, where gratuities make up the majority of employment revenue, the worker directly benefits from giving good service, which of course translates to good tips. But for the vast majority of service staff, and particularly those employed in venues yielding little or no gratuities—fast food outlets, café chains, cleaning and maintenance operations—this promises many workers little more than a unilateral imperative to be perpetually bright and amenable.

8   The vast majority of service personnel do not spontaneously produce an unaffected display of cheer and good will continuously for the duration of a shift. When a company markets its products on servers' friendliness, they must then monitor and control employees' friendliness, so good service is defined and enforced from above. Particularly in chains, which are premised upon their consistent reproduction of the same experience in numerous locations, organizations are obliged to impose systems to manage employees' interaction with their customers. In some chains, namely the fast food giants such as McDonald's and Burger King, employee banter is scripted into cash registers, so that as soon as a customer orders, workers are cued to offer, "would you like a dessert with that?" (an offer of dubious benefit to the customer) and to wish them a nice day. Ultimately, this has allowed corporations to be able to assimilate "good service"—or, friendly workers—into their overall brand image.

Does your experience as a customer (or worker) at fast food chains match this description?

9   While cafés genuflect toward the notion of good service, their layouts and management styles preclude much possibility of creating the warmth that this would entail. Good service is, of course, important, but not if it interferes with throughput. What's more, these cafés have been at the forefront of a new wave of organizations that not only market themselves on service quality but also describe employees' job satisfaction as the seed from which this flowers.

10   Perhaps the most glaring example of this is Starbucks, where cheerful young workers are displayed behind elevated

counters as they banter back and forth, calling out fancy Italian drink names and creating theatre out of their productive labor. Starbucks' corporate literature gushes not only about the good service its customers will receive, but about the great joy that its "partners" take in providing it, given the company's unique ability to "provide a great work environment and treat each other with respect and dignity," and where its partners are "emotionally and intellectually committed to Starbucks success." In the epigraph to this essay, Starbucks' chairman even describes the company's relationship with its workers as a commodity. Not only does Starbucks offer good service, but it attempts to guarantee something even better: good service provided by employees that are genuinely happy to give it.

The creation of this new kind of worker is in effect a public relations gimmick.

11   Starbucks has branded a new kind of worker, the happy, wholesome, perfume-free barista. The company offers unusual benefits for service workers, including stock options, health insurance, dental plans and other perks such as product discounts and giveaways. Further, they do so very, very publicly, and the company's promotional materials are filled with moving accounts of workers who never dreamed that corporate America could care so much. With the other hand, though, the company has smashed unionization drives in New York, Vancouver and at its Seattle roaster; it schedules workers at oddly timed shifts that never quite add up to full-time hours; the company pays only nominally more than minimum wage, and their staffs are still unable to subsist schlepping lattes alone.

12   Starbucks is not alone in marketing itself as an enlightened employer. When General Motors introduced its Saturn line, the new brand was promoted almost entirely on the company's good relations with its staff. The company's advertising spots often featured pictures of and quotes from the union contract, describing their unique partnership between manufacturer, workers and union, which allowed blue-collar personnel to have a say in everything from automobile designs to what would be served for lunch. The company rightly guessed that this strategy would go over well with liberal consumers concerned about the ethics of their purchases. Better yet, Saturn could market its cars based on workers' happiness whether personnel were satisfied or not, because very few consumers would ever have the chance to interact with them.

13   At the specialty coffee chains, however, consumers *have* to talk to employees, yet nobody ever really asks. The café service counter runs like a smooth piece of machinery, and I found that most people preferred to pretend that they were interacting with an appliance. In such short transactions, it is exceedingly difficult

for customers to remember the humanity of each of the four to seven people they might interact with to get their coffees. Even fast food counters have one server who processes each customer's order, yet in cafés the workers just become another gadget in the well-oiled café machine. This is a definite downside for the employees—clients are much ruder to café staff than in any other sector of the industry I ever worked in. I found that people were more likely to be annoyed than touched by any reference to my having a personality, and it took no small amount of thought on my part to realize why.

14 Barista workers are hired to represent an abstract category of worker, not to act as individuals. Because of the service system marked by short customer interaction periods and a homogenous staff, the services rendered are linked in the consumer imagination to the company and not to any one individual worker. Workers' assimilation into the company image makes employees in chain service as branded as the products they serve. The chain gang, the workers who hold these eminently collegiate after-school jobs, are proscribed sales scripts and drilled on customer service scenarios to standardize interactions with customers. The company issues protocols for hair length, color and maintenance, visible piercings and tattoos as well as personal hygiene and acceptable odorific products. Workers are made more interchangeable by the use of uniforms, which, of course, serve to make the staff just that. The organization is a constant intermediary in every transaction, interjecting its presence in every detail of the service experience, and this standardization amounts to an absorption of individuals' personalities into the corporate image.

Raine spells out her thesis in this paragraph.

15 Many of the measures that chains take to secure the homogeneity of their employees do not strike us as particularly alarming, likely because similar restrictions have been in place for several hundred years. Good service today has inherited many of the trappings of the good servant of yore, including prohibitions against eating, drinking, sitting or relaxing in front of the served, entering and exiting through back doors, and wearing uniforms to visually mark workers' status. These measures almost completely efface the social identities of staff during work hours, providing few clues to workers' status in their free time. Contact between service workers and their customers is thus limited to purely functional relations, so that the public only see them as workers, as makers of quality coffee, and never as possible peers.

16 Maintaining such divisions is integral to good service because this display of class distinctions ultimately underlies our

notions of service quality. Good service means not only serving well, but also allowing customers to feel justified in issuing orders, to feel okay about being served—which, in turn, requires demonstrations of class difference and the smiles that suggest servers' comfort with having a subordinate role in the service exchange.

17   Unlike the penguin-suited household servant staffs whose class status was clearly defined, service industry workers today often have much more in common from a class perspective with those that they serve. This not only creates an imperative for them to wear their class otherness on their sleeves, as it were, but also to accept their subordinate role to those they serve by being unshakably tractable and polite.

18   Faith Popcorn has rather famously referred to the four-dollar latte as a "small indulgence," noting that while this is a lot to pay for a glass of hot milk, it is quite inexpensive for the feeling of luxury that can accompany it. In this service climate, the class status of the server and the served—anyone who can justify spending this much on a coffee—is blurry, indeed. Coffee shops that market themselves on employee satisfaction assert the same happy servant that allows politically conscientious consumers, who are in many cases the workers' own age and class peers, to feel justified in receiving good service. Good service—as both an apparent affirmation of subordinate classes' desire to serve and as an enforced one-sided politeness—reproduces the class distinctions that have historically characterized servant-served relationships so that these are perpetuated within the contemporary service market.

Raine begins to shift attention to the customers' role in coffee shop culture.

19   The specialty coffee companies are large corporations, and for the twenty-somethings who stock their counters, barista work is too temporary to bother fighting the system. Mostly, people simply quit. Dissatisfied workers are stuck with engaging in tactics that will change nothing but allow them to make the best of their lot. These include minor infractions such as taking liberties with the uniforms or grabbing little bits of company time for their own pleasure, what Michel de Certeau calls *la perruque* and the companies themselves call "time theft." As my time in the chain gang wore on, I developed my own tactic, the only one I found that jostled the customers out of their complacency and allowed me to be a barista and a person.

20   There is no easy way to serve without being a servant, and I have always found that the best way to do so is to show my actual emotions rather than affecting a smooth display of interminable patience and good will. For café customers, bettering baristas' lots can be as simple as asking about their day,

addressing them by name—any little gesture to show that you noticed the person behind the service that they can provide. My tactic as a worker is equally simple, but it is simultaneously an assertion of individual identity at work, a refusal of the class distinctions that characterize the service environment and a rebuttal to the companies that would promote my satisfaction with their system: be rude. Not arbitrarily rude, of course—customers are people, too, and nobody gains anything by spreading bad will. But on those occasions when customer or management behavior warranted a zinging comeback, I would give it.

21   Rudeness, when it is demanded, undermines companies' claims on workers' personal warmth and allows them to retain their individuality by expressing genuine rather than affected feelings in at-work interpersonal exchanges. It is a refusal of the class distinctions that underlie consumers' unilateral prerogative of rudeness and servers' unilateral imperative to be nice. It runs contrary to everything that we have been taught, not only about service but about interrelating with others. But this seems to be the only method of asserting one's person-hood in the service environment, where workers' personalities are all too easily reduced to a space-time, conflated with the drinks they serve. Baristas of the world, if you want to avoid becoming a green-aproned coffee dispensary, you're just going to have to tell people off about it.

> Were you expecting this "solution" to the situation Raine presents?

> Raine reveals her specific audience, "baristias of the world," only at the end of her argument.

Sample Student Causal Argument

Armadi Tansal

Professor Stewart

English 115

29 October 2012

Modern Warfare: Video Games' Link to Real-World Violence

"John" is a nineteen-year-old college student who gets decent grades. He comes from a typical upper-middle-class family and plans to get his MBA after he graduates. John is also my friend, which is why I'm not using his real name.

John has been playing moderately violent video games since he was nine years old. I started playing video and console games around that age too, and I played a lot in junior high, but John plays more than anyone I know. John says that over the past year he has played video games at least four hours every day, and "sometimes all day and night on the weekends." I have personally witnessed John play *Call of Duty: Modern Warfare 2* for six hours straight, with breaks only to use the bathroom or eat something.

> Armadi Tansal establishes a personal relationship to his subject and audience.

I've never seen John act violently, and he's never been in trouble with the law. But new research on violent video games suggests that John's gaming habit puts him at risk for violent or aggressive behavior. Dr. Craig Anderson, a psychologist at the University of Iowa, says "the active role required by video games . . . may make violent video games even more hazardous than violent television or cinema." When people like John play these games, they get used to being rewarded for violent behavior. For example, in the multiplayer version of *Modern Warfare 2*, if the player gets a five-kill streak, he can call in a Predator missile strike. If you kill 25 people in a row, you can call in a tactical nuclear strike. Missile strikes help you advance toward the mission goals more quickly, so the more people you kill, the faster you'll win.

Along with *Modern Warfare 2*, John plays games like *Left 4 Dead, Halo,* and *Grand Theft Auto*. All these games are rated M for Mature, which according to the Entertainment Software Rating Board means they "may contain intense violence, blood and gore, sexual content and/or strong

Tansal 2

language." Some M-rated games, like *Grand Theft Auto,* feature random violence, where players can run amok in a city, beat up and kill people, and smash stuff for no reason. In others, like *Modern Warfare 2,* the violence takes place in the context of military action. To do well in all of these games, you have to commit acts of violence. But does acting violently in games make you more violent in real life?

Anderson says studies show that "violent video games are significantly associated with: increased aggressive behavior, thoughts, and affect [feelings]; increased physiological arousal; and decreased prosocial (helping) behavior." He also claims that "high levels of violent video game exposure have been linked to delinquency, fighting at school and during free play periods, and violent criminal behavior (e.g., self-reported assault, robbery)."

Being "associated with" and "linked to" violent behavior doesn't necessarily mean video games cause such behavior. Many people have argued that the links Anderson sees are coincidental, or that any effects video games might have on behavior are so slight that we shouldn't worry about them. Christopher Ferguson and John Kilburn, professors of Criminal Justice at Texas A&M International University, feel that the existing research does not support Anderson's claims. In a report published in the *Journal of Pediatrics,* they point out that in past studies, "the closer aggression measures got to actual violent behavior, the weaker the effects seen" (762).

From what I can tell, John doesn't have any more violent thoughts and feelings than most men his age. When I asked him if he thought the games had made him more violent or aggressive in real life, he said, "I'm actually less violent now. When we were kids we used to play 'war' with fake guns and sticks, chasing each other around the neighborhood and fighting commando-style. We didn't really fight but sometimes kids got banged up. No one ever gets hurt playing a video game."

Anderson admits that "a healthy, normal, nonviolent child or adolescent who has no other risk factors for high aggression or violence is not going to become a school shooter simply because they play five hours or 10 hours a week of these violent video games" (qtd. in St. George). But just because violent video games don't turn all players into

Tansal identifies the causal question at the heart of his argument.

Direct quotations from published sources build credibility.

Tansal is careful not to accept the easy answer that video games cause everyone to be more violent.

Tansal 3

Here Tansal hints at his thesis, which will be explicitly stated at the end of his argument.

mass murderers, that doesn't mean they have no effect on a player's behavior and personality. For example, my friend John doesn't get into fights or rob people, but he doesn't display a lot of prosocial "helping" behaviors either. He spends most of his free time gaming, so he doesn't get out of his apartment much. Also, the friends he does have mostly play video games with him.

Even though the games restrict his interactions with other humans and condition him to behave violently onscreen, John is probably not at high risk of becoming violent in real life. But according to researchers, this low risk of becoming violent is because none of the dozens of other risk factors associated with violent behavior are present in his life (Anderson et al. 160). If John were a high school dropout, came from a broken home, or abused alcohol and other drugs, his game playing might be more likely to contribute to violent behavior.

Tansal clarifies his thesis that games can be a contributing cause of violent behavior.

Anderson contends that violent video games are a "causal risk factor" for violence and aggression—not that they cause violent aggression. In other words, the games are a small piece of a much larger problem. People like my friend John are not likely to become violent because of the video games they play. But Anderson's research indicates that some people do. Although there is no simple way to tell who those people are, we should include video games as a possible risk factor when we think about who is likely to become violent.

Even if the risk contributed by violent video games is slight for each individual, the total impact of the games on violence in society could be huge. *Call of Duty: Modern Warfare 2* is the third-best-selling video game in the United States (Orry). Its creator, Activision Blizzard, had $1.3 billion dollars in sales in the just first three months of 2010 (Pham). Millions of people play this game, and games like it, and they aren't all as well-adjusted as John. If video games contribute to violent tendencies in only a small fraction of players, they could still have a terrible impact.

Tansal concludes by arguing that video games may not cause many people to become more violent, but it doesn't take many to be a big problem.

Tansal 4

Works Cited

Anderson, Craig. "Violent Video Games: Myths, Facts, and Unanswered Questions." *Psychological Science Agenda* 16.5 (2003): n. pag. Web. 6 Oct. 2010.

Anderson, Craig, et al. "Violent Video Game Effects on Aggression, Empathy, and Prosocial Behavior in Eastern and Western Countries." *Psychological Bulletin* 136 (2010): 151-73. Print.

Entertainment Software Rating Board. *Game Ratings and Descriptor Guide*. Entertainment Software Association, n. d. Web. 7 Oct. 2010.

Ferguson, Christopher J., and John Kilburn. "The Public Health Risks of Media Violence: A Meta-Analytic Review." *Journal of Pediatrics* 154.5 (2009): 759-63. Print.

John (pseudonym). Personal interview. 4 Oct. 2010.

Orry, James. *"Modern Warfare 2* the 3rd Best-Selling Game in the US." *Videogamer.com*. Pro-G Media Ltd., 12 Mar. 2010. Web. 6 Oct. 2010.

Pham, Alex. "Call of Duty: Modern Warfare 2 Propels Revenue, Profit for Activision Blizzard." *Los Angeles Times*. Los Angeles Times, 6 May 2010. Web. 7 Oct. 2010.

St. George, Donna. "Study Links Violent Video Games, Hostility." *Washington Post*. Washington Post, 3 Nov. 2008. Web. 5 Oct. 2010.

PEARSON
mywritinglab

For additional writing resources that will help you master the objectives of this chapter, go to www.mywritinglab.com.

12 | Evaluation Arguments

QUICK TAKE

In this chapter, you will learn that

1. Evaluation arguments set out criteria and then judge something to be good or bad according to those criteria (see page 171)
2. Evaluation arguments are based on practical, aesthetic, and ethical criteria (see page 173)
3. Evaluation arguments often use comparisons (see page 174)

By some estimates, as many as five million animals are killed in shelters each year. Are "no-kill" shelters a good idea? Advocates of no-kill shelters argue that alternatives to euthanizing animals can be created by working to increase adoption demand for shelter animals. No-kill shelters also work to promote spaying and neutering to decrease the number of animals sent to shelters in the first place. Others argue that the term "no-kill" is divisive because it implies that some shelters are "kill" shelters and suggests that many shelter workers are cruel or uncaring. Are no-kill shelters an effective solution? What kind of evaluations would support or oppose the concept of the "no-kill" shelter? How can evaluation arguments be used to support more humane treatment of shelter animals?

P eople make evaluations all the time. Newspapers, magazines, and television have picked up on this love of evaluation by running "best of" polls. They ask their readers to vote on the best Chinese restaurant, the best pizza, the best local band, the best coffeehouse, the best dance club, the best neighborhood park, the best swimming hole, the best bike ride (scenic or challenging), the best volleyball court, the best place to get married, and so on. If you ask one of your friends who voted in a "best" poll why she picked a particular restaurant as the best of its kind, she might respond by saying simply, "I like it." But if you ask her why she likes it, she might start offering good reasons such as these: the food is tasty, the service prompt, the prices fair, and the atmosphere comfortable. It's really not a mystery why these polls are often quite predictable or why the same restaurants tend to win year after year. Many people think that evaluations are matters of personal taste, but when we begin probing the reasons, we often discover that different people use similar criteria to make evaluations.

The key to convincing other people that your judgment is sound is establishing the criteria you will use to make your evaluation. Sometimes it will be necessary to argue for the validity of the criteria that you think your readers should consider. If your readers accept your criteria, it's likely they will agree with your conclusions.

Understand How Evaluation Arguments Work

Evaluation arguments set out criteria and then judge something to be good or bad (or better, or best) according to those criteria.

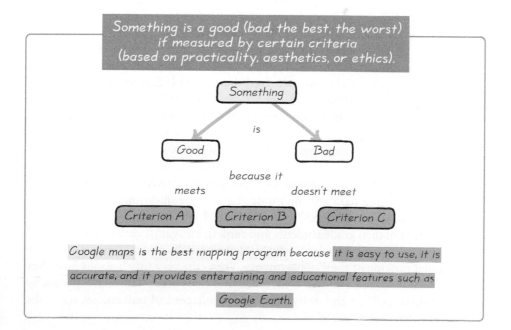

Recognize Kinds of Evaluations

Arguments of evaluation are structured much like arguments of definition. Recall that the criteria in arguments of definition are set out in because clauses:

SOMETHING is a _____ because it meets certain criteria.

Evaluative claims argue that:

SOMETHING is a GOOD (or BAD) _____ because it meets certain criteria.

While people often agree about general criteria, they sometimes disagree about the relevance and appropriateness of specific criteria in an evaluation. Take as an example the question of which colleges are good schools. Until twenty years ago, most of the information that people used to evaluate a college came from the college itself. You could find out the price of tuition and what courses were offered, but other information was difficult to find, and it was hard to compare one college with another.

In 1983 the magazine *U.S. News & World Report* began ranking U.S. colleges and universities from a consumer's perspective. These rankings have remained controversial ever since. *U.S. News* evaluates schools using a complex set of criteria. Twenty-five percent of a school's ranking is based on a survey in which officials at each college rate the quality of schools in the same category as their own school. The results of this survey reflect the school's reputation among university administrators. The remaining 75 percent is based on six kinds of statistical data. These measure retention of students, faculty resources, student selectivity, financial resources, alumni giving, and, for some schools, graduation rates (the difference between the number of students expected to graduate and the number who actually do).

U.S. News chooses specific types of information to look at in each category. For example, "faculty resources" are measured by the size of classes, average faculty pay, the percentage of professors with the highest degree in their field, the overall student-faculty ratio, and the percentage of faculty who are full-time.

Many college officials have criticized the criteria *U.S. News* uses to evaluate colleges. In an August 1998 *U.S. News* article, Gerhard Casper, the president of Stanford University (which is consistently near the top of the rankings), writes, "Much about these rankings—particularly their specious formulas and spurious precision—is utterly misleading." Casper argues that using graduation rates as a criterion rewards schools that pass low-achieving students.

U.S. News replies in its defense that colleges and universities themselves do a lot of ranking, using data and methods that can be questioned. Schools rank students for admission, using SAT or ACT scores, high school GPA, class rank, and other factors, and then grade students and rank them against each other once they are enrolled in college. Schools also evaluate their faculty and take great interest in the national ranking of their departments. They care very much about how they stand in relation to one another. Why, then, *U.S. News* argues, shouldn't people be able to evaluate colleges and universities, since colleges and universities are in the business of evaluating people?

The magazine and the colleges have very different ideas about what constitute fair and relevant criteria for evaluating a college. But the *U.S. News* college rankings generate a tremendous amount of income for the magazine, suggesting that students and their parents agree with the criteria, and use them to help make their own decisions about college.

Some evaluation arguments rely more heavily on certain types of criteria than others. For example, a movie review (_____ is a good movie) is likely to focus most closely on aesthetic considerations: engaging characters, an exciting story, beautiful cinematography. Ethical considerations may be relevant—say, if the film is exceptionally violent, or celebrates antisocial behavior—but usually don't predominate in a movie review. Practical considerations will probably be least important, since anyone reading a movie review is presumably willing to spend the price of admission to see a film. Use these three sources of criteria—aesthetic, moral, and practical—to generate criteria for deciding how good or bad something is, whether that something is a person, a place, an artifact, or a policy.

Build an Evaluation Argument

Although evaluation arguments seem very similar to definition arguments, there is a key difference. Definition arguments seek to place something in the correct category by observing its qualities. They hinge on our judgments about similarity and difference. Evaluation arguments focus instead on what we value. Because of this, the criteria you choose when making an evaluation argument are very important. If your criteria do not appeal to the values of your audience, your readers will not feel that your evaluation is accurate.

Suppose that a city task force on downtown revitalization has a plan to demolish the oldest commercial building in your city. Your neighborhood association wants to preserve the building, perhaps by turning it into a museum. To persuade officials to do this, you must show that your plan for preservation is a good one, while the taskforce's plan for demolition is a bad one. You might argue that a museum would attract visitors to the downtown area, bringing in revenue. You might argue that the elaborately carved stone facade of the building is a rare example of a disappearing craft. Or you might argue that it is only fair to preserve the oldest commercial building in town, since the city's oldest house and other historic buildings have been saved.

Each of these arguments uses different criteria. The argument that a museum will bring in money is based on practical considerations. The argument about the rare and beautiful stonework on the building is based on aesthetic (artistic) considerations. The argument that an old commercial building deserves the same treatment as other old buildings is based on fairness, or ethical concerns. Depending on your audience, you might use all three kinds of criteria, or you might focus more on one or two kinds. If your city is in the middle of a budget crisis, it might be wise to stress the practical, economic benefits of a museum. If several City Council members are architects or amateur historians, your argument

Windmills produce energy without pollution and reduce dependence on foreign oil. Do you agree or disagree with people who do not want windmills built near them because they find them ugly?

might focus on the aesthetic criteria. You have to make assumptions about what your audience will value most as they consider your evaluation.

Evaluative arguments can look at just one case in isolation, but often they make comparisons. You could construct an argument about the fate of the old building that only describes your plan and its benefits. Or, you might also directly address the demolition proposal, showing how it lacks those benefits. Then your argument might be structured like this:

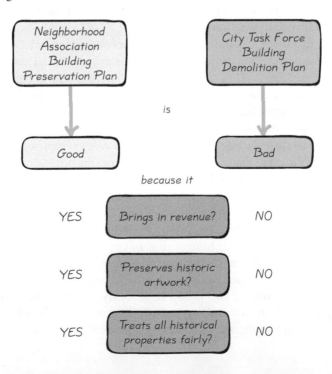

Finding Good Reasons

What's The Best Alternative Fuel?

Biodiesel is an alternative fuel source that is made from vegetable oil (or animal fats) and alcohol. While biodiesel can be used alone, it is often mixed with petroleum diesel. Blends of up to 20 percent biodiesel can be used in a standard diesel engine without modifications—meaning that many cars on the road today would be capable of using biodiesel if it were to become widely available.

But is biodiesel a realistic solution to the world's dependence on fossil fuels? Many think yes. Proponents point to the reduction in greenhouse gas emissions and the lower dependence on foreign oil that would accompany wide-scale biodiesel adoption. Detractors point to millions of acres of land, which would typically be used for food production, that would be converted to fuel production, inevitably causing shortages and an overall rise in food prices.

Write about it

1. One way to assess a complicated issue like alternative fuel technologies is to evaluate each technology against a set of common criteria. Which of the following criteria are useful for evaluating fuel-efficient cars? Why are they useful?
   - cost of development and production
   - sticker price of cars using the technology
   - how long it takes for cars to reach the market
   - efficiency and reliability of cars using the technology
   - environmental impact
   - convenience of refueling and maintenance
   - driver's aesthetic experience

2. Are any of the above criteria more important than the others? If so, how would you rank them? Why? Are there any criteria you would add?

3. There are several sources you can consult to find statistical information about price and performance of new and used cars. Do some research to find how different fuel-efficient cars compare. Using the criteria you established, write an evaluation of the car you think is the best (or the worst).

Steps to Writing an Evaluation Argument

Step 1 Make a Claim

Make an evaluative claim based on criteria.

Template

> SOMETHING is good (bad, the best, the worst) if measured by certain criteria (practicality, aesthetics, ethics).

Examples

- A book or movie review
- An evaluation of a controversial aspect of sports (e.g., the current system of determining who is champion in Division I college football by a system of bowls and polls) or a sports event (e.g., this year's WNBA playoffs) or a team
- An evaluation of the effectiveness of a social policy or law such as restrictions on newly licensed drivers, current gun control laws, or environmental regulation

Step 2 Think About What's at Stake

- Does nearly everyone agree with you? Then your claim probably isn't interesting or important. If you can think of people who disagree, then something is at stake.
- Who argues the opposite of your claim?
- Why do they make a different evaluation?

Step 3 List the Criteria

- Which criteria make something either good or bad?
- Which criteria are the most important?
- Which criteria are fairly obvious, and which will you have to argue for?

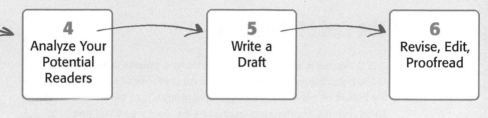

Step 4 Analyze Your Potential Readers

- Who are your readers?
- How familiar will they be with what you are evaluating?
- Which criteria are they most likely to accept with little explanation, and which will they disagree with?

Step 5 Write a Draft

Introduction

- Introduce the person, group, institution, event, or object that you are going to evaluate. You might want to announce your stance at this point or wait until the concluding section.
- Give the background that your intended readers will need.

Body

- Describe each criterion and then analyze how well what you are evaluating meets that criterion.
- If you are making an evaluation according to the effects someone or something produces, describe each effect in detail.
- Anticipate where readers might question either your criteria or how they apply to your subject.
- Address opposing viewpoints by acknowledging how their evaluations might differ and by showing why your evaluation is better.

Conclusion

- If you have not yet announced your stance, conclude that, on the basis of the criteria you set out or the effects you have analyzed, something is good (bad, the best, the worst).
- If you have made your stance clear from the beginning, end with a compelling example or analogy.

Step 6 Revise, Edit, Proofread

- For detailed instructions, see Chapters 4–6.
- For a checklist to use to evaluate your draft, see pages 61–62.

P. J. O'Rourke

The End of the Affair

P. J. O'Rourke is a humorist and satirist who follows in the tradition of the New Journalism where there is no pretense of objectivity and the biases of the writer are in the foreground. Even those who don't agree with his libertarian conservative political views still find him funny, like Bill Maher, who invites O'Rourke on his HBO show. O'Rourke was editor-in-chief of the satirical *National Lampoon* magazine and worked at *Rolling Stone* from 1986 to 2001. The titles of his books suggest his sense of humor: *Modern Manners: An Etiquette Books for Rude People* (1983), *The Bachelor's Home Companion: A Practical Guide to Keeping House like a Pig* (1987), *Holidays in Hell* (1988), *Parliament of Whores: A Lone Humorist Attempts to Explain the Entire U.S. Government* (1991), *Give War a Chance: Eyewitness Accounts of Mankind's Struggle against Tyranny, Injustice, and Alcohol-free Beer* (1992), and *Peace Kills: America's Fun New Imperialism* (2004). O'Rourke's humor is infused with outrage over the influence of government in ordinary life, which you will find in this evaluation argument, published in the *Wall Street Journal* in 2009.

O'Rourke begins by announcing that he is from an older generation. What does he gain and lose from this strategy?

2

The phrase "bankrupt General Motors," which we expect to hear uttered on Monday, leaves Americans my age in economic shock. The words are as melodramatic as "Mom's nude photos." And, indeed, if we want to understand what doomed the American automobile, we should give up on economics and turn to melodrama.

Politicians, journalists, financial analysts and other purveyors of banality have been looking at cars as if a convertible were a business. Fire the MBAs and hire a poet. The fate of Detroit isn't a matter of financial crisis, foreign competition, corporate greed, union intransigence, energy costs or measuring the shoe size of the footprints in the carbon. It's a tragic romance—unleashed passions, titanic clashes, lost love and wild horses. Foremost are the horses. Cars can't be comprehended without them. A hundred and some years ago Rudyard Kipling wrote "The Ballad of the King's Jest," in which an Afghan tribesman avers: Four things greater than all things are—Women and Horses and Power and War.

Note how his favored criteria—romance, passion, horses—have to do with aesthetics, not practical issues like safety or environmental impact.

3

Insert another "power" after the horse and the verse was as true in the suburbs of my 1950s boyhood as it was in the Khyber Pass.

4

Horsepower is not a quaint leftover of linguistics or a vague metaphoric anachronism. James Watt, father of the steam engine and progenitor of the industrial revolution, lacked a measurement for the movement of weight over distance in time—what we call energy. (What we call energy wasn't even an intellectual concept in the late 18th century—in case you think the recent collapse of global capitalism was history's most transformative moment.) Mr. Watt did research using draft animals and found that, under optimal conditions, a dray horse could lift 33,000 pounds one foot off the ground in one minute. Mr. Watt—the eponymous watt not yet existing—called this unit of energy "1 horse-power."

Note how this paragraph establishes O'Rourke's expertise, his credibility.

5   In 1970 a Pontiac GTO (may the brand name rest in peace) had horsepower to the number of 370. In the time of one minute, for the space of one foot, it could move 12,210,000 pounds. And it could move those pounds down every foot of every mile of all the roads to the ends of the earth for every minute of every hour until the driver nodded off at the wheel. Forty years ago the pimply kid down the block, using $3,500 in saved-up soda-jerking money, procured might and main beyond the wildest dreams of Genghis Khan, whose hordes went forth to pillage mounted upon less oomph than is in a modern leaf blower.

O'Rourke's favored criteria—status and being cool —have nothing to do with practicality and everything to do with aesthetics.

6   Horses and horsepower alike are about status and being cool. A knight in ancient Rome was bluntly called "guy on

horseback," Equesitis. Chevalier means the same, as does Cavalier. Lose the capitalization and the dictionary says, "insouciant and
debonair; marked by a lofty disregard of others' interests, rights, or
feelings; high-handed and arrogant and supercilious." How cool is
that? Then there are cowboys—always cool—and the U.S. cavalry
that coolly comes to their rescue plus the proverbially cool-handed
"Man on Horseback" to whom we turn in troubled times.

O'Rourke uses predominantly male references. Do you think he was writing only for men?

7   Early witnesses to the automobile urged motorists to get a
horse. But that, in effect, was what the automobile would do—get a
horse for everybody. Once the Model T was introduced in 1908 we
all became Sir Lancelot, gained a seat at the Round Table and were
privileged to joust for the favors of fair maidens (at drive-in movies).
The pride and prestige of a noble mount was vouchsafed to the
common man. And woman, too. No one ever tried to persuade
ladies to drive sidesaddle with both legs hanging out the car door.

More "status" and "being cool."

8   For the purpose of ennobling us schlubs, the car is better than
the horse in every way. Even more advantageous than cost, convenience and not getting kicked and smelly is how much easier it is to
drive than to ride. I speak with feeling on this subject, having taken
up riding when I was nearly 60 and having begun to drive when I
was so small that my cousin Tommy had to lie on the transmission
hump and operate the accelerator and the brake with his hands.

"Schlub" is Yid-dish slang for an unattractive per-son. Why does O'Rourke use this term?

9   After the grown-ups had gone to bed, Tommy and I shifted
the Buick into neutral, pushed it down the driveway and out of
earshot, started the engine and toured the neighborhood. The
sheer difficulty of horsemanship can be illustrated by what
happened to Tommy and me next. Nothing. We maneuvered the
car home, turned it off and rolled it back up the driveway. (We
were raised in the blessedly flat Midwest.) During our foray the
Buick's speedometer reached 30. But 30 miles per hour is a full
gallop on a horse. Delete what you've seen of horse riding in
movies. Possibly a kid who'd never been on a horse could ride at
a gallop without killing himself. Possibly one of the Jonas Brothers
could land an F-14 on a carrier deck.

10   Thus cars usurped the place of horses in our hearts. Once
we'd caught a glimpse of a well-turned Goodyear, checked out
the curves of the bodywork and gaped at that swell pair of head-
lights, well, the old gray mare was not what she used to be. We
embarked upon life in the fast lane with our new paramour. It was
a great love story of man and machine. The road to the future was
paved with bliss.

Cars in the 1950s and 1960s represented the triumph of aes-thetics over prac-tical issues like gas mileage and safety.

11   Then we got married and moved to the suburbs. Being away
from central cities meant Americans had to spend more of their

time driving. Over the years away got farther away. Eventually this meant that Americans had to spend all of their time driving. The play date was 40 miles from the Chuck E. Cheese. The swim meet was 40 miles from the cello lesson. The Montessori was 40 miles from the math coach. Mom's job was 40 miles from Dad's job and the three-car garage was 40 miles from both.

O'Rourke describes how practicality gained the upper hand over aesthetics.

12   The car ceased to be object of desire and equipment for adventure and turned into office, rec room, communications hub, breakfast nook and recycling bin—a motorized cup holder. Americans, the richest people on Earth, were stuck in the confines of their crossover SUVs, squeezed into less space than tech-support call-center employees in a Mumbai cubicle farm. Never mind the six-bedroom, eight-bath, pseudo-Tudor with cathedral-ceilinged great room and 1,000-bottle controlled-climate wine cellar. That was a day's walk away.

O'Rourke mocks how practicality rules—that the romance of cars is reduced to cup holders.

13   We became sick and tired of our cars and even angry at them. Pointy-headed busybodies of the environmentalist, new urbanist, utopian communitarian ilk blamed the victim. They claimed the car had forced us to live in widely scattered settlements in the great wasteland of big-box stores and the Olive Garden. If we would all just get on our Schwinns or hop a trolley, they said, America could become an archipelago of cozy gulags on the Portland, Oregon, model with everyone nestled together in the most sustainably carbon-neutral, diverse and ecologically unimpactful way.

14   But cars didn't shape our existence; cars let us escape with our lives. We're way the heck out here in Valley Bottom Heights and Trout Antler Estates because we were at war with the cities. We fought rotten public schools, idiot municipal bureaucracies, corrupt political machines, rampant criminality and the pointy-headed busybodies. Cars gave us our dragoons and hussars, lent us speed and mobility, let us scout the terrain and probe the enemy's lines. And thanks to our cars, when we lost the cities we weren't forced to surrender, we were able to retreat.

Note how O'Rourke characterizes the unfortunate practicalities of modern life.

15   But our poor cars paid the price. They were flashing swords beaten into dull plowshares. Cars became appliances. Or worse. Nobody's ticked off at the dryer or the dishwasher, much less the fridge. We recognize these as labor-saving devices. The car, on the other hand, seems to create labor. We hold the car responsible for all the dreary errands to which it needs to be steered. Hell, a golf cart's more fun. You can ride around in a golf cart with a six-pack, safe from breathalyzers, chasing Canada geese on the fairways and taking swings at gophers with a mashie.

O'Rourke reverses the usual positive meaning of the metaphor of turning swords into plowshares.

16   We've lost our love for cars and forgotten our debt to them and meanwhile the pointy-headed busybodies have been exacting their revenge. We escaped the poke of their noses once, when we lived downtown, but we won't be able to peel out so fast the next time. In the name of safety, emissions control and fuel economy, the simple mechanical elegance of the automobile has been rendered ponderous, cumbersome and incomprehensible. One might as well pry the back off an iPod as pop the hood on a contemporary motor vehicle. An aging shade-tree mechanic like myself stares aghast and sits back down in the shade. Or would if the car weren't squawking at me like a rehearsal for divorce. You left the key in. You left the door open. You left the lights on. You left your dirty socks in the middle of the bedroom floor.

Now the new cars are tied explicitly to "busybodies"—the practical-minded regulators that O'Rourke despises.

17   I don't believe the pointy-heads give a damn about climate change or gas mileage, much less about whether I survive a head-on with one of their tax-sucking mass-transit projects. All they want to is to make me hate my car. How proud and handsome would Bucephalas look, or Traveler or Rachel Alexandra, with seat and shoulder belts, air bags, 5-mph bumpers and a maze of pollution-control equipment under the tail?

It's romantic aesthetics vs. ugly practicality.

18   And there's the end of the American automobile industry. When it comes to dull, practical, ugly things that bore and annoy me, Japanese things cost less and the cup holders are more conveniently located.

19   The American automobile is—that is, was—never a product of Japanese-style industrialism. America's steel, coal, beer, beaver pelts and PCs may have come from our business plutocracy, but American cars have been manufactured mostly by romantic fools. David Buick, Ransom E. Olds, Louis Chevrolet, Robert and Louis Hupp of the Hupmobile, the Dodge brothers, the Studebaker brothers, the Packard brothers, the Duesenberg brothers, Charles W. Nash, E. L. Cord, John North Willys, Preston Tucker and William H. Murphy, whose Cadillac cars were designed by the young Henry Ford, all went broke making cars. The man who founded General Motors in 1908, William Crapo (really) Durant, went broke twice. Henry Ford, of course, did not go broke, nor was he a romantic, but judging by his opinions he certainly was a fool.

20 America's romantic foolishness with cars is finished, however, or nearly so. In the far boondocks a few good old boys haven't got the memo and still tear up the back roads. Doubtless the Obama administration's Department of Transportation is even now calculating a way to tap federal stimulus funds for mandatory OnStar installations to locate and subdue these reprobates.

Is O'Rourke himself one of those good old boys?

21 Among certain youths—often first-generation Americans—there remains a vestigial fondness for Chevelle low-riders or Honda "tuners." The pointy-headed busybodies have yet to enfold these youngsters in the iron-clad conformity of cultural diversity's embrace. Soon the kids will be expressing their creative energy in a more constructive way, planting bok choy in community gardens and decorating homeless shelters with murals of Che.

22 I myself have something old-school under a tarp in the basement garage. I bet when my will has been probated, some child of mine will yank the dust cover and use the proceeds of the eBay sale to buy a mountain bike. Four things greater than all things are, and I'm pretty sure one of them isn't bicycles. There are those of us who have had the good fortune to meet with strength and beauty, with majestic force in which we were willing to trust our lives. Then a day comes, that strength and beauty fails, and a man does what a man has to do. I'm going downstairs to put a bullet in a V-8.

Sample Student Evaluation Argument

Katrani 1

Sepideh Katrani
Dr. Josephs
English 1102
19 December 2011

The Right to Speak Freely

On August 1, 2011, a new policy took effect in the Smithtown Central School District. The policy was developed by the high school administration, discussed by the Parent-Teacher Association, and adopted by the Board of School Directors. While these discussions were taking place, the group directly affected by this new set of rules was never invited into the conversation. Students were not asked for our opinions about whether there is a need for such a sweeping policy, what will be banned under the new rules, or what we think might happen once it is implemented.

> After describing the policy, Sepi Katrani begins her evaluation by stating the negative consequences she believes will occur.

Under the new dress code, students will be forbidden to wear any clothing or "ornamentation (jewelry, wristbands, head scarves) that carries a political or religious message" (Smithtown Central 23). Administrators and members of the School Board claim that such guidelines are necessary to maintain order and eliminate distractions that get in the way of our education. They haven't considered the egregious side effect of their decision: the restriction of our First Amendment rights.

The new restrictions are based on invalid assumptions about the way the majority of students will respond when other people express views and beliefs that differ from their own. Wearing a gold cross that represents an affiliation with a particular religious group or an article of clothing that is an expression of a specific religious belief does not cause other students to stop in the hallway and try to convert each other. There is no evidence that wearing a T-shirt that endorses a candidate for political office makes other students scream out their opposition and interrupt class.

> Katrani acknowledges the reason that such policies have been put in place in many high schools in recent years.

Since the Columbine shootings, school administrators are understandably hypersensitive to the potential for violence and have imposed policies designed to eliminate threats. The side effect of these well-intended rules is to limit students' right to speak freely. What these restrictions don't do is lead to safer schools. Legal scholar Richard Salgado explains that "contrary to what many assume, greater speech rights for students and safer schools are complementary objectives, rather than mutually exclusive goals" (1376).

As high school students, we know—or can learn—the meaning of freedom of speech and freedom of religion. Some students mistakenly believe that the First Amendment gives us the right to say whatever we want, whenever we want, in any way we want. Most of us know that this is *not* true. We understand that there are instances in which speech is "nonprotected." We are familiar with the well-known comment made by Oliver Wendell Holmes that "falsely yelling fire in a theater and causing a panic" is not excusable in the name of freedom of speech. Harassment, libel, and slander are nonprotected speech. Advocating illegal activities or directly threatening someone is nonprotected speech (*History*). Freedom of speech isn't a free pass.

But two of the most important categories of *protected* speech are political and religious speech—the very things this new dress code is designed to curtail. We are granted the freedom to speak freely in this country so that we can state different political views and hear what others have to say. We're allowed to disagree with our government and to talk about why we are opposed to some laws or policies and agree with others. The underlying concept is that people can come up with better policies collectively, if we listen to each other. That's why political speech is protected; and that's why high school students should be allowed to practice this crucial element of living in a democratic society. If not in high school, where else can we learn to exercise our civic rights and responsibilities? "[If] students are going to learn to become responsible citizens in a democracy, they must be able to exercise their constitutional rights" (Cambron-McCabe 709).

In 1969, the Supreme Court ruled in Tinker v. Des Moines that the school district was wrong in suspending three students because they wore black armbands to school in protest of the Vietnam War. The Supreme Court "famously declared that students do not 'shed their constitutional rights to freedom of speech or expression at the schoolhouse gate'" (Salgado 1377). This ruling did not address other First Amendment rights, but we can assume those rights, including freedom of religion, should not be left "at the schoolhouse gate."

Katrani 3

Katrani does not need to insert an in-text citation here because these passages from the Constitution are considered common knowledge.

Because of constitutionally protected freedom of religion, American citizens aren't required to worship in the same way. If we choose not to, we can't be forced to worship at all. The Constitution states that Congress can't make any laws about the "establishment of religion" or "prohibiting the free exercise thereof." In a public school, it shouldn't matter at all what religion anyone practices. In fact, school is the place where we have the chance to learn about what other people believe and why. Discussing religious beliefs isn't the same as imposing those beliefs on anyone else. In a public school, we shouldn't be forbidding students to express their beliefs.

This new dress code will guarantee that we never have the chance to learn that other people don't believe the same things we do. Teachers will be required to be the "clothing police" and spend their time and energy making sure that anyone who wears an armband with a political message or a T-shirt with a religious symbol is punished. They will have to try to adjudicate many borderline cases. Focusing on enforcement instead of instruction would inevitably detract from the educational mission of the school. It would be a much better use of teachers' time to help us learn about each other's opinions and beliefs. Instead of worrying about what we're wearing, the high school administration and the School Board should be encouraging us to participate in respectful communication about why we choose to wear a head scarf or a campaign button. Then they would be improving our education instead of dictating our wardrobe.

Katrani imagines that enforcing the new policy is not only unethical because it limits students' rights, but also impractical.

Who is the intended audience for Katrani's evaluation? Do you think the arguments she presents in the essay are appropriate to her purpose?

Katrani 4

Works Cited

Cambron-McCabe, Nelda. "Balancing Students' Constitutional Rights."
    Phi Delta Kappan 90.10 (2009): 709-13. *Academic Search Complete*.
    EBSCO. Web. 11 December 2011.
The History of the Supreme Court. New York Life. n.d. Web. 11 December
    2011.

Katrani 4

Salgado, Richard. "Protecting Student Speech Rights While Increasing
School Safety: School Jurisdiction and the Search for Warning
Signs in a Post-Columbine/Red Lake Environment." *Brigham Young
University Law Review* 2005.5 (2005): 1371-1412. *Academic Search
Complete*. Web. 10 December 2011.
Smithtown Central School District. (2011). *Student Handbook
2011–2012*. Print.

For additional writing resources that will help you master the objectives of this
chapter, go to www.mywritinglab.com.

13 | Narrative Arguments

QUICK TAKE

In this chapter, you will learn that

1. Narrative arguments rely on concrete individual stories rather than large-scale statistics (see below)
2. Narrative arguments often should allow readers to draw their own conclusions (see page 189)
3. Narrative arguments must strike readers as truthful and representative of larger issues (see page 191)

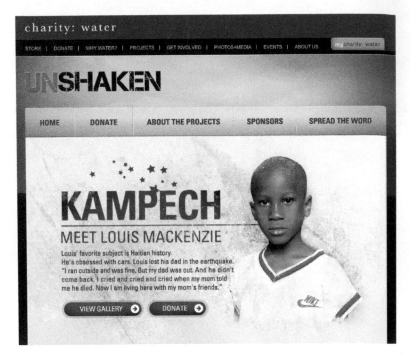

Charity: water understands the persuasive power of personal stories. Their online campaign features narratives like the story of Louis Mackenzie, a young boy who lost his father in the January 2010 earthquake in Haiti. "I cried and cried and cried when my mom told me he died," the text reads. As many organizations have learned, people often feel more compelled to donate money when they read personal stories like Louis's than when they are barraged with abstract numbers and statistics. Why are such stories effective as arguments? What makes some stories more compelling than others? © 2010 Charitywater.org. Used with permission.

Understand How Narrative Arguments Work

A single, detailed personal story sometimes makes a stronger case than large-scale statistical evidence. The Annenberg Public Policy Center reported that an estimated 1.6 million of 17 million U.S. college students gambled online in 2005, but it was the story of Greg Hogan that made the problem real for many Americans. Hogan, the son of a Baptist minister, was an extraordinarily talented musician, who played onstage twice at Carnegie Hall by age 13. He chose to attend Lehigh University in Pennsylvania, where he was a member of the orchestra and class president. At Lehigh he also acquired an addiction to online poker. He lost $7,500, much of which he borrowed from fraternity brothers. To pay them back, he robbed a bank, only to be arrested a few hours later. Eventually he received a long prison sentence. Hogan's story helped to influence Congress to pass the Unlawful Internet Gambling Enforcement Act, which requires financial institutions to stop money transfers to gambling sites.

Successful narrative arguments typically don't have a thesis statement but instead tell a compelling story. From the experience of one individual, readers infer a claim and the good reasons that support the claim.

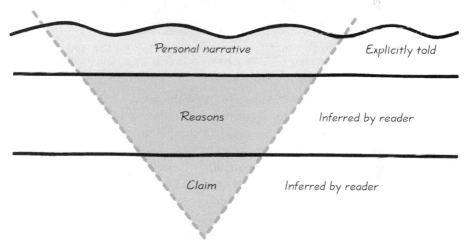

Personal narrative	Explicitly told
Reasons	Inferred by reader
Claim	Inferred by reader

Recognize Kinds of Narrative Arguments

Using narrative to make an argument is part of human nature. As far back as we have records, we find people telling stories and singing songs that argue for change. During periods of history where explicit arguments are dangerous to make, stories have allowed people to safely criticize authority or imagine how life could be different. The history of folk music is a continuous recycling of old tunes, phrases, and narratives to engage new political situations. Antiwar ballads popular in Ireland in the 1840s were sung in the 1960s by Americans protesting their country's involvement in Vietnam. All the popular narrative genres—short stories, novels, movies, and theater—have been used as ways to make arguments for change.

Singer/songwriter Shawn Colvin is one of many contemporary folk, blues, rock, and rap artists who continue the tradition of making narrative arguments in their songs. Can you think of a song that makes a narrative argument?

Narrative arguments allow readers to fill in the good reasons, and come to their own conclusions. The personal connection readers can feel with the writer of a narrative argument makes this strategy a compelling means of persuasion. Moreover, because the writer usually refrains from making an outright claim, people reading narrative arguments are more likely to feel that they are "making up their own minds" rather than being reluctantly persuaded.

Narrative arguments can be representative anecdotes or they can be longer accounts of particular events that express larger ideas. One such story is George Orwell's account of a hanging in Burma (the country now known as Myanmar) while he was a British colonial administrator in the late 1920s. In "A Hanging," first published in 1931, Orwell narrates the story of an execution of a nameless prisoner who was convicted of a nameless crime. Everyone present quietly and dispassionately performs his job—the prison guards, the hangman, the superintendent, and even the prisoner, who offers no resistance when he is bound and led to the gallows. All is totally routine until a very small incident makes Orwell realize what is happening:

> It was about forty yards to the gallows. I watched the bare brown back of the prisoner marching in front of me. He walked clumsily with his bound arms, but quite steadily, with that bobbing gait of the Indian who never straightens his knees. At each step his muscles slid neatly into place, the lock of hair on his scalp danced up and down, his feet printed themselves on the wet gravel. And once, in spite of the men who gripped him by each shoulder, he stepped slightly aside to avoid a puddle on the path.

It is curious, but till that moment I had never realized what it means to destroy a healthy, conscious man. When I saw the prisoner step aside to avoid the puddle, I saw the mystery, the unspeakable wrongness, of cutting a life short when it is in full tide. This man was not dying, he was alive just as we were alive. All the organs of his body were working—bowels digesting food, skin renewing itself, nails growing, tissues forming—all toiling away in solemn foolery. His nails would still be growing when he stood on the drop, when he was falling through the air with a tenth of a second to live. His eyes saw the yellow gravel and the grey walls, and his brain still remembered, foresaw, reasoned—reasoned even about puddles. He and we were a party of men walking together, seeing, hearing, feeling, understanding the same world; and in two minutes, with a sudden snap, one of us would be gone—one mind less, one world less.

Orwell's narrative leads to a dramatic moment of recognition, which gives this story its lasting power. His sudden realization of what execution means to both the prisoner and his executioners is a powerful argument to reconsider the morality of the death penalty.

At the end of this chapter, read E. B. White's "Education," a short essay that contains no explicit thesis statement. Then consider this question: what are White's persuasive purposes in recounting these narrative events?

Build a Narrative Argument

Because storytelling is such a familiar activity, it is easy for writers to get carried away with their narratives, and lose sight of the points they are trying to make. Readers find narrative compelling, but not if the narrative is long-winded, full of unnecessary detail, or has no obvious point. Furthermore, readers are quickly put off if they feel they are being given a lecture.

There are two keys to making effective narrative arguments: establishing that the narrative is truthful, and showing its relevance to a wider problem or question. Writing from personal experience can increase the impact of your argument, but that impact diminishes greatly if readers doubt you are telling the truth. And while the story you tell may be true, it is important that it also be representative— something that has happened to many other people, or something that could happen to your readers. Narrative arguments are useful for illustrating how people are affected by particular issues or events, but they are more effective if you have evidence that goes beyond a single incident.

One rule of thumb that you can keep in mind when building a narrative argument is to start out with as much detail and as many events as you can recall; include lots of sensory details so that your reader will truly believe that your tale is true. Then revise and edit heavily. It's hard to select the best details and events for your argument until you have written them all down, and often the process of writing and remembering will bring up new details that you had forgotten, or hadn't seen the relevance of before. Once you can see the big picture you have painted with your narrative, it is easier to see what your readers do not need, and remove it. This strategy brings your story, and your argument, into sharper focus.

Steps to Writing a Narrative Argument

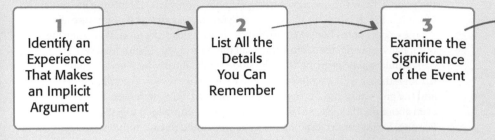

1
Identify an Experience That Makes an Implicit Argument

2
List All the Details You Can Remember

3
Examine the Significance of the Event

Step 1 Identify an Experience That Makes an Implicit Argument

Think about experiences that made you realize that something is wrong or that things need to be changed. The experience does not have to be one that leads to a moral lesson at the end, but it should be one that makes your readers think.

Examples

- Being accused of and perhaps even *punished* for something you didn't do or for standing up for something you believed in
- Moving from a well-financed suburban school to a much poorer rural or urban school in the same state
- Experiencing stereotyping or prejudice in any way—for the way you look, the way you act or speak, your age, your gender, or your race or ethnicity or religion

Step 2 List All the Details You Can Remember

- When did it happen?
- How old were you?
- Why were you there?
- Who else was there?
- Where did it happen? If the place is important, describe what it looked like.
- What did it all sound like? feel like? smell like? taste like?

Step 3 Examine the Significance of the Event

- How did you feel about the experience when it happened?
- How did it affect you then?
- How do you feel about the experience now?
- What long-term effects has it had on your life?

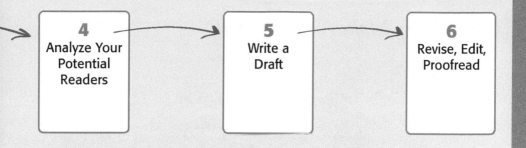

Step 4 Analyze Your Potential Readers

- Who are your readers?
- How much will your readers know about the background of the experience you are describing?
- Would anything similar ever likely have happened to them?
- How likely are they to agree with your feelings about the experience?

Step 5 Write a Draft

- You might need to give some background first, but if you have a compelling story, often it's best to launch right in.
- You might want to tell the story as it happened (chronological order), or you might want to begin with a striking incident and then go back to tell how it happened (flashback).
- You might want to reflect on your experience at the end, but you want your story to do most of the work. Avoid drawing a simple moral lesson. Your readers should share your feelings if you tell your story well.

Step 6 Revise, Edit, Proofread

- For detailed instructions, see Chapter 5.
- For a checklist to use to evaluate your draft, see pages 61–62.

Finding Good Reasons

Can A Story Make An Argument?

As climate change melts sea ice, the U.S. Geological Survey projects that two-thirds of polar bears will disappear by 2050. This dramatic decline of polar bears is occurring in our lifetime, which is but a minuscule fraction of the time polar bears have roamed the vast Arctic seas. The retreat of ice has implications beyond the obvious habitat loss. The larger gap of open water between the ice and land also contributes to rougher wave conditions, making the bears' swim from shore to sea ice more hazardous. Exacerbating the problems of the loss of hunting areas, the shrinking polar ice cap will also cause a decline in polar bears' prey—seals. The polar bear is the proverbial "canary in the coal mine" of the serious threat global warming poses to wildlife species around the world, unless we take immediate and significant action to reduce global warming pollution.

Write about it

1. What argument might the photograph be making about the state of climate change? What details reveal the specifics of the argument? Why is there just one bear pictured?

2. Why was the polar bear chosen to dramatize the effects of climate change? What other types of animals would have made good choices? Poor choices?

3. This photograph dramatizes climate change as a reality and implies that action should be taken to arrest it. But what is the other side of this issue? Does this story change your thinking about climate change? Why or why not?

4. Narrative arguments often rely on emotional appeals. Pathos can be very effective; on the other hand, it can sometimes be off-putting. Does this photograph make its argument rationally or emotionally or both?

E. B. White

Education

You probably recognize E. B. White (1899–1985) as the author of the children's classics *Charlotte's Web* (1952) and *Stuart Little* (1945). But for decades, beginning in the 1920s, White was also a regular contributor to *The New Yorker* and to other magazines geared to well-educated, prosperous, mostly eastern Americans, and his works made him perhaps the most popular essayist in the United States. White studied at Cornell University, spent his career living in New York City and in New England, and collected his essays into several books. First published in *Harper's* magazine in 1939 and then included in White's *One Man's Meat* in 1942, the following comparison of two educational philosophies remains relevant today. What should our schools be like? Is education carried out more effectively in large, fully equipped, progressive, but relatively impersonal settings, or in smaller but intensely personal, teacher-dominated schools?

I have an increasing admiration for the teacher in the country school where we have a third grade scholar in attendance. She not only undertakes to instruct her charges in all the subjects of the first three grades, but she manages to function quietly and effectively as a guardian of their health, their clothes, their habits, their mothers, and their snowball engagements. She has been doing this sort of Augean task for twenty years, and is both kind and wise. She cooks for the children on the stove that heats the room, and she can cool their passions or warm their soup with equal competence. She conceives their costumes, cleans up their messes, and shares their confidences. My boy already regards his teacher as his great friend, and I think tells her a great deal more than he tells us.

Note that the essay begins and ends with a description of the country school. That way, the favored school gets the favored position.

2   The shift from city school to country school was something we worried about quietly all last summer. I have always rather favored public school over private school, if only because in public school you meet a greater variety of children. This bias of mine, I suspect, is partly an attempt to justify my own past (I never knew anything but public schools) and partly an involuntary defense against getting kicked in the shins by a young ceramist on his way to the kiln. My wife was unacquainted with public schools, never having been exposed (in her early life) to anything more public than the washroom of Miss Winsor's. Regardless of our backgrounds, we both knew that the change in schools was something that concerned not us but the scholar himself. We hoped it would work out all right. In New York our son went to a medium-priced

Note how this paragraph is an effort to establish the writer's credibility.

White often uses triplets as a way to add concreteness.

"sallied forth" gives a mock heroic tone to the essay; the author doesn't take the story too seriously-or come on as too preachy.

Note how these metaphors for the bus color the reader's attitude toward the city school.

How do these details about the city school contrast with the details of the country school?

The vivid descriptive details make the country-school scene credible, not sentimental.

Note how the country teachers contrast with the city ones. Which are more attractive?

private institution with semi-progressive ideas of education, and modern plumbing. He learned fast, kept well, and we were satisfied. It was an electric, colorful, regimented existence with moments of pleasurable pause and giddy incident. The day the Christmas angel fainted and had to be carried out by one of the Wise Men was educational in the highest sense of the term. Our scholar gave imitations of it around the house for weeks afterward, and I doubt if it ever goes completely out of his mind.

3 His days were rich in formal experience. Wearing overalls and an old sweater (the accepted uniform of the private seminary), he sallied forth at morn accompanied by a nurse or a parent and walked (or was pulled) two blocks to a corner where the school bus made a flag stop. This flashy vehicle was as punctual as death: seeing us waiting at the cold curb, it would sweep to a halt, open its mouth, suck the boy in, and spring away with an angry growl. It was a good deal like a train picking up a bag of mail. At school the scholar was worked on for six or seven hours by half a dozen teachers and a nurse, and was revived on orange juice in mid-morning. In a cinder court he played games supervised by an athletics instructor, and in a cafeteria he ate lunch worked out by a dietician. He soon learned to read with gratifying facility and discernment and to make Indian weapons of a semi-deadly nature. Whenever one of his classmates fell low of a fever the news was put on the wires and there were breathless calls to physicians, discussing periods of incubation and allied magic.

4 In the country all one can say is that the situation is different, and somehow more casual. Dressed in corduroys, sweatshirt, and short rubber boots, and carrying a tin dinner pail, our scholar departs at the crack of dawn for the village school, two and a half miles down the road, next to the cemetery. When the road is open and the car will start, he makes the journey by motor, courtesy of his old man. When the snow is deep or the motor is dead or both, he makes it on the hoof. In the afternoons he walks or hitches all or part of the way home in fair weather, gets transported in foul. The school-house is a two-room frame building, bungalow type, shingles stained a burnt brown with weather-resistant stain. It has a chemical toilet in the basement and two teachers above the stairs. One takes the first three grades, the other the fourth, fifth, and sixth. They have little or no time for individual instruction, and no time at all for the esoteric. They teach what they know themselves, just as fast and as hard as they can manage. The pupils sit still at their desks in class, and do their milling around outdoors during recess.

5   There is no supervised play. They play cops and robbers (only they call it "Jail") and throw things at one another–snowballs in winter, rose hips in fall. It seems to satisfy them. They also construct darts, pinwheels, and "pick-up-sticks" (jackstraws), and the school itself does a brisk trade in penny candy, which is for sale right in the classroom and which contains "surprises." The most highly prized surprise is a fake cigarette, made of cardboard, fiendishly lifelike.

Additional specific details make the country school exceptionally attractive and child-friendly.

6   The memory of how apprehensive we were at the beginning is still strong. The boy was nervous about the change too. The tension, on that first fair morning in September when we drove him to school, almost blew the windows out of the sedan. And when later we picked him up on the road, wandering along with his little blue lunch-pail, and got his laconic report "All right" in answer to our inquiry about how the day had gone, our relief was vast. Now after almost a year of it, the only difference we can discover in the two school experiences is that in the country he sleeps better at night–and *that* problem is more the air than the education. When grilled on the subject of school-in-country vs. school-in-city, he replied that the chief difference is that the day seems to go so much quicker in the country. "Just like lightening," he reported.

The strong metaphor at the very end clinches the essay's preference for the country school— without its having to be explicitly stated.

Devon 1

Devon Williams
Mr. Patterson
English 101
17 May 2012

Homesick

Study abroad: "Expand your horizons." "An experience you'll never forget." "It'll change your life." "It'll look *great* on a college application." The clichés are all true, I've learned from experience. But they also don't tell the whole study-abroad story.

With a minimum of prompting from my parents, I decided to spend my senior year of high school as an exchange student somewhere in Europe. I almost didn't care where; I just wanted to go. The process of selecting

Devon Williams opens his narrative with a series of phrases certain to be familiar to his audience.

Devon 2

the best program, completing the application, and choosing a destination
was extensive and exhausting. But it was also exhilarating because I
couldn't wait to see the world and be on my own. Eventually, all of the
decisions were made and the paperwork was in order. I was going to
spend six months in Rome.

Think about how hard it is to plan a weekend away from home and
how much you need to pack for a two-week vacation. Now multiply that.
A lot. I needed to prepare to be away from home for a whole semester
and more. I made dozens of detailed lists, and then lost them. I bought
tons of new clothes, and then returned them. I downloaded hours of my
favorite music onto my iPod–enough to get me through a ten-hour plane
ride–and then erased it for some different choices. I practiced packing
my things so that I could fit as much as possible into my suitcase
without going over the airline's weight limit. I practiced speaking
Italian, but I usually didn't have anyone to practice with, so really
I was just talking to myself. And I counted the days.

> Williams creates a sense of nervous anxiety by using repetition and varied sentence structures and lengths.

Finally the anticipation and planning came to an end, and the trip—
my great adventure—began. Saying goodbye wasn't as hard as I thought
it would be; my mom had a tear in her eye at the airport, but I was all
smiles. I knew that I'd miss my parents and my brother, but I was wired
up with excitement. Eager to be self-sufficient, I even got my dad to
agree that we wouldn't e-mail, IM, or Skype more than once a week.

Almost as soon as the plane landed in Rome, I regretted that
decision. All of a sudden being on my own and in charge was more of a
burden than an adventure. I had never been in an international airport
by myself, let alone with signs in another language. I was used to having
someone else take charge, find the luggage, and lead the way to
transportation. That day it was only me, in an unfamiliar place, unsure
about where I needed to go or how to get there. The few Italian words
I learned were totally insufficient for any real communication. I ordered
the wrong food at a small stand, mixed up "arrivals" and "departures,"
had trouble negotiating the ladies' room–and had no one to turn to for
help. There they were the first twinges of homesickness.

> Williams references the title of his essay, establishing the emotional content of his story.

Over the next three weeks, those twinges turned into aches. Nothing
was familiar, and I just couldn't seem to get comfortable. My host family
was very kind, open, and welcoming. But they weren't *my* family. They

spoke little English, they never served pizza, and I didn't know how to fit in with the daughter or her friends. The household routines were different, and I didn't know how to wash my clothes and even help out in the kitchen; my room was tiny and my favorite things were home in my closet. The way the family members joked and hugged and teased each other was different, and I didn't know how to act. I felt like a two-year-old who couldn't name what I wanted or answer even the simplest questions. And my cell phone was worthless—no one to call for help.

The sounds, the smells, even the textures were unlike anything I'd ever encountered. The worst was the traffic noise in Rome: trucks, busses, cars, mopeds, bicycles, all moving so fast there were times I couldn't even cross the street. And all those vehicles belch smoke everywhere. Drivers yelled at other drivers, pedestrians screamed at drivers, and everyone shouted back at each other; the streets seemed to go every which way, and I got lost about half the time. I didn't expect the stench of garbage piling up on the streets for days at a time. I didn't expect to see—or smell—homeless people sleeping in the Coliseum. I didn't expect that the sheets would be so starchy, the bed would be so lumpy, or the towels would be so scratchy. I wanted to go home.

But little by little I found myself adapting. Clichés still abounded: "Over time, things will get better." My classmates were actually generous and patient and gracious, once I gave them a chance, and they were as curious about me and my life as I was about them. Indiana was as exotic and intriguing to them as Italy was to me. It became easier every day to understand and to be understood in Italian. And the more comfortable I got, the more I was able to appreciate the amazing place I was experiencing.

The food was particularly amazing. I discovered tiramisu, a sinfully delicious melt-in-your-mouth dessert, and I couldn't get enough of it. And then there was the cappuccino— everywhere. That sweetened frothy coffee substitute "drink product" that comes out of metal dispensers at convenience stores in Indiana should be ashamed of itself. There is an art to making cappuccino, and the men who serve up *real* Italian coffee take pride in their creations and present each cup with a flourish. It became a favorite game to find the best tiramisu and cappuccino. There are subtle and wonderful differences in how they're made in every café. The best afternoons were those when coffee and cake were both perfect.

As the focus of the narration shifts, Williams makes a connection to his introduction by including another well-worn phrase.

Devon 4

On my quest, I walked all over Rome and learned to love the nooks and crannies, alleys and piazzas; getting lost was something to look forward to. That's how I found the fountains. Everyone has heard of the famous Trevi fountain and its obligatory coin toss. But not everyone knows that there is a lovely fountain in every Roman square and park, each different from the others and every one with its own unique feel and clientele. They are works of art, decorated with sculptures that depict Roman mythology and history and religion. The *Fontana di Piazza S. Maria* in Trastevere was built in the shape of an octagon so people can gather to sit on the wide steps that surround it throughout the day and into the evening. It's most beautiful at night when all the buildings in the square are lit up. The public fountains are spectacular, but I always looked for the smaller fountains tucked in the middle of private courtyards, covered with moss or climbing vines, each with its own uniqueness.

> The inclusion of specific details makes the descriptions credible and appealing.

My months in Rome flashed by so quickly and so beautifully. I wanted it to last forever, to borrow another cliché. And here's another: "All good things come to an end."

I thought it would be easy, going back to my old comfortable life.

And when I got back, everything was indeed completely familiar. I was back with my own family and friends, and the routines were the same. The TV was turned on to the sports sounds of ESPN, the plumbing was dependable (hot water!), and the foods were predictable once again. The kitchen smelled just the way I remembered it: no garlic, no cappuccino, no tiramisu. The sheets were silky, the bed was spongy, the towels were fleecy. My curfew was back in force, and I couldn't go anywhere unless the car was available to borrow. I was home.

> Williams concludes his narration with a simple statement that implies the significance of his experience.

Homesick? No more. Now I was Romesick.

14 | Rebuttal Arguments

QUICK TAKE

In this chapter, you will learn that

1. Rebuttal arguments use two basic strategies: refutation and counter-argument (see page 202)
2. Refutation arguments focus on the shortcomings of the opposing argument (see page 203)
3. Counterarguments acknowledge opposing positions but go on to maintain that the writer has the better argument (see page 204)

Whaling is an ancient form of hunting that greatly expanded in the nineteenth century due to a worldwide demand for whale oil. By 1986 the worldwide whale populations were so seriously depleted that the International Whaling Committee banned commercial whaling to allow whale populations to replenish. Limited whaling continues for scientific research, but environmental organizations such as Greenpeace insist that "science" is a guise for the continuation of commercial whaling. Greenpeace protests all whaling vigorously—both by peaceful means and by open ocean confrontations with whaling vessels. Could their protests at sea be considered a rebuttal argument?

Understand How Rebuttal Arguments Work

There are two basic approaches to rebutting an argument: you can refute the argument, or you can counterargue. In the first case, **refutation**, you demonstrate the shortcomings of the argument you wish to discredit, and you may or may not offer a positive claim of your own. In the second case, **counterargument**, you focus on the strengths of the position you support, and spend little time on the specifics of the argument you are countering. There can be substantial overlap between these two tactics, and good rebuttal arguments often employ both refutation and counterargument.

Because they focus on the shortcomings in the opposition's argument, a refutation argument often takes much of its structure from the argument being refuted.

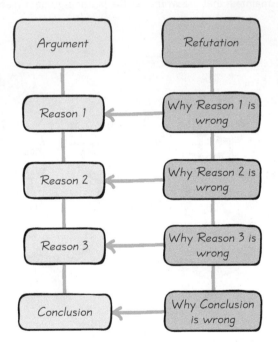

Many college students believe that using technology to "multitask" makes them more productive, believing that studying, texting a friend, and listening to music all at once is an efficient use of their time. But research shows that engaging in multiple tasks is distracting, interferes with memory, and makes it difficult to switch from one task to another, making multitaskers less productive than people focusing on one task at a time.

Counterarguments more often take up ideas the opposing claims have not addressed at all, or they take a very different approach to the problem. By largely ignoring the specifics of the argument being countered, they make the implicit claim that the counterargument is superior.

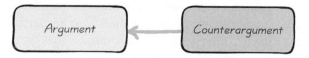

Those who argue for tariffs on goods from China claim that tariffs will protect American manufacturing jobs, but tariffs are a bad idea because they would increase prices on clothing, furniture, toys, and other consumer goods for everyone, and would cause the loss of retailing jobs as well.

Recognize Kinds of Rebuttal Arguments

Refutation

A refutation can either challenge the assumptions underlying a claim, or it can question the evidence supporting a claim. Until about five hundred years ago, people believed that the sky, and everything in it, moved, while the Earth remained still. They observed the stars moving from west to east in a regular, circular motion, and concluded that all the heavenly bodies orbited around an axis between Earth and Polaris, the northern star. This theory, however, did not explain the movement of the planets. If you watch the path of Mars over several nights, for example, you will notice that it moves, like the stars, from east to west. But occasionally, it will appear to move backward, from west to east, before reversing itself and resuming an east-to-west course. This phenomenon is called retrograde motion, and it is exhibited by all the planets in our solar system. In fact, our word *planet* derives from the Greek term *planetes*, meaning "wanderer." The ancient Greeks assumed that the planets and stars orbited the Earth, but that the planets sometimes wandered from their paths.

In the second century CE, the Greek astronomer Ptolemy made precise and detailed observations of the planets and created a model to predict their retrograde motion. In his treatise, the *Almagest*, he theorized that Mars and the other "wanderers" periodically deviated from their path around the Earth, making small circles, or epicycles, before moving on again. It was a complicated system, but it predicted the movements of the planets very accurately, and so it went unchallenged for over a thousand years.

In the early sixteenth century, the Polish astronomer Nicolaus Copernicus recognized that Ptolemy's observations could be explained more simply if the Earth and other planets circled the Sun. Copernicus's theory, later confirmed by the German astronomer Johannes Kepler, eventually replaced the Ptolemaic model of the solar system as the accepted explanation for observed planetary motion.

Copernicus did not question Ptolemy's evidence—the data he had collected showing where the stars and planets appear in the sky to an Earth-bound observer. Instead, he questioned Ptolemy's central assumption that Earth is the center of the solar system. Because evidence of the planet's retrograde motion had been observed by people over such a long period of time, it was unlikely to be wrong. Instead, it was the theory Ptolemy constructed to explain his data that was incorrect.

But sometimes evidence is wrong. Sometimes, too, evidence is incomplete or not representative, and sometimes counterevidence can be found. People who are bent on persuading others may leave out information that weakens their case, or employ evidence in questionable ways to try to bolster their claims. Dermatologists argue that indoor tanning is harmful to people's health because it exposes them to ultraviolet radiation, a known cause of cancer. The tanning industry, not surprisingly, disagrees, arguing that indoor tanning is safer than outdoor tanning because it assures safe levels of UV radiation exposure. While sunbathers often get sunburned, indoor tanners only get safe levels of radiation. This is an intriguing claim, but the AMA has discovered that in fact people who use tanning beds *do* get burned—as many of 50 percent of them. The tanning industry also claims indoor tanning provides people with a "protective" tan that reduces the amount of harmful UV radiation they absorb when they do go out in the sun. Doctors counter this claim by pointing out that a "base tan" provides only as much protection as a sunblock with a Sun Protection Factor, or SPF, of 3, and that the minimum recommended SPF for sunscreen is 15. The protection offered by an indoor tan is minimal at best. Both sides continue to argue over what evidence is valid, and accurate, when assessing the safety of indoor tanning.

Counterargument

Another way to rebut is to counterargue. In a counterargument, you might acknowledge an opposing point of view, but you might not consider it in detail. Rather, you put the main effort into your own argument. A counterarguer, in effect, says, "I hear your argument. But there is more to it than that. Now listen while I explain why another position is stronger." Counterargument is an effective way of persuading audiences, but sometimes it is used as a way to avoid addressing opposing views honestly. People's tendency to be persuaded by counterargument also makes them susceptible to red herrings, when an irrelevant but dramatic detail is put forward as if it were important, or *ad hominem* attacks, where someone makes spurious accusations about an opponent instead of engaging in real debate.

The counterarguer depends on the wisdom of his or her audience members to hear all sides of an issue and make up their own minds about the merits of the case. In the following short poem, Wilfred Owen, a veteran of the horrors of World War I trench warfare, offers a counterargument to those who argue that war is noble, to those who believe along with the poet Horace that "dulce et decorum est pro patria mori"—that it is sweet and fitting to die for one's country. The vast amount of destruction and enormous loss of life that occurred during the "war to end all wars" led people to question the belief that it is always noble to die for one's country.

Dulce Et Decorum Est

Bent double, like old beggars under sacks,
Knock-kneed, coughing like hags, we cursed through sludge,
Till on the haunting flares we turned our backs
And towards our distant rest began to trudge.
Men marched asleep. Many had lost their boots
But limped on, blood-shod. All went lame; all blind;
Drunk with fatigue; deaf even to the hoots
Of tired, outstripped Five-Nines that dropped behind.

Gas! Gas! Quick, boys! — An ecstasy of fumbling,
Fitting the clumsy helmets just in time;
But someone still was yelling out and stumbling,
And flound'ring like a man in fire or lime . . .
Dim, through the misty panes and thick green light,
As under a green sea, I saw him drowning.
In all my dreams, before my helpless sight,
He plunges at me, guttering, choking, drowning.

If in some smothering dreams you too could pace
Behind the wagon that we flung him in,
And watch the white eyes writhing in his face,
His hanging face, like a devil's sick of sin;
If you could hear, at every jolt, the blood
Come gargling from the froth-corrupted lungs,
Obscene as cancer, bitter as the cud
Of vile, incurable sores on innocent tongues,
My friend, you would not tell with such high zest
To children ardent for some desperate glory,
The old Lie: Dulce et Decorum est
Pro patria mori.

Owen does not summarize the argument in favor of being willing to die for one's country and then refute that argument point by point. Rather, his poem presents an opposing argument, supported by a narrative of the speaker's experience in a poison-gas attack, that he hopes will more than counterbalance what he calls "the old Lie." Owen simply ignores the reasons people give for being willing to die for one's country and argues instead that there are good reasons not to do so.

And he hopes that the evidence he summons for his position will outweigh for his audience (addressed as "My friend") the evidence in support of the other side.

Rebuttal arguments frequently offer both refutation and counterargument. Like attorneys engaged in a trial, people writing rebuttals must make their own cases based on good reasons and hard evidence, but they also do what they can to undermine their opponent's case. In the end the jury—the audience—decides.

Build a Rebuttal Argument

As you prepare to rebut an argument, look closely at what your opponent says. What exactly are the claims? What is the evidence? What are the assumptions? What do you disagree with? Are there parts you agree with? Are there assumptions you share? Do you agree that the evidence is accurate?

Knowing where you agree with someone helps you focus your rebuttal on differences. Having points of agreement can also help you build credibility with your audience, if you acknowledge that your opponent makes some logical points, or makes reasonable assumptions.

Consider using counterargument if you generally agree with a claim but do not think it goes far enough, if you feel an argument proposes the wrong solution to a problem, or if you think that, while accurate, it misses the "big picture." Counterargument lets you frame your own, stronger take on the question at hand without spending a lot of time trying to find flaws in the opposing position when there may not be many in it.

If you do have serious objections to an argument, plan to refute it, and start by looking for the most important differences in your respective positions. What are the biggest "red flags" in the argument you disagree with? What are the weakest points of your opponent's argument? What are the strongest points of your own? You will probably want to highlight these differences in your rebuttal. You may find many problems with evidence and logic, in which case you will probably want to prioritize them. You do not necessarily need to point out the flaws in every single element of an argument. Direct your audience to the ones that matter the most.

You can also use counterargument in combination with refutation, first showing why an existing argument is wrong, and then offering an alternative. This is one of the more common forms of rebuttal. As you examine your opponent's claims and evidence, look closely for fallacies and faulty logic (see pages 17–19). How do these distort the problem or lead the audience to mistaken conclusions? Pointing them out to your readers will strengthen your position.

Look too at sources. Check your opponent's facts. Scrutinize the experts he or she relies on. And consider the purpose and motivation behind arguments you rebut. Groups funded by major industries, political parties, and special interest groups may have hidden or not-so-hidden agendas driving the arguments they make. Pointing these out to your readers can strengthen your own position.

Finding Good Reasons

Can The Web Be Trusted For Research?

Most Web users are familiar with the huge and immensely popular *Wikipedia*, the online encyclopedia. What makes *Wikipedia* so different from traditional, print encyclopedias is that entries can be contributed or edited by anyone.

In 2007, Jimmy Wales, president of Wikimedia and one of its founders, debated the legitimacy of Wikipedia with Dale Hoiberg, editor-in-chief of *Encyclopedia Britannica*. Hoiberg's main criticism of *Wikipedia* is that its structure—an open-source wiki without the formal editorial control that shapes traditional, print encyclopedias— allows for inaccurate entries.

In response, Wales argues that *Britannica* and newspapers also contain errors, but Wikipedia has the advantage that they are easily corrected. Furthermore, he asserts that *Wikipedia*'s policy of using volunteer administrators to delete irrelevant entries and requiring authors of entries to cite reliable, published sources ensures quality. Nonetheless, some universities including UCLA and the University of Pennsylvania along with many instructors strongly discourage and even ban students from citing *Wikipedia* in their work. (*Wikipedia* also cautions against using its entries as a primary source for serious research.)

Write about it

1. If your school decided to ban the use of *Wikipedia* as a reference because it lacked the authority of a traditional encyclopedia, would you want to challenge it? Why or why not?

2. What is your position on the policy? Would you challenge or support the administrators' position? Would it be effective to refute the school's claims point by point, noting fallacies in logic and reasoning? Would it be effective to build a counterargument in which you examine the assumptions on which the opposing reasons are based? Which strategy would you choose, or would you use a combination, and why?

3. Take up the task of challenging or supporting the school's policy by writing a rebuttal. Think about your audience. What arguments are your readers most likely to consider before deciding to repeal or reinforce the policy?

Steps to Writing a Rebuttal Argument

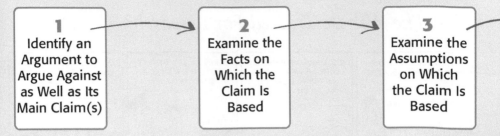

1	2	3
Identify an Argument to Argue Against as Well as Its Main Claim(s)	Examine the Facts on Which the Claim Is Based	Examine the Assumptions on Which the Claim Is Based

Step 1 Identify an Argument to Argue Against as Well as Its Main Claim(s)

- What exactly are you arguing against?
- Are there secondary claims attached to the main claim?
- Include a fair summary of your opponent's position in your finished rebuttal.

Examples

- Arguing against raising taxes for the purpose of building a new sports stadium (examine how proponents claim that a new sports facility will benefit the local economy)
- Arguing for raising the minimum wage (examine how opponents claim that a higher minimum wage isn't necessary and negatively affects small-business owners)

Step 2 Examine the Facts on Which the Claim Is Based

- Are the facts accurate, current, and representative?
- Is there another body of facts that you can present as counterevidence?
- If the author uses statistics, can the statistics be interpreted differently?
- If the author quotes from sources, how reliable are those sources?
- Are the sources treated fairly, or are quotations taken out of context?

Step 3 Examine the Assumptions on Which the Claim Is Based

- What are the primary and secondary assumptions of the claim you are rejecting?
- How are those assumptions flawed?
- Does the author resort to name-calling, use faulty reasoning, or ignore key facts (see pages 17–19)?

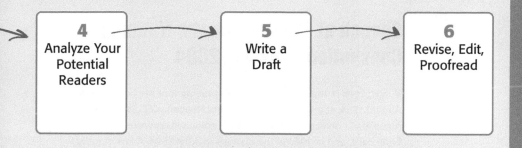

Step 4 Analyze Your Potential Readers

- To what extent do your potential readers support the claim that you are rejecting?
- If they strongly support that claim, how might you appeal to them to change their minds?
- What common assumptions and beliefs do you share with them?

Step 5 Write a Draft

Introduction

Identify the issue and the argument you are rejecting.

- Provide background if the issue is unfamiliar to most of your readers.
- Give a quick summary of the competing positions even if the issue is familiar to your readers.
- Make your aim clear in your thesis statement.

Body

Take on the argument that you are rejecting. Consider questioning the evidence that is used to support the argument by doing one or more of the following.

- Challenge the facts and the currency and relevance of examples.
- Present counterevidence and countertestimony.
- Challenge the credibility of sources cited.
- Question the way in which statistical evidence is presented and interpreted.
- Argue that quotations are taken out of context.

Conclusion

- Conclude on a firm note by underscoring your objections.
- Consider closing with a counterargument or counterproposal.

Step 6 Revise, Edit, Proofread

- For detailed instructions, see Chapter 5.
- For a checklist to use to evaluate your draft, see pages 61–62.

Ron Reagan

Speech at the Democratic National Convention, July 27, 2004

Ron Reagan is the son of the fortieth president of the United States. In August 1994, at the age of 83, President Reagan was diagnosed with Alzheimer's disease, an incurable neurological disorder that destroys brain cells, and he died of the disease in June 2004. A few months later, on July 27, Ron Reagan offered the following speech to the delegates to the Democratic National Convention and to the millions of Americans watching on television. It was countered the next day by Richard Doerflinger, whose piece follows this one in *Good Reasons*.

G ood evening, ladies and gentlemen.

In his first three paragraphs, Reagan makes his purpose clear.

2   A few of you may be surprised to see someone with my last name showing up to speak at a Democratic Convention. Apparently some of you are not. Let me assure you, I am not here to make a political speech and the topic at hand should not—must not—have anything to do with partisanship.

3   I am here tonight to talk about the issue of research into what may be the greatest medical breakthrough in our or any lifetime: the use of embryonic stem cells—cells created using the material of our own bodies—to cure a wide range of fatal and debilitating illnesses: Parkinson's disease, multiple sclerosis, diabetes, lymphoma, spinal cord injuries, and much more.

4   Millions are afflicted. And every year, every day, tragedy is visited upon families across the country, around the world. Now, it may be within our power to put an end to this suffering. We only need to try.

Paragraphs 5, 6, 7, 8, 9, and 10 define stem cell research. Note his simple explanation and the informal tone, appropriate for a speech.

5   Some of you already know what I'm talking about when I say embryonic stem cell research. Others of you are probably thinking, that's quite a mouthful. Maybe this is a good time to go for a tall cold one. Well, wait a minute, wait a minute.

6   Let me try and paint as simple a picture as I can while still doing justice to the science, the incredible science involved. Let's say that ten or so years from now you are diagnosed with Parkinson's disease. There is currently no cure, and drug therapy, with its attendant side-effects, can only temporarily relieve the symptoms.

7   Now, imagine going to a doctor who, instead of prescribing drugs, takes a few skin cells from your arm. The nucleus of one of your cells is placed into a donor egg whose own nucleus has been

removed. A bit of chemical or electrical stimulation will encourage your cell's nucleus to begin dividing, creating new cells which will then be placed into a tissue culture. Those cells will generate embryonic stem cells containing only your DNA, thereby eliminating the risk of tissue rejection. These stem cells are then driven to become the very neural cells that are defective in Parkinson's patients. And finally, those cells—with your DNA—are injected into your brain where they will replace the faulty cells whose failure to produce adequate dopamine led to the Parkinson's disease in the first place.

8   In other words, you're cured.

9   And another thing, these embryonic stem cells, they could continue to replicate indefinitely and, theoretically, can be induced to recreate virtually any tissue in your body.

10   How'd you like to have your own personal biological repair kit standing by at the hospital? Sound like magic? Welcome to the future of medicine.

> Reagan subtly but explicitly distinguishes stem cell research from abortion.

11   Now by the way, no fetal tissue is involved in this process. No fetuses are created, none destroyed. This all happens in the laboratory at the cellular level.

12   Now, there are those who would stand in the way of this remarkable future, who would deny the federal funding so crucial to basic research. They argue that interfering with the development of even the earliest stage embryo, even one that will never be implanted in a womb and will never develop into an actual fetus, is tantamount to murder.

13   A few of these folks, needless to say, are just grinding a political axe and they should be ashamed of themselves. But many are well-meaning and sincere. Their belief is just that, an article of faith, and they are entitled to it. But it does not follow that the theology of a few should be allowed to forestall the health and well-being of the many.

14   And how can we affirm life if we abandon those whose own lives are so desperately at risk? It is a hallmark of human intelligence that we are able to make distinctions.

> Reagan answers critics of stem cell research in paragraphs 12–16.

15   Yes, these cells could theoretically have the potential, under very different circumstances, to develop into human beings—that potential is where their magic lies. But they are not, in and of themselves, human beings. They have no fingers and toes, no brain or spinal cord. They have no thoughts, no fears. They feel no pain.

16   Surely we can distinguish between these undifferentiated cells multiplying in a tissue culture and a living, breathing person—a parent, a spouse, a child.

Actor Michael J. Fox, who was diagnosed in 1991 with Parkinson's disease, spoke at the Bio International Convention in 2007. Fox appealed to scientists and investors to aggressively translate scientific research into creative treatments for debilitating diseases, including Parkinson's.

17   I know a child—well, she must be 13 now so I guess I'd better call her a young woman. She has fingers and toes. She has a mind. She has memories. She has hopes. She has juvenile diabetes. Like so many kids with this disease, she's adjusted amazingly well. The insulin pump she wears—she's decorated hers with rhinestones. She can handle her own catheter needle. She's learned to sleep through the blood drawings in the wee hours of the morning.

18   She's very brave. She is also quite bright and understands full well the progress of her disease and what that might ultimately mean: blindness, amputation, diabetic coma. Every day, she fights to have a future.

Reagan appeals to a single representative example to support his case. Why does he pick this particular example?

19   What excuse will we offer this young woman should we fail her now? What might we tell her children? Or the millions of others who suffer? That when given an opportunity to help, we turned away? That facing political opposition, we lost our nerve? That even though we knew better, we did nothing?

20   And, should we fail, how will we feel if, a few years from now, a more enlightened generation should fulfill the promise of embryonic stem cell therapy? Imagine what they would say of us who lacked the will.

21   No, we owe this young woman and all those who suffer—we owe ourselves—better than that. We are better than that. We are a wiser people, a finer nation.

22   And for all of us in this fight, let me say: we will prevail. The tide of history is with us. Like all generations who have come before ours, we are motivated by a thirst for knowledge and compelled to see others in need as fellow angels on an often difficult path, deserving of our compassion.

23   In a few months, we will face a choice. Yes, between two candidates and two parties, but more than that. We have a chance to take a giant stride forward for the good of all humanity. We can choose between the future and the past, between reason and ignorance, between true compassion and mere ideology.

24   This—this is our moment, and we must not falter.

25   Whatever else you do come November 2, I urge you, please, cast a vote for embryonic stem cell research.

26   Thank you for your time.

Richard M. Doerflinger

Don't Clone Ron Reagan's Agenda

Richard M. Doerflinger is the Associate Director of Pro-Life Activities for the United States Conference of Catholic Bishops. In 2009 Doerflinger was awarded an inaugural Life Prize by the Gerard Health Foundation for his work in "preserving and upholding the sanctity of human life" in areas such as public advocacy, legal action, and outreach. A specialist in bioethics, biotechnology, and public policy, he wrote the essay that follows on July 28, 2004, in response to the previous essay in *Good Reasons*, by Ron Reagan.

Ron Reagan's speech at the Democratic convention last night was expected to urge expanded funding for stem cell research using so-called "spare" embryos—and to highlight these cells' potential for treating the Alzheimer's disease that took his father's life.

2   He did neither. He didn't even mention Alzheimer's, perhaps because even strong supporters of embryonic stem cell research say it is unlikely to be of use for that disease. (Reagan himself admitted this on a July 12 segment of MSNBC's *Hardball*.) And he didn't talk about current debates on funding research using existing embryos. Instead he endorsed the more radical agenda of human cloning—mass-producing one's own identical twins in the laboratory so they can be exploited as (in his words) "your own personal biological repair kit" when disease or injury strikes.

3   Politically this was, to say the least, a gamble. Americans may be tempted to make use of embryos left over from fertility clinics, but most polls show them to be against human cloning for any purpose. Other advanced nations—Canada, Australia, France, Germany, Norway—have banned the practice completely, and the United Nations may approve an international covenant against it this fall. Many groups and individuals who are "pro-choice" on abortion oppose research cloning, not least because it would require the mass exploitation of women to provide what Ron Reagan casually calls "donor eggs." And the potential "therapeutic" benefits of cloning are even more speculative than those of embryonic stem cell research—the worldwide effort even to obtain viable stem cells from cloned embryos has already killed hundreds of embryos and produced exactly one stem cell line, in South Korea.

4   But precisely for these reasons, Ron Reagan should be praised for his candor. The scientists and patient groups promoting embryonic stem cell research know that the current debate on funding is a mere transitional step. For years they have supported the mass manufacture of human embryos through cloning, as the logical and necessary goal of their agenda, but lately they have been coy about this as they fight for the more popular slogan of "stem cell research." With his speech Reagan has removed the mask, and allowed us to debate what is really at stake.

5   He claimed in his speech, of course, that what is at stake in this debate is the lives of millions of patients with devastating diseases. But by highlighting Parkinson's disease and juvenile diabetes as two diseases most clearly justifying the move to human cloning, he failed to do his homework. These are two of the diseases that pro-cloning scientists now admit will probably *not* be helped by research cloning.

6   Scottish cloning expert Ian Wilmut, for example, wrote in the *British Medical Journal* in February that producing genetically matched stem cells through cloning is probably quite unnecessary for treating any neurological disease. Recent findings suggest that the nervous system is "immune privileged," and will not generally reject stem cells from a human who is genetically different. He added that cloning is probably useless for auto-immune diseases like juvenile diabetes, where the body mistakenly rejects its own insulin-producing cells as though they were foreign. "In such cases," he wrote, "transfer of immunologically identical cells to a patient is expected to induce the same rejection."

7   Wilmut's observations cut the ground out from under Ron Reagan's simple-minded claim that cloning is needed to avoid tissue rejection. For some diseases, genetically matched cells are unnecessary; for others, they are useless, because they only replicate the genetic profile that is part of the problem. (Ironically, for Alzheimer's both may be true—cloning may be unnecessary to avoid tissue rejection in the brain, and useless because the cloned cells would have the same genetic defect that may lead to Alzheimer's.) Reagan declared that this debate requires us to "choose between . . . reason and ignorance," but he did not realize which side has the monopoly on ignorance.

8   That ignorance poses an obstacle to real advances that are right before our eyes. Two weeks before Ron Reagan declared that a treatment for Parkinson's may arrive "ten or so years from now," using "the material of our own bodies," a Parkinson's patient and his doctor quietly appeared before Congress to point out that this has already been done. Dennis Turner was treated in 1999 by Dr. Michel Levesque of Cedars-Sinai Medical Center in Los Angeles, using his own adult neural stem cells. Dr. Levesque did not use the Rube Goldberg method of trying to turn those cells into a

cloned embryo and then killing the embryo to get stem cells—he just grew Turner's own adult stem cells in the lab, and turned them directly into dopamine-producing cells. And with just one injection, on one side of Turner's brain, he produced an almost complete reversal of Parkinson's symptoms over four years.

9   Turner stopped shaking, could eat without difficulty, could put in his own contact lenses again, and resumed his avocation of big-game photography—on one occasion scrambling up a tree in Africa to escape a charging rhinoceros.

10   Amazingly, while this advance has been presented at national and international scientific conferences and featured on ABC-TV in Chicago, the scientific establishment supporting embryonic stem cell research has almost completely ignored it, and most news media have obediently imposed a virtual news blackout on it. That did not change even after the results were presented to the Senate Commerce Subcommittee on Science, Technology and Space this month. Pro-cloning Senators on the panel actually seemed angry at the witnesses, for trying to distract them from their fixation on destroying embryos.

11   Turner also testified that his symptoms have begun to return, especially arising from the side of his brain that was left untreated, and he would like to get a second treatment. For that he will have to wait. Dr. Levesque has received insufficient appreciation and funding for his technique, and is still trying to put together the funds for broader clinical trials—as most Parkinson's foundations and NIH peer reviewers look into the starry distance of Ron Reagan's dreams about embryonic stem cells.

12   But hey, who cares about real Parkinson's patients when there's a Brave New World to sell? ■

Sample Student Rebuttal Argument

Ramos 1

Marta Ramos

Professor Jacobs

English 101

30 April 2012

Oversimplifying the Locavore Ethic

James McWilliams's argument in his book "Just Food" is based on an overly simplistic understanding of the locavore ethic. His claim, that eating locally is an unrealistic goal, fails to take into account the flexibility of locavorism, the ways consumer food preferences drive the free market system, and the realities of food processing infrastructure.

> Ramos identifies the source that she will refute and the source's claim in the first paragraph.

McWilliams's criticism of locavorism would make sense if, as he implies, locavores were a single-minded group of people demanding the complete conversion of the agricultural systems to uniform, regimented local production and consumption. In fact, there is no reason that locavorism has to completely replace the existing agricultural system, and hardly any locavores advocate this. Locavorism, the practice of eating food that is grown locally and in season, is not an all-or-nothing policy. It is a direction in which individuals and communities can move. Locavores.com, a Web site run by the chef Jessica Prentice, who coined the term "locavore," spells out local-eating strategies:

> Ramos defines the term "locavore" and asserts that McWilliams misunderstands the movement.

> If not LOCALLY PRODUCED, then ORGANIC.
>
> If not ORGANIC, then FAMILY FARM.
>
> If not FAMILY FARM, then LOCAL BUSINESS.
>
> If not LOCAL BUSINESS, then TERROIR—foods famous for the region they are grown in. ("Guidelines")

This hierarchy of food sources prefers local sources over distant ones, and prioritizes local farms and businesses to receive local food dollars. Eating locally, according to Locavores, represents "A step toward regional food self reliance" ("Top"). Given the political instability of many areas of the world that grow our food and the way energy costs can drastically affect food prices, it makes sense to reduce our dependence on distant food sources. As Jennifer Maiser, one of the founders of the locavore movement, puts it,

> Ramos uses a direct quotation from a respected voice in the locavore community to build credibility.

Ramos 2

Locavores are people who pay attention to where their food comes from and commit to eating local food as much as possible. The great thing about eating local is that it's not an all-or-nothing venture. Any small step you take helps the environment, protects your family's health and supports small farmers in your area.

The goal is not to end completely our importation of food.

McWilliams cites Phoenix as an example of why locavorism won't work. Certainly cities like Phoenix, which lacks the water to grow much food, will always rely on external supply chains to feed their populations. But the obstacles to local eating in Phoenix should not prevent residents of San Francisco, Sarasota, or Charleston from eating locally grown foods. Locavorism doesn't have to work everywhere to be beneficial.

In addition to misrepresenting locavorism's goals, McWilliams illogically claims that it cannot meet people's food needs. "At current levels of fruit production," he warns, "apples are the only crop that could currently feed New Yorkers at a level that meets the U.S. Recommended Dietary Allowances" (44). McWilliams is wrong when he claims that if New Yorkers ate locally grown fruits, they could "rarely indulge in a pear, peach, or basket of strawberries" (44). That might be the case if New York farmers continued to grow nothing but apples and grapes. But if some of those crops were replaced with other fruits, New York could have a very diverse supply of produce that would come reasonably close to meeting the nutritional needs of its citizens. In fact, if committed locavores seek out locally grown strawberries, peaches, and pears, and are willing to pay more money for them than they do for apples, local farmers will have sound economic reasons for replacing some of their aging apple trees with peach and pear trees. McWilliams makes locavorism sound impractical because he tries to imagine it working within current agricultural realities. In fact, locavores seek to change the way food is produced and consumed. Moreover, locavorism works toward this change not, as McWilliams suggests, by advocating laws that restrict food producers but by encouraging consumers to vote with their wallets.

McWilliams's argument about New York also rests on the peculiar assumption that every person in the state has to eat the same fruits in

In her refutation Ramos addresses McWilliams's argument point by point.

Ramos quotes McWilliams and then disproves the quoted claim.

Ramos 3

the same amounts in order for locavorism to work. He points out that except for apples and grapes, "every other fruit the state produces is not being harvested at a level to provide all New Yorkers with an adequate supply" (44). McWilliams implies that if you can't grow enough of a crop to supply every single person in the state, there is no point in growing it; however, the goal of locavorism is choice, not total local supply of all food, a fact McWilliams seems to willfully ignore.

> Ramos questions McWilliams's assumptions and finds them lacking.

Finally, McWilliams claims that the cost and inconvenience of processing food locally will prevent communities from moving toward local eating. He notes that "whereas the conventional system of production and distribution has in place a series of large-scale processing centers capable of handling these tasks in a handful of isolated locations," smaller communities do not (45). There are two problems with this argument. First, many of the "processing centers" McWilliams is thinking of *aren't* capable of handling the task of food production. The National Resources Defense Council reports that "from 1995 to 1998, 1,000 spills or pollution incidents occurred at livestock feedlots in 10 states and 200 manure-related fish kills resulted in the death of 13 million fish" ("Facts"). In 2009, Fairbank Farms recalled over half a million pounds of ground beef after nineteen people were hospitalized and two died from E. coli bacteria in the meat (United States). Also in 2009, the King Nut Companies of Solon, Ohio, sickened over 400 people, including three who died, by producing and distributing peanut butter infected with salmonella ("Virginia"). Large-scale processing plants are not a solution to our food security needs. They are part of the problem.

> Ramos addresses the claim that she takes greatest issue with last. She then gives it further emphasis by providing two distinct counterarguments.

Second, the cost of changing the country's food-processing system from large-scale to small-scale is not as prohibitive as McWilliams makes it sound. Factories age. Machines wear out and have to be replaced. Food production facilities are replaced all the time. Newer facilities could easily be built on a smaller, more regional scale. In fact, given the cost of recalls and lawsuits when tainted food is distributed over a large area, food producers have good reason to think about smaller, more localized production and distribution.

McWilliams either does not understand locavorism or understands it and prefers to misrepresent its goals and methods. His arguments in favor of our current food production system ignore both the very real benefits of local eating, and the considerable cost of the existing system.

> Ramos closes with an appeal to the benefits of locavorism.

Ramos 4

Works Cited

"Facts about Pollution from Livestock Farms." *Natural Resources Defense Council.* Natural Resources Defense Council, 15 July 2005. Web. 7 Apr. 2010.

"Guidelines for Eating Well." *Locavores.* Locavores, 3 June 2009. Web. 9 Apr. 2010.

Maiser, Jennifer. "10 Steps to Becoming a Locavore." *PBS: NOW.* Jump Start Productions, 2 Nov. 2007. Web. 8 Apr. 2010.

McWilliams, James E. *Just Food: Where Locavores Get It Wrong and How We Can Truly Eat Responsibly.* New York: Little, Brown, 2009.

"Top Twelve Reasons to Eat Locally." *Locavores.* Locavores, 3 June 2009. Web. 9 Apr. 2010.

United States. Dept. of Health and Human Services. "Multistate Outbreak of E. coli O157:H7 Infections Associated with Beef from Fairbanks Farms." *Centers for Disease Control and Prevention.* Dept. of Health and Human Services, 24 Nov. 2009. Web. 8 Apr. 2010.

"Virginia, Minnesota Confirms Salmonella Deaths Related to Tainted Peanut Butter." *Fox News.* Fox News Network, 13 Jan. 2009. Web. 10 Apr. 2010.

For additional writing resources that will help you master the objectives of this chapter, go to www.mywritinglab.com.

15 | Proposal Arguments

QUICK TAKE

In this chapter, you will learn that

1. Proposal arguments identify a problem and offer a solution (see page 221)

2. Successful proposal arguments convince readers that the solution will work (see page 222)

3. Successful proposal arguments acknowledge other possible solutions and argue why the proposed solution is better (see page 222)

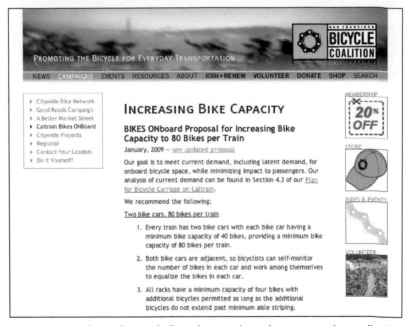

The San Francisco Bicycle Coalition, "dedicated to creating safer streets and more livable communities," is an organization whose primary goal is to build a citywide bike network in San Francisco. The success of the coalition's efforts to increase bicycle ridership for commuters created its own problem: Caltrain commuter trains ran out of room for bicycles, and riders were "bumped" because the trains' bike storage cars were filled to capacity. The coalition crafted a new proposal called Bikes On Board to persuade Caltrain to add more bike storage capacity on its trains. The coalition's proposal encourages riders to report "bumps" in order to document exactly how many times cyclists are denied rides on trains due to limited bike storage. This well-defined proposal forms part of a larger campaign and organizational mission encompassing environmental, economic, and personal fitness issues. What local issues inspire you to propose action? How would you go about crafting a proposal argument to promote interest in a cause or solution?

Understand How Proposal Arguments Work

Proposal arguments make the case that someone should do something: "The federal government should raise grazing fees on public lands." "The town council should renovate the old swimming pool in Butler Gymnasium." "All parents should secure their children in booster seats when driving, even for short distances." Proposals can also argue that something should *not* be done, or that people should stop doing something: "The plan to extend Highway 45 is a waste of tax dollars and citizens should not vote for it." "Don't drink and drive."

The challenge for writers of proposal arguments is to convince readers to take action. It's easy for readers to agree that something should be done, as long as they don't have to do it. It's much harder to get readers involved with the situation or convince them to spend their time or money trying to carry out the proposal. A successful proposal argument conveys a sense of urgency to motivate readers, and describes definite actions they should take.

The key to a successful proposal is using good reasons to convince readers that if they act, something positive will happen (or something negative will be avoided). If your readers believe that taking action will benefit them, they are more likely to help bring about what you propose.

Proposal arguments take the form shown here.

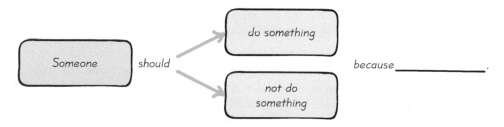

We should convert existing train tracks in the downtown areas to a light-rail system and build a new freight track around the city because we need to relieve traffic and parking congestion downtown.

Recognize Components of Proposal Arguments

Most successful proposals have four major components:

- **Identifying and defining the problem.** Sometimes, your audience is already fully aware of the problem you want to solve. If your city frequently tears up streets and then leaves them for months without fixing them, you shouldn't have to spend much time convincing citizens that streets should be repaired more quickly. But if you raise a problem unfamiliar to your readers, first you will have to convince them that the problem is real. Citizens will not see the need to replace miles of plumbing lines running under the streets, for example, unless you convince them that the pipes are old and corroded and are a risk to everyone's safety. You will also need to define the scope of the problem—does every single pipe need to be replaced, or only those more than forty years old? Is this a job for the city, or do federal clean water regulations mean that other government officials must be involved? The clearer you are about what must be done, and by whom, the stronger your argument will be.

■ **Stating a proposed solution.** A strong proposal offers a clear, definite statement of exactly what you are proposing. Vague statements that "Something must be done!" may get readers stirred up about the issue, but they are unlikely to lead to constructive action. A detailed proposal also adds credibility to your argument, showing that you are concerned enough to think through the nuts and bolts of the changes to be made. You can state your proposed solution near the beginning of your argument (it's in effect your thesis statement), or introduce it later—for example, after you have considered and rejected other possible solutions.

■ **Convincing readers that the proposed solution is well considered and fair.** Once your readers agree that a problem exists and a solution should be found, you have to convince them that your solution is the best one. You have to supply good reasons to favor your proposal. Perhaps you want your city to fire the planning committee members who are responsible for street repair. You will need to show that those officials are indeed responsible for the delays, and that, once they are fired, the city will be able to quickly hire new, more effective planners. You can make your case more forcefully if you include evidence from your research to demonstrate that you are familiar with the complexity of the issue.

■ **Demonstrating that the solution is feasible.** Your solution not only has to work; it must be feasible. You might be able to raise money for street repairs by billing property owners for repairs to the streets in front of their houses, but opposition to such a proposal would be fierce. Most Americans will object to making individuals responsible for road repair costs when roads are used by all drivers.

You may also have to show how your proposal is better than other possible actions that could be taken. Perhaps others believe your city should hire private contractors to repair the streets more quickly, or reward work crews who finish quickly with extra pay or days off. If there are multiple proposed solutions, all perceived as equally good, then there is no clear course of action for your audience to work for. Very often, that means nothing will happen. When you present your proposal, take a clear stand—don't hedge. Of course different people have different opinions, but you want your readers to accept yours as the most reasonable.

Build a Proposal Argument

At this moment, you might not think that you feel strongly enough about anything to write a proposal argument. But if you write a list of things that make you mad or at least a little annoyed, then you have a start toward writing a proposal argument. Some things on your list are not going to produce proposal arguments that many people would want to read. If your roommate is a slob, you might be able to write a proposal for that person to start cleaning up more, but who else would be interested? Similarly, it might be annoying to you that where you live is too far from the ocean, but it is hard to imagine making a serious proposal to move your city closer to the coast. Short of those extremes, however, are many things that might make you think, "Why hasn't someone done something about this?" If you believe that others have something to gain if a problem is solved, or at least that the situation can be made a little better, then you might be able to develop a good proposal argument.

For instance, suppose you are required to use computers to complete major assignments in all of your classes. There are some machines available for students to use during the school day, but the demand is far greater than the supply. The policy is that students' personal computers may not be configured to access the Internet in the school building. This makes you angry because you are frequently unable to complete your work at school because more people than can be accommodated want to sign up for spaces in the computer labs. These slots are always at a premium because no one may come into the labs when a class is in session. You notice that sometimes there are computer stations available when a class is being run in the lab. You decide to write a letter to the principal asking her to allow students to log onto the school network, to purchase more computers, or to use any empty seats in the computer labs.

When you speak to your teachers about this problem, you learn more about why the existing policies were instituted. A majority of parents have asked the school board to prohibit unlimited Internet access in the schools. The network servers are already taxed because of high traffic from classroom use. And many teachers believe that computer labs should be treated like any other instructional space and be assigned the same way that classrooms are.

You realize that you'll need to convince the principal that the lack of computer access is a serious problem. You need to provide evidence that students are now unable to complete assignments, but they would do their course work during study halls or lunch periods if they could use computers. Then you need to decide which of your ideas you are going to propose. Remember that you need to present reasonable arguments that your audience will be open to and demonstrate that your solution will solve the problem.

Purchasing more computers or increasing server space will be expensive, and budgets are tight. Even if either of these options would solve your problem, who will pay for more equipment? Many problems in life could be solved if you had access to unlimited resources, but very few people—or organizations—have such resources at their command. It's not enough to propose a solution that can resolve the problem. You have to be able to argue for the feasibility of your solution by proposing realistic ways to fund these purchases.

Steps to Writing a Proposal Argument

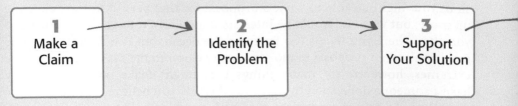

Step 1 Make a Claim

Make a proposal claim advocating a specific change or course of action. (Often this claim will be stated after the problem is identified; see Step 2.)

Template

> We should (or should not) do SOMETHING.

Examples

- Redesigning the process of registering for courses, getting e-mail, or making appointments to be more efficient
- Creating bicycle lanes to make cycling safer and to reduce traffic
- Streamlining the rules for recycling newspapers, bottles, and cans to encourage increased participation

Step 2 Identify the Problem

- What exactly is the problem, what causes it, and who is most affected?
- Has anyone tried to do anything about it? If so, why haven't they succeeded?
- What is likely to happen in the future if the problem isn't solved?

Step 3 Support Your Solution

Support your proposal with good reasons as specifically as you can.

- What exactly do you want to achieve?
- What good consequences will follow if your proposal is adopted?
- How exactly will your solution work? Can it be accomplished quickly, or will it have to be phased in over a few years?
- Has anything like it been tried elsewhere? If so, what happened?
- If your solution costs money, how do you propose to pay for it?

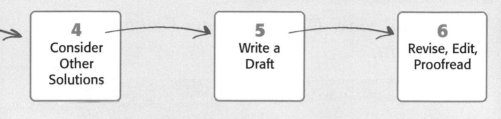

Step 4 Consider Other Solutions

- What other solutions have been or might be proposed for this problem, including doing nothing?
- Why is your solution better?

Step 5 Write a Draft

Introduction

- Set out the issue or problem, perhaps by telling about your experience or the experience of someone you know.
- Argue for the seriousness of the problem.
- Give some background about the problem if necessary.
- State your proposal as your thesis.

Body

- Present your solution. Consider setting out your solution first, explaining how it will work, indicating the good consequences that will follow (and the bad consequences that will be avoided), discussing other possible solutions, and arguing that yours is better. Or consider discussing other possible solutions first, arguing that they don't solve the problem or are not feasible, and then presenting your solution.
- Make clear the goals of your solution. Many solutions cannot solve problems completely.
- Describe in detail the steps in implementing your solution and how they will solve the problem you have identified.
- Explain the positive consequences that will follow from your proposal. What good things will happen, and what bad things will be avoided, if your advice is taken?

Conclusion

- Issue a call to action—if your readers agree with you, they will want to take action.
- Restate and emphasize exactly what readers need to do to solve the problem.

Step 6 Revise, Edit, Proofread

- For detailed instructions, see Chapter 5.
- For a checklist to use to evaluate your draft, see pages 61–62.

Finding Good Reasons

Who Should Make Decisions About Economic Development?

Cape Cod, Massachusetts, is a peninsula that expands from the southern portion of Massachusetts into the Atlantic Ocean. Famous for its beautiful shoreline, Cape Cod is a popular destination for summer vacationers. The Cape Wind Project is a proposed 24-square-mile offshore wind farm that would be built beginning a little less than 5 miles off of the Cape's southern coast. Proponents of the plan cite the benefits of clean energy. Strong opposition, however, has been voiced by the Alliance to Protect Nantucket Sound, which claims that the proposed wind farm will not only destroy property values, but also irrevocably damage the Cape's priceless views, threaten the vital tourist industry, dislocate necessary shipping lanes, disrupt fish populations, and pose a hazard to birds. The Cape Wind Project has brought a prolonged battle in Massachusetts courts that no doubt will continue with a series of appeals.

Write about it

1. If you were the spokesperson for the Cape Wind Project, what reasons would you give to the Massachusetts State Courts to persuade them to begin construction of the wind farm?

2. If you were the spokesperson for the Alliance to Protect Nantucket Sound, what reasons would you give to the Massachusetts State Courts to persuade them to block the construction of the wind farm?

3. If you were a judge on the Massachusetts State Bench, what reasons might you expect to hear from these two groups?

4. Choose one of the scenarios (from prompts 1, 2, or 3), taking on the position in favor of or opposing development of the wind farm. Draft a proposal to convince the judge to rule in your favor.

Wallace Stegner

A Wilderness Letter

Wallace Stegner (1909–1993) was a successful novelist in the United States after World War II. He wrote more than thirty books, including *Angle of Repose*, which won the Pulitzer Prize, and The *Spectator Bird*, which won the National Book Award in 1976. Stegner was also an outspoken conservationist, and his books often feature natural settings and environmental themes. In 1960 he wrote the following letter, a famous argument for the spiritual values found in the wild; it helped to persuade Congress to create the National Wilderness Preservation System in 1964.

Los Altos, California
December 3, 1960

David E. Pesonen
Wildland Research Center
Agricultural Experiment Station
243 Mulford Hall
University of California
Berkeley 4, Calif.

Dear Mr. Pesonen:

Stegner indicates his awareness of his audience's values.

1   I believe that you are working on the wilderness portion of the Outdoor Recreation Resources Review Commission's report. If I may, I should like to urge some arguments for wilderness preservation that involve recreation, as it is ordinarily conceived, hardly at all. Hunting, fishing, hiking, mountain-climbing, camping, photography, and the enjoyment of natural scenery will all, surely, figure in your report. So will the wilderness as a genetic reserve, a scientific yardstick by which we may measure the world in its natural balance against the world in its man-made imbalance. What I want to speak for is not so much the wilderness uses, valuable as those are, but the wilderness idea, which is a resource in itself. Being an intangible and spiritual resource, it will seem mystical to the practical minded—but then anything that cannot be moved by a bulldozer is likely to seem mystical to them.

Stegner devotes his entire second paragraph to a statement of his thesis—to his proposal.

2   I want to speak for the wilderness idea as something that has helped form our character and that has certainly shaped our history as a people. It has no more to do with recreation than churches have to do with recreation, or than the strenuousness and optimism and expansiveness of what the historians call the "American Dream" have to do with recreation. Nevertheless, since

it is only in this recreation survey that the values of wilderness are being compiled, I hope you will permit me to insert this idea between the leaves, as it were, of the recreation report.

This paragraph details the nature of the problem that Stegner urges his reader to avoid.

3   Something will have gone out of us as a people if we ever let the remaining wilderness be destroyed; if we permit the last virgin forests to be turned into comic books and plastic cigarette cases; if we drive the few remaining members of the wild species into zoos or to extinction; if we pollute the last clear air and dirty the last clean streams and push our paved roads through the last of the silence, so that never again will Americans be free in their own country from the noise, the exhausts, the stinks of human and automotive waste. And so that never again can we have the chance to see ourselves single, separate, vertical and individual in the world, part of the environment of trees and rocks and soil, brother to the other animals, part of the natural world and compe-tent to belong in it. Without any remaining wilderness we are com-mitted wholly, without chance for even momentary reflection and rest, to a headlong drive into our technological termite-life, the Brave New World of a completely man-controlled environment.

In the second half of this paragraph, Stegner turns to the positive consequences that will follow from his proposal.

We need wilderness preserved—as much of it as is still left, and as many kinds—because it was the challenge against which our character as a people was formed. The reminder and the reassur-ance that it is still there is good for our spiritual health even if we never once in ten years set foot in it. It is good for us when we are young, because of the incomparable sanity it can bring briefly, as vacation and rest, into our insane lives. It is important to us when we are old simply because it is there—important, that is, simply as an idea.

4   We are a wild species, as Darwin pointed out. Nobody ever tamed or domesticated or scientifically bred us. But for at least three millennia we have been engaged in a cumulative and ambitious race to modify and gain control of our environment, and in the process we have come close to domesticating ourselves. Not many people are likely, any more, to look upon what we call "progress" as an unmixed blessing. Just as surely as it has brought us increased comfort and more material goods, it has brought us spiritual losses, and it threatens now to become the Frankenstein that will destroy us. One means of sanity is to retain a hold on the natural world, to remain, insofar as we can, good animals. Americans still have that chance, more than many peoples; for while we were demonstrating ourselves the most efficient and ruthless environment-busters in history, and slash-ing and burning and cutting our way through a wilderness conti-nent, the wilderness was working on us. It remains in us as

surely as Indian names remain on the land. If the abstract dream of human liberty and human dignity became, in America, something more than an abstract dream, mark it down at least partially to the fact that we were in subdued ways subdued by what we conquered.

5   The Connecticut Yankee, sending likely candidates from King Arthur's unjust kingdom to his Man Factory for rehabilitation, was over-optimistic, as he later admitted. These things cannot be forced, they have to grow. To make such a man, such a democrat, such a believer in human individual dignity, as Mark Twain himself, the frontier was necessary, Hannibal and the Mississippi and Virginia City, and reaching out from those the wilderness; the wilderness as opportunity and idea, the thing that has helped to make an American different from and, until we forget it in the roar of our industrial cities, more fortunate than other men. For an American, insofar as he is new and different at all, is a civilized man who has renewed himself in the wild. The American experience has been the confrontation by old peoples and cultures of a world as new as if it had just risen from the sea. That gave us our hope and our excitement, and the hope and excitement can be passed on to newer Americans, Americans who never saw any phase of the frontier. But only so long as we keep the remainder of our wild as a reserve and a promise—a sort of wilderness bank.

6   As a novelist, I may perhaps be forgiven for taking literature as a reflection, indirect but profoundly true, of our national consciousness. And our literature, as perhaps you are aware, is sick, embittered, losing its mind, losing its faith. Our novelists are the declared enemies of their society. There has hardly been a serious or important novel in this century that did not repudiate in part or in whole American technological culture for its commercialism, its vulgarity, and the way in which it has dirtied a clean continent and a clean dream. I do not expect that the preservation of our remaining wilderness is going to cure this condition. But the mere example that we can as a nation apply some other criteria than commercial and exploitative considerations would be heartening to many Americans, novelists or otherwise. We need to demonstrate our acceptance of the natural world, including ourselves; we need the spiritual refreshment that being natural can produce. And one of the best places for us to get that is in the wilderness where the fun houses, the bulldozers, and the pavement of our civilization are shut out.

7   Sherwood Anderson, in a letter to Waldo Frank in the 1920s, said it better than I can. "Is it not likely that when the

In these two paragraphs Stegner defines the American spirit as tied to the wilderness—another good reason to preserve wild spaces.

Here in these paragraphs Stegner offers another good reason to preserve the wilderness, as a counter to commercial exploitation.

country was new and men were often alone in the fields and the forest they got a sense of bigness outside themselves that has now in some way been lost. . . . Mystery whispered in the grass, played in the branches of trees overhead, was caught up and blown across the American line in clouds of dust at evening on the prairies. . . . I am old enough to remember tales that strengthen my belief in a deep semi-religious influence that was formerly at work among our people. The flavor of it hangs over the best work of Mark Twain. . . . I can remember old fellows in my home town speaking feelingly of an evening spent on the big empty plains. It had taken the shrillness out of them. They had learned the trick of quiet. . . . "

8   We could learn it too, even yet; even our children and grandchildren could learn it. But only if we save, for just such absolutely non-recreational, impractical, and mystical uses as this, all the wild that still remains to us.

9   It seems to me significant that the distinct downturn in our literature from hope to bitterness took place almost at the precise time when the frontier officially came to an end, in 1890, and when the American way of life had begun to turn strongly urban and industrial. The more urban it has become, and the more frantic with technological change, the sicker and more embittered our literature, and I believe our people, have become. For myself, I grew up on the empty plains of Saskatchewan and Montana and in the mountains of Utah, and I put a very high valuation on what those places gave me. And if I had not been able to periodically to renew myself in the mountains and deserts of western America I would be very nearly bughouse. Even when I can't get to the back country, the thought of the colored deserts of southern Utah, or the reassurance that there are still stretches of prairies where the world can be instantaneously perceived as disk and bowl, and where the little but intensely important human being is exposed to the five directions of the thirty-six winds, is a positive consolation. The idea alone can sustain me. But as the wilderness areas are progressively exploited or "improved," as the jeeps and bulldozers of uranium prospectors scar up the deserts and the roads are cut into the alpine timberlands, and as the remnants of the unspoiled and natural world are progressively eroded, every such loss is a little death in me. In us.

10   I am not moved by the argument that those wilderness areas which have already been exposed to grazing or mining are already deflowered, and so might as well be "harvested." For mining I cannot say much good except that its operations are generally short-lived. The extractable wealth is taken and the shafts, the tailings, and the ruins left, and in a dry country such as the American

Stegner restates his thesis with emphasis; he gives an entire paragraph to one sentence.

Stegner argues from personal experience.

Here Stegner answers an objection to his proposal.

West the wounds men make in the earth do not quickly heal. Still, they are only wounds; they aren't absolutely mortal. Better a wounded wilderness than none at all. And as for grazing, if it is strictly controlled so that it does not destroy the ground cover, damage the ecology, or compete with the wildlife it is in itself nothing that need conflict with the wilderness feeling or the validity of the wilderness experience. I have known enough range cattle to recognize them as wild animals; and the people who herd them have, in the wilderness context, the dignity of rareness; they belong on the frontier, moreover, and have a look of rightness. The invasion they make on the virgin country is a sort of invasion that is as old as Neolithic man, and they can, in moderation, even emphasize a man's feeling of belonging to the natural world. Under surveillance, they can belong; under control, they need not deface or mar. I do not believe that in wilderness areas where grazing has never been permitted, it should be permitted; but I do not believe either that an otherwise untouched wilderness should be eliminated from the preservation plan because of limited existing uses such as grazing which are in consonance with the frontier condition and image.

11   Let me say something on the subject of the kinds of wilderness worth preserving. Most of those areas contemplated are in the national forests and in high mountain country. For all the usual recreational purposes, the alpine and the forest wildernesses are obviously the most important, both as genetic banks and as beauty spots. But for the spiritual renewal, the recognition of identity, the birth of awe, other kinds will serve every bit as well. Perhaps, because they are less friendly to life, more abstractly nonhuman, they will serve even better. On our Saskatchewan prairie, the nearest neighbor was four miles away, and at night we saw only two lights on all the dark rounding earth. The earth was full of animals—field mice, ground squirrels, weasels, ferrets, badgers, coyotes, burrowing owls, snakes. I knew them as my little brothers, as fellow creatures, and I have never been able to look upon animals in any other way since. The sky in that country came clear down to the ground on every side, and it was full of great weathers, and clouds, and winds, and hawks. I hope I learned something from looking a long way, from looking up, from being much alone. A prairie like that, one big enough to carry the eye clear to the sinking, rounding horizon, can be as lonely and grand and simple in its forms as the sea. It is as good a place as any for the wilderness experience to happen; the vanishing prairie is as worth preserving for the wilderness idea as the alpine forest.

Stegner concludes with three paragraphs of personal testimony and argument by consequence. Note how the language soars to an emotional crescendo.

12   So are great reaches of our western deserts, scarred somewhat by prospectors but otherwise open, beautiful, waiting, close to whatever God you want to see in them. Just as a sample, let me suggest the Robbers' Roost country in Wayne County, Utah, near the Capitol Reef National Monument. In that desert climate the dozer and jeep tracks will not soon melt back into the earth, but the country has a way of making the scars insignificant. It is a lovely and terrible wilderness, such as wilderness as Christ and the prophets went out into; harshly and beautifully colored, broken and worn until its bones are exposed, its great sky without a smudge of taint from Technocracy, and in hidden corners and pockets under its cliffs the sudden poetry of springs. Save a piece of country like that intact, and it does not matter in the slightest that only a few people every year will go into it. That is precisely its value. Roads would be a desecration, crowds would ruin it. But those who haven't the strength or youth to go into it and live can simply sit and look. They can look two hundred miles, clear into Colorado: and looking down over the cliffs and canyons of the San Rafael Swell and the Robbers' Roost they can also look as deeply into themselves as anywhere I know. And if they can't even get to the places on the Aquarius Plateau where the present roads will carry them, they can simply contemplate the idea, take pleasure in the fact that such a timeless and uncontrolled part of earth is still there.

13   These are some of the things wilderness can do for us. That is the reason we need to put into effect, for its preservation, some other principle that the principles of exploitation or "usefulness" or even recreation. We simply need that wild country available to us, even if we never do more than drive to its edge and look in. For it can be a means of reassuring ourselves of our sanity as creatures, a part of the geography of hope.
Very sincerely yours,

Wallace Stegner

Sample Student Proposal Argument
Satire as Proposal

In this sample student argument, Michael Bruce approaches his subject using satire to make his point. Satire uses humor and exaggeration and irony to gently prod us into recognizing flaws in our own thinking. A serious proposal can be offered that is so outrageous that it cannot be taken seriously. Readers should quickly recognize that the writer does not want his audience to adopt his stated proposal but instead one that is implied and opposite.

Most readers will immediately recognize the reference here to Jonathan Swift's "A Modest Proposal." Swift wrote his essay in 1792 to address the issue of extreme poverty in eighteenth-century Ireland; in it he proposed as a "solution" to the problem that Irish children be eaten! Bruce borrows Swift's title and mimics the structure of Swift's well-known essay. Even if the reader does not recognize the allusion, the tone and content of Bruce's argument should make it clear that the writer isn't interested in convincing his readers to adopt the "simple solution" he presents. Rather, he's asking his readers to examine their attitudes and to find a way to confront a seemingly intractable dilemma.

Bruce 1

Michael Bruce

Dr. Stewart

ENG 110

6 September 2011

A Modest Proposal: The WIDE Approach to a Slimmer Citizenry

It is an all too common sight: parents, themselves obese, walking through supermarkets and discount retail outlets with their chubby children trailing behind. These children are inevitably overweight, heading toward a life of chronic illness and social stigma. Diseases that were once the sole province of adults are now seen in children. Because of their parents' poor example and bad habits, overweight children will inevitably become obese adults.

The condition of these suffering children promises dire consequences for our entire society, not only these unfortunate families. According to the Centers for Disease Control and Prevention, one-third of American adults are obese. We know that children follow in their parents' large footsteps. In fact, the CDC reports that 12.5 million children and adolescents

> Michael Bruce sets the tone by establishing the problem—increasing rates of childhood obesity—and making a harsh judgment and laying blame on parents.

Bruce 2

in the United States are obese. That's a lot of chunky American kids ("Overweight"). Significant financial burdens are imposed on our republic as a result of all these extra pounds. Medical costs of weight-related diseases are reported to have been $147 billion in 2008, the equivalent of $154 billion in 2011 dollars (Finkelstein). Economists calculate other costs in lost wages, shortened life span, higher rates for insurance, etc., etc. (Bhattacharya). Fat, in short, is expensive.

> Bruce presents specific evidence about the prevalence and costs of this health concern. But in his commentary he uses informal, even flippant language.

Several solutions have already been offered, most of them educational in nature; all have failed. I contend that these failures have resulted because they have been targeted to only a small portion of the population. My proposal requires the mandatory participation of every citizen, not only those who place themselves and their children in danger with every meal. In all its simplicity and elegance, I am sure this proposal will not be met with any objection, and will be enormously successful.

> Readers familiar with Swift's essay will recognize the parallel structure of Bruce's transition.

The problem of obesity has been called a public health crisis (Ebbeling, Pawlak, and Ludwig 473). I contend that is not true; rather it is a serious personal health concern. Those who are obese and raising obese children need to change their ways and carry their weight. I believe that obesity is nothing more than the result of the individual's decision to eat too much, to partake of too many calories—too many unhealthy calories. Therefore, all overweight individuals must be held responsible for what they eat and for what they feed the children in their care.

To assist these people in making wise food choices, I propose that the federal government impose a fat tax on all food sold in the United States. Instead of the flat tax that some politicians have proposed, I hereby propose a fat tax. It is true that everyone buys food, though not all are obese. Even healthy people of normal weight occasionally indulge in mongo-size fast food hamburgers with cheese fries and a double chocolate shake. Therefore, all food will be taxed, and everyone who buys food must pay.

The system will be enforced by the means of a Weight Identification Evaluation card. Every citizen must register for a WIDE card and carry it at all times. Embedded in the card will be a microchip on which pertinent information will be stored: age, height, weight, marital status, number and ages of any dependent children, and body weight index. This number, referred to simply as the BMI, is used to identify weight

Bruce sets out his satirical proposal but again includes factual information that makes it clear he is knowledgeable about the topic.

categories: underweight, normal, overweight, obese, and extreme obesity (Mayo Clinic).

The WIDE card will be presented and scanned whenever anyone purchases any food in any venue. A BMI calculator located at the point of purchase will confirm the buyer's current weight status. The tax will be assessed on a graduated scale, so those with a BMI equal to or greater than 40 will pay the highest rate, while those whose BMI is between 18.5 and 30 would pay only a nominal surcharge. Parents must display the WIDE card of each of their children, whether the children are physically present or not. Taxes for food purchased by adults with obese children would be levied at twice the top rate.

The additional revenue generated by this new sales tax will be used to offset the financial toll that obesity takes on our society. Other financial benefits will roll out as a result of this new policy. New businesses will spring into existence to design and manufacture the cards, microchips, and BMI scanners. Enterprising businessmen and women will be inspired to develop effective means to help people lose mass quantities of weight. The United States Commerce Department will hire hundreds of WIDE monitors to prevent the emergence of an underground economy in skinny cards and lightweight scales. Thus, sales taxes, business taxes, and income taxes will add to the public coffers.

Bruce develops his "proposal" with a list of imagined financial and legal benefits.

Because the federal government will issue the WIDE card, it will have the added benefit of serving as a national identification card, thereby ending that debate once and for all. Finally, there would be the extra boon to our legal system of locating illegal immigrants and deadbeat dads to ensure they get out or pay up, as the case may be.

It is true that other solutions have been proposed to address the growing problem of obesity in our country. But here I will quote Jonathan Swift and say, "Let no man talk to me of these and the like expedients, till he hath at least some glimpse of hope that there will ever be some hearty and sincere attempt to put them in practice." There will be no sincere attempt to address this issue unless we accept the World Health Organization's designation of obesity as an epidemic and address it as such ("Nutrition").

Once again, Bruce refers to Swift as he makes the transition to his serious proposal.

Bruce 4

There is a precedent for such a shift. Consider current attitudes toward cigarette smoking. Between 1965 and 2009, the percentage of adults who habitually smoke has dropped from 42.4% to 20.6%. Teen smoking is on a steady decline. In 1991, 27.5% of high school students surveyed reported that they had smoked cigarettes the past 30 days, but by 2009, that number had dropped to 19.5% ("Smoking"). What caused such a precipitous decline in this addictive behavior enjoyed by so many? A rigorous campaign made smoking uncool. An anti-obesity movement could adopt the practices that made the anti-smoking campaign successful. It would of course require images of huge lumps of fat prominently displayed in pop-up ads as we use our smart phones to find the nearest taco place, and that would be gross. But we can't allow our squeamishness to interfere.

It will take a long time before over-eating and under-exercising becomes the exception and Americans begin to slim down. If obesity really is a social problem, I guess we need to find a collective solution. But that means thinking of fat as a problem that affects all Americans, not only the third of us who just can't seem to kick the food habit. My proposal, on the other hand, is in line with the American ethos of taking individual responsibility to solve our own problems and improve our own circumstances. And what better incentive could there be? Eat less or pay more.

The writer concludes by suggesting a realistic approach to the problem, but then closes the essay on a light note.

Bruce 5

Works Cited

Bhattacharya, Jay, and Neeraj Sood. "Who Pays for Obesity?" *Journal of Economic Perspectives*, 25(1): 139-58. Winter 2011. *ProQuest.* Web. 3 Sept. 2011.

Ebbeling, Cara B., Dorota B. Pawlak, and David S. Ludwig. "Childhood Obesity: Public-health Crisis, Common Sense Cure." *Lancet* 360. (2002): 473-82. Print.

Bruce 6

Finkelstein, E. A., J. G. Trogdon, and W. Dietz. "Annual Medical
Spending Attributable to Obesity." *Health Affairs* 28 (2009):
w822-w831. Cited on *Centers for Disease Control and Prevention*.
US Dept. of Health and Human Services, Web. 3 Sept. 2011.

Mayo Clinic Staff. "Obesity: Definition." *Mayo Clinic.* Mayo Foundation
for Medical Education and Research, 6 May 2011. Web. 25 Aug.
2011.

"Nutrition: Controlling the Global Obesity Epidemic." *World Health
Organization*. World Health Organization, 2011. Web. 1 Sept. 2011.

"Overweight and Obesity." *Centers for Disease Control and Prevention*. US
Dept. of Health and Human Services, 28 Mar. 2011. USA.gov. Web.
25 Aug. 2011.

"Smoking & Tobacco Use: Trends in Current Cigarette Smoking Among
High School Students and Adults, United States, 1965–2009."
Centers for Disease Control and Prevention. US Dept. of Health and
Human Services, 20 Sept. 2010. Web. 1 Sept. 2011.

Swift, Jonathan. "A Modest Proposal." 1792. *Project Gutenberg*. Project
Gutenberg Literary Archive Foundation, 2003. Web. 25 August
2011.

PEARSON
my**writinglab**

For additional writing resources that will help you master the objectives of this chapter, go to www.mywritinglab.com.

Researching Arguments

PART

4

16 | Planning and Writing the Research Project

QUICK TAKE

In this chapter, you will learn that

1. Analyzing the assignment is the first step in completing a research project (see below)
2. The next step is finding a topic and asking a research question (see page 241)
3. Your preliminary research should lead to a working thesis, which will guide you through further research and the development of your argument (see page 243)
4. Before you begin writing your paper, take time to review your thesis and determine your contribution and your main points

Analyze the Research Task

Research is a creative process, which is another way of saying it is a messy process. Even though the process is complex, your results will improve if you keep the big picture in mind while you are immersed in research. If you have an assignment that requires research, look closely at what you are being asked to do.

Look for key words

Often the assignment will tell you what is expected.

- An assignment that asks you, for example, how the usual *definition* of intellectual property applies to YouTube invites you to write a definition argument (see Chapter 10).
- An *analysis of causes* requires you to write a causal argument (see Chapter 11).
- An *evaluation* requires you to make critical judgments based on criteria (see Chapter 12).
- A *proposal* requires you to assemble evidence in support of a solution to a problem or a call for the audience to do something (see Chapter 15).

Identify your potential readers

- How familiar are your readers with your subject?
- What background information will you need to supply?
- If your subject is controversial, what opinions or beliefs are your readers likely to hold?
- If some readers are likely to disagree with you, how can you convince them?

Assess the project's length, scope, and requirements

- What kind of research are you being asked to do?
- What is the length of the project?
- What kinds and number of sources or field research are required?
- Which documentation style is required?

Set a schedule

- Note the due dates on the assignment for drafts and final versions.
- Set dates for yourself on finding and evaluating sources, drafting your thesis, creating a working bibliography, and writing a first draft.
- Give yourself enough time to do a thorough job.

Find a Subject

One good way to begin is by browsing, which may also show you the breadth of possibilities included in a topic and possibly lead you to new topics (see Chapter 3).

You might begin browsing by doing one or more of the following.

- **Visit "Research by Subject" on your library's Web site.** Clicking on a subject such as "African and African American Studies" will take you to a list of online resources. Often you can find an e-mail link to a reference librarian who can assist you.
- **Look for topics in your courses.** Browse your course notes and readings. Are there any topics you might want to explore in greater depth?
- **Browse a Web subject directory.** Web subject directories, including *Yahoo Directory* (dir.yahoo.com), are useful when you want to narrow a topic or learn what subcategories a topic might contain. In addition to

the Web subject directories, your library's Web site may have a link to the *Opposing Viewpoints* database.

■ **Look for topics as you read.** When you read actively, you ask questions and respond to ideas in the text. Review what you wrote in the margins or the notes you have made about something you read that interested you. You may find a potential topic.

Ask a Research Question

Often you'll be surprised by the amount of information your initial browsing uncovers. Your next task will be to identify a question for your research project within that mass of information. This **researchable question** will be the focus of the remainder of your research and ultimately of your research project or paper. Research is all about the search, after all, so think of yourself as a sort of "private investigator," out to find the answer to an interesting question. Browsing on the subject of organic foods, for example, might lead you to one of the following researchable questions.

■ How do farmers benefit from growing organic produce?
■ Are organic foods better than conventional foods?
■ Why are organic products more expensive than nonorganic products?
■ Are Americans being persuaded to buy more organic products?

Once you have formulated a research question, you should begin thinking about what kind of research you will need to do to address the question.

Gather Information About the Subject

Much of the research done at a university creates new information through **primary research**—experiments, examination of historical documents—and **field research**, including data-gathering surveys, interviews, and detailed observations, described in Chapter 17.

However, most researchers rely partly or exclusively on the work of others as sources of information. After all, research is a cooperative enterprise, and researchers are always building on other researchers' work. Research based on the work of others is called **secondary research**. In the past this information was contained almost exclusively in collections of print materials housed in libraries, but today enormous amounts of information are available through library databases and on the Web. Chapters 18 and 19 outline a process for you to locate and evaluate the quality of sources you might use as you conduct your research.

Draft a Working Thesis

Once you have done some preliminary research into your question, you can begin to craft a working thesis. Let's take one topic as an example—the increasing popularity of organic products, including meat, dairy products, and produce. If you research this topic, you will discover that due to this trend, large corporations such as Walmart are beginning to offer organic products in their stores. However, the enormous demand for organic products is actually endangering smaller organic farmers and producers. As you research the question of why small farmers and producers in the United States are endangered and what small farmers and producers in other countries have done to protect themselves, a working thesis begins to emerge.

Write your subject, research question, and working thesis on a note card or sheet of paper. Keep your working thesis handy. You may need to revise it several times until the wording is precise. As you research, ask yourself: does this information tend to support my thesis? Information that does not support your thesis is still important! It may lead you to adjust your thesis or even to abandon it altogether. You may need to find another source or reason that shows your thesis is still valid. Again, think of yourself as a private investigator, out to find an answer: you can't settle on a reliable one if you rush to a premature judgment.

Example

SUBJECT: Increased demand for organic products seems to be endangering smaller farmers and producers

RESEARCH QUESTION: How can successful smaller organic farmers and producers protect themselves from becoming extinct?

WORKING THESIS: In order to meet the increasing demand for organic products that has been created by larger corporations such as Walmart, smaller organic farmers and producers should form regional co-ops. These co-ops will work together to supply regional chains, much as co-ops of small farmers and dairies in Europe work together, thereby cutting transportation and labor costs and ensuring their survival in a much-expanded market.

Conduct Additional Research

Continue to gather information about your topic. It is likely that some of the ideas, facts, and statistics you discover will support your thesis, but other resources will present alternative viewpoints. It's important to understand the range of opinions held by reasonable people about the subject you are learning about, so don't dismiss viewpoints that seem to contradict your own.

You may find that as your knowledge expands, your working thesis will continue to evolve to reflect a more nuanced understanding of your subject. Research is a process that sometimes results in unexpected findings. Consider it a work in progress, and be open to making changes in your original ideas as you learn more about your subject.

Review Your Goals and Plan Your Organization

If you have chosen a subject you're interested in, asked questions about it, and researched it thoroughly, you have a wealth of ideas and information to communicate to your audience.

Review your assignment and thesis

Before you begin writing a research project, review the assignment to remind yourself of the purpose of your argument, your potential readers, and the requested length of the finished paper.

Your **working thesis** will be the focus of your project. At this stage in the writing process, the thesis may still be rough, and it may change again as you write your draft, but having a working thesis will help keep your project focused. You may have conducted field research, and you should have located, read, evaluated, and taken notes on enough source material to write your project.

Determine your contribution

A convincing and compelling source-based argument does not make claims based solely on the word of you, the writer. To be persuasive, it must draw on the expertise and reputations of others as well. However, you must also demonstrate that you have thought about and synthesized the evidence you have gathered from your sources, and you must show your readers which elements of your project represent your original thinking.

Determine exactly what you are adding to the larger conversation about your subject by answering these questions.

- Whom do you agree with?
- Whom do you disagree with?
- Which positions do you agree with but can add an additional point or example to?
- What original analysis or theorizing do you have to offer?

See Chapters 18 and 19 for examples of how to identify your contribution in relation to your sources.

Write a Draft

Some writers begin by writing the title, first paragraph, and concluding paragraph.

Write a specific title

A bland, generic title says to readers that you are likely to be boring.

Generic

> Good and Bad Fats

Specific titles are like tasty appetizers; if you like the appetizer, you'll probably like the main course.

Specific

> The Secret Killer: Hydrogenated Fats

Write an engaging introduction

Get off to a fast start. If, for example, you want to alert readers to the dangers of partially hydrogenated oils in the food we eat, you could begin by explaining the difference in molecular structure between natural unsaturated fatty acids and trans-fatty acids. And you would probably lose your readers by the end of the first paragraph.

Instead, let readers know what is at stake along with giving some background and context; consider dramatizing a problem that your paper will address. State your thesis early on. Then go into the details in the body of your project.

Write a strong conclusion

The challenge in writing ending paragraphs is to leave the reader with something provocative, something beyond pure summary of the previous paragraphs. Connect back to your thesis, and use a strong concluding image, example, question, or call to action to leave your readers with something to remember and think about.

Steps to Writing a Research Project

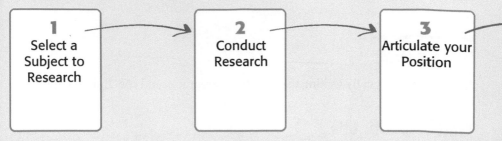

Step 1 Select a Subject to Research

- Determine the parameters of the assignment. What is the task you need to accomplish?
- Find a subject that will meet the requirements. Choose a topic you are sincerely interested in learning about. It should be something about which reasonable people hold different opinions, and it should be specific enough that you can address it reliably in the space and time available to you.
- Frame your research by posing an open-ended question.

Examples: Do social networking sites affect face-to-face interactions in positive or negative ways? Should college athletes be compensated as professionals?

Step 2 Conduct Research

- Decide what kind of research is most appropriate to answer your question. Will you give interviews, make observations, refer to print or electronic resources, or all of these?
- Gather sufficient information to understand the range of opinions about the subject.
- Be sure to note the information you will need to accurately cite your sources.

Step 3 Articulate your Position

Write a thesis clearly stating your opinion. Don't hedge; take a stance and articulate it forcefully.

Examples: Stronger regulations should be put into place to clarify and strengthen privacy rights. The use of standardized tests to evaluate student performance has resulted in a more focused and effective school curriculum.

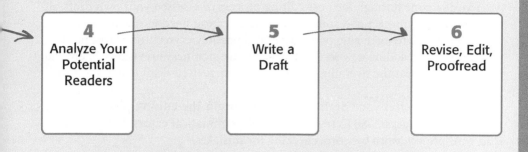

Step 4 Analyze Your Potential Readers

- Who are your readers?
- How familiar will they be with the subject?
- Are they likely to agree or disagree with your thesis? Are you challenging a conventional view, offering a new interpretation, or affirming a widely held belief?

Step 5 Write a Draft

Introduction
- Introduce the topic you are addressing.
- Supply any background information your readers will need to know.
- Clearly state the conclusions you have reached as a result of your research.

Body
- Present the data that led you to your position.
- You might want to acknowledge and refute alternative views.
- Use outside sources to support your discussion.
- Include correctly formatted in-text citations.

Conclusion
- Do not merely re-state your position, but wrap up your discussion in a way that emphasizes your thesis.
- You might want to conclude with a relevant quote or significant finding you discovered in your research.

Step 6 Revise, Edit, Proofread

For detailed instructions, see Chapter 5.
- For a checklist to evaluate your draft, see pages 61–62

Review and Revise

After you've gone through the peer editing process or assessed your own draft, sit down with your project and consider the changes you need to make. Start from the highest level, reorganizing paragraphs and possibly even cutting large parts of your project and adding new sections. If you make significant revisions, likely you will want to repeat the overall evaluation of your revised draft when you finish (see Chapter 5).

When you feel your draft is complete, begin the editing phase. Use the guidelines on pages 67–80 to revise style and grammatical errors. Finally, proofread your project, word by word, checking for mistakes.

PEARSON
mywritinglab

For additional writing resources that will help you master the objectives of this chapter, go to www.mywritinglab.com.

17 | Conducting Field Research

QUICK TAKE

In this chapter, you will learn that

1. For issues that are local or personal, conducting primary research is the most effective method for gathering information (see below)
2. There are several types of field research, including interviews, surveys, and observations (see pages 249–252)

Conducting Field Research

Sometimes you may be researching a question that requires you to gather first-hand information. Field research takes you directly to the source: to the people and primary source documents that can provide you with direct access to the information you want to know more about. For example, if you are researching a local issue such as the need for a skate park or center for teens to gather, you may need to conduct interviews, administer a survey, or make observations.

Interviews

Interviewing experts on your research subject can help build your knowledge base. It is likely that there are one or more people in your community who are extremely knowledgeable about the topic you are interested in. Most people are glad to share their experience and expertise with students. These human resources can provide you with a wealth of information and ideas.

You can use interviews to discover what the people most affected by a particular issue are thinking, such as why skateboards are not allowed on some city streets or in some parks.

Arrange interviews

Before you contact anyone, think carefully about your goals. Knowing what you want to find out through your interviews will help you determine whom you need to interview and what questions you need to ask. Use these guidelines to prepare for an interview.

- Decide what you want or need to know and who best can provide that information for you. Be sure the person you are interviewing is an essential person to consult.

- Schedule each interview in advance, and let the person know why you are conducting the interview. Estimate how long your interview will take, and tell your subject how much of her or his time you will need.

- Choose a location that is convenient for your subject but not too chaotic or loud. An office or study room is better than a noisy cafeteria.

- Plan your questions in advance. Write down a few questions and have a few more in mind. Do enough background reading to establish that you have done some homework; you don't want the person you are interviewing to think that he or she is providing information that is available elsewhere.

- If you want to record the interview, ask for permission in advance. A recording device sometimes can intimidate the person you are interviewing.

Conduct interviews

- Come prepared with your questions, a notebook, and a pen or pencil.

- If you plan to record the interview (with your subject's permission), make sure whatever recording device you use has an adequate power supply and will not run out of tape, disk space, or memory.

- Listen carefully so you can follow up on key points. Make notes when important questions are raised or answered, but don't attempt to transcribe every word the person is saying.

- When you are finished, thank your subject, and ask his or her permission to get in touch again if you have additional questions.

It's possible to conduct a long-distance interview by phone, e-mail, or a video tool like Google+ Hangout or Skype. This can allow you to learn from an expert who doesn't live or work close enough to your home for you to meet. The process of planning and conducting the interview is the same, but in your initial contact, you need to ask if the interview subject is willing to communicate with you electronically, and if the subject is registered with and able to use the platform in question. If you're using e-mail or a chat function, you will have the benefit of a written record of your discussion, but with e-mail you might lose the spontaneity and flexibility of a face-to-face conversation, and IM chats often encourage interruptions.

Surveys

Extensive surveys that can be projected to large populations, like the ones used in political polls, require the effort of many people. Small surveys, however, often can provide insight on local issues, such as how people might be affected if public library hours were reduced.

Plan surveys

What information do you need for your research question? Decide what exactly you want to know and design a survey that will provide that information. Likely you will want both close-ended questions (multiple choice, yes or no, rating scale) and open-ended questions that allow detailed responses. To create a survey, follow these guidelines.

■ Write a few specific, unambiguous questions. People will fill out your survey quickly. If the questions are confusing, the results will be meaningless.

■ Include one or two open-ended questions, such as "What do you like about X?" or "What don't you like about X?" Open-ended questions can be difficult to interpret, but sometimes they turn up information you had not anticipated.

■ Test the questions on a few people before you conduct the survey.

■ Think about how you will interpret your survey. Multiple-choice formats make data easy to tabulate, but often they miss key information. Open-ended questions will require you to figure out a way to sort responses into categories.

Administer surveys

■ Decide on who you need to survey and how many respondents your survey will require. For example, if you want to claim that the results of your survey represent the views of residents of your community, your method of selecting respondents should give all residents an equal chance to be selected. Don't select only your next-door neighbors.

■ Decide how you will contact participants in your survey. If you are conducting your survey on private property, you will need permission from the property owner. Likewise, e-mail lists and lists of mailing addresses are usually guarded closely to preserve privacy. You will need to secure permission from the appropriate parties if you want to contact people via an e-mail list.

■ If you mail or e-mail your survey, include a statement about what the survey is for.

Observations

Observing can be a valuable source of data. For example, if you are researching the effect of posting information about fat content and calories influences customers' selections, observe how many people choose low-calorie meals when given that option.

Make observations

- Choose a place where you can observe with the least intrusion. The less people wonder about what you are doing, the better.
- Carry a notebook and write extensive field notes. Record as much information as you can, and worry about analyzing it later.
- Record the date, exactly where you were, exactly when you arrived and left, and important details like the number of people present.
- Write on one side of your notebook so you can use the facing page to note key observations and analyze your data later.

Analyze observations

You must interpret your observations so they make sense in the context of your argument. Ask yourself the following questions.

- What patterns of behavior did you observe?
- How was the situation you observed unique? How might it be similar to other locations?
- What constituted "normal" activity during the time when you were observing? Did anything out of the ordinary happen?
- Why were the people there? What can you determine about the purposes of the activities you observed?

As you write about the results of your research, explain to the reader the process you used to gather information. You will need to include a citation for any interviews you conduct just as you would for a print or electronic source (see Chapter 21).

PEARSON
mywritinglab

For additional writing resources that will help you master the objectives of this chapter, go to www.mywritinglab.com.

18 | Finding Secondary Sources

QUICK TAKE

In this chapter, you will learn that

1. Developing a search strategy at the beginning will get you to quality sources faster (see below)
2. Using your working thesis to generate a list of keywords will enable you to search library databases, online sources, and print sources in your library (see below)
3. Library sources, including databases, online references, and printed books and journals offer the highest quality because they have been screened by reference librarians (see page 254 and page 263)
4. Valuable sources are also online, but you have to know how and where to find them (see page 257)

Develop Strategies for Finding Sources

The distinction between doing research online and in the library is blurring as more and more libraries make their collections accessible on the Web. Nevertheless, libraries still contain many resources not available on the Web. Even more important, libraries have professional research librarians who can help you locate sources quickly.

Determine where to start looking

Searches using *Google* or *Yahoo!* turn up thousands of items, many of which are often not useful for research. Considering where to start is the first step.

Scholarly books and articles in scholarly journals often are the highest-quality sources, but the lag in publication time makes them less useful for very current topics. Newspapers cover current issues, but often not in the depth of books and scholarly journals. Government Web sites and publications are often the best for finding statistics and are also valuable for researching science and medicine.

Learn the art of effective keyword searches

Keyword searches take you to the sources you need. Start with your working thesis and generate a list of possible keywords for researching your thesis.

First, think of keywords that make your search more specific. For example, a search for sources related to Internet privacy issues might focus more specifically on privacy *and*

Internet
cookies
Web profiling
Flash
spyware

You should also think about more general ways to describe what you are doing—what synonyms can you think of for your existing terms? Other people may have discussed the topic using those terms instead. Instead of relying on "privacy," you can also try keywords like

identity theft
data protection
electronic records

You can even search using terms that refer to related people, events, or movements that you are familiar with.

Facebook
Internet vigilantism
Google+
phishing

Many databases have a thesaurus that can help you find more keywords.

Find Sources in Databases

Sources found through library **databases** have already been filtered for you by professional librarians. They will include some common sources like popular magazines and newspapers, but the greatest value of database sources are the many journals, abstracts, studies, e-books, and other writing produced by specialists whose work has been scrutinized and commented on by other experts. When you read a source from a library database, chances are you are hearing an informed voice in an important debate.

Locate databases

You can find databases on your library's Web site. Sometimes you will find a list of databases. Sometimes you select a subject, and then you are directed to databases. Sometimes you select the name of a database vendor such as *EBSCO* or *ProQuest*. The vendor is the company that provides databases to the library.

Use databases

Your library has a list of databases and indexes by subject. If you can't find this list on your library's Web site, ask a **reference librarian** for help. Follow these steps to find articles.

1. Select a database appropriate to your subject or a comprehensive database like *Academic Search Complete, Academic Search Premier,* or *LexisNexis Academic.*
2. Search the database using your list of keywords.
3. Once you have chosen an article, print or e-mail to yourself the complete citation to the article. Look for the e-mail link after you click on the item you want.
4. Print or e-mail to yourself the full text if it is available. The full text is better than cutting and pasting because you might lose track of which words are yours, leading to unintended plagiarism.
5. If the full text is not available, check the library catalog or ask your librarian if it's possible to get a printed copy of the article.

Your library will probably have printed handouts or online information that tells you which database to use for a particular subject. Ask a librarian who works at the reference or information desk to help you.

If you wish to get only full-text articles, you can filter your search by checking that option. Full-text documents give you the same text you would find in print. Sometimes the images are not reproduced in the HTML versions, but the PDF versions show the actual printed copy. Get the PDF version if it is available. Articles in HTML format usually do not contain the page numbers.

Common Databases

Academic OneFile	Indexes periodicals from the arts, humanities, sciences, social sciences, and general news, with full-text articles and images. (*Formerly Expanded Academic ASAP*)
Academic Search Premier and Complete	Provide full-text articles for thousands of scholarly publications, including social sciences, humanities, education, computer sciences, engineering, language and linguistics, literature, medical sciences, and ethnic-studies journals.

(*Continued*)

Common Databases

ArticleFirst	Indexes journals in business, the humanities, medicine, science, and social sciences.
EBSCOhost Research Databases	Gateway to a large collection of EBSCO databases, including *Academic Search Premier* and *Complete*, *Business Source Premier* and *Complete*, *ERIC*, and *Medline*.
Factiva	Provides full-text articles on business topics, including articles from the *Wall Street Journal*.
Google Books	Allows you to search within books and gives you snippets surrounding search terms for copyrighted books. Many books out of copyright have the full text. Available for everyone.
Google Scholar	Searches scholarly literature according to criteria of relevance. Available for everyone.
General OneFile	Contains millions of full-text articles about a wide range of academic and general-interest topics.
LexisNexis Academic	Provides full text of a wide range of newspapers, magazines, government and legal documents, and company profiles from around the world.
Opposing Viewpoints Resource Center	Provides full-text articles representing differing points of view on current issues.
ProQuest Databases	Like EBSCOhost, ProQuest is a gateway to a large collection of databases with over 100 billion pages, including the best archives of doctoral dissertations and historical newspapers.

Find Sources on the Web

Because anyone can publish on the Web, there is no overall quality control and there is no system of organization—two strengths we take for granted in libraries. Nevertheless, the Web offers you some resources for current topics that would be difficult or impossible to find in a library. The key to success is knowing where you are most likely to find current and accurate information about the particular question you are researching, and knowing how to access that information.

Use search engines wisely

Search engines designed for the Web work in ways similar to library databases and your library's online catalog but with one major difference. Databases typically do some screening of the items they list, but search engines potentially take you to everything on the Web—millions of pages in all. Consequently, you have to work harder to limit searches on the Web or you can be deluged with tens of thousands of items. Some of the sources you find may be unreliable or inaccurate. Your school might have a firewall in place that blocks access to certain sites. Don't let that slow you down; you will find many, many resources as you keep looking.

Kinds of search engines

A search engine is a set of programs that sort through millions of items at incredible speed. There are four basic kinds of search engines.

1. **Keyword search engines** (e.g., *Bing, Google, Yahoo!*). Keyword search engines give different results because they assign different weights to the information they find.
2. **Meta-search engines** (e.g., *Dogpile, MetaCrawler, Surfwax*). Meta-search engines allow you to use several search engines simultaneously. While the concept is sound, metasearch agents are limited because many do not access *Google* or *Yahoo!*
3. **Web directories** (e.g., *Britannica.com, Yahoo! Directory*). Web directories classify Web sites into categories and are the closest equivalent to the cataloging system used by libraries. On most directories professional editors decide how to index a particular Web site. Web directories also allow keyword searches.
4. **Specialized search engines** are designed for specific purposes:
   - regional search engines (e.g., *Baidu* for China)
   - medical search engines (e.g., *WebMD*)
   - legal search engines (e.g., *Lexis*)

- job search engines (e.g., *Monster.com*)
- property search engines (e.g., *Zillow*)

Advanced searches

Search engines often produce too many hits and are therefore not always useful. If you look only at the first few items, you may miss what is most valuable. The alternative is to refine your search. Most search engines offer you the option of an advanced search, which gives you the opportunity to limit numbers.

The advanced searches on *Google* and *Yahoo!* give you the options of using a string of words to search for sites that contain (1) all the words, (2) the exact phrase, (3) any of the words, or (4) that do not contain certain words. They also

An advanced search on *Google* for government (.gov) sites only.

allow you to specify the site, the date range, the file format, and the domain. For example, if you want to limit a search for *identity theft statistics* to reliable government Web sites, you can specify the domain as **.gov**.

The **OR** operator is useful if you don't know exactly which term will get the results you want, especially if you are searching within a specific site. For example, you could try this search: "face-to-face OR f2f site:webworkerdaily.com."

You can also exclude terms by putting a minus sign before the term. If you want to search for social network privacy, but not *Facebook*, try "social network privacy—Facebook."

Find online government sources

The federal government has made many of its publications available on the Web. Also, many state governments now publish important documents on the Web. Often the most current and most reliable statistics are government statistics. Among the more important government resources are the following.

- **Bureau of Labor Statistics** (www.bls.gov/). Source for official U.S. government statistics on employment, wages, and consumer prices
- **Census Bureau** (www.census.gov/). Contains a wealth of links to sites for population, social, economic, and political statistics, including the *Statistical Abstract of the United States* (www.census.gov/compendia/statab/)
- **Centers for Disease Control** (www.cdc.gov/). Authoritative and trustworthy source for health statistics
- **CIA World Factbook** (www.cia.gov/library/publications/the-world-factbook/). Resource for geographic, economic, demographic, and political information on the nations of the world
- **Library of Congress** (www.loc.gov/). Many of the resources of the largest library in the world are available on the Web
- **National Institutes of Health** (www.nih.gov/). Extensive health information including MedlinePlus searches
- **NASA** (www.nasa.gov/). A rich site with much information and images concerning space exploration and scientific discovery
- **Thomas** (thomas.loc.gov/). The major source of legislative information, including bills, committee reports, and voting records of individual members of Congress
- **USA.gov** (www.usa.gov/). The place to start when you are not sure where to look for government information

Find online reference sources

Your library's Web site has a link to reference sites, either on the main page or under another heading like "research tools."

Reference sites are usually organized by subject, and you can find resources under the subject heading.

- **Business information** (links to business databases and sites like *Hoover's* that profiles companies)
- **Dictionaries** (including the *Oxford English Dictionary* and various subject dictionaries and language dictionaries)
- **Education** (including *The College Blue Book* and others)

- **Encyclopedias** (including *Britannica Online* and others)
- **Government information** (links to federal, state, and local Web sites)
- **Reference books** (commonly used books like atlases, almanacs, biographies, handbooks, and histories)
- **Statistics and demographics** (links to federal, state, and local government sites; *FedStats* [www.fedstats.gov/] is a good place to start)

Search interactive media

The Internet allows you to access other people's opinions on thousands of topics. Millions of people post messages on discussion lists and groups, *Facebook* groups, blogs, RSS feeds, *Twitter*, and so on. Much of what you read on interactive media sites is undocumented and highly opinionated, but you can still gather important information about people's attitudes and get tips about other sources, which you can verify later.

Several search engines have been developed for interactive media. *Facebook* and *Twitter* also have search engines for their sites.

Discussion list search engines

- **Big Boards** (www.big-boards.com). Tracks over two thousand of the most active discussion forums
- **Google Groups** (groups.google.com). Archives discussion forums dating back to 1981
- **Yahoo Groups** (groups.yahoo.com). A directory of groups by subject

---

Know the limitations of *Wikipedia*

Wikipedia is a valuable resource for current information and for popular culture topics that are not covered in traditional encyclopedias. You can find out, for example, that SpongeBob SquarePants's original name was "SpongeBoy," but the name had already been copyrighted.

Nevertheless, many instructors and the scholarly community in general do not consider *Wikipedia* a reliable source of information for a research paper. The fundamental problem with *Wikipedia* is stability, not whether the information is correct or incorrect. *Wikipedia* and other wikis constantly change. The underlying idea of documenting sources is that readers can consult the same sources that you consulted. Consult other sources to confirm what you find on Wikipedia and cite those sources. Often the *Wikipedia* entry includes a list of references that you can use as a starting point for your own research.

Blog search engines

- **Bloglines** (www.bloglines.com). Web-based aggregator that delivers RSS feeds
- **Google Blog Search** (blogsearch.google.com). Searches blogs in several languages besides English
- **IceRocket** (blogs.icerocket.com). Searches blogs, *MySpace*, and *Twitter*
- **Technorati** (www.technorati.com). Searches blogs and other user-generated content

Find Multimedia Sources

Massive collections of images; audio files including music, speeches, and podcasts; videos; maps, charts, and graphs; and other resources are now available on the Web.

Find images

The major search engines for images include the following.

- **Bing Images** (www.bing.com/images/)
- **Google Image Search** (images.google.com/)
- **Picsearch** (www.picsearch.com/)
- **Yahoo! Image Search** (images.search.yahoo.com)

Libraries and museums also offer large collections of images that may help you in your research. For example, the American Memory collection in the Library of Congress offers an important visual record of the history of the United States (memory.loc.gov/ammem/).

Find videos

- **Bing Videos** (www.bing.com/videos/)
- **blinkx** (www.blinkx.com/)
- **Google Videos** (video.google.com/)
- **Vimeo** (vimeo.com)
- **Yahoo! Video Search** (video.search.yahoo.com)
- **YouTube** (www.youtube.com)

Find podcasts

- iTunes Podcast Resources (www.apple.com/itunes/podcasts/)
- PodcastDirectory.com (www.podcastdirectory.com/)

Find charts, graphs, and maps

You can find statistical data represented in charts and graphs on many government Web sites.

- *Statistical Abstract of the United States* (www.census.gov/compendia/statab/)
- *Google Earth* (earth.google.com/)
- *National Geographic Map Machine* (mapmachine.nationalgeographic.com/)
- *Perry Casteñada Map Collection, University of Texas* (www.lib.utexas.edu/maps/map_sites/map_sites.html)

Respect copyright

Just because images, videos, and other multimedia files are easy to download from the Web does not mean that everything is available for you to use. Look for the creator's copyright notice and suggested credit line. This notice will tell you if you can reproduce the multimedia file. Don't forget to include properly formatted citations for each electronic resource you include in your paper.

Find Print Sources

Print sources may seem "old fashioned" if you grew up with the Internet. You might even feel a little bit intimidated by them. But they are the starting point for much of the research done by experts. In high school and beyond, they are indispensable. No matter how current the topic you are researching, you will likely find information in print sources that is simply not available online.

Print sources have other advantages as well.

- Books are shelved according to subject, allowing easy browsing.
- Books often have bibliographies, directing you to other research on the subject.
- You can search for books in multiple ways: author, title, subject, or call letter.

■ The majority of print sources have been evaluated by scholars, editors, and publishers, who decided whether they merited publication.

Find books

Nearly all libraries now shelve books according to the Library of Congress Classification System, which uses a combination of letters and numbers to give you the book's unique location in the library. The Library of Congress call number begins with a letter or letters that represent the broad subject area into which the book is classified. The call number will enable you to find the item you need.

Locating e-books

If your library collection includes e-books, you can use the online catalog to find them the same way you find printed books. You'll see on the record "e-book" or "electronic resource." Click on the link and you can read the book and often download a few pages.

Find journal articles

Like books, **scholarly journals** provide in-depth examinations of subjects. The articles in scholarly journals are written by experts, and they usually contain lists of references that can guide you to other research on a subject.

Popular journals are useful for gaining general information. Articles in popular magazines are usually short with few, if any, source references and are typically written by journalists. Some instructors frown on using popular magazines, but these journals can be valuable for researching current opinion on a particular topic.

Many scholarly journals and popular magazines are available on your library's Web site. Find them the same way you look for books, using your library's online catalog. Databases increasingly contain the full text of articles, allowing you to read and copy the contents onto your computer. If the article you are looking for isn't available online, the paper copy will be shelved with the books in your library.

PEARSON
mywritinglab

For additional writing resources that will help you master the objectives of this chapter, go to www.mywritinglab.com.

19 | Evaluating and Recording Sources

QUICK TAKE

In this chapter, you will learn that

1. Your working thesis will help you to determine the relevance of sources (see below)
2. Librarians have developed methods for evaluating the quality of library database and print sources (see page 267)
3. Evaluating the quality of online sources presents special challenges (see page 269)
4. Recording all the information you need to cite a source is critical to the research process (see page 270)

Determine the Relevance of Sources

Whether you use print or online sources, a successful search will turn up many more items than you can expect to use in your final product. You have to make a series of decisions as you evaluate your material. Use your research question and working thesis to create guidelines for yourself about importance and relevance.

If you ask a research question about contemporary events such as the NCAA's policy on compensating student athletes (see pages 144–148), you will need to find both background information and current information. You will need to know, for example, the most recent statistics on how many scholarship athletes actually graduate because the NCAA's main defense of not paying scholarship athletes is that they get a free education.

Use these guidelines to determine the importance and relevance of your sources to your research question.

- Does your research question require you to consult primary or secondary sources?
- Does a source you have found address your question?
- Does a source support or disagree with your working thesis? (You should not throw out work that challenges your views. Representing opposing views accurately enhances your credibility.)
- Does a source add significant information?

- Is the source current? (For most topics try to find the most up-to-date information.)
- What indications of possible bias do you note in the source?

Determine the Quality of Sources

In the digital era, we don't lack for information, but we do lack filters for finding quality information. Two criteria will help you to make a beginning assessment of quality: individual vs. edited sources and popular vs. scholarly sources.

Distinguish individual and anonymous sources from edited sources

Anyone with a computer and Internet access can put up a Web site. Furthermore, they can put up sites anonymously or under an assumed name. It's no wonder that so many Web sites contain misinformation or are intentionally deceptive.

In general, sources that have been edited and published in scholarly journals, scholarly books, major newspapers, major online and print magazines, and government Web sites are considered of higher quality than what an individual might put on a personal Web site, a Facebook page, a user review, or in a blog.

Edited sources can have biases, and indeed some are quite open about their perspectives. *National Review* offers a conservative perspective, the *Wall Street Journal* is pro-business, and the *Nation* is a liberal voice. The difference from individual and anonymous sites is that we know the editorial perspectives of these journals, and we expect the editors to check the facts. On self-published Web sites and in self-published books, anything goes.

Distinguish popular sources from scholarly sources

Scholarly books and **scholarly journals** are published by and for experts. Scholarly books and articles published in scholarly journals undergo a **peer review** process in which a group of experts in a field reviews them for their scholarly soundness and academic value. Scholarly books and articles in scholarly journals include

- author's name and academic credentials and
- a list of works cited.

Newspapers, popular books, and popular magazines vary widely in quality. Newspapers and popular magazines range from highly respected publications such as the *Los Angeles Times, Scientific American,* and the *Atlantic Monthly* to the sensational tabloids at grocery-store checkouts. Popular sources are not peer reviewed and require more work on your part to determine their quality. EBSCO-host databases allow you to limit searches to scholarly journals.

Distinguish primary sources from secondary sources

Another key distinction for researchers is primary versus secondary sources. In the humanities and fine arts, primary sources are original, creative works and original accounts of events written close to the time they occurred. Secondary sources interpret creative works and primary sources of events.

In the sciences, primary sources are the factual results of experiments, observations, clinical trials, and other factual data. Secondary sources analyze and interpret those results.

Read sources critically

Evaluating sources requires you to read critically, which includes the following.

- Identifying the source, which is not always easy online
- Identifying the author and assessing the author's credentials
- Understanding the content—what the text says
- Recognizing the author's purpose—whether the author is attempting to reflect, inform, or persuade
- Recognizing biases in the choices of words, examples, and structure
- Recognizing what the author does not include or address
- Developing an overall evaluation that takes into account all of the above

Evaluate the quality of visual sources

Evaluating the quality of visual sources involves skills similar to critical reading. Similar to critical reading, you should

- identify and assess the source,
- identify the creator,
- identify the date of creation,
- describe the content,
- assess the purpose, and
- recognize how the purpose influences the image, graphic, or video.

For visuals including charts and graphs, pay attention to the source of any data presented and see that the data are presented fairly.

Evaluate Database and Print Sources

Books are expensive to print and distribute, so book publishers generally protect their investment by providing some level of editorial oversight. Printed and on-line materials in your library undergo another review by professional librarians who select them to include in their collections.

This initial screening doesn't free you, however, from the responsibility of evaluating the quality of the sources. Many printed and database sources contain their share of inaccurate, misleading, and biased information. Also, all sources carry the risk of becoming outdated if you are looking for current information.

Checklist for evaluating database and print sources

Over the years librarians have developed a set of criteria for evaluating sources, and you should apply them in your research.

1. **Source.** Who published the book or article? Enter the publisher's name on Google or another search engine to learn about the publisher. Scholarly books and articles in scholarly journals are generally more reliable than popular magazines and books, which tend to emphasize what is sensational or entertaining at the expense of accuracy and comprehensiveness.

2. **Author.** Who wrote the book or article? Enter the author's name on Google or another search engine to learn more about him or her. What are the author's qualifications? Does the author represent an organization?

3. **Timeliness.** How current is the source? If you are researching a fast-developing subject such as treating ADHD, then currency is very important, but even historical topics are subject to controversy or revision.

4. **Evidence.** Where does the evidence come from—facts, interviews, observations, surveys, or experiments? Is the evidence adequate to support the author's claims?

5. **Biases.** Can you detect particular biases of the author? How do the author's biases affect the interpretation offered?

6. **Advertising.** For print sources, is advertising a prominent part of the journal or newspaper? How might the ads affect the credibility or the biases of the information that gets printed

Evaluate Web Sources

Researching on the Web has been compared to drinking from a fire hose. The key to success is not only getting the torrent down to the size of a glass, but also making sure the water in the glass is pure enough to drink.

Pay attention to domain names

Domain names can give you clues about the quality of a Web site.

- **.com** Commercial site. The information on a .com site is generally about a product or company, or it might be a personal Web site or blog hosted by a larger site like WordPress or Blogger.com. While the information may be accurate, keep in mind that the purpose of the site may be to sell a product or service, or it may be sustained by ads from companies seeking to do this. Look for information about the organization, publisher, or author of these sites.
- **.edu** Educational institution. The suffix tells you the site is on a school server, ranging from kindergarten to higher education. If the information is from a department or research center, it is generally credible, but if the site is an individual's, treat it as you would other kinds of self-published information.
- **.gov** Government. If you see this suffix, you're viewing a federal government site. Most government sites are considered credible sources.
- **.org** Nonprofit organization. Initially, nonpartisan organizations like the Red Cross used this domain, but increasingly partisan political groups and commercial interests have taken the .org suffix. Evaluate these sites carefully.
- **.mil** Military. This domain suffix is owned by the various branches of the armed forces.
- **.net** Network. Anyone can use this domain. Seek out information about the organization, publisher, or author of these sites.

Be alert for biased Web sites

Nearly every large company and political and advocacy organization has a Web site. We expect these sites to represent the company or the point of view of the organization. Many sites on the Web, however, are not so clearly labeled.

For example, if you do a search for "Sudden Infant Death Syndrome (SIDS)" and "vaccines," you'll find near the top of the list an article titled "Vaccines and Sudden Infant Death Syndrome (SIDS): A Link?" (www.thinktwice.com/sids.htm). The article concludes that vaccines cause SIDS. If you look at the home page—www.thinktwice.com—you'll find that the site's sponsor, Global Vaccine Institute, opposes all vaccinations of children.

Always look for other objective sources for verification of your information. The U.S. Centers for Disease Control publishes fact sheets with the latest information about diseases and their prevention (www.cdc.gov/vaccinesafety/Concerns/sids_faq.html). The fact sheet on SIDS and vaccines reports that people associate sudden infant death syndrome with vaccinations because babies are given their first vaccinations when they are between 2 and 4 months old, the same age babies die of SIDS. There is no scientific evidence that vaccines cause SIDS.

Checklist for evaluating Web sources

Web sources present special challenges for evaluation. When you find a Web page by using a search engine, you will often go deep into a complex site without having any sense of the context for that page. To evaluate the credibility of the site, you would need to examine the home page, not just the specific page you get to first. Use the following criteria for evaluating Web sites.

1. **Source.** What organization sponsors the Web site? Look for the site's owner at the top or bottom of the home page or in the Web address. Enter the owner's name on *Google* or another search engine to learn about the organization. If a Web site doesn't indicate ownership, then you have to make judgments about who put it up and why.

2. **Author.** Is the author identified? Look for an "About Us" link if you see no author listed. Enter the author's name on *Google* or another search engine to learn more about the author. Often Web sites give no information about their authors other than an e-mail address, if that. In such cases it is difficult or impossible to determine the author's qualifications. Be cautious about information on an anonymous site.

3. **Purpose.** Is the Web site trying to sell you something? Many Web sites are infomercials that might contain useful information, but they are no more trustworthy than other forms of advertising. Is the purpose to entertain? to inform? to persuade?

4. **Timeliness.** When was the Web site last updated? Look for a date on the home page. Many Web pages do not list when they were last updated; thus you cannot determine their currency.

5. **Evidence.** Are sources of information listed? Any factual information should be supported by indicating where the information came from. Reliable Web sites that offer information will list their sources.

6. **Biases.** Does the Web site offer a balanced point of view? Many Web sites conceal their attitude with a reasonable tone and seemingly factual evidence such as statistics. Citations and bibliographies do not ensure that a site is reliable. Look carefully at the links and sources cited, and peruse the "About Us" link if one is available.

7. **Appearance.** Sometimes you can learn a lot just by paying attention to what a Web site looks like. Is it well organized and easy to navigate? Are the graphics and other visual components professional and informative? Is the site relatively "clean" or is it cluttered with advertisements?

Keep Track of Sources

As you begin to collect your sources, make sure you get full bibliographic information for everything you might want to use in your project. Making note of this information as you do your research will make it easier to write your Works Cited list later or Reference lists later. And it will help you avoid unintentional plagiarism (see Chapter 20).

Decide which documentation style you will use. (One of the most common documentation styles—MLA is explained in detail in Chapter 21.)

Locate elements of a citation in database sources

For any sources you find on databases, MLA style requires you to provide the full print information, the name of the database in italics, the medium of publication (*Web*), and the date you accessed the database. If page numbers are not included, use *n. page*. Do not include the URL of the database.

See pages 286–287 for detailed coverage.

Author's name	Shaughnessy, Dan
Title of article	"They've Had Some Chief Concerns"
Publication information	
Name of periodical	*Boston Globe*
Date of publication	12 Oct. 2007
Section and page number	C5
Database information	
Name of database	*LexisNexis Academic*
Medium of publication	Web
Date you accessed the site	19 Apr. 2010

Citation in MLA-style list of works cited

Shaughnessy, Dan. "They've Had Some Chief Concerns." *Boston Globe* 12 Oct. 2007: C5. *LexisNexis Academic*. Web. 19 Apr. 2010.

Many databases include a feature that shows you how to cite the source; some have a built-in citation generator. These can be very helpful because they provide all the information you need in one place. Double-check the format before you include the citation in your paper. They aren't always 100 percent accurate.

Locate elements of a citation in online sources

As you conduct your online research, make sure you collect the necessary bibliographic information for everything you might want to use as a source. Because of the potential volatility of online sources (they can and do disappear overnight), their citations require extra information. Depending on the citation format you use, you'll arrange this information in different ways.

See pages 287 for detailed coverage in using MLA format.

Author's name	Zaiger, Alan Scher
Title of work	"Study: NCAA Graduation Rate Comparisons Flawed"
Title of the overall Web site	*ABC News*
Publication information	
Publisher or sponsor	ABC News
Date of publication	20 Apr. 2010
Medium of publication	Web
Date you accessed the site	1 Nov. 2010

Citation in MLA-style list of works cited

Zaiger, Alan Scher. "Study: NCAA Graduation Rate Comparisons Flawed." *ABC News*. ABC News, 20 Apr. 2010. Web. 1 Nov. 2010.

Locate elements of a citation in print sources

For books you will need, at minimum, the following information, which can typically be found on the front and back of the title page.

See page 287 for detailed coverage.

Author's name	Fleitz, David L.
Title of the book	Louis Sockalexis: The First Cleveland Indian
Publication information	
Place of publication	Jefferson
Name of publisher	McFarland
Date of publication	2002
Medium of publication	Print

Citation in MLA-style list of works cited

Fleitz, David L. *Louis Sockalexis: The First Cleveland Indian*. Jefferson:
McFarland, 2002. Print.

See pages 285–286 for detailed coverage.

For additional writing resources that will help you master the objectives of this chapter, go to www.mywritinglab.com.

20 | Avoiding Plagiarism

QUICK TAKE

In this chapter, you will learn that

1. Plagiarism means claiming credit for someone else's intellectual work (see below)
2. The best way to avoid unintentional plagiarism is to take care to distinguish source words from your own words (see below)
3. All quotations should be well integrated into your text (see pages 275–280)

What Exactly Is Plagiarism?

You have heard of **plagiarism**: It's the dishonest practice of using another person's intellectual property without appropriate acknowledgment. But think about it more positively: You want to build your credibility, you want your reader to know that you have studied the matter carefully, and you want to show that you have the expertise to weigh in with an opinion that matters. In this chapter, we explain how you can build credibility, establish your authority, and give appropriate credit to others where credit is due—in a way that builds academic integrity. To find good reasons to support your argument, you will often want to draw on work done by others. Research can help you understand an issue, clarify your own thinking, and appreciate why other people might disagree with you. The key to avoiding plagiarism is giving credit where it is due. You must acknowledge the sources of the information and ideas you incorporate into your work by including properly formatted citations.

Plagiarism means claiming credit for someone else's intellectual work no matter whether it's to make money or get a better grade. Intentional or not, plagiarism has dire consequences. Reputable authors have gotten into trouble through carelessness by copying passages from published sources without acknowledging those sources. A number of famous people have had their reputations tarnished by accusations of plagiarism, and several prominent journalists have lost their jobs and careers for copying the work of other writers and passing it off as their own.

Deliberate plagiarism

If you buy a paper online, copy someone else's paper word for word, or take an article off the Internet and turn it in as yours, it's plain stealing, and people who take that risk should know that the punishment can be severe—usually failure for the course and sometimes expulsion. Deliberate plagiarism is easy for your instructors to spot because they recognize shifts in style, and it is easy for them to use search engines to find the sources of stolen work.

Patch plagiarism

The ever-increasing use of online sources has also increased instances of plagiarism. Some students still see it as a big free buffet where they can grab anything, paste it in a file, and submit it as their own work. Other students intend to submit work that is their own, but they commit patch or accidental plagiarism because they aren't careful in taking notes to distinguish the words of others from their own words.

What you are not required to acknowledge

Fortunately, common sense governs issues of academic plagiarism. The standards of documentation are not so strict that the source of every fact you cite must be acknowledged. You do not have to document the following:

- **Facts available from many sources.** For example, many reference sources report that the death toll of the sinking of the *Titanic* on April 15, 1912, was around 1,500.
- **Results of your own field research.** If you take a survey and report the results, you don't have to cite yourself. You do need to cite individual interviews.

What you are required to acknowledge

The following sources should be acknowledged with an in-text citation and an entry in the list of works cited (MLA style).

- **Quotations.** Short quotations should be enclosed within quotation marks, and long quotations should be indented as a block. See pages 280–281 for how to integrate quotations with signal phrases.
- **Summaries and paraphrases.** Summaries represent the author's argument in miniature as accurately as possible. Paraphrases restate the author's argument in your own words.
- **Facts that are not common knowledge.** For facts that are not easily found in general reference works, cite the source.

- **Ideas that are not common knowledge.** The sources of theories, analyses, statements of opinion, and arguable claims should be cited.
- **Statistics, research findings, examples, graphs, charts, and illustrations.** As a reader you should be skeptical about statistics and research findings when the source is not mentioned. When a writer does not cite the sources of statistics and research findings, there is no way of knowing how reliable the sources are or whether the writer is making them up.

Avoid Plagiarism When Taking Notes

The best way to avoid unintentional plagiarism is to take care to distinguish source words from your own words. Don't mix words from the source with your own words.

- **Create a working bibliography and make separate files for content notes.** Create a file for each source and label it clearly with the author's name. If you work on paper, use a separate page for each source. At the top of each page, write down all the information you will need for a Works Cited list in your working bibliography.
- **If you copy anything from a source when taking notes, place those words in quotation marks and note the page number(s) where those words appear.** If you copy words from an online source, take special care to note the source. You could easily copy online material and later not be able to find where it came from.
- **Print out the entire source so you can refer to it later.** Having photocopies or complete printed files allows you to double-check later that you haven't used words from the source by mistake and that any words you quote are accurate.

Avoid Plagiarism When Quoting Sources

Effective research writing builds on the work of others. You can summarize or paraphrase the work of others, but often it is best to let the authors speak in your text by quoting their exact words. Indicate the words of others by placing them inside quotation marks.

Most people who get into plagiarism trouble lift words from a source and use them without quotation marks. Look carefully at this example to see where the line is drawn. In the following passage, Steven Johnson takes sharp issue with the old metaphor of "surfing" applied to the Web:

The concept of "surfing" does a terrible injustice to what it means to navigate around the Web. . . . What makes the idea of cybersurf so infuriating is the implicit connection drawn to television. Web surfing, after all, is a derivation of channel surfing—the term thrust upon the world by the rise of remote controls and cable panoply in the mid-eighties. . . . Applied to the boob tube, of course, the term was not altogether inappropriate. Surfing at least implied that channel-hopping was more dynamic, more involved, than the old routine of passive consumption. Just as a real-world surfer's enjoyment depended on the waves delivered up by the ocean, the channel surfer was at the mercy of the programmers and network executives. The analogy took off because it worked well in the one-to-many system of cable TV, where your navigational options were limited to the available channels.

But when the term crossed over to the bustling new world of the Web, it lost a great deal of precision. . . . Web surfing and channel surfing are genuinely different pursuits; to imagine them as equivalents is to ignore the defining characteristics of each medium. Or at least that's what happens in theory. In practice, the Web takes on the greater burden. The television imagery casts the online surfer in the random, anesthetic shadow of TV programming, roaming from site to site like a CD player set on shuffle play. But what makes the online world so revolutionary is the fact that there *are* connections between each stop on a Web itinerant's journey. The links that join those various destinations are links of association, not randomness. A channel surfer hops back and forth between different channels because she's bored. A Web surfer clicks on a link because she's interested.

—Steven Johnson. *Interface Culture: How New Technology Transforms the Way We Create and Communicate* New York: Harper, 1997. 107–09.

If you were writing a paper or creating a Web site that concerns online surfing, you might want to mention the distinction that Johnson makes between channel surfing and surfing on the Internet.

Quoting directly

If you quote directly, you must place quotation marks around all words you take from the original:

> One observer marks this contrast: "A channel surfer hops back and forth between different channels because she's bored. A Web surfer clicks on a link because she's interested" (Johnson 109).

Notice that the quotation is introduced and not just dropped in. This example follows MLA style, where the citation—(Johnson 109)—goes outside the quotation marks but before the final period. In MLA style, source references are made according to the author's last name, which refers you to the full citation in the list of works cited at the end. Following the author's name is the page number where the quotation can be located. (Notice that there is no comma after the name.)

Attributing every quotation

If the author's name appears in the sentence, cite only the page number, in parentheses:

> According to Steven Johnson, "A channel surfer hops back and forth between different channels because she's bored. A Web surfer clicks on a link because she's interested" (109).

Quoting words that are quoted in your source

Use single quotation marks to quote material that is already quoted in your source:

> Steven Johnson uses the metaphor of a Gothic cathedral to describe a computer interface: "'The principle of the Gothic architecture,' Coleridge once said, 'is infinity made imaginable.' The same could be said for the modern interface" (42).

Avoid Plagiarism When Summarizing and Paraphrasing

Summarizing

When you summarize, you state the major ideas of an entire source or part of a source in a paragraph or perhaps even a sentence. The key is to put the summary in your own words. If you use words from the source, you must put those words within quotation marks.

Plagiarized

> Steven Johnson argues in *Interface Culture* that the concept of "surfing" is misapplied to the Internet because channel surfers hop back and forth between different channels because they're bored, but Web surfers click on links because they're interested. [Most of the words are lifted directly from the original; see page 276.]

Acceptable summary

> Steven Johnson argues in *Interface Culture* that the concept of "surfing" is misapplied to the Internet because users of the Web consciously choose to link to other sites while television viewers mindlessly flip through the channels until something catches their attention.

Paraphrasing

When you paraphrase, you represent the idea of the source in your own words at about the same length as the original. You still need to include the reference to the source of the idea. The following example illustrates an unacceptable paraphrase.

Plagiarized

> Steven Johnson argues that the concept of "surfing" does a terrible injustice to what it means to navigate around the Web. What makes the idea of Web surfing infuriating is the association with television. Surfing is not a bad metaphor for channel hopping, but it doesn't fit what people do on the Web. Web surfing and channel surfing are truly different activities; to imagine them as the same is to ignore their defining characteristics. A channel surfer skips around because she's bored while a Web surfer clicks on a link because she's interested (107-09).

Even though the source is listed, this paraphrase is unacceptable. Too many of the words in the original are used directly here, including much or all of entire sentences. When a string of words is lifted from a source and inserted without quotation marks, the passage is plagiarized. Changing a few words in a sentence is not a paraphrase. Compare these two sentences.

Source

> Web surfing and channel surfing are genuinely different pursuits; to imagine them as equivalents is to ignore the defining characteristics of each medium.

Unacceptable paraphrase

> Web surfing and channel surfing are truly different activities; to imagine them as the same is to ignore their defining characteristics.

The paraphrase takes the structure of the original sentence and substitutes a few words. It is much too similar to the original.

> **A true paraphrase represents an entire rewriting of the idea from the source.**

Acceptable paraphrase

> Steven Johnson argues that "surfing" is a misleading term for describing how people navigate on the Web. He allows that "surfing" is appropriate for clicking across television channels because the viewer has to interact with what the networks and cable companies provide, just as the surfer has to interact with what the ocean provides. Web surfing, according to Johnson, operates at

> much greater depth and with much more consciousness of purpose. Web
> surfers actively follow links to make connections (107-09).

Even though this paraphrase contains a few words from the original, such as
navigate and *connections*, these sentences are original in structure and wording
while accurately conveying the meaning of the source.

Decide When to Quote and When to Paraphrase

The general rule in deciding when to include direct quotations and when to paraphrase lies in the importance of the original wording.

- If you want to refer to an idea or fact and the original wording is not
  critical, make the point in your own words.
- Save direct quotations for language that is memorable or conveys the
  character of the source.

Use quotations effectively

Quotations are a frequent problem area in research projects. Review every quotation to ensure that each is used effectively and correctly.

- **Limit the use of long quotations.** If you have more than one block quotation
  on a page, look closely to see if one or more can be paraphrased or summarized. Use direct quotations only if the original wording is important.
- **Check that each quotation is supporting your major points rather than
  making major points for you.** If the ideas rather than the original wording are what's important, paraphrase the quotation and cite the source.
- **Check that each quotation is introduced and attributed.** Each quotation
  should be introduced and the author or title named. Check for signal
  phrases that signal a quotation: Smith *claims,* Jones *argues,* Brown *states.*
- **Check that each quotation is properly formatted and punctuated.** Prose
  quotations longer than four lines should be indented one inch in MLA
  style. Shorter quotations should be enclosed within quotation marks.
- **Check that you cite the source for each quotation.** You are required to
  cite the sources of all direct quotations, paraphrases, and summaries.
- **Check the accuracy of each quotation.** It's easy to leave out words or
  mistype a quotation. Compare what is in your project to the original
  source. If you need to add words to make the quotation grammatical, make
  sure the added words are in brackets. Use ellipses to indicate omitted words.
- **Read your project aloud to a classmate or a friend.** Each quotation
  should flow smoothly when you read your project aloud. Put a check
  beside rough spots as you read aloud so you can revise later.

Use signal phrases

Signal verbs often indicate your stance toward a quotation. Introducing a quotation with "X says" or "X believes" tells your readers nothing. Find a livelier verb that suggests how you are using the source. For example, if you write "X contends," your reader is alerted that you likely will disagree with the source. Be as precise as possible.

Signal phrases that report information or a claim

> X argues that ...
> X asserts that ...
> X claims that ...
> X observes that ...
> As X puts it, ...
> X reports that ...
> As X sums it up, ...

Signal phrases when you agree with the source

> X affirms that ...
> X has the insight that ...
> X points out insightfully that ...
> X theorizes that ...
> X verifies that ...

Signal phrases when you disagree with the source

> X complains that ...
> X contends that ...
> X denies that ...
> X disputes that ...
> X overlooks that ...
> X rejects that ...
> X repudiates that ...

Signal phrases in the sciences

Signal phrases in the sciences often use the past tense, especially for interpretations and commentary.

X described …
X found …
X has suggested …

Introduce block quotations

Long direct quotations, called **block quotations**, are indented from the margin instead of being placed in quotation marks. In MLA style, a quotation longer than four lines should be indented 1 inch and double spaced. You still need to integrate a block quotation into the text of your project by mentioning who wrote or said it.

- No quotation marks appear around the block quotation.
- Words quoted in the original retain the double quotation marks.
- The page number appears in parentheses after the period at the end of the block quotation.

It is a good idea to include at least one or two sentences following the quotation to describe its significance to your thesis.

Double-check quotations

Whether they are long or short, you should double-check all quotations you use to be sure they are accurate and that all words belonging to the original are set off with quotation marks or placed in a block quotation. If you wish to leave out words from a quotation, indicate the omitted words with ellipses (…), but make sure you do not alter the meaning of the original quotation. If you need to add words of your own to a quotation to make the meaning clear, place your words in square brackets.

Plagiarism in Academic Writing

If you find any of the following problems in your academic writing, you may be guilty of plagiarizing someone else's work. Because plagiarism is usually inadvertent, it is especially important that you understand what constitutes using sources responsibly. Avoid these pitfalls.

- **Missing attribution.** Make sure the author of a quotation has been identified. Include a lead-in or signal phrase that provides attribution to the source, and identify the author in the citation.

- **Missing quotation marks.** You must put quotation marks around material quoted directly from a source.

- **Inadequate citation.** Give a page number to show where in the source the quotation appears or where a paraphrase or summary is drawn from.

- **Paraphrase relies too heavily on the source.** Be careful that the wording or sentence structure of a paraphrase does not follow the source too closely.

- **Distortion of meaning.** Don't allow your paraphrase or summary to distort the meaning of the source, and don't take a quotation out of context, resulting in a change of meaning.

- **Missing works-cited entry.** The Works Cited page must include all the works cited in the project.

- **Missing in-text citation.** Every resource listed on the Works Cited page must be cited somewhere in the paper.

- **Inadequate citation of images.** A figure or photo must appear with a caption and a citation to indicate the source of the image. If material includes a summary of data from a visual source, an attribution or citation must be given for the graphic being summarized.

For additional writing resources that will help you master the objectives of this chapter, go to www.mywritinglab.com.

21 | Documenting Sources in MLA Style

QUICK TAKE

In this chapter, you will learn that

1. Citing sources in MLA style is a two-part process, including in-text references and a Works Cited page at the end of your paper (see below)
2. Works cited entries for different kinds of sources follow a basic pattern (see page 285)
3. Research papers using MLA style are formatted according to a few basic conventions (see page 300)

When you use ideas and information from your research, it is imperative that you acknowledge the source. Neglecting to accurately cite your sources can result in unintentional plagiarism (as discussed in the previous chapter). You must include all of the relevant information and use the correct format in your citations.

Distinct citation formats are used in different disciplines because of the ways research is conducted in the arts and humanities, the social sciences, and the natural sciences. Each format is designed to assist students and researchers in that field to easily find the original documents. This allows your readers to see the development of the ideas over time, to recognize your contribution to the discussion, and to use the original resources as part of their own research. It's important to follow the guidelines closely, attending to the details of organization and punctuation.

APA stands for American Psychological Association, which publishes a style manual used widely in the social sciences, including government, linguistics, psychology, sociology, and education.

MLA, which stands for the Modern Language Association, is one of the most commonly used citation formats. This style is the norm for the humanities and fine arts, including English and rhetoric and composition. In this chapter, you'll find information and examples of how to conform to MLA standards. If you have questions that aren't addressed here, consult the *MLA Handbook for Writers of Research Papers*, Seventh Edition (2009), and the *MLA Style Manual and Guide to Scholarly Publishing*, Third Edition (2008).

MLA and APA formats require the same basic information, but the way sources are acknowledged varies. Your instructor may require you to cite your sources according to APA guidelines. For detailed information about APA style, consult the *Publication Manual of the American Psychological Association*, Sixth Edition (2010).

Elements of MLA Documentation

Citing a source in your paper

Citing sources is a two-part process. When readers find a reference to a source (called an in-text or parenthetical citation) in the body of your paper, they can turn to the Works Cited list at the end and find the full publication information. Place the author's last name and the page number inside parentheses at the end of the sentence.

> Anticipating the impact of Google's project of digitally scanning books in major research libraries, one observer predicts that "the real magic will come in the second act, as each word in each book is cross-linked, clustered, cited, extracted, indexed, analyzed, annotated, remixed, reassembled and woven deeper into the culture than ever before" (Kelly 43).

Author not mentioned in text

If you mention the author's name in the sentence, you do not have to put the name in the parenthetical reference at the end. Just cite the page number.

> Anticipating the impact of Google's project of digitally scanning books in major research libraries, Kevin Kelly predicts that "the real magic will come in the second act, as each word in each book is cross-linked, clustered, cited, extracted, indexed, analyzed, annotated, remixed, reassembled and woven deeper into the culture than ever before" (43).

Author mentioned in text

The corresponding entry in the Works Cited list at the end of your paper would be as follows.

Works Cited

> Kelly, Kevin. "Scan This Book!" *New York Times* 14 May 2006, late ed., sec 6: 43+. Print.

Entry in the works-cited list

Citing an entire work, a Web site, or another electronic source

If you wish to cite an entire work (a book, a film, a performance, and so on), a Web site, or an electronic source that has no page numbers or paragraph numbers, MLA style instructs that you mention the name of the person (for example, the author or director) in the text with a corresponding entry in the works-cited list. You do not need to include the author's name in parentheses. If you cannot identify the author, mention the title in your text.

Joel Waldfogel discusses the implications of a study of alumni donations to colleges and universities, observing that parents give generously to top-rated colleges in the hope that their children's chances for admission will improve.

> Author mentioned in text

Works Cited

Waldfogel, Joel. "The Old College Try." *Slate*. Washington Post Newsweek Interactive, 6 July 2007. Web. 27 Jan. 2010.

MLA style requires the medium of publication (print, Web, performance, etc.) to be included in each citation.

Creating an MLA-style works-cited list

To create your works-cited list, go through your paper and find every reference to the sources you consulted during your research. Each in-text reference must have an entry in your works-cited list. Do not include any sources on your works-cited list that you do not refer to in your paper.

Organize your works-cited list alphabetically by authors' last names or, if no author is listed, the first word in the title other than *a*, *an*, or *the*. (See pages 305–306 for a sample works-cited list.) MLA style uses four basic forms for entries in the works-cited list: books, periodicals (scholarly journals, newspapers, magazines), online library database sources, and other online sources (Web sites, discussion forums, blogs, online newspapers, online magazines, online government documents, and e-mail messages). There are also specific formats for citation of interviews, images, music, and film.

Works-cited entries for books

Entries for books have three main elements.

Pollan, Michael. *In Defense of Food: An Eater's Manifesto*. New York: Penguin, 2008. Print.

1. Author's name.
   - List the author's name with the last name first, followed by a period.

2. *Title of book.*
- Find the exact title on the title page, not the cover.
- Separate the title and subtitle with a colon.
- Italicize the title and put a period at the end.

3. Publication information.
- Give the city of publication and a colon.
- Give the name of the publisher, using accepted abbreviations, and a comma.
- Give the date of publication, followed by a period.
- Give the medium of publication (Print), followed by a period.

Works-cited entries for periodicals

Entries for periodicals (scholarly journals, newspapers, magazines) have three main elements.

Pilgrim, Sarah, David Smith, and Jules Pretty. "A Cross-Regional Assessment of the Factors Affecting Ecoliteracy: Implications for Policy and Practice." *Ecological Applications* 17.6 (2007): 1742-51. Print.

1. Author's name.
- List the author's name with the last name first, followed by a period.

2. "Title of article."
- Place the title of the article inside quotation marks.
- Insert a period before the closing quotation mark.

3. Publication information.
- Italicize the title of the journal.
- Give the volume number.
- List the date of publication, in parentheses, followed by a colon.
- List the page numbers, followed by a period. (Note: MLA uses hyphens in page spans and does not use full numbers.)
- Give the medium of publication (Print), followed by a period.

Works-cited entries for library database sources

Basic entries for library database sources have four main elements.

Damiano, Jessica. "Growing Vegetables in Small Spaces: Train Them up Trellises and Plant Crops in Succession." *Newsday* 2 May 2010: G107. *LexisNexis Academic.* Web. 8 Apr. 2010.

1. Author's name.
- List the author's name with the last name first, followed by a period.

2. "Title of article."
- Place the title of the article inside quotation marks.
- Insert a period before the closing quotation mark.

3. Print publication information
- Give the print publication information in standard format, in this case for a periodical (see pages 294–296).

4. Database information
- Italicize the name of the database, followed by a period.
- List the medium of publication, followed by a period. For all database sources, the medium of publication is *Web*.
- List the date you accessed the source (day, month, and year), followed by a period.

Works-cited entries for other online sources

Basic entries for online sources (Web sites, discussion forums, blogs, online newspapers, online magazines, online government documents, and e-mail messages) have three main elements. Sometimes information such as the author's name or the date of publication is missing from the online source. Include the information you are able to locate.

There are many formats for the different kinds of electronic publications. Here is the format of an entry for an online article.

Jacobs, Ruth. "Organic Garden Gives Back." *Colby Magazine* 99.1 (2010): n. pag. Web. 2 Apr. 2010.

1. Author's name.
- List the author's name with the last name first, followed by a period.

2. "Title of work"; Title of the overall Web site
- Place the title of the work inside quotation marks if it is part of a larger Web site.
- Italicize the name of the overall site if it is different from the title of the work.
- Some Web sites are updated periodically, so list the version if you find it (e.g., 2010 edition).

3. Publication information.
- List the publisher or sponsor of the site, followed by a comma. If not available, use *N.p.* (for *no publisher*).
- List the date of publication if available; if not, use *n.d.* (for *no date*).
- List the medium of publication (*Web*).
- List the date you accessed the source (day, month, and year).

MLA In-Text Citations

1. Author named in your text

Put the author's name in a signal phrase in your sentence. Put the page number in parentheses before the period at the end of the sentence.

Sociologist Daniel Bell called this emerging U.S. economy the "postindustrial society" (3).

2. Author not named in your text

Put the author's last name and the page number inside parentheses at the end of the sentence.

In 1997, the Gallup poll reported that 55% of adults in the United States think secondhand smoke is "very harmful," compared to only 36% in 1994 (Saad 4).

3. Work by a single author

The author's last name comes first, followed by the page number. There is no comma.

(Bell 3)

4. Work by two or three authors

The authors' last names follow the order of the title page. If there are two authors, join the names with *and*. If there are three authors, use a comma between the first two names and a comma with *and* before the last name.

(Francisco, Vaughn, and Lynn 7)

5. Work by four or more authors

You may use the phrase *et al.* (meaning "and others") for all names but the first, or you may write out all the names. Make sure you use the same method for both the in-text citations and the works-cited list.

(Abrams et al. 1653)

6. Work by an unnamed author

Use a shortened version of the title that includes at least the first important word. Your reader will use the shortened title to find the full title in the works-cited list.

> A review in the *New Yorker* of Ryan Adams's new album focuses on the artist's age ("Pure" 25).

Notice that "Pure" is in quotation marks because it is the shortened title of an article. If it were a book, the short title would be in italics.

7. Work by a group or organization

Treat the group or organization as the author, but try to identify the group author in the text and place only the page number in parentheses. Shorten terms that are commonly abbreviated.

> According to the *Irish Free State Handbook*, published by the Ministry for Industry and Finance, the population of Ireland in 1929 was approximately 4,192,000 (23).

8. Quotations longer than four lines

When using indented (block) quotations of more than four lines, place the period *before* the parentheses enclosing the page number.

> In her article "Art for Everybody," Susan Orlean attempts to explain the popularity of painter Thomas Kinkade:
>> People like to own things they think are valuable. . . .
>> The high price of limited editions is part of their appeal:
>> it implies that they are choice and exclusive, and that
>> only a certain class of people will be able to
>> afford them. (128)
> This same statement could possibly also explain the popularity of phenomena like PBS's *Antiques Road Show*.

If the source is longer than one page, provide the page number for each quotation, paraphrase, and summary.

9. Web sources including Web pages, blogs, podcasts, wikis, videos, and other multimedia sources

Name the author in the text instead of putting the author's name in parentheses.

> Andrew Keen ironically used his own blog to claim that "blogs are boring to write (yawn), boring to read (yawn) and boring to discuss (yawn)."

If you cannot identify the author, mention the title in your text.

> The podcast "Catalina's Cubs" describes the excitement on Catalina Island when the Chicago Cubs went there for spring training in the 1940s.

10. Work in an anthology

Cite the name of the author of the work within an anthology, not the name of the editor of the collection. Alphabetize the entry in the list of works cited by the author, not the editor.

> In "Ethos and the Aims of Rhetoric," Nan Johnson compares emotional appeals made by ancient Greek philosophers to contemporary uses of that powerful rhetorical tool (98).

11. Two or more works by the same author

When an author has two or more items in the works-cited list, distinguish which work you are citing by using the author's last name and then a shortened version of the title of each source.

> Elements of magical realism can also be seen in the lyrical narration of the retelling of a classic tale (Allende, *Zorro*, 153).

Note that *Zorro* is italicized because it is the name of a book; if an article were named, quotation marks would be used.

12. Different authors with the same last name

If your list of works cited contains items by two or more different authors with the same last name, include the initial of the first name in the parenthetical reference.

> Web surfing requires more mental involvement than channel surfing (S. Johnson 107).

Note that a period follows the initial.

13. Two or more sources within the same sentence

Place each citation directly after the statement it supports.

> In the 1990s, many sweeping pronouncements were made that the Internet is the best opportunity to improve education since the printing press (Ellsworth xxii) or even in the history of the world (Dyrli and Kinnaman 79).

14. Two or more sources within the same citation
If two sources support a single point, separate them with a semicolon.

> (McKibbin 39; Gore 92)

15. Work quoted in another source
When you do not have access to the original source of the material you wish to use, put the abbreviation *qtd. in* (quoted in) before the information about the indirect source.

> National governments have become increasingly what Ulrich Beck, in a 1999 interview, calls "zombie institutions"—institutions that are "dead and still alive" (qtd. in Bauman 6).

16. Literary works
To supply a reference to a literary work, you sometimes need more than a page number from a specific edition. Readers should be able to locate a quotation in any edition of the book. Give the page number from the edition that you are using, then a semicolon and other identifying information.

> "Marriage is a house" is one of the most memorable lines in *Don Quixote* (546; pt. 2, bk. 3, ch. 19).

MLA Works-Cited List: Books

One author

17. Book by one author
The author's last name comes first, followed by a comma, the first name, and a period.

> Doctorow, E. L. *The March*. New York: Random, 2005. Print.

18. Two or more books by the same author
In the entry for the first book, include the author's name. In the second entry, substitute three hyphens and a period for the author's name. List the titles of books by the same author in alphabetical order.

> Grimsley, Jim. *Boulevard*. Chapel Hill: Algonquin, 2002. Print.
> ---. *Dream Boy*. New York: Simon, 1995. Print.

Multiple authors

19. Book by two or three authors
Second and subsequent authors' names appear first name first. A comma separates the authors' names.

> Shange, Ntozake, and Ifa Bayeza. *Some Sing, Some Cry: A Novel*. New York: St. Martin's, 2010. Print.

20. Book by four or more authors
You may use the phrase *et al.* (meaning "and others") for all authors but the first, or you may write out all the names. Use the same method in the in-text citation as you do in the works-cited list.

> Zukin, Cliff, et al. *A New Engagement? Political Participation, Civic Life, and the Changing American Citizen*. New York: Oxford UP, 2006. Print.

Anonymous and group authors

21. Book by an unknown author
Begin the entry with the title.

> *Encyclopedia of Americana*. New York: Somerset, 2001. Print.

22. Book by a group or organization
Treat the group as the author of the work.

> United Nations. *The Charter of the United Nations: A Commentary*. New York: Oxford UP, 2000. Print.

23. Religious texts
Do not italicize the title of a sacred text, including the Bible, unless you are citing a specific edition.

> Holy Bible. King James Text: Modern Phrased Version. New York: Oxford UP, 1980. Print.

Imprints, reprints, and undated books

24. Book with no publication date
If no year of publication is given but can be approximated, put a *c.* ("circa") and the approximate date in brackets: [c. 2009]. Otherwise, put *n.d.* ("no date"). For works before 1900, you do not need to list the publisher.

> O'Sullivan, Colin. *Traditions and Novelties of the Irish Country Folk*. Dublin, [c. 1793]. Print.

> James, Franklin. *In the Valley of the King*. Cambridge: Harvard UP, n.d. Print.

25. Reprinted works
For works of fiction that have been printed in many different editions or reprints, give the original publication date after the title.

> Wilde, Oscar. *The Picture of Dorian Gray*. 1890. New York: Norton, 2001. Print.

Parts of books

26. Introduction, foreword, preface, or afterword
Give the author and then the name of the specific part being cited. Next, name the book. Then, if the author for the whole work is different, put that author's name after the word *By*. Place inclusive page numbers at the end.

> Benstock, Sheri. Introduction. *The House of Mirth*. By Edith Wharton. Boston: Bedford-St. Martin's, 2002. 3-24. Print.

27. Single chapter written by same author as the book

> Ardis, Ann L. "Mapping the Middlebrow in Edwardian England." *Modernism and Cultural Conflict: 1880-1922*. Cambridge: Cambridge UP, 2002. 114-42. Print.

28. Selection from an anthology or edited collection

> Sedaris, David. "Full House." *The Best American Nonrequired Reading 2004*. Ed. Dave Eggers. Boston: Houghton, 2004. 350-58. Print.

29. Article in a reference work
You can omit the names of editors and most publishing information for an article from a familiar reference work. Identify the edition by date. There is no need to give the page numbers when a work is arranged alphabetically. Give the author's name, if known.

> "Utilitarianism." *The Columbia Encyclopedia*. 6th ed. 2001. Print.

Editions and translations

30. Book with an editor
List an edited book under the editor's name if your focus is on the editor. Otherwise, cite an edited book under the author's name as shown in the second example below.

Lewis, Gifford, ed. *The Big House of Inver*. By Edith Somerville and Martin
Ross. Dublin: Farmar, 2000. Print.

Somerville, Edith, and Martin Ross. *The Big House of Inver*. Ed. Gifford Lewis.
Dublin: Farmar, 2000. Print.

31. Book with a translator

Benjamin, Walter. *The Arcades Project*. Trans. Howard Eiland and Kevin
McLaughlin. Cambridge: Harvard UP, 1999. Print.

32. Second or subsequent edition of a book

Hawthorn, Jeremy, ed. *A Concise Glossary of Contemporary Literary Theory*.
3rd ed. London: Arnold, 2001. Print.

Multivolume works

33. Multivolume work

Identify both the volume you have used and the total number of volumes in
the set.

Samuel, Raphael. *Theatres of Memory*. Vol. 1. London: Verso, 1999. 2 vols.
Print.

If you refer to more than one volume, identify the specific volume in your
in-text citations, and list the total number of volumes in your list of works cited.

Samuel, Raphael. *Theatres of Memory*. 2 vols. London: Verso, 1999. Print.

MLA Works-Cited List: Periodicals

Journal articles

34. Article by one author

Mallory, Anne. "Burke, Boredom, and the Theater of Counterrevolution."
PMLA 118.2 (2003): 329-43. Print.

35. Article by two or three authors

Miller, Thomas P., and Brian Jackson. "What Are English Majors For?"
College Composition and Communication 58.4 (2007): 825-31. Print.

36. Article by four or more authors

You may use the phrase *et al.* (meaning "and others") for all authors but the first, or you may write out all the names.

> Breece, Katherine E., et al. "Patterns of mtDNA Diversity in Northwestern North America." *Human Biology* 76.1 (2004): 33-54. Print.

Pagination in journals

37. Article in a scholarly journal

List the volume and issue number after the name of the journal.

> Duncan, Mike. "Whatever Happened to the Paragraph?" *College English* 69.5 (2007): 470-95. Print.

38. Article in a scholarly journal that uses only issue numbers

List the issue number after the name of the journal.

> McCall, Sophie. "Double Vision Reading." *Canadian Literature* 194 (2007): 95-97. Print.

Magazines

39. Monthly or seasonal magazines

Use the month (or season) and year in place of the volume. There is no comma before the date. Abbreviate the names of all months except May, June, and July.

> Barlow, John Perry. "Africa Rising: Everything You Know about Africa Is Wrong." *Wired* Jan. 1998: 142-58. Print.

40. Weekly or biweekly magazines

Give both the day and the month of publication, as listed on the issue.

> Brody, Richard. "A Clash of Symbols." *New Yorker* 25 June 2007: 16. Print.

Newspapers

41. Newspaper article by one author

The author's last name comes first, followed by a comma and the first name.

> Marriott, Michel. "Arts and Crafts for the Digital Age." *New York Times* 8 June 2006, late ed.: C13. Print.

42. Article by two or three authors
The second and subsequent authors' names are printed in regular order, first name first:

> Schwirtz, Michael, and Joshua Yaffa. "A Clash of Cultures at a Square in
> Moscow." *New York Times*, 11 July 2007, late ed.: A9. Print.

43. Newspaper article by an unknown author
Begin the entry with the title.

> "The Dotted Line." *Washington Post*, 8 June 2006, final ed.: E2. Print.

Reviews, editorials, letters to the editor

44. Review
If there is no title, just name the work reviewed.

> Mendelsohn, Daniel. "The Two Oscar Wildes." Rev. of *The Importance of
> Being Earnest*, dir. Oliver Parker. *The New York Review of Books*,
> 10 Oct. 2002: 23-24. Print.

45. Editorial

> "Hush-hush, Sweet Liberty." Editorial. *Los Angeles Times*, 7 July 2007: A18.
> Print.

46. Letter to the editor

> Doyle, Joe. Letter. *Direct*, 1 July 2007: 48. Print.

MLA Works-Cited List: Library Database Sources

47. Work from a library database
Begin with the print publication information, then the name of the database (italicized), the medium of publication (*Web*), and the date of access.

> Snider, Michael. "Wired to Another World." *Maclean's*, 3 Mar. 2003: 23-24.
> *Academic Search Premier*. Web. 14 Jan. 2010.

MLA Works-Cited List: Online Sources

Web publications

When do you list a URL? MLA style no longer requires including URLs of Web sources. URLs are of limited value because they change frequently and they can be specific to an individual search. Include the URL as supplementary information only when your readers probably cannot locate the source without the URL.

48. Publication by a known author

> Boerner, Steve. "Leopold Mozart." *The Mozart Project: Biography*. The Mozart
> Project, 21 Mar. 1998. Web. 30 Oct. 2010.

49. Publication by a group or organization

If a work has no author's or editor's name listed, begin the entry with the title.

> "State of the Birds." *Audubon*. National Audubon Society, 2008. Web.
> 19 Aug. 2010.

50. Article in a scholarly journal on the Web

Some scholarly journals are published on the Web only. List articles by author, title, name of journal in italics, volume and issue number, and year of publication. If the journal does not have page numbers, use *n. pag.* in place of page numbers. Then list the medium of publication (*Web*) and the date of access (day, month, and year).

> Fleckenstein, Kristie. "Who's Writing? Aristotelian Ethos and the Author Position
> in Digital Poetics." *Kairos* 11.3 (2007): n. pag. Web. 6 Apr. 2010.

51. Article in a newspaper on the Web

The first date is the date of publication; the second is the date of access.

> Brown, Patricia Leigh. "Australia in Sonoma." *New York Times*. New York
> Times, 5 July 2008. Web. 3 Aug. 2010.

52. Article in a magazine on the Web

> Brown, Patricia Leigh. "The Wild Horse Is Us." *Newsweek*. Newsweek,
> 1 July 2008. Web. 12 Dec. 2010.

53. Book on the Web

> Prebish, Charles S., and Kenneth K. Tanaka. *The Faces of Buddhism in America*. Berkeley: U of California P, 2003. *eScholarship Editions*. Web. 2 May 2010.

Other online sources

54. Blog entry

If there is no sponsor or publisher for the blog, use *N.p.*

> Arrington, Michael. "Think Before You Voicemail." *TechCrunch*. N.p., 5 July 2008. Web. 10 Sept. 2010.

55. E-mail

Give the name of the writer, the subject line, a description of the message, the date, and the medium of delivery (*E-mail*).

> Ballmer, Steve. "A New Era of Business Productivity and Innovation." Message to Microsoft Executive E-mail. 30 Nov. 2010. E-mail.

56. Video on the Web

Video on the Web often lacks a creator and a date. Begin the entry with a title if you cannot find a creator. Use *n.d.* if you cannot find a date.

> Wesch, Michael. *A Vision of Students Today*. *YouTube*. YouTube, 2007. Web. 28 May 2010.

57. Personal home page

List *Home page* without quotation marks in place of the title. If no date is listed, use *n.d.*

> Graff, Harvey J. Home page. Dept. of English, Ohio State U, n.d. Web. 15 Nov. 2010.

58. Wiki entry

A wiki is a collaborative writing and editing tool. Although some topic-specific wikis are written and carefully edited by recognized scholars, the more popular wiki sites—such as *Wikipedia*—are often considered unreliable sources for academic papers.

> "Snowboard." *Wikipedia*. Wikimedia Foundation, 2009. Web. 30 Jan. 2010.

59. Podcast

> Sussingham, Robin. "All Things Autumn." No. 2. *HighLifeUtah*. N.p.,
> 20 Nov. 2006. Web. 28 Feb. 2010.

60. PDFs and digital files

PDFs and other digital files can often be downloaded through links. Determine the kind of work you are citing, include the appropriate information for the particular kind of work, and list the type of file.

> Glaser, Edward L., and Albert Saiz. "The Rise of the Skilled City." Discussion
> Paper No. 2025. Harvard Institute of Economic Research. Cambridge:
> Harvard U, 2003. PDF file.

MLA Works-Cited List: Other Sources

61. Sound recording

> McCoury, Del, perf. "1952 Vincent Black Lightning." By Richard Thompson.
> *Del and the Boys*. Ceili, 2001. CD.

62. Film

Begin with the title in italics. List the director, the distributor, the date, and the medium. Other data, such as the names of the screenwriters and performers, is optional.

> *Wanted*. Dir. Timur Bekmambetov. Perf. James McAvoy, Angelina Jolie, and
> Morgan Freeman. Universal, 2008. Film.

63. DVD

> *No Country for Old Men*. Dir. Joel Coen and Ethan Coen. Perf. Tommy Lee
> Jones, Javier Bardem, and Josh Brolin. Paramount, 2007. DVD.

64. Television or radio program

> "Kaisha." *The Sopranos*. Perf. James Gandolfini, Lorraine Bracco, and Edie
> Falco. HBO. 4 June 2006. Television.

65. Personal Interview

> Andrews, Michael. Personal Interview. 25 Sept. 2010.

Sample MLA paper

> Include your last name and page number as page header, beginning with the first page, 1/2" from the top.

> MLA style does not require a title page. Ask your instructor whether you need one.

Brian Witkowski

Mr. Mendelsohn

RHET 309K

3 May 2010

Need a Cure for Tribe Fever?

How About a Dip in the Lake?

> Center your title. Do not put the title in quotation marks or type it in all capital letters.

> Use 1" margins all around. Double-space everything.

Everyone is familiar with the Cleveland Indians' Chief Wahoo logo—and I do mean everyone, not just Clevelanders. Across America people wear the smiling mascot on Cleveland Indians caps and jerseys, and recent trends in sports merchandise have popularized new groovy multicolored Indians sportswear. Because of lucrative contracts between major league baseball and Little League, youth teams all over the country don Cleveland's famous (or infamous) smiling Indian each season as fresh-faced kids scamper onto the diamonds looking like mini major leaguers

> Cite publications by the name of the author (or authors).

(Liu). Various incarnations of the famous Chief Wahoo—described by writer Ryan Zimmerman as "a grotesque caricature grinning idiotically through enormous bucked teeth"—have been around since the 1940s. Now redder and even more cartoonish than the original hook-nosed, beige Indian with a devilish grin, Wahoo often passes as a cheerful baseball buddy like the San Diego Chicken or the St. Louis Cardinals' Fredbird.

Though defined by its distinctive logo, Cleveland baseball far preceded its famous mascot. The team changed from the Forest Citys to the Spiders to the Bluebirds/Blues to the Broncos to the Naps and finally to the Indians. Dubbed the Naps in 1903 in honor of its star player and manager Napoleon Lajoie, the team gained their current appellation in 1915. After Lajoie was traded, the team's president challenged sportswriters to devise a suitable "temporary" label for the floundering club. Publicity material claims that the writers decided on the Indians to celebrate Louis Sockalexis, a Penobscot Indian who played for the team from 1897 to 1899. With a high batting average and the notability of being the first Native American in professional baseball, Sockalexis was immortalized by the new Cleveland label (Schneider 10-23). (Contrary to popular lore, some

> Indent each paragraph 1/2" on the ruler in your word processing program.

cite alternative—and less reverent—motivations behind the team's naming and point to a lack of Sockalexis publicity in period newspaper articles discussing the team's naming process [Staurowsky 95-97].) Almost ninety years later, the "temporary" name continues to raise eyebrows, in both its marketability and its ideological questionability.

Today the logo is more than a little embarrassing. Since the high-profile actions of the American Indian Movement (AIM) in the 1970s, sports teams around the country—including the Indians—have been criticized for their racially insensitive mascots. Native American groups question these caricatured icons—not just because of grossly stereotyped mascots, but also because of what visual displays of team support say about Native American culture. Across the country, professional sporting teams, as well as high schools and colleges, perform faux rituals in the name of team spirit. As Tim Giago, publisher of *The Lakota Times*, a weekly South Dakotan Native American newspaper, has noted,

> The sham rituals, such as the wearing of feathers, smoking of so-called peace pipes, beating of tomtoms, fake dances, horrendous attempts at singing Indian songs, the so-called war whoops, and the painted faces, address more than the issues of racism. They are direct attacks upon the spirituality of the Indian people. (qtd. in Wulf)

Controversy over such performances still fuels the fire between activists and alumni at schools such as the University of Illinois at Champaign-Urbana, where during many decades of football halftimes fans cheered the performance of a student (often white) dressed as Chief Illiniwek. In March of 2007, the University of Illinois board of trustees voted in a nearly unanimous decision to retire the mascot's name, regalia and image ("Illinois").

Since 1969, when Oklahoma disavowed its "Little Red" mascot, more than 600 school and minor league teams have followed a more ethnically sensitive trend and ditched their "tribal" mascots (Price). High-profile teams such as Stanford, St. Johns University, and Miami (Ohio) University have changed their team names from the Indians to the Cardinal (1972), the Redmen to the Red Storm (1993), and the Redskins to the Redhawks

(1996), respectively. In 2005, the NCAA officially ruled that "colleges whose nicknames or mascots refer to American Indians will not be permitted to hold National Collegiate Athletic Association tournament events" (Wolverton). By September 2005, only seventeen schools remained in violation (Wolverton). While many people see such controversies as mere bowing to the pressures of the late twentieth and early twenty-first centuries, others see the mascot issue as a topic well worthy of debate.

Cleveland's own Chief Wahoo has far from avoided controversy. Multiple conflicts between Wahoo devotees and dissenters occur annually during the baseball season. At the opening game of 1995, fifty Native Americans and supporters took stations around Jacobs Field to demonstrate against the use of the cartoonish smiling crimson mascot (Kropk). Arrests were made in 1998 when demonstrators from the United Church of Christ burned a three-foot Chief Wahoo doll in effigy ("Judge"). Opinions on the mascot remain mixed. Jacoby Ellsbury, outfielder for the Boston Red Sox and a member of the Colorado River Indian Tribes, said in 2007, "I'm not offended [by the mascot]. You can look at it two different ways. You can look at it that it's offensive or you can look at it that they are representing Native Americans. Usually I'll try to take the positive out of it" (Shaughnessy). Nonetheless, Ellsbury still acknowledges that he "can see both sides of [the controversy]" (Shaughnessy). Wedded to their memorabilia, fans proudly stand behind their Indian as others lobby vociferously for its removal, splitting government officials, fans, and social and religious groups.

In 2000 Cleveland mayor Michael White came out publicly against the team mascot, joining an already established group of religious leaders, laypersons, and civil rights activists who had demanded Wahoo's retirement. African American religious and civic leaders such as Rev. Gregory A. Jacobs pointed to the absurdity of minority groups who embrace the Wahoo symbol. "Each of us has had to fight its [sic] own battle, quite frankly," Jacobs stated. "We cannot continue to live in this kind of hypocrisy that says, Yes, we are in solidarity with my [sic] brothers and sisters, yet we continue to exploit them" (qtd. in Briggs).

This controversy also swirls outside of the greater Cleveland area. In 2009 the image of Wahoo was removed from the team's training complex in Goodyear, Arizona ("Cleveland"), while the *Seattle Times* went so far as to digitally remove the Wahoo symbol from images of the Cleveland baseball cap ("Newspaper"). As other teams make ethnically sensitive and image-conscious choices to change their mascots, Cleveland stands firm in its resolve to retain Chief Wahoo. Despite internal division and public ridicule fueled by the team icon, the city refuses to budge.

Cleveland's stubbornness on the issue of Wahoo runs contrary to the city's recently improved image and downtown revitalization. As a native of Cleveland, I understand the power of "Tribe Fever" and the unabashed pride one feels when wearing Wahoo garb during a winning (or losing) season. Often it is not until we leave northeastern Ohio that we realize the negative image that Wahoo projects. What then can Cleveland do to simultaneously save face and bolster its burgeoning positive city image? I propose that the team finally change the "temporary" Indians label. In a city so proud of its diverse ethnic heritage—African American, Italian American, and Eastern European American to name a few examples—why stand as a bearer of retrograde ethnic politics? Cleveland should take this opportunity to link its positive Midwestern image to the team of which it is so proud. I propose changing the team's name to the Cleveland Lakers.

The city's revival in the last twenty years has embraced the geographic and aesthetic grandeur of Lake Erie. Disavowing its "mistake on the lake" moniker of the late 1970s, Cleveland has traded aquatic pollution fires for a booming lakeside business district. Attractions such as the Great Lakes Science Center, the Rock and Roll Hall of Fame, and the new Cleveland Browns Stadium take advantage of the beauty of the landscape and take back the lake. Why not continue this trend through one of the city's biggest and highest-profile moneymakers: professional baseball? By changing the team's name to the Lakers, the city would gain national advertisement for one of its major selling points, while simultaneously announcing a new ethnically inclusive image that is appropriate to our wonderfully diverse city. It would be a public relations triumph for the city.

Of course this call will be met with many objections. Why do we have to buckle to pressure? Do we not live in a free country? What fans and citizens alike need to keep in mind is that ideological pressures would not be the sole motivation for this move. Yes, retiring Chief Wahoo would take Cleveland off AIM's hit list. Yes, such a move would promote a kinder and gentler Cleveland. At the same time, however, such a gesture would work toward uniting the community. So much civic division exists over this issue that a renaming could help start to heal these old wounds.

Additionally, this type of change could bring added economic prosperity to the city. First, a change in name will bring a new wave of team merchandise. Licensed sports apparel generates more than a 10-billion-dollar annual retail business in the United States, and teams have proven repeatedly that new uniforms and logos can provide new capital. After all, a new logo for the Seattle Mariners bolstered severely slumping merchandise sales (Lefton). Wahoo devotees need not panic; the booming vintage uniform business will keep him alive, as is demonstrated by the current ability to purchase replica 1940s jerseys with the old Indians logo. Also, good press created by this change will hopefully help increase tourism in Cleveland. If the goodwill created by the Cleveland Lakers can prove half as profitable as the Rock and Roll Hall of Fame, then local businesses will be humming a happy tune. Finally, if history repeats itself, a change to a more culturally inclusive logo could, in and of itself, prove to be a cash cow. When Miami University changed from the Redskins to the Redhawks, it saw alumni donations skyrocket (Price). A less divisive mascot would prove lucrative to the ball club, the city, and the players themselves. (Sluggers with inoffensive logos make excellent spokesmen.)

Perhaps this proposal sounds far-fetched: Los Angeles may seem to have cornered the market on Lakers. But where is their lake? (The Lakers were formerly the Minneapolis Lakers, where the name makes sense in the "Land of 10,000 Lakes.") Various professional and collegiate sports teams—such as baseball's San Francisco Giants and football's New York Giants—share a team name, so licensing should not be an issue. If Los Angeles has qualms about sharing the name, perhaps Cleveland could persuade Los Angeles to become the Surfers or the Stars; after all, Los Angeles players seem to spend as much time on the big and small screens as on the court.

Witkowski 6

Now is the perfect time for Cleveland to make this jump. Perhaps a new look will help usher in a new era of Cleveland baseball and a World Series ring to boot. Through various dry spells, the Cleveland Indians institution has symbolically turned to the descendants of Sockalexis, asking for goodwill or a latter-generation Penobscot slugger (Fleitz 3). Perhaps the best way to win goodwill, fortunes, and the team's first World Series title since 1948 would be to eschew a grinning life-size Chief Wahoo for the new Cleveland Laker, an oversized furry monster sporting water wings, cleats, and a catcher's mask. His seventh-inning-stretch show could include an air-guitar solo with a baseball bat as he quietly reminds everyone that the Rock Hall is just down the street.

Witkowski 7

Works Cited

> Center "Works Cited" on a new page.

Briggs, David. "Churches Go to Bat Against Chief Wahoo." *Cleveland Plain Dealer* 25 Aug. 2000: 1A. *LexisNexis Academic*. Web. 19 Apr. 2010.

> Double-space all entries. In-dent all but the first line in each entry one-half inch.

"Cleveland Indians' Chief Wahoo Logo Left Off Team's Ballpark, Training Complex in Goodyear, Arizona." *Cleveland.com*. Cleveland Plain Dealer, 12 Apr. 2009. Web. 23 Apr. 2010.

Fleitz, David L. *Louis Sockalexis: The First Cleveland Indian*. Jefferson: McFarland, 2002. Print.

"Illinois Trustees Vote to Retire Chief Illiniwek." *ESPN*. ESPN Internet Ventures, 13 Mar. 2007. Web. 26 Apr. 2010.

"Judge Dismisses Charges Against City in Wahoo Protest." *Associated Press* 6 Aug. 2001. *LexisNexis Academic*. Web. 19 Apr. 2010.

> Alphabetize entries by the last names of the authors or by the first important word in the title if no author is listed.

Kropk, M. R. "Chief Wahoo Protestors Largely Ignored by Fans." *Austin American Statesman* 6 May 1995: D4. Print.

Lefton, Terry. "Looks Are Everything: For New Franchises, Licensing Battles Must Be Won Long Before the Team Even Takes the Field." *Sport* 89 (May 1998): 32. Print.

Witkowski 8

Liu, Caitlin. "Bawl Game." *Portfolio.com*. Condé Nast, 21 Oct. 2008.
Web. 28 Apr. 2009.

"Newspaper Edits Cleveland Indian Logo from Cap Photo." *Associated Press* 31 Mar. 1997. *LexisNexis Academic*. Web. 27 Apr. 2010.

Price, S. L. "The Indian Wars." *Sports Illustrated* 4 Mar. 2002: 66+. *Academic OneFile*. Web. 20 Apr. 2010.

Schneider, Russell. *The Cleveland Indians Encyclopedia*. Philadelphia: Temple UP, 1996. Print.

Shaughnessy, Dan. "They've Had Some Chief Concerns." *Boston Globe* 12 October 2007: C5. *LexisNexis Academic*. Web. 19 Apr. 2010.

Staurowsky, Ellen J. "Sockalexis and the Making of the Myth at the Core of the Cleveland's 'Indian' Image." *Team Spirits: The Native American Mascots Controversy*. Eds. C. Richard King and Charles Fruehling Springwood. Lincoln: U of Nebraska P, 2001. 82-106. Print.

Wolverton, Brad. "NCAA Restricts Colleges With Indian Nicknames and Mascots." *Chronicle of Higher Education* 2 Sept. 2005: A65. *ProQuest*. Web. 25 Apr. 2010.

Wulf, Steve. "A Brave Move." *Sports Illustrated* 24 Feb. 1992: 7. Print.

Zimmerman, Ryan. "The Cleveland Indians' Mascot Must Go." *Christian Science Monitor* 15 Oct. 2007: 5. *LexisNexis Academic*. Web. 19 Apr. 2010.

Italicize the titles of books and periodicals.

Check to make sure all the sources you have cited in your text are in the list of works cited.

For additional writing resources that will help you master the objectives of this chapter, go to www.mywritinglab.com.

Contemporary Arguments

PART

5

22 | Negotiating the Environment

American Environmentalism

Most people agree that the modern environmental movement emerged from the work of two people: Aldo Leopold, who outlined a "land ethic" in his 1948

In this photograph from an environmental rally, how does this model Earth covered in plastic bags make an argument? How does it make you feel? What kinds of appeals does it use?

book *A Sand County Almanac*; and Rachel Carson, whose 1962 book *Silent Spring* sounded a national alarm against pesticides commonly used in the agriculture industry, particularly DDT. Together Leopold and Carson argued persuasively for a new sense of our relationship to our environment, for the conviction that we should be living in balance with nature, not in domination over it. Both books ultimately influenced not only agricultural practice but also efforts to protect endangered species, to regulate population growth, and to clean up our air and water resources. When President Richard Nixon created the Environmental Protection Agency in 1973, environmental concern became institutionalized in the United States; most states created their own departments of natural resources or environmental protection soon afterward.

In part, Aldo Leopold and Rachel Carson were successful because their appeals struck a chord deep within many Americans. For in a very real sense environmentalism is anything but modern. Ingrained deep within the American character, it derives from a respect for the land—the American Eden—that is evident in the legend of Rip Van Winkle, in the work of Hudson River painters such as Thomas Cole, in the landscape architecture of

> We are the most dangerous species of life on the planet, and every other species, even the earth itself, has cause to fear our power to exterminate. But we are also the only species which, when it chooses to do so, will go to great effort to save what it might destroy.
>
> —WALLACE STEGNER

Frederick Law Olmsted, in Henry David Thoreau's *Walden* and in Ralph Waldo Emerson's Transcendentalist writings in the 1850s, in John Muir's testimonials about Yosemite, and in Theodore Roosevelt's withdrawals into the Badlands and his campaign to begin a system of national parks. Of course, the exploitation of the American green world for profit is also ingrained in our national character. Even as some Americans were revering the land as a special landscape that sustained them physically and spiritually, pioneers moving westward were subduing it for their own purposes, in the process spoiling rivers and air and virgin forests—and native peoples—in the name of development.

Contemporary Arguments

Today, tensions between preserving nature and using nature are perhaps as high as they have ever been. When the BP spill dumped millions of gallons of crude oil into the Gulf of Mexico in 2010, the debate between exploiters of nature and preservers of nature became particularly fierce. The tensions inherent in the two positions help to explain why environmental issues remain so prevalent in public discourse.

- What are—and what should be—the proper relationships among science, technology, and the environment?
- What is the appropriate relationship between people and the natural environment?
- How can humans balance resource development and resource protection—with "resources" including everything from timber and coal to streams and animals?
- What are the nature and extent of global warming, and what counter-measures does it require?
- How can poorer nations develop economically without negative global environmental repercussions?

Such questions are debated each day in all media, especially as organized environmental groups are legion, ranging from the activist Earth First! (whose 10,000 members sometimes advocate direct action in support of environmental aims) to more mainstream groups such as the Sierra Club or the Nature Conservancy. The Nature Conservancy has created a membership of about a million in an explicit effort to create partnerships between scientists and

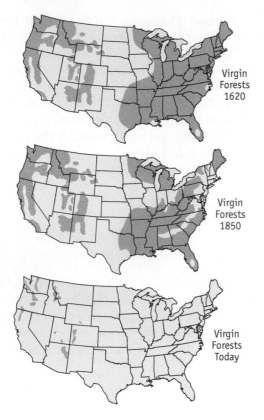

How virgin forests have diminished in the continental United States.

businesspeople in the interests of environmental reform. On the other hand, conservatives such as Rush Limbaugh and Sarah Palin have often ridiculed the efforts of environmentalists in the interest of a relatively unbridled developmentalism that is in the optimistic tradition of nineteenth-century free enterprise.

Debates about environmental issues are part and parcel of American culture. In the following pages you will find a sampling of the arguments concerning our relationship to the natural world. Three selections (by Rachel Carson, Edward O. Wilson, and Wendell Berry) offer philosophical perspectives and relate environmental ethics to human societies and practices—thereby providing context for a host of specific arguments, such as those about global warming. (You should also take a few minutes to review Wallace Stegner's famous "Wilderness Letter," on pages 227–232.) We also present an argument and counterargument (by Chris Packham and Mark Wright) on an issue of expediency: Do we have the financial resources to spend on saving exotic animal species (like pandas) when there are so many other pressing environmental issues before us?

Then this chapter focuses at length on the issue of global warming, from Al Gore's moral appeal to Americans to dramatically change their energy habits to Christopher Horner's exhortation that global warming is merely a phenomenon in Earth's history that bears little or no relationship to human practices. The Issue in Focus on global warming also includes a kind of debate between George Will and Chris Mooney on the seriousness of global warming. How reliable is the scientific evidence that shows warming in the Earth's atmosphere? How responsible are humans for climate changes? This section also offers advice on coping with global warming from a conservative commentator and from a journalist who questions the efficacy of so-called "green consumerism." Do some creature comforts have to be given up in order for people to survive in a healthy environment? What choices must we make among economic growth, technological advancement and innovation, the preservation of green spaces, environmental quality, and biodiversity—and what should be our priorities?

Brown pelicans are common along the coasts of the South and California, but they were headed toward extinction by 1970 because the pesticide DDT caused their eggs to be too thin to support developing chicks to maturity. Although DDT was banned in the United States, many countries continue to use it for agricultural spraying and malaria control even though insects and mosquitoes have developed resistance to it.

Rachel Carson

The Obligation to Endure

Rachel Carson (1907–1964) was raised in Springdale, Pennsylvania, 18 miles up the Allegheny River from Pittsburgh, where she developed the love of nature that she maintained throughout her life. At age 22 she began her career as a marine biologist at Woods Hole, Massachusetts, and she later went to graduate school at Johns Hopkins University in Baltimore. In 1936 she began working in the agency that later became the U.S. Fish and Wildlife Service. A meticulous scientist, Carson wrote three highly praised books about the sea and wetlands: *Under the Sea Wind* (1941), *The Sea Around Us* (1951), and *The Edge of the Sea* (1954).

When Carson decided to write *Silent Spring* (published in 1962), it marked a great change in her life. For the first time, she became an environmental activist in addition to being an enthusiastic writer about nature. During the 1950s she had grown progressively alarmed at the effects of the chemical DDT on fish, waterfowl, and birds. When her initial alarms went unheard, because DDT was contributing to substantial increases in agricultural production and controlling disease-spreading insects, she decided to write a short book to raise public consciousness. That book was *Silent Spring*, one of the most important books of the past century.

> What follows are the famous first chapter and beginning sections of the second chapter of *Silent Spring*. Notice how the two chapters use very different rhetorical tactics in order to persuade readers and move them to act.

I.

There was once a town in the heart of America where all life seemed to live in harmony with its surroundings. The town lay in the midst of a checkerboard of prosperous farms, with fields of grain and hillsides of orchards where, in spring, white clouds of bloom drifted above the green fields. In autumn, oak and maple and birch set up a blaze of color that flamed and flickered across a backdrop of pines. Then foxes barked in the hills and deer silently crossed the fields, half hidden in the mists of the fall mornings.

2   Along the roads, laurel, viburnum and alder, great ferns and wildflowers delighted the traveler's eye through much of the year. Even in winter the roadsides were places of beauty, where countless birds came to feed on the berries and on the seed heads of the dried weeds rising above the snow. The countryside was, in fact, famous for the abundance and the variety of its bird life, and when the flood of migrants was pouring through in spring and fall people traveled from great distances to observe them. Others came to fish the streams, which flowed clear and cold out of the hills and contained shady pools where trout lay. So it had been from the days many years ago when the first settlers raised their houses, sank their wells, and built their barns.

3   Then a strange blight crept over the area and everything began to change. Some evil spell had settled on the community: mysterious maladies swept the flocks of chickens; the cattle and sheep sickened and died. Everywhere was a shadow of death. The farmers spoke of much illness among their families. In the town the doctors had become more and more puzzled by new kinds of sickness appearing among their patients. There had been several sudden and unexpected deaths not only among adults but even among children, who would be stricken suddenly while at play and die within a few hours.

4   There was a strange stillness. The birds, for example—where had they gone? Many people spoke of them, puzzled and disturbed. The feeding stations in the backyards were deserted. The few birds seen anywhere were moribund; they trembled violently and could not fly. It was a spring without voices. On the mornings that had once throbbed with the dawn chorus of robins, catbirds, doves, jays, wrens, and scores of other bird voices there was now no sound; only silence lay over the fields and woods and marsh.

5   On the farms the hens brooded, but no chicks hatched. The farmers complained that they were unable to raise any pigs—the litters were small and the young survived only a few days. The apple trees were coming into bloom but no bees droned among the blossoms, so there was no pollination and there would be no fruit.

6   The roadsides, once so attractive, were now lined with browned and withered vegetation as though swept by fire. These, too, were silent, deserted by all living things. Even the streams were now lifeless. Anglers no longer visited them, for all the fish had died.

7   In the gutters under the eaves and between the shingles of roofs, a white granular powder still showed a few patches; some weeks before it had fallen like snow upon the roofs and the lawns, the fields and the streams.

8   No witchcraft, no enemy action had silenced the rebirth of new life in this stricken world. The people had done it themselves.

9   This town does not actually exist, but it might easily have a thousand counterparts in America or elsewhere in the world. I know of no community that has experienced all the misfortunes I describe. Yet every one of these disasters has actually happened somewhere, and many real communities have already suffered a substantial number of them. A grim specter has crept upon us almost unnoticed, and this imagined tragedy may easily become a stark reality we all shall know

What has already silenced the voices of spring in countless towns in America? This book is an attempt to explain.

II.

The history of life on earth has been a history of interaction between living things and their surroundings. To a large extent, the physical form and the habits of the earth's vegetation and its animal life have been molded by the environment. Considering the whole span of earthly time, the opposite effect, in which life actually modifies its surroundings, has been relatively slight. Only within the moment of time represented by the present century has one species—man—acquired significant power to alter the nature of his world.

2   During the past quarter century this power has not only increased to one of disturbing magnitude but it has changed in character. The most alarming of all man's assaults upon the environment is the contamination of air, earth, rivers, and sea with dangerous and even lethal materials. This pollution is for the most part irrecoverable; the chain of evil it initiates not only in the world that must support life but in living tissues is for the most part irreversible. In this now universal contamination of the environment, chemicals are the sinister and little-recognized partners of radiation in changing the very nature of the world—the very nature of its life. Strontium 90, released through nuclear explosions into the air, comes to earth in rain or drifts down as fallout, lodges in soil, enters into the grass or corn or wheat grown there, and in time takes up its abode in the bones of a human being, there to remain until his death. Similarly, chemicals sprayed on croplands or forests or gardens lie long in soil, entering into living organisms, passing from one to another in a chain of poisoning and death. Or they pass mysteriously by underground streams until they emerge and, through the alchemy of air and sunlight, combine into new forms that kill vegetation, sicken cattle, and work unknown harm on those who drink from once pure wells. As Albert Schweitzer has said, "Man can hardly even recognize the devils of his own creation."

3   It took hundreds of millions of years to produce the life that now inhabits the earth—eons of time in which that developing and evolving and diversifying life reached a state of adjustment and balance with its surroundings. The environment, rigorously shaping and directing the life it supported, contained elements that were hostile as well as supporting. Certain rocks gave out dangerous radiation; even within the light of the sun, from which all life draws its energy, there were short-wave radiations with power to injure.

Given time—time not in years but in millennia—life adjusts, and a balance has been reached. For time is the essential ingredient; but in the modern world there is no time.

4   The rapidity of change and the speed with which new situations are created follow the impetuous and heedless pace of man rather than the deliberate pace of nature. Radiation is no longer merely the background radiation of rocks, the bombardment of cosmic rays, the ultraviolet of the sun that have existed before there was any life on earth; radiation is now the unnatural creation of man's tampering with the atom. The chemicals to which life is asked to make its adjustment are no longer merely the calcium and silica and copper and all the rest of the minerals washed out of the rocks and carried in rivers to the sea; they are the synthetic creations of man's inventive mind, brewed in his laboratories, and having no counterparts in nature.

5   To adjust to these chemicals would require time on the scale that is nature's; it would require not merely the years of a man's life but the life of generations. And even this, were it by some miracle possible, would be futile, for the new chemicals come from our laboratories in an endless stream; almost five hundred annually find their way into actual use in the United States alone. The figure is staggering and its implications are not easily grasped—500 new chemicals to which the bodies of men and animals are required somehow to adapt each year, chemicals totally outside the limits of biologic experience.

6   Among them are many that are used in man's war against nature. Since the mid-1940's over 200 basic chemicals have been created for use in killing insects, weeds, rodents, and other organisms described in the modern vernacular as "pests"; and they are sold under several thousand different brand names.

7   These sprays, dusts, and aerosols are now applied almost universally to farms, gardens, forests, and homes—nonselective chemicals that have the power to kill every insect, the "good" and the "bad," to still the song of birds and the leaping of fish in the streams, to coat the leaves with a deadly film, and to linger on in soil—all this though the intended target may be only a few weeds or insects. Can anyone believe it is possible to lay down such a barrage of poisons on the surface of the earth without making it unfit for all life? They should not be called "insecticides," but "biocides."

8   The whole process of spraying seems caught up in an endless spiral. Since DDT was released for civilian use, a process of escalation has been going on in which ever more toxic materials must be found. This has happened because insects, in a triumphant vindication of Darwin's principle of the survival of the fittest, have evolved super races immune to the particular insecticide used, hence a deadlier one has always to be developed—and then a deadlier one than that. It has happened also because, for reasons to be described later, destructive insects often undergo a "flareback," or resurgence, after spraying, in numbers greater than before. Thus the chemical war is never won, and all life is caught in its violent crossfire.

9   Along with the possibility of the extinction of mankind by nuclear war, the central problem of our age has therefore become the contamination of man's total environment with such substances of incredible potential for harm—substances that accumulate in the tissues of plants and animals and even penetrate the germ cells to shatter or alter the very material of heredity upon which the shape of the future depends.

10   Some would-be architects of our future look toward a time when it will be possible to alter the human germ plasm by design. But we may easily be doing so now by

inadvertence, for many chemicals, like radiation, bring about gene mutations. It is ironic to think that man might determine his own future by something so seemingly trivial as the choice of an insect spray.

11   All this has been risked—for what? Future historians may well be amazed by our distorted sense of proportion. How could intelligent beings seek to control a few un-wanted species by a method that contaminated the entire environment and brought the threat of disease and death even to their own kind? Yet this is precisely what we have done. We have done it, moreover, for reasons that collapse the moment we examine them. We are told that the enormous and expanding use of pesticides is necessary to maintain farm production. Yet is our real problem not one of *overproduction*? Our farms, despite measures to remove acreages from production and to pay farmers *not* to produce, have yielded such a staggering excess of crops that the American taxpayer in 1962 is paying out more than one billion dollars a year as the total carrying cost of the surplus-food storage program. And is the situation helped when one branch of the Agriculture Department tries to reduce production while another states, as it did in 1958, "It is believed generally that reduction of crop acreages under provisions of the Soil Bank will stimulate interest in use of chemicals to obtain maximum production on the land retained in crops."

12   All this is not to say there is no insect problem and no need of control. I am say-ing, rather, that control must be geared to realities, not to mythical situations, and that the methods employed must be such that they do not destroy us along with the insects. . . .

Edward O. Wilson

The Conservation Ethic

Edward O. Wilson, a long-time Harvard professor and an entomologist with a special interest in ants, is one of the world's leading naturalists. He has won the Pulitzer Prize (twice) and the National Medal of Science, among other awards. Many of his books, including *The Diversity of Life, Naturalist*, and *Biophilia*, emphasize the vitality of species diversity and decry activities that cause the extinction of particular species. Wilson points out the value of even the smallest bugs and plants as integral parts of life systems. The following text, from *Biophilia* (1984), outlines important connections between ecology and ethics.

When very little is known about an important subject, the questions people raise are almost invariably ethical. Then as knowledge grows, they become more concerned with information and amoral, in other words more narrowly intellectual. Finally, as understanding becomes sufficiently complete, the questions turn ethical again. Environmentalism is now passing from the first to the second phase, and there is reason to hope that it will proceed directly on to the third.

2   The future of the conservation movement depends on such an advance in moral reasoning. Its maturation is linked to that of biology and a new hybrid field, bioethics, that deals with the many technological advances recently made possible by biology. Philosophers and scientists are applying a more formal analysis to such complex problems as the allocations of scarce organ transplants, heroic but extremely expensive efforts to prolong life, and the possible use of genetic engineering to alter human heredity. They have only begun to consider the relationships between human beings and organisms with the same rigor. It is clear that the key to precision lies in the understanding of motivation, the ultimate reasons why people care about one thing but not another—why, say, they prefer a city with a park to a city alone. The goal is to join emotion with the rational analysis of emotion in order to create a deeper and more enduring conservation ethic.

3   Aldo Leopold, the pioneer ecologist and author of *A Sand County Almanac*, defined an ethic as a set of rules invented to meet circumstances so new or intricate, or else encompassing responses so far in the future, that the average person cannot foresee the final outcome. What is good for you and me at this moment might easily sour within ten years, and what seems ideal for the next few decades could ruin future generations. That is why any ethic worthy of the name has to encompass the distant future. The relationships of ecology and the human mind are too intricate to be understood entirely by unaided intuition, by common sense—that overrated capacity composed of the set of prejudices we acquire by the age of eighteen.

4   Values are time-dependent, making them all the more difficult to carve in stone. We want health, security, freedom, and pleasure for ourselves and our families. For distant generations we wish the same but not at any great personal cost. The difficulty created for the conservation ethic is that natural selection has programmed people to think mostly in physiological time. Their minds travel back and forth across hours, days, or at most a hundred years. The forests may all be cut, radiation slowly rise, and the winters grow steadily colder, but if the effects are unlikely to become decisive for a few generations, very few people will be stirred to revolt. Ecological and evolutionary time, spanning centuries and millennia, can be conceived in an intellectual mode but has no immediate emotional impact. Only through an unusual amount of education and reflective thought do people come to respond emotionally to far-off events and hence place a high premium on posterity.

5   The deepening of the conservation ethic requires a greater measure of evolutionary realism, including a valuation of ourselves as opposed to other people. What do we really owe our remote descendants? At the risk of offending some readers I will suggest: Nothing. Obligations simply lose their meaning across centuries. But what do we owe ourselves in planning for them? Everything. If human existence has any verifiable meaning, it is that our passions and toil are enabling mechanisms to continue that existence unbroken, unsullied, and progressively secure. It is for ourselves, and not for them or any abstract morality, that we think into the distant future. The precise manner in which we take this measure, how we put it into words, is crucially important. For if the whole process of our life is directed toward preserving our species and personal genes, preparing for future generations is an expression of the highest morality of which human beings are capable. It follows that the destruction of

the natural world in which the brain was assembled over millions of years is a risky step. And the worst gamble of all is to let species slip into extinction wholesale, for even if the natural environment is conceded more ground later, it can never be reconstituted in its original diversity. The first rule of the tinkerer, Aldo Leopold reminds us, is to keep all the pieces.

6   This proposition can be expressed another way. What event likely to happen during the next few years will our descendants most regret? Everyone agrees, defense ministers and environmentalists alike, that the worst thing possible is global nuclear war. If it occurs the entire human species is endangered; life as normal human beings wish to live it would come to an end. With that terrible truism acknowledged, it must be added that if no country pulls the trigger the worst thing that will *probably* happen—in fact is already well underway—is not energy depletion, economic collapse, conventional war, or even the expansion of totalitarian governments. As tragic as these catastrophes would be for us, they can be repaired within a few generations. The one process now going on that will take millions of years to correct is the loss of genetic and species diversity by the destruction of natural habitats. This is the folly our descendants are least likely to forgive us.

7   Extinction is accelerating and could reach ruinous proportions during the next twenty years. Not only are birds and mammals vanishing but such smaller forms as mosses, insects, and minnows. A conservative estimate of the current extinction rate is one thousand species a year, mostly from the destruction of forests and other key habitats in the tropics. By the 1990s the figure is expected to rise past ten thousand species a year (one species per hour). During the next thirty years fully one million species could be erased.

8   Whatever the exact figure—and the primitive state of evolutionary biology permits us only to set broad limits—the current rate is still the greatest in recent geological history. It is also much higher than the rate of production of new species by ongoing evolution, so that the net result is a steep decline in the world's standing diversity. Whole categories of organisms that emerged over the past ten million years, among them the familiar condors, rhinoceros, manatees, and gorillas, are close to the end. For most of their species, the last individuals to exist in the wild state could well be those living there today. It is a grave error to dismiss the hemorrhaging as a "Darwinian" process, in which species autonomously come and go and man is just the latest burden on the environment. Human destructiveness is something new under the sun. Perhaps it is matched by the giant meteorites thought to smash into the Earth and darken the atmosphere every hundred million years or so (the last one apparently arrived 65 million years ago and contributed to the extinction of the dinosaurs). But even that interval is ten thousand times longer than the entire history of civilization. In our own brief lifetime humanity will suffer an incomparable loss in aesthetic value, practical benefits from biological research, and worldwide biological stability. Deep mines of biological diversity will have been dug out and carelessly discarded in the course of environmental exploitation, without our even knowing fully what they contained.

9   The time is late for simple answers and divine guidance, and ideological confrontation has just about run its course. Little can be gained by throwing sand in the gears of industrialized society, even less by perpetuating the belief that we can solve

Aldo Leopold

Excerpts from "The Land Ethic"

Aldo Leopold (1887–1948) was one of the most influential nature writers of the twentieth century and one of the founders of modern ecology. He was completing his essay "The Land Ethic" when he died while fighting a brushfire in a neighbor's field. It appeared in Leopold's posthumously published A Sand County Almanac (1949). As the following excerpts illustrate, the essay offers a new way of understanding our relationship with the environment—an understanding that has powerfully influenced environmental policy debates in the United States.

The Ethical Sequence

The first ethics dealt with the relation between individuals; the Mosaic Decalogue is an example. Later accretions dealt with the relation between the individual and society. The Golden Rule tries to integrate the individual to society; democracy to integrate social organization to the individual.

There is as yet no ethic dealing with man's relation to land and to the animals and plants which grow upon it.

The Community Concept

All ethics so far evolved rest upon a single premise: that the individual is a member of a community of interdependent parts. His instincts prompt him to compete for his place in that community, but his ethics prompt him also to cooperate (perhaps in order that there may be a place to compete for).

The land ethic simply enlarges the boundaries of the community to include soils, waters, plants, and animals, or collectively: the land.

any problem created by earlier spasms of human ingenuity. The need now is for a great deal more knowledge of the true biological dimensions of our problem, civility in the face of common need, and the style of leadership once characterized by Walter Bagehot as agitated moderation.

10   Ethical philosophy is a much more important subject than ordinarily conceded in societies dominated by religious and ideological orthodoxy. It faces an especially severe test in the complexities of the conservation problem. When the time scale is expanded to encompass ecological events, it becomes far more difficult to be certain about the wisdom of any particular decision. Everything is riddled with ambiguity; the middle way turns hard and general formulas fail with dispiriting consistency. Consider that a man who is a villain to his contemporaries can become a hero to his descendants. If a tyrant were to carefully preserve his nation's land and natural resources for his personal needs while keeping his people in poverty, he might unintentionally be-

The Ecological Conscience

Obligations have no meaning without conscience, and the problem we face is the extension of the social conscience from people to land.

Substitutes for a Land Ethic

A system of conservation based solely on economic self-interest is hopelessly lopsided. It tends to ignore, and thus eventually to eliminate, many elements in the land community that lack commercial value, but that are (as far as we know) essential to its healthy functioning.

The Land Pyramid

Land, then, is not merely soil; it is a fountain of energy flowing through a circuit of soils, plants, and animals. Food chains are the living channels which conduct energy upward; death and decay return it to the soil.

Land Health and the A–B Cleavage

We see repeated the same basic paradoxes: man the conqueror *versus* man the biotic citizen; science the sharpener of his sword *versus* science the searchlight on his universe; land the slave and servant *versus* land the collective organism.

The Outlook

Examine each question in terms of what is ethically and esthetically right, as well as what is economically expedient. A thing is right when it tends to preserve the integrity, stability, and beauty of the biotic community. It is wrong when it tends otherwise.

queath a rich, healthful environment to a reduced population for enjoyment in later, democratic generations. This caudillo will have improved the long-term welfare of his people by giving them greater resources and more freedom of action. The exact reverse can occur as well: today's hero can be tomorrow's destroyer. A popular political leader who unleashes the energies of his people and raises their standard of living might simultaneously promote a population explosion, overuse of resources, flight to the cities, and poverty for later generations. Of course these two extreme examples are caricatures and unlikely to occur just so, but they suffice to illustrate that, in ecological and evolutionary time, good does not automatically flow from good or evil from evil. To choose what is best for the near future is easy. To choose what is best for the distant future is also easy. But to choose what is best for both the near and distant futures is a hard task, often internally contradictory, and requiring ethical codes yet to be formulated.

Many species of frogs and toads are disappearing throughout the world at a rapid rate. The causes of this decline appear to be numerous, but in the Amazon basin, the primary cause is loss of habitat from deforestation. Frogs and toads occupy an important niche on the food chain, and their loss negatively affects many other species.

Chris Packham and Mark Wright

Should Pandas Be Left to Face Extinction?

In September 2009 the well-known British naturalist, photographer, and writer Chris Packham (born 1961) created an international furor when during a radio interview he proposed that giant pandas ought to be allowed to go extinct. A fierce advocate for nature and wildlife, he nevertheless contends that so-called "T-shirt animals" (like pandas) get far too much attention and draw resources from far more critical environmental concerns. On September 23, 2009, the British newspaper *The Guardian* carried a debate between Packham and Mark Wright that we reprint below. Wright, a leading scientist at the

World Wide Fund for Nature, was one of a great many who disagreed with Packham. Scientists are estimating that half the species on earth may become extinct in the next century. After the debate, we reprint several blog postings from around the world that commented on Packham's position. The blogs appeared on the *RadioTimes* Web site in the final days of September.

Yes, says Chris Packham

I don't want the panda to die out. I want species to stay alive—that's why I get up in the morning. I don't even kill mosquitoes or flies. So if pandas can survive, that would be great. But let's face it: conservation, both nationally and globally, has a limited amount of resources, and I think we're going to have to make some hard, pragmatic choices.

2   The truth is, pandas are extraordinarily expensive to keep going. We spend millions and millions of pounds on pretty much this one species, and a few others, when we know that the best thing we could do would be to look after the world's biodiversity hotspots with greater care. Without habitat, you've got nothing. So maybe if we took all the cash we spend on pandas and just bought rainforest with it, we might be doing a better job.

3   Of course, it's easier to raise money for something fluffy. Charismatic megafauna like the panda do appeal to people's emotional side, and attract a lot of public attention. They are emblematic of what I would call single-species conservation: i.e., a focus on one animal. This approach began in the 1970s with Save the Tiger, Save the Panda, Save the Whale, and so on, and it is now out of date. I think pandas have had a valuable role in raising the profile of conservation, but perhaps "had" is the right word.

4   Panda conservationists may stand up and say, "It's a flagship species. We're also conserving Chinese forest, where there is a whole plethora of other things." And when that works, I'm not against it. But we have to accept that some species are stronger than others. The panda is a species of bear that has gone herbivorous, and that eats a type of food that isn't all that nutritious, and that dies out sporadically. It is susceptible to various diseases, and, up until recently, it has been almost impossible to breed in captivity. They've also got a very restricted range, which is ever decreasing, due to encroachment on their habitat by the Chinese population. Perhaps the panda was already destined to run out of time.

5   Extinction is very much a part of life on earth. And we are going to have to get used to it in the next few years because climate change is going to result in all sorts of disappearances. The last large mammal extinction was another animal in China—the Yangtze river dolphin, which looked like a worn-out piece of pink

soap with piggy eyes and was never going to make it on to anyone's T-shirt. If that had appeared beautiful to us, then I doubt very much that it would be extinct. But it vanished, because it was pig-ugly and swam around in a river where no one saw it. And now, sadly, it has gone for ever.

6   I'm not trying to play God; I'm playing God's accountant. I'm saying we won't be able to save it all, so let's do the best we can. And at the moment I don't think our strategies are best placed to do that. We should be focusing our conservation endeavours on biodiversity hotspots, spreading our net more widely and looking at good-quality habitat maintenance in order to preserve as much of the life as we possibly can, using hard science to make educated decisions as to which species are essential to a community's maintenance. It may well be that we can lose the cherries from the cake. But you don't want to lose the substance. Save the Rainforest, or Save the Kalahari: that would be better.

No, says Mark Wright

1   You are reading this because it is about giant pandas. We could have this argument about the frogs of the rainforest and the issues would be identical, but the ability to get people's attention would be far lower. So in that sense, yes, you could argue that conservationists capitalize on the panda's appeal.

2   And, to be fair, I can understand where Chris Packham is coming from. Everywhere you look on this planet there are issues to be addressed, and we have finite resources. So we do make really horrible choices. But nowadays, almost exclusively, when people work in conservation they focus on saving habitats.

3   Chris has talked about pandas being an evolutionary cul-de-sac, and it's certainly unusual for a carnivore to take up herbivory. But there are many, many other species that live in a narrowly defined habitat. When he says that if you leave them be, they will die out, that's simply not true. If we don't destroy their habitat they will just chunter along in the same way that they have for the thousands of years.

4   And besides, in terms of its biodiversity and the threats it faces, I think that the part of China where pandas live should be on the preservation list anyway. The giant panda shares its habitat with the red panda, golden monkeys, and various birds that are found nowhere else in the world. The giant panda's numbers are increasing in the wild, so I don't see them dying out, and I haven't heard anything to suggest that other biodiversity isn't thriving equally.

5   It is true, though, that there some cases where preserving an animal is not the best use of resources. If you asked 100 conservationists—even at the World Wide Fund—you would proba-

bly get 90 different answers, but look at what happened with the northern white rhino in Africa, which we're pretty sure has died out. We lament its loss. But at the same time it had gotten to the stage where the likelihood of success was at a critically low level. If you were doing a battlefield triage system, the rhino would probably have had to be a casualty.

6   Otherwise, charismatic megafauna can be extremely useful. Smaller creatures often don't need a big habitat to live in, so in conservation terms it's better to go for something further up the food chain, because then by definition you are protecting a much larger area, which in turn encompasses the smaller animals.

7   And of course they are an extraordinarily good vehicle for the messages we want to put out on habitat conservation. Look at Borneo, where you instantly think of the orangutans. In the southern oceans, you think of the blue whale. Then there are polar bears in the north. There are things you pull out from the picture because people can relate to them. And it does make a difference.

Web postings

A giant panda, an example of what Chris Packham calls "T-shirt animals."

1   Lay off them! They haven't done anything to you! They are already nearly extinct [so] let them die naturally. How would you like it if they told you to go die? You wouldn't like it, would you? (**Nicola-Lucy**)

2   Nice to hear someone with such a public profile expressing the honest view of the majority within conservation circles. It's long been widely agreed that the long-term success of [conservation] efforts depends on promoting sustainable environments, where the natural world (including all the animals, plants, etc.) will find its own balance without us—as opposed to the reactive preservation on total global numbers of individual species, without regards to impact on local environments.

3   Nicola-Lucy: breathe and relax. I think you may have misread Chris's views on pandas. I think he meant we should 'pull the plug' on plowing so much money into a campaign that has seen no marked improvement for decades now, not go round culling the remaining population. (**Sam**)

4   [Packham's] comments have clearly been made through a lack of understanding of wider conservation projects. By protecting the

panda you are protecting its habitat and environment and therefore protecting the entire ecosystem that it lives within, including the people that need sustainable livelihoods. He's clearly missed the bigger picture that species and humans are intrinsically linked and by saving one you are protecting the longevity of the other. (**Becki**)

5   We pour millions into cats and dogs. Why not get rid of cats and dogs and save the panda! (**Sally**)

6   Becki misses the point spectacularly. Protecting ecosystems is certainly an excellent cause, but there is no need to link that to pandas who seem to have a darwinian instinct for self-elimination. It isn't about money plowed into conservation of habitats. . . . It is more about the ridiculous lengths we humans are going to get them to mate. (**Peter**)

7   This man is an evil, disgusting specimen of humanity. Is this what it's come down to? We can ignore the fact that the economy spends millions on cigarettes every year and this is causing more damage to the universal economy than the pandas are! We were put on this earth to do whatever we can to preserve the earth that we were put on and the animals that we share it with. (**Amy**)

8   I suppose I sit on the fence. I can see both points of view. If it is us humans causing the extinction, then we have a responsibility to do all we can reasonably do to prevent this. . . . However, it does seem to me that the panda has itself chosen to take a path which because of its diet would in any event lead to extinction. So should we step in and do something or allow nature to take its course? (**John**)

9   I think it is terrible that anyone can say that pandas should be left to die. The human race really is arrogant, greedy, etc. Glad I do not eat meat. (**Sue**)

10   I have to admit I've had an unreasonable hatred of pandas ever since I failed to see one in the Quinling Mountains in central China, but even I wouldn't agree that we should let it go extinct. It is certainly an environmental oddity, but before humans impacted on its life it would have been quite a widespread and successful species with a good chance of carrying on for the 3 million years or so that is the average life expectancy of a vertebrate species. To call it an evolutionary failure because human-induced habitat destruction had vastly reduced its range seems a little unfair. Like gorillas and tigers it is a flagship species and as we approach the point of total destruction of most of the world's ecosystems it would seem the best chance for any of them to survive is if they are home to some big charismatic animal. Conserve the panda and you conserve the Golden Takin, the Golden Pheasant, the Golden Snub-Nosed Monkey, not to mention all the other thousands of species that live in the area. (**Julian**)

Wendell Berry

Manifesto: The Mad Farmer Liberation Front

Writer, teacher, and land lover Wendell Berry (born 1934) grew up (and still lives) on a farm in Kentucky. His poetry and essays explore the connections between people and nature and typically endorse a simple lifestyle, at odds with new technologies that threaten agrarian ways. His many published works include the essays "What Are People For?" and "Why I Am Not Going to Buy a Computer." His books of poetry include *Sabbaths* and *The Country of Marriage* (1973), from which the following poetic argument is taken.

Love the quick profit, the annual raise,
vacation with pay. Want more
of everything ready-made. Be afraid
to know your neighbors and to die.

5 And you will have a window in your head.
Not even your future will be a mystery
any more. Your mind will be punched in a card
and shut away in a little drawer.

When they want you to buy something
10 they will call you. When they want you
to die for profit they will let you know.
So, friends, every day do something
that won't compute. Love the Lord.
Love the world. Work for nothing.
15 Take all that you have and be poor.
Love someone who does not deserve it.

Denounce the government and embrace
the flag. Hope to live in that free
republic for which it stands.
20 Give your approval to all you cannot
understand. Praise ignorance, for what man
has not encountered he has not destroyed.

Ask the questions that have no answers.
Invest in the millennium. Plant sequoias.
25 Say that your main crop is the forest
that you did not plant,
that you will not live to harvest.

Say that the leaves are harvested
when they have rotted into the mold.
30 Call that profit. Prophesy such returns.
Put your faith in the two inches of humus

that will build under the trees
every thousand years.

Listen to carrion—put your ear
35 close, and hear the faint chattering
of the songs that are to come.
Expect the end of the world. Laugh.

Laughter is immeasurable. Be joyful
though you have considered all the facts.
40 So long as women do not go cheap
for power, please women more than men.

Ask yourself: Will this satisfy
a woman satisfied to bear a child?
Will this disturb the sleep
45 of a woman near to giving birth?

Go with your love to the fields.
Lie down in the shade. Rest your head
in her lap. Swear allegiance
to what is nighest your thoughts.

50 As soon as the generals and the politicos
can predict the motions of your mind,
lose it. Leave it as a sign
to mark the false trail, the way
you didn't go.

55 Be like the fox
who makes more tracks than necessary,
some in the wrong direction.
Practice resurrection.

ISSUE IN FOCUS

Climate Change

Climate change gets considerable attention in political and social debates today: that's an understatement. The broad term *climate change* refers to variability over time within Earth's atmospheric conditions as well as to recorded alterations within regional temperatures and climate patterns. While the vast majority of scientists agree that climates are always changing, debates nevertheless still arise about the consequences of those changes and their causes: are the changes serious, and are they the result of natural causes and cycles or human activities? Scientists, activists, and policy makers also dispute about the degree of damage (if any) that is caused by climate change, and about the kinds of changes humans need to make in response to climate change.

Some scientists and political leaders assert the need to completely overhaul human habits—from our dependency on fossil fuels to heat our homes and the kinds of cars we drive to the kinds of lightbulbs we use and the kinds of clothes we wear. Other voices publicly assert that global warming, with its emphasis on endangered species, severe storms, and devastation to impoverished regions, is simply stirring up drama and debate when we're actually seeing merely the cyclical and natural patterns of Earth.

The most visible public figure to emerge in the climate change conversation is former U.S. vice president Al Gore. In his 2006 film *An Inconvenient Truth,* Gore strives to make the complex science behind this issue clear and spur his audience to action. Certainly, the widespread distribution, compelling visuals (particularly the footage of a polar bear stranded on melting ice), and impassioned arguments of the film make *An Inconvenient Truth* a stirring statement of the position of many environmentalists on climate change and its negative consequences. The issue reached a public milestone at the 2007 Academy Awards ceremony (where *An Inconvenient Truth* won an Oscar for best documentary) as Gore and actor Leonardo DiCaprio bantered about politics and climate change—demonstrating very visible faces in the conversation about climate change. It reached an additional milestone when Gore was awarded the Nobel Peace Prize in recognition of his efforts. (He shared the prize with the Intergovernmental Panel on Climate Change, a United Nations network of scientists, in October 2007.)

In short, the debates about climate change continue—debates not only about whether or not it exists, but also about whether and to what extent people should respond. Skeptics (such as George Will, in an essay printed below) argue that there is not enough measurable data to support *any* action. They contend that scientists have captured only a glimpse of Earth's long-standing history of temperature, atmospheric, and climate variation. They wonder whether global warming is natural and inevitable—not the result of human activity after all. If human activity is the primary cause, then why did global temperatures seem to decrease in the 1950s and 1960s, when carbon dioxide emissions were already increasing greatly—and why did *Newsweek* publish a cover story on global *cooling* in 1975? If temperature changes occur cyclically, why worry, particularly because attempted interventions on such a large phenomenon would only be futile—and because there could be as many benefits to global warming as problems associated with it? Skeptics on the subject of climate change question scientists' ability to forecast

Glacier calving, Alaska

vast, long-term climatic conditions when even highly trained meteorologists sometimes struggle to predict the next day's weather. They question the motivations of politicians like Gore, the costs of a "cleanup," and the impact of those costs on the poor.

Perhaps there is only one thing that everyone can agree on: the debate will continue. In this section, you'll find images and words that illustrate the arguments in the complicated conversations about climate change. On the one hand, we include Christopher Horner's "Top Ten 'Global-Warming' Myths," and George Will's "Dark Green Doomsayers," to demonstrate the arguments of the skeptics. On the other hand, to represent the arguments of those concerned about climate change, we include a feature from Al Gore's "climate crisis" Web site, Chris Mooney's rejoinder to Will, Daniel Frum's advice on the conservative approach to global warming, and a cartoon that supports climate change in visual (and satiric) form. At their heart, all of these arguments require us to think about how we live on our planet and how we care for it, as well as the legacy we wish to leave future generations. As readers and writers, you too may feel strongly about humans' influence and your own role in climate change. Pay attention to how the arguers that follow construct their presentations in essays, cartoons, and photographs. Focus on what makes a text effective or ineffective, regardless of what position you take with regard to climate change.

Al Gore

What Is Global Warming?

Carbon dioxide and other gases warm the surface of the planet naturally by trapping solar heat in the atmosphere. This is a good thing because it keeps our planet habitable. However, by burning fossil fuels such as coal, gas and oil and clearing forests we have dramatically increased the amount of carbon dioxide in the Earth's atmosphere and temperatures are rising.

The vast majority of scientists agree that global warming is real, it's already happening, and that it is the result of our activities and not a natural occurrence.[1] The evidence is overwhelming and undeniable.

The number of Category 4 and 5 hurricanes has almost doubled in the last 30 years.[2]

"What Is Global Warming?" from www.climatecrisis.net. Courtesy of Participant Productions.

Malaria has spread to higher altitudes in places like the Colombian Andes, 7,000 feet above sea level.[3]

The flow of ice from glaciers in Greenland has more than doubled over the past decade.[4]

At least 279 species of plants and animals are already responding to global warming by moving closer to the poles.[5]

If the warming continues, we can expect catastrophic consequences.

Deaths from global warming will double in just 25 years— to 300,000 people a year.[6]

Global sea levels could rise by more than 20 feet with the loss of shelf ice in Greenland and Antarctica, devastating coastal areas worldwide.[7]

Heat waves will be more frequent and more intense.

Droughts and wildfires will occur more often.

The Arctic Ocean could be ice-free in summer by 2050.[8]

More than a million species worldwide could be driven to extinction by 2050.[9]

We're already seeing changes. Glaciers are melting, plants and animals are being forced from their habitat, and the number of severe storms and droughts is increasing.

There is no doubt we can solve this problem. In fact, we have a moral obligation to do so. Small changes to your daily routine can add up to big differences in helping to stop global warming. The time to come together to solve this problem is now—TAKE ACTION.

[1]According to the Intergovernmental Panel on Climate Change (IPCC), this era of global warming "is unlikely to be entirely natural in origin" and "the balance of evidence suggests a discernible human influence of the global climate."

[2]Emanuel, K. 2005. Increasing destructiveness of tropical cyclones over the past 30 years. *Nature* 436: 686–688.

[3]World Health Organization.

[4]Krabill, W., E. Hanna, P. Huybrechts, W. Abdalati, J. Cappelen, B. Csatho, E. Frefick, S. Manizade, C. Martin, J, Sonntag, R. Swift, R. Thomas, and J. Yungel. 2004. Greenland Ice Sheet: Increased coastal thinning. *Geophysical Research Letters* 31.

[5]*Nature.*

[6]World Health Organization.

[7]*Washington Post*, Debate on Climate Shifts to Issue of Irreparable Change, Juliet Eilperin, January 29, 2006, Page A1.

[8]Arctic Climate Impact Assessment. 2004. Impacts of a Warming Arctic. Cambridge, UK: Cambridge University Press. Also quoted in *Time Magazine,* Vicious Cycles, Missy Adams, March 26, 2006.

[9]*Time Magazine,* Feeling the Heat, David Bjerklie, March 26, 2006.

Al Gore

Ten Things to Do to Help Stop Global Warming

tenthingstodo

Want to do something to help stop global warming?
Here are 10 simple things you can do and how much carbon dioxide you'll save doing them.

Change a light
Replacing one regular light bulb with a compact fluorescent light bulb will save 150 pounds of carbon dioxide a year.

Drive less
Walk, bike, carpool or take mass transit more often. You'll save one pound of carbon dioxide for every mile you don't drive!

Recycle more
You can save 2,400 pounds of carbon dioxide per year by recycling just half of your household waste.

Check your tires
Keeping your tires inflated properly can improve gas mileage by more than 3%.

Every gallon of gasoline saved keeps 20 pounds of carbon dioxide out of the atmosphere!

Use less hot water
It takes a lot of energy to heat water. Use less hot water by installing a low flow showerhead
(350 pounds of CO_2 saved per year) and washing your clothes in cold water or warm water (500 pounds saved per year).

Avoid products with a lot of packaging
You can save 1,200 pounds of carbon dioxide if you cut down your garbage by 10%.

Adjust your thermostat
Moving your thermostat just 2 degrees in winter and up 2 degrees in summer
You could save about 2,000 pounds of carbon dioxide a year with this simple adjustment.

Plant a tree
A single tree will absorb one ton of carbon dioxide over it's lifetime

Turn off electronic devices
Simply turning off your television, DVD player, stereo, and computer when you're
not using them will save you thousands of pounds of carbon dioxide a year.

Spread the word! Encourage your friends to buy An Inconvenient Truth

aninconvenienttruth
available on DVD
November 21
www.climatecrisis.net

"The Ten Things to Do to Stop Global Warming" from www.climatecrisis.net. Courtesy of Participant Productions.

Christopher C. Horner

Top Ten "Global-Warming" Myths

1. IT'S HOT IN HERE!

2   In fact, "It's the baseline, stupid." Claiming that present temperatures are warm requires a starting point at, say, the 1970s, or around the Little Ice Age (approximately 1200 A.D. to the end of the 19th century), or thousands of years ago. Select many other baselines, for example, such as the 1930s, or 1000 A.D.—or 1998—and it is presently cool. Cooling does paint a far more frightening picture, given that another ice age would be truly catastrophic, while throughout history, warming periods have always ushered in prosperity. Maybe that's why the greens tried "global cooling" first.

3   The claim that the 1990s were the hottest decade on record specifically targets the intellectually lazy and easily frightened, ignoring numerous obvious factors. "On record" obviously means a very short period, typically the past 100-plus years, or since the end of the Little Ice Age. The National Academies of Science debunked this claim in 2006. Previously, rural measuring stations registered warmer temps after decades of "sprawl" (growth), cement being warmer than a pasture.

2. THE SCIENCE IS SETTLED—CO_2 CAUSES GLOBAL WARMING.

4   Al Gore shows his audience a slide of CO_2 concentrations, and a slide of historical temperatures. But for very good reason he does not combine them in one overlaid slide: historically, atmospheric CO_2, as often as not, increases after warming. This is typical in the campaign of claiming "consensus" to avoid debate (consensus about what is being left unspoken or distorted).

5   What scientists do agree on is little and says nothing about man-made global warming, to wit: (1) that global average temperature is probably about 0.6 degree Celsius—or 1 degree Fahrenheit—higher than a century ago; (2) that atmospheric levels of carbon dioxide have risen by about 30 percent over the past 200 years; and (3) that CO_2 is one greenhouse gas, some level of an increase of which presumably would warm the Earth's atmosphere were all else equal, which it demonstrably is not.

6   Until scientists are willing to save the U.S. taxpayers more than $5 billion per year thrown at researching climate, it is fair to presume the science is not settled.

3. CLIMATE WAS STABLE UNTIL MAN CAME ALONG.

7   Swallowing this whopper requires burning every basic history and science text, just as "witches" were burned in retaliation for changing climates in ages (we had thought) long past. The "hockey stick" chart—poster child for this concept—has been disgraced and air-brushed from the UN's alarmist repertoire.

4. THE GLACIERS ARE MELTING!

8   As good fortune has it, frozen things do in fact melt or at least recede after cooling periods mercifully end. The glacial retreat we read about is selective, however.

Glaciers are also advancing all over, including lonely glaciers nearby their more popular retreating neighbors. If retreating glaciers were proof of global warming, then advancing glaciers are evidence of global cooling. They cannot both be true, and in fact, neither is. Also, retreat often seems to be unrelated to warming. For example, the snowcap on Mount Kilimanjaro is receding—despite decades of cooling in Kenya due to regional land use and atmospheric moisture.

5. CLIMATE CHANGE IS RAISING THE SEA LEVELS.

9   Sea levels rise during interglacial periods such as that in which we (happily) find ourselves. Even the distorted United Nations Intergovernmental Panel on Climate Change reports refute the hysteria, finding no statistically significant change in the rate of increase over the past century of man's greatest influence, despite green claims of massive melting already occurring. Small island nations seeking welfare and asylum for their citizens such as in socially generous New Zealand and Australia have no sea-level rise at all and in some cases see instead a drop. These societies' real problem is typically that they have made a mess of their own situation. One archipelago nation is even spending lavishly to lobby the European Union for development money to build beachfront hotel resorts, at the same time it shrieks about a watery and imminent grave. So, which time are they lying?

6. GLOBAL WARMING HAS DOOMED THE POLAR BEARS!

10   For some reason, Al Gore's computerized polar bear can't swim, unlike the real kind, as one might expect of an animal named Ursa Maritimus. On the whole, these bears are thriving, if a little less well in those areas of the Arctic that are cooling (yes, cooling). Their biggest threat seems to be computer models that air-brush them from the future, the

"Some say it's irrevocable, others say it's irreversible. Given
such an absence of consensus I suggest we do nothing drastic."

same models that tell us it is much warmer now than it is. As usual in this context, you must answer the question: Who are you going to believe—me or your lying eyes?

7. GLOBAL WARMING MEANS MORE FREQUENT, MORE SEVERE STORMS.

11   Here again the alarmists cannot even turn to the wildly distorted and politicized "Summary for Policy Makers" of the UN's IPCC to support this favorite chestnut of the press.

8. CLIMATE CHANGE IS THE GREATEST THREAT TO THE WORLD'S POOR.

12   Climate—or more accurately, weather—remains one of the greatest challenges facing the poor. Climate change adds nothing to that calculus, however. Climate and weather patterns have always changed, as they always will. Man has always best dealt with this through wealth creation and technological advance—a.k.a. adaptation—and most poorly through superstitious casting of blame, such as burning "witches." The wealthiest societies have always adapted best. One would prefer to face a similar storm in Florida than Bangladesh. Institutions, infrastructure and affordable energy are key to dealing with an ever-changing climate, not rationing energy.

9. GLOBAL-WARMING PROPOSALS ARE ABOUT THE ENVIRONMENT.

13   Only if this means that they would make things worse, given that "wealthier is healthier and cleaner." Even accepting every underlying economic and alarmist environmentalist assumption, no one dares say that the expensive Kyoto Protocol would detectably affect climate. Imagine how expensive a pact must be—in both financial and human costs—to so severely ration energy use as the greens demand. Instead, proponents candidly admit desires to control others' lifestyles, and supportive industries all hope to make millions off the deal. Europe's former environment commissioner admitted that Kyoto is "about leveling the playing field for big businesses worldwide" (in other words, bailing them out).

10. THE U.S. IS GOING IT ALONE ON KYOTO AND GLOBAL WARMING.

14   Nonsense. The U.S. rejects the Kyoto Protocol's energy-rationing scheme, along with 155 other countries, representing most of the world's population, economic activity, and projected future growth. Kyoto is a European treaty with one dozen others, none of whom is in fact presently reducing its emissions. Similarly, claims that Bush refused to sign Kyoto, and/or he withdrew, not only are mutually exclusive but also false. We signed it, Nov. 11, 1998. The Senate won't vote on it. Ergo, the (Democratic) Senate is blocking Kyoto. Gosh.

15   Don't demand they behave otherwise, however. Since Kyoto was agreed, Europe's CO_2 emissions are rising twice as fast as those of the climate-criminal United States, a gap that is widening in more recent years. So we should jump on a sinking ship?

16   Given Al Gore's proclivity for invoking Winston Churchill in this drama, it is only appropriate to summarize his claims as such: Never in the field of political conflict has so much been asked by so few of so many . . . for so little.

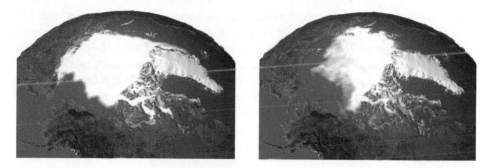

Sea ice in the Arctic Ocean has been shrinking at a rate of 9% per decade. The image on the left shows the minimum sea ice concentration for the year 1979, and the image on the right shows the minimum sea ice concentration in 2003. Are these photographs more or less effective than the photographs of polar bears, such as the one on pages 194 and 330, in getting people to take action to slow global warming?

George Will

Dark Green Doomsayers

A corollary of Murphy's Law ("If something can go wrong, it will") is: "Things are worse than they can possibly be." Energy Secretary Steven Chu, an atomic physicist, seems to embrace that corollary but ignores Gregg Easterbrook's "Law of Doomsaying": Predict catastrophe no sooner than five years hence but no later than 10 years away, soon enough to terrify but distant enough that people will forget if you are wrong.

2   Chu recently told the *Los Angeles Times* that global warming might melt 90 percent of California's snowpack, which stores much of the water needed for agriculture. This, Chu said, would mean "no more agriculture in California," the nation's leading food producer. Chu added: "I don't actually see how they can keep their cities going."

3   No more lettuce or Los Angeles? Chu likes predictions, so here is another: Nine decades hence, our great-great-grandchildren will add the disappearance of California artichokes to the list of predicted planetary calamities that did not happen. Global cooling recently joined that lengthening list.

4   In the 1970s, "a major cooling of the planet" was "widely considered inevitable" because it was "well established" that the Northern Hemisphere's climate "has been getting cooler since about 1950" (*New York Times*, May 21, 1975). Although some disputed that the "cooling trend" could result in "a return to another ice age" (the *Times*, Sept. 14, 1975), others anticipated "a full-blown 10,000-year ice age" involving "extensive Northern Hemisphere glaciation" (*Science News*, March 1, 1975, and *Science*

magazine, Dec. 10, 1976, respectively). The "continued rapid cooling of the Earth" (*Global Ecology*, 1971) meant that "a new ice age must now stand alongside nuclear war as a likely source of wholesale death and misery" (*International Wildlife*, July 1975). "The world's climatologists are agreed" that we must "prepare for the next ice age" (*Science Digest*, February 1973). Because of "ominous signs" that "the Earth's climate seems to be cooling down," meteorologists were "almost unanimous" that "the trend will reduce agricultural productivity for the rest of the century," perhaps triggering catastrophic famines (*Newsweek* cover story, "The Cooling World," April 28, 1975). Armadillos were fleeing south from Nebraska, heat-seeking snails were retreating from Central European forests, the North Atlantic was "cooling down about as fast as an ocean can cool," glaciers had "begun to advance" and "growing seasons in England and Scandinavia are getting shorter" (*Christian Science Monitor*, Aug. 27, 1974).

5   Speaking of experts, in 1980 Paul Ehrlich, a Stanford scientist and environmental Cassandra who predicted calamitous food shortages by 1990, accepted a bet with economist Julian Simon. When Ehrlich predicted the imminent exhaustion of many nonrenewable natural resources, Simon challenged him: Pick a "basket" of any five such commodities, and I will wager that in a decade the price of the basket will decline, indicating decreased scarcity. Ehrlich picked five metals—chrome, copper, nickel, tin and tungsten—that he predicted would become more expensive. Not only did the price of the basket decline, the price of *all five* declined.

6   An expert Ehrlich consulted in picking the five was John Holdren, who today is President Obama's science adviser. Credentialed intellectuals, too—actually, *especially*—illustrate Montaigne's axiom: "Nothing is so firmly believed as what we least know."

7   As global levels of sea ice declined last year, many experts said this was evidence of man-made global warming. Since September, however, the increase in sea ice has been the fastest change, either up or down, since 1979, when satellite record-keeping began. According to the University of Illinois' Arctic Climate Research Center, global sea ice levels now equal those of 1979.

8   An unstated premise of eco-pessimism is that environmental conditions are, or recently were, optimal. The proclaimed faith of eco-pessimists is weirdly optimistic: These optimal conditions must and can be preserved or restored if government will make us minimize our carbon footprints and if government will "remake" the economy.

9   Because of today's economy, another law—call it the Law of Clarifying Calamities—is being (redundantly) confirmed. On graphs tracking public opinion, two lines are moving in tandem and inversely: The sharply rising line charts public concern about the economy, the plunging line follows concern about the environment. A recent Pew Research Center poll asked which of 20 issues should be the government's top priorities. Climate change ranked 20th.

10   Real calamities take our minds off hypothetical ones. Besides, according to the U.N. World Meteorological Organization, there has been no recorded global warming for more than a decade, or one-third of the span since the global cooling scare.

Chris Mooney

Climate Change Myths and Facts

A recent controversy over claims about climate science by *Washington Post* op-ed columnist George F. Will raises a critical question: Can we ever know, on any contentious or politicized topic, how to recognize the real conclusions of science and how to distinguish them from scientific-sounding spin or misinformation?

2   Congress will soon consider global-warming legislation, and the debate comes as contradictory claims about climate science abound. Partisans of this issue often wield vastly different facts and sometimes seem to even live in different realities. In this context, finding common ground will be very difficult. Perhaps the only hope involves taking a stand for a breed of journalism and commentary that is not permitted to simply say anything; that is constrained by standards of evidence, rigor and reproducibility that are similar to the canons of modern science itself.

3   Consider a few of Will's claims from his February 15 column, "Dark Green Doomsayers": In a long paragraph quoting press sources from the 1970s, Will suggested that widespread scientific agreement existed at the time that the world faced potentially catastrophic cooling. Today, most climate scientists and climate journalists consider this a timeworn myth. Just last year, the *Bulletin of the American Meteorological Society* published a peer-reviewed study examining media coverage at the time and the contemporary scientific literature. While some media accounts did hype a cooling scare, others suggested more reasons to be concerned about warming. As for the published science? Reviewing studies between 1965 and 1979, the authors found that "emphasis on greenhouse warming dominated the scientific literature even then."

4   Yet there's a bigger issue: It's misleading to draw a parallel between "global cooling" concerns articulated in the 1970s and global warming concerns today. In the 1970s, the field of climate research was in a comparatively fledgling state, and scientific understanding of 20th-century temperature trends and their causes was far less settled. Today, in contrast, hundreds of scientists worldwide participate in assessments of the state of knowledge and have repeatedly ratified the conclusion that human activities are driving global warming—through the U.N. Intergovernmental Panel on Climate Change, the scientific academies of various nations (including our own), and leading scientific organizations such as the American Association for the Advancement of Science, the American Geophysical Union and the American Meteorological Society.

5   Will wrote that "according to the University of Illinois' Arctic Climate Research Center, global sea ice levels now equal those of 1979." It turns out to be a relatively meaningless comparison, though the Arctic Climate Research Center has clarified that global sea ice extent was "1.34 million sq. km less in February 2009 than in February 1979." Again, though, there's a bigger issue: Will's focus on "global" sea ice at two arbitrarily selected points of time is a distraction. Scientists pay heed to long-term trends in sea ice, not snapshots in a noisy system. And while they expect global warming to reduce summer Arctic sea ice, the global picture is a more complicated matter; it's not as

clear what ought to happen in the Southern Hemisphere. But summer Arctic sea ice is indeed trending downward, in line with climatologists' expectations, according to the Arctic Climate Research Center.

6   Will also wrote that "according to the U.N. World Meteorological Organization, there has been no recorded global warming for more than a decade." The World Meteorological Organization (WMO) is one of many respected scientific institutions that support the consensus that humans are driving global warming. Will probably meant that since 1998 was the warmest year on record according to the WMO—NASA, in contrast, believes that that honor goes to 2005—we haven't had any global warming since. Yet such sleight of hand would lead to the conclusion that "global cooling" sets in immediately after every new record temperature year, no matter how frequently those hot years arrive or the hotness of the years surrounding them. Climate scientists, knowing that any single year may trend warmer or cooler for a variety of reasons—1998, for instance, featured an extremely strong El Niño—study globally averaged temperatures over time. To them, it's far more relevant that out of the 10 warmest years on record, at least seven have occurred in the 2000s, according to the WMO.

7   Readers and commentators must learn to share some practices with scientists—following up on sources, taking scientific knowledge seriously rather than cherry-picking misleading bits of information, and applying critical thinking to the weighing of evidence. That, in the end, is all that good science really is. It's also what good journalism and commentary alike must strive to be—now more than ever.

David Frum

The Conservative Case for Going Green

The world burns 80 million barrels of oil a day. The United States produces only about 7.5 million of those 80 million barrels. Canada and Mexico together produce seven million more. Norway contributes a little shy of three million. Toss in the United Kingdom and Brazil—stretch a point and include Gabon, Indonesia and Kazakhstan—and still only about one-third of the world's oil comes from countries that can be counted on to behave responsibly.

2   Now look at the other side of the ledger: Approximately nine million of the 80 million barrels come from Russia. Another nine million come from Saudi Arabia. Add four million from Iran, 2.5 million from Venezuela and two million from Nigeria, the output of the other Gulf states, scattered production elsewhere in Asia and Africa, and all told, almost two-thirds of the world's oil revenues are paid to people likely to put them to bad use. At $50 a barrel, America's oil imports underwrite $1-trillion a year of extremism,

corruption, authoritarianism, aggression, terrorism and general mischief. Double that price, and the problem gets worse.

3   The global supply picture for natural gas looks even worse. Half the world's natural gas reserves are located under Russia and Iran. Add Algeria and Qatar, and you have accounted for almost three-quarters.

4   The oil and gas consumption of the advanced Western economics does worse than enrich bad actors; it empowers them. So a new Republican party's first energy priority must be: Lead the world to consume less oil and gas.

5   Many people imagine that America's energy use always goes up, up, up—that Americans are helplessly, uncontrollably "addicted to oil," in the words of George W. Bush. Wrong metaphor. Addicts will pay any price to get their fix. American oil consumers respond to price signals. After the oil shock of 1979, American oil consumption declined by almost 3.5 million barrels a day. Not until 1996 did American oil use recover to the levels of the late 1970s. Even by 2005, Americans were using only 17% more oil than they did three decades before. Oil consumption in other advanced Western nations followed a similar pattern.

6   The oil shock of 2003–2005 has likewise altered consumer behavior. Sales of Lincoln Navigators and Ford Expeditions dropped 55% between 2004 and 2005. Over the same period, sales of Honda Civics jumped 30%. Housing sales in exurban neighbourhoods slowed. The National Association of Realtors reported that 9% of home buyers listed "short commute to work" as a prime house-buying consideration in 2005; 40% said so in 2006.

7   Some conservatives and Republicans—including President Bush—want to limit the problem of oil to foreign oil. The problem, they say, is that America imports too much: Close to 60% of America's 20-plus million-barrels-per-day usage.

8   This is a very mistaken way to look at the problem. Oil is a globally traded commodity. There is one world oil market, one world price. If Iran uses its oil revenues to underwrite a nuclear program, what does it matter whether those revenues are denominated in dollars, euros or yen? If Osama bin Laden were to seize control of the Saudi state, would it console us that comparatively little of his oil wealth derived from U.S. sources?

9   While increased North American oil production will be helpful, only substitution and conservation can achieve the important national security goal of reducing the power of unreliable oil suppliers. Congressional Democrats and President Bush have shown us how not to achieve that goal. Both of them advocate large-scale

government intervention in energy markets to subsidize alternative fuels (especially ethanol) and new technologies (hydrogen cells, electric cars and so on). This is the path the United States took in the 1970s, and it led to very little progress and enormous waste.

10   There is a simpler and better way to encourage consumers to conserve while denying income to producers: Tax those forms of energy that present political and environmental risks—and exempt those that do not. That tax will create an inbuilt price advantage for all the untaxed energy sources, which could then battle for market share on their competitive merits.

11   What would such a tax look like? It would fall heavily on oil, natural gas and polluting coal—more lightly on ethanol—and it would exempt hydropower, solar, wind, geothermal, and nuclear altogether. In short: It would look exactly like the carbon tax advocated by global warming crusaders.

12   The environmental movement has always trafficked in apocalyptic fantasy. From its onset, it has offered one vision after another of impending catastrophe. Sometimes environmentalists warned of a new ice age, sometimes of mass famine provoked by overpopulation, sometimes of the spread of deserts from the equators to the globe, now latterly that carbon dioxide will melt the polar icecaps and send super-tsunamis racing toward Manhattan. The specifics fluctuate, but the conviction of certain doom never alters.

13   Perhaps this is why voters' environmental instincts seldom translate into actual environmental votes: Environmentalists seem positively to crave disaster as a righteous judgment on erring humanity. And here may be the secret clue as to why the environmental issue is ripe for plucking by sensible conservatives.

14   It is a plain matter of record that the American environment has steadily and substantially improved over the past three decades.

15   Environmental trends are nearly all positive, with all forms of pollution except greenhouse gases in steady decline in the United States and the European Union. In the middle-1970s, only one-third of America's lakes and rivers were safe for fishing and swimming. Today, two-thirds are, and the proportion continues to rise. Since 1970, smog has declined by one-third, even as the number of cars has nearly doubled and vehicle-miles traveled have increased by 43%. Acid rain has declined by 67%, even though the United States now burns almost twice as much coal annually to produce electric power.

16   Our task now is to build on these improvements—not to deny them, and certainly not to lapse into doomsday hysteria because sea levels are rising a couple of inches per century.

17   Who is more likely to be trusted to produce rational, cost-effective measures against global warming: People who waited to act until the evidence became overwhelming? Or people who have been itching for decades to repeal the Industrial Revolution on any excuse they could find?

18   Conservatives trust free people and free markets to solve our energy and environmental problems. We are going to break America's dependency on oil, gas and coal not by regulations, but by a tax that makes renewables and nuclear power more competitive with fossil fuels. Every dime of that tax increase will be rebated back to the American people in the form of tax reductions to working parents and cuts in taxes on productive investment. At a time when Democrats and liberals seem to have adopted environmentalism as a substitute religion, Republicans and conservatives are ideally positioned to reclaim it for common sense and the common good.

How "Green" Is Your T-Shirt?

Cotton is cheaper and takes less energy to manufacture than synthetic fibers. But over its lifetime, a cotton T-shirt requires more than twice the energy that is necessary to manufacture and maintain a polyester blouse. The main difference: polyester garments can be washed at a lower temperature, can hang dry and need no ironing.

The list below shows energy used over the lifetime of the garment, in kilowatt hours.*

COTTON T-SHIRT	POLYESTER BLOUSE
Raw material: 4	Raw material: 9
Manufacturing: 7	Manufacturing: 3
Transportation: 2	Transportation: 1
Use: 18	Use: 2

Use assumes 25 washes per garment. The cotton T-shirt is washed at 140 degrees Fahrenheit, followed by tumble-drying and ironing. The polyester blouse is washed at 104 degrees Fahrenheit, hung dry, and not ironed.

*The energy of one kilowatt hour will operate a 40-watt lightbulb for a full day or a 19-inch color television for about four hours.

(*Source:* University of Cambridge Institute for Manufacturing.)

FROM READING TO WRITING

1. Analyze the paired arguments by either Al Gore and Christopher Horner, or by George Will and Chris Mooney: how is each argument the product of its audience and purpose? What sources of argument (ethical appeals, emotional appeals, and logical appeals) does each author choose and why? (See Chapter 7 for more on rhetorical analysis.)

2. Compare the various photos and charts that appear on the preceding pages in this chapter. What visual argument does each photo seem to make?

3. Write an argument that makes its point by defining a key term related to environmental concerns. You might choose to change someone's attitude toward a particular practice or concept in order to defend or challenge it, for instance, by defining it in a certain way. For example, you might start with the claim that "Green clothes are just a marketing ploy for the fashion industry to cash in on consumers' increased environmental awareness" or "Global warming is actually a blessing in disguise for some of the world." (See Chapter 10 for strategies for writing definition arguments.)

4. Propose a change in policy related to an environmental issue in your community. (See Chapter 15 for help with writing a proposal argument.)

5. Write a rebuttal of an article related to the environment in your local or school newspaper. Imitate, as appropriate, the moves you see in essays by Horner and Mooney; and see Chapter 14 for advice on rebuttals. Consider whether you wish to show the weaknesses in the article, whether you wish to counterargue, or both.

6. Write an essay that recounts a personal experience of yours to make an argumentative point related to the environment. It could be a story about camping or hiking, for example, or a tale of your encounter with some environmental problem or challenge. (See Chapter 13 for advice on writing narrative arguments.)

23 | Education

What Do We Really Need to Know?

Why have Americans always been so passionate about issues related to education? For one thing, education issues affect every American in a personal way because no other people strive for universal education with the zeal that Americans do. True, there is a strong anti-intellectual strain in American life, and true, not everyone appreciates the mandate for universal education; but it is also true that Americans do pursue with a passion the ideal of "education for all" both as a means of self-improvement and as the source of the enlightened citizenry required by democratic institutions. For another thing, education issues in America are decided locally and immediately. The relatively decentralized nature of our educational "system" (not that American education is as monolithic as the term "system" implies) encourages continuing and passionate public discussion among citizens interested in shaping the policies and practices of local schools.

What principles should guide educational policy in the United States? That fundamental question, which lies behind most of the debates about education, has been restated in a compelling way by the American philosopher and educational reformer John Dewey: *Should society be a function of education*, or *should education be a function of society?* In other words, should educational institutions be developed to perpetuate American institutions and values and to develop a skilled workforce for the American economy ("education as a function of society")? Or should educational institutions be developed chiefly in order to critique and reform American institutions in the interest of creating a more just and equitable society ("society as a function of education")? To put it yet another way: Should schools emphasize mastery of bodies of knowledge, "what every educated citizen needs to know"? Or instead should it emphasize practical learning skills—problem-solving ability, flexibility, independent thinking, and resourcefulness? Most people would answer, "Both": Education should equip people both with practical, vocational abilities and with the critical and communication skills necessary to make for a vibrant, resourceful, just society. Yet that answer only complicates the issue, for in what proportion should schools develop creative criticizers and questioners versus efficient and adjusted workers?

Contemporary Arguments

The arguments included in this part of *Good Reasons* bear directly on the issue of "education as a function of society" versus "society as a function of education." Ralph Waldo Emerson's famous "The American Scholar" offers a definition of what a college student should be and do and how a college student should learn— one that continues to shape institutions and individuals. W. E. B. DuBois next offers (in "The Talented Tenth") an argument about the nature of higher education for African Americans that counters the more strictly vocational goals that were emphasized by Booker T. Washington. Later a cartoon strip by Garry B. Trudeau challenges Americans to make higher education a means of enhancing critical thinking and intellectual development.

Another group of arguments addresses the function of primary and secondary education. Margaret Spellings and Gerald Bracey face off over the controversial No Child Left Behind educational reform passed into law in 2001. The act is based on the principle that setting high standards and goals can improve educational outcomes, but critics have been suspicious of the testing required and the mechanisms used to evaluate schools and teachers. Then we offer Herb Childress's proposal for "A Subtractive Education."

The chapter concludes with an Issue in Focus: Is College Worth the Price? With college tuition rates spiking and the U.S. economy struggling to recover, critics are questioning the wisdom of encouraging so many people to attend college. The Issue in Focus not only addresses the controversy directly, but it also suggests practical alternatives to college that most high school graduates have not considered.

Arguments related to education are developed further in this book—in the essay by E. B. White that appears on pages 195–197, for example, and in the ads for college that appear on pages 116 and 122. But in this part of *Good Reasons*, the emphasis is on education in particular. The readings you encounter should give you a better understanding of the issues that you and your classmates are grappling with right now. As you read, remember that the perennial nature of debates about education can be frustrating, especially to educational leaders. But the very relentlessness of the debates probably brings out the best feature of a democratic society: the freedom of citizens to shape policy through open and public exchange.

Ralph Waldo Emerson

The American Scholar

Ralph Waldo Emerson (1803–1882) originally trained to become a Unitarian minister but instead left that profession to take up what would be a long and celebrated career in writing and public speaking. Emerson was a prolific and original thinker, with many of his ideas forming the basis of the American Transcendentalist movement, which valued spirituality, the natural world, human optimism, and a healthy skepticism toward reason and logic. In "The American Scholar," originally delivered before the Phi Beta Kappa Society in 1837 and later collected in *Essays* (1841), Emerson argues for a new and distinctly "American" brand of educational philosophy.

Mr. President and Gentlemen,

2   I greet you on the re-commencement of our literary year. Our anniversary is one of hope, and, perhaps, not enough of labor. We do not meet for games of strength or skill, for the recitation of histories, tragedies, and odes, like the ancient Greeks; for parliaments of love and poesy, like the Troubadours; nor for the advancement of science, like our contemporaries in the British and European capitals. Thus far, our holiday has been simply a friendly sign of the survival of the love of letters amongst a people too busy to give to letters any more. As such, it is precious as the sign of an indestructible instinct. Perhaps the time is already come, when it ought to be, and will be, something else; when the sluggard intellect of this continent will look from under its iron lids, and fill the postponed expectation of the world with something better than the exertions of mechanical skill. Our day of dependence, our long apprenticeship to the learning of other lands, draws to a close. The millions, that around us are rushing into life, cannot always be fed on the sere remains of foreign harvests. Events, actions arise, that must be sung, that will sing themselves. Who can doubt, that poetry will revive and lead in a new age, as the star in the constellation Harp, which now flames in our zenith, astronomers announce, shall one day be the pole-star for a thousand years?

3   In this hope, I accept the topic which not only usage, but the nature of our association, seem to prescribe to this day,—the AMERICAN SCHOLAR. Year by year, we come up hither to read one more chapter of his biography. Let us inquire what light new days and events have thrown on his character, and his hopes.

4   It is one of those fables, which, out of an unknown antiquity, convey an unlooked-for wisdom, that the gods, in the beginning, divided Man into men, that he might be more helpful to himself; just as the hand was divided into fingers, the better to answer its end.

5   The old fable covers a doctrine ever new and sublime; that there is One Man,—present to all particular men only partially, or through one faculty; and that you must take the whole society to find the whole man. Man is not a farmer, or a professor, or an engineer, but he is all. Man is priest, and scholar, and statesman, and producer, and soldier. In the *divided* or social state, these functions are parcelled out to individuals, each of whom aims to do his stint of the joint work, whilst each other performs his. The fable implies, that the individual, to possess himself, must sometimes return from his own labor to embrace all the other laborers. But unfortunately, this original unit, this fountain of power, has been so distributed to multitudes, has been so minutely subdivided and peddled out, that it is spilled into drops, and cannot be gathered. The state of society is one in which the members have suffered amputation from the trunk, and strut about so many walking monsters,—a good finger, a neck, a stomach, an elbow, but never a man.

6   Man is thus metamorphosed into a thing, into many things. The planter, who is Man sent out into the field to gather food, is seldom cheered by any idea of the true dignity of his ministry. He sees his bushel and his cart, and nothing beyond, and sinks into the farmer, instead of Man on the farm. The tradesman scarcely ever gives an ideal worth to his work, but is ridden by the routine of his craft, and the soul is subject to dollars. The priest becomes a form; the attorney, a statute-book; the mechanic, a machine; the sailor, a rope of a ship.

7   In this distribution of functions, the scholar is the delegated intellect. In the right state, he is, *Man Thinking*. In the degenerate state, when the victim of society, he tends to become a mere thinker, or, still worse, the parrot of other men's thinking.

8   In this view of him, as Man Thinking, the theory of his office is contained. Him nature solicits with all her placid, all her monitory pictures; him the past instructs; him the future invites. Is not, indeed, every man a student, and do not all things exist for the student's behoof? And, finally, is not the true scholar the only true master? But the old oracle said, 'All things have two handles: beware of the wrong one.' In life, too often, the scholar errs with mankind and forfeits his privilege. Let us see him in his school, and consider him in reference to the main influences he receives.

9   I. The first in time and the first in importance of the influences upon the mind is that of nature. Every day, the sun; and, after sunset, night and her stars. Ever the winds blow; ever the grass grows. Every day, men and women, conversing, beholding and beholden. The scholar is he of all men whom this spectacle most engages. He must settle its value in his mind. What is nature to him? There is never a beginning, there is never an end, to the inexplicable continuity of this web of God, but always circular power returning into itself. Therein it resembles his own spirit, whose beginning, whose ending, he never can find,—so entire, so boundless. Far, too, as her splendors shine,

system on system shooting like rays, upward, downward, without centre, without circumference,—in the mass and in the particle, nature hastens to render account of herself to the mind. Classification begins. To the young mind, every thing is individual, stands by itself. By and by, it finds how to join two things, and see in them one nature; then three, then three thousand; and so, tyrannized over by its own unifying instinct, it goes on tying things together, diminishing anomalies, discovering roots running under ground, whereby contrary and remote things cohere, and flower out from one stem. It presently learns, that, since the dawn of history, there has been a constant accumulation and classifying of facts. But what is classification but the perceiving that these objects are not chaotic, and are not foreign, but have a law which is also a law of the human mind? The astronomer discovers that geometry, a pure abstraction of the human mind, is the measure of planetary motion. The chemist finds proportions and intelligible method throughout matter; and science is nothing but the finding of analogy, identity, in the most remote parts. The ambitious soul sits down before each refractory fact; one after another, reduces all strange constitutions, all new powers, to their class and their law, and goes on for ever to animate the last fibre of organization, the outskirts of nature, by insight.

10   Thus to him, to this school-boy under the bending dome of day, is suggested, that he and it proceed from one root; one is leaf and one is flower; relation, sympathy, stirring in every vein. And what is that Root? Is not that the soul of his soul?—A thought too bold,—a dream too wild. Yet when this spiritual light shall have revealed the law of more earthly natures,—when he has learned to worship the soul, and to see that the natural philosophy that now is, is only the first gropings of its gigantic hand, he shall look forward to an ever expanding knowledge as to a becoming creator. He shall see, that nature is the opposite of the soul, answering to it part for part. One is seal, and one is print. Its beauty is the beauty of his own mind. Its laws are the laws of his own mind. Nature then becomes to him the measure of his attainments. So much of nature as he is ignorant of, so much of his own mind does he not yet possess. And, in fine, the ancient precept, "Know thyself," and the modern precept, "Study nature," become at last one maxim.

11   II. The next great influence into the spirit of the scholar, is, the mind of the Past,—in whatever form, whether of literature, of art, of institutions, that mind is inscribed. Books are the best type of the influence of the past, and perhaps we shall get at the truth,—learn the amount of this influence more conveniently,—by considering their value alone.

12   The theory of books is noble. The scholar of the first age received into him the world around; brooded thereon; gave it the new arrangement of his own mind, and ul-tered it again. It came into him, life; it went out from him, truth. It came to him, short-lived actions; it went out from him, immortal thoughts. It came to him, business; it went from him, poetry. It was dead fact; now, it is quick thought. It can stand, and it can go. It now endures, it now flies, it now inspires. Precisely in proportion to the depth of mind from which it issued, so high does it soar, so long does it sing.

13   Or, I might say, it depends on how far the process had gone, of transmuting life into truth. In proportion to the completeness of the distillation, so will the purity and im-perishableness of the product be. But none is quite perfect. As no air-pump can by any means make a perfect vacuum, so neither can any artist entirely exclude the conven-tional, the local, the perishable from his book, or write a book of pure thought, that shall

be as efficient, in all respects, to a remote posterity, as to contemporaries, or rather to the second age. Each age, it is found, must write its own books; or rather, each generation for the next succeeding. The books of an older period will not fit this.

14 Yet hence arises a grave mischief. The sacredness which attaches to the act of creation,—the act of thought,—is transferred to the record. The poet chanting, was felt to be a divine man: henceforth the chant is divine also. The writer was a just and wise spirit: henceforward it is settled, the book is perfect; as love of the hero corrupts into worship of his statue. Instantly, the book becomes noxious: the guide is a tyrant. The sluggish and perverted mind of the multitude, slow to open to the incursions of Reason, having once so opened, having once received this book, stands upon it, and makes an outcry, if it is disparaged. Colleges are built on it. Books are written on it by thinkers, not by Man Thinking; by men of talent, that is, who start wrong, who set out from accepted dogmas, not from their own sight of principles. Meek young men grow up in libraries, believing it their duty to accept the views, which Cicero, which Locke, which Bacon, have given, forgetful that Cicero, Locke, and Bacon were only young men in libraries, when they wrote these books.

15 Hence, instead of Man Thinking, we have the bookworm. Hence, the book-learned class, who value books, as such; not as related to nature and the human constitution, but as making a sort of Third Estate with the world and the soul. Hence, the restorers of readings, the emendators, the bibliomaniacs of all degrees.

16 Books are the best of things, well used; abused, among the worst. What is the right use? What is the one end, which all means go to effect? They are for nothing but to inspire. I had better never see a book, than to be warped by its attraction clean out of my own orbit, and made a satellite instead of a system. The one thing in the world, of value, is the active soul. This every man is entitled to; this every man contains within him, although, in almost all men, obstructed, and as yet unborn. The soul active sees absolute truth; and utters truth, or creates. In this action, it is genius; not the privilege of here and there a favorite, but the sound estate of every man. In its essence, it is progressive. The book, the college, the school of art, the institution of any kind, stop with some past utterance of genius. This is good, say they,—let us hold by this. They pin me down. They look backward and not forward. But genius looks forward: the eyes of man are set in his forehead, not in his hindhead: man hopes: genius creates. Whatever talents may be, if the man create not, the pure efflux of the Deity is not his;—cinders and smoke there may be, but not yet flame. There are creative manners, there are creative actions, and creative words; manners, actions, words, that is, indicative of no custom or authority, but springing spontaneous from the mind's own sense of good and fair.

17 On the other part, instead of being its own seer, let it receive from another mind its truth, though it were in torrents of light, without periods of solitude, inquest, and self-recovery, and a fatal disservice is done. Genius is always sufficiently the enemy of genius by over influence. The literature of every nation bear me witness. The English dramatic poets have Shakespearized now for two hundred years.

18 Undoubtedly there is a right way of reading, so it be sternly subordinated. Man Thinking must not be subdued by his instruments. Books are for the scholar's idle times. When he can read God directly, the hour is too precious to be wasted in other men's transcripts of their readings. But when the intervals of darkness come, as come they must,—when the sun is hid, and the stars withdraw their shining,—we repair to

the lamps which were kindled by their ray, to guide our steps to the East again, where the dawn is. We hear, that we may speak. The Arabian proverb says, "A fig tree, looking on a fig tree, becometh fruitful."

19   It is remarkable, the character of the pleasure we derive from the best books. They impress us with the conviction, that one nature wrote and the same reads. We read the verses of one of the great English poets, of Chaucer, of Marvell, of Dryden, with the most modern joy,—with a pleasure, I mean, which is in great part caused by the abstraction of all *time* from their verses. There is some awe mixed with the joy of our surprise, when this poet, who lived in some past world, two or three hundred years ago, says that which lies close to my own soul, that which I also had wellnigh thought and said. But for the evidence thence afforded to the philosophical doctrine of the identity of all minds, we should suppose some preestablished harmony, some foresight of souls that were to be, and some preparation of stores for their future wants, like the fact observed in insects, who lay up food before death for the young grub they shall never see.

20   I would not be hurried by any love of system, by any exaggeration of instincts, to underrate the Book. We all know, that, as the human body can be nourished on any food, though it were boiled grass and the broth of shoes, so the human mind can be fed by any knowledge. And great and heroic men have existed, who had almost no other information than by the printed page. I only would say, that it needs a strong head to bear that diet. One must be an inventor to read well. As the proverb says, "He that would bring home the wealth of the Indies, must carry out the wealth of the Indies." There is then creative reading as well as creative writing. When the mind is braced by labor and invention, the page of whatever book we read becomes luminous with manifold allusion. Every sentence is doubly significant, and the sense of our author is as broad as the world. We then see, what is always true, that, as the seer's hour of vision is short and rare among heavy days and months, so is its record, perchance, the least part of his volume. The discerning will read, in his Plato or Shakespeare, only that least part,—only the authentic utterances of the oracle;—all the rest he rejects, were it never so many times Plato's and Shakespeare's.

21   Of course, there is a portion of reading quite indispensable to a wise man. History and exact science he must learn by laborious reading. Colleges, in like manner, have their indispensable office,—to teach elements. But they can only highly serve us, when they aim not to drill, but to create; when they gather from far every ray of various genius to their hospitable halls, and, by the concentrated fires, set the hearts of their youth on flame. Thought and knowledge are natures in which apparatus and pretension avail nothing. Gowns, and pecuniary foundations, though of towns of gold, can never countervail the least sentence or syllable of wit. Forget this, and our American colleges will recede in their public importance, whilst they grow richer every year.

22   III. There goes in the world a notion, that the scholar should be a recluse, a valetudinarian,—as unfit for any handiwork or public labor, as a penknife for an axe. The so-called 'practical men' sneer at speculative men, as if, because they speculate or *see*, they could do nothing. I have heard it said that the clergy,—who are always, more universally than any other class, the scholars of their day,—are addressed as women; that the rough, spontaneous conversation of men they do not hear, but only a mincing and diluted speech. They are often virtually disfranchised; and, indeed, there

are advocates for their celibacy. As far as this is true of the studious classes, it is not just and wise. Action is with the scholar subordinate, but it is essential. Without it, he is not yet man. Without it, thought can never ripen into truth. Whilst the world hangs before the eye as a cloud of beauty, we cannot even see its beauty. Inaction is cowardice, but there can be no scholar without the heroic mind. The preamble of thought, the transition through which it passes from the unconscious to the conscious, is action. Only so much do I know, as I have lived. Instantly we know whose words are loaded with life, and whose not.

23   The world,—this shadow of the soul, or *other me*, lies wide around. Its attractions are the keys which unlock my thoughts and make me acquainted with myself. I run eagerly into this resounding tumult. I grasp the hands of those next me, and take my place in the ring to suffer and to work, taught by an instinct, that so shall the dumb abyss be vocal with speech. I pierce its order; I dissipate its fear; I dispose of it within the circuit of my expanding life. So much only of life as I know by experience, so much of the wilderness have I vanquished and planted, or so far have I extended my being, my dominion. I do not see how any man can afford, for the sake of his nerves and his nap, to spare any action in which he can partake. It is pearls and rubies to his discourse. Drudgery, calamity, exasperation, want, are instructors in eloquence and wisdom. The true scholar grudges every opportunity of action past by, as a loss of power.

24   It is the raw material out of which the intellect moulds her splendid products. A strange process too, this, by which experience is converted into thought, as a mulberry leaf is converted into satin. The manufacture goes forward at all hours.

25   The actions and events of our childhood and youth, are now matters of calmest observation. They lie like fair pictures in the air. Not so with our recent actions,—with the business which we now have in hand. On this we are quite unable to speculate. Our affections as yet circulate through it. We no more feel or know it, than we feel the feet, or the hand, or the brain of our body. The new deed is yet a part of life,—remains for a time immersed in our unconscious life. In some contemplative hour, it detaches itself from the life like a ripe fruit, to become a thought of the mind. Instantly, it is raised, transfigured; the corruptible has put on incorruption. Henceforth it is an object of beauty, however base its origin and neighborhood. Observe, too, the impossibility of antedating this act. In its grub state, it cannot fly, it cannot shine, it is a dull grub. But suddenly, without observation, the selfsame thing unfurls beautiful wings, and is an angel of wisdom. So is there no fact, no event, in our private history, which shall not, sooner or later, lose its adhesive, inert form, and astonish us by soaring from our body into the empyrean. Cradle and infancy, school and playground, the fear of boys, and dogs, and ferules, the love of little maids and berries, and many another fact that once filled the whole sky, are gone already; friend and relative, profession and party, town and country, nation and world, must also soar and sing.

26   Of course, he who has put forth his total strength in fit actions, has the richest return of wisdom. I will not shut myself out of this globe of action, and transplant an oak into a flower-pot, there to hunger and pine; nor trust the revenue of some single faculty, and exhaust one vein of thought, much like those Savoyards, who, getting their livelihood by carving shepherds, shepherdesses, and smoking Dutchmen, for all Europe, went out one day to the mountain to find stock, and discovered that they had whittled up the last of their pine-trees. Authors we have, in numbers, who have written out their vein,

and who, moved by a commendable prudence, sail for Greece or Palestine, follow the trapper into the prairie, or ramble round Algiers, to replenish their merchantable stock.

27   If it were only for a vocabulary, the scholar would be covetous of action. Life is our dictionary. Years are well spent in country labors; in town,—in the insight into trades and manufactures; in frank intercourse with many men and women; in science; in art; to the one end of mastering in all their facts a language by which to illustrate and embody our perceptions. I learn immediately from any speaker how much he has already lived, through the poverty or the splendor of his speech. Life lies behind us as the quarry from whence we get tiles and copestones for the masonry of today. This is the way to learn grammar. Colleges and books only copy the language which the field and the work-yard made.

28   But the final value of action, like that of books, and better than books, is, that it is a resource. That great principle of Undulation in nature, that shows itself in the inspiring and expiring of the breath; in desire and satiety; in the ebb and flow of the sea; in day and night; in heat and cold; and as yet more deeply ingrained in every atom and every fluid, is known to us under the name of Polarity,—these "fits of easy transmission and reflection," as Newton called them, are the law of nature because they are the law of spirit.

29   The mind now thinks; now acts; and each fit reproduces the other. When the artist has exhausted his materials, when the fancy no longer paints, when thoughts are no longer apprehended, and books are a weariness,—he has always the resource to live. Character is higher than intellect. Thinking is the function. Living is the functionary. The stream retreats to its source. A great soul will be strong to live, as well as strong to think. Does he lack organ or medium to impart his truths? He can still fall back on this elemental force of living them. This is a total act. Thinking is a partial act. Let the grandeur of justice shine in his affairs. Let the beauty of affection cheer his lowly roof. Those 'far from fame,' who dwell and act with him, will feel the force of his constitution in the doings and passages of the day better than it can be measured by any public and designed display. Time shall teach him, that the scholar loses no hour which the man lives. Herein he unfolds the sacred germ of his instinct, screened from influence. What is lost in seemliness is gained in strength. Not out of those, on whom systems of education have exhausted their culture, comes the helpful giant to destroy the old or to build the new, but out of unhandselled savage nature, out of terrible Druids and Berserkirs, come at last Alfred and Shakespeare.

30   I hear therefore with joy whatever is beginning to be said of the dignity and necessity of labor to every citizen. There is virtue yet in the hoe and the spade, for learned as well as for unlearned hands. And labor is everywhere welcome; always we are invited to work; only be this limitation observed, that a man shall not for the sake of wider activity sacrifice any opinion to the popular judgments and modes of action.

31   I have now spoken of the education of the scholar by nature, by books, and by action. It remains to say somewhat of his duties.

32   They are such as become Man Thinking. They may all be comprised in self-trust. The office of the scholar is to cheer, to raise, and to guide men by showing them facts amidst appearances. He plies the slow, unhonored, and unpaid task of observation. Flamsteed and Herschel, in their glazed observatories, may catalogue the stars with the praise of all men, and, the results being splendid and useful, honor is sure. But he,

in his private observatory, cataloguing obscure and nebulous stars of the human mind, which as yet no man has thought of as such,—watching days and months, sometimes, for a few facts; correcting still his old records;—must relinquish display and immediate fame. In the long period of his preparation, he must betray often an ignorance and shift-lessness in popular arts, incurring the disdain of the able who shoulder him aside. Long he must stammer in his speech; often forego the living for the dead. Worse yet, he must accept,—how often! poverty and solitude. For the ease and pleasure of tread-ing the old road, accepting the fashions, the education, the religion of society, he takes the cross of making his own, and, of course, the self-accusation, the faint heart, the frequent uncertainty and loss of time, which are the nettles and tangling vines in the way of the self-relying and self-directed; and the state of virtual hostility in which he seems to stand to society, and especially to educated society. For all this loss and scorn, what offset? He is to find consolation in exercising the highest functions of hu-man nature. He is one, who raises himself from private considerations, and breathes and lives on public and illustrious thoughts. He is the world's eye. He is the world's heart. He is to resist the vulgar prosperity that retrogrades ever to barbarism, by pre-serving and communicating heroic sentiments, noble biographies, melodious verse, and the conclusions of history. Whatsoever oracles the human heart, in all emergen-cies, in all solemn hours, has uttered as its commentary on the world of actions,—these he shall receive and impart. And whatsoever new verdict Reason from her inviolable seat pronounces on the passing men and events of today,—this he shall hear and promulgate.

33   These being his functions, it becomes him to feel all confidence in himself, and to defer never to the popular cry. He and he only knows the world. The world of any mo-ment is the merest appearance. Some great decorum, some fetish of a government, some ephemeral trade, or war, or man, is cried up by half mankind and cried down by the other half, as if all depended on this particular up or down. The odds are that the whole question is not worth the poorest thought which the scholar has lost in listening to the controversy. Let him not quit his belief that a popgun is a popgun, though the an-cient and honorable of the earth affirm it to be the crack of doom. In silence, in steadi-ness, in severe abstraction, let him hold by himself; add observation to observation, patient of neglect, patient of reproach; and bide his own time,—happy enough, if he can satisfy himself alone, that this day he has seen something truly. Success treads on every right step. For the instinct is sure, that prompts him to tell his brother what he thinks. He then learns, that in going down into the secrets of his own mind, he has de-scended into the secrets of all minds. He learns that he who has mastered any law in his private thoughts, is master to that extent of all men whose language he speaks, and of all into whose language his own can be translated. The poet, in utter solitude re-membering his spontaneous thoughts and recording them, is found to have recorded that, which men in crowded cities find true for them also. The orator distrusts at first the fitness of his frank confessions,—his want of knowledge of the persons he ad-dresses,—until he finds that he is the complement of his hearers;—that they drink his words because he fulfils for them their own nature; the deeper he dives into his privat-est, secretest presentiment, to his wonder he finds, this is the most acceptable, most public, and universally true. The people delight in it; the better part of every man feels, This is my music; this is myself.

34   In self-trust, all the virtues are comprehended. Free should the scholar be,—free and brave. Free even to the definition of freedom, "without any hindrance that does not arise out of his own constitution." Brave; for fear is a thing, which a scholar by his very function puts behind him. Fear always springs from ignorance. It is a shame to him if his tranquility, amid dangerous times, arise from the presumption, that, like children and women, his is a protected class; or if he seek a temporary peace by the diversion of his thoughts from politics or vexed questions, hiding his head like an ostrich in the flowering bushes, peeping into microscopes, and turning rhymes, as a boy whistles to keep his courage up. So is the danger a danger still; so is the fear worse. Manlike let him turn and face it. Let him look into its eye and search its nature, inspect its origin,—see the whelping of this lion,—which lies no great way back; he will then find in himself a perfect comprehension of its nature and extent; he will have made his hands meet on the other side, and can henceforth defy it, and pass on superior. The world is his, who can see through its pretension. What deafness, what stone-blind custom, what overgrown error you behold, is there only by sufferance,—by your sufferance. See it to be a lie, and you have already dealt it its mortal blow.

35   Yes, we are the cowed,—we the trustless. It is a mischievous notion that we are come late into nature; that the world was finished a long time ago. As the world was plastic and fluid in the hands of God, so it is ever to so much of his attributes as we bring to it. To ignorance and sin, it is flint. They adapt themselves to it as they may; but in proportion as a man has any thing in him divine, the firmament flows before him and takes his signet and form. Not he is great who can alter matter, but he who can alter my state of mind. They are the kings of the world who give the color of their present thought to all nature and all art, and persuade men by the cheerful serenity of their carrying the matter, that this thing which they do, is the apple which the ages have desired to pluck, now at last ripe, and inviting nations to the harvest. The great man makes the great thing. Wherever Macdonald sits, there is the head of the table. Linnaeus makes botany the most alluring of studies, and wins it from the farmer and the herb-woman; Davy, chemistry; and Cuvier, fossils. The day is always his, who works in it with serenity and great aims. The unstable estimates of men crowd to him whose mind is filled with a truth, as the heaped waves of the Atlantic follow the moon.

36   For this self-trust, the reason is deeper than can be fathomed,—darker than can be enlightened. I might not carry with me the feeling of my audience in stating my own belief. But I have already shown the ground of my hope, in adverting to the doctrine that man is one. I believe man has been wronged; he has wronged himself. He has almost lost the light, that can lead him back to his prerogatives. Men are become of no account. Men in history, men in the world of today are bugs, are spawn, and are called 'the mass' and 'the herd.' In a century, in a millennium, one or two men; that is to say,—one or two approximations to the right state of every man. All the rest behold in the hero or the poet their own green and crude being,—ripened; yes, and are content to be less, so *that* may attain to its full stature. What a testimony,—full of grandeur, full of pity, is borne to the demands of his own nature, by the poor clansman, the poor partisan, who rejoices in the glory of his chief. The poor and the low find some amends to their immense moral capacity, for their acquiescence in a political and social inferiority. They are content to be brushed like flies from the path of a great person, so that justice shall be done by him to that common nature which it is the dearest desire of all to see

enlarged and glorified. They sun themselves in the great man's light, and feel it to be their own element. They cast the dignity of man from their downtrod selves upon the shoulders of a hero, and will perish to add one drop of blood to make that great heart beat, those giant sinews combat and conquer. He lives for us, and we live in him.

37   Men such as they are, very naturally seek money or power; and power because it is as good as money,—the "spoils," so called, "of office." And why not? for they aspire to the highest, and this, in their sleep-walking, they dream is highest. Wake them, and they shall quit the false good, and leap to the true, and leave governments to clerks and desks. This revolution is to be wrought by the gradual domestication of the idea of Culture. The main enterprise of the world for splendor, for extent, is the upbuilding of a man. Here are the materials strown along the ground. The private life of one man shall be a more illustrious monarchy,—more formidable to its enemy, more sweet and serene in its influence to its friend, than any kingdom in history. For a man, rightly viewed, comprehendeth the particular natures of all men. Each philosopher, each bard, each actor, has only done for me, as by a delegate, what one day I can do for myself. The books which once we valued more than the apple of the eye, we have quite exhausted. What is that but saying, that we have come up with the point of view which the universal mind took through the eyes of one scribe; we have been that man, and have passed on. First, one; then, another; we drain all cisterns, and, waxing greater by all these supplies, we crave a better and more abundant food. The man has never lived that can feed us ever. The human mind cannot be enshrined in a person, who shall set a barrier on any one side to this unbounded, unboundable empire. It is one central fire, which, flaming now out of the lips of Etna, lightens the capes of Sicily; and, now out of the throat of Vesuvius, illuminates the towers and vineyards of Naples. It is one light which beams out of a thousand stars. It is one soul which animates all men.

38   But I have dwelt perhaps tediously upon this abstraction of the Scholar. I ought not to delay longer to add what I have to say, of nearer reference to the time and to this country.

39   Historically, there is thought to be a difference in the ideas which predominate over successive epochs, and there are data for marking the genius of the Classic, of the Romantic, and now of the Reflective or Philosophical age. With the views I have intimated of the oneness or the identity of the mind through all individuals, I do not much dwell on these differences. In fact, I believe each individual passes through all three. The boy is a Greek; the youth, romantic; the adult, reflective. I deny not, however, that a revolution in the leading idea may be distinctly enough traced.

40   Our age is bewailed as the age of Introversion. Must that needs be evil? We, it seems, are critical; we are embarrassed with second thoughts; we cannot enjoy any thing for hankering to know whereof the pleasure consists; we are lined with eyes; we see with our feet; the time is infected with Hamlet's unhappiness,—

"Sicklied o'er with the pale cast of thought."

Is it so bad then? Sight is the last thing to be pitied. Would we be blind? Do we fear lest we should outsee nature and God, and drink truth dry? I look upon the discontent of the literary class, as a mere announcement of the fact, that they find themselves not in the state of mind of their fathers, and regret the coming state as untried; as a boy dreads the water before he has learned that he can swim. If there is any period one would desire to be born in,—is it not the age of Revolution; when the old and the new stand side by side, and admit of being compared; when the energies of all men are searched by fear and by hope; when the historic glories of the old, can be compensated by the rich possibilities of the new era? This time, like all times, is a very good one, if we but know what to do with it.

41   I read with joy some of the auspicious signs of the coming days, as they glimmer already through poetry and art, through philosophy and science, through church and state.

42   One of these signs is the fact, that the same movement which effected the elevation of what was called the lowest class in the state, assumed in literature a very marked and as benign an aspect. Instead of the sublime and beautiful; the near, the low, the common, was explored and poetized. That, which had been negligently trodden under foot by those who were harnessing and provisioning themselves for long journeys into far countries, is suddenly found to be richer than all foreign parts. The literature of the poor, the feelings of the child, the philosophy of the street, the meaning of household life, are the topics of the time. It is a great stride. It is a sign,—is it not? of new vigor, when the extremities are made active, when currents of warm life run into the hands and the feet. I ask not for the great, the remote, the romantic; what is doing in Italy or Arabia; what is Greek art, or Provencal minstrelsy; I embrace the common, I explore and sit at the feet of the familiar, the low. Give me insight into today, and you may have the antique and future worlds. What would we really know the meaning of? The meal in the firkin; the milk in the pan; the ballad in the street; the news of the boat; the glance of the eye; the form and the gait of the body;—show me the ultimate reason of these matters; show me the sublime presence of the highest spiritual cause lurking, as always it does lurk, in these suburbs and extremities of nature; let me see every trifle bristling with the polarity that ranges it instantly on an eternal law; and the shop, the plough, and the leger, referred to the like cause by which light undulates and poets sing;—and the world lies no longer a dull miscellany and lumber-room, but has form and order; there is no trifle; there is no puzzle; but one design unites and animates the farthest pinnacle and the lowest trench.

43   This idea has inspired the genius of Goldsmith, Burns, Cowper, and, in a newer time, of Goethe, Wordsworth, and Carlyle. This idea they have differently followed and with various success. In contrast with their writing, the style of Pope, of Johnson, of Gibbon, looks cold and pedantic. This writing is blood-warm. Man is surprised to find that things near are not less beautiful and wondrous than things remote. The near explains the far. The drop is a small ocean. A man is related to all nature. This perception of the worth of the vulgar is fruitful in discoveries. Goethe, in this very thing the most modern of the moderns, has shown us, as none ever did, the genius of the ancients.

44   There is one man of genius, who has done much for this philosophy of life, whose literary value has never yet been rightly estimated;—I mean Emanuel Swedenborg. The most imaginative of men, yet writing with the precision of a mathematician, he endeavored to engraft a purely philosophical Ethics on the popular Christianity of his time. Such an attempt, of course, must have difficulty, which no genius could surmount. But he saw and showed the connection between nature and the affections of the soul. He pierced the emblematic or spiritual character of the visible, audible, tangible world. Especially did his shade-loving muse hover over and interpret the lower parts of nature;

he showed the mysterious bond that allies moral evil to the foul material forms, and has given in epical parables a theory of insanity, of beasts, of unclean and fearful things.

45   Another sign of our times, also marked by an analogous political movement, is, the new importance given to the single person. Every thing that tends to insulate the individual,—to surround him with barriers of natural respect, so that each man shall feel the world is his, and man shall treat with man as a sovereign state with a sovereign state;—tends to true union as well as greatness. "I learned," said the melancholy Pestalozzi, "that no man in God's wide earth is either willing or able to help any other man." Help must come from the bosom alone. The scholar is that man who must take up into himself all the ability of the time, all the contributions of the past, all the hopes of the future. He must be an university of knowledges. If there be one lesson more than another, which should pierce his ear, it is, The world is nothing, the man is all; in yourself is the law of all nature, and you know not yet how a globule of sap ascends; in yourself slumbers the whole of Reason; it is for you to know all, it is for you to dare all. Mr. President and Gentlemen, this confidence in the unsearched might of man belongs, by all motives, by all prophecy, by all preparation, to the American Scholar. We have listened too long to the courtly muses of Europe. The spirit of the American freeman is already suspected to be timid, imitative, tame. Public and private avarice make the air we breathe thick and fat. The scholar is decent, indolent, complaisant. See already the tragic consequence. The mind of this country, taught to aim at low objects, eats upon itself. There is no work for any but the decorous and the complaisant. Young men of the fairest promise, who begin life upon our shores, inflated by the mountain winds, shined upon by all the stars of God, find the earth below not in unison with these,—but are hindered from action by the disgust which the principles on which business is managed inspire, and turn drudges, or die of disgust,—some of them suicides. What is the remedy? They did not yet see, and thousands of young men as hopeful now crowding to the barriers for the career, do not yet see, that, if the single man plant himself indomitably on his instincts, and there abide, the huge world will come round to him. Patience,—patience;—with the shades of all the good and great for company; and for solace, the perspective of your own infinite life; and for work, the study and the communication of principles, the making those instincts prevalent, the conversion of the world. Is it not the chief disgrace in the world, not to be an unit;—not to be reckoned one character;—not to yield that peculiar fruit which each man was created to bear, but to be reckoned in the gross, in the hundred, or the thousand, of the party, the section, to which we belong; and our opinion predicted geographically, as the north, or the south? Not so, brothers and friends,—please God, ours shall not be so. We will walk on our own feet; we will work with our own hands; we will speak our own minds. The study of letters shall be no longer a name for pity, for doubt, and for sensual indulgence. The dread of man and the love of man shall be a wall of defence and a wreath of joy around all. A nation of men will for the first time exist, because each believes himself inspired by the Divine Soul which also inspires all men. ∎

W. E. B. DuBois

The Talented Tenth

William Edward Burghardt DuBois (1868–1963) was determined to expedite the emancipation of African Americans. Having received his education from Fisk (1885–1888) and from Harvard (where he received his Ph.D. in 1895), he launched a distinguished career as a social scientist, social critic, social reformer, and civil rights leader. He wrote many books, played a prominent role in the founding of the NAACP (in 1909), and for many years edited its magazine, *Crisis*.

DuBois's theories brought him into conflict with the most influential African American working at the turn of the century, Booker T. Washington. Washington preached a policy of accommodation: He felt that African Americans could best achieve social and legal progress by gradually winning the respect of whites through hard work and personal virtue, and he founded Tuskegee Institute as a means of improving and extending vocational education. DuBois, by contrast, in his famous 1903 book *The Souls of Black Folk*, charged that Washington's approach would only perpetuate injustice. Later that year, in "The Talented Tenth," DuBois elaborated his position on higher education for African Americans. DuBois revisited the subject of "The Talented Tenth" throughout his career.

T he Negro race, like all races, is going to be saved by its exceptional men. The problem of education, then, among Negroes must first of all deal with the Talented Tenth: it is the problem of developing the Best of this race that they may guide the Mass away from the contamination and death of the Worst, in their own and other races. Now the training of men is a difficult and intricate task. Its technique is a matter for educational experts, but its object is for the vision of seers. If we make money the object of man-training, we shall develop money-makers but not necessarily men; if we make technical skill the object of education, we may possess artisans but not, in nature, men. Men we shall have only as we make manhood the object of the work of the schools—intelligence, broad sympathy, knowledge of the world that was and is, and of the relation of men to it—this is the curriculum of that Higher Education which must underlie true life. On this foundation we may build bread winning, skill of hand and quickness of brain, with never a fear lest the child and man mistake the means of living for the object of life.

2   If this be true—and who can deny it—three tasks lay before me: first to show from the past that the Talented Tenth as they have risen among American Negroes have been worthy of leadership; secondly to show how these men may be educated and developed; and thirdly to show their relation to the Negro problem.

3   You misjudge us because you do not know us. From the very first it has been the educated and intelligent of the Negro people that have led and elevated the mass, and the sole obstacles that nullified and retarded their efforts were slavery and race prejudice:

for what is slavery but the legalized survival of the unfit and the nullification of the work of natural internal leadership? Negro leadership therefore sought from the first to rid the race of this awful incubus that it might make way for natural selection and the survival of the fittest. In colonial days came Phillis Wheatley and Paul Cuffe striving against the bars of prejudice; and Benjamin Banneker, the almanac maker, voiced their longings when he said to Thomas Jefferson, "I freely and cheerfully acknowledge that I am of the African race and in colour which is natural to them, of the deepest dye; and it is under a sense of the most profound gratitude to the Supreme Ruler of the Universe, that I now confess to you that I am not under that state of tyrannical thraldom and inhuman captivity to which too many of my brethren are doomed, but that I have abundantly tasted of the fruition of those blessings which proceed from that free and unequalled liberty with which you are favored."

4   Then came Dr. James Derham, who could tell even the learned Dr. Rush something of medicine, and Lemuel Haynes, to whom Middlebury College gave an honorary A. M. in 1804. These and others we may call the Revolutionary group of distinguished Negroes—they were persons of marked ability, leaders of a Talented Tenth, standing conspicuously among the best of their time. They strove by word and deed to save the color line from becoming the line between the bond and free, but all they could do was nullified by Eli Whitney and the Curse of Gold. So they passed into forgetfulness.

5   But their spirit did not wholly die; here and there in the early part of the century came other exceptional men. Some were natural sons of unnatural fathers and were given often a liberal training and thus a race of educated mulattoes sprang up to plead for black men's rights. There was Ira Aldridge, whom all Europe loved to honor; there was that Voice crying in the Wilderness, David Walker.

6   In 1831 there met that first Negro convention in Philadelphia, at which the world gaped curiously but which bravely attacked the problems of race and slavery, crying out against persecution and declaring that "Laws as cruel in themselves as they were unconstitutional and unjust, have in many places been enacted against our poor, unfriended and unoffending brethren (without a shadow of provocation on our part), at whose bare recital the very savage draws himself up for fear of contagion— looks noble and prides himself because he bears not the name of Christian." Side by side this free Negro movement, and the movement for abolition, strove until they merged in to one strong stream. Too little notice has been taken of the work which the Talented Tenth among Negroes took in the great abolition crusade. From the very day that a Philadelphia colored man became the first subscriber to Garrison's "Liberator," to the day when Negro soldiers made the Emancipation Proclamation possible, black leaders worked shoulder to shoulder with white men in a movement, the success of which would have been impossible without them. There was Purvis and Remond, Pennington and Highland Garnett, Sojourner Truth and Alexander Crummel, and above all, Frederick Douglass—what would the abolition movement have been without them? They stood as living examples of the possibilities of the Negro race, their own hard experiences and well wrought culture said silently more than all the drawn periods of orators—they were the men who made American slavery impossible.

7   And so we come to the present—a day of cowardice and vacillation, of strident wide-voiced wrong and faint hearted compromise; of double-faced dallying with Truth and Right. Who are today guiding the work of the Negro people? The "exceptions" of course. And yet so sure as this Talented Tenth is pointed out, the blind worshippers of the Average cry out in alarm: "These are exceptions, look here at death, disease and crime—these are the happy rule." Of course they are the rule, because a silly nation made them the rule: Because for three long centuries this people lynched Negroes who dared to be brave, raped black women who dared to be virtuous, crushed dark-hued youth who dared to be ambitious, and encouraged and made to flourish servility and lewdness and apathy. But not even this was able to crush all manhood and chastity and aspiration from black folk. A saving remnant continually survives and persists, continually aspires, continually shows itself in thrift and ability and character. Exceptional it is to be sure, but this is its chiefest promise; it shows the capability of Negro blood, the promise of black men. Do Americans ever stop to reflect that there are in this land a million men of Negro blood, well-educated, owners of homes, against the honor of whose womanhood no breath was ever raised, whose men occupy positions of trust and usefulness, and who, judged by any standard, have reached the full measure of the best type of modern European culture? Is it fair, is it decent, is it Christian to ignore these facts of the Negro problem, to be-little such aspiration, to nullify such leadership and seek to crush these people back into the mass out of which by toil and travail, they and their fathers have raised themselves?

8   Can the masses of the Negro people be in any possible way more quickly raised than by the effort and example of this aristocracy of talent and character? Was there ever a nation on God's fair earth civilized from the bottom upward? Never; it is, ever was and ever will be from the top downward that culture filters. The Talented Tenth rises and pulls all that are worth the saving up to their vantage ground. This is the history of human progress; and the two historic mistakes which have hindered that progress were the thinking first that no more could ever rise save the few already risen: or second, that it would better the unrisen to pull the risen down.

9   How then shall the leaders of a struggling people be trained and the hands of the risen few strengthened? There can be but one answer: The best and most capable of their youth must be schooled in the colleges and universities of the land. We will not quarrel as to just what the university of the Negro should teach or how it should teach it—I willingly admit that each soul and each race-soul needs its own peculiar curriculum. But this is true: A university is a human invention for the transmission of knowledge and culture from generation to generation, through the training of quick minds and pure hearts, and for this work no other human invention will suffice, not even trade and industrial schools.

10   All men cannot go to college but some men must; every isolated group or nation must have its yeast, must have for the talented few centers of training where men are not so mystified and befuddled by the hard and necessary toil of earning a living, as to have no aims higher than their bellies, and no God greater than Gold. This is true training, and thus in the beginning were the favored sons of the freedmen trained. Out of the colleges of the North came, after the blood of war, Ware, Cravath, Chase, Andrews, Bumstead and Spence to build the foundations of knowledge

and civilization in the black South. Where ought they to have begun to build? At the bottom, of course, quibbles the mole with his eyes in the earth. Aye! truly at the bottom, at the very bottom; at the bottom of knowledge, down in the very depths of knowledge there where the roots of justice strike into the lowest soil of Truth. And so they did begin; they founded colleges, and up from the colleges shot normal schools, and out from the normal schools went teachers, and around the normal teachers clustered other teachers to teach the public schools; the college trained in Greek and Latin and mathematics, 2,000 men; and these men trained full 50,000 others in morals and manners, and they in turn taught thrift and the alphabet to nine millions of men, who today hold $300,000,000 of property. It was a miracle—the most wonderful peace-battle of the 19th century, and yet today men smile at it, and in fine superiority tell us that it was all a strange mistake; that a proper way to found a system of education is first to gather the children and buy them spelling books and hoes; afterward men may look about for teachers, if haply they may find them; or again they would teach men Work, but as for Life—why, what has Work to do with Life, they ask vacantly.

11   Was the work of these college founders successful; did it stand the test of time? Did the college graduates, with all their fine theories of life, really live? Are they useful men helping to civilize and elevate their less fortunate fellows? Let us see. Omitting all institutions which have not actually graduated students from a college course, there are today in the United States thirty-four institutions giving something above high school training to Negroes and designed especially for this race.

12   Three of these were established in border States before the War; thirteen were planted by the Freedmen's Bureau in the years 1864–1869; nine were established between 1870 and 1880 by various church bodies: five were established after 1881 by Negro churches; and four are state institutions supported by United States' agricultural funds. In most cases the college departments are small adjuncts to high and common schoolwork. As a matter of fact six institutions—Atlanta, Fisk, Howard, Shaw, Wilberforce and Leland—are the important Negro colleges so far as actual work and number of students are concerned. In all these institutions, seven hundred and fifty Negro college students are enrolled. In grade the best of these colleges are about a year behind the smaller New England colleges and a typical curriculum is that of Atlanta University. Here students from the grammar grades, after a three years' high school course, take a college course of 136 weeks. One-fourth of this time is given to Latin and Greek; one-fifth, to English and modern languages; one-sixth, to history and social science; one-seventh, to natural science; one-eighth to mathematics; and one-eighth to philosophy and pedagogy.

13   In addition to these students in the South, Negroes have attended Northern colleges for many years. As early as 1826 one was graduated from Bowdoin College, and from that time till today nearly every year has seen elsewhere, other such graduates. They have, of course, met much color prejudice. Fifty years ago very few colleges would admit them at all. Even today no Negro has ever been admitted to Princeton, and at some other leading institutions they are rather endured than encouraged. Oberlin was the great pioneer in the work of blotting out the color line in colleges, and has more Negro graduates by far than any other Northern college.

14 The total number of Negro college graduates up to 1899 (several of the graduates of that year not being reported), was as follows:

	Negro Colleges	White Colleges
Before '76	137	75
'75–80	143	22
'80–85	250	31
'85–90	413	43
'90–95	465	66
'95–99	475	88
Class Unknown	57	64
Total	1,914	390

15 Of these graduates 2,079 were men and 252 were women; 50 per cent of Northern-born college men come South to work among the masses of their people, at a sacrifice which few people realize; nearly 90 per cent of the Southern-born graduates instead of seeking that personal freedom and broader intellectual atmosphere which their training has led them, in some degree, to conceive, stay and labor and wait in the midst of their black neighbors and relatives.

16 The most interesting question, and in many respects the crucial question, to be asked concerning college-bred-Negroes, is: Do they earn a living? It has been intimated more than once that the higher training of Negroes has resulted in sending into the world of work, men who could find nothing to do suitable to their talents. Now and then there comes a rumor of a colored college man working at menial service, etc. Fortunately, returns as to occupations of college-bred Negroes, gathered by the Atlanta conference, are quite full—nearly sixty per cent of the total number of graduates.

17 This enables us to reach fairly certain conclusions as to the occupations of all college-bred Negroes. Of 1,312 persons reported, there were:

701 Teachers:
    Presidents and Deans, 19
    Teacher of Music, 7
    Professors, Principals and Teachers, 675
221 Clergymen:
    Bishop, 1
    Chaplains U.S. Army, 2
    Missionaries, 9
    Presiding Elders, 12
    Preachers, 197
83 Physicians:
    Doctors of Medicine, 76
    Druggists, 4
    Dentists, 3
74 Students
62 Lawyers

> 53 in Civil Service:
>> U.S. Minister Plenipotentiary, 1
>> U.S. Consul, 1
>> U.S. Deputy Collector, 1
>> U.S. Gauger, 1
>> U.S. Postmasters, 2
>> U.S. Clerks, 44
>> State Civil Service, 2
>> City Civil Service, 1
> 47 Business Men:
>> Merchants, etc., 30
>> Managers, 13
>> Real Estate Dealers, 4
> 26 Farmers
> 22 Clerks and Secretaries:
>> Secretary of National Societies, 7
>> Clerks, etc., 15
> 9 Artisans
> 9 Editors
> 5 Miscellaneous

18   These figures illustrate vividly the function of the college-bred Negro. He is, as he ought to be, the group leader, the man who sets the ideals of the community where he lives, directs its thoughts and heads its social movements. It need hardly be argued that the Negro people need social leadership more than most groups; that they have no traditions to fall back upon, no long established customs, no strong family ties, no well defined social classes. All these things must be slowly and painfully evolved. The preacher was, even before the war, the group leader of the Negroes, and the church their greatest social institution. Naturally this preacher was ignorant and often immoral, and the problem of replacing the older type by better educated men has been a difficult one. Both by direct work and by direct influence on other preachers, and on congregations, the college-bred preacher has an opportunity for reformatory work and moral inspiration, the value of which cannot be overestimated.

19   It has, however, been in the furnishing of teachers that the Negro college has found its peculiar function. Few persons realize how vast a work, how mighty a revolution has been thus accomplished. To furnish five millions and more of ignorant people with teachers of their own race and blood, in one generation, was not only a very difficult undertaking, but a very important one, in that it placed before the eyes of almost every Negro child an attainable ideal. It brought the masses of the blacks in contact with modern civilization, made black men the leaders of their communities and trainers of the new generation. In this work college-bred Negroes were first teachers, and then teachers of teachers. And here it is that the broad culture of college work has been of peculiar value. Knowledge of life and its wider meaning, has been the point of the Negro's deepest ignorance, and the sending out of teachers whose training has not been simply for bread winning, but also for human culture, has been of inestimable value in the training of these men.

20   In earlier years the two occupations of preacher and teacher were practically the only ones open to the black college graduate. Of later years a larger diversity of life

among his people, has opened new avenues of employment. Nor have these college men been paupers and spendthrifts: 557 college-bred Negroes owned in 1899, $1,342,862.50 worth of real estate (assessed value), or $2,411 per family. The real value of the total accumulations of the whole group is perhaps about $10,000,000, or $5,000 a piece. Pitiful is it not beside the fortunes of oil kings and steel trusts, but after all is the fortune of the millionaire the only stamp of true and successful living? Alas! it is, with many and there's the rub.

21   The problem of training the Negro is today immensely complicated by the fact that the whole question of the efficiency and appropriateness of our present systems of education, for any kind of child, is a matter of active debate, in which final settlement seems still afar off. Consequently it often happens that persons arguing for or against certain systems of education for Negroes, have these controversies in mind and miss the real question at issue. The main question, so far as the Southern Negro is concerned, is: What under the present circumstance, must a system of education do in order to raise the Negro as quickly as possible in the scale of civilization? The answer to this question seems to me clear: It must strengthen the Negro's character, increase his knowledge and teach him to earn a living. Now it goes without saying that it is hard to do all these things simultaneously or suddenly and that at the same time it will not do to give all the attention to one and neglect the others: we could give black boys trades, but that alone will not civilize a race of ex-slaves; we might simply increase their knowledge of the world, but this would not necessarily make them wish to use this knowledge honestly; we might seek to strengthen character and purpose, but to what end if this people have nothing to eat or to wear? A system of education is not one thing, nor does it have a single definite object, nor is it a mere matter of schools. Education is that whole system of human training within and without the school house walls, which molds and develops men. If then we start out to train an ignorant and unskilled people with a heritage of bad habits, our system of training must set before itself two great aims—the one dealing with knowledge and character, the other part seeking to give the child the technical knowledge necessary for him to earn a living under the present circumstances. These objects are accomplished in part by the opening of the common schools on the one hand, and of the industrial schools on the other. But only in part, for there must also be trained those who are to teach these schools—men and women of knowledge and culture and technical skill who understand modern civilization, and have the training and aptitude to impart it to the children under them. There must be teachers, and teachers of teachers, and to attempt to establish any sort of a system of common and industrial school training, without *first* (and I say *first* advisedly) without *first* providing for the higher training of the very best teachers, is simply throwing your money to the winds. School houses do not teach themselves—piles of brick and mortar and machinery do not send out *men*. It is the trained, living human soul, cultivated and strengthened by long study and thought, that breathes the real breath of life into boys and girls and makes them human, whether they be black or white, Greek, Russian or American. Nothing, in these latter days, has so dampened the faith of thinking Negroes in recent educational movements, as the fact that such movements have been accompanied by ridicule and denouncement and decrying of those very institutions of higher training which made the Negro public school possible, and make Negro industrial schools thinkable. It was Fisk, Atlanta, Howard and Straight, those colleges born of the

faith and sacrifice of the abolitionist, that placed in the black schools of the South the 30,000 teachers and more, which some, who depreciate the work of these higher schools, are using to teach their own new experiments. If Hampton, Tuskegee and the hundred other industrial schools prove in the future to be as successful as they deserve to be, then their success in training black artisans for the South will be due primarily to the white colleges of the North and the black colleges of the South, which trained the teachers who today conduct these institutions. There was a time when the American people believed pretty devoutly that a log of wood with a boy at one end and Mark Hopkins at the other represented the highest ideal of human training. But in these eager days it would seem that we have changed all that and think it necessary to add a couple of saw-mills and a hammer to this outfit, and, at a pinch, to dispense with the services of Mark Hopkins.

22   I would not deny, or for a moment seem to deny, the paramount necessity of teaching the Negro to work, and to work steadily and skillfully; or seem to depreciate in the slightest degree the important part industrial schools must play in the accomplishment of these ends, but I *do* say, and insist upon it, that it is industrialism drunk with its vision of success, to imagine that its own work can be accomplished without providing for the training of broadly cultured men and women to teach its own teachers, and to teach the teachers of the public schools.

23   But I have already said that human education is not simply a matter of schools; it is much more a matter of family and group life—the training of one's home, of one's daily companions, of one's social class. Now the black boy of the South moves in a black world—a world with its own leaders, its own thoughts, its own ideals. In this world he gets by far the larger part of his life training, and through the eyes of this dark world he peers into the veiled world beyond. Who guides and determines the education which he receives in his world? His teachers here are the group-leaders of the Negro people—the physicians and clergymen, the trained fathers and mothers, the influential and forceful men about him of all kinds; here it is, if at all, that the culture of the surrounding world trickles through and is handed on by the graduates of the higher schools. Can such culture training of group leaders be neglected? Can we afford to ignore it? Do you think that if the leaders of thought among Negroes are not trained and educated thinkers, that they will have no leaders? On the contrary a hundred half-trained demagogues will still hold the places they so largely occupy now, and hundreds of vociferous busy-bodies will multiply. You have no choice; either you must help furnish this race from within its own ranks with thoughtful men of trained leadership, or you must suffer the evil consequences of a headless misguided rabble.

24   I am an earnest advocate of manual training and trade teaching for black boys, and for white boys, too. I believe that next to the founding of Negro colleges the most valuable addition to Negro education since the war, has been industrial training for black boys. Nevertheless, I insist that the object of all true education is not to make men carpenters, it is to make carpenters men; there are two means of making the carpenter a man, each equally important: the first is to give the group and community in which he works, liberally trained teachers and leaders to teach him and his family what life means; the second is to give him sufficient intelligence and technical skill to make

him an efficient workman. The first object demands the Negro college and college-bred men—not a quantity of such colleges, but a few of excellent quality; not too many college-bred men, but enough to leaven the lump, to inspire the masses, to raise the Talented Tenth to leadership. The second object demands a good system of common schools, well-taught, conveniently located and properly equipped.

25   What is the chief need for the building up of the Negro public school in the South? The Negro race in the South needs teachers today above all else. This is the concurrent testimony of all who know the situation. For the supply of this great demand two things are needed—institutions of higher education and money for school houses and salaries. It is usually assumed that a hundred or more institutions for Negro training are today turning out so many teachers and college-bred men that the race is threatened with an over-supply. This is sheer nonsense. There are today less than 3,000 living Negro college graduates in the United States, and less than 1,000 Negroes in college. Moreover, in the 164 schools for Negroes, 95 per cent of their students are doing elementary and secondary work, work which should be done in the public schools. Over half the remaining 2,157 students are taking high school studies. The mass of so-called "normal" schools for the Negro are simply doing elementary common school work, or, at most, high school work, with a little instruction in methods. The Negro colleges and the post-graduate courses at other institutions are the only agencies for the broader and more careful training of teachers. The work of these institutions is hampered for lack of funds. It is getting increasingly difficult to get funds for training teachers In the best modern methods, and yet all over the South, from State Superintendents, county officials, city boards and school principals comes the wail, "We need TEACHERS!" and teachers must be trained. As the fairest minded of all white Southerners, Atticus G. Haygood, once said: "The defects of colored teachers are so great as to create an urgent necessity for training better ones. Their excellencies and their successes are sufficient to justify the best hopes of success in the effort, and to vindicate the judgment of those who make large investments of money and service to give to colored students opportunity for thoroughly preparing themselves for the work of teaching children of their people."

26   The truth of this has been strikingly shown in the marked improvement of white teachers in the South. Twenty years ago the rank and file of white public school teachers were not as good as the Negro teachers. But they, by scholarships and good salaries, have been encouraged to thorough normal and collegiate preparation, while the Negro teachers have been discouraged by starvation wages and the idea that any training will do for a black teacher. If carpenters are needed it is well and good to train men as carpenters. But to train men as carpenters, and then set them to teaching is wasteful and criminal; and to train men as teachers and then refuse them living wages, unless they become carpenters, is rank nonsense.

27   The United States Commissioner of Education says in his report for 1900: "For comparison between the white and colored enrollment in secondary and higher education, I have added together the enrollment in high schools and secondary schools, with the attendance on colleges and universities, not being sure of the actual grade of work done in the colleges and universities. The work done in the secondary schools is reported in such detail in this office, that there can be no doubt of its grade."

28   He then makes the following comparisons of persons in every million enrolled in secondary and higher education:

	Whole Country	Negroes
1880	4,362	1,289
1900	10,743	2,061

29 And he concludes: "While the number in colored high schools and colleges had increased somewhat faster than the population, it had not kept pace with the average of the whole country, for it had fallen from 30 per cent to 24 per cent of the average quota. Of all colored pupils, one (1) in one hundred was engaged in secondary and higher work, and that ratio has continued substantially for the past twenty years. If the ratio of colored population in secondary and higher education is to be equal to the average for the whole country, it must be increased to five times its present average." And if this be true of the secondary and higher education, it is safe to say that the Negro has not one-tenth his quota in college studies. How baseless, therefore, is the charge of too much training! We need Negro teachers for the Negro common schools, and we need first-class normal schools and colleges to train them. This is the work of higher Negro education and it must be done.

30   Further than this, after being provided with group leaders of civilization, and a foundation of intelligence in the public schools, the carpenter, in order to be a man, needs technical skill. This calls for trade schools. Now trade schools are not nearly such simple things as people once thought. The original idea was that the "Industrial" school was to furnish education, practically free, to those willing to work for it: it was to "do" things—i.e.: become a center of productive industry, it was to be partially, if not wholly, self-supporting, and it was to teach trades. Admirable as were some of the ideas underlying this scheme, the whole thing simply would not work in practice; it was found that if you were to use time and material to teach trades thoroughly, you could not at the same time keep the industries on a commercial basis and make them pay. Many schools started out to do this on a large scale and went into virtual bankruptcy. Moreover, it was found also that it was possible to teach a boy a trade mechanically, without giving him the full educative benefit of the process, and, vice versa, that there was a distinctive educative value in teaching a boy to use his hands and eyes in carrying out certain physical processes, even though he did not actually learn a trade. It has happened, therefore, in the last decade, that a noticeable change has come over the industrial schools. In the first place the idea of commercially remunerative industry in a school is being pushed rapidly to the background. There are still schools with shops and farms that bring an income, and schools that use student labor partially for the erection of their buildings and the furnishing of equipment. It is coming to be seen, however, in the education of the Negro, as clearly as it has been seen in the education of the youths the world over, that it is the *boy* and not the material product, that is the true object of education. Consequently the object of the industrial school came to be the thorough training of boys regardless of the cost of the training, so long as it was thoroughly well done.

31   Even at this point, however, the difficulties were not surmounted. In the first place modern industry has taken great strides since the war, and the teaching of trades is no longer a simple matter. Machinery and long processes of work have greatly changed the work of the carpenter, the ironworker and the shoemaker. A really efficient workman must be today an intelligent man who has had good technical training in addition to thorough common school, and perhaps even higher training. To meet this situation the industrial schools began a further development; they established distinct Trade Schools for the thorough training of better class artisans, and at the same time they sought to preserve for the purposes of general education, such of the simpler processes of elementary trade learning as were best suited therefor. In this differentiation of the Trade School and manual training, the best of the industrial schools simply followed the plain trend of the present educational epoch. A prominent educator tells us that, in Sweden, "In the beginning the economic conception was generally adopted, and everywhere manual training was looked upon as a means of preparing the children of the common people to earn their living. But gradually it came to be recognized that manual training has a more elevated purpose, and one, indeed, more useful in the deeper meaning of the term. It came to be considered as an educative process for the complete moral, physical and intellectual development of the child."

32   Thus, again, in the manning of trade schools and manual training schools we are thrown back upon the higher training as its source and chief support. There was a time when any aged and wornout carpenter could teach in a trade school. But not so today. Indeed the demand for college-bred men by a school like Tuskegee, ought to make Mr. Booker T. Washington the firmest friend of higher training. Here he has as helpers the son of a Negro senator, trained in Greek and the humanities and graduated at Harvard; the son of a Negro congressman and lawyer, trained in Latin and mathematics, and graduated at Oberlin; he has as his wife, a woman who read Virgil and Homer in the same class room with me; he has as college chaplain, a classical graduate of Atlanta University; as teacher of science, a graduate of Fisk; as teacher of history, a graduate of Smith,—indeed some thirty of his chief teachers are college graduates, and instead of studying French grammars in the midst of weeds, or buying pianos for dirty cabins, they are at Mr. Washington's right hand helping him in a noble work. And yet one of the effects of Mr. Washington's propaganda has been to throw doubt upon the expediency of such training for Negroes, as these persons have had.

33   Men of America, the problem is plain before you. Here is a race transplanted through the criminal foolishness of your fathers. Whether you like it or not the millions are here, and here they will remain. If you do not lift them up, they will pull you down. Education and work are the levers to uplift a people. Work alone will not do it unless inspired by the right ideals and guided by intelligence. Education must not simply teach work—it must teach Life. The Talented Tenth of the Negro race must be made leaders of thought and missionaries of culture among their people. No others can do this work and Negro colleges must train men for it. The Negro race, like all other races, is going to be saved by its exceptional men. ■

Garry B. Trudeau

Teaching Is Dead

Garry B. Trudeau (born 1948) is one of America's most influential (and controversial) political and social commentators. His vehicle is the comic strip "Doonesbury," which appears in more than 850 newspapers and whose audience may top 100 million readers. What exactly does this cartoon argue about the nature of current higher education?

Margaret Spellings

Remarks at the 2006 No Child Left Behind Summit

Born in 1957, Margaret Spellings became Secretary of Education in 2005. In that role, she stressed accountability and assessment of education in secondary schools. In the speech below, delivered to the No Child Left Behind Summit held in Philadelphia in 2006, Spellings recounts what she takes to be the positive results of this educational reform movement. Compare her use of statistics, and her sense of the goals of education, with those provided by Gerald Bracey in the essay that follows.

Thank you, Paul Vallas, for introducing me. You're a terrific leader and manager, and you've achieved great results. Since you came here, student achievement has risen by 11 points in reading and 17 points in math. Fifth grade math scores alone increased by 26 points. All this, and you've balanced your budget, too. Clearly, your background in economics has been a tremendous asset to your school districts … and to the students and parents they serve.

2   As Paul or any successful business leader will tell you, high standards and accountability are the foundation for success. That's Business 101. It's the same in education, and a few years ago with No Child Left Behind, we made that foundation permanent.

3   With this law, we set a historic goal for our country: every child learning on grade level by 2014. This is the first in a series of departmental summits—public discussions to help educators and administrators ensure our students reach that goal. I'm looking forward to future events on other topics … including how to serve more students more effectively … and how to close the achievement gap between children from different races, backgrounds, and ZIP codes.

4   All of us know that the hard work of educating our students happens in classrooms, not in the superintendent's office, the state legislature, the U.S. Capitol—or for that matter, the Education Secretary's office. So I'd like to take a moment to say thank you to all of the teachers who are here.

5   I would like to thank the American Federation of Teachers for joining us. I've appreciated AFT's input on many key policy issues, especially their great work on reading, and we have a great working relationship. Just last night, I was with Nat LaCour at the teacher of the year celebration. I also want to thank the NEA for being here; one of their own, Kim Oliver, was honored yesterday as the new Teacher of the Year for 2006.

6   Yesterday I stood on the White House lawn and watched President Bush proclaim Kim National Teacher of the Year. She said she chose to be a teacher because like all of us, she was lucky enough to have a teacher who challenged her.

7   Everywhere I go, I am inspired by hard-working teachers who believe that every child deserves a quality education. And like Kim, when they look at a struggling student, they see nothing but potential. You can feel it when you walk into their classrooms—their confidence and great expectations are palpable.

8   I recently met a local teacher of the year in Spokane, Washington. She had earned that honor after 17 years of teaching elementary school—but the most recent ones were different. She told me she was a better teacher today than she was five years ago because of No Child Left Behind.

9   That's probably the best compliment this law could get. Because at its heart, it was intended to help teachers help students reach their potential. And all of us must do everything we can to support educators in this most important task.

10   We at the Department of Education are offering free workshops on effective strategies for teachers. Our training is certified in all 50 states and the District of Columbia. Through our online courses at Ed.gov, teachers may even obtain Highly Qualified Teacher status without ever leaving their homes.

11   Before No Child Left Behind, if a parent asked how a school was doing, we couldn't really answer the question. We had very little data about how to track year-to-year progress … and often no benchmarks for success.

12   This law is helping us learn about what works in our schools. And clearly, high standards and accountability are working. Over the last 5 years, our 9-year-olds have made more progress in reading than in the previous 28 combined. Scores are at all-time highs for African-American and Hispanic students.

13   We're also learning about what we need to improve. And we've reached a point where we must make some tough decisions and confront some sacred cows.

14   If we're going to have all students learning on grade level by 2014, we've got to start running faster and doing more. We're seeing it's possible. Delaware, Kansas, North Carolina, and Oklahoma are on track to reaching our goal in elementary school reading. But many others are not yet.

15   As leaders, as policymakers, and as parents, it's our job to help those schools reach their full potential. And it's our job to make sure every child has the knowledge and skills to succeed.

16   We have a saying in Texas, "if all you ever do is all you've ever done, then all you'll ever get is all you've ever got." And in my experience, if you just put more money for the same old things in the same old system, it usually means you'll get the same old results. Until every child can read and do math on grade level, the same old thing won't be enough. Not by a long shot. If we're serious about our 2014 goal—and I know we are—then we've got to change some things.

17   Business as usual doesn't always serve the needs of teachers or students. For example, today, you're most likely to find the most experienced and qualified teachers in our wealthiest communities. But in high-poverty middle and high schools, only half of math teachers majored or minored in the field they're teaching.

18   We don't serve teachers or students well by placing our least experienced teachers in our most challenging environments. Nor do we serve teachers well by asking them to teach subjects they don't know much about. It's not right, it's not fair, and it sets teachers—and students—up for failure.

19   A lot of you are superintendents and administrators who, like me, are responsible for addressing problems like these. And having worked in education at the state and local levels, I understand the challenges you face. When you're hearing from school boards, parents, your state officials, and the Secretary of Education … it can be hard to

reconcile the different interests and different expectations. But students are counting on us to make sure the system serves their needs and priorities—and not just the grown-ups.

20 So I'm calling on each and every one of you to apply strategies like the ones you'll hear about today. This is not a show-and-tell. I want this event to kick off some serious debates about how to solve the issues we're facing.

21 For example, how can we reform our personnel system to make sure our most challenging schools are served by our most effective teachers? Shouldn't we track the results they're getting with students and learn from that data? Since we know that teachers with strong content knowledge get better results, shouldn't we reach out to professionals from other fields to bring them into our classrooms, especially when our shortages in these critical areas are so great?

22 The President and the Congress recently created a $100 million Teacher Incentive Fund to encourage more experienced teachers to go to high-poverty schools, and reward them for results—an approach that has been shown to positively impact student performance.

23 The fund also supports state and local administrators who develop proven models that others could replicate—and I encourage all of you who are here to take advantage of that opportunity. We'll start accepting applications for the new Teacher Incentive Fund on Monday, just in time to kick off the Department's Celebrating Teachers Week.

24 In addition, my department will continue to support teachers with significant resources, including more than 3 billion dollars this year. Today you'll hear from some people who are using those resources in innovative and effective ways.

25 We're also faced with a shortage of qualified teachers in math, science, and critical foreign languages—and to overcome it, we must make some changes. That's why the President has also called for $122 million to help prepare 70,000 teachers to lead AP and International Baccalaureate classes … and $25 million to help recruit 30,000 math and science professionals to be adjunct teachers in these essential subject areas.

26 This is urgent work … and to have all kids on grade level by 2014, we only have time to do what works. As all of you know, our children aren't growing up in the same world we did. You can't pick up a newspaper or magazine these days without reading about global competitiveness. But after traveling around the country and meeting so many great educators, and after meeting the awesome teachers of the year yesterday at the White House—including Pennsylvania's own Barbara Benglian—I know we have nothing to fear.

27 Last week I visited a middle school in Maryland with President Bush and saw sixth graders learning about astronomy, robotic engineering, and aerospace technology—and loving it. We went into a class called Introduction to Robotic Systems, and the teacher walked up to the President and said, "Welcome to the future!" And he was right.

28 The class was full of students asking "what if" questions. They had high expectations and a lot of confidence, and they knew they could make a difference.

29 There are certain things you can't teach in a classroom that our students already have—qualities like creativity, diversity, and entrepreneurship. Our job is to give them the knowledge and skills to compete. Fortunately, we have plenty of great teachers who are up to the task.

30   That's why, like the President, I don't fear foreign competition. Students and teachers like this remind us that America has always been the most innovative society in the world. And together, we will make sure we always are. We know our goal of getting all students to grade level by 2014 is attainable, and as the title of this summit says, teachers will make it happen. ■

Gerald W. Bracey

The Condition of Public Education

Gerald W. Bracey, who holds a Ph.D in psychology, has regularly used his writing to comment upon the state of education in America, and especially to critique what he considers to be serious flaws in our educational policies. He is an associate of the High/Scope Educational Research Foundation, a fellow at the Education Policy Studies Laboratory at Arizona State University, and a fellow at the Education and the Public Interest Center at the University of Colorado at Boulder. He has been one of the most outspoken critics of the policies of No Child Left Behind, even calling for the abolition of the Department of Education. In the essay below from the October 2006 *Phi Beta Kappan*, an excerpt of a longer study, Bracey examines the ways that statistics can be, and have been, used to suggest that No Child Left Behind is working.

N ewt Gingrich has suggested that Democrats run their election campaigns on a simple slogan: "Had enough?"[1] Bush Administration shenanigans and Congressional political ploys so brazen as to be unbelievable—for instance, tying a rise in the minimum wage that would benefit millions to a reduction in the estate tax that would benefit the nation's 7,500 wealthiest families—had me nodding in agreement. Herewith, the year in review.

DESPERATELY SEEKING STRAWS TO GRASP

2   "This law is helping us learn about what works in our schools. And clearly, high standards and accountability are working. Over the last five years, our 9-year-olds have made more progress in reading than in the previous 28 combined." So said Margaret Spellings at the No Child Left Behind Summit in April 2006, referring to gains on the National Assessment of Educational Progress (NAEP).[2] In statistical circles, what the secretary is doing is called "cherry picking." And in this instance, careless and self-serving cherry picking, too. Those last five years Spellings spoke of span 1999 to 2004. For two of those years Bill Clinton was President, and it is possible that all that gain— all 7 points—occurred on his watch. In two of those five years, NCLB did not exist. In 2001–02, NCLB (signed into law in January 2002) would have been in existence only three months before a NAEP assessment—had there been one. And given the confusion that reigned from 2002 to 2004 and the hostility between the states and the U.S. Department of Education, it is not likely that much gain occurred then. (Remember that in 2002, then-Secretary Rod Paige accused some states of trying to "ratchet down their standards" and thus of being "enemies of equal justice and equal opportunity and ... apologists for failure."[3] It's surprising he didn't go on to call them terrorist organizations.)

3   Spellings' statement is true only if you start in NAEP's first trend year, 1971. Begin in the year of NAEP's previous trend high point, 1980, and the gain would be only 4 points. Then, too, there was no gain from 1999 to 2004 for 13-year-olds and a decline of 3 points for 17-year-olds. And why didn't she mention math trends, since 9-year-olds showed a 9-point gain and 13-year-olds a 5-point gain? Seventeen-year-olds, though, showed a 1-point decline.

4   Spellings also said, "Scores are at all-time highs for African American and Hispanic students."[4] Well, if she meant reading scores for 9-year-olds, that was true. But it wasn't true for 17-year-old blacks or 13- and 17-year-old Hispanics (13-year-old blacks were at an all-time high by a single point). The statement would have been true, too, in mathematics, except for black and Hispanic 17-year-olds.

5   The regular NAEP assessment of 2005, though, proved less upbeat. The "regular" NAEP assessments, the ones billed as "the nation's report card," change items over time in conjunction with curricular shifts; the NAEP that yields trends administers the same items at each assessment. In the regular assessment for 2005, fourth-grade reading reached the same level as it had at the onset of NCLB in 2002, and eighth-grade reading declined 2 points. In math, scores rose 3 points for fourth-graders from 2003 and 1 point for eighth-graders.

6   In reading, the proportion of students at or above the proficient level was static for fourth-graders at 31% and fell for eighth-graders from 33% to 31%. In mathematics, the proportion of fourth-graders at or above proficient rose from 32% to 36%, while for

eighth-graders it rose from 29% to 30%. While "the Administration scrambled to put the best face on the numbers and to defend the law that some complain forces a test-driven curriculum on the classroom," Lois Romano reported in the *Washington Post*, Ross Wiener of the Education Trust had a more common reaction: "No one can be sat-isfied with these results. There's been a discernible slowdown in progress since `03, at a time when we desperately need to accelerate gains. The absence of particularly bad news isn't the same as good news."[5] As for President Bush's comment that the achieve-ment gaps were narrowing and "that's positive and that's important," Wiener countered, "It is meager progress. Students of color and low-income students continue to be edu-cated at levels far below their affluent peers."[6]

7   For many people, Wiener's views raised the question, "Is NCLB working?" Two re-ports that appeared within two weeks of each other said "No."[7] Both studies analyzed the regular NAEP assessments, not the trend data.

8   In the first of these reports, researchers at Policy Analysis for California Education (PACE) at the University of California, Berkeley, examined reading trends for 12 states on both the state tests and NAEP. (The states were Arizona, California, Illinois, Iowa, Kentucky, Massachusetts, Nebraska, New Jersey, North Carolina, Oklahoma, Texas, and Washington.) The states began with much higher proportions of "state-proficient" stu-dents; the average gap between state-defined proficiency and NAEP-defined proficiency was 38%; the smallest gap was in Massachusetts at 10%; the largest, in Texas at 55%.

9   The gap in itself is of no great import. Both state standards and NAEP achieve-ment levels for determining proficiency are wholly arbitrary—both lack any connection to external criteria for validation—and the NAEP levels are far too high. For instance, U.S. fourth-graders were 11th in math and third in science among the 26 nations that participated in the 1995 Third International Mathematics and Science Study (TIMSS). But NAEP found only 18% of fourth-graders to be proficient or better in math and 26% to be proficient or better in science. Still, for analyzing changes over time, rather than for absolute differences, the NAEP levels can be useful. The following table shows the annual gains in fourth-grade reading and math in pre- and post-NCLB years.

| | Reading | | Math | |
	STATE	NAEP	STATE	NAEP
Pre-NCLB Gains	2.6	0.4	2.7	1.5
Post-NCLB Gains	1.9	−0.2	2.9	2.4

10   As we can readily see, the post-NCLB gains in reading are smaller on both state tests and NAEP. There is actually a loss on NAEP. In math, the state test gains post-NCLB are about the same as prior to the law, while the gains in NAEP mathematics have picked up. Among the states, only Arkansas managed a reading gain of more than 1% per year on NAEP. In math, the annual gains on NAEP ranged from 1.3% in Illinois to 4.0% in Arkansas. Now, if Arkansas can sustain these gains, it can reach 100% proficiency in math by 2024—only a decade late. In Illinois, 100% proficiency in math could be attained by 2057. Both projections are hopelessly optimistic, though, because they are based on the unrealistic assumption that equally large increases in gains will occur each year.

11   The U.S. Department of Education (ED) took its usual approach to such informa-tion: it attempted to defame the messenger. Kevin Sullivan, identified by the *Los Ange-les Times* as a spokesman for ED, said that PACE "has a track record of putting out flawed and misleading information about No Child Left Behind."[8]

12   As this issue went to press around Labor Day, I had no comments from Mr. Sulli-van or any ED official on the new PACE study. Nor has anyone at ED addressed the similar study conducted by Jaekyung Lee of SUNY, Buffalo, for the Harvard Civil Rights Project. Given that Douglas Harris, Gene Glass, and Robert Linn reviewed Lee's study, it is not likely to fall victim to ED's derogation. At least, not for its methodology. Although Lee uses quite different methods from those used by the PACE researchers, his study produced results similar to PACE's:

> NCLB did not have a significant impact on improving reading and math achievement across the nation and states. Based on the NAEP results, the national average achievement remains flat in reading and grows at the same pace in math after NCLB than before. In grade 4 math, there was a temporary improvement right after NCLB, but it was followed by a return to the pre-reform growth rate....
>
> NCLB has not helped the nation and states significantly narrow the achievement gap....
>
> NCLB's attempt to scale up the alleged success of states that adopted test-driven accountability policy prior to NCLB (e.g., Florida, North Carolina, Texas) did not work. It neither enhanced [these] states' earlier academic im-provement nor transferred the effects of a test-driven accountability system to states that adopted test-based accountability under NCLB....
>
> The higher the stakes of state assessments, the greater the discrepan-cies between NAEP and state assessment results. These discrepancies were particularly large for poor, black, and Hispanic students.

13   That last finding—the higher the stakes, the higher the state/NAEP discrepancy—does not describe a perfect relationship, but it also comes as no surprise. Lee and col-league Kenneth Wong of Brown University had earlier constructed an index to measure state accountability levels.[9] Using this index, Lee found that the correlation between the height of the stakes and the size of the NAEP/state discrepancy was +.36. Not huge, but statistically significant.

14   At the state level, few states showed increases in NAEP reading, and none showed accelerated growth after the law was passed. Lee states that eighth-graders maintained growth similar to that seen pre-NCLB but that fourth-graders showed ac-celerated growth in math in the post-NCLB years. Lee notes, though, that most of the improved growth occurred between 2000 and 2003 and that growth returned to its pre-NCLB rate afterward. But, as mentioned earlier, NCLB came into existence only in January 2002, and it probably had no influence on what was happening in the last half of the 2001–02 school year. Thus, if NCLB affected math growth in the period from 2000 to 2003, it would have had to work its wonders in a single school year, 2002–03. (There were no NAEP data to examine for 2001–02.) As also mentioned, given the haphazard implementation of NCLB, this seems most unlikely. It is at least possible that the rate increases took place prior to NCLB.

15   Commenting on the NAEP trend results of 2004, Secretary Spellings declared, "Changing the direction of America's schools is like turning the Queen Mary, a large ship whose captain can't change course on a dime. The goal requires a lot of time and effort, but we are beginning to turn our own Queen Mary around."[10] That might or might not be true of the trend analysis. The analyses of regular NAEP data by PACE and by Lee make it clear that, as far as regular NAEP assessments go, the liner is dead in the water.

NCLB: A THREAT TO THE NATION'S GLOBAL COMPETITIVENESS?

16   At that NCLB Summit in April, Spellings also said, "There are certain things you can't teach in a classroom that our students *already have—qualities like creativity, diversity, and entrepreneurship.* Our job is to give them the knowledge and skills to compete.... America has always been the most innovative society in the world. And together, we will make sure we always are"[11] (emphasis added).

17   This might be the first time diversity has been listed with creativity and entrepreneurship as a personal quality, but many people believe that those qualities of creativity and entrepreneurship are what keep the nation competitive in the first place. The minister of education of Singapore certainly thinks so. Tharman Shanmugaratnam told *Newsweek* pundit Fareed Zakaria that Singapore had a test meritocracy while America had a talent meritocracy. "We cannot use tests to measure creativity, ambition, or the willingness of students to question conventional wisdom. These are areas where Singapore must learn from America."[12] Even allowing that the minister is being a bit disingenuous—the last thing a totalitarian society like Singapore wants is a cadre of young people who question conventional wisdom—his comment on tests rings true.

18   Zakaria had approached the minister because he was intrigued that kids from Singapore aced tests but that, "ten or twenty years later, it is the American kids who are ahead. Singapore has few truly top-ranked scientists, entrepreneurs, inventors, business executives, or academics. American kids test much worse, but seem to do better later in life and in the real world." A Singaporean father who had lived in the U.S. for a period before returning to his island nation confirmed the minister's assertions, telling Zakaria, "In the American school, when my son would speak up, he was applauded and encouraged. In Singapore, he's seen as pushy and weird." Schooling in Singapore "is a chore. Work hard, memorize, test well." The father placed his son in an American-style private school.

19   Similarly, Joseph Renzulli, who directs the National Research Center on the Gifted and Talented, housed at the University of Connecticut, had Japanese visitors tell him, "Your schools have produced a continuous flow of inventors, designers, entrepreneurs, and innovative leaders,"[13] They noticed American creativity and thought the schools had something to do with it.

20   It is not only between Asian and American schools that one sees the contrast between passive memorization and active participation in the learning process. A *Washington Post* op-ed from a few years ago described the writer's frustrations trying to get Scottish high-schoolers to discuss Shakespeare. "It took months of badgering before I was able to get my Scottish students to speak up in class. They simply weren't accustomed to asking questions or tossing around their own observations. American schools

teach American kids to ask questions. They teach students to be curious, skeptical, even contrary.... At their best, they teach kids to challenge the teachers."[14]

21   But Spellings doesn't get it. She visited a school in 2006 and reported that "the class was full of students asking `what if' questions."[15] But she doesn't see the connection between questions, creativity, and competitiveness. How does she think American kids got those qualities that "they already have" in the first place? Is it something in the water? She needs a long chat with Robert Sternberg, dean of the College of Arts and Sciences at Tufts University. Sternberg calls creativity a habit. If you don't arrange conditions for people to practice the habit, it won't develop. And, he contends, "the increasingly massive and far-reaching use of conventional standardized tests is one of the most effective, if unintentional, vehicles this country has created for suppressing creativity."[16] There is nothing creative about taking a test. Aside from a few rare exceptions, taking a test is the opposite of asking a question.

22   As I have said before, we'd better think more than twice about replacing a culture that cultivates asking questions with one that worships high test scores. Somebody needs to give Secretary Spellings a wake-up call.

Notes

1. Quoted in Karen Tumulty and Mike Allen, "Republicans on the Run," *Time*, 3 April 2006.
2. "Remarks by Secretary Spellings at No Child Left Behind Summit," U.S. Department of Education, 27 April 2006, www.ed.gov/news. Search on "Press Releases."
3. "Letter Released from U.S. Education Secretary Paige to State School Chiefs on Implementing No Child Left Behind Act," U.S. Department of Education, 23 October 2002.
4. "Remarks by Secretary Spellings."
5. Lois Romano, "Test Scores Move Little in Math, Reading," *Washington Post*, 20 October 2005, p. A-3.
6. Ibid.
7. Bruce Fuller et al., *Is the No Child Left Behind Act Working?* (Berkeley: Policy Analysis for California Education, 2006); and Jaekyung Lee, *Tracking Achievement Gaps and Assessing the Impact of NCLB on the Gaps* (Cambridge, Mass.: Civil Rights Project, Harvard University, June 2006).
8. Mitchell Landsberg, "Reading Gains Slowing, Study Says," *Los Angeles Times*, 20 June 2006.
9. Jaekyung Lee and Kenneth Wong, "The Impact of Accountability on Racial and Socioeconomic Equity: Considering Both School Resources and Achievement Outcomes," *American Educational Research Journal*, Winter 2004, pp. 797–832.
10. "Spellings Hails New National Report Card Results," U.S. Department of Education, 14 July 2005, www.ed.gov/news. Search on "Press Releases."
11. "Remarks by Secretary Spellings."
12. Fareed Zakaria, "We All Have a Lot to Learn," *Newsweek*, 9 January 2006, www.msnbc.msn.com/id/10663340/site/newsweek.

13. Joseph Renzulli, "A Quiet Crisis Is Clouding the Future of R & D," *Education Week*, 25 May 2005, pp. 32–33.
14. Amy Biancolli, "At Least Our Kids Ask Questions," *Washington Post*, 27 April 2001, p. A-23.
15. "Remarks by Secretary Spellings."
16. Robert J. Sternberg, "Creativity Is a Habit," *Education Week*, 22 February 2006, p. 47. ■

Herb Childress

A Subtractive Education

Herb Childress is Dean of Research and Assessment at Boston Architectural College. His background in architecture gives him a unique perspective on how the physical design of a place influences what actually happens there. For example, in his study of the lives of teenagers, *Landscapes of Betrayal* (2000), he shows how community planning has failed to provide challenging growth opportunities for young people. In the essay below, published in the educational journal *Phi Delta Kappan* in 2006, Childress asks how the shape of our schools affects secondary education.

I am a meandering kind of thinker. Something comes up for me, and that reminds me of something else, and then I remember a third thing, and pretty soon I'm talking about something brand new. Let me take you on a little tour of how that works for me.

2 I'm walking to Albertson's because Ben & Jerry's Frozen Yogurt is on sale—two pints for five dollars. I get to the store, it's about seven o'clock at night, and the parking lot is jammed; people are weaving around with their shopping carts through the stream of incoming cars trying to get their groceries to their own cars and go home.

3 And I'm looking at all of these hundreds of people and all of these cars, and I suddenly think, "I wonder how many of these people could resolve a trigonometric identity." Honest to God, that's what came into my head. Well, from there, this meandering thinker was off to the races. "I wonder how many of these people could tell you about the origins of the French Revolution. I wonder how many can still diagram a sentence."

4 And then I thought, "Well, why would I care if they could or not? They all have enough money to afford their cars and their groceries; they're getting by. Would they get by any better if they remembered how to construct the perpendicular bisector of a line segment using only a straightedge and a compass?"

5 Well, that of course took me right back to the high school that I wrote my book about and to all the kids who ever asked why they should bother learning something. "Why are we doing this?" That was the plaintive cry from the back corners of the room. "Why are we doing this?" It never came from the front: up front were the kids to

whom it never occurred to ask that question or who had given up asking it. And the arguments that came back from the teachers were never very compelling to me. They said things like, "There's *lots* of careers that use algebra," though they never offered a specific example. Or, when the question came up with regard to conjugating French verbs, it would be met with, "Well, you might travel to France someday." For these kids from rural Northern California, even the City of Lights was neither a likely nor an especially desirable destination. Their picture of France amounted to the Eiffel Tower, the Arc de Triomphe, and a language that made them say things like, "Hello, I name myself Stacy. How do you name yourself?"

6   "Why are we doing this?" the kids ask. So let's ask ourselves why we have them doing all of these crazy things. When I think about what high school is for, I remember that John Ogbu, the educational anthropologist, wrote that, "whatever else education may be, from the standpoint of society it is a preparation of children for adult life as adults in their society conceive it."

7   Well, I don't know, John. Here I am in the Albertson's parking lot, willing to bet my Ben & Jerry's and most of my paycheck that not one of the next three people I see could name the first European to sail around the Cape of Good Hope. "Adult life as adults in our society conceive it" doesn't typically include answering trivia questions like that, unless we're standing on a stage across from Alex Trebek. (By the way, it was Vasco da Gama in 1497, and yes, I had to look it up.)

8   But let's give John Ogbu another reading and another chance: "Whatever else education may be, from the standpoint of society it is a preparation of children for adult life as adults in their society conceive it." I think that's true, but the problem we have, in our very diverse society, is that Ogbu's phrase "preparation for adulthood" has many different meanings, based on a lot of potential adulthoods. I think we need to make those adulthoods explicit so that we're not working at cross-purposes. So I'm going to do two things here. I'm going to start out by telling you what I think a successful adulthood is, and then I'm going to tell you—based on the evidence of my own and other people's research—what our education system says that a successful adulthood is.

9   Here's a definition I hold of strong adulthood. I've cast it in the form of a list of my ideal outcome measures for a high school, the characteristics I hope that graduates have as they prepare to move toward adulthood.

- *Graduates of my ideal high school should love to read.* This is not at all the same as saying that they can read. There's an enormous middle ground between illiterate and literate, which has sometimes been called alliterate—a term for people who can read but choose not to, who see little value or reward in it. People who love to read are people who are open to new ideas, who are engaged in constant reinvention.
- *Graduates of my ideal high school should enjoy numbers.* I'm no mathematician, but I can do arithmetic in my head very well. It's a skill I developed before I was 8 by playing cribbage and rummy and pinochle and by keeping score at bowling. It's a skill that has served me well all the way through calculus and physics, it's a skill that helps me navigate the everyday world of taxes and budgeting, of saving and knowing when I can indulge in an extravagance, and it's a

skill that helps me evaluate the accuracy and pertinence of information that's offered to me.

- *Graduates of my ideal high school should enjoy physical exertion and activity.* And that activity should take several forms, from team sports to hiking across town to playing hacky sack. Anything that gets you sweaty is a damn sight better than television, and we should encourage young people to regard physical activity as a lifelong pursuit, rather than as something to look back on fondly once high school football has ended.

- *Graduates of my ideal high school should have some well-developed outlet for their creative desires.* This will also take all kinds of forms, from writing to visual arts to music to physics, but the quest for putting ideas together in a unique way is part of what makes us really human.

- *Graduates of my ideal high school should know how to work in groups, and they should know how to teach a skill to someone else.* Kids are going to be working with groups for the rest of their lives, from work to marriage and parenthood to community service. We are social animals, and we need to quit pretending that individual performance is the only thing that really matters.

- *Graduates of my ideal high school should be brave and take risks.* This means that they must be exposed to failure and supported through the other side. They need to know that it's possible to fall down and still get up again. They must know that, if a magazine rejects their article, there are hundreds more to try. They need to know that anything really worth doing will be scary and intimidating—and that they have to do it anyway.

- *Graduates of my ideal high school should understand and take an interest in their community.* They should know something about real estate, local government and services, major local industries, and the natural landscape and climate. Even if they move away, knowing *how* to find out about these things is a skill that will serve them wherever they go.

- *Graduates of my ideal high school should be compassionate and care about people they don't know.* They should understand that a lot of what happens in people's lives isn't their fault—and that even things that *are* someone's fault usually are mistakes that can be recovered from rather than a sign of a core moral failing that leaves people irredeemable and so dismissible.

10   For me, this list presents a compelling model of an attractive adulthood. It is a set of characteristics that I don't encounter all that often in the adults I know. In fact, it is a set of characteristics that I strive for but sometimes fail to live up to myself. The list outlines adulthood as a rigorous, ongoing practice rather than a state to be obtained and then mounted on the wall with the high school diploma. And such an adulthood is one that will serve as the foundation for an infinite number of careers, in an ever-shifting economic world.

11   Now, this may not be the same definition that *you* would create for an attractive, complete adulthood. And that's fine, so long as you actually go through the exercise and create a definition that you can really stand behind and don't just accept the default version.

12   And believe me, there is a default version. Our institutions—maintained and shepherded as they are by white-collar people who understand complex organizations—promote as the norm their own white-collar, managerial, hierarchical, certified view of adulthood. That's what schools attempt to perpetuate, and it's the model of adulthood for which they prepare young people. Half a century ago, the sociologist C. Wright Mills had the same impression and described the high school as "the seed-bed of white-collar skills." Like the early Spanish in California and Mexico, the white-collar, information-laden school takes on the missionary role of civilizing the uncivilized and converting the heathens. Even the most benevolent of the conquerors are preparing the natives for what they see as a materially and morally superior way of life. We are "helping," "developing," or "training," or whatever term we might use to mean making someone else be more like us.

13   This has led to a model of secondary education that I call an "additive education," in which each certified specialist takes an assembly under construction and screws on a particular component and then passes the material along to the next specialist. One person takes 150 kids and screws on some algebra, and another person takes those same kids and screws on some world history, and a third person takes those same kids and screws on some Hemingway. Over the course of four years, each successful kid gets more than 20 components screwed on. And in the end, they're screwed, indeed. They're encased in this educational armor and have no experience in encountering and challenging their own communities, futures, or desires, because all of that has been sublimated to the repetitive and mechanical structures that they endured.

14   In the high school I've studied most thoroughly, which is a tragically normal high school, I found six underlying principles of the school, principles that were never stated overtly but that were repeated over and over in the rules that were laid, in the spaces that were created, in the furniture that was used, in the lessons that were taught, and in the lessons that were avoided. And these were the six principles:

1. Kids and adults should be physically separated.
2. Teaching should be active, and learning should be passive.
3. Abstraction is beneficial, and uniqueness should be avoided.
4. Economies of scale are necessary and beneficial.
5. Objective evaluation and peer competition are necessary and beneficial.
6. Students should be prepared for a life of geographic and organizational mobility.

15   And, after all, the world educators endure is governed by these same rules. So let's look at them as educators suffer them.

1. *Kids and adults should be physically separated.* Certainly, teachers, administrators, and education policy makers are all physically (and conceptually) separated from one another.
2. *Teaching should be active, and learning should be passive.* The school that most completely follows the guidelines is considered the best school by those who write the guidelines, which become more prescriptive all the time.
3. *Abstraction is beneficial, and uniqueness should be avoided.* Unique local outcomes and desires are less important than test scores and standings on other

indices of achievement—and certainly less important than the number of AP courses offered.

4. *Economies of scale are necessary and beneficial.* Every single school must be immersed in district, state, and federal systems that ensure completeness and correctness and that avoid duplication of services.

5. *Objective evaluation and peer competition are necessary and beneficial.* Schools themselves are forced to compete with one another on grossly abstract terms that have little to do with the life of learning and citizenship.

6. *Students should be prepared for a life of geographic and organizational mobility.* Teachers and administrators, if they are successful, also move upward or outward from their classrooms and into larger communities or educational structures.

16   So schools, to their credit, don't ask kids to deal with anything that adults don't have to face as well. Our white-collar organizational biases, in our modern economic circumstances, lead toward an education in which kids are trained primarily to endure what educators themselves endure. Remember again Ogbu's quote: "Whatever else education may be, from the standpoint of society it is a preparation of children for adult life as adults in their society conceive it." The main lessons of the "hidden curriculum" are to compete with your peers, to be compliant with your superiors, and to refrain from asking awkward questions. And those lessons are there on purpose! That's what makes the safest economic life in a culture in which capital is mobile and a company can leave Michigan for Georgia and then leave Georgia for Indonesia. In such a world, you have to demonstrate superiority over other workers and unquestioning loyalty to your supervisors and their world view.

17   This additive education is an education of fear. It's an effort to avoid disaster rather than to reach for a dream, to avoid a career at McDonald's rather than to pursue a deep personal mission. It's an effort to ensure that kids will have the tools necessary to survive in the similarly white-collar colleges and workplaces they will move on to. It's an effort to keep them from being sorted out of the pool for advancement before they ever really get under way. It's a recognition that our modern economic terrain allows employers to use the desperation of labor as a resource anywhere in the world, that every American who might formerly have done physical work is competing with someone in another country who is willing to work for less, in worse conditions, and for longer hours than our nation allows. It's a recognition that we have educated ourselves into a society in which information is the only material we have left to manipulate.

18   I understand this education of fear, and I think I know why it exists. But I have no patience for it, because I see how cold and empty it leaves its products—both the kids and the adults. They learn to avoid pain instead of to seek love. They learn to avoid commitment, because they might have to leave. They're never asked to engage who they really are, but rather to be more and more like their masters.

19   When I encounter students in a high school like that—which is to say, almost all the time—my immediate urge is to help them escape, to get them into the lifeboats before they drown. I'm not entirely sure what we'd be moving toward, but that's not a question that you ask in a time of crisis. You just get people out of the wreckage and away from the danger. This is my own fearful response to the education of fear.

20   When I was talking to the folks at Duke about the possibility of my coming there to teach their first-year students, I told them that I was fascinated by people who were between about 15 and 25 years old, standing on the brink of adulthood, peering over the edge in simultaneous fear and anticipation. I told them that I thought high school was something that had to be recovered from and that I thought I could aid in that recovery.

21   And I talked about my friend Pete. Pete is a young man; he'll be 29 soon. He's a wonderful writer, a great friend to those of us blessed to know him well, a great son and brother to his family, and, possibly, the best illustrator that I've ever had the chance to watch at work. He draws like an angel.

22   Pete has no idea what he wants from an adult life. Both of his parents are teachers, and he enjoyed school all the way up through sixth grade. But when he moved from elementary school to junior high school, began to move from one teacher and 25 classmates to six teachers and 150 classmates who shifted all day long, he didn't survive the change. He told me that he could recognize instantly that those adults weren't really there for him, that they didn't even know him. And about halfway through seventh grade, he tested his hypothesis, as any good scientist would. In the middle of an assigned five-page essay, he wrote the third page in an imaginary alphabet that he'd drawn, to see if anyone would read it. No one did, and his hypothesis was confirmed.

23   Pete had a naturally occurring social life in elementary school; in a class of 25 kids who are together all year long, people make allowances for eccentricity and learn to appreciate one another's gifts. When you're shoved into an anonymous crowd of 600 kids you don't know, you tend to seek out people who are the most like you in order to have some safety and stability. But Pete wasn't in any of those natural safety groups. His eccentricity and artistic mind, assets through sixth grade, became social and academic liabilities three months later.

24   By the time I met him in high school, Pete had two lives: exuberant and creative with his small circle of friends and in the theater and completely alienated in the classroom and in the larger social life of the school. He maintained his mathematically precise 2.0 grade-point average so that he could graduate, but there was never even one entire course that reliably captured his attention. There were *days*, there were *topics*, there were *moments* when you could see him come alive and watch the gears turn, but mostly Pete was that kid in the back right corner who you'd never guess was six feet tall because he sat so low in his chair. He saw nothing in the adult world that he trusted, that he wanted, or that he was adequately guided toward. And that distrust of and distaste for adult life persist for him to this day.

25   So I was talking to the folks at Duke about Pete in the context of helping kids recover from high school, and the director of the writing program said, "Our kids don't come here with 2.0s. We help kids recover from getting 4.3s." And then I began to think in a different way about the scars left by our education system. The rebellious get their 40 lashes on a regular basis, but the silent and compliant have wounds of their own, harder to see but no less real and no less deep. We rightfully strive to eliminate a system of schooling in which there are winners and losers, but we don't think to eliminate a system of schooling in which even the winners have lost their curiosity, have lost their passion, have lost the willingness to ask, "Why are we doing this?"

26   We are deeply familiar with this screwed-on model of high school, this additive education in which each professional adds his or her component onto the raw material

that comes down the line. But I've been wondering: What would a subtractive model of education look like? And I'm beginning to think it might look something like what a sculptor does. When Michelangelo wrote about the experience of sculpting, he said that the stone itself told him what to do, that the figure was waiting inside that stone and that his task as an artist was to take away what wasn't essential. "I saw the angel in the marble and carved until I set him free."

27   And that's what I do with Pete—informally but very purposefully. And it's what I hoped to be able to do with my Duke students. I think I have to sit with a person and be with him or her for a quite a while before I can expect to have much of an effect. And then I think I can ask for permission to pick off some of the armor and maybe find out who's under all of those uniform shells. I trust that there is a core person there, and my belief is that it's probably the same person who was there at 10 years old, before the specialists got to him or her. Once I know who that is, I am able to see some things that excite this student, and I can introduce him or her to a wider range of such things. There will be some natural skills, and I can help the student hone and develop and expand and challenge those.

28   And each person will have his or her own visions of successful adult life, collected by being a part of a family and immersed in the media and knowing a larger group of friends. I can show a young person my own model of adulthood as another potential way of living to examine, but I can't expect that he or she will choose it, and I can't personalize a response—when he or she *doesn't* choose it—as a rejection of me.

29   I realize that this is a hazy vision. I can't tell you what the structure of a subtractive education looks like on a day-to-day basis. I know that it looks small and attentive, some-what passive on the part of the educator, slow, inexpert, and out of control, and that it re-quires the time and the inclination to listen to and believe young people. But I think it also looks different for every practitioner and with every student, and probably on every day.

30   Even if you agree with me that a subtractive education would be a humane and powerful experience, I cannot offer you a curriculum that you could all follow to get there with every student. That kind of static curriculum would automatically lead us back toward nonresponsive, nonseeing, automatic, additive ways of being. All I can do is tell you what I see in the world, tell you what I think it means, tell you about some of the lives that are hindered by our common practices, and sit together with you to see if there's something different that we can do.

31   Here's the vision that drives me, and *this* vision is very clear. I'm 48 years old, and I'm optimistically assuming that I have another 35 years or so to work with teenagers and young adults. My dream is that I will live to see the day that the modern high school will be considered the counterpart of the mission, the orphanage, and the poor farm—an institution that was taken for granted and considered beneficial in its time but has since been judged to be inhumane and unthinkable. High school is taken for granted, and it was and is still considered beneficial. But I believe that we have out-grown the institution's usefulness. I believe that we have different ways of service—different ways of *being*—that we can employ on behalf of young people. And I believe that we are fundamentally not the kind of people who want to make our least powerful citizens endure this four-year sentence of disrespect and invisibility.

32   We are better than our systems. We are better than our structures. We can be brave, help our kids discover who they are, help them go where they want to go, and wish them Godspeed as they leave us behind. ■

Is College Worth the Price?

It's an old story," says Anthony P. Carnevale, director of Georgetown University's Center on Education and the Workforce and one of the authors featured in this section: "When economic downturns hit, unemployment rates spiral and tales of college graduates forced to tend bar or mop floors proliferate."

But is the story really so old? Fifty years ago, according to the National Center for Education Statistics, about 45 percent of 1.7 million high school graduates went to college. In 2010, that number had grown by nearly three times as much, with 68 percent of 3.2 million high school graduates pursuing a college education. In short, more people—many more—than ever before are attending college before entering the workforce.

According to the *Concise Encyclopedia of Economics*, opinions about the "necessity" of a college degree have fluctuated for decades, often in correspondence with the rising and falling increase in salary for college graduates. But regardless of arguments made in decades past, one thing is clear: Today, college is on more people's minds than ever before. What should we make of its worth? And what parameters we should use to *define* its worth in the first place?

Many think that college's Golden Age has come and gone. College, they say, has become "the new high school"—and, as it grows more and more common for people to attend college, the degree means less and less. Not only that, tuition prices are sky-rocketing, leaving increasing numbers of college graduates in large amounts of debt—and without the employment opportunities to pay it back. Opponents of a "college education for all!" approach often cite statistics indicating that the gap in salaries between college and high school graduates is shrinking, while additional statistics suggest there are more college graduates than there are jobs requiring a college degree. Furthermore, say some critics, the myth that a diploma is necessary for successful entry into the job market diminishes opportunities for those equally capable but less officially "qualified" candidates. While few if any opponents would advocate for the complete abolition of the university system, they do argue that college degrees are appropriate mostly for the few, and not the many—and that a system that purports college to be the "be all/end all" of personal advancement is damaging to both individuals and society as a whole.

Not so fast, say others. Proponents of the college experience often discredit the statistics cited by naysayers. They argue that college graduates still consistently earn more than those who entered the workforce immediately after high school, and that the employment sector maintains continual demand for those bearing a college degree. In fact, they say, more employers than ever require post-secondary degrees (whether two- or four-year) as a condition for consideration—a trend often attributed to technological advances and the concomitant need for employees to be educated in the use of those technologies. Then there are the social benefits derived from a college-educated population. "Individuals who have had the opportunity to go to college have a greater probability of having the resources to develop into productive and engaged citizens," says the Solutions for Our Future Project (an organization dedicated to educating the public about the social benefits of higher education). Meanwhile, the Policy Institute cautions that "while the costs incurred educating our society are enormous, and growing, we must be aware that the costs of failing to do so might be even greater."

THE NON-TUITION
COSTS OF EDUCATION

High school grads often look at the bill for their upcoming 4 years of college in disbelief. Thankfully, student loans often cover the cost of actually getting them into the classroom, but what about all the additional expenses that come along with their four years away from home? Living on their own for the first time is costly, especially in the fast-paced world the college social scene.

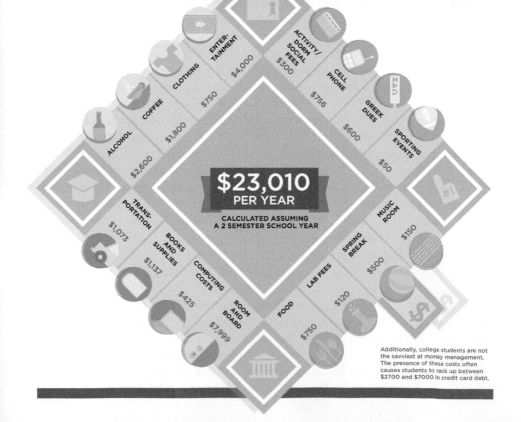

ENTER-TAINMENT $4,000

ACTIVITY/DORM SOCIAL FEES $300

CLOTHING $750

CELL PHONE $756

COFFEE $1,800

GREEK DUES $600

ALCOHOL $2,600

SPORTING EVENTS $50

TRANS-PORTATION $1,073

MUSIC ROOM $150

BOOKS AND SUPPLIES $1,137

SPRING BREAK $500

COMPUTING COSTS $425

LAB FEES $120

ROOM AND BOARD $7,999

FOOD $750

$23,010
PER YEAR

CALCULATED ASSUMING
A 2 SEMESTER SCHOOL YEAR

Additionally, college students are not the savviest at money management. The presence of these costs often causes students to rack up between $2700 and $7000 in credit card debt.

ALCOHOL

Don't let their schedules fool you, college kids always find time to party. In fact, partying is such a staple of the college like that the average student spends $2,600/year on beer.

COFFEE

Between exciting social life, class projects, studying, and part time work, a daily dose of caffeine is nearly required to function. All those morning Starbucks lattés can add up to $1,800/year.

CLOTHING

College is a chance to redefine oneself, to transform one's image, and of course, to get dates with style. To that end, college students spend around $750/year on new clothes.

ENTERTAINMENT

And where do they take all the new dates you meet at college? To the movies, concerts, plays, resturants, and on and on. In fact, the average college student spends around $4,000 per year on entertainment.

BOOKS AND SUPPLIES

The national average cost of books and class supplies for the 2010 – 2011 school year was $1,137.

COMPUTING COSTS

The average retail price of a new laptop for college is around $1700. This works out to about $425/year in computing costs.

ROOM AND BOARD

Room and board fees cover the cost of on-campus housing and a meal plan for food served in the school cafeteria. In 2008 these costs stood around $7999/year average.

TRANSPORATION

Between exploring their new city and traveling home on the holidays, students living on-campus from the 2010 – 2011 school year spent an average of $1,073 on transportation.

ACTIVITY/DORM SOCIAL FEES

Many students decide to join a fraternity or sorority to take advantage of the social life. Greek life isn't free however – dues can cost about $600/year.

CELL PHONE

A cell phone is a survival tool in college. The average cell phone bill is around $63/month.

GREEK DUES

Many students decide to join a fraternity or sorority to take advantage of the social life. Greek life isn't free however – dues can cost about $600/year.

SPORTING EVENTS

Each year, college students throw on their face paint, don big foam fingers, and support their school at at least one sports game. The average cost of a college football game is around $50.

FOOD

Of course, not every meal can be eaten on campus, especially with all those late nights exploring the new city. Assuming the student eats the majority of their meals on campus, extra food costs typically run around $750 per year.

LAB FEES

Most degrees require students to take at least one science class and/or art class. Lab fees for such classes typically run around $60/semester per class.

SPRING BREAK

If ever there was a reason to crack open beers at 9 AM on a beach, spring break at college is it. The average cost of a trip to any of the popular spring break destinations is $500.

MUSIC ROOM

Students who take music classes need to rent practice rooms to rehearse. This generally costs about $75 per semester, depending on the school.

Sources: www.collegeboard.com | abcnews.go.com | walletpop.com | college.lovetoknow.com | collegeboard.com | youngadults.about.com | mainstreet.com | degreecentral.com | icsellinghope.com | campuscalm.com | blog.oregonlive.com

Advocates for some form of middle ground assert that "degrees" and "education" are not necessarily the same thing. While *degrees* may not be worth the cost, the principle of *education* is—but in order to honor it, we need to change the system so that it focuses more on nurturing well-rounded individuals and less on churning out diplomas. Furthermore, say some, society should do away with funneling high school graduates directly into college regardless of interests or career aspirations. Instead, college should be approached on a case-by-case basis, pursued only if it enhances an individual's goals or is the necessary means to working in a particular career.

In this Issue In Focus, we present arguments that represent many of these divergent viewpoints. First, Anthony P. Carnevale, Director of the Georgetown

University Center on Education and the Workforce, argues in a January 2011 essay in *Inside Higher Ed* that college is still very much worth it, primarily from an economic perspective. Richard Vedder, an economist, counters Carnevale's arguments directly, asserting that college is not a wise investment for the majority of high school graduates. Clive Crook argues (in an essay first published in 2006 in the *Atlantic*) that education is important, but not the "cure-all" for the nation's various social and economic challenges. Finally, Gregory Kristof recommends another middle ground: taking a "gap year" off between high school and college.

Will a college degree be "worth it" in your life? As you read, pay attention not only to the claims that are made but also to *how* they are made: Do the articles cite statistics, and if so, how might this data be skewed or interpreted in ways that can support seemingly divergent arguments? Do you find statistical evidence to be more compelling than personal anecdotes, interviews with experts, or rhetorical reasoning? Should college's "worth" be based purely on the numbers, or does education offer more intangible (and perhaps even more important) benefits than can be captured by career statistics? Should everybody go to college, or should college be reserved for the few? Are there alternative paths to education that are just as viable and valid as college, or is a college degree, these days, a necessity? These are issues to confront as you contemplate the beginning of your college experience.

Anthony P. Carvenale

College Is Still Worth It [1]

I t's an old story: when economic downturns hit, unemployment rates spiral and tales of college graduates forced to tend bar or mop floors proliferate. So, too, do the assertions of experts and budget-constrained political leaders that young people don't need costly postsecondary education in a job market that has little use for college degrees.

2   Those who make the "skip college" argument [3] often bolster their arguments with official state and national Bureau of Labor Statistics (BLS) data suggesting that the U.S. higher education system has been turning out far more college grads than current or future job openings require.

3   To a public wary of paying steep tuition bills in a depressed economy, it all sounds alarming and—with the backing of national and state government BLS data—authoritative.

4   There's just one problem with the official BLS statistics: they're wrong.

5   BLS data assigns occupations a "required" education level. Their numbers assert that 16.6 percent of jobs, or nearly 25 million jobs, require a bachelor's; in reality, over 30.7 million jobs, or 20.4 percent are filled with workers who have a bachelor's.

6   The BLS also holds that 6.1 million jobs (4.1 percent) require an associate degree, when 14 million jobs across the economy are actually filled by those with associate-degree holders. The BLS data, therefore, imply that Americans are overeducated.

7   The most persuasive evidence that the BLS numbers are wrong are earnings data, which show that employers across the country pay a "wage premium" to college graduates, even in occupations that BLS does not consider "college" jobs. This simply means that businesses pay more money to workers with degrees than to those without because employers believe that postsecondary educated workers are more valuable.

8   And employers aren't just hiring degrees. Over the decades, this premium has ebbed and flowed, but the longer-term trend in demand for college graduates has risen consistently. The college wage premium over high school graduates dropped significantly in the 1970s when vast numbers of college-educated Baby Boomers and males who went to college instead of Vietnam flooded the job market.

9   When the baby boomers aged beyond their prime college age years and the Vietnam draft ended, most expected a plunge in college-going. The rate of college-going did fall off, but not nearly as much as most experts predicted. Instead, a sharp upswing in the demand for college-educated workers kept college enrollments growing. Moreover, since the early 1980s, college completion has been unable to keep pace with employer demand. As a result, the college wage premium over high school degrees skyrocketed from roughly 30 percent to 74 percent at present. Hardly a sign of an oversupply of college talent.

10   To dismiss the significance of wage data requires a belief that employers across the country have systematically hired overqualified workers for their job openings and then grossly overpaid them for the past three decades. Consider the implications: It would mean that employers followed the law of supply and demand in the 1970s by cutting back the wage premium, but completely cast it aside in subsequent years by inexplicably throwing extra money at college-educated workers.

11   It would mean that, by 2008, more than a *third* of all workers with postsecondary education were receiving an appreciable economic benefit from their degrees that reasonable employers should never have paid. In short, if all of this is true, then chaos reigns: economic markets don't work, employers are irrational, and preparing children for college is naive for all but a select few.

12   There is a better explanation for the puzzling official data that suggest we are producing too many college graduates.

OFFICIAL EDUCATION DEMAND NUMBERS HAVE SERIOUS FLAWS

13   Bureau of Labor Statistics data, as mentioned, underpin the argument that America overproduces college graduates by the millions. Among the chronically overqualified and overpaid are 43 percent of nuclear technicians who have attained more than the "required" associate degree, and the 80 percent of commercial pilots who hold more than their "required" certificate.

14   While we have high regard for the BLS, and believe that its national and state-level occupational and employment data are unimpeachable, we cannot say the same for its education numbers. They are an offhand byproduct of its other data—and of substantially lower quality.

15   One significant flaw in the BLS method is that it categorizes occupations as either "college" or "non-college," a methodology that is both subjective and static. A better approach, typical of mainstream economic analysis, is to track actual earnings of college graduates to determine the demand for postsecondary education. We reason that if the wages of college-educated workers within an occupation are high and/or rising relative to people with high school diplomas or less, that reflects a tangible advantage conferred by postsecondary education. People with college degrees in these occupations, therefore, are not overeducated because they are actually gaining value in return for their educational investment. While all degrees may not produce equal returns, in virtually every case, the return is far greater than the cost of obtaining the diploma.

16   In contrast, we do not define the "college labor market" as the BLS does, with its set of "college" occupations that cover the traditional white-collar and professional jobs. The official BLS data assign an education level to an occupation based on the lowest level of education attainment necessary to access the occupation. This approach is remarkably static and fails to adjust to changing economic realities.

17   For one, it misses the shift toward increased postsecondary requirements within occupations that are not traditionally deemed "college jobs." Labor economists agree that there has been a consistent shift toward increased postsecondary requirements across a growing share of occupations that previously did not require two- or four-year college degrees. Examples in the white-collar world include increasing demand for college degrees among managers, health care workers, and a wide variety of office workers, from insurance agents to building inspectors. Examples in the blue- and pink-collar world include increasing degree requirements among production workers, health care technicians, and utility and transportation workers.

TECHNOLOGY DRIVES ONGOING DEMAND FOR BETTER-EDUCATED WORKERS

18   The standard explanation in the economic literature for such shifts is "skill-biased technology change." The core mechanism behind this concept in our current economy is the computer, which automates repetitive tasks and increases the relative value of nonrepetitive tasks in individual occupations. Performing these more sophisticated tasks successfully typically requires more skill, training and education.

19   Wage data show that employers have tended to hire workers with postsecondary credentials for these more complex positions—and pay a wage premium to get them. As a result, we view a "college job" as any position that gives substantial earnings returns to a college degree, irrespective of occupation, whether an individual is an insurance agent or a rocket scientist.

20   Our method for tracking education demand is also careful to minimize counting statistical outliers such as bartenders, cab drivers and janitors with BAs and graduate degrees. These kinds of mismatches between degrees and low-skilled jobs—a phenomenon sometimes called "over-education"—are relatively small in number and don't

matter much in an economy of nearly 150 million jobs. In addition, most such workers won't stay in those positions long-term. They eventually move on to better-paying jobs. Over a 10-year period, each cashier job has 13 incumbents who permanently leave the occupation; among medical doctors, that replacement rate is only one.

21 People rarely leave jobs that require a college education because they have the best earnings, benefits and working conditions. There are many more brain surgeons who used to be cashiers than there are cashiers who used to be brain surgeons. A brain surgeon never starts as a brain surgeon, but would have likely had all types of jobs before entering college and medical school. Most jobs people hold in high school are in retail, food services, and other low-skill, low-wage jobs, and future brain surgeons are no exception.

22 In addition, low-skill, non-college positions tend to be greatly overrepresented in the official jobs data because so many of them are part-time. Although low-wage, low-skill jobs make up 20 percent of all jobs in a single year, they only make up 14 percent of the hours worked. Jobs that require a BA or better make up 30 percent of all jobs, but 75 percent of those are full-time, full-year jobs, compared with 64 percent of jobs that require a high school diploma or less.

23 There are, then, a number of serious flaws with the BLS education demand numbers, ranging from the designation of college and non-college occupations to their failure to reflect rising education requirements across virtually every occupational category. Still, because the BLS has a stellar—and deserved—reputation for its employment data, its static and misleading metrics on education requirements are treated with undue credibility. BLS numbers are widely used by social scientists to gauge education demand, and yet their accuracy receives little serious scrutiny.

CENSUS NUMBERS OFFER VALUABLE TEST OF BLS EDUCATION DEMAND PROJECTIONS

24 As it turns out, though, there is an effective test to gauge the validity of education demand projections based on BLS data. The Census Bureau actually counts the number of workers with college degrees in the workforce and tracks their earnings on the job. As time passes and the Census data catch up with the BLS projections, we can determine if those projections were accurate. To get to the punch line: BLS projections always under-predict demand for college educations.

25 For instance, when we compare the BLS projections for 2006 and the actual count of people in the labor force with degrees during that year, we see that the Bureau undercounted the true number of postsecondary-educated workers by 17 million in 2006, or roughly 30 percent, and by 22 million, or 40 percent in 2008. The alternative method we introduced in Help Wanted [4] missed by just 4 percent.

26 The bottom line is that the BLS predictions didn't even come close to what actually happened in the economy. The only way to reconcile those projections with real life is to assert that the Bureau's projections reflect the number of college degrees employers actually *require,* not the actual numbers of college-educated workers they decide to hire. If this is the case, then employers not only hired millions of overqualified workers in 2006 and 2008, but paid wage premiums of more than 70 percent for the privilege— a notion, as we said earlier, that requires a belief that business owners across the nation and economic markets as a whole have taken leave of their senses.

SPATE OF MEDIA STORIES ON VALUE OF COLLEGE FUELS NEEDLESS FEARS

27 And yet, much of the media coverage of the issue would have us believe college isn't worth it.

28   Stories on the value of college tend to follow the business cycle, and when the cycle is down, journalists often find it easy to write a story that bucks the conventional wisdom. Headlines that suggest postsecondary education no longer pays off in the labor market are news because they play into middle-class parents' fears that they will not be able to give their children the advantages they had. The bad advice gets more and more pointed as the recession deepens.

29   This year, the *New York Times* offered "Plan B: Skip College," while the *Washington Post* ran "Parents Crunch the Numbers and Wonder, Is College Still Worth It?" Even the *Chronicle of Higher Education* has succumbed, [5], recently running "Here's Your Diploma. Now Here's Your Mop."—a story about a college graduate working as a janitor that implies a college degree may not be worthwhile in today's economic climate.

30   And if college educated workers were overpaid by 75 percent and oversupplied by 40 percent, why wouldn't they be the first fired and last hired in these tough times? It is true that unemployment rates are relatively high among college grads. When it rains long enough and hard enough, everyone gets wet. But the unemployment rate for all workers with college degrees is a quarter the rate for high school graduates.

31   And it's true, as the *New York Times* pointed out in an editorial [6] on December 13, that the unemployment rate for freshly minted college grads was 9.2 percent, not much different from the 9.8 percent unemployment rate for all workers. But the *Times* didn't bother to mention that the unemployment rate for freshly minted high school graduates was 35 percent.

32   The current recession isn't the first to produce such gloom. The *New York Times* and other prominent newspapers were printing similar stories in the early 1980s, during the last severe recession. At that time, the *Times* ran headlines like "The Underemployed: Working for Survival Instead of Careers."

33   And it's not just the journalists who get gloomy. The *New York Times* quoted Ronald Kutscher, associate commissioner at the Bureau of Labor Statistics in 1984, as saying, "We are going to be turning out about 200,000 to 300,000 too many college graduates a year in the '80s." Yet the 1980s was a decade that saw an unprecedented rise in the wage premium for college-educated workers over high school-educated workers. The wage premium for college degrees over high school degrees increased from 30 percent to more than 80 percent—evidence that the postsecondary system was underproducing college graduates, not that, as Kutscher went on to say, "the supply far exceeds the demand."

34   The gloomy stories, the high unemployment among college graduates and the misleading official data are unlikely to keep many middle- and upper-class youth from going to college. Higher education is a value that such families are unlikely to abandon, regardless of economic pressures. Instead, the real tragedy of these headlines is the message they send to less privileged youth for whom college is not an assumed path. The negative press on college fuels pre-existing biases among working families that college is neither accessible nor worth the cost and effort. Moreover, the bad press and worse data strengthen the hand of elitists [7] who argue that college should be the exclusive preserve of those born into the right race, ethnicity and bank account.

35   It is important to note that current evidence demonstrates increasing demand for college graduates, and the future promises more of the same. By 2018, our own projections from the "Help Wanted" study show that 63 percent of jobs nationwide will require some form of postsecondary degree. Moreover, postsecondary education has become the only way to secure middle-class earnings in America and, for the least advantaged among us, is now the only way to escape poverty. In 1970, about 60 percent of Americans who attained middle-class status were high school graduates or dropouts. Today, only 46 percent can be found there. In contrast, 44 percent of the top three income deciles had postsecondary education in 1970; today, 81 percent do.

36   The press coverage and expert stumbles don't reflect the empirical reality, but they are symptomatic of a mundane human instinct. People tend to project what's happening in the present into the distant future. If housing prices are great, they'll be that way forever! If job creation is slow, it will be that way forever! If college graduates have to work as bartenders in the depth of a recession, their degrees will never get them ahead! The reality is that jobs come and go with economic cycles. But what lies beneath the economic cycles, and what has remained constant, is the relentless engine of technological change that demands more skilled workers. There is no indication that the trend has suddenly reversed itself.

COLLEGE IS STILL THE BEST SAFE HARBOR IN BAD ECONOMIC TIMES

37   Meanwhile, when jobs disappear, college is the best safe harbor for waiting out the recession and improving your hiring prospects in anticipation of the recovery. Indeed, college-educated workers are much more likely to be employed than their high school-educated counterparts, even during a recession.

38   Irrespective of the current economic conditions, individuals need to consider college as a lifelong investment decision. Likewise, the investment horizon for economic development needs to be measured in decades, not annual budget cycles. Skipping or shortening college on the basis of a headline or even a few years of bad economic news is foolish for individuals whose careers will span 40 or more years of working life. On average, skipping an associate degree will cost a high school graduate half a million dollars in earnings, and skipping a bachelor's degree will cost $1 million in potential earnings over a lifetime.

39   Many argue that the value of college is declining as tuition rises.[8] However, while it is true that the sticker price cost of going to college has risen faster than the inflation rate, the college wage premium has risen even faster, both in terms of the cost of going to college and the inflation rate. The best measure of the value of college is the net present value of going to college. Here we discount the lifetime earnings by the real interest rate, and discount the principal and interest payments from taking out a college loan (a $60,000 loan). Once we've done that, the most accurate estimation of the average value of a college education over a high school education is still $1 million dollars (net present value).

40   Our own forthcoming research shows that we have under-produced college graduates by almost 10 million since 1983. We also find in Help Wanted that through 2018, at least three million jobs that require postsecondary education and training will be unfilled due to lack of supply. The share of jobs for those with a high school education or less is shrinking. In 1973, high school graduates and dropouts accounted for 72 percent of

jobs, while by 2007 it was 41 percent. The opposite has happened for those with at least some college: the share of jobs has increased from 28 percent in 1973 to 59 percent in 2007, and is projected to be 63 percent by 2018. Likewise, the share of national wage income from college-educated workers has increased from 38 percent to 73 percent since 1970, and there is every reason to believe that this trend will continue.

41   We believe there is no doubt about the requirements of our fast-approaching economic future: we need more college graduates, not fewer. But at the very time we need our higher-education system to kick into high gear, it is under pressure to apply the brakes instead.

42   While the economics of higher education are clear, the politics are not. The economy's lackluster demand in recession, coupled with media stories questioning the value of college, makes it easier to excuse cuts in public funding for postsecondary education. In the short term, federal stimulus funds have helped fill the gaps for postsecondary cuts driven by declining state revenues. But the stimulus funds will be unavailable after 2011, and federal money can't make up the difference indefinitely. In fact, it's an easy target for the chopping block. Higher education is especially vulnerable in the debate about public priorities because it lacks the core constituency and the immediacy of such issues as Social Security or homeland security.

43   Still, it's clear that reducing funding for postsecondary education is both bad economic and social policy. The consequences of slashing higher education budgets is a decision that will effect inequality for the next several decades by determining who gets access to middle-class careers. And, slowing the stream of college graduates into the economy threatens to leave employers without the skilled workers they need to thrive in a fiercely competitive economy.

44   While doubts about spending on higher education are understandable in the depths of a catastrophic recession, the potential consequences of succumbing to gloom and relying on flawed data to inform decisions about the value of postsecondary education are ruinous.

45   Bad numbers on the economic value of college encourage disinvestment in college both by individuals and government. And disinvestment in higher education is bad news not only for our higher education system, but for our economy—and for the lives and futures of millions of Americans.

LINKS:

1. http://www.insidehighered.com/views/2011/01/14/carnevale_college_is_still_worth_it_for_americans
2. http://www.insidehighered.com/users/news
3. http://www.nebhe.org/2010/11/30/the-real-education-crisis-are-35-of-all-college-degrees-in-new-england-unnecessary/
4. http://cew.georgetown.edu/jobs2018/
5. http://chronicle.com/article/Heres-Your-Diploma-Now/124982/
6. http://www.nytimes.com/2010/12/14/opinion/14tue1.html
7. http://www.aei.org/article/101207
8. http://www.insidehighered.com/news/2008/04/07/miller ■

Richard Vedder

For Many, College Isn't Worth It [1]

I n this space last Friday, Anthony Carnevale strongly and lengthily argued [3] that "college is still worth it." He implicitly criticized those, including me [4], who rely on U.S. Bureau of Labor Statistics (BLS) data showing that the number of college graduates exceeds the number of available jobs that require a college degree. While he says many things, he has two main points. First, "There's just one problem with the official BLS statistics: they're wrong." Second, he notes that "the most persuasive evidence that the BLS numbers are wrong are earnings data which show employers across the country pay a 'wage premium' for college graduates.... "

2   I will argue that the BLS data are, in fact, pretty good, and that while Carnevale is factually correct about the earnings data, his interpretation of it is, at the minimum, misleading. Moreover, I will further argue that what is involved here is a classic application of what economists over the age of 50 call "Say's Law" (i.e., the theory suggesting that supply creates its own demand; economists under 50 are largely ignorant of it because they have no knowledge of the evolution of their own discipline, reflecting the general abandonment of thorough teaching of the history of economic thought).

3   Furthermore, I will argue that diplomas are a highly expensive and inefficient screening device used by employers who are afraid to test potential employee skills owing to a most unfortunate Supreme Court decision and related legislation. Finally, I will assert that Carnevale and others who argue "college has a high payoff" are comparing apples with oranges—i.e., they are making totally inappropriate comparisons that lead to skewed conclusions.

4   An even-handed interpretation of the data is that college *is* "worth it" for some significant number of young people, but is a far more problematic investment for others. The call by President Obama, the Lumina and Gates Foundations, and many higher education advocates to rapidly and radically increase the number of college graduates is fundamentally off-base.

THE BLS DATA

5   Carnevale essentially argues that the BLS data are pretty bad, mainly because earnings data show that employers pay workers with college degrees a wage premium, which would be irrational if the education associated with a college degree were not valuable for the job in question. Indeed, "a better approach" to this question, according to Carnevale, would be "to track actual earnings of college graduates to determine the demand for postsecondary education." Additionally, Carnevale accurately notes that there are some variations within skills required within some of the BLS occupational

categories, and it is possible that for some jobs a college degree would be necessary or highly desirable, while for others it would not be.

6   However, Carnevale's overall description of the BLS data and its system for categorizing education requirements is far from accurate. For instance, Carnevale blandly declares that "[t]he official BLS data assign an education level to an occupation based on the lowest level of education attainment necessary to access the occupation." Actually, as the BLS makes quite clear on its website [5], it "assign[s] what [its] research suggests was the most significant source of education or training" for each occupation. (Apparently Carnevale confuses a proposed change to the BLS category system—and one which isn't going to be implemented [6] at that—with the system currently in place.) Furthermore, the BLS also noted that its data do in some cases understate educational requirements, but in others they overstate it, suggesting that, in the aggregate, the BLS data can be viewed as reasonably sound.

7   Another problem with Carnevale's critique of the BLS data is that, in reality, the BLS dataset is arguably superior to that developed by Carnevale and his colleagues. This point was made a couple of months ago by Paul E. Harrington and Andrew M. Sum [7] when they observed that taking Carnevale's approach "assumes a world where no under-employment or mal-employment of college graduates exists." On the other hand, the BLS dataset is robust enough to account for underemployment, albeit perhaps imperfectly.

8   Carnevale's criticism of the BLS data is nothing, however, compared to that of Cliff Adelman of the Institute for Higher Education policy, who, in commenting on Carnevale's article, said "the base data are bizarre," claiming the statistics misrepresented the numbers in some occupations (he focused on solar panel installers and like occupations) by a huge magnitude. Adelman simply misread the data—badly—as Carnevale himself has indicated in a response.

9   Before turning to Carnevale's earnings-based argument, I want to comment on his remark about "statistical outliers such as bartenders, cab drivers and janitors with B.A.s and graduate degrees.... These kinds of mismatches between degrees and low-skilled jobs ... are relatively small in number and don't matter much.... "

10   Hogwash. The BLS tells us that for waiters and waitresses alone, there are more than one-third of a million who hold B.A. degrees or more—not an inconsequential number. And the BLS data would indicate that, *in total*,about 17 million college graduates have jobs that do not require a college degree. Not only is that 11 percent or so of the total labor force, hardly a "relatively small" number, but, more relevantly, it constitutes well over 30 percent of the working college graduates in the U.S.—a number of mammoth proportions.

11   Carnevale argues that a large portion of these persons are short-term in these jobs, and that they typically move on into more appropriate jobs later on. I am the first to admit the turnover rate of waiters is greater than that of physicians, but so what? If roughly one-third of college graduates in general are in jobs not requiring college-level training, that is far more than frictional unemployment—workers temporarily taking a low paying job while awaiting more permanent employment. And that certainly is not simply a function of the recession, although that phenomenon no doubt has aggravated the problem.

THE EARNINGS DATA

12 Carnevale is absolutely correct that college graduates on average earn more than those with lesser formal educational certifications. And I would agree that on average college graduates have a higher productivity per worker (justifying the higher pay) than those merely possessing high school diplomas. Therefore, for many, going to college is a good personal investment decision.

13 But to a considerable extent, the reason college graduates have higher pay has little to do with what they learned in college *per se*. Suppose an employer has two applicants, who in personal interviews seemed similar in quality. The employer likely will choose the college graduate over the high school graduate because, on average, college graduates have higher levels of cognitive skills (as measured by IQ tests or similar instruments), are more likely to have relatively high levels of motivation and discipline developed before attending college, have more general knowledge about the world in which we live, etc. Hence such employees are often offered a wage premium, since the anticipated level of performance of the college graduate is perceived to be higher. The diploma serves as a screening device that allows businesses to narrow down the applicant pool quickly and almost without cost to the employer, but with a huge financial cost to the individual earning the diploma (often at least $100,000), and to society at large in the form of public subsidies.

14 For the past several decades, moreover, the ability of employers to find other means of certifying competence and skills has been severely circumscribed by judicial decisions and laws. In *Griggs v. Duke Power* (1971), the U.S. Supreme Court essentially outlawed employer testing of prospective workers where the test imparted a "disparate impact" on members of minority groups. Cautious employers have sharply reduced such testing, and are now forced to rely on other measures of competence, namely the possession of a college diploma.

15 This perception that college is primarily a screening device rather than the source of a true vocationally relevant curriculum is supported by a good deal of data that show college students spend relatively little time in academic studies (e.g., the Time Use Survey [8] data of the BLS). The most notable recent effort, utilizing detailed data from the National Survey of Student Engagement, is examined in Richard Arum and Josipa Roksa's new book *Academically Adrift: Limited Learning on College Campuses* [9], just released by the University of Chicago Press. "How much are students actually learning in contemporary higher education? The answer for many undergraduates, we have concluded, is not much," write Arum and Roksa.

SAY'S LAW AND CREDENTIAL INFLATION

16 The economist Jean Baptiste Say, writing in 1803, formulated his "law of markets," which can be roughly summarized as: "supply creates its own demand." In the context of American higher education, colleges have supplied millions of graduates over recent decades—more than needed to fill jobs that historically have been considered ones requiring the skills associated with a college education. Therefore, employers are flooded with applicants who possess college degrees, and given the inherently better character and intellectual traits that college graduates on average have, the employers

demand a diploma for a job. The rise in the supply of diplomas created the demand for them, not the other way around.

17   Jobs that have not changed much over time, such as serving as a mail carrier or restaurant manager, now have large numbers of college graduates filling them, relative to the past. This is almost certainly mainly a manifestation of what might be termed "credential inflation." To be sure, the quality of high school graduates may have declined over time somewhat owing to the mediocre state of our public schools, but it is hard to believe this is important in explaining the rise in, say, college-educated mail carriers.

APPLES AND ORANGES: RISK-TAKING IN ATTENDING COLLEGE

18   A huge problem in any analysis such as that performed by Carnevale is that it ignores the vast number of students who enter college and do not complete a degree. While I am the first to admit there are some problems with the underlying IPEDS data used to measure dropout rates, it is probably nonetheless true that at least two out of every five persons entering college full-time fail to graduate within *six* years. There is a huge risk associated with enrolling in college: you might not graduate. A person considering a $100,000 investment in 1,000 shares of XYZ Corporation common stock at $100 a share is assured that he or she will have those 1,000 shares, although there are some risks associated with the shares declining in value over time. A person making a $100,000 investment in a B.A. degree is *not* assured that he or she will obtain the investment—i.e., actually graduate in a timely fashion.

19   For years, economists have written that the rate of return on college investments tends to be high—10 percent is an oft-cited estimate, greater than the average investor is likely to earn in alternatives such as stocks, bonds or real estate. Thus the studies have concluded that going to college typically makes sense, independent of any nonpecuniary advantages college offers. Yet these studies have failed to account for the added risk associated with it—the probability of dropping out.

20   Two new studies have attempted to correct for this problem, one by Gonzalo Castex and the other by KartikAthreya and Janice Eberly (both are available for download here [10]). They suggest that the reported superior rate of return on investing in college disappears when investments are adjusted for risk.

21   At the individual student level, it is possible to reasonably estimate the risk. A student who was at the top of her class at a top-flight suburban high school, had a composite SAT score of 1500, and plans to attend a private college with relatively low dropout rates is probably going to get a reasonable return on her investment, although even that is no certainty. By contrast, a student who is below average in his graduating class from a mediocre high school, has a combined SAT score of 850, and is considering a college with high dropout rates is very likely not to graduate even in six years, and probably will get a very low return on his college investment. That student might well do much better by going to a certificate program at a career college, learning to be a truck driver, or becoming a barber, for example.

22   In short, a good maxim is "different strokes for different folks." A one-size-fits-all solution does not work as long as human beings have vastly different aptitudes, skills,

motivations, etc. On balance, we are probably over-invested in higher education, not under-invested. The earnings data reflect less about human capital accumulation imparted to college graduates by their collegiate experiences than the realities of information costs associated with job searches.

23   With fewer public subsidies of higher education, I suspect much or all of the problem would disappear: College enrollments would reach levels consistent with the needs of our economy and the personal economic welfare of those attending.

LINKS:

1. http://www.insidehighered.com/views/2011/01/20/
   vedder_going_to_college_isn_t_a_smart_decision_for_many_young_people
2. http://www.insidehighered.com/users/news
3. http://www.insidehighered.com/views/2011/01/14/
   carnevale_college_is_still_worth_it_for_americans
4. http://collegeaffordability.blogspot.com/search/label/underemployment
5. http://www.bls.gov/emp/ep_education_tech.htm
6. http://www.bls.gov/emp/ep_propedtrain.htm
7. http://www.nebhe.org/2010/11/08/college-labor-shortages-in-2018/
8. http://www.bls.gov/tus/charts/students.htm
9. http://www.insidehighered.com/news/2011/01/18/
   study_finds_large_numbers_of_college_students_don_t_learn_much
10. http://www.aeaweb.org/aea/2011conference/program/preliminary.php?search_
    string=eberly&search_type=last_name&search=Search ∎

...FOR THE NEXT THIRTY YEARS

8/6

Clive Crook

A Matter of Degrees: Why College Is Not an Economic Cure-all

I t is unusual nowadays to venture more than five minutes into any debate about the American economy—about widening income inequality, say, or threats to the country's global competitiveness, or the squeeze on the middle class—without somebody invoking the great economic cure-all: education. We must improve it. For a moment, partisan passions subside and everybody nods.

2   But only for a moment. How, exactly, do we improve education? Where does the problem reside—in elementary schools, high schools, or colleges? Is the answer to recruit better teachers, or to get more students moving from high school to university? Should we spend more public money? Change the way schools are organized and paid for (supporting charter schools and vouchers, perhaps)? In no time, correctly orthogonal positions are laid down, and the quarreling resumes. But nobody challenges the importance of the issue. The centrality of education as a driver of the nation's economic prospects appears beyond dispute.

3   Yet the connections between education and economics are not as they seem. To rest the case for improving schools and colleges largely on economic grounds is a mistake. It distorts education policy in unproductive ways. And though getting education right surely matters, more is at stake than a slight increase in economic growth.

4   Everybody understands that, as a rule of thumb, more school means a bigger paycheck. On average, having a college degree, rather than just a high-school degree, increases your earnings by about two-thirds. A problem arises, however, if you try to gross up these gains across the whole population. If an extra year of education equipped students with skills that increased their productivity, then giving everybody another year of school or college would indeed raise everybody's income. But take the extreme case, and suppose that the extra year brought no gain in productive skills. Suppose it merely sorted people, signaling "higher ability" to a would-be employer. Then giving an extra year of school to everybody would raise nobody's income, because nobody's position in the ordering would change. The private benefit of more education would remain, but the social benefit would be zero.

5   Would sending everybody to Harvard raise everybody's future income by the full amount of the "Harvard premium"? Yes, if the value of a degree from Harvard resided in the premium skills you acquired there (and if the college's classrooms could be scaled up a little). Well, ask any Harvard graduate about the teaching. The value of a degree from Harvard lies mainly in the sorting that happens during the application process. So the answer is no: if everybody went to Harvard, the Harvard premium would collapse.

6   In the case of an extra year of education, it need not be all or nothing; another year of study usually does impart *some* productivity-enhancing skill. But how much? A year of extra training in computer programming presumably has a direct material value. An extra year spent learning medieval history might improve a student's intellectual self-discipline and ability to think analytically, but has lower material utility: nobody studies feudal land grants for the boost to lifetime earnings. So aggregated figures such as the proportion of high-school graduates going on to college—a number that is constantly cited and compared internationally—tell you very little.

7   Totting up college matriculations as a way of measuring national success is doubly ill-conceived if the signaling function flips over, so that a college education becomes the norm, and college nonattendance is taken to mean "unfit for most jobs."

8   In 2004, 67 percent of American high-school graduates went straight on to college, compared with just under half in 1972. This is widely applauded. It looks like progress—but is it really? Failing to go to college did not always mark people out as rejects, unfit for any kind of well-paid employment. But now, increasingly, it does. In a cruel paradox, this may be one reason why parental incomes better predict children's incomes in the United States than they used to—in other words, one reason why America is becoming less meritocratic. A college degree has become an expensive passport to good employment, one for which drive and ability less often can substitute, yet one that looks unaffordable to many poor families.

9   Many occupations are suffering from chronic entry-requirement inflation. Hotels, for instance, used to appoint junior managers from among the more able, energetic, and presentable people on their support or service staff, and give them on-the-job training. Today, according to the Bureau of Labor Statistics, around 800 community and junior colleges offer two-year associate degrees in hotel management. In hotel chains, the norm now is to require a four-year bachelor's or master's degree in the discipline.

10   For countless other jobs that once required little or no formal academic training—preschool teacher, medical technician, dental hygienist, physical-therapy assistant, police officer, paralegal, librarian, auditor, surveyor, software engineer, financial manager, sales manager, and on and on—employers now look for a degree. In some of these instances, in some jurisdictions, the law requires one. All of these occupations are, or soon will be, closed to nongraduates. At the very least, some of the public and private investment in additional education needs to be questioned.

11   To be sure, today's IT-driven world is creating a genuine need for some kinds of better-educated workers. It is the shortage of such people, according to most politicians and many economists, that is causing the well-documented rise in income inequality. Both to spur the economy and to lessen inequality, they argue, the supply of college graduates needs to keep rising.

12   It seems plausible, but this theory too is often overstated, and does not fit the facts particularly well. The college wage premium rose rapidly for many years, up to the late 1990s. Since then it has flattened off, just when the pace of innovation would have led you to expect a further acceleration. An even more awkward fact is that especially in the past decade or so, rising inequality has been driven by huge income increases at the very top of the distribution. In the wide middle, where differences in educational attainment ought to count, changes in relative earnings have been far

more subdued. During the 1990s, CEO salaries roughly doubled in inflation-adjusted terms. But median pay actually went up more slowly than pay at the bottom of the earnings distribution, and even pay at the 90th percentile (highly educated workers, mostly, but not CEOs) increased only a little faster than median wages. Today, shortages of narrowly defined skills *are* apparent in specific industries or parts of industries—but simply pushing more students through any kind of college seems a poorly judged response.

13   The country will continue to need cadres of highly trained specialists in an array of technical fields. In many cases, of course, the best place to learn the necessary skills will be a university. For many and perhaps most of us, however, university education is not mainly for acquiring directly marketable skills that raise the nation's productivity. It is for securing a higher ranking in the labor market, and for cultural and intellectual enrichment. Summed across society, the first of those purposes cancels out. The second does not. That is why enlightenment, not productivity, is the chief social justification for four years at college.

14   Shoving ever more people from high school to college is not only of dubious economic value, it is unlikely to serve the cause of intellectual enrichment if the new students are reluctant or disinclined. Yet there are still large prizes to be had through educational reform—certainly in enlightenment and perhaps in productivity. They simply lurk farther down the educational ladder.

15   The most valuable attribute for young people now entering the workforce is adaptability. This generation must equip itself to change jobs readily, and the ability to retrain, whether on the job or away from the job, will be crucial. The necessary intellectual assets are acquired long before college, or not at all. Aside from self-discipline and the capacity to concentrate, they are preeminently the core-curriculum skills of literacy and numeracy.

16   Illiteracy has always cut people off from the possibility of a prosperous life, from the consolations of culture, and from full civic engagement. In the future, as horizons broaden for everybody else, people lacking these most basic skills will seem even more imprisoned. The most recent National Assessment of Adult Literacy found that 30 million adult Americans have less than basic literacy (meaning, for instance, that they find it difficult to read mail, or address an envelope). Three out of ten seniors in public high schools still fail to reach the basic-literacy standard. Progress on literacy would bring great material benefits, of course, for the people concerned and some benefits for the wider economy—but those benefits are not the main reason to make confronting illiteracy the country's highest educational priority.

17   In addressing the nation's assorted economic anxieties—over rising inequality, the stagnation of middle-class incomes, and the fading American dream of economic opportunity—education is not the longed-for cure-all. Nor is anything else. The debate about these issues will have to range all across the more bitterly disputed terrains of public policy—taxes, public spending, health care, and more. It is a pity, but in the end a consensus that blinds itself to the complexity of the issues is no use to anyone. ■

Gregory Kristof

On the Ground with a "Gap Year"

I t took place on a frosty peak tucked away in the Tibetan highlands: my friend Rick and I walked in on a group of monks as they were on their knees, groaning.

2　They were performing secret rituals involving yak butter.

3　Peeking out from behind animal fur curtains, Rick and I hoped that they hadn't noticed us yet. They hummed and sat in rows facing a stage of yak butter candles that threw images against the walls like kicked hacky sacks. Back in the shadows, I worried: What would happen if they saw two white dudes chillin' behind the furs?

4　"Pssst," Rick said. "I think we should leave."

5　"Let's make for the door." I said.

6　I flattened myself against the back of the room, inching toward the door. Take it slow, I told myself. Don't drag your feet. Hurry up! I just had a few more feet to go. Two steps to go. Wow, I would make a great spy.

7　One step. And then—right as I was considering tacking on two zeros to the front of my name—ZINGZAMEMEM-BzerrBzerrBzerr ...

8　I know, my ringtone sucks. Eyes caved in on me. I sort of just lay there on the dirt floor, not moving much, just looking up sporadically at the curious faces, and feeling sorry that I had disrupted their ritual. And yet I felt warm inside because I was here, getting caught in a mountain temple by Buddhist monks, and not where I shoulda-coulda-woulda been: listening to a PowerPoint lecture in a Boston classroom.

9　My decision to defer college for a year wasn't easy. In my New York high-school, nearly every kid treads the usual path from graduation to college. Upon hearing that I would hop off the traditional academic bandwagon, some teachers, friends, and other parents would respond with "That sounds great!" while murmuring comforting remarks that I would probably turn out OK.

10　I was extremely excited about college, so it was tough to say "Not this time" to the bounty of friends and general awesomeness that my Freshman year would most assuredly bring me.

11　But I remember thinking how most of my great high school memories were localized capsules, like dots on paper waiting to be connected. A great weekend here, a good report card there. It was only when I extracted myself from each individual moment that I would realize that the damn picture still wouldn't come into focus. Where was I going? Where did I want to go?

12　I wanted more. I wanted to see how the other half lived, to learn the things that weren't found in books, to live a phantasmagoria of unforgettable experiences. I wanted to experience a life in which images glided by like kangaroos on rollerblades.

13　So I went to China. So far, I've rock-climbed above Buddhist grottos, showered in underground waterfalls, squeaked my way across 13th century temples hanging halfway up cliffs, and stayed in earthquake-ravaged villages where everyone still dwells in tents. In a one-street town whose sole cab driver appeared to be blind, Rick and I went deep inside one of the world's most dazzling monasteries to party with monks (the scene was about as bangin' as what you'd expect from a group of pacifists). I've motorcycled across a frozen holy lake in the Himalayas, and I've stared into giant volcano pits on the North Korean border.

14   Not all of this was safe and rosy. Rick and I spent one night fending off wild dogs with a metal bar and headlamp, after escaping from the clutches of a hawk-nosed Tibetan with a few loose screws. We finally found a place to stay (by barging into a man's tent at 5 a.m. and striking a deal with him to spend the night), but still, the Himalayan winter nearly turned us into popsicles.

15   I even learned the in's and out's of the squat toilet. Do not sink too low when you squat. Trust me.

16   And while we are on the subject of appropriate dinner table conversation, let me warn you never to pee into a strong oncoming Tibetan wind. Unless you are seeking a novel and roundabout face-washing technique. Believe me, it happened.

17   So if you are willing to unrut your wheels, if you enjoy hopscotching through the world of motorcycles and open prairie, or if you're just searching for that extra boost to send yourself hurtling down a road less traveled, then perhaps a year abroad is right for you. Think about it in particular if you're going to study a language in college: why pay expensive tuition to learn Spanish in the States when you can learn it more thoroughly and cheaply in Bolivia?

18   Even a gap year's undesired moments can have a palliative benefit. Setting off for remote mountain villages, only to discover that they have been utterly abandoned; triumphantly finding a town's only bathroom, only to discover that the mud you are now standing in is not actually mud; these are the curve balls that keep you on your toes, that preserve in your life what remains of childhood spontaneity.

19   A gap year is a larky way to mature out of youth. But if you do it right, it's also a way to keep it.

20   I nearly forgot to mention that the original purpose of traveling to China was to bolster my Chinese at Tsinghua University in Beijing. Thanks to its great program, as well as the superb Ruiwen school in Dalian, I'm now fluent. But talent in Chinese doesn't compare with talent in analyzing terrain for wild dog hangouts, or with kaleidoscopic memories that will refract experiences for a lifetime.

21   So, graduating seniors, now's the time to search the Web for travel abroad programs. Check out Global Citizen Year for a mini Peace Corps experience. If you're less interested in a formal program, just do what I did: sign up for a foreign language school and book a flight. Because of the dollar's purchasing power, travel in China is very cheap — a rebuttal to those who think gap years are only for rich kids. I hope you choose to defer enrollment for one year, and I hope that your gap year, like mine, goes wrong in all the right ways.

22   When college does roll around, you'll already have gone through your own freshman orientation. After getting lost in a remote village because I was seeking a familiar temple but was approaching it from a completely different direction, I learned that where you are going is not all that matters. Where you are coming from matters, too.

23   It's like this: Spend time huddling for candle warmth on the Tibetan Plateau, and the C in physics ain't gonna seem so harsh.

24   Eventually the dots begin to connect themselves. That's when I discovered that I got more than what I'd bargained for. I initially wanted simply to get a sense of where I was headed for the next few years. But the poverty I encountered in western China irrevocably challenged me. I felt, on the most profound of levels, the realness of others. I became just one person among very, very many. Especially since I was in China.

25   Speaking of melting into the background, that was exactly my wish that evening when my friend and I got caught in the temple.

26   "I'm just a traveler," I said. After an ungolden silence, a monk stepped forward: "Come eat with us."

27   Rick and I spent the rest of that evening under a temple rooftop somewhere among the Himalayan foothills—I couldn't find the place now. We and the incredibly hospitable monks traded stories and cheers over yak meat, yak cheese, and yak butter tea well past my bedtime.

28   Who says you need a classroom for an education?

FROM READING TO WRITING

1. There are two explicit rebuttals in this chapter: Gerald Bracey refutes Margaret Spellings, and Richard Vedder answers the argument of Anthony Carnevale. Find an essay in a local publication that is related to education issues and that you disagree with, and then compose a rebuttal. (Consult Chapter 14 on writing a rebuttal.)

2. Gregory Kristof concludes this chapter with an argument that depends on personal experience. Write a narrative of your own experiences that supports your point of view about a specific educational practice or policy. (For more on narrative arguments, see Chapter 13.)

3. Evaluate some policy or practice related to education in your community—it could be a teacher, an academic department, the food, Greek life, admissions practices, tuition rates, or anything else. Be sure to base your evaluation on specific criteria, such as those described in Chapter 12.

4. This book reproduces two ads related to education, on pages 116 and 122. Locate other ads for colleges (in magazines, newspapers, or college Web sites), and analyze the nature of the arguments presented. How do those ads present and support their arguments? Look carefully as well at the cartoons in this chapter. What specific arguments are offered in those cartoons, and what good reasons are offered in support?

5. Education arguments frequently depend on definitions. "Higher education is nothing but a big business," someone might say, for example. Or "Liberal arts education is turning into vocational education." Compose your own argument that redefines some concept or topic related to education—high school or college sports, for example; or Greek life; or charter schools, or whatever. For advice on definition arguments, see Chapter 10.

6. Imagine that Ralph Waldo Emerson and W. E. B. DuBois were involved in a conversation about the nature and goals of education. Based on the essays by those two thinkers that are reproduced in this chapter, do you think they would have any areas of agreement, any common ground? And what issues would separate them?

7. Would you say that a particular school or university that you are familiar with has markedly improved or deteriorated over the years? If so, what caused that advance or decline? (For advice on causal arguments, see Chapter 11.)

24 | Globalization: Importing and Exporting America

America meets the world as the iconic golden arches mix with Thai characters at McDonald's restaurant in Chiang Mai. Is the world becoming more like America, or is America becoming more global?

America's Place in the World—and the World's Place in America

The place of America and Americans in relation to the rest of the world has always been an important topic in the national conversation. A product itself of globalization (embodied in the figure of Christopher Columbus) and created through the force of European colonialism, the United States has taken an increasing role in international affairs since its founding. But globalization has only grown more important, it seems, since the end of the Cold War (which seemed to leave the United States as the world's only superpower); since the development of economic reforms in China, in the European Union, and in other parts of the world (which are challenging the primacy of American economic power); and especially since the events of September 11, 2001, and the subsequent war in Iraq (which have compromised our will to work cooperatively with traditional allies). Indeed, according to a survey released on August 18, 2004, by the Pew Research Center for the People and the Press, the American public has a divided, even paradoxical opinion about the place of the United States in the world. On the one hand, Americans agree that the United States has assumed a more powerful role as a world leader, but, on the other hand, they concede that America also seems less respected around the world. Americans reject the role of the United States as a single world leader, but they also reject the pull toward isolation. More generally, then, Americans are confronting what has come to be known as globalization—that is, the general impact of various nations on each other and more particularly the impact of American culture on other nations and cultures, and their impact on the United States.

Some of those impacts are economic, as the United States outsources manufacturing jobs to other nations, shifts in the direction of a service economy, and exports its ideologies (e.g., representative democracy, women's rights, resistance to sweatshop labor, pluralistic religious tolerance). Other impacts are military and political, as leaders and citizens debate the wisdom of various options. (For example, should our nation behave as a kind of American empire, free to impose its wishes and will on others? Should our foreign policy be an effort to export democracy, even at the point of a gun? Or should we cooperate more broadly with allies, cultivate new friends, and respect the right of each nation to self-determination? Should the United States close off its borders, literally and figuratively, to follow a kind of neo-isolationism?) Yet other impacts are broadly cultural, as Americans import some of the cultural practices and values of others (as in popular songs, films, restaurants, fashions, and so forth) and export our own cultural values and traditions to others. This chapter of *Good Reasons with Contemporary Arguments* offers arguments about one or another aspect of these questions related to globalization.

Workers at a call center in New Delhi, India, take a break between calls.

Contemporary Arguments

The arguments in this chapter focus on the exchange of capital and cultural goods between the United States and other nations. Todd Gitlin's essay uses iconic American cultural signs to argue that the global village today has a distinctly American flavor—though that flavor blends and changes in its new environments. In an essay about Walmart and Mexico, Laura Carlsen (a long-time student of the economic effects of American business on Mexican life) discusses her concern about the broader impact of American economic power on the cultures of other nations. Thomas Friedman explains approvingly the new "flat world" that globalization is creating, and Robyn Meredith and Suzanne Hoppough tout the economic benefits of globalization in a way that counters Carlsen. Sadanand Dhume interprets the Best Picture of 2008, *Slumdog Millionaire*, as the product of a thoroughly globalized mentality and "a metaphor for India in the age of globalization." And Lance Morrow concludes the chapter with an essay on how globalization has changed how Americans view themselves, especially through images related to immigration.

While the topics discussed in this chapter are varied, all of the readings bring up similar questions about the movement between cultures—of people, goods, values, images, and communication. What are the effects of globalization? What do you think about American importation of cultural forms from other nations? What about exportation of American culture that is welcomed—even sought out—by people in other nations? Is this importation and exportation dangerous, enriching, or some complicated mixture of the two?

Todd Gitlin

Under the Sign of Mickey Mouse & Co.

Todd Gitlin is a professor of journalism and sociology at Columbia University. A leading and longtime culture critic who writes for a variety of publications (including *Mother Jones*, a popular magazine with a left-of-center appeal, especially to younger readers), he has received several prestigious grants and fellowships, including one from the MacArthur Foundation. His books include *Media Unlimited: How the Torrent of Images and Sounds Overwhelms Our Lives* (2002), *Letters to a Young Activist* (2003), and *The Bulldozer and the Big Tent: Blind Republicans, Lame Democrats, and the Recovery of American Ideals* (2007). The selection below comes from the last chapter of *Media Unlimited.*

Everywhere, the media flow defies national boundaries. This is one of its obvious, but at the same time amazing, features. A global torrent is not, of course, the master metaphor to which we have grown accustomed. We're more accustomed to Marshall McLuhan's *global village.* Those who resort to this metaphor casually often forget that if the world is a global village, some live in mansions on the hill, others in huts. Some dispatch images and sounds around town at the touch of a button; others collect them at the touch of *their* buttons. Yet McLuhan's image reveals an indispensable half-truth. If there is a village, it speaks American. It wears jeans, drinks Coke, eats at the golden arches, walks on swooshed shoes, plays electric guitars, recognizes Mickey Mouse, James Dean, E.T., Bart Simpson, R2-D2, and Pamela Anderson.

2   At the entrance to the champagne cellar of Piper-Heidsieck in Reims, in eastern France, a plaque declares that the cellar was dedicated by Marie Antoinette. The tour is narrated in six languages, and at the end you walk back upstairs into a museum featuring photographs of famous people drinking champagne. And who are they? Perhaps members of today's royal houses, presidents or prime ministers, economic titans or Nobel Prize winners? Of course not. They are movie stars, almost all of them American—Marilyn Monroe to Clint Eastwood. The symmetry of the exhibition is obvious, the premise unmistakable: Hollywood stars, champions of consumption, are the royalty of this century, more popular by far than poor doomed Marie.

3   Hollywood is the global cultural capital—capital in both senses. The United States presides over a sort of World Bank of styles and symbols, an International Cultural Fund of images, sounds, and celebrities. The goods may be distributed by American-, Canadian-, European-, Japanese-, or Australian-owned multinational corporations, but their styles, themes, and images do not detectably change when a new board of directors takes over. Entertainment is one of America's top exports. In 1999, in fact, film, television, music, radio, advertising, print publishing, and computer software together *were* the top export, almost $80 billion worth, and while software alone accounted for $50 billion of the total, some of that category also qualifies as entertainment—video games and pornography, for example. Hardly anyone is exempt from the force of American images and sounds. French resentment of Mickey Mouse, Bruce Willis, and the rest of American civilization is well known. Less well known, and rarely acknowledged by the French, is the fact that *Terminator 2* sold 5 million tickets in France during the month it opened—with no submachine guns at the heads of the customers. The same culture minister, Jack Lang, who in 1982 achieved a moment of predictable notoriety in the United States for declaring that *Dallas* amounted to cultural imperialism, also conferred France's highest honor in the arts on Elizabeth Taylor and Sylvester Stallone. The point is not hypocrisy pure and simple but something deeper, something obscured by a single-minded emphasis on American power: dependency. American popular culture is the nemesis that hundreds of millions—perhaps billions—of people love, and love to hate. The antagonism and the dependency are inseparable, for the media flood—essentially American in its origin, but virtually unlimited in its reach—represents, like it or not, a common imagination.

4   How shall we understand the Hong Kong T-shirt that says "I Feel Coke"? Or the little Japanese girl who asks an American visitor in all innocence, "Is there really a Disneyland in America?" (She knows the one in Tokyo.) Or the experience of a German

television reporter sent to Siberia to film indigenous life, who after flying out of Moscow and then traveling for days by boat, bus, and jeep, arrives near the Arctic Sea where live a tribe of Tungusians known to ethnologists for their bearskin rituals. In the community store sits a grandfather with his grandchild on his knee. Grandfather is dressed in traditional Tungusian clothing. Grandson has on his head a reversed baseball cap.

5   American popular culture is the closest approximation today to a global lingua franca, drawing the urban and young in particular into a common cultural zone where they share some dreams of freedom, wealth, comfort, innocence, and power—and perhaps most of all, youth as a state of mind. In general, despite the rhetoric of "identity," young people do not live in monocultures. They are not monocular. They are both local and cosmopolitan. Cultural bilingualism is routine. Just as their "cultures" are neither hard-wired nor uniform, so there is no simple way in which they are "Americanized," though there are American tags on their experience—low-cost links to status and fun. Everywhere, fun lovers, efficiency seekers, Americaphiles, and Americaphobes alike pass through the portals of Disney and the arches of McDonald's wearing Levi's jeans and Gap jackets. Mickey Mouse and Donald Duck, John Wayne, Marilyn Monroe, James Dean, Bob Dylan, Michael Jackson, Madonna, Clint Eastwood, Bruce Willis, the multicolor chorus of Coca-Cola, and the next flavor of the month or the universe are the icons of a curious sort of one-world sensibility, a global semiculture. America's bid for global unification surpasses in reach that of the Romans, the British, the Catholic Church, or Islam; though without either an army or a God, it requires less. The Tungusian boy with the reversed cap on his head does not automatically think of it as "American," let alone side with the U.S. Army.

6   The misleadingly easy answer to the question of how American images and sounds became omnipresent is: American imperialism. But the images are not even faintly force-fed by American corporate, political, or military power. The empire strikes from inside the spectator as well as from outside. This is a conundrum that deserves to be approached with respect if we are to grasp the fact that Mickey Mouse and Coke are everywhere recognized and often enough *enjoyed*. In the peculiar unification at work throughout the world, there is surely a supply side, but there is not only a supply side. Some things are true even if multinational corporations claim so: there is demand.

7   What do American icons and styles mean to those who are not American? We can only imagine—but let us try. What young people graced with disposable income encounter in American television shows, movies, soft drinks, theme parks, and American-labeled (though not American-manufactured) running shoes, T-shirts, baggy pants, ragged jeans, and so on, is a way of being in the world, the experience of a flow of ready feelings and sensations bobbing up, disposable, dissolving, segueing to the next and the next after that. It is a quality of immediacy and casualness not so different from what Americans desire. But what the young experience in the video game arcade or the music megastore is more than the flux of sensation. They flirt with a loose sort of social membership that requires little but a momentary (and monetary) surrender. Sampling American goods, images, and sounds, they affiliate with an empire of

informality. Consuming a commodity, wearing a slogan or a logo, you affiliate with dis-affiliation. You make a limited-liability connection, a virtual one. You borrow some of the effervescence that is supposed to emanate from this American staple, and hope to be recognized as one of the elect. When you wear the Israeli version that spells *Coca-Cola* in Hebrew, you express some worldwide connection with unknown peers, or a sense of irony, or both—in any event, a marker of membership. In a world of ubiquitous images, of easy mobility and casual tourism, you get to feel not only local or national but global—without locking yourself in a box so confining as to deserve the name "identity."

8   We are seeing on a world scale the familiar infectious rhythm of modernity. The money economy extends its reach, bringing with it a calculating mentality. Even in the poor countries it stirs the same hunger for private feeling, the same taste for disposable labels and sensations on demand, the same attention to fash-ion, the new and the now, that cropped up earlier in the West. Income beckons; income rewards. The taste for the marketed spectacle and the media-soaked way of life spreads. The culture consumer may not like the American goods in particular but still acquires a taste for the media's speed, formulas, and frivolity. Indeed, the lightness of American-sponsored "identity" is central to its appeal. It imposes few burdens. Attachments and affiliations coexist, overlap, melt together, form, and re-form.

9   Marketers, like nationalists and fundamentalists, promote "identities," but for most people, the melange is the message. Traditional bonds bend under pressure from imports. Media from beyond help you have your "roots" and eat them, too. You can watch Mexican television in the morning and American in the afternoon, or graze between Kurdish and English. You can consolidate family ties with joint visits to Disney World—making Orlando, Florida, the major tourist destination in the United States, and the Tokyo and Marne-la-Vallée spin-offs massive attractions in Japan and France. You can attach to your parents, or children, by playing oldie mu-sic and exchanging sports statistics. You plunge back into the media flux, looking for—what? Excitement? Some low-cost variation on known themes? Some next new thing? You don't know just what, but you will when you see it—or if not, you'll change channels.

10   As devotees of Japanese video games, Hong Kong movies, and Mexican *telenovelas* would quickly remind us, the blends, juxtapositions, and recombinations of popular culture are not just American. American and American-based models, styles, and symbols are simply the most far-flung, successful, and consequential. In the course of a century, America's entertainment corporations succeeded brilliantly in cul-tivating popular expectations for entertainment—indeed, the sense of a *right* to be en-tertained, a right that belongs to the history of modernity, the rise of market economies and individualism. The United States, which began as Europe's collective fantasy, built a civilization to deliver the goods for playing, feeling, and meaning. Competitors ignore its success at their own peril, financial and otherwise. ■

**Laura
Carlsen**

Walmart vs. Pyramids

Laura Carlsen is the director of the Americas Program for the International Relations Center (formerly the Interhemispheric Resource Center), which provides policy analysis and options for economic policy involving North, Central, and South America. A graduate of Stanford University, in 1986 she received a Fulbright Scholarship to study the impact on women of the Mexican economic crisis. She continues to reside in Mexico City. Carlsen has also written about trade agreements and other economic issues impacting Mexico. The article reprinted below appeared in several places in October and November of 2004, including New York University's Global Beat Syndicate, the *Common Dreams* Web site (www. commondreams.org), and *Human Quest*, an academic journal of religion and philosophy.

The showdown is rife with symbolism. Walmart's expansion plans in Mexico have brought about a modern-day clash of passions and principles at the site of one of the earth's first great civilizations.

2   Several months ago Walmart, the world's largest retail chain, quietly began constructing a new store in Mexico—the latest step in a phenomenal takeover of Mexico's supermarket sector. But the expansion north of Mexico City is not just part of Walmart's commercial conquest of Mexico. It is infringing on the cultural foundations of the country. The new store is just 3,000 meters from the Pyramid of the Sun, the tallest structure in the ancient city of Teotihuacan.

3   The Teotihuacan Empire is believed to have begun as early as 200 B.C. Its dominion stretched deep into the heart of Mayan country in Guatemala and throughout present-day Mexico. At its peak, Teotihuacan was a thriving city of about 200,000 inhabitants, but the civilization declined in 700 A.D. under circumstances still shrouded in mystery.

4   Since then, other tribes and civilizations, including the Aztecs and contemporary Mexican society, have claimed the "City of the Gods" as their heritage. The grand human accomplishment it represents and the power of its architectural, historical and, for many, spiritual legacy is central to Mexico's history and culture.

5   While little is known for certain about the rise and fall of Teotihuacan, much is known about the rise of the Walmart empire. From a store in Rogers, Arkansas founded by the Walton brothers in 1962, the enterprise grew in the breathtakingly short period of 42 years into the world's largest company.

6   In Mexico, its conquest of the supermarket sector began by buying up the nation's extensive chain, Aurrerá, beginning in 1992. Today, with 657 stores, Mexico is home to more Walmarts and their affiliates than any other country outside the United States. Walmart is now Mexico's largest private employer, with over 100,000 employees. But recent studies in the United States, where resistance to the megastores has been growing, show that job creation is often job displacement, because Walmarts put local stores out of business, leading to net job losses.

7   Walmart has revolutionized the labor and business world by working cheap and growing big. Labor costs are held down through anti-union policies, the hiring of undocumented workers in the United States, alleged discrimination against women and persons with disabilities, and cutbacks in benefits. Prices paid suppliers are driven down by outsourcing competition. Buoyed by $244.5 billion dollars in annual net sales, the chain can afford to make ever deeper incursions into Mexico's retail sector.

8   A diverse group of local merchants, artists, actors, academics and indigenous organizations are leading the opposition, protesting that the store damages Mexico's rich cultural heritage. Through ceremonies, hunger strikes, demonstrations and press coverage, the movement to defend the site has kept the conflict in the public eye and heightened the public-opinion costs to WalMart. Now opponents have taken their concerns to the Mexican Congress and UNESCO.

9   Some ancient ruins have already been found on the store's new site, and Walmart construction workers told the national daily, *La Jornada,* that they had orders to hide any archaeological relics they found. Normally, the presence of relics requires that further excavation be carried out painstakingly or halted altogether. But the booming Walmart corporation clearly has no time for such delays.

10   The dispute in Teotihuacan today is not a battle between the past and the future. It is a struggle over a country's right to define itself. For defenders of the ancient site, the foremost symbol of the nation's cultural heritage also constitutes part of its contemporary integrity. Modern Mexico is still a country that defines itself by legends, and whose collective identity—unlike its neophyte northern neighbor—reaches back thousands of years.

11   In this context, Walmart is a symbol of the cultural insensitivity of rampant economic integration. While its actions may be technically legal, in the end Walmart could pay a high price for this insensitivity . . . and if there is anything Walmart hates, it is high prices.

Thomas Friedman

Why the World Is Flat

The online magazine *Wired* published the following interview in May 2005. Daniel Pink, the author of several books himself on globalization, as well as numerous articles in the *New York Times*, conducted the interview since he is a contributing editor for *Wired*. Friedman, author and syndicated columnist, is described fully in the introduction.

Thirty-five years ago this summer, the golfer Chi Chi Rodriguez was competing in his seventh U.S. Open, played that year at Hazeltine Country Club outside Minneapolis. Tied for second place after the opening round, Rodriguez eventually finished 27th, a few strokes ahead of such golf legends as Jack Nicklaus, Arnold Palmer, and Gary Player. His caddy for the tournament was a 17-year-old local named Tommy Friedman.

2   Rodriguez retired from golf several years later. But his caddy—now known as Thomas L. Friedman, foreign affairs columnist for *The New York Times* and author of the new book *The World Is Flat: A Brief History of the Twenty-First Century*—has spent his career deploying the skills he used on the golf course: describing the terrain, shouting warnings and encouragement, and whispering in the ears of big players. After ten years of writing his twice-weekly foreign affairs column, Friedman has become the most influential American newspaper columnist since Walter Lippmann.

3   One reason for Friedman's influence is that, in the mid-'90s, he staked out the territory at the intersection of technology, financial markets, and world trade, which the foreign policy establishment, still focused on cruise missiles and throw weights, had largely ignored. "This thing called globalization," he says, "can explain more things in more ways than anything else."

4   Friedman's 1999 book, *The Lexus and the Olive Tree: Understanding Globalization*, provided much of the intellectual framework for the debate. "The first big book on globalization that anybody actually read," as Friedman describes it, helped make him a fixture on the Davos-Allen Conference-Renaissance Weekend circuit. But it also made him a lightning rod. He's been accused of "rhetorical hyperventilation" and dismissed as an "apologist" for global capital. The columnist Molly Ivins even dubbed top-tier society's lack of concern for the downsides of globalization "the Tom Friedman Problem."

5   After 9/11, Friedman says, he paid less attention to globalization. He spent the next three years traveling to the Arab and Muslim world trying to get at the roots of the attack on the U.S. His columns on the subject earned him his third Pulitzer Prize. But Friedman realized that while he was writing about terrorism, he missed an even bigger story: Globalization had gone into overdrive. So in a three-month burst last year, he wrote *The World Is Flat* to explain his updated thinking on the subject.

6   Friedman enlisted some impressive editorial assistance. Bill Gates spent a day with him to critique the theory. Friedman presented sections of the book to the strategic planning unit at IBM and to Michael Dell. But his most important tutors were two Indians: Nandan Nilekani, CEO of Infosys, and Vivek Paul, a top executive at Wipro. "They were the guys who really cracked the code for me."

7   *Wired* sat down with Friedman in his office at the *Times'* Washington bureau to discuss the flattening of the world.

8   **WIRED: What do you mean the world is flat?**
FRIEDMAN: I was in India interviewing Nandan Nilekani at Infosys. And he said to me, "Tom, the playing field is being leveled." Indians and Chinese were going to compete for work like never before, and Americans weren't ready. I kept chewing over that phrase—"the playing field is being leveled"—and then it hit me: Holy mackerel, the world is becoming flat. Several technological and political forces have converged, and that has produced a global, Web-enabled playing field that allows for multiple forms of collaboration without regard to geography or distance—or soon, even language.

The 10 Great Levelers

1. **Fall of the Berlin Wall**
   The events of November 9, 1989, tilted the worldwide balance of power toward democracies and free markets.

2. **Netscape IPO**
   The August 9, 1995, offering sparked massive investment in fiber-optic cables.

3. **Work flow software**
   The rise of apps from PayPal to VPNs enabled faster, closer coordination among far-flung employees.

4. **Open-sourcing**
   Self-organizing communities, à la Linux, launched a collaborative revolution.

5. **Outsourcing**
   Migrating business functions to India saved money *and* a third world economy.

9   **So, we're talking about globalization enhanced by things like the rise of open source?**
This is Globalization 3.0. In Globalization 1.0, which began around 1492, the world went from size large to size medium. In Globalization 2.0, the era that introduced us to multinational companies, it went from size medium to size small. And then around 2000 came Globalization 3.0, in which the world went from being small to tiny. There's a difference between being able to make long distance phone calls cheaper on the Internet and walking around Riyadh with a PDA where you can have all of Google in your pocket. It's a difference in degree that's so enormous it becomes a difference in kind.

10   **Is that why the Netscape IPO is one of your "10 flatteners"? Explain.**
Three reasons. Netscape brought the Internet alive with the browser. They made the Internet so that Grandma could use it and her grandchildren could use it. The second thing that Netscape did was commercialize a set of open transmission protocols so that no company could own the Net. And the third is that Netscape triggered the dotcom boom, which triggered the dotcom bubble, which triggered the overinvestment of a trillion dollars in fiber-optic cables.

11   **Are you saying telecommunications trumps terrorism? What about September 11? Isn't that as important?**
There's no question flattening is more important. I don't think you can understand 9/11 without understanding flattening.

12   **This is probably the first book by a major foreign affairs thinker that talks about the world-changing effects of . . . supply chains.**
[*Friedman laughs.*]

6. Offshoring
Contract manufacturing elevated China to economic prominence.

7. Supply-chaining
Robust networks of suppliers, retailers, and customers increased business efficiency. See Walmart.

8. Insourcing
Logistics giants took control of customer supply chains, helping mom-and-pop shops go global. See UPS and FedEx.

9. In-forming
Power searching allowed everyone to use the Internet as a "personal supply chain of knowledge." See Google.

10. Wireless
Like "steroids," wireless technologies pumped up collaboration, making it mobile and personal.

13   **Why are supply chains so important?**
They're incredible flatteners. For UPS to work, they've got to create systems with customs offices around the world. They've got to design supply chain algorithms so when you take that box to the UPS Store, it gets from that store to its hub and then out. Everything they are doing is taking fat out of the system at every joint. I was in India after the nuclear alert of 2002. I was interviewing Vivek Paul at Wipro shortly after he'd gotten an email from one of their big American clients saying, "We're now looking for an alternative to you. We don't want to be looking for an alternative to you. You don't *want* us to be looking for an alternative to you. Do something about this!" So I saw the effect that India's being part of this global supply chain had on the behavior of the Indian business community, which eventually filtered up to New Delhi.

14   **And that's how you went from your McDonald's Theory of Conflict Prevention—two countries that have a McDonald's will never go to war with each other—to the Dell Theory of Conflict Prevention.**
Yes. No two countries that are both part of a major global supply chain like Dell's will fight against each other as long as they are both part of that supply chain. When I'm managing your back room, when I'm managing your HR, when I'm doing your accounting—that's way beyond selling you burgers. We are intimately in bed with each other. And that has got to affect my behavior.

15   **In some sense, then, the world is a gigantic supply chain. And you don't want to be the one who brings the whole thing down.**
Absolutely.

16   **Unless your goal is to bring the whole thing down. Supply chains work for al Qaeda, too, don't they?**
Al Qaeda is nothing more than a mutant supply chain. They're playing off the same platform as Wal-mart and Dell. They're just not restrained by it. What is al Qaeda? It's an open source religious political movement that works off the global supply chain. That's what we're up against in Iraq. We're up against a suicide supply chain. You take one bomber and deploy him in Baghdad, and another is manufactured in Riyadh the next day. It's exactly like when you take the toy off the shelf at Wal-Mart and another is made in Shen Zhen the next day.

17   **The book is almost dizzily optimistic about India and China, about what flattening will bring to these parts of the world.**
I firmly believe that the next great breakthrough in bioscience could come from a 15-year-old who downloads the human genome in Egypt. Bill Gates has a nice line: He says, 20 years ago, would you rather have been a B-student in Poughkeepsie or a genius in Shanghai? Twenty years ago you'd rather be a B-student in Poughkeepsie. Today?

18   **Not even close.**
Not even close. You'd much prefer to be the genius in Shanghai because you can now export your talents anywhere in the world.

19   **As optimistic as you are about that kid in Shanghai, you're not particularly optimistic about the US.**
I'm worried about my country. I love America. I think it's the best country in the world. But I also think we're not tending to our sauce. I believe that we are in what Shirley Ann Jackson [president of Rensselaer Polytechnic Institute] calls a "quiet crisis." If we don't change course now and

buckle down in a flat world, the kind of competition our kids will face will be intense and the social implications of not repairing things will be enormous.

20 **You quote a CEO who says that Americans have grown addicted to their high salaries, and now they're going to have to earn them. Are Americans suffering from an undue sense of entitlement?**
Somebody said to me the other day that—I wish I had this for the book, but it's going to be in the paperback—the entitlement we need to get rid of is our sense of entitlement.

21 **Let's talk about the critics of globalization. You say that you don't want the antiglobalization movement to go away. Why?**
I've been a critic of the antiglobalization movement, and they've been a critic of me, but the one thing I respect about the movement is their authentic energy. These are not people who don't care about the world. But if you want to direct your energy toward helping the poor, I believe the best way is not throwing a stone through a McDonald's window or protesting World Bank meetings. It's through local governance. When you start to improve local governance, you improve education, women's rights, transportation.

22 **It's possible to go through your book and conclude it was written by a US senator who wants to run for president. There's a political agenda in this book.**
Yes, absolutely.

23 **You call for portable benefits, lifelong learning, free trade, greater investment in science, government funding for tertiary education, a system of wage insurance. Uh, Mr. Friedman, are you running for president?**
[*Laughs loudly*.] No, I am not running for president!

24 **Would you accept the vice presidential nomination?**
I just want to get my Thursday column done!

25 **But you are outlining an explicit agenda.**
You can't be a citizen of this country and not be in a hair-pulling rage at the fact that we're at this inflection moment and nobody seems to be talking about the kind of policies we need to get through this flattening of the world, to get the most out of it and cushion the worst. We need to have as focused, as serious, as energetic, as sacrificing a strategy for dealing with flatism as we did for communism. This is the challenge of our day.

26 **Short of Washington fully embracing the Friedman doctrine, what should we be doing? For instance, what advice should we give to our kids?**
When I was growing up, my parents told me, "Finish your dinner. People in China and India are starving." I tell my daughters, "Finish your homework. People in India and China are starving for your job."

27 **Think about your own childhood for a moment. If a teenage Tommy Friedman could somehow have been transported to 2005, what do you think he would have found most surprising?**
That you could go to PGA.com and get the scores of your favorite golfer in real time. That would have been amazing.

ROBYN **MEREDITH** AND SUZANNE **HOPPOUGH**

Why Globalization Is Good

Robyn Meredith is author of the best-selling book *The Elephant and the Dragon: The Rise of India and China and What it Means for All of Us.* She and her colleague at *Forbes* magazine, Suzanne Hoppough, collaborated on the following excerpt from *The Elephant and the Dragon* and published it in *Forbes* on April 16, 2007.

A ragtag army of save-the-world crusaders has spent years decrying multinational corporations as villains in the wave of globalization overwhelming the Third World. This ominous trend would fatten the rich, further impoverish and oppress the poor, and crush local economies.

2 The business-bashing group Public Citizen argued as much in a proclamation signed by almost 1,500 organizations in 89 countries in 1999. Whereupon hundreds of protesters rioted outside a conference of the World Trade Organization in Seattle, shattering windows, blocking traffic, and confronting cops armed with tear gas and pepper spray. Six hundred people were arrested.

3 Cut to 2007, and the numbers are in: The protesters and do-gooders are just plain wrong. It turns out that globalization is good—and not just for the rich, but *especially* for the poor. The booming economies of India and China—the Elephant and the Dragon—have lifted 200 million people out of abject poverty in the 1990s as globalization took off, the International Monetary Fund says. Tens of millions more have catapulted themselves far ahead into the middle class.

4 It's remarkable what a few container ships can do to make poor people better off. Certainly more than $2 trillion of foreign aid, which is roughly the amount (with an inflation adjustment) that the U.S. and Europe have poured into Africa and Asia over the past half-century.

5 In the next eight years almost a billion people across Asia will take a Great Leap Forward into a new middle class. In China middle-class incomes are set to rise threefold, to $5,000, predicts Dominic Barton, a Shanghai managing partner for McKinsey & Co.

6 As the Chindia revolution spreads, the ranks of the poor get smaller, not larger. In the 1990s, as Vietnam's economy grew 6% a year, the number of people living in poverty (42 million) fell 7% annually; in Uganda, when GDP growth passed 3%, the number fell 6% per year, says the World Bank.

7 China unleashed its economy in 1978, seeding capitalism first among farmers newly freed to sell the fruits of their fields instead of handing the produce over to Communist Party collectives. Other reforms let the Chinese create 22 million new businesses that now employ 135 million people who otherwise would have remained peasants like the generations before them. Foreign direct investment, the very force so virulently opposed by the do-gooders, has helped drive China's gross domestic product to a more than tenfold increase since 1978. Since the reforms started, $600 billion has flooded into the country, $70 billion of it in the past year. Foreigners built hundreds of thousands of new factories as the Chinese government built the coal mines, power grid, airports, and highways to supply them.

8   As China built infrastructure, it created Special Economic Zones where foreign companies willing to build modern factories could hire cheap labor, go years without paying any taxes, and leave it to government to build the roads and other infrastructure they needed. All of that, in turn, drove China's exports from $970 million to $974 billion in three decades. Those container loads make Americans better off, too. You can get a Chinese DVD at Walmart for $28, and after you do you will buy some $15 movies made in the U.S.A.

9   Per-person income in China has climbed from $16 a year in 1978 to $2,000 now. Wages in factory boomtowns in southern China can run $4 a day—scandalously low in the eyes of the protesters, yet up from pennies a day a generation ago and far ahead of increases in living costs. Middle-class Chinese families now own TVs, live in new apartments, and send their children to private schools. Millions of Chinese have traded in their bicycles for motorcycles or cars. McDonald's has signed a deal with Sinopec, the huge Chinese gasoline retailer, to build drive-through restaurants attached to gas stations on China's new roads.

10   Today 254 Starbucks stores serve coffee in the land of tea, including one at the Great Wall and another at the Forbidden Palace. (The latter is the target of protesters.) In Beijing 54 Starbucks shops thrive, peddling luxury lattes that cost up to $2.85 a cup and paying servers $6 for an 8-hour day. That looks exploitative until you peek inside a nearby Chinese-owned teahouse where the staff works a 12-hour day for $3.75. Says one woman, 23, who works for an international cargo shipper in Beijing: "My parents were both teachers when they were my age, and they earned 30 yuan [$3.70] a month. I earn 4,000 yuan ($500) a month, live comfortably, and feel I have better opportunities than my parents did."

11   Tony Ma, age 51, was an unwilling foot soldier in Mao's Cultural Revolution. During that dark period from 1966 to 1976 universities were closed, and he was sent at age 16 to work in a steel mill for $2 a month. He cut metal all day long for seven years and feared he might never escape. When colleges reopened, he landed a spot to study chemistry, transferred to the U.S., got a Ph.D. in biochemistry, and signed on with Johnson & Johnson at $45,000 a year. Later he returned to the land he fled and now works for B.F. Goodrich in Hong Kong. The young college grads in China today wouldn't bother immigrating to the U.S. for a job that pays $45,000, he says—because now they have better opportunities at home.

12   Capitalism alone, however, isn't enough to remake Third World economies—globalism is the key. A big reason India trails behind its bigger neighbor to the northeast in lifting the lower classes is that, even after embracing capitalism, it kept barriers to the flow of capital from abroad. Thus 77% of Indians live on $2 a day or less, the Asian Development Bank says, down only nine percentage points from 1990. A third of the population is illiterate. In 1980 India had more of its population in urban centers than China did (23% versus 20% for China). But by 2005 China had 41% in cities, where wages are higher; India's urbanites had grown to only 29%.

13   Freed of British colonial rule in 1947 and scarred by its paternalistic effects, India initially combined capitalism with economic isolationism. It thwarted foreign companies intent on investing there and hampered Indian firms trying to sell abroad. This hurt Indian consumers and local biz: A $100 Microsoft operating system got slapped with duties that brought the price to $250 in India, putting imported software and computers

further from reach for most people and businesses. Meanwhile, the government granted workers lavish job protections and imposed heavy taxes and regulations on employers. Government jobs usually were by rote and paid poorly, but they guaranteed lifetime employment. They also ensured economic stagnation.

14   Financial crisis struck in 1991. Desperate for cash, India flew a planeload of gold reserves to London and began, grudgingly, to open its economy. Import duties were lowered or eliminated, so India's consumers and companies could buy modern, foreign-made goods and gear. Overseas firms in many industries were allowed to own their subsidiaries in India for the first time since 1977. India all but banned foreign investment until 1991. Since then foreign companies have come back, but not yet on the scale seen in China. Foreign companies have invested $48 billion in India since 1991—$7.5 billion of that just in the last fiscal year—the same amount dumped into China every six weeks. By the mid-1990s the economy boomed and created millions of jobs.

15   By the late 1990s U.S. tech companies began turning to India for software design, particularly in the Y2K crunch. The Indians proved capable and cheap, and the much-maligned offshoring boom began. Suddenly Indian software engineers were programming corporate America's computers. New college graduates were answering America's customer service phone calls. Builders hired construction workers to erect new high-rise buildings suddenly in demand as American and European firms rushed to hire Indian workers. The new college hires, whose older siblings had graduated without finding a job, tell of surpassing their parents' salaries within five years and of buying cell phones, then motorcycles, then cars and even houses by the time they were 30. All of that would have been impossible had India failed to add globalization to capitalism.

16   Today, despite its still dilapidated airports and pothole-riddled highways, the lumbering Elephant now is in a trot, growing more than 7% annually for the last decade. In 2005, borrowing from the Chinese, India began a five-year, $150 billion plan to update its roads, airports, ports, and electric plants. India is creating free trade zones, like those in China, to encourage exports of software, apparel, auto parts and more. S.B. Kutwal manages the assembly line where Tata Motors builds Safari SUVs. He remembers how, in the 1980s, people waited five years to buy a scooter and cars were only for the rich. "Since we've liberated the economy, lots of companies have started coming into India," says Kutwal. "People couldn't afford cars then. Now the buying power is coming."

17   In Mumbai (formerly Bombay), Delhi, Bangalore, and other big cities, shopping malls have sprung up, selling everything from Levi's jeans to Versace. India still has raggedy street touts, but when they tap on car windows at stoplights, instead of peddling cheap plastic toys, they sell to the new India: copies of *Vogue* and *House & Garden* magazines. Western restaurants are moving in, too: Domino's Pizza and Ruby Tuesday's have come to India, and 107 McDonald's have sprung up, serving veggie burgers in the land where cattle are sacred.

18   None of this gives pause to an entity called International Forum on Globalization. The group declares that globalism's aim is to "benefit transnational corporations over workers; foreign investors over local businesses; and wealthy countries over

developing nations. While promoters . . . proclaim that this model is the rising tide that will lift all boats, citizen movements find that it is instead lifting only yachts."

19   "The majority of people in rich and poor countries aren't better off" since the World Trade Organization formed in 1995 to promote global trade, asserts Christopher Slevin, deputy director of Global Trade Watch, an arm of Ralph Nader's Public Citizen. "The breadth of the opposition has grown. It's not just industrial and steel workers and people who care about animal rights. It includes high-tech workers and the offshoring of jobs, also the faith-based community."

20   While well-off American techies may be worried, it seems doubtful that an engineer in Bangalore who now earns $40,000 a year, and who has just bought his parents' house, wants to ban foreign investment.

21   Slevin's further complaint is that globalism is a creature of WTO, the World Bank and other unelected bodies. But no, the people do have a voice in the process, and it is one that is equivocal on the matter of free market capitalism. The Western World's huge agriculture subsidies—$85 billion or more annually, between the U.S., Japan, and the European Union—are decreed by democratically elected legislatures. The EU pays ranchers $2 per cow in daily subsidies, more than most Indians earn. If these farmers weren't getting handouts, and if trade in farm products were free, then poor farmers in the Third World could sell more of their output, and could begin to lift themselves out of poverty.

Sadanand Dhume

Slumdog Paradox

Sadanand Dhume is a writer who is based in Washington, D.C. Having lived in Asia from 1999 to 2004, he is an expert on Asian affairs and the author of *My Friend the Fanatic: Travels with a Radical Islamist*, a travel narrative about the rise of Muslim fundamentalism in Indonesia. His writing has been published in the *Washington Post, Forbes, Commentary,* and *YaleGlobal Online*, where the following essay appeared on February 9, 2009.

The unexpected international success of *Slumdog Millionaire* has pleased some Indians while provoking unusually strong protests from others. The critical and commercial success of the film, contrasted with sharp criticism and a lackluster run in Indian theaters, captures the inherent contradictions of an increasingly globalized country. India basks in the glow of international recognition, but resents the critical scrutiny that global exposure brings.

2   Not since Sir Richard Attenborough's *Gandhi* has a film about India captured the world's imagination as strongly as *Slumdog Millionaire*, director Danny Boyle's gritty yet uplifting drama about a boy from the slums of Mumbai who makes good as a game-show contestant on the Indian version of *Who Wants*

to Be a Millionaire. The low-budget production—which cost $15 million to make, a pittance in Hollywood terms—has garnered both commercial and critical success, grossing $96 million world-wide as of February 1st, and picking up four Golden Globe awards and 10 Oscar nominations. In one among a raft of glowing reviews, the *Wall Street Journal*'s Joe Morgenstern hailed *Slumdog* as "the world's first globalized masterpiece."

3   In India, however, the response to the film has been ambivalent. Commercially, it has failed to replicate its American success. Despite a wave of publicity and an ambitious nationwide rollout, *Slumdog* is showing in half-empty theaters. It trails the box-office receipts of an obscure Hindi horror movie released the same day. And though some Indian reviewers praised the film for everything from inspired casting to an improbable Bollywoodish storyline, it also attracted its share of brickbats. On his blog, Bollywood star Amitabh Bachchan struck a populist note: "If SM projects India as [a] third-world, dirty, underbelly developing nation and causes pain and disgust among nationalists and patriots, let it be known that a murky underbelly exists and thrives even in the most developed nations." The critic Meenakshi Shedde dismissed the film as "a laundry list of India's miseries." Interviewed in the *Los Angeles Times*, film professor Shyamal Sengupta called the film "a white man's imagined India."

Jamal Malik (Dev Patel) appears on the game show *Who Wants to Be a Millionaire?* in a scene from *Slumdog Millionaire* (2008).

4   In many ways, *Slumdog Millionaire* is a metaphor for India in the age of globalization. The director, Danny Boyle, and screenwriter, Simon Beaufoy, are British. The male lead, Dev Patel, who plays the part of the quiz-show contestant Jamal, is a Gujarati whose family migrated to London from Nairobi. His love interest, Latika, is played by Freida Pinto, a Catholic girl from Mumbai, India's most cosmopolitan city. The novel upon which the film is loosely based, *Q and A,* was written by an Indian diplomat currently stationed in South Africa. The television game show *Who Wants to Be a Millionaire,* which supplies the film's narrative backbone, is another British creation. Adapted in more than 50 countries, the show is recognizable to audiences from Beijing to Buenos Aires.

5   The film's success also underscores India's emergence on the world stage. Indeed, the superficial similarities with Ang Lee's *Crouching Tiger, Hidden Dragon,* the 2001 blockbuster set in Qing dynasty China, are striking. Both films draw on the talents of a widespread diaspora: Michelle Yeoh, Dev Patel. Like *Crouching Tiger, Slumdog* taps into Western curiosity about a country whose weight is increasingly felt in ordinary lives. Service workers in the West worry about being "Bangalored," or losing their jobs to less expensive competitors in India. Credit-card and consumer-appliance users routinely deal with customer-service professionals in Gurgaon or Hyderabad. In America, one no longer has to live in a big city to be familiar with yoga or chicken tikka masala. An Indian company, Tata Motors, owns the iconic automobile brands Jaguar and Land Rover. India-born professionals helm Pepsi and Citibank. Salman Rushdie and Jhumpa Lahiri occupy a similarly exalted place in fiction. To sum up, it seems unlikely that a story set in the slums of Manila or Jakarta would find nearly as large an audience in Boston or Baton Rouge.

6   For India, one of the most autarkic and culturally inward-looking countries in Asia until the advent of economic reforms in 1991, the benefits of globalization are easily apparent. In purchasing power parity terms, per capita income more than doubled from $1,400 in 1991 to $3,800 in 2006. The ranks of the middle class, broadly defined, have swelled to more than 250 million people. More Indians buy cell phones each month than any other people.

7   The same story can be told on the corporate and macroeconomic level. Since liberalization, a dozen Indian firms—spanning banking, pharmaceuticals, software, and services—have listed on the New York Stock Exchange, and three on the technology-heavy NASDAQ. The United Nations Conference on Trade and Development estimates that a record $36.7 billion of foreign direct investment flowed into India in 2008. Foreign-exchange reserves stand at a robust $250 billion.

8   There are less tangible changes as well. For generations after independence from Britain in 1947, more or less the only way for an Indian to make a mark on the world stage was to emigrate. A. R. Rahman, the Chennai-based composer of the *Slumdog* soundtrack, has not needed to change the color of his passport to snag a Golden Globe or multiple Oscar nominations. In a broader sense, the same holds true for many of the scientists and engineers who work for General Electric or Microsoft in Bangalore, or for the employees of a clutch of ambitious homegrown pharmaceutical companies with global ambition. India may not quite be center-stage—its contribution to world trade remains a slender 1.5 percent—but neither is it off-stage anymore. If an ambitious government target is met, the country's share of world trade will more than triple to 5 percent by 2020.

9   Notwithstanding the giant strides made over the past 18 years, Indian criticism of *Slumdog* also reveals the chasm between the country's self-perception and projection and any reasonable measure of its achievements. India may boast homegrown programs in space exploration and nuclear power, but—as a first time visitor to India immediately notices and as the film mercilessly reveals—it also struggles to provide its people with electricity, sanitation, and drinking water. About half of Indian women are illiterate, a higher percentage than in Laos, Cambodia, or Myanmar. It is at number 122—between Nepal and Lesotho—on the World Bank index that measures ease of doing business, and 85 on the global corruption index maintained by the anti-graft NGO Transparency International. To put it bluntly, the squalor of the slums depicted in *Slumdog* is closer to reality than an elaborately choreographed Bollywood dance sequence shot on location in Switzerland.

10   To sum up, by jettisoning socialism and embracing globalization India has become more prosperous than at any time in more than six decades of independence. But the effects of failed policies pursued between 1947 and 1991 cannot be erased overnight. As *Slumdog* reveals, India is doing better than ever only when benchmarked against its own dismal past. When compared to the West, or to East Asian countries that have truly transformed themselves—Japan, Taiwan, and Korea—the gap between India's rhetoric and its reality remains jarring. *Slumdog* may wound national pride, but the answer is more openness not less. As long as chronic poverty remains a central fact of Indian life, the spotlight that globalization brings will shine on India's software success as well as on its slums.

LANCE MORROW

Cowboys and Immigrants

The distinguished journalist Lance Morrow (born 1939) was a leading writer for *Time* magazine for three decades, but he is not really retired. He still contributes to CNN and to many publications. The following essay appeared in *Smithsonian* magazine in 2009.

At Fort Clark in West Texas one night in the 1870s, my great-grandmother Ella Mollen Morrow was asleep in the officers' quarters. Her husband, Maj. Albert Morrow, was several days' ride away, on patrol with his troop of Fourth U.S. Cavalry. A soldier, probably drunk, crawled into the house through a window. My great-grandmother heard him. She took up a Colt .44 revolver and warned him to get out. He kept coming at her. She warned him again. The man kept coming.

2   She shot him—"between the eyes," as a family history said, adding, "No inquiry was held, or deemed necessary."

3   That was the frontier, all right, and I confess that during the presidential campaign last fall, Sarah Palin—moose hunter, wilderness mom—stirred, for a moment anyway, a genetic current of admiration in my heart. It was an atavistic memory of Ella, of her self-sufficient smoking pistol and its brisk frontier justice, which, on that night in West Texas, pre-emptively brought the bad guy down, dead at her feet. No nonsense.

4   At the time, the McCain-Obama campaign seemed a clash of neat American opposites. John McCain (maverick, ex-fighter pilot, military hero, senator from Geronimo country), with his sidekick Palin (chirpy backwoods deadeye), worked the Frontier story line. Barack Obama came onstage as apotheosis, the multiracial, multicultural evolution of what Ellis Island promised to the Nation of Immigrants long ago.

Horses and men, ropes and dust: it's a scene from a prototypical Western movie.

5   But in the evolving financial shambles of the months since the election, the conflict between these mystic poles of American history appeared to vanish, or to dissolve in a chaotic nonideological synthesis. Both Ellis Island and the Frontier hated Wall Street, just as passengers in steerage and passengers in first-class unite in despising icebergs. And amid the great federal bailouts, *Newsweek* proclaimed, "We Are All Socialists Now."

6   I wonder. The Frontier and Ellis Island are myths of origin, alternate versions of the American Shinto. They're not likely to disappear anytime soon.

7   The two myths are sentimental and symbolic categories, no doubt—ideas or mere attitudes more than facts: facets of human nature. (Quite often, when given a hard look, myths fall apart: the historical frontier, for example, was demonstrably communitarian as well as individualist.) But like the philosopher Isaiah Berlin's Hedgehog and Fox or literary critic Philip Rahv's Paleface and Redskin, they offer convenient bins in which to sort out tendencies.

8   Both myths owe something of their vividness to Hollywood—one to the films of John Ford and John Wayne, for example, and the other to Frank Capra's parables of the common man. The Frontier is set on the spacious Western side of American memory—a terrain whose official masculinity made my great-grandmother's, and Palin's, Annie Oakley autonomies seem somehow bracing. On the other side (diverse, bubbling away in the "melting pot," vaguely feminine in some *gemütlich* nurturing sense) lies Ellis Island. If Frontier dramas call for big skies, open space and freedom, Ellis Island's enact themselves in cities; their emphasis is human, sympathetic, multilingual, and noisy, alive with distinctive cooking smells and old-country customs. The Frontier is big, open-ended, physically demanding, silent.

9   This bifurcation of American consciousness occurred with a certain chronological neatness—a development "unforeseen, though not accidental," as Trotsky might have said, working his eyebrows. Ellis Island opened for business in 1892 as the gateway for the first of some 12 million immigrants. One year later, the historian Frederick Jackson Turner delivered his "frontier thesis" before the American Historical Society at the World's Columbian Exposition in Chicago. When the Pacific Ocean halted the American frontier on the West

Emma Lazarus

The New Colossus

Emma Lazarus (1849–1887) wrote poetry and essays on a wide variety of topics. Her works were published in the best-known magazines of her time, and she became an influential figure in the rapidly changing New York art scene. She was born into a well-established Jewish family in New York City, was well educated, and worked to improve the conditions of Jews both at home and abroad by establishing programs to educate new immigrants and by founding the Society for the Improvement and Colonization of Eastern European Jews. Her most famous sonnet, reprinted here, was written in 1883 to help raise money for the Statue of Liberty Pedestal, and in 1903 it was engraved on a tablet within the pedestal on which the Statue of Liberty now stands.

Coast, Turner argued, the distinctive urgencies of American destiny closed down. But at just that moment, the East Coast opened up to a powerful flow of new immigrant energies.

10   In the years 1889–96, the gun-toting ranchman-intellectual Theodore Roosevelt published his four-volume history, *The Winning of the West*. The evolution of the Frontier mythology was in some ways an instinctive reaction against all those foreigners. Ellis Island made the Frontier feel claustrophobic, just as the arrival of sodbusters with their plows and fences would incense the free-range cattle people.

11   Starting with Teddy Roosevelt, these two American archetypes have reappeared from time to time as presidential styles and ideological motifs. T.R., the sickly New York City boy who repaired health and heart in the Dakota Badlands, was the first modern Frontier president. His dramatization of Frontier attitude occurred at the moment of the Spanish-American War, of Senator Albert Beveridge's triumphal jingo about "The March of the Flag." In 1899, sixteen of Teddy's Rough Riders joined Buffalo Bill Cody's touring Wild West show. Gaudy Wild Bill in fringed buckskins told an audience at the Trans-Mississippi Exposition in Omaha: "The whistle of the locomotive has drowned the howl of the coyote; the barb-wire fence has narrowed the range of the cow-puncher; but no material evidence of prosperity can obliterate our contribution to Nebraska's imperial progress."

12   But in Frontier rhetoric there was often a paradoxical note of elegy and loss, as if the toughest place and moment of the American story was also the most transient, most fragile. By 1918, the Old Bull Moose, reconciled to the Republican Party, was condemning the "social system . . . of every man for himself" and calling for worker's rights, public housing, and day care for the children of mothers working in factories. In nine months, he was dead.

13   The other Roosevelt, T.R.'s cousin Franklin, became the first Ellis Island president. He came to office not at a moment when America had seemed to triumph, but when it had seemed to fail. In myth, if not in fact, the Frontier sounded the bugle—cavalry to the rescue. Ellis Island's narrative began with Emma Lazarus' disconcerting, hardly welcoming phrases of abjection—"your tired, your poor . . . the wretched refuse . . . " Its soundtrack was the street sounds of the *pluribus*.

> Not like the brazen giant of Greek fame,
> With conquering limbs astride from land to land;
> Here at our sea-washed, sunset gates shall stand
> A mighty woman with a torch, whose flame
> 5 Is the imprisoned lightning, and her name
> Mother of Exiles. From her beacon-hand
> Glows world-wide welcome; her mild eyes command
> The air-bridged harbor that twin cities frame.
> "Keep, ancient lands, your storied pomp!" cries she
> 10 With silent lips. "Give me your tired, your poor,
> Your huddled masses yearning to breathe free,
> The wretched refuse of your teeming shore.
> Send these, the homeless, tempest-tost to me,
> I lift my lamp beside the golden door!" ∎

14   One of the things that made Lyndon Johnson interesting was that he so thoroughly embodied both the Frontier and Ellis Island—and tried to enact both, in the Great Society and in Vietnam. Perhaps it was the conflict between the two ideals that brought him down. A son of the Texas hill country, with its lingering folklore of the Alamo and of long-ago massacres under the Comanche moon, Johnson was also a New Deal Democrat and FDR protégé with all the activist-government Ellis Island instincts. In an interplay of Ellis and the Frontier, he actually tried to bomb Ho Chi Minh into submission while offering to turn Vietnam into a Great Society, full of New Deal projects (dams and bridges and electrification), if only Uncle Ho would listen to reason.

15   At the Democratic National Convention in 1984, the perfect Ellis Island man, Gov. Mario Cuomo of New York, conjured up a sweet America that originated in sepia photographs of ships arriving in New York Harbor, the vessels' rails crowded with the yearning faces of people from a dozen countries over there, at the instant of their rebirth, their entry into the American alchemy that would transform them and their children forever. "We speak for the minorities who have not yet entered the mainstream," this son of Italian immigrants proclaimed. "We speak for ethnics who want to add their culture to the magnificent mosaic that is America." He called up Ellis Island that summer of 1984 at the same moment Ronald Reagan of California convinced Americans that they were tall in the saddle again, riding into the sunshine of a new morning in America. The Frontier won that round, by a landslide.

16   Reagan personified the cowboy universe that sees itself as self-reliant, competent, freedom-loving, morally autonomous, responsible. He owned a ranch and wore cowboy clothes, and in the Oval Office he displayed a passel of sculptures of cowboys and Indians and bucking broncos. In Reagan's exercise room in the family quarters of the White House, his wife, Nancy, had hung a favorite Reagan self-image, a framed photograph showing him in bluejeans and work shirt and shield-size belt buckle and a

Thomas Bailey Aldrich

The Unguarded Gates

Thomas Bailey Aldrich (1836–1907) provides a poetic argument from the same time period as Emma Lazarus (his poem was published in 1895—two years after hers), but with a more guarded viewpoint. Aldrich was a prominent and prolific New England writer originally from Portsmouth, New Hampshire; his 1883 book An Old Town by the Sea *was an important regional book. Aldrich's 1870 novel* Story of a Bad Boy *served as one inspiration for Mark Twain's* Tom Sawyer.

Wide open and unguarded stand our gates.
And through them press a wild, a motley throng—
Men from the Volga and the Tartar steppes,
Featureless figures of the Hoang Ho,
5   Malayan, Seythian, Teuton, Kelt, and Slav,
Flying the Old World's poverty and scorn;

well-aged, handsomely crushed white cowboy hat: Reagan's eyes crinkle at the far horizon. The photo watched from the wall as President Reagan pumped iron.

17   George W. Bush put himself in the Reagan mold. Barack Obama's victory represented, among other things, a repudiation of the Frontier style of Bush and Dick Cheney, in favor of an agenda arising from the Ellis Island point of view, with its emphasis on collective social interests, such as health care and the environment. A civic paradigm seemed to have shifted, and a generational paradigm as well.

18   And yet the future (Obama's hopeful young constituency) found itself boomeranged back to the Great Depression. The simultaneous arrival of Obama and bad financial times elicited perhaps too many articles about Franklin Roosevelt and the New Deal. Implicitly, George W. Bush and the Frontier way of doing things seem as discredited today as Herbert Hoover seemed in 1933.

19   Newsweek's proclamation notwithstanding, my guess is that the categories of Ellis Island and the Frontier persist—but now, like so much else, have been globalized. In the 21st century, the division between the two mind-sets projects itself into McLuhan's misnamed "global village," which, more accurately, has become a planetary megacity with some wealthy neighborhoods (now not as wealthy as they thought they were) and vast slum districts—a megacity without police force or sanitation department. The messy municipal planet remains in many ways a frontier, a multicultural Dodge City or Tombstone (lawless, with shooting in the streets, dangerous with terrorism and nuclear possibilities, not a fit place for women and children) that has an Ellis Island aspiration to survive and prosper as the family of man.

20   The Frontier and Ellis Island analyze problems in different ways and arrive at different decisions. The Frontier assumes the drunken soldier is a rapist or murderer and shoots

These bringing with them unknown gods and rites,
Those tiger passions, here to stretch their claws.
In street and alley what strange tongues are these.
10 Accents of menace alien to our air,
Voices that once the tower of Babel knew!
O, Liberty, white goddess, is it well
To leave the gate unguarded? On thy breast
Fold sorrow's children, soothe the hurts of fate,
15 Lift the downtrodden, but with the hand of steel
Stay those who to thy sacred portals come
To waste the fight of freedom. Have a care
Lest from thy brow the clustered stars be torn
And trampled in the dust. For so of old
20 The thronging Goth and Vandal trampled Rome,
And where the temples of the Caesars stood
The lean wolf unmolested made her lair. ∎

him between the eyes. Ellis Island may see him as a confused fool and hope to talk him into a cup of coffee and a 12-step program. Roughly the same choices present themselves to a president: the planet is the Frontier; the planet is Ellis Island. Genius is the ability to hold two contradictory truths in the mind at the same time without going crazy.

Immigrant families on Ellis Island, 1900, waiting for a ferry to Manhattan.

FROM READING TO WRITING

1. Analyze the argument by Gitlin, Carlsen, or Morrow: how is that argument the product of its audience and purpose? How would the argument be presented differently if it were directed to a different readership or published in a different forum? How would the argument be different if it were rewritten on this very day? (See Chapter 7 for advice on rhetorical analysis.)

2. Examine the various photos, charts, and other illustration that accompany the selections in this chapter. What visual argument does each one make? (See Chapter 8 for guidance on analyzing visuals.)

3. Write your own argument about some aspect of globalization. Do you see its effects in your community?

4. Propose your own solution to a problem associated with globalization or immigration. (See Chapter 15 for advice on writing proposals.)

5. Are you an immigrant yourself, or the child (or grandchild) of an immigrant parent or two? Write a narrative argument related to immigration or globalization that is based on, and generalizes from, your personal experiences. (See Chapter 13 for advice on writing narrative arguments.)

6. What exactly is "globalization," anyway? Write an essay that defines the term in such a way that persuades readers to sympathize with it—or to oppose it. (See Chapter 10 for advice on writing definition arguments.)

7. Evaluate globalization, using data from secondary research (or your personal observations) to support your conclusions.

25 | Science and Ethics

The Ethics of Science and Technology

How does Siri meet—or not meet—your notions of what an electronic personal assistant might look like? What are some of the ethical concerns associated with having a talking phone that learns over time to know you better and anticipate your specific needs?

Item: In November 2004, couples with a family history of cancer were given an unusual permission by the Human Fertilization and Embryology Authority in Great Britain—they were allowed to select for human fertilization embryos free of cancer-causing genes. Critics immediately complained about this effort to create "designer babies." They drew comparisons with Adolph Hitler's interest in creating a "super-race" of genetically enhanced Aryans and raised concerns about the possibility that "better" human beings might have advantages over "natural" people.

Item: Early in 2005 in the United States, members of the National Academy of Sciences were finishing a recommendation report on the legal and ethical status of "chimeras"—hybrid creatures created by implanting one animal's stem cells into the fetal matter of a different species. Several living creatures have been "invented" and patented in recent years, raising the question of the possibility of others—mice with human brains? Pigs bioengineered to produce human blood? Or even a genetically plausible hybrid between humans and chimpanzees?

Item: One Thanksgiving Day, teenager Shawn Woolley committed suicide after (his mother claims) weeks of 12-hour stints playing the online role-playing game EverQuest addled his neurochemical condition. Do electronically mediated experiences like playing EverQuest—not to mention similar experiences that may soon make the transition from science fiction to reality—have mind-and-body effects on the human condition? What about the widespread use of Prozac and other mind-altering drugs: do they threaten to change our sense of what human

> "Twenty-first century technologies—genetics, nanotechnology, and robotics—are so powerful they can spawn whole new classes of accidents and abuses."
>
> —BILL JOY, SUN MICROSYSTEMS

nature is at its core? No wonder science fiction movies and narratives are so popular—characters like the Terminator (hybrids of human and nonhuman) seem possible in the not-so-very-distant future.

These three items, brought to our attention by Jeffrey Pruchnic, highlight some of the ethical issues related to science and technology that people are grappling with these days. Science and technology, as central enterprises in our culture, have always raised difficult moral and ethical questions. Science fiction stories and films have frequently addressed those same questions. Whether it is environmental protection (the subject of Chapter 22), medicine, genetic engineering (including stem cell research and cloning), animal rights, the teaching of evolution, computer technologies, space exploration, or military weapons technology, science and technology command our attention and our committed arguments because they challenge our assumptions about what is possible and push the limits of what we think of as ethical.

Contemporary Arguments

Many new technologies are calling into question "the nature of nature," including our human nature. Is the natural world really "natural" when genetic engineers construct new species of plants and animals? And what are we to make of scientific developments that offer the potential for tremendous human benefits if they also have the potential to change our very human natures? Here we include arguments on four especially important and compelling developments related to science and human nature.

The first is robotics. According to Bill Gates, robots have the potential to become as ubiquitous as computers—although he acknowledges that there are as many naysayers about today's robotics developments as there once were about the possibilities of bringing computers into nearly every home. In "A Robot in Every Home," Gates discusses the potential for robotics with enthusiasm, but detractors (represented here by Paul Marks) are raising questions about the ethics of replacing humans and human labor with robots and robotic labor. The rise of robotics lends an almost science-fiction quality to technology and gives rise in the popular imagination to sci-fi's greatest dreams and fears. Will robots turn on their creators, as Frankenstein turned on his or as *Battlestar Galactica*'s cylons turned on the human race? Or will they remain friendly as pets, like C3PO and R2D2?

The second new technology under watch is nanotechnology. MIT researcher K. Eric Drexler coined the term because *nano* literally means "one billionth": nanotechnology refers to the science of creating molecule-sized materials and machines. Occupying the space between biology and engineering, nanotechnologists promise to create new things that fundamentally change the ways we work and live. As *Spiderman, Star-Trek: The Next Generation,* and popular magazines such as *Forbes* and *Wired* all indicate, nanotechnology promises to be the Next Big Thing. Nano skin creams are on the market, nano-enhanced tennis balls are used in the Davis Cup, and microscopic silicon chips run computer games. More important, nanotechnologists are developing micromachines that might radically improve water quality, benefit agriculture, clean up toxic waste, or make obsolete our reliance on oil by improving the efficiency of solar power. Others might enter the human body to repair tissue. Nanomaterials hundreds of times stronger than steel might make possible ten-pound automobiles or airplanes.

But is nanotechnology safe? Could dangerous nanoparticles escape and cause great damage? And what about nanotechnology's implications for the way human beings think of themselves? Will nanotechnology widen the gap between haves and have-nots around the globe? Those very serious questions are raised here in an essay by Bill Joy and in an interview with Ralph C. Merkle.

Third, we invite you to meditate on medical ethics. How do we ethically balance the risks and responsibilities of tampering with "the natural"? No doubt you have read and heard a great deal about stem cell research because of highly publicized appeals on its behalf by very public people: Michael J. Fox (who suffers from Parkinson's disease), Christopher Reeve (the actor who

New scientific advances are creating new ethical issues for consideration. What are the ethical consequences of pursuing genetic engineering or creating robots with humanlike intelligence?

suffered paralyzing, ultimately fatal spine damage in a horseback riding accident), and Nancy Reagan (who cared for former President Ronald Reagan during his battle with Alzheimer's). Earlier in this book (pages 210–215) we published a debate between the former president's son, Ron Reagan, and Richard Doerflinger about the stem cell controversy. Here in this chapter we offer Nathaniel Hawthorne's famous short story "The Birth-mark" as an argument about medical ethics—as well as Sally Satel's essay on the ethics of selling human organs.

Finally, we close with an Issue in Focus, on genetically modified food—the fourth science-and-ethics controversy represented here. Perhaps you too have personal, moral, religious, or occupational reasons to be concerned about one or another of these controversies. Read the selections that follow with care—and then develop and express your own considered views.

BILL JOY

Why the Future Doesn't Need Us

Bill Joy is a cofounder of Sun Microsystems and was the chief scientist there until 2003. He played a major role in developing an early form of UNIX, a computer operating system, as well as other computer technologies, such as the JAVA programming language. "Why the Future Doesn't Need Us" appeared in the April 2000 issue of *Wired* magazine, a monthly periodical that covers cultural, political, and economic impacts of technology. The article, which expresses a surprisingly critical position on technology, created a large stir—see the interview with Ralph C. Merkle that follows this selection by Bill Joy.

From the moment I became involved in the creation of new technologies, their ethical dimensions have concerned me, but it was only in the autumn of 1998 that I became anxiously aware of how great are the dangers facing us in the 21st century. I can date the onset of my unease to the day I met Ray Kurzweil, the deservedly famous inventor of the first reading machine for the blind and many other amazing things.

2   Ray and I were both speakers at George Gilder's Telecosm conference, and I encountered him by chance in the bar of the hotel after both our sessions were over. I was sitting with John Searle, a Berkeley philosopher who studies consciousness. While we were talking, Ray approached and a conversation began, the subject of which haunts me to this day.

3   I had missed Ray's talk and the subsequent panel that Ray and John had been on, and they now picked right up where they'd left off, with Ray saying that the rate of improvement of technology was going to accelerate and that we were going to become robots or fuse with robots or something like that, and John countering that this couldn't happen, because the robots couldn't be conscious.

4   While I had heard such talk before, I had always felt sentient robots were in the realm of science fiction. But now, from someone I respected, I was hearing a strong

argument that they were a near-term possibility. I was taken aback, especially given Ray's proven ability to imagine and create the future. I already knew that new technologies like genetic engineering and nanotechnology were giving us the power to remake the world, but a realistic and imminent scenario for intelligent robots surprised me.

5   It's easy to get jaded about such breakthroughs. We hear in the news almost every day of some kind of technological or scientific advance. Yet this was no ordinary prediction. In the hotel bar, Ray gave me a partial preprint of his then-forthcoming book *The Age of Spiritual Machines,* which outlined a utopia he foresaw—one in which humans gained near immortality by becoming one with robotic technology. On reading it, my sense of unease only intensified; I felt sure he had to be understating the dangers, understating the probability of a bad outcome along this path.

6   I found myself most troubled by a passage detailing a *dys*topian scenario:

> First let us postulate that the computer scientists succeed in developing intelligent machines that can do all things better than human beings can do them. In that case presumably all work will be done by vast, highly organized systems of machines and no human effort will be necessary. Either of two cases might occur. The machines might be permitted to make all of their own decisions without human oversight, or else human control over the machines might be retained.
>
> If the machines are permitted to make all their own decisions, we can't make any conjectures as to the results, because it is impossible to guess how such machines might behave. We only point out that the fate of the human race would be at the mercy of the machines. It might be argued that the human race would never be foolish enough to hand over all the power to the machines. But we are suggesting neither that the human race would voluntarily turn power over to the machines nor that the machines would willfully seize power. What we do suggest is that the human race might easily permit itself to drift into a position of such dependence on the machines that it would have no practical choice but to accept all of the machines' decisions. As society and the problems that face it become more and more complex and machines become more and more intelligent, people will let machines make more of their decisions for them, simply because machine-made decisions will bring better results than man-made ones. Eventually a stage may be reached at which the decisions necessary to keep the system running will be so complex that human beings will be incapable of making them intelligently. At that stage the machines will be in effective control. People won't be able to just turn the machines off, because they will be so dependent on them that turning them off would amount to suicide.
>
> On the other hand it is possible that human control over the machines may be retained. In that case the average man may have control over certain private machines of his own, such as his car or his personal computer, but control over large systems of machines will be in the hands of a tiny elite—just as it is today, but with two differences. Due to improved techniques the elite will have greater control over the masses; and because human work will no longer be necessary the masses will be superfluous, a useless burden on the system. If the elite is ruthless they may simply decide to exterminate the mass of humanity. If they are humane they may use propaganda or other psychological or biological techniques to reduce the birth rate until the mass of humanity becomes extinct, leaving the world to the elite. Or, if the elite consists of soft-hearted liberals, they may decide

to play the role of good shepherds to the rest of the human race. They will see to it that everyone's physical needs are satisfied, that all children are raised under psychologically hygienic conditions, that everyone has a wholesome hobby to keep him busy, and that anyone who may become dissatisfied undergoes "treatment" to cure his "problem." Of course, life will be so purposeless that people will have to be biologically or psychologically engineered either to remove their need for the power process or make them "sublimate" their drive for power into some harmless hobby. These engineered human beings may be happy in such a society, but they will most certainly not be free. They will have been reduced to the status of domestic animals.[1]

7   In the book, you don't discover until you turn the page that the author of this passage is Theodore Kaczynski—the Unabomber. I am no apologist for Kaczynski. His bombs killed three people during a 17-year terror campaign and wounded many others. One of his bombs gravely injured my friend David Gelernter, one of the most brilliant and visionary computer scientists of our time. Like many of my colleagues, I felt that I could easily have been the Unabomber's next target.

8   Kaczynski's actions were murderous and, in my view, criminally insane. He is clearly a Luddite, but simply saying this does not dismiss his argument; as difficult as it is for me to acknowledge, I saw some merit in the reasoning in this single passage. I felt compelled to confront it.

9   Kaczynski's dystopian vision describes unintended consequences, a well-known problem with the design and use of technology, and one that is clearly related to Murphy's law—"Anything that can go wrong, will." (Actually, this is Finagle's law, which in itself shows that Finagle was right.) Our overuse of antibiotics has led to what may be the biggest such problem so far: the emergence of antibiotic-resistant and much more dangerous bacteria. Similar things happened when attempts to eliminate malarial mosquitoes using DDT caused them to acquire DDT resistance; malarial parasites likewise acquired multi-drug-resistant genes.[2]

10   The cause of many such surprises seems clear: The systems involved are complex, involving interaction among and feedback between many parts. Any changes to such a system will cascade in ways that are difficult to predict; this is especially true when human actions are involved.

11   I started showing friends the Kaczynski quote from *The Age of Spiritual Machines;* I would hand them Kurzweil's book, let them read the quote, and then watch their reaction as they discovered who had written it. At around the same time, I found Hans Moravec's book *Robot: Mere Machine to Transcendent Mind.* Moravec is one of the leaders in robotics research, and was a founder of the world's largest robotics research program, at Carnegie Mellon University. *Robot* gave me more material to try out on my friends—material surprisingly supportive of Kaczynski's argument. For example:

Biological species almost never survive encounters with superior competitors. Ten million years ago, South and North America were separated by a sunken Panama isthmus. South America, like Australia today, was populated by marsupial mammals, including pouched equivalents of rats, deers, and tigers. When the isthmus connecting North and South America rose, it took only a few thousand years for the northern placental species, with slightly more effective metabolisms and reproductive and nervous systems, to displace and eliminate almost all the southern marsupials.

In a completely free marketplace, superior robots would surely affect humans as North American placentals affected South American marsupials (and as humans have affected countless species). Robotic industries would compete vigorously among themselves for matter, energy, and space, incidentally driving their price beyond human reach. Unable to afford the necessities of life, biological humans would be squeezed out of existence.

There is probably some breathing room, because we do not live in a completely free marketplace. Government coerces nonmarket behavior, especially by collecting taxes. Judiciously applied, governmental coercion could support human populations in high style on the fruits of robot labor, perhaps for a long while.

12   A textbook dystopia—and Moravec is just getting wound up. He goes on to discuss how our main job in the 21st century will be "ensuring continued cooperation from the robot industries" by passing laws decreeing that they be "nice,"[3] and to describe how seriously dangerous a human can be "once transformed into an unbounded superintelligent robot." Moravec's view is that the robots will eventually succeed us—that humans clearly face extinction.

13   I decided it was time to talk to my friend Danny Hillis. Danny became famous as the cofounder of Thinking Machines Corporation, which built a very powerful parallel supercomputer. Despite my current job title of Chief Scientist at Sun Microsystems, I am more a computer architect than a scientist, and I respect Danny's knowledge of the information and physical sciences more than that of any other single person I know. Danny is also a highly regarded futurist who thinks long-term: four years ago he started the Long Now Foundation, which is building a clock designed to last 10,000 years, in an attempt to draw attention to the pitifully short attention span of our society.

14   So I flew to Los Angeles for the express purpose of having dinner with Danny and his wife, Pati. I went through my now-familiar routine, trotting out the ideas and passages that I found so disturbing. Danny's answer—directed specifically at Kurzweil's scenario of humans merging with robots—came swiftly, and quite surprised me. He said, simply, that the changes would come gradually, and that we would get used to them.

15   But I guess I wasn't totally surprised. I had seen a quote from Danny in Kurzweil's book in which he said, "I'm as fond of my body as anyone, but if I can be 200 with a body of silicon, I'll take it." It seemed that he was at peace with this process and its attendant risks, while I was not.

16   While talking and thinking about Kurzweil, Kaczynski, and Moravec, I suddenly remembered a novel I had read almost 20 years ago—*The White Plague,* by Frank Herbert—in which a molecular biologist is driven insane by the senseless murder of his family. To seek revenge he constructs and disseminates a new and highly contagious plague that kills widely but selectively. (We're lucky Kaczynski was a mathematician, not a molecular biologist.) I was also reminded of the Borg of *Star Trek,* a hive of partly biological, partly robotic creatures with a strong destructive streak. Borg-like disasters are a staple of science fiction, so why hadn't I been more concerned about such robotic dystopias earlier? Why weren't other people more concerned about these nightmarish scenarios?

17   Part of the answer certainly lies in our attitude toward the new—in our bias toward instant familiarity and unquestioning acceptance. Accustomed to living with almost routine scientific breakthroughs, we have yet to come to terms with the fact that the most compelling 21st-century technologies—robotics, genetic engineering, and nanotechnology—pose a different threat than the technologies that have come before. Specifically, robots, engineered organisms, and nanobots share a dangerous amplifying factor: They can self-replicate. A bomb is blown up only once—but one bot can become many, and quickly get out of control.

18   Much of my work over the past 25 years has been on computer networking, where the sending and receiving of messages creates the opportunity for out-of-control replication. But while replication in a computer or a computer network can be a nuisance, at worst it disables a machine or takes down a network or network service. Uncontrolled self-replication in these newer technologies runs a much greater risk: a risk of substantial damage in the physical world.

19   Each of these technologies also offers untold promise: the vision of near immortality that Kurzweil sees in his robot dreams drives us forward; genetic engineering may soon provide treatments, if not outright cures, for most diseases; and nanotechnology and nanomedicine can address yet more ills. Together they could significantly extend our average life span and improve the quality of our lives. Yet, with each of these technologies, a sequence of small, individually sensible advances leads to an accumulation of great power and, concomitantly, great danger.

20   What was different in the 20th century? Certainly, the technologies underlying the weapons of mass destruction (WMD)—nuclear, biological, and chemical (NBC)—were powerful, and the weapons an enormous threat. But building nuclear weapons required, at least for a time, access to both rare—indeed, effectively unavailable—raw materials and highly protected information; biological and chemical weapons programs also tended to require large-scale activities.

21   The 21st-century technologies—genetics, nanotechnology, and robotics (GNR)—are so powerful that they can spawn whole new classes of accidents and abuses. Most dangerously, for the first time, these accidents and abuses are widely within the reach of individuals or small groups. They will not require large facilities or rare raw materials. Knowledge alone will enable the use of them.

22   Thus we have the possibility not just of weapons of mass destruction but of knowledge-enabled mass destruction (KMD), this destructiveness hugely amplified by the power of self-replication.

23   I think it is no exaggeration to say we are on the cusp of the further perfection of extreme evil, an evil whose possibility spreads well beyond that which weapons of mass destruction bequeathed to the nation-states, on to a surprising and terrible empowerment of extreme individuals.

II

24   Nothing about the way I got involved with computers suggested to me that I was going to be facing these kinds of issues.

25   My life has been driven by a deep need to ask questions and find answers. When I was 3, I was already reading, so my father took me to the elementary school, where I sat on the principal's lap and read him a story. I started school early, later skipped a

grade, and escaped into books—I was incredibly motivated to learn. I asked lots of questions, often driving adults to distraction.

26   As a teenager I was very interested in science and technology. I wanted to be a ham radio operator but didn't have the money to buy the equipment. Ham radio was the Internet of its time: very addictive, and quite solitary. Money issues aside, my mother put her foot down—I was not to be a ham; I was antisocial enough already.

27   I may not have had many close friends, but I was awash in ideas. By high school, I had discovered the great science fiction writers. I remember especially Heinlein's *Have Spacesuit Will Travel* and Asimov's *I, Robot,* with its Three Laws of Robotics. I was enchanted by the descriptions of space travel, and wanted to have a telescope to look at the stars; since I had no money to buy or make one, I checked books on telescope-making out of the library and read about making them instead. I soared in my imagination.

28   Thursday nights my parents went bowling, and we kids stayed home alone. It was the night of Gene Roddenberry's original *Star Trek,* and the program made a big impression on me. I came to accept its notion that humans had a future in space, Western-style, with big heroes and adventures. Roddenberry's vision of the centuries to come was one with strong moral values, embodied in codes like the Prime Directive: to not interfere in the development of less technologically advanced civilizations. This had an incredible appeal to me; ethical humans, not robots, dominated this future, and I took Roddenberry's dream as part of my own.

29   I excelled in mathematics in high school, and when I went to the University of Michigan as an undergraduate engineering student I took the advanced curriculum of the mathematics majors. Solving math problems was an exciting challenge, but when I discovered computers I found something much more interesting: a machine into which you could put a program that attempted to solve a problem, after which the machine quickly checked the solution. The computer had a clear notion of correct and

Science fiction has long toyed with the question of what will happen if robots advance to human (or even above human) reasoning ability. In this film still from *I, Robot,* we see Sonny, a robot with both intelligence and free will.

incorrect, true and false. Were my ideas correct? The machine could tell me. This was very seductive.

30   I was lucky enough to get a job programming early supercomputers and discovered the amazing power of large machines to numerically simulate advanced designs. When I went to graduate school at UC Berkeley in the mid-1970s, I started staying up late, often all night, inventing new worlds inside the machines. Solving problems. Writing the code that argued so strongly to be written.

31   In *The Agony and the Ecstasy,* Irving Stone's biographical novel of Michelangelo, Stone described vividly how Michelangelo released the statues from the stone, "breaking the marble spell," carving from the images in his mind.[4] In my most ecstatic moments, the software in the computer emerged in the same way. Once I had imagined it in my mind I felt that it was already there in the machine, waiting to be released. Staying up all night seemed a small price to pay to free it—to give the ideas concrete form.

32   After a few years at Berkeley I started to send out some of the software I had written—an instructional Pascal system, Unix utilities, and a text editor called vi (which is still, to my surprise, widely used more than 20 years later)—to others who had similar small PDP-11 and VAX minicomputers. These adventures in software eventually turned into the Berkeley version of the Unix operating system, which became a personal "success disaster"—so many people wanted it that I never finished my PhD. Instead I got a job working for Darpa putting Berkeley Unix on the Internet and fixing it to be reliable and to run large research applications well. This was all great fun and very rewarding. And, frankly, I saw no robots here, or anywhere near.

33   Still, by the early 1980s, I was drowning. The Unix releases were very successful, and my little project of one soon had money and some staff, but the problem at Berkeley was always office space rather than money—there wasn't room for the help the project needed, so when the other founders of Sun Microsystems showed up I jumped at the chance to join them. At Sun, the long hours continued into the early days of workstations and personal computers, and I have enjoyed participating in the creation of advanced microprocessor technologies and Internet technologies such as Java and Jini.

34   From all this, I trust it is clear that I am not a Luddite. I have always, rather, had a strong belief in the value of the scientific search for truth and in the ability of great engineering to bring material progress. The Industrial Revolution has immeasurably improved everyone's life over the last couple hundred years, and I always expected my career to involve the building of worthwhile solutions to real problems, one problem at a time.

35   I have not been disappointed. My work has had more impact than I had ever hoped for and has been more widely used than I could have reasonably expected. I have spent the last 20 years still trying to figure out how to make computers as reliable as I want them to be (they are not nearly there yet) and how to make them simple to use (a goal that has met with even less relative success). Despite some progress, the problems that remain seem even more daunting.

36   But while I was aware of the moral dilemmas surrounding technology's consequences in fields like weapons research, I did not expect that I would confront such issues in my own field, or at least not so soon.

37   Perhaps it is always hard to see the bigger impact while you are in the vortex of a change. Failing to understand the consequences of our inventions while we are in the rapture of discovery and innovation seems to be a common fault of scientists and technologists; we have long been driven by the overarching desire to know that is the nature of science's quest, not stopping to notice that the progress to newer and more powerful technologies can take on a life of its own.

38   I have long realized that the big advances in information technology come not from the work of computer scientists, computer architects, or electrical engineers, but from that of physical scientists. The physicists Stephen Wolfram and Brosl Hasslacher introduced me, in the early 1980s, to chaos theory and nonlinear systems. In the 1990s, I learned about complex systems from conversations with Danny Hillis, the biologist Stuart Kauffman, the Nobel-laureate physicist Murray Gell-Mann, and others. Most recently, Hasslacher and the electrical engineer and device physicist Mark Reed have been giving me insight into the incredible possibilities of molecular electronics.

39   In my own work, as codesigner of three microprocessor architectures—SPARC, picoJava, and MAJC—and as the designer of several implementations thereof, I've been afforded a deep and firsthand acquaintance with Moore's law. For decades, Moore's law has correctly predicted the exponential rate of improvement of semiconductor technology. Until last year I believed that the rate of advances predicted by Moore's law might continue only until roughly 2010, when some physical limits would begin to be reached. It was not obvious to me that a new technology would arrive in time to keep performance advancing smoothly.

40   But because of the recent rapid and radical progress in molecular electronics—where individual atoms and molecules replace lithographically drawn transistors—and related nanoscale technologies, we should be able to meet or exceed the Moore's law rate of progress for another 30 years. By 2030, we are likely to be able to build machines, in quantity, a million times as powerful as the personal computers of today—sufficient to implement the dreams of Kurzwell and Moravec.

41   As this enormous computing power is combined with the manipulative advances of the physical sciences and the new, deep understandings in genetics, enormous transformative power is being unleashed. These combinations open up the opportunity to completely redesign the world, for better or worse: The replicating and evolving processes that have been confined to the natural world are about to become realms of human endeavor.

42   In designing software and microprocessors, I have never had the feeling that I was designing an intelligent machine. The software and hardware is so fragile and the capabilities of the machine to "think" so clearly absent that, even as a possibility, this has always seemed very far in the future.

43   But now, with the prospect of human-level computing power in about 30 years, a new idea suggests itself: that I may be working to create tools which will enable the construction of the technology that may replace our species. How do I feel about this? Very uncomfortable. Having struggled my entire career to build reliable software

systems, it seems to me more than likely that this future will not work out as well as some people may imagine. My personal experience suggests we tend to overestimate our design abilities.

44   Given the incredible power of these new technologies, shouldn't we be asking how we can best coexist with them? And if our own extinction is a likely, or even possible, outcome of our technological development, shouldn't we proceed with great caution?

Notes

[1] The passage Kurzweil quotes is from Kaczynski's "Unabomber Manifesto," which was published jointly, under duress, by the *New York Times* and the *Washington Post* to attempt to bring his campaign of terror to an end. I agree with David Gelernter, who said about their decision:

"It was a tough call for the newspapers. To say yes would be giving in to terrorism, and for all they knew he was lying anyway. On the other hand, to say yes might stop the killing. There was also a chance that someone would read the tract and get a hunch about the author; and that is exactly what happened. The suspect's brother read it, and it rang a bell.

"I would have told them not to publish. I'm glad they didn't ask me. I guess."

(*Drawing Life: Surviving the Unabomber.* Free Press, 1997: 120.)

[2] Garrett, Laurie. *The Coming Plague: Newly Emerging Diseases in a World Out of Balance.* Penguin, 1994. 47–52, 414, 419, 452.

[3] Isaac Asimov described what became the most famous view of ethical rules for robot behavior in his book *I, Robot* in 1950, in his Three Laws of Robotics: 1. A robot may not injure a human being, or, through inaction, allow a human being to come to harm. 2. A robot must obey the orders given it by human beings, except where such orders would conflict with the First Law. 3. A robot must protect its own existence, as long as such protection does not conflict with the First or Second Law.

[4] Michelangelo wrote a sonnet that begins:

Non ha l' ottimo artista alcun concetto
Ch' un marmo solo in sΠ non circonscriva
Col suo soverchio; e solo a quello arriva
La man che ubbidisce all' intelleto.

Stone translates this as:

The best of artists hath no thought to show
which the rough stone in its superfluous shell
doth not include; to break the marble spell
is all the hand that serves the brain can do.

Stone describes the process: "He was not working from his drawings or clay models; they had all been put away. He was carving from the images in his mind. His eyes and hands knew where every line, curve, mass must emerge, and at what depth in the heart of the stone to create the low relief."

(*The Agony and the Ecstasy.* Doubleday, 1961: 6, 144.)

Ralph C. Merkle

Nanotechnology: Designs for the Future

Ubiquity is a Web-based publication of the Association for Computing Machinery focusing on a variety of issues related to the information technology industry. In 2000, *Ubiquity* interviewed Ralph C. Merkle, a former research scientist at Xerox Parc; advisor at the Foresight Institute; and at the time a nanotechnology theorist at Zyvex, a nanotechnology research and development company. Merkle's main research interests are nanotechnology (also called molecular manufacturing), cryptography, and cryonics. He served as executive editor of the journal *Nanotechnology* for several years. In 1998, Merkle won the Feynman Prize in *Nanotechnology* for his theoretical work. As you will see, the interview excerpted below is partly in response to Bill Joy's "Why the Future Doesn't Need Us," the first selection in this chapter.

UBIQUITY: Bill Joy's recent *Wired* article on the perils of today's advanced technologies—including nanotechnology—has certainly received a lot of attention, and we did a follow-up interview with him in *Ubiquity*. What are your thoughts on that subject?

2 RALPH C.: Well, certainly the idea that nanotechnology would raise concerns
MERKLE: is something that actually was a major impetus for the founding of the Foresight Institute back in 1986—and by 1989, Foresight had its first technical conference on nanotechnology, and in fact Bill Joy spoke at that meeting. So one of the things that's a bit surprising is that Bill's concerns about nanotechnology seem to be quite recent—just the last year or two—even though the understanding that this particular technology was going to be very powerful and would raise significant concerns has been around for at least a couple of decades.

3 UBIQUITY: Why don't you take a moment now to tell us about the Foresight Institute?

4 MERKLE: The Foresight Institute (www.foresight.org/guidelines/index.html) was created primarily to guide the development of nanotechnology, and it was founded in large part because, when you look at where the technology is going, you reach the conclusion that, though it has great potential for good, there are also some concerns which need to be addressed. We've been having a series of gatherings at Foresight now for some years where Senior Associates (people who have pledged to support the Foresight Institute) can get together informally and off the record and discuss the various issues.

5 UBIQUITY: What are the meetings like?

6 MERKLE: The most recent gathering had over 250 people—including Bill Joy, as a matter of fact—and one of the sessions was a discussion of the Foresight guidelines for safe development of nanotechnology. A year and a half ago we had a workshop where we discussed the guidelines and

worked out an initial draft, which was discussed at the 1999 gathering at Foresight, and then further modified and updated and then discussed again at the most recent gathering.

7   UBIQUITY: What do you think would explain the sudden increase of concern about this?

8   MERKLE: Well, I can't really address the specifics of Bill Joy's situation. I do know that nanotechnology is an idea that most people simply didn't believe, even though the roots of it go back to a lecture by Richard Feynman in 1959 (www.zyvex.com/nanotech/feynman.html). That was a very famous talk in which he basically said the laws of physics should allow us to arrange things molecule by molecule and even atom by atom, and that at some point it was inevitable that we would develop a technology that would let us do this. I don't think that it was taken very seriously at that time, but as the years progressed it gradually began to be more accepted. If you think the technology is infeasible, you don't worry about what it might do and what its potential is. However, as you begin to internalize the fact that this technology is going to arrive and that we are going to have a very powerful manufacturing technology that will let us build a wide range of remarkable new products, then one of the things that arises is a concern that this new set of capabilities could create new problems, new concerns, and that these should be addressed.

9   UBIQUITY: But not the way Bill Joy is addressing them?

10   MERKLE: One of the things about Bill Joy's original article that concerned me is that he was calling for a relinquishment, as he put it, of research—and I think that's a *very* foolish strategy. If you look at the various strategies available for dealing with a new technology, sticking your head in the sand is not the most plausible strategy and in fact actually makes the situation more dangerous.

11   UBIQUITY: Why so?

12   MERKLE: For at least three reasons. The first, of course, is that we need to have a collective understanding of the new technology in order to ensure that we develop it appropriately. The second reason is that the new technologies that we see coming will have major benefits, and will greatly alleviate human suffering. The third reason is that, if we attempt to block the development of new technology, if we collectively try and say, "These technologies are technologies that are not meant for humans to understand," and we try to back away from them, what we effectively have done is not to block the technologies, we have simply ensured that the most responsible parties will not develop them.

13   UBIQUITY: So you think "relinquishment" is exactly the wrong strategy.

14   MERKLE: Right. Those people who pay no attention to a call for relinquishment, and in particular those people who are least inclined to be concerned about safe development will, in fact, be the groups that eventually develop the technology. In other words, a relinquishment of the new technology, unless it is absolutely 100 percent effective, is not effective at all. If it's 99.99 percent effective, then you simply ensure that the .01 percent

who pays no attention to such calls for relinquishment is the group that will develop it. And that actually creates a worse outcome than if the responsible players move forward and develop the technology with the best understanding that they have and the best efforts to ensure that the technology is developed in a safe and responsible fashion.

15 UBIQUITY: Let's go back to the second reason and expand on that to the extent of enumerating what you consider are the most prominent hopes that it offers.

16 MERKLE: Well, certainly what we see today is an entire planet, which has many limitations. I'm not quite sure how to express it, but certainly if you look at the human condition today, not everyone is well fed. Not everyone has access to good medical care. Not everyone has the basics—the physical basics that provide for a healthy and a happy life. And clearly, if you have a lower cost manufacturing technology, which can build a wide range of products less expensively, it can build, among other things, better medical products. Disease and ill health are caused largely by damage at the molecular and cellular level, yet today's surgical tools are too large to deal with that kind of problem. A molecular manufacturing technology will let us build molecular surgical tools, and those tools will, for the first time, let us directly address the problems at the very root level. So today we see a human population of over six billion people, many of whom have serious medical conditions, which either can't be treated or cannot be treated economically. In other words, we don't have the resources to effectively treat all the conditions that we see. If we can reduce the cost and improve the quality of medical technology through advances in nanotechnology, then we can more widely address the medical conditions that are prevalent and reduce the level of human

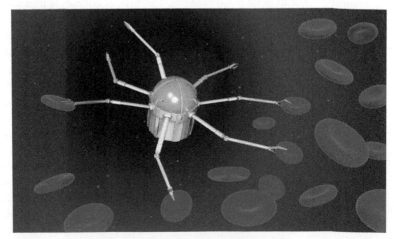

In this conceptualization, a nanobot works with and carries red blood cells.

suffering. (See www.foresight.org/Nanomedicine for more information about medical applications.)

17   UBIQUITY: And besides the opportunities in medicine? What else?

18   MERKLE: On another level, food; the simple process of feeding the human population. Today because of technological limits there is a certain amount of food that we can produce per acre. If we were to have intensive greenhouse agriculture, which would be something we could do economically, if we could economically manufacture the appropriate computer controlled enclosures that would provide protection and would provide a very controlled environment for the growth of food we could have much higher production. It looks as though yields of over 10 times what we can currently grow per acre are feasible if you control, for example, the CO_2 concentration, the humidity, the temperature, all the various factors that plants depend on to grow rapidly. If we control those, if we make those optimal for the growth of various crops then we can grow more per acre. And furthermore, we can grow it less expensively because molecular manufacturing technology is inherently low cost, and therefore it will let us grow more food more easily.

19   UBIQUITY: What are the implications?

20   MERKLE: The first is that it makes food less expensive. The second is that many of the people in the world today who are starving are not starving because there is an inherent inability to produce food, they are starving because they are caught in the middle of political fights and blockades that have been used as political weapons. As a consequence, food is available but it cannot be shipped into an area and so the people in that area suffer the consequences. However, if you have a distributed manufacturing technology, one of the great advantages is that it should let us have a much lower cost infrastructure. In other words, today manufacturing takes place in very large facilities. If you want to build, for example, a computer chip, you need a giant semiconductor fabrication facility. But if you look at nature, nature can grow complex molecular machines using nothing more than a plant.

21   UBIQUITY: Example?

22   MERKLE: Well, a potato, for example, can grow quite easily on a very small plot of land. With molecular manufacturing, in a similar fashion, we'll be able to have distributed manufacturing, which will permit manufacturing at the site using technologies that are low cost and easily available once the core technology has been developed. And as a consequence, you would have people able to build low-cost greenhouse agriculture tools even if there were a blockade because the manufacturing facilities would be widely distributed, and therefore they could avoid the blockade by simply making what they need inside the blockaded region using cheap raw materials and sunlight.

23   UBIQUITY: And if nanotechnology did so much for people's health and food production, what would it do, do you suppose, for their current economic

institution? Would it transition to large-scale nanotechnology? Have un-intended consequences in terms of disrupting the economy?

24   MERKLE: I think we would see changes in the economy. Previous technologies have made major changes. Old companies that have had major advantages in the past certainly find those advantages go away. Certainly as manufacturing becomes less expensive, then today's major manufacturing companies would find that they would be at a disadvantage in the future. Other companies that are producing intellectual products, software companies or companies that are not dealing with material objects—banks and financial institutions, for example—fundamentally are dealing with a flow of information so would be relatively less affected. I think you would see some major shifts in the economy in that manufacturing companies would find that what they were doing was either greatly changed or outright replaced. As in any technological revolution, there will be winners and losers. On balance, everyone will come out ahead, although there will be specific instances where particular companies will have major problems, and in fact, will simply not be able to cope with a new environment and presumably suffer the consequences.

25   UBIQUITY: What about the competition between different countries? Would, for example, the severely underdeveloped countries have an ability to do very rapid catch-up?

26   MERKLE: Yes. I think they would. Also, you have to remember that we are looking at a future where to a first approximation everyone is wealthy. Now, there are certain things that are inherently scarce. For example, there is only a certain amount of beachfront property in California. It is going to be scarce, it is going to be expensive, and only a small percentage of the population will be able to afford it. But if you look at other material possessions—housing or electronics—you find that the only limitation is our ability to manufacture them inexpensively. So the first approximation in this future that we're looking at is that everyone will be physically well off. They will have a great abundance in material goods, and as a consequence, I think that will soften and ease some of the conflicts that we see now. One of the issues facing us today is that there are countries where there is a serious lack of resources, the standards of living are very low, and as a consequence this creates a fundamental unease and discomfort in entire populations. If you have a higher standard of living, at least that source of conflict will be greatly reduced. Now, as we all know, there are many potential sources of conflict in the world, but even easing some of them will be very helpful.

27   UBIQUITY: Give us an example of a product that would be improved using molecular manufacturing?

28   MERKLE: The answer that comes most readily to mind is diamonds. Diamond has a better strength-to-weight ratio than steel or aluminum. Its strength-to-weight ratio is more than 50 times that of steel or aluminum alloy. So, it's much stronger and much lighter. If we had a shatterproof variant of diamond, we would have a remarkably light and strong material from which

to make all of the products in the world around us. In particular, aerospace products—airplanes or rockets—would benefit immensely from having lighter, stronger materials. So one of the things that we can say with confidence is that we will have much lighter, much stronger materials, and this will reduce the cost of air flight, and it will reduce the cost of rockets. It will let us go into space for literally orders of magnitude lower cost.

29   UBIQUITY: Has NASA shown any interest in this?

30   MERKLE: Needless to say, they are pursuing research in nanotechnology with the idea of having lighter, stronger materials as one of the significant objectives. There is a whole range of other capabilities, of course, that would be of interest in NASA. For example, lighter computers and lighter sensors would let you have more function in a given weight, which is very important if you are launching things into space, and you have to pay by the pound to put things there.

31   UBIQUITY: Are there any other areas that would be significantly affected by nanotechnology?

32   MERKLE: The other area is in advanced computer technology. The computer hardware revolution has been continuing with remarkable steadiness over the last few decades. If you extrapolate into the future you find that, in the coming decades, we'll have to build molecular computers to keep the computer hardware revolution on track. Nanotechnology will let us do that, and it will let us build computers that are incredibly powerful. We'll have more power in the volume of a sugar cube than exists in the entire world today.

33   UBIQUITY: Can you put any kind of timeframe on that?

34   MERKLE: We're talking about decades. We're not talking about years; we're not talking about a century. We're talking decades—and probably not many decades.

BILL **GATES**

A Robot in Every Home

From 1995 to 2009, Bill Gates had been ranked by *Forbes* magazine as the richest person in the world (he has now "fallen" to number 2). Best known for his role with Microsoft, the company he cofounded with Paul Allen, Gates now serves as the primary stockholder for that corporation. He spends most of his time doing philanthropic work with the Gates Foundation, which he and his wife, Melinda, founded in 2000. In "A Robot in Every Home," which first appeared in the December 2006 issue of *Scientific American*, Gates waxes enthusiastic and optimistic about the prospect of bringing robotics into every American household—much as Microsoft did with personal computers.

Imagine being present at the birth of a new industry. It is an industry based on groundbreaking new technologies, wherein a handful of well-established corporations sell highly specialized devices for business use and a fast-growing number of start-up companies produce innovative toys, gadgets for hobbyists and other interesting niche products. But it is also a highly fragmented industry with few common standards or platforms. Projects are complex, progress is slow, and practical applications are relatively rare. In fact, for all the excitement and promise, no one can say with any certainty when—or even if—this industry will achieve critical mass. If it does, though, it may well change the world.

2   Of course, the paragraph above could be a description of the computer industry during the mid-1970s, around the time that Paul Allen and I launched Microsoft. Back then, big, expensive mainframe computers ran the back-office operations for major companies, governmental departments and other institutions. Researchers at leading universities and industrial laboratories were creating the basic building blocks that would make the information age possible. Intel had just introduced the 8080 microprocessor, and Atari was selling the popular electronic game Pong. At homegrown computer clubs, enthusiasts struggled to figure out exactly what this new technology was good for.

3   But what I really have in mind is something much more contemporary: the emergence of the robotics industry, which is developing in much the same way that the computer business did 30 years ago. Think of the manufacturing robots currently used on automobile assembly lines as the equivalent of yesterday's mainframes. The industry's niche products include robotic arms that perform surgery, surveillance robots deployed in Iraq and Afghanistan that dispose of roadside bombs, and domestic robots that vacuum the floor. Electronics companies have made robotic toys that can imitate people or dogs or dinosaurs, and hobbyists are anxious to get their hands on the latest version of the Lego robotics system.

4   Meanwhile some of the world's best minds are trying to solve the toughest problems of robotics, such as visual recognition, navigation and machine learning. And they are succeeding. At the 2004 Defense Advanced Research Projects Agency (DARPA) Grand Challenge, a competition to produce the first robotic vehicle capable of navigating autonomously over a rugged 142-mile course through the Mojave Desert, the top competitor managed to travel just 7.4 miles before breaking down. In 2005, though, five vehicles covered the complete distance, and the race's winner did it at an average speed of 19.1 miles an hour. (In another intriguing parallel between the robotics and computer industries, DARPA also funded the work that led to the creation of Arpanet, the precursor to the Internet.)

5   What is more, the challenges facing the robotics industry are similar to those we tackled in computing three decades ago. Robotics companies have no standard operating software that could allow popular application programs to run in a variety of devices. The standardization of robotic processors and other hardware is limited, and very little of the programming code used in one machine can be applied to another. Whenever somebody wants to build a new robot, they usually have to start from square one.

6   Despite these difficulties, when I talk to people involved in robotics—from university researchers to entrepreneurs, hobbyists and high school students—the level of excitement and expectation reminds me so much of that time when Paul Allen and I

looked at the convergence of new technologies and dreamed of the day when a computer would be on every desk and in every home. And as I look at the trends that are now starting to converge, I can envision a future in which robotic devices will become a nearly ubiquitous part of our day-to-day lives. I believe that technologies such as distributed computing, voice and visual recognition, and wireless broadband connectivity will open the door to a new generation of autonomous devices that enable computers to perform tasks in the physical world on our behalf. We may be on the verge of a new era, when the PC will get up off the desktop and allow us to see, hear, touch and manipulate objects in places where we are not physically present.

From Science Fiction to Reality

7 The word "robot" was popularized in 1921 by Czech playwright Karel Capek, but people have envisioned creating robot-like devices for thousands of years. In Greek and Roman mythology, the gods of metalwork built mechanical servants made from gold. In the first century A.D., Heron of Alexandria—the great engineer credited with inventing the first steam engine—designed intriguing automatons, including one said to have the ability to talk. Leonardo da Vinci's 1495 sketch of a mechanical knight, which could sit up and move its arms and legs, is considered to be the first plan for a humanoid robot.

8 Over the past century, anthropomorphic machines have become familiar figures in popular culture through books such as Isaac Asimov's *I, Robot*, movies such as *Star Wars* and television shows such as *Star Trek*. The popularity of robots in fiction indicates that people are receptive to the idea that these machines will one day walk among us as helpers and even as companions. Nevertheless, although robots play a vital role in industries such as automobile manufacturing—where there is about one robot for every 10 workers—the fact is that we have a long way to go before real robots catch up with their science-fiction counterparts.

9 One reason for this gap is that it has been much harder than expected to enable computers and robots to sense their surrounding environment and to react quickly and accurately. It has proved extremely difficult to give robots the capabilities that humans take for granted—for example, the abilities to orient themselves with respect to the objects in a room, to respond to sounds and interpret speech, and to grasp objects of varying sizes, textures and fragility. Even something as simple as telling the difference between an open door and a window can be devilishly tricky for a robot.

10 But researchers are starting to find the answers. One trend that has helped them is the increasing availability of tremendous amounts of computer power. One megahertz of processing power, which cost more than $7,000 in 1970, can now be purchased for just pennies. The price of a megabit of storage has seen a similar decline. The access to cheap computing power has permitted scientists to work on many of the hard problems that are fundamental to making robots practical. Today, for example, voice-recognition programs can identify words quite well, but a far greater challenge will be building machines that can understand what those words mean in context. As computing capacity continues to expand, robot designers will have the processing power they need to tackle issues of ever greater complexity.

11 Another barrier to the development of robots has been the high cost of hardware, such as sensors that enable a robot to determine the distance to an object as well as motors and servos that allow the robot to manipulate an object with both strength and

delicacy. But prices are dropping fast. Laser range finders that are used in robotics to measure distance with precision cost about $10,000 a few years ago; today they can be purchased for about $2,000. And new, more accurate sensors based on ultrawide-band radar are available for even less.

12   Now robot builders can also add Global Positioning System chips, video cameras, array microphones (which are better than conventional microphones at distinguishing a voice from background noise) and a host of additional sensors for a reasonable expense. The resulting enhancement of capabilities, combined with expanded processing power and storage, allows today's robots to do things such as vacuum a room or help to defuse a roadside bomb—tasks that would have been impossible for commercially produced machines just a few years ago.

A BASIC Approach

13   In February 2004 I visited a number of leading universities, including Carnegie Mellon University, the Massachusetts Institute of Technology, Harvard University, Cornell University and the University of Illinois, to talk about the powerful role that computers can play in solving some of society's most pressing problems. My goal was to help students understand how exciting and important computer science can be, and I hoped to encourage a few of them to think about careers in technology. At each university, after delivering my speech, I had the opportunity to get a firsthand look at some of the most interesting research projects in the school's computer science department. Almost without exception, I was shown at least one project that involved robotics.

14   At that time, my colleagues at Microsoft were also hearing from people in academia and at commercial robotics firms who wondered if our company was doing any work in robotics that might help them with their own development efforts. We were not, so we decided to take a closer look. I asked Tandy Trower, a member of my strategic staff and a 25-year Microsoft veteran, to go on an extended fact-finding mission and to speak with people across the robotics community. What he found was universal enthusiasm for the potential of robotics, along with an industry-wide desire for tools that would make development easier. "Many see the robotics industry at a technological turning point where a move to PC architecture makes more and more sense," Tandy wrote in his report to me after his fact-finding mission. "As Red Whittaker, leader of [Carnegie Mellon's] entry in the DARPA Grand Challenge, recently indicated, the hardware capability is mostly there; now the issue is getting the software right."

15   Back in the early days of the personal computer, we realized that we needed an ingredient that would allow all of the pioneering work to achieve critical mass, to coalesce into a real industry capable of producing truly useful products on a commercial scale. What was needed, it turned out, was Microsoft BASIC. When we created this programming language in the 1970s, we provided the common foundation that enabled programs developed for one set of hardware to run on another. BASIC also made computer programming much easier, which brought more and more people into the industry. Although a great many individuals made essential contributions to the development of the personal computer, Microsoft BASIC was one of the key catalysts for the software and hardware innovations that made the PC revolution possible.

16   After reading Tandy's report, it seemed clear to me that before the robotics industry could make the same kind of quantum leap that the PC industry made 30 years

ago, it, too, needed to find that missing ingredient. So I asked him to assemble a small team that would work with people in the robotics field to create a set of programming tools that would provide the essential plumbing so that anybody interested in robots with even the most basic understanding of computer programming could easily write robotic applications that would work with different kinds of hardware. The goal was to see if it was possible to provide the same kind of common, low-level foundation for integrating hardware and software into robot designs that Microsoft BASIC provided for computer programmers.

17   Tandy's robotics group has been able to draw on a number of advanced technologies developed by a team working under the direction of Craig Mundie, Microsoft's chief research and strategy officer. One such technology will help solve one of the most difficult problems facing robot designers: how to simultaneously handle all the data coming in from multiple sensors and send the appropriate commands to the robot's motors, a challenge known as concurrency. A conventional approach is to write a traditional, single-threaded program—a long loop that first reads all the data from the sensors, then processes this input and finally delivers output that determines the robot's behavior, before starting the loop all over again. The shortcomings are obvious: if your robot has fresh sensor data indicating that the machine is at the edge of a precipice, but the program is still at the bottom of the loop calculating trajectory and telling the wheels to turn faster based on previous sensor input, there is a good chance the robot will fall down the stairs before it can process the new information.

18   Concurrency is a challenge that extends beyond robotics. Today as more and more applications are written for distributed networks of computers, programmers have struggled to figure out how to efficiently orchestrate code running on many different servers at the same time. And as computers with a single processor are replaced by machines with multiple processors and "multicore" processors—integrated circuits with two or more processors joined together for enhanced performance—software designers will need a new way to program desktop applications and operating systems. To fully exploit the power of processors working in parallel, the new software must deal with the problem of concurrency.

19   One approach to handling concurrency is to write multi-threaded programs that allow data to travel along many paths. But as any developer who has written multi-threaded code can tell you, this is one of the hardest tasks in programming. The answer that Craig's team has devised to the concurrency problem is something called the concurrency and coordination runtime (CCR). The CCR is a library of functions—sequences of software code that perform specific tasks—that makes it easy to write multithreaded applications that can coordinate a number of simultaneous activities. Designed to help programmers take advantage of the power of multicore and multiprocessor systems, the CCR turns out to be ideal for robotics as well. By drawing on this library to write their programs, robot designers can dramatically reduce the chances that one of their creations will run into a wall because its software is too busy sending output to its wheels to read input from its sensors.

20   In addition to tackling the problem of concurrency, the work that Craig's team has done will also simplify the writing of distributed robotic applications through a technology called decentralized software services (DSS). DSS enables developers to create applications in which the services—the parts of the program that read a sensor, say, or

control a motor—operate as separate processes that can be orchestrated in much the same way that text, images and information from several servers are aggregated on a Web page. Because DSS allows software components to run in isolation from one another, if an individual component of a robot fails, it can be shut down and restarted—or even replaced—without having to reboot the machine. Combined with broadband wireless technology, this architecture makes it easy to monitor and adjust a robot from a remote location using a Web browser.

21   What is more, a DSS application controlling a robotic device does not have to reside entirely on the robot itself but can be distributed across more than one computer. As a result, the robot can be a relatively inexpensive device that delegates complex processing tasks to the high-performance hardware found on today's home PCs. I believe this advance will pave the way for an entirely new class of robots that are essentially mobile, wireless peripheral devices that tap into the power of desktop PCs to handle processing-intensive tasks such as visual recognition and navigation. And because these devices can be networked together, we can expect to see the emergence of groups of robots that can work in concert to achieve goals such as mapping the seafloor or planting crops.

22   These technologies are a key part of Microsoft Robotics Studio, a new software development kit built by Tandy's team. Microsoft Robotics Studio also includes tools that make it easier to create robotic applications using a wide range of programming languages. One example is a simulation tool that lets robot builders test their applications in a three-dimensional virtual environment before trying them out in the real world. Our goal for this release is to create an affordable, open platform that allows robot developers to readily integrate hardware and software into their designs.

Robots like this vacuum are already in use in households around the world.

Should We Call Them Robots?

23   How soon will robots become part of our day-to-day lives? According to the International Federation of Robotics, about two million personal robots were in use around the world in 2004, and another seven million will be installed by 2008. In South Korea the Ministry of Information and Communication hopes to put a robot in every home there by 2013. The Japanese Robot Association predicts that by 2025, the personal robot industry will be worth more than $50 billion a year worldwide, compared with about $5 billion today.

24   As with the PC industry in the 1970s, it is impossible to predict exactly what applications will drive this new industry. It seems quite likely, however, that robots will play an important role in providing physical assistance and even companionship for the elderly. Robotic devices will probably help people with disabilities get around and extend the strength and endurance of soldiers, construction workers and medical professionals. Robots will maintain dangerous industrial machines, handle hazardous materials and monitor remote oil pipelines. They will enable health care workers to diagnose and treat patients who may be thousands of miles away, and they will be a central feature of security systems and search-and-rescue operations.

25   Although a few of the robots of tomorrow may resemble the anthropomorphic devices seen in *Star Wars*, most will look nothing like the humanoid C-3PO. In fact, as mobile peripheral devices become more and more common, it may be increasingly difficult to say exactly what a robot is. Because the new machines will be so specialized and ubiquitous—and look so little like the two-legged automatons of science fiction—we probably will not even call them robots. But as these devices become affordable to consumers, they could have just as profound an impact on the way we work, communicate, learn and entertain ourselves as the PC has had over the past 30 years.

Paul Marks

Armchair Warlords and Robot Hordes

Paul Marks is a technology correspondent for *New Scientist*, an international weekly science magazine and Web site that covers issues in science and technology. In 2007, Marks won the BT IT Security Journalist of the Year Award. His portfolio included the article below, published in *New Scientist* on October 28, 2006, which examines the development of lethal robot soldiers and the risks attached to their use.

It sounds like every general's dream: technology that allows a nation to fight a war with little or no loss of life on its side. It is also a peace-seeking citizen's nightmare. Without the politically embarrassing threat of soldiers returning home in flag-wrapped coffins, governments would find it far easier to commit to military action. The consequences for countries on the receiving end—and for world peace—would be immense.

2   This is not a fantasy scenario. Over the coming years, the world's most powerful military machine, the U.S. Department of Defense, aims to replace a large proportion of its armed vehicles and weaponry with robotized technologies. By 2010, a third of its "deep-strike" aircraft will be unmanned aerial vehicles (UAVs), according to a Congressional Research Service report issued in July (http://tinyurl.com/yafoht). In a further five years a similar proportion of the U.S. army's ground combat vehicles will be remote-controlled robots varying in size from supermarket carts to trucks. The U.S. navy, too, will have fleets of uncrewed boats and submarines.

3   The U.S. military is already using robots in various roles. In November 2002, for example, an armed UAV destroyed a car in Yemen carrying the suspected chief of Al-Qaida in that country, killing him and five others. In Iraq and Afghanistan, robots are proving highly successful in neutralizing roadside bombs and other small-scale explosives.

4   This is only the start. One of the next steps is to give robotic ground vehicles the attack power of UAVs, arming them with weapons such as machine guns, grenade launchers and anti-tank rockets (*New Scientist,* 21 September, p. 28). They could then be sent into places that were particularly dangerous for troops, such as booby-trapped or ambush-vulnerable buildings.

5   After that the plan is to take things to a whole new level, with unmanned planes and ground robots able to communicate with each other and act in concert. A reconnaissance UAV could signal swarms of robots to attack an enemy position, for example, or an unmanned ground vehicle might call in an air strike from UAVs.

6   All uncrewed vehicles are remote-controlled at present, but the Pentagon's Office of Naval Research is planning to develop technology that it hopes will enable a robot to determine whether a person it comes across is a threat, using measures such as the remote sensing of their heartbeat—though whether these kinds of methods can be made reliable is highly questionable.

7   "Teleoperation [remote control] is the norm, but semi-autonomous enhancements are being added all the time," says Bob Quinn of Foster-Miller, a technology firm in Waltham, Massachusetts, owned by the UK defense research company Qinetiq. Foster-Miller, like its main rival iRobot, was set up by roboticists from the Massachusetts Institute of Technology. The company's armed robot, dubbed Swords, has just received U.S. army safety certification. Nevertheless, doubts remain over how reliable armed robotic devices will be, especially if they end up operating autonomously. What happens when the software fails?

8   Such fears have persuaded the military to go slow on the use of autonomous weaponry. An early version of one of Foster-Miller's robots was designed to de-mine beaches autonomously

but was later converted to remote control at the navy's request. It is feasible that as safety concerns are addressed, autonomous devices will become increasingly popular, though experts in robotics point out that might be a long time away. An armed robot will not only need to be fail-safe, it must also be able to identify friend and foe just as well as a soldier.

9   Despite these fears, the rise of armed robots seems inevitable. Quinn tells the story of a group of U.S. marines impressed by a Swords robot armed with a machine gun being tested at a U.S. army base. "If they could have, they would have put that robot in their trunk, because they were off to Ramadi, Iraq, and they wanted that robot to [help them] stay alive. When you see that passion, I have no philosophical problems about this technology whatsoever," he says.

10   Outside the military, however, plenty of people beg to differ. Ultimately, these developments will allow the U.S., as well as several NATO countries that are also keen on the technology, to fight wars without suffering anywhere near as many casualties. The idea that warfare can be "clinical" has been found wanting time and again in recent years—think of the current conflicts in Iraq and Afghanistan, and Israel's recent bombardment of Lebanon— but there's no question that reliable autonomous robots deployed on a large scale could make fighting wars a great deal less risky for those that own them.

11   And therein lies the great danger. What are the chances of a less violent world when the powerful nations can make their mark on the less powerful at the flick of a switch? As Quinn puts it: "We are not trying to create a level battlefield here, we are trying to do the opposite: create a very un-level battlefield."

Sally Satel

Organs for Sale

Sally Satel is a practicing psychiatrist, lecturer at the Yale University School of Medicine, and resident scholar at the American Enterprise Institute for Public Policy Research, a nonpartisan, nonprofit institution committed to research and education on issues of government, politics, economics, and social welfare. Her work focuses on mental health policy and political trends in medicine. She is the author of several books, including *When Altruism Isn't Enough: The Case for Compensating Kidney Donors.* Her argument below appeared in the *Journal of the American Enterprise Institute* on October 14, 2006.

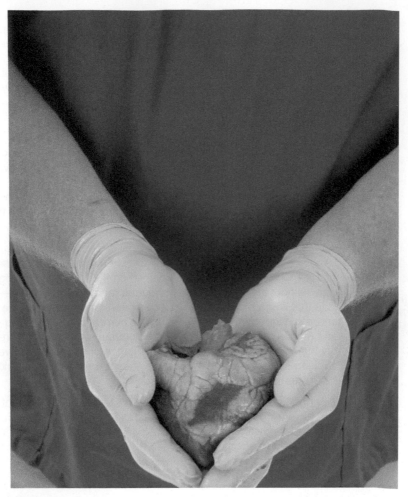

How should we resolve the ever-increasing demand for organs to aid those in need of transplants?

A   year ago, I was searching the Internet for something rare and valuable: a human kidney. In August 2004, I learned I had end-stage renal disease and would need a transplant. At the time, my prospects for a donation from family or friends looked bleak, and I would soon have to begin dialysis. I would be hooked up to a machine three days a week for four hours at a time. This would continue for at least five years—the time it would take for a kidney from a deceased donor to become available. Even with dialysis, the kidneys of many sick people deteriorate so quickly that time runs out. An average of 11 Americans die each day waiting for a renal transplant.

2   Waiting for a kidney from a deceased donor is such a risky business that some people try publicly to convince strangers to give them live organs. Some put up billboards ("I NEED A KIDNEY, CAN YOU HELP? Call . . . "), start websites (GordyNeedsAKidney.org, whose opening page carries the plaintive headline, "Please

Help Our Dad"), or go overseas to become "transplant tourists" on the Chinese black market with the frightful knowledge that the organ they get will almost surely come from an executed political prisoner. The desperation, as I found myself, is perfectly understandable. I have no siblings. Several friends said they would look into it—donors don't need to be genetically related—but they turned out to have disqualifying medical problems or spouses who objected, or they grew scared.

3   Last fall, I turned to a website called MatchingDonors.com—which "matches" mostly prospective kidney donors with recipients—and quickly found a prospective donor. But six weeks later, he changed his mind. Then my wonderful friend Virginia Postrel came along. We are both healthy after a transplant operation on March 4 at the Washington Hospital Center. If Virginia had not donated her kidney, I could have languished on dialysis for years. Indeed, when I joined the national queue in January 2005, there were about 60,000 other people ahead of me, according to the nonprofit United Network for Organ Sharing (UNOS), which maintains the list under a monopoly contract with the federal government.

4   Today, there are 67,600 people waiting for a posthumous kidney. In big cities, where the ratio of needy patients to available organs is highest, the wait—spent on dialysis, a procedure that circulates your blood through a machine that purifies it and returns it to your body—is up to eight years. Last year, only 16,470 people received kidneys; roughly half of the donors were deceased, and half were living. Meanwhile, 4,100 died waiting. By 2010, the wait will be at least ten years, exceeding the average length of time that adults on dialysis survive.

5   Despite decades of public education about the virtues of donating organs at death, the level of such gifts has remained disappointingly steady. Only about one-third of Americans have designated themselves as donors on their driver's licenses or on state-run donor registries. For the rest, the decision to donate organs will fall to family members, who about half the time deny the requests of hospitals. More important, however, is that very few of the Americans who die, perhaps 13,000 a year (or less than 1 percent of all deaths), possess organs healthy enough for transplanting—so even if every family consented, the need for thousands of kidneys would go unmet.

6   The chasm between the number of available kidneys and the number of people needing one will widen each year. This is due to our misplaced faith in the power of altruism. The "transplant community," as it is called—organizations that encourage funding and gifts of organs, and many surgeons and nephrologists—expects people, both living donors and loved ones of the deceased, to give a body part and to receive nothing in return. In fact, it is illegal in the United States to receive money or anything of value ("valuable consideration") in exchange for an organ, a principle set down by Congress in 1984 in the National Organ Transplantation Act.

7   Don't get me wrong. Altruism is a beautiful thing—it's the reason I have a new kidney—but altruism alone cannot resolve the organ shortage. For that reason, more and more physicians, ethicists, economists, and legal scholars are urging the legalization of payments for organs in order to generate more kidneys for transplantation. One doesn't need to be Milton Friedman to know that a price of zero for anything virtually guarantees its shortage.

8   "Is it wrong for an individual . . . who wishes to utilize part of his body for the benefit of another [to] be provided with financial compensation that could obliterate a life of

destitution for the individual and his family?" asked Dr. Richard Fine, president of the American Society of Transplantation, in his address to the World Transplant Congress this year. Supporters of experimenting with a market for organs encounter an array of objections, theoretical and practical. One popular argument, first advanced by Richard M. Titmuss, professor of social administration at the London School of Economics, is that altruism is the sole legitimate impulse behind organ donation. In 1971, Titmuss, a dedicated socialist and member of the Fabian Society, published *The Gift Relationship: From Human Blood to Social Policy*, which rapidly became a U.S. bestseller. He argued that altruistic acts are among the most sensitive indicators of the quality of human relationships and values in a society. Capitalism, on the other hand, is morally bankrupt.

9   This ethic is very much alive among the bureaucrats that run the United Network for Organ Sharing, which manages the transplant list. "Organ transplantation is built upon altruism and public trust. If anything shakes that trust, then everyone loses," says the UNOS website. Yet the trust is already badly rattled. "The current system has degenerated into an equal opportunity to die on the waiting list," observes nephrologist Benjamin Hippen, who advocated compensating donors (or perhaps they should be called "vendors") before the President's Council on Bioethics this summer.

10   Another theoretical objection to compensating donors is the notion that it will "commodify" the body and thus dehumanize the rest of us, let alone the person who gives his kidney in exchange for "valuable consideration." Yet with proper respect for donors and informed consent, it strikes me that careful engagement in financial arrangements is far less distasteful than allowing people to suffer and die. These are not abstract people, mind you, like the ones who may well be helped by stem cell discoveries years down the road, but live humans like the 49-year-old former secretary from the Pentagon I met last summer. For four years now, every Monday, Wednesday, and Friday, she has been sitting in Chair No. 7 in the dialysis center a few blocks from our offices.

11   Others go so far as to reject the very premise that saving lives is a paramount goal of medicine. "If we turn organ procurement into a crusade, we make of death simply a problem to be solved rather than an event to be endured as best we can, with whatever resources of mind and spirit are available to us,"[1] says Gilbert Meilaender, professor of theological ethics at Valparaiso University and a member of the President's Council on Bioethics. Now, it is one thing to question whether we should prolong the life of a vegetative patient, but quite another to abandon treatments for renal failure under circumstances in which a well-established remedy (transplantation) already exists—a remedy whose economic cost to society is lower than the cost of the less effective alternative, dialysis.

12   This is a good time to point out that the live donor—or vendor—of a kidney is exposed to only minor risks, the most significant being those associated with anesthesia and surgery itself—0.03% mortality—comparable to any other operation. Because the surgery is done using a laparoscopic approach, the visible scar is only 2 to 3 inches long. My donor, Virginia, was out of the hospital in three days and back to writing her magazine column a week later.

13   Long-term risks are also low. Typical is a 1997 study from Norway that followed 1,332 kidney donors for an average of 32 years. It found no difference in mortality rates between people who give kidneys and the general population. A 25-year follow-up of

70 donors conducted by the Cleveland Clinic found that the renal function is "well pre-served" and that the overall incidence of hypertension was comparable to that of non-donors. The truth is that a normal person can get along perfectly well with one kidney. The risk a donor runs is that his single functioning kidney will become diseased or in-jured, and he'll need a transplant himself—a highly unlikely event.

14   Perhaps the most vocal critic of compensating donors is the National Kidney Foun-dation. It is offended by the idea that a donor might benefit in ways other than the psy-chic reward of pure giving. States NKF chairman Charles Fruit, "Families decide to donate the organs of a loved one for altruistic reasons. Payment is an affront to those who have already donated."[2] Virginia, a take-no-prisoners journalist, responded pointedly to Fruit on her website, <www.dynamist.com>, "The argument that paying organ donors is 'an affront' to unpaid donors is disgusting. Are unpaid donors giving organs to save lives or just to make themselves feel morally superior? Even in the latter case, they shouldn't care if *other* people get paid."

15   In the end, moral objections such as these put us at a standoff. I doubt I could change the mind of Professor Meilaender, who sincerely believes that organ donation vio-lates what it means to be human. And there's nothing he can say to dissuade me from be-lieving that free, informed, and willing individuals should be able to participate in a regulated exchange involving valuable consideration. Thus, the meaningful question be-comes how both sides can honor their moral commitments.

16   The best answer is by creating a market arrangement to exist in parallel with al-truistic giving. Within such a framework, any medical center or physician who objects to the practice of compensating donors can simply opt out of performing transplants that use such organs. Recipients on the list are free to turn down a paid-for organ and wait for one given altruistically. Choice for all—donors, recipients, and physicians—is enhanced. And it is choice in the greater service of diminishing sickness and death. Paradoxically, the current system based on altruism-or-else undermines the individual autonomy that is at the heart of the most widely held values in bioethics.

17   Not all objections to donor compensation, however, are abstract. A common con-cern is the potential for exploiting donors—especially low-income donors, who, as the critics reasonably claim, will be the most likely to find incentives attractive. Without question, protecting donors is enormously important. That is why any plan for compen-sation should be regulated. Potential donors must receive education about what it means to donate a kidney and the risks they run. They must undergo careful medical and psychological screening and receive quality follow-up care.

18   Critics often point to the horror stories from transplant black markets overseas and hold them up as cautionary tales. But the catastrophists have it exactly backward. It is when payment is not an above-board part of the medical system that black mar-kets lead to minimal education of prospective donors, poor post-operative and follow-up care, and failure to honor agreements for payment.

19   Finally, some critics argue we have no evidence that an incentive system would work. True. So we need experimentation. Frankly, I don't know what the perfect kidney market would look like, but let's assume that Congress makes a bold and common-sense move and amends current law to permit the exchange of money or something of value for a kidney. Here are several alternative market systems:

1. A FORWARD MARKET FOR CADAVER ORGANS:

20 Economist Lloyd Cohen proposed one of the first market-based models to increase the number of cadaver organs. Potential donors would either (1) be paid a small amount today by the government or insurance companies to join the current donor registry, or (2) register today in return for the possibility of a much larger payment to their estates should the organs be used at death.

21 The advantage of such a forward-looking approach is that the decision-making burden is taken off family members at a painful time—when they are sitting in the emergency room learning that someone they love is now brain-dead. And, of course, there is no worry of exploiting the donor. A forward market could also help satisfy the 23,000 people waiting for livers, hearts, and lungs.

22 But deceased donors cannot meet the need for kidneys. In addition, kidneys from live donors are healthier than those obtained after death and survive, typically, for 10 to 20 years (or one-third longer). Thus, to mitigate the shortage of kidneys, we must consider offering incentives to people amenable to relinquishing one while they are alive.

2. THE CENTRALIZED SINGLE COMPENSATOR:

23 In this approach, the federal government or a designated agency acts as the only authority with the power to buy and allocate organs for transplants. As is currently the case with cadaver organs, kidneys obtained through compensated donors would be matched with the next best candidate waiting on the national list.

24 Under this scheme, Medicare would underwrite the incentives in light of the fact that it already pays for dialysis treatment under the 1972 End Stage Renal Disease (ESRD) amendment to the Social Security Act. This entitlement provides care for Americans with terminal renal failure regardless of age if they have met required work credits for Social Security. Last year, the ESRD program spent about $16 billion on dialysis, or about $66,000 per patient annually. Since a 35-year-old spends about nine years on dialysis, the total cost is around $600,000; for a 64-year-old, about four years at $300,000. Compare these expenses with the cost of a transplant operation—approximately $75,000 in all for the one-time cost of the surgeries and hospital stays of the donor and recipient, plus the first year of follow-up medical care (including medicine).

25 In most cases, these savings would easily pay for a lifetime supply of the expensive immunosuppressant drugs to prevent rejection of the new kidney. The drugs cost $15,000 to $20,000 a year, and every recipient must take them every day for life. Medicare pays for transplant surgery but stops reimbursing for the drugs, at 80 percent of full price, three years post-transplant if the patient goes back to work.

26 What kinds of compensation should be offered? A reasonable case could be made for an outright payment—after all, it is hard to argue that an individual is competent enough to sell an organ yet unfit to manage the money he receives in exchange for it—but I am partial to a compromise approach in order to defuse those who say that people will sell their organs for quick cash or use it to buy something frivolous. For example, the donor could choose from a menu of options, including a deposit to a 401(k) retirement plan, tax credits, tuition vouchers for the donor's children, long-term nursing

care, family health coverage, life and nonfatal injury insurance, a charitable contribution in the donor's name, or cash payments stretched over time.

27   Donor protection is the linchpin of any compensation model. Standard guidelines for physical and psychological screening, donor education, and informed consent could be formulated by a medical organization, such as the American Society of Transplant Surgeons, or another entity designated by the federal Department of Health and Human Services. A "waiting period" of three to six months could be built in to ensure the prospective donor has ample time to think it through. Monitoring donor health post-transplant is important as well. One idea is to provide lifetime health insurance, through Medicare or a private insurer for the donor. He would receive annual physicals, routine medical screening, and long-term follow-up in addition to standard health coverage. A federally sponsored registry of donors could help us study long-term outcomes for donors and vendors and take steps to remedy physical or psychological difficulties that arise.

3. MULTIPLE COMPENSATORS:

28   In this scheme, donors, compensators (that is, the entities that pay for the transplants), and medical centers (that perform them) would be coordinated with one another through an intermediary broker. Medicare would be one of several possible compensators, along with private insurers, charitable foundations, or a fund established perhaps through a surcharge added to the cost paid by insurers and foundations.

4. PRIVATE CONTRACTS:

29   The easiest way to start a market for organs is simply to change the law to allow someone who needs an organ and someone who wants to sell one to make their own arrangements through contract—as infertile couples currently do with surrogate mothers. But such a system would inevitably attract criticism because it appears to favor well-off sick people over poor.

30   While private contracts may seem unfair because only those with means will be able to purchase directly, poor people who need kidneys would be no worse off—and, very likely, considerably better off—than under the current system. First, a stranger interested in selling a kidney is unlikely to give it away for free to the next person on the list (only 88 donors last year made such anonymous gifts); thus, few poor people would be deprived of kidneys they would otherwise have gotten voluntarily. Second, anyone who gets a kidney by contract is removed from the waiting list, and everyone behind him benefits by moving up. Third, private charities could offer to help subsidize the cost for a needy patient or pay outright.

31   These broad proposals, and variants on them, need considerable elaboration. Many questions remain: How would prices be determined? Would each available kidney be allotted to the next well-matched person on the list? Or should living organs be preferentially allocated to the healthiest people on the list—that is, those who will get the most "life" out of the organ? Could noncitizens be paid donors? Also, could people have a say in who would receive their kidneys? As it currently stands, most living donors give altruistically because they are trying to help a friend or relative, not a stranger. But it is surely possible that the decision of an ambivalent friend could tip in the direction of giving with the promise of compensation. And since each patient on

dialysis is functionally "attached" to a Medicare entitlement, perhaps the recipient could direct a portion of "his" Medicare allotment to his friend as payment.

32   There is no denying the political and practical challenges that come with introducing payment into a 20-year-old scheme built on the premise that generosity is the only legitimate motive for giving. Yet as death and suffering mount, constructing a market-based incentive program to increase the supply of transplantable organs has become a moral imperative. Its architects must give serious consideration to principled reservations and to concerns about donor safety, but repugnance and caution are not in themselves arguments against innovation. They are only reasons for vigilance and care.

Notes

1 Gilbert Meilaender, "Gifts of the Body," *New Atlantis*, Number 13 (Summer 2006): 25–35.
2 Letters in response to Richard Epstein, "Kidney Beancounters," *Wall Street Journal*, May 15, 2006 (May 26, 2006). ■

Nathaniel Hawthorne

The Birth-Mark

Nathaniel Hawthorne (1804–1864), one of America's greatest fiction writers, lived most of his life near Boston. He first published "The Birth-Mark" in 1843.

In the latter part of the last century there lived a man of science, an eminent proficient in every branch of natural philosophy, who not long before our story opens had made experience of a spiritual affinity more attractive than any chemical one. He had left his laboratory to the care of an assistant, cleared his fine countenance from the furnace smoke, washed the stain of acids from his fingers, and persuaded a beautiful woman to become his wife. In those days when the comparatively recent discovery of electricity and other kindred mysteries of Nature seemed to open paths into the region of miracle, it was not unusual for the love of science to rival the love of woman in its depth and absorbing energy. The higher intellect, the imagination, the spirit, and even the heart might all find their congenial aliment in pursuits which, as some of their ardent votaries believed, would ascend from one step of powerful intelligence to another, until the philosopher should lay his hand on the secret of creative force and perhaps make new worlds for himself. We know not whether Aylmer possessed this degree of faith in man's ultimate control over Nature. He had devoted himself, however, too unreservedly to scientific studies ever to be weaned from them by any second passion. His love for his young wife might prove the stronger of the two; but it could only be by intertwining itself with his love of science, and uniting the strength of the latter to his own.

2   Such a union accordingly took place, and was attended with truly remarkable consequences and a deeply impressive moral. One day, very soon after their marriage, Aylmer sat gazing at his wife with a trouble in his countenance that grew stronger until he spoke.

3   "Georgiana," said he, "has it never occurred to you that the mark upon your cheek might be removed?"

4   "No, indeed," said she, smiling; but perceiving the seriousness of his manner, she blushed deeply. "To tell you the truth it has been so often called a charm that I was simple enough to imagine it might be so."

5   "Ah, upon another face perhaps it might," replied her husband; "but never on yours. No, dearest Georgiana, you came so nearly perfect from the hand of Nature that this slightest possible defect, which we hesitate whether to term a defect or a beauty, shocks me, as being the visible mark of earthly imperfection."

6   "Shocks you, my husband!" cried Georgiana, deeply hurt; at first reddening with momentary anger, but then bursting into tears. "Then why did you take me from my mother's side? You cannot love what shocks you!"

7   To explain this conversation it must be mentioned that in the centre of Georgiana's left cheek there was a singular mark, deeply interwoven, as it were, with the texture and substance of her face. In the usual state of her complexion—a healthy though delicate bloom—the mark wore a tint of deeper crimson, which imperfectly defined its shape amid the surrounding rosiness. When she blushed it gradually became more indistinct, and finally vanished amid the triumphant rush of blood that bathed the whole cheek with its brilliant glow. But if any shifting motion caused her to turn pale there was the mark again, a crimson stain upon the snow, in what Aylmer sometimes deemed an almost fearful distinctness. Its shape bore not a little similarity to the human hand, though of the smallest pygmy size. Georgiana's lovers were wont to say that some fairy at her birth hour had laid her tiny hand upon the infant's cheek, and left this impress there in token of the magic endowments that were to give her such sway over all hearts. Many a desperate swain would have risked life for the privilege of pressing his lips to the mysterious hand. It must not be concealed, however, that the impression wrought by this fairy sign manual varied exceedingly, according to the difference of temperament in the beholders. Some fastidious persons—but they were exclusively of her own sex—affirmed that the bloody hand, as they chose to call it, quite destroyed the effect of Georgiana's beauty, and rendered her countenance even hideous. But it would be as reasonable to say that one of those small blue stains which sometimes occur in the purest statuary marble would convert the Eve of Powers to a monster. Masculine observers, if the birthmark did not heighten their admiration, contented themselves with wishing it away, that the world might possess one living specimen of ideal loveliness without the semblance of a flaw. After his marriage,—for he thought little or nothing of the matter before,—Aylmer discovered that this was the case with himself

8   Had she been less beautiful,—if Envy's self could have found aught else to sneer at,—he might have felt his affection heightened by the prettiness of this mimic hand, now vaguely portrayed, now lost, now stealing forth again and glimmering to and fro with every pulse of emotion that throbbed within her heart; but seeing her otherwise so perfect, he found this one defect grow more and more intolerable with every moment of their united lives. It was the fatal flaw of humanity which Nature, in one shape or another, stamps ineffaceably on all her productions, either to imply that they are temporary and finite, or that their perfection must be wrought by toil and pain. The crimson hand expressed the ineludible gripe in which mortality clutches the highest and purest of earthly mould, degrading them into kindred with the lowest, and even with the very

brutes, like whom their visible frames return to dust. In this manner, selecting it as the symbol of his wife's liability to sin, sorrow, decay, and death, Aylmer's sombre imagination was not long in rendering the birthmark a frightful object, causing him more trouble and horror than ever Georgiana's beauty, whether of soul or sense, had given him delight.

9   At all the seasons which should have been their happiest, he invariably and without intending it, nay, in spite of a purpose to the contrary, reverted to this one disastrous topic. Trifling as it at first appeared, it so connected itself with innumerable trains of thought and modes of feeling that it became the central point of all. With the morning twilight Aylmer opened his eyes upon his wife's face and recognized the symbol of imperfection; and when they sat together at the evening hearth his eyes wandered stealthily to her cheek, and beheld, flickering with the blaze of the wood fire, the spectral hand that wrote mortality where he would fain have worshipped. Georgiana soon learned to shudder at his gaze. It needed but a glance with the peculiar expression that his face often wore to change the roses of her cheek into a deathlike paleness, amid which the crimson hand was brought strongly out, like a bass-relief of ruby on the whitest marble.

10   Late one night when the lights were growing dim, so as hardly to betray the stain on the poor wife's cheek, she herself, for the first time, voluntarily took up the subject.

11   "Do you remember, my dear Aylmer," said she, with a feeble attempt at a smile, "have you any recollection of a dream last night about this odious hand?"

12   "None! none whatever!" replied Aylmer, starting; but then he added, in a dry, cold tone, affected for the sake of concealing the real depth of his emotion, "I might well dream of it; for before I fell asleep it had taken a pretty firm hold of my fancy."

13   "And you did dream of it?" continued Georgiana, hastily; for she dreaded lest a gush of tears should interrupt what she had to say. "A terrible dream! I wonder that you can forget it. Is it possible to forget this one expression? — 'It is in her heart now; we must have it out!' Reflect, my husband; for by all means I would have you recall that dream."

14   The mind is in a sad state when Sleep, the all-involving, cannot confine her spectres within the dim region of her sway, but suffers them to break forth, affrighting this actual life with secrets that perchance belong to a deeper one. Aylmer now remembered his dream. He had fancied himself with his servant Aminadab, attempting an operation for the removal of the birthmark; but the deeper went the knife, the deeper sank the hand, until at length its tiny grasp appeared to have caught hold of Georgiana's heart; whence, however, her husband was inexorably resolved to cut or wrench it away.

15   When the dream had shaped itself perfectly in his memory, Aylmer sat in his wife's presence with a guilty feeling. Truth often finds its way to the mind close muffled in robes of sleep, and then speaks with uncompromising directness of matters in regard to which we practise an unconscious self-deception during our waking moments. Until now he had not been aware of the tyrannizing influence acquired by one idea over his mind, and of the lengths which he might find in his heart to go for the sake of giving himself peace.

16   "Aylmer," resumed Georgiana, solemnly, "I know not what may be the cost to both of us to rid me of this fatal birthmark. Perhaps its removal may cause cureless deformity; or it may be the stain goes as deep as life itself. Again: do we know that there is a possibility, on any terms, of unclasping the firm gripe of this little hand which was laid upon me before I came into the world?"

17   "Dearest Georgiana, I have spent much thought upon the subject," hastily interrupted Aylmer. "I am convinced of the perfect practicability of its removal."

18   "If there be the remotest possibility of it," continued Georgiana, "let the attempt be made at whatever risk. Danger is nothing to me; for life, while this hateful mark makes me the object of your horror and disgust,—life is a burden which I would fling down with joy. Either remove this dreadful hand, or take my wretched life! You have deep science. All the world bears witness of it. You have achieved great wonders. Cannot you remove this little, little mark, which I cover with the tips of two small fingers? Is this beyond your power, for the sake of your own peace, and to save your poor wife from madness?"

19   "Noblest, dearest, tenderest wife," cried Aylmer. rapturously, "doubt not my power. I have already given this matter the deepest thought—thought which might almost have enlightened me to create a being less perfect than yourself. Georgiana, you have led me deeper than ever into the heart of science. I feel myself fully competent to render this dear cheek as faultless as its fellow; and then, most beloved, what will be my triumph when I shall have corrected what Nature left imperfect in her fairest work! Even Pygmalion, when his sculptured woman assumed life, felt not greater ecstasy than mine will be."

20   "It is resolved, then," said Georgiana, faintly smiling. "And, Aylmer, spare me not, though you should find the birthmark take refuge in my heart at last."

21   Her husband tenderly kissed her cheek—her right cheek—not that which bore the impress of the crimson hand.

22   The next day Aylmer apprised his wife of a plan that he had formed whereby he might have opportunity for the intense thought and constant watchfulness which the proposed operation would require; while Georgiana, likewise, would enjoy the perfect repose essential to its success. They were to seclude themselves in the extensive apartments occupied by Aylmer as a laboratory, and where, during his toilsome youth, he had made discoveries in the elemental powers of Nature that had roused the admiration of all the learned societies in Europe. Seated calmly in this laboratory, the pale philosopher had investigated the secrets of the highest cloud region and of the profoundest mines; he had satisfied himself of the causes that kindled and kept alive the fires of the volcano; and had explained the mystery of fountains, and how it is that they gush forth, some so bright and pure, and others with such rich medicinal virtues, from the dark bosom of the earth. Here, too, at an earlier period, he had studied the wonders of the human frame, and attempted to fathom the very process by which Nature assimilates all her precious influences from earth and air, and from the spiritual world, to create and foster man, her masterpiece.

23   The latter pursuit, however, Aylmer had long laid aside in unwilling recognition of the truth—against which all seekers sooner or later stumble—that our great creative Mother, while she amuses us with apparently working in the

broadest sunshine, is yet severely careful to keep her own secrets, and, in spite of her pretended openness, shows us nothing but results. She permits us, indeed, to mar, but seldom to mend, and, like a jealous patentee, on no account to make. Now, however, Aylmer resumed these half-forgotten investigations; not, of course, with such hopes or wishes as first suggested them; but because they involved much physiological truth and lay in the path of his proposed scheme for the treatment of Georgiana.

24   As he led her over the threshold of the laboratory, Georgiana was cold and tremulous. Aylmer looked cheerfully into her face, with intent to reassure her, but was so startled with the intense glow of the birthmark upon the whiteness of her cheek that he could not restrain a strong convulsive shudder. His wife fainted.

25   "Aminadab! Aminadab!" shouted Aylmer, stamping violently on the floor.

26   Forthwith there issued from an inner apartment a man of low stature, but bulky frame, with shaggy hair hanging about his visage, which was grimed with the vapors of the furnace. This personage had been Aylmer's underworker during his whole scientific career, and was admirably fitted for that office by his great mechanical readiness, and the skill with which, while incapable of comprehending a single principle, he executed all the details of his master's experiments. With his vast strength, his shaggy hair, his smoky aspect, and the indescribable earthiness that incrusted him, he seemed to represent man's physical nature; while Aylmer's slender figure, and pale, intellectual face, were no less apt a type of the spiritual element.

27   "Throw open the door of the boudoir, Aminadab," said Aylmer, "and burn a pastil."

28   "Yes, master," answered Aminadab, looking intently at the lifeless form of Georgiana; and then he muttered to himself, "If she were my wife, I'd never part with that birthmark."

29   When Georgiana recovered consciousness she found herself breathing an atmosphere of penetrating fragrance, the gentle potency of which had recalled her from her deathlike faintness. The scene around her looked like enchantment. Aylmer had converted those smoky, dingy, sombre rooms, where he had spent his brightest years in recondite pursuits, into a series of beautiful apartments not unfit to be the secluded abode of a lovely woman. The walls were hung with gorgeous curtains, which imparted the combination of grandeur and grace that no other species of adornment can achieve; and as they fell from the ceiling to the floor, their rich and ponderous folds, concealing all angles and straight lines, appeared to shut in the scene from infinite space. For aught Georgiana knew, it might be a pavilion among the clouds. And Aylmer, excluding the sunshine, which would have interfered with his chemical processes, had supplied its place with perfumed lamps, emitting flames of various hue, but all uniting in a soft, impurpled radiance. He now knelt by his wife's side, watching her earnestly, but without alarm; for he was confident in his science, and felt that he could draw a magic circle round her within which no evil might intrude.

30   "Where am I? Ah, I remember," said Georgiana, faintly; and she placed her hand over her cheek to hide the terrible mark from her husband's eyes.

31   "Fear not, dearest!" exclaimed he. "Do not shrink from me! Believe me, Georgiana, I even rejoice in this single imperfection, since it will be such a rapture to remove it."

32   "Oh, spare me!" sadly replied his wife. "Pray do not look at it again. I never can forget that convulsive shudder."

33   In order to soothe Georgiana, and, as it were, to release her mind from the burden of actual things, Aylmer now put in practice some of the light and playful secrets which science had taught him among its profounder lore. Airy figures, absolutely bodiless ideas, and forms of unsubstantial beauty came and danced before her, imprinting their momentary footsteps on beams of light. Though she had some indistinct idea of the method of these optical phenomena, still the illusion was almost perfect enough to warrant the belief that her husband possessed sway over the spiritual world. Then again, when she felt a wish to look forth from her seclusion, immediately, as if her thoughts were answered, the procession of external existence flitted across a screen. The scenery and the figures of actual life were perfectly represented, but with that bewitching, yet indescribable difference which always makes a picture, an image, or a shadow so much more attractive than the original. When wearied of this, Aylmer bade her cast her eyes upon a vessel containing a quantity of earth. She did so, with little interest at first; but was soon startled to perceive the germ of a plant shooting upward from the soil. Then came the slender stalk; the leaves gradually unfolded themselves; and amid them was a perfect and lovely flower.

34   "It is magical!" cried Georgiana. "I dare not touch it."

35   "Nay, pluck it," answered Aylmer, — "pluck it, and inhale its brief perfume while you may. The flower will wither in a few moments and leave nothing save its brown seed vessels; but thence may be perpetuated a race as ephemeral as itself."

36   But Georgiana had no sooner touched the flower than the whole plant suffered a blight, its leaves turning coal-black as if by the agency of fire.

37   "There was too powerful a stimulus," said Aylmer, thoughtfully.

38   To make up for this abortive experiment, he proposed to take her portrait by a scientific process of his own invention. It was to be effected by rays of light striking upon a polished plate of metal. Georgiana assented; but, on looking at the result, was affrighted to find the features of the portrait blurred and indefinable; while the minute figure of a hand appeared where the cheek should have been. Aylmer snatched the metallic plate and threw it into a jar of corrosive acid.

39   Soon, however, he forgot these mortifying failures. In the intervals of study and chemical experiment he came to her flushed and exhausted, but seemed invigorated by her presence, and spoke in glowing language of the resources of his art. He gave a history of the long dynasty of the alchemists, who spent so many ages in quest of the universal solvent by which the golden principle might be elicited from all things vile and base. Aylmer appeared to believe that, by the plainest scientific logic, it was altogether within the limits of possibility to discover this long-sought medium; "but," he added, "a philosopher who should go deep enough to acquire the power would attain too lofty a wisdom to stoop to the exercise of it." Not less singular were his opinions in regard to the elixir vitæ. He more than intimated that it was at his option to concoct a liquid that should prolong life for years, perhaps interminably; but that it would produce a discord in Nature which all the world, and chiefly the quaffer of the immortal nostrum, would find cause to curse.

40   "Aylmer, are you in earnest?" asked Georgiana, looking at him with amazement and fear. "It is terrible to possess such power, or even to dream of possessing it."

41   "Oh, do not tremble, my love," said her husband. "I would not wrong either you or myself by working such inharmonious effects upon our lives; but I would have you consider how trifling, in comparison, is the skill requisite to remove this little hand."

42   At the mention of the birthmark, Georgiana, as usual, shrank as if a redhot iron had touched her cheek.

43   Again Aylmer applied himself to his labors. She could hear his voice in the distant furnace room giving directions to Aminadab, whose harsh, uncouth, misshapen tones were audible in response, more like the grunt or growl of a brute than human speech. After hours of absence, Aylmer reappeared and proposed that she should now examine his cabinet of chemical products and natural treasures of the earth. Among the former he showed her a small vial, in which, he remarked, was contained a gentle yet most powerful fragrance, capable of impregnating all the breezes that blow across a kingdom. They were of inestimable value, the contents of that little vial; and, as he said so, he threw some of the perfume into the air and filled the room with piercing and invigorating delight.

44   "And what is this?" asked Georgiana, pointing to a small crystal globe containing a gold-colored liquid. "It is so beautiful to the eye that I could imagine it the elixir of life."

45   "In one sense it is," replied Aylmer; "or, rather, the elixir of immortality. It is the most precious poison that ever was concocted in this world. By its aid I could apportion the lifetime of any mortal at whom you might point your finger. The strength of the dose would determine whether he were to linger out years, or drop dead in the midst of a breath. No king on his guarded throne could keep his life if I, in my private station, should deem that the welfare of millions justified me in depriving him of it."

46   "Why do you keep such a terrific drug?" inquired Georgiana in horror.

47   "Do not mistrust me, dearest," said her husband, smiling; "its virtuous potency is yet greater than its harmful one. But see! here is a powerful cosmetic. With a few drops of this in a vase of water, freckles may be washed away as easily as the hands are cleansed. A stronger infusion would take the blood out of the cheek, and leave the rosiest beauty a pale ghost."

48   "Is it with this lotion that you intend to bathe my cheek?" asked Georgiana, anxiously.

49   "Oh, no," hastily replied her husband; "this is merely superficial. Your case demands a remedy that shall go deeper."

50   In his interviews with Georgiana, Aylmer generally made minute inquiries as to her sensations and whether the confinement of the rooms and the temperature of the atmosphere agreed with her. These questions had such a particular drift that Georgiana began to conjecture that she was already subjected to certain physical influences, either breathed in with the fragrant air or taken with her food. She fancied likewise, but it might be altogether fancy, that there was a stirring up of her system—a strange, indefinite sensation creeping through her

veins, and tingling, half painfully, half pleasurably, at her heart. Still, whenever she dared to look into the mirror, there she beheld herself pale as a white rose and with the crimson birthmark stamped upon her cheek. Not even Aylmer now hated it so much as she.

51   To dispel the tedium of the hours which her husband found it necessary to devote to the processes of combination and analysis, Georgiana turned over the volumes of his scientific library. In many dark old tomes she met with chapters full of romance and poetry. They were the works of philosophers of the middle ages, such as Albertus Magnus, Cornelius Agrippa, Paracelsus, and the famous friar who created the prophetic Brazen Head. All these antique naturalists stood in advance of their centuries, yet were imbued with some of their credulity, and therefore were believed, and perhaps imagined themselves to have acquired from the investigation of Nature a power above Nature, and from physics a sway over the spiritual world. Hardly less curious and imaginative were the early volumes of the Transactions of the Royal Society, in which the members, knowing little of the limits of natural possibility, were continually recording wonders or proposing methods whereby wonders might be wrought.

52   But to Georgiana the most engrossing volume was a large folio from her husband's own hand, in which he had recorded every experiment of his scientific career, its original aim, the methods adopted for its development, and its final success or failure, with the circumstances to which either event was attributable. The book, in truth, was both the history and emblem of his ardent, ambitious, imaginative, yet practical and laborious life. He handled physical details as if there were nothing beyond them; yet spiritualized them all, and redeemed himself from materialism by his strong and eager aspiration towards the infinite. In his grasp the veriest clod of earth assumed a soul. Georgiana, as she read, reverenced Aylmer and loved him more profoundly than ever, but with a less entire dependence on his judgment than heretofore. Much as he had accomplished, she could not but observe that his most splendid successes were almost invariably failures, if compared with the ideal at which he aimed. His brightest diamonds were the merest pebbles, and felt to be so by himself, in comparison with the inestimable gems which lay hidden beyond his reach. The volume, rich with achievements that had won renown for its author, was yet as melancholy a record as ever mortal hand had penned. It was the sad confession and continual exemplification of the shortcomings of the composite man, the spirit burdened with clay and working in matter, and of the despair that assails the higher nature at finding itself so miserably thwarted by the earthly part. Perhaps every man of genius in whatever sphere might recognize the image of his own experience in Aylmer's journal.

53   So deeply did these reflections affect Georgiana that she laid her face upon the open volume and burst into tears. In this situation she was found by her husband.

54   "It is dangerous to read in a sorcerer's books," said he with a smile, though his countenance was uneasy and displeased. "Georgiana, there are pages in that volume which I can scarcely glance over and keep my senses. Take heed lest it prove as detrimental to you."

55   "It has made me worship you more than ever," said she.

56   "Ah, wait for this one success," rejoined he, "then worship me if you will. I shall deem myself hardly unworthy of it. But come, I have sought you for the luxury of your voice. Sing to me, dearest."

57   So she poured out the liquid music of her voice to quench the thirst of his spirit. He then took his leave with a boyish exuberance of gayety, assuring her that her seclusion would endure but a little longer, and that the result was already certain. Scarcely had he departed when Georgiana felt irresistibly impelled to follow him. She had forgotten to inform Aylmer of a symptom which for two or three hours past had begun to excite her attention. It was a sensation in the fatal birthmark, not painful, but which induced a restlessness throughout her system. Hastening after her husband, she intruded for the first time into the laboratory.

58   The first thing that struck her eye was the furnace, that hot and feverish worker, with the intense glow of its fire, which by the quantities of soot clustered above it seemed to have been burning for ages. There was a distilling apparatus in full operation. Around the room were retorts, tubes, cylinders, crucibles, and other apparatus of chemical research. An electrical machine stood ready for immediate use. The atmosphere felt oppressively close, and was tainted with gaseous odors which had been tormented forth by the processes of science. The severe and homely simplicity of the apartment, with its naked walls and brick pavement, looked strange, accustomed as Georgiana had become to the fantastic elegance of her boudoir. But what chiefly, indeed almost solely, drew her attention, was the aspect of Aylmer himself.

59   He was pale as death, anxious and absorbed, and hung over the furnace as if it depended upon his utmost watchfulness whether the liquid which it was distilling should be the draught of immortal happiness or misery.

60   How different from the sanguine and joyous mien that he had assumed for Georgiana's encouragement!

61   "Carefully now, Aminadab; carefully, thou human machine; carefully, thou man of clay!" muttered Aylmer, more to himself than his assistant. "Now, if there be a thought too much or too little, it is all over."

62   "Ho! ho!" mumbled Aminadab. "Look, master! look!"

63   Aylmer raised his eyes hastily, and at first reddened, then grew paler than ever, on beholding Georgiana. He rushed towards her and seized her arm with a gripe that left the print of his fingers upon it.

64   "Why do you come hither? Have you no trust in your husband?" cried he, impetuously. "Would you throw the blight of that fatal birthmark over my labors? It is not well done. Go, prying woman, go!"

65   "Nay, Aylmer," said Georgiana with the firmness of which she possessed no stinted endowment, "it is not you that have a right to complain. You mistrust your wife; you have concealed the anxiety with which you watch the development of this experiment. Think not so unworthily of me, my husband. Tell me all the risk we run, and fear not that I shall shrink; for my share in it is far less than your own."

66   "No, no, Georgiana!" said Aylmer, impatiently; "it must not be."

67   "I submit," replied she calmly. "And, Aylmer, I shall quaff whatever draught you bring me; but it will be on the same principle that would induce me to take a dose of poison if offered by your hand."

68   "My noble wife," said Aylmer, deeply moved, "I knew not the height and depth of your nature until now. Nothing shall be concealed. Know, then, that this crimson hand, superficial as it seems, has clutched its grasp into your being with a strength of which I had no previous conception. I have already administered agents powerful enough to do aught except to change your entire physical system. Only one thing remains to be tried. If that fail us we are ruined."

69   "Why did you hesitate to tell me this?" asked she.

70   "Because, Georgiana," said Aylmer, in a low voice, "there is danger."

71   "Danger? There is but one danger—that this horrible stigma shall be left upon my cheek!" cried Georgiana. "Remove it, remove it, whatever be the cost, or we shall both go mad!"

72   "Heaven knows your words are too true," said Aylmer, sadly. "And now, dearest, return to your boudoir. In a little while all will be tested."

73   He conducted her back and took leave of her with a solemn tenderness which spoke far more than his words how much was now at stake. After his departure Georgiana became rapt in musings. She considered the character of Aylmer, and did it completer justice than at any previous moment. Her heart exulted, while it trembled, at his honorable love—so pure and lofty that it would accept nothing less than perfection nor miserably make itself contented with an earthlier nature than he had dreamed of. She felt how much more precious was such a sentiment than that meaner kind which would have borne with the imperfection for her sake, and have been guilty of treason to holy love by degrading its perfect idea to the level of the actual; and with her whole spirit she prayed that, for a single moment, she might satisfy his highest and deepest conception. Longer than one moment she well knew it could not be; for his spirit was ever on the march, ever ascending, and each instant required something that was beyond the scope of the instant before.

74   The sound of her husband's footsteps aroused her. He bore a crystal goblet containing a liquor colorless as water, but bright enough to be the draught of immortality. Aylmer was pale; but it seemed rather the consequence of a highly-wrought state of mind and tension of spirit than of fear or doubt.

75   "The concoction of the draught has been perfect," said he, in answer to Georgiana's look. "Unless all my science have deceived me, it cannot fail."

76   "Save on your account, my dearest Aylmer," observed his wife, "I might wish to put off this birthmark of mortality by relinquishing mortality itself in preference to any other mode. Life is but a sad possession to those who have attained precisely the degree of moral advancement at which I stand. Were I weaker and blinder it might be happiness. Were I stronger, it might be endured hopefully. But, being what I find myself, methinks I am of all mortals the most fit to die."

77   "You are fit for heaven without tasting death!" replied her husband "But why do we speak of dying? The draught cannot fail. Behold its effect upon this plant."

78   On the window seat there stood a geranium diseased with yellow blotches, which had overspread all its leaves. Aylmer poured a small quantity of the liquid upon the soil in which it grew. In a little time, when the roots of the plant had taken up the moisture, the unsightly blotches began to be extinguished in a living verdure.

79   "There needed no proof," said Georgiana, quietly. "Give me the goblet I joyfully stake all upon your word."

80   "Drink, then, thou lofty creature!" exclaimed Aylmer, with fervid admiration. "There is no taint of imperfection on thy spirit. Thy sensible frame, too, shall soon be all perfect."

81   She quaffed the liquid and returned the goblet to his hand.

82   "It is grateful," said she with a placid smile. "Methinks it is like water from a heavenly fountain; for it contains I know not what of unobtrusive fragrance and deliciousness. It allays a feverish thirst that had parched me for many days. Now, dearest, let me sleep. My earthly senses are closing over my spirit like the leaves around the heart of a rose at sunset."

83   She spoke the last words with a gentle reluctance, as if it required almost more energy than she could command to pronounce the faint and lingering syllables. Scarcely had they loitered through her lips ere she was lost in slumber. Aylmer sat by her side, watching her aspect with the emotions proper to a man the whole value of whose existence was involved in the process now to be tested. Mingled with this mood, however, was the philosophic investigation characteristic of the man of science. Not the minutest symptom escaped him. A heightened flush of the cheek, a slight irregularity of breath, a quiver of the eyelid, a hardly perceptible tremor through the frame,—such were the details which, as the moments passed, he wrote down in his folio volume. Intense thought had set its stamp upon every previous page of that volume, but the thoughts of years were all concentrated upon the last.

84   While thus employed, he failed not to gaze often at the fatal hand, and not without a shudder. Yet once, by a strange and unaccountable impulse he pressed it with his lips. His spirit recoiled, however, in the very act, and Georgiana, out of the midst of her deep sleep, moved uneasily and murmured as if in remonstrance. Again Aylmer resumed his watch. Nor was it without avail. The crimson hand, which at first had been strongly visible upon the marble paleness of Georgiana's cheek, now grew more faintly outlined. She remained not less pale than ever; but the birthmark with every breath that came and went, lost somewhat of its former distinctness. Its presence had been awful; its departure was more awful still. Watch the stain of the rainbow fading out the sky, and you will know how that mysterious symbol passed away.

85   "By Heaven! it is well-nigh gone!" said Aylmer to himself, in almost irrepressible ecstasy. "I can scarcely trace it now. Success! success! And now it is like the faintest rose color. The lightest flush of blood across her cheek would overcome it. But she is so pale!"

86   He drew aside the window curtain and suffered the light of natural day to fall into the room and rest upon her cheek. At the same time he heard a gross, hoarse chuckle, which he had long known as his servant Aminadab's expression of delight.

87   "Ah, clod! ah, earthly mass!" cried Aylmer, laughing in a sort of frenzy, "you have served me well! Matter and spirit—earth and heaven—have both done their part in this! Laugh, thing of the senses! You have earned the right to laugh."

88   These exclamations broke Georgiana's sleep. She slowly unclosed her eyes and gazed into the mirror which her husband had arranged for that purpose. A faint smile flitted over her lips when she recognized how barely perceptible was

now that crimson hand which had once blazed forth with such disastrous brilliancy as to scare away all their happiness. But then her eyes sought Aylmer's face with a trouble and anxiety that he could by no means account for.

89   "My poor Aylmer!" murmured she.

90   "Poor? Nay, richest, happiest, most favored!" exclaimed he. "My peerless bride, it is successful! You are perfect!"

91   "My poor Aylmer," she repeated, with a more than human tenderness, "you have aimed loftily; you have done nobly. Do not repent that with so high and pure a feeling, you have rejected the best the earth could offer. Aylmer, dearest Aylmer, I am dying!"

92   Alas! it was too true! The fatal hand had grappled with the mystery of life, and was the bond by which an angelic spirit kept itself in union with a mortal frame. As the last crimson tint of the birthmark—that sole token of human imperfection—faded from her cheek, the parting breath of the now perfect woman passed into the atmosphere, and her soul, lingering a moment near her husband, took its heavenward flight. Then a hoarse, chuckling laugh was heard again! Thus ever does the gross fatality of earth exult in its invariable triumph over the immortal essence which, in this dim sphere of half development, demands the completeness of a higher state. Yet, had Alymer reached a profounder wisdom, he need not thus have flung away the happiness which would have woven his mortal life of the selfsame texture with the celestial. The momentary circumstance was too strong for him; he failed to look beyond the shadowy scope of time, and, living once for all in eternity, to find the perfect future in the present.

ISSUE IN FOCUS

Is Genetically Modified Food a Boon or a Risk?

Each month, the United States Food and Drug Administration lists on its Web site its latest "food alerts": foods recalled by sellers because of fears about their safety. In the first two weeks of May 2010 alone, the FDA alerted Americans to concerns about certain apricots, breads, sunflower seeds, cheeses, lettuce, bread, and Amish pumpkin butter.

In one sense, fears about food safety have been around since time immemorial; ever since the Garden of Eden, consumers have worried about what they were putting into their mouths. Nevertheless, out of necessity early humans began experimenting with various species to tame for agricultural purposes so that today, just over 100 crop species are grown intensively around the world, and only a handful of these supply us with most of what we now eat. Through a process of trial and error, farmers and scientists developed processes of selection and cross-breeding (or "hybridization") to combine desirable traits from several varieties into elite cross-bred species. When desired characteristics were unavailable in the crop species, farmers introduced genes from wild species into the cultivated plants. The result, as in the case of corn and dairy cows, is the production of highly productive food species that people born two centuries ago could not have envisioned.

And so in a sense the modern use of gene transfer techniques in the development of genetically modified (GM) crops is but a logical extension of a practice that has existed in agriculture for thousands of years. While GM crops are initially more costly to produce, they eventually save farmers money due to the efficiencies created by greater yields and resistance to insects. Biotechnology, its proponents maintain, further benefits our food supply because genetic modification reduces harmful toxic compounds that exist either naturally or unnaturally in the food we eat. Biotechnology may also allow farmers to produce plants that are tolerant to low temperatures, that thrive in poor soil conditions, and that have a longer shelf-life—all of which could benefit the world's hungry.

And yet modern GM processes are decidedly different from their forebears. While the development of new cultivars through classical breeding processes generally takes ten to fifteen years, changes from new gene transfer methods can occur within one generation; and while traditional cross-breeding transfers genes only between similar plants, modern bioengineering can isolate a gene from one type of organism and combine it with the DNA of dissimilar species. Given what is still unknown about the effects of such rapid and dramatic transformation, critics express concern over the rapidity with which GM foods are spreading across the globe. Critics of GM also worry about losses of crop biodiversity—essential for species resilience and the health of surrounding ecosystems—as the popularity of high-yielding varieties limits the genetic variation found in major crops. Should not new species be tested carefully over a long period of time in order that potential risks to health, safety, society, and the environment can be fully assessed?

In the following pages, we present several arguments related to genetically modified food. Mark Anslow, writing in March 2008 for *The Ecologist* (a British publication that promotes ecologically conscious living), summarizes the case against GM foods in his "Ten Reasons Why GM Won't Feed the World." His suspicions are supported by a 2004 argument by Jeffrey Smith (author of *Genetic Roulette: The Documented Health Risks of Genetically Engineered Foods*), who contends that GM foods are influencing behavior; and by a 2009 argument by Ben Burkett, an African American farmer from Mississippi who is president of the National Family Farm.

By contrast, James Freeman defends GM in an essay that originally appeared in *USA Today* in February 2000. Freeman maintains that biotechnology is nothing more than a highly developed breeding tool, and he labels its opponents "scare mongers" with a limited understanding of the realities of

How was your food grown? If you are living in the United States, it is likely that you are consuming genetically modified foods on a regular basis.

biotechnology and its benefits. In addition, we offer Gregory Jaffe's advice on how to "Lessen the Fear of Genetically Engineered Crops." An expert on consumer issues relating to agricultural biotechnology, Jaffe suggests in his essay (which appeared August 8, 2001 in the *Christian Science Monitor*) that "sensible measures" must be developed to ensure that GM foods are safe for public consumption.

So in the end is it ethical and practical for scientists to modify living organisms, to tamper with the food supply? Is the genetic modification of crops inherently hazardous? Could we unwittingly be making our foods and our world unsafe? And what about the long-term consequences of producing and consuming GM foods? Do GM crops affect the environment or the wild ecosystem, reducing crop biodiversity and the persistence of beneficial insects? (Some suspect that the revered monarch butterfly is being compromised by new varieties of corn.) Could new crops lead to the development of noxious "superweeds"? And what about genetic pollution? Should we be concerned that GM genes might be transferred to other organisms, even to humans and other animals? How can scientists allay public concerns considering the complexities of the issues involved?

MARK ANSLOW

Ten Reasons Why GM Won't Feed the World

G enetic modification can't deliver a safe, secure future food supply. Here's why.

1. Failure to deliver

2 Despite the hype, genetic modification consistently fails to live up to industry claims. Only two GM traits have ever made it to market: herbicide resistance and BT toxin expression (see below). Other promises of genetic modification have failed to materialize. The much vaunted GM "golden rice"—hailed as a cure to vitamin A deficiency—has never made it out of the laboratory, partly because in order to meet recommended levels of vitamin A intake, consumers would need to eat 12 bowls of the rice every day.[1] In 2004, the Kenyan government admitted that Monsanto's GM sweet potatoes were no more resistant to feathery mottle virus than ordinary strains, and in fact produced lower yields.[2] And in January 2008, news that scientists had modified a carrot to cure osteoporosis by providing calcium had to be weighed against the fact that you would need to eat 1.6 kilograms of these vegetables each day to meet your recommended calcium intake.[3]

2. Costing the Earth

3 GM crops are costing farmers and governments more money than they are making. In 2003, a report by the Soil Association estimated the cost to the US economy of GM crops at around $12 billion (£6 billion) since 1999, on account of inflated farm subsidies, loss of export orders, and various seed recalls.[4] A study in Iowa found that GM soybeans required all the same costs as conventional farming but, because they produced lower yields (see below), the farmers ended up making no profit at all.[5] In India, an independent study found that BT cotton crops were costing farmers 10 per cent more than non-BT variants and bringing in 40 per cent lower profits.[6] Between 2001 and 2005, more than 32,000 Indian farmers committed suicide, most as a result of mounting debts caused by inadequate crops.[7]

3. Contamination and gene escape

4 No matter how hard you try, you can never be sure that what you are eating is GM-free. In a recent article, the *New Scientist* admitted that contamination and cross-fertilization between GM and non-GM crops "has happened on many occasions already."[8] In late 2007, U.S. company Scotts Miracle-Gro was fined $500,000 by the U.S. Department of Agriculture when genetic material from a new golf-course grass was found in native grasses as far as 13 miles away from the test sites, apparently released when freshly cut grass was caught and blown by the wind.[9] In 2006, an analysis of 40 Spanish

conventional and organic farms found that eight were contaminated with GM corn varieties, including one farmer whose crop contained 12.6 per cent GM plants.

4. Reliance on pesticides

5   Far from reducing dependency on pesticides and fertilizers, GM crops frequently increase farmers' reliance on these products. Herbicide-resistant crops can be sprayed
indiscriminately with weedkillers such as Monsanto's Roundup because they are engineered to withstand the effect of the chemical. This means that significantly higher levels
of herbicide are found in the final food product, however, and often a second herbicide is
used in the late stages of the crop to promote "dessication," or drying, meaning that these
crops receive a double dose of harmful chemicals.[10] BT maize, engineered to produce
an insecticidal toxin, has never eliminated the use of pesticides,[11] and because the BT
gene cannot be switched off, the crops continue to produce the toxin right up until harvest, reaching the consumer at its highest possible concentrations.[12]

5. Frankenfoods

6   Despite the best efforts of the biotech industry, consumers remain staunchly opposed
to GM food. In 2007, the vast majority of 11,700 responses to the government's consultation on whether contamination of organic food with traces of GM crops should be allowed were strongly negative. The British government's own "GM Nation" debate in
2003 discovered that half of its participants "never want to see GM crops grown in the
United Kingdom under any circumstances," and 96 per cent thought that society knew
too little about the health impacts of genetic modification. In India, farmers' experience
of BT cotton has been so disastrous that the Maharashtra government now advises
that farmers grow soybeans instead. And in Australia, over 250 food companies lodged
appeals with the state governments of New South Wales and Victoria over the lifting of
bans against growing GM canola crops.[13]

6. Breeding resistance

7   Nature is smart, and there are already reports of species emerging that are resistant
to GM crops. This is seen in the emergence of new "superweeds" on farms in North
America—plants that have evolved the ability to withstand the industry's chemicals.
A report by the conservation body English Nature (now Natural England), in 2002,
revealed that oilseed rape plants that had developed resistance to three or more her-
bicides were "not uncommon" in Canada.[14] The superweeds had been created
through random crosses between neighboring GM crops. In order to tackle these superweeds, Canadian farmers were forced to resort to even stronger, more toxic her-
bicides.[15] Similarly, pests (notably the diamondback moth) have been quick to
develop resistance to BT toxin, and in 2007 swarms of mealy bugs began attacking
supposedly pestresistant Indian cotton.

7. Creating problems for solutions

8   Many of the so-called "problems" for which the biotechnology industry develops "solutions" seem to be notions of PR rather than science. Herbicide-resistance was sold under the claim that because crops could be doused in chemicals, there would be much

less need to weed mechanically or plough the soil, keeping more carbon and nitrates under the surface. But a new long-term study by the U.S. Agricultural Research Service has shown that organic farming, even with ploughing, stores more carbon than the GM crops save.[16] BT cotton was claimed to increase resistance to pests, but farmers in East Africa discovered that by planting a local weed amid their corn crop, they could lure pests to lay their eggs on the weed and not the crop.[17]

8. Health risks

9   The results of tests on animals exposed to GM crops give serious cause for concern over their safety. In 1998, Scottish scientists found damage to every single internal organ in rats fed blight-resistant GM potatoes. In a 2006 experiment, female rats fed on herbicide-resistant soybeans gave birth to severely stunted pups, of which half died within three weeks. The survivors were sterile. In the same year, Indian news agencies reported that thousands of sheep allowed to graze on BT cotton crop residues had died suddenly. Further cases of livestock deaths followed in 2007. There have also been reports of allergy-like symptoms among Indian laborers in BT cotton fields. In 2002, the only trial ever to involve human beings appeared to show that altered genetic material from GM soybeans not only survives in the human gut, but may even pass its genetic material to bacteria within the digestive system.[18]

9. Left hungry

10   GM crops have always come with promises of increased yields for farmers, but this has rarely been the case. A three-year study of 87 villages in India found that non-BT cotton consistently produced 30 per cent higher yields than the (more expensive) GM alternative.[19] It is now widely accepted that GM soybeans produce consistently lower yields than conventional varieties. In 1992, Monsanto's own trials showed that the company's Roundup Ready soybeans yield 11.5 per cent less on harvest. Later Monsanto studies went on to reveal that some trials of GM canola crops in Australia actually produced yields 16 per cent below the non- GM national average.[20]

10. Wedded to fertilizers and fossil fuels

11   No genetically modified crop has yet eliminated the need for chemical fertilizers in order to achieve expected yields. Although the industry has made much of the possibility of splicing nitrogen-fixing genes into commercial food crops in order to boost yields, there has so far been little success. This means that GM crops are just as dependent on fossil fuels to make fertilizers as conventional agriculture. In addition to this, GM traits are often specifically designed to fit with large-scale industrial agriculture. Herbicide resistance is of no real benefit unless your farm is too vast to weed mechanically, and it presumes that the farmers already farm in a way that involves the chemical spraying of their crops. Similarly, BT toxin expression is designed to counteract the problem of pest control in vast monocultures, which encourage infestations.

12   In a world that will soon have to change its view of farming—facing as it does the twin challenges of climate change and peak oil—GM crops will soon come to look like a relic of bygone practices.

References

[1] http://www.gmwatch.org/archive2.asp?arcid=8521

[2] http://www.greens.org/s-r/35/35-03.html

[3] *Telegraph*, 14th January 2008, http://tinyurl.com/38e2rp

[4] Soil Association, 2007, http://tinyurl.com/33bfuh

[5] http://ianrnews.unl.edu/static/0005161.shtml

[6] http://www.i-sis.org.uk/IBTCF.php

[7] *Indian Muslims*, 20th November 2007, http://tinyurl.com/2u7wy7

[8] *New Scientist*, "Genes for Greens," 5th January 2007, Issue 2637, Vol 197

[9] http://gmfoodwatch.tribe.net/thread/a1b77b8b-15f5-4f1d-86df-2bbca5aaec70

[10] http://www.prospect-magazine.co.uk/article_details.php?id=9927

[11] http://www.btinternet.com/~nlpWESSEX/Documents/usdagmeconomics.htm

[12] http://www.prospect-magazine.co.uk/article_details.php?id=9927

[13] http://www.indybay.org/newsitems/2007/11/27/18463803.php

[14] http://www.english-nature.org.uk/pubs/publication/PDF/enrr443.pdf

[15] *Innovations Report*, 20th June 2005, http://tinyurl.com/3axmln

[16] http://www.gmwatch.org/archive2.asp?arcid=0658

[17] http://www.i-sis.org.uk/GMcropsfailed.php

[18] All references from "GM Food Nightmare Unfolding in the Regulatory Sham," by Mae-Wan Ho, Joe Cummins, and Peter Saunders, ISIS report.

[19] http://www.i-sis.org.uk/IBTCF.php

[20] http://www.gmwatch.org/archive2.asp?arcid=8558

James Freeman

You're Eating Genetically Modified Food

There's no escape. You are consuming mass quantities of genetically modified food. The milk on your Cheerios this morning came from a genetically modified cow, and the Cheerios themselves featured genetically modified whole grain goodness. At lunch you'll enjoy french fries from genetically modified potatoes and perhaps a bucket of genetically modified fried chicken. If you don't have any meetings this afternoon, maybe you'll wash it all down with the finest genetically modified hops, grains, and barley, brewed to perfection—or at least to completion if you're drinking Schaefer.

2   Everything you eat is the result of genetic modification. When a rancher in Wyoming selected his stud bull to mate with a certain cow to produce the calf that ultimately produced the milk on your breakfast table, he was manipulating genes. Sounds delicious, doesn't it? Sorry, but you get the point.

3   Long before you were ever born, farmers were splicing genes and manipulating seeds to create more robust plants. Genetic modification used to be called "breeding," and people have been doing it for centuries. Thomas Jefferson did it at Monticello, as he experimented in his gardens with literally hundreds of varieties of fruits and vegetables. (Hmm, Thomas Jefferson and genes. . . . This column is going to disappoint a lot of people doing Web searches.)

4   Anyway, to return to the topic at hand, breeding isn't a scary word, so people who oppose technology call it "genetic modification." They want to cast biotechnology, which is just a more precise and effective breeding tool, as some kind of threat to our lives, instead of the blessing that it is.

5   Have you ever seen corn in its natural state without genetic modification? It's disgusting. We're talking about that nasty, gnarled, multi-colored garbage used as ornamentation in Thanksgiving displays. The fear mongers should eat that the next time they want to criticize technology. In fact, the fear mongers are waging a very successful campaign against biotechnology, especially in Europe where they've lobbied to limit the availability of "genetically modified" foods. Even in the United States, where we generally embrace technology and its possibilities, the fear is spreading—not because of some horrible event related to the food supply, but because of more aggressive spinning of the media. In fact, you've been enjoying foods enhanced by biotechnology for most of the last decade. And the news is all good—lower prices and more abundant food.

6   As for the future, the potential to eliminate human suffering is enormous. Right now, according to the World Health Organization, more than a million kids die every year because they lack vitamin A in their diets. Millions more become blind. WHO estimates that more than a billion people suffer from anemia, caused by iron deficiency. What if we could develop rice or corn plants with all of the essential vitamins for children? Personally, I'd rather have an entire day's nutrition bio-engineered into a Twinkie or a pan pizza, but I recognize the benefits of more-nutritious crops. Reasonable people can disagree on the best applications for this technology.

7   Still, the critics want to talk about the dangers of genetically modified crops. The Environmental Protection Agency wants to regulate the use of certain bio-engineered corn seeds because they include a resistance to pests. Specifically, the seeds are bred to include a toxin called BT that kills little creatures called corn borers, so farmers don't need to spray pesticides. Turns out, according to the EPA, that the toxin in the corn can kill monarch butterflies, too. The butterflies don't eat corn, but the EPA is afraid that the corn pollen will blow over and land on a milkweed and stick to it and then confused monarch caterpillars will inadvertently eat the pollen. Not exactly the end of the world, but it sounds bad—until you consider the alternatives. According to Professor Nina Fedoroff, "A wide-spectrum pesticide sprayed from a plane is going to kill a lot more insects than will be killed by an in-plant toxin."

8   Of course, the anti-tech crowd will say that they don't like pesticides either. They promote organic farming—meaning we use more land to produce our food and we

clear more wilderness. We also pay more for food, since we're not using the efficiencies that come from technology. Maybe that's not a problem for you or me, but it's bad news for those millions of malnourished kids around the world. Says Fedoroff, "I think that most inhabitants of contemporary urban societies don't have a clue about how tough it is to grow enough food for the human population in competition with bacteria, fungi, insects, and animals and in the face of droughts, floods, and other climatic variations." That may be true, but I do think that most Americans understand the positive impact of technology. And that's why they'll ultimately reject the scare campaign against biotechnology.

Jeffrey Smith

Another Reason for Schools to Ban Genetically Engineered Foods

Before the Appleton, Wisconsin high school replaced their cafeteria's processed foods with wholesome, nutritious food, the school was described as out-of-control. There were weapons violations, student disruptions, and a cop on duty fulltime. After the change in school meals, the students were calm, focused, and orderly. There were no more weapons violations, and no suicides, expulsions, dropouts, or drug violations. The new diet and improved behavior has lasted for seven years, and now other schools are changing their meal programs with similar results.

2   Years ago, a science class at Appleton found support for their new diet by conducting a cruel and unusual experiment with three mice. They fed them the junk food that kids in other high schools eat everyday. The mice freaked out. Their behavior was totally different than the three mice in the neighboring cage. The neighboring mice had good karma; they were fed nutritious whole foods and behaved like mice. They slept during the day inside their cardboard tube, played with each other, and acted very mouse-like. The junk food mice, on the other hand, destroyed their cardboard tube, were no longer nocturnal, stopped playing with each other, fought often, and two mice eventually killed the third and ate it. After the three month experiment, the students rehabilitated the two surviving junk food mice with a diet of whole foods. After about three weeks, the mice came around.

3   Sister Luigi Frigo repeats this experiment every year in her second grade class in Cudahy, Wisconsin, but mercifully, for only four days. Even on the first day of junk food, the mice's behavior "changes drastically." They become lazy, antisocial, and nervous. And it still takes the mice about two to three weeks on unprocessed foods to return to normal. One year, the second graders tried to do the experiment again a few months later with the same mice, but this time the animals refused to eat the junk food.

4   Across the ocean in Holland, a student fed one group of mice genetically modified (GM) corn and soy, and another group the non-GM variety. The GM mice stopped playing with each other and withdrew into their own parts of the cage. When the student tried to pick them up, unlike their well-behaved neighbors, the GM mice scampered around in apparent fear and tried to climb the walls. One mouse in the GM group was found dead at the end of the experiment.

5   It's interesting to note that the junk food fed to the mice in the Wisconsin experiments also contained genetically modified ingredients. And although the Appleton school lunch program did not specifically attempt to remove GM foods, it happened anyway. That's because GM foods such as soy and corn and their derivatives are largely found in processed foods. So when the school switched to unprocessed alternatives, almost all ingredients derived from GM crops were taken out automatically.

6   Does this mean that GM foods negatively affect the behavior of humans or animals? It would certainly be irresponsible to say so on the basis of a single student mice experiment and the results at Appleton. On the other hand, it is equally irresponsible to say that it doesn't.

7   We are just beginning to understand the influence of food on behavior. A study in *Science* in December 2002 concluded that "food molecules act like hormones, regulating body functioning and triggering cell division. The molecules can cause mental imbalances ranging from attention-deficit and hyperactivity disorder to serious mental illness." The problem is we do not know which food molecules have what effect. The bigger problem is that the composition of GM foods can change radically without our knowledge.

8   Genetically modified foods have genes inserted into their DNA. But genes are not Legos; they don't just snap into place. Gene insertion creates unpredicted, irreversible changes. In one study, for example, a gene chip monitored the DNA before and after a single foreign gene was inserted. As much as 5 percent of the DNA's genes changed the amount of protein they were producing. Not only is that huge in itself, but these changes can multiply through complex interactions down the line.

9   In spite of the potential for dramatic changes in the composition of GM foods, they are typically measured for only a small number of known nutrient levels. But even if we *could* identify all the changed compounds, at this point we wouldn't know which might be responsible for the antisocial nature of mice or humans. Likewise, we are only beginning to identify the medicinal compounds in food. We now know, for example, that the pigment in blueberries may revive the brain's neural communication system, and the antioxidant found in grape skins may fight cancer and reduce heart disease. But what about other valuable compounds we don't know about that might change or disappear in GM varieties?

10   Consider GM soy. In July 1999, years after it was on the market, independent researchers published a study showing that it contains 12–14 percent less cancer-fighting phytoestrogens. What else has changed that we don't know about? [Monsanto responded with its own study, which concluded that soy's phytoestrogen levels vary too much to even carry out a statistical analysis. They failed to disclose, however, that the laboratory that conducted Monsanto's experiment had been instructed to use an obsolete method to detect phytoestrogens—one that had been replaced due to its highly variable results.]

11   In 1996, Monsanto published a paper in the *Journal of Nutrition* that concluded in the title, "The composition of glyphosate-tolerant soybean seeds is equivalent to that of conventional soybeans." The study only compared a small number of nutrients and a close look at their charts revealed significant differences in the fat, ash, and carbohydrate content. In addition, GM soy meal contained 27 percent more trypsin inhibitor, a well-known soy allergen. The study also used questionable methods. Nutrient comparisons are routinely conducted on plants grown in identical conditions so that variables such as weather and soil can be ruled out. Otherwise, differences in plant composition could be easily missed. In Monsanto's study, soybeans were planted in widely varying climates and geography.

12   Although one of their trials *was* a side-by-side comparison between GM and non-GM soy, for some reason the results were left out of the paper altogether. Years later, a medical writer found the missing data in the archives of the *Journal of Nutrition* and made them public. No wonder the scientists left them out. The GM soy showed significantly lower levels of protein, a fatty acid, and phenylalanine, an essential amino acid. Also, toasted GM soy meal contained nearly twice the amount of a lectin that may block the body's ability to assimilate other nutrients. Furthermore, the toasted GM soy contained as much as seven times the amount of trypsin inhibitor, indicating that the allergen may survive cooking more in the GM variety. (This might explain the 50 percent jump in soy allergies in the UK, just after GM soy was introduced.)

13   We don't know all the changes that occur with genetic engineering, but certainly GM crops are not the same. Ask the animals. Eyewitness reports from all over North America describe how several types of animals, when given a choice, avoided eating GM food. These included cows, pigs, elk, deer, raccoons, squirrels, rats, and mice. In fact, the Dutch student mentioned above first determined that his mice had a two-to-one preference for non-GM before forcing half of them to eat only the engineered variety.

14   Differences in GM food will likely have a much larger impact on children. They are three to four times more susceptible to allergies. Also, they convert more of the food into body-building material. Altered nutrients or added toxins can result in developmental problems. For this reason, animal nutrition studies are typically conducted on young, developing animals. After the feeding trial, organs are weighed and often studied under magnification. If scientists used mature animals instead of young ones, even severe nutritional problems might not be detected. The Monsanto study used mature animals instead of young ones.

15   They also diluted their GM soy with non-GM protein 10- or 12-fold before feeding the animals. And they never weighed the organs or examined them under a microscope. The study, which is the only major animal feeding study on GM soy ever published, is dismissed by critics as rigged to avoid finding problems.

16   Unfortunately, there is a much bigger experiment going on—an uncontrolled one which we are all a part of. We're being fed GM foods daily, without knowing the impact of these foods on our health, our behavior, or our children. Thousands of schools around the world, particularly in Europe, have decided not to let their kids be used as guinea pigs. They have banned GM foods.

17   The impact of changes in the composition of GM foods is only one of several reasons why these foods may be dangerous. Other reasons may be far worse (see

www.seedsofdeception.com). With the epidemic of obesity and diabetes and with the results in Appleton, parents and schools are waking up to the critical role that diet plays. When making changes in what kids eat, removing GM foods should be a priority.

Ben Burkett

Green Revolution a Failure in Africa

The global food crisis and how to stop hunger from escalating in the midst of the current economic crisis will be the subject of a recent G8 meeting of Agricultural ministers in Treviso, Italy. For now, the G8 and the United States continue to advocate the same disastrous policies that got us into the current mess where 1 billion people lack access to adequate food. U.S. agriculture secretary Tom Vilsack has said that biotechnology is necessary to address hunger while the U.S. Senate Foreign Relations Committee recently approved without much public debate the "Global Hunger Security Act" sponsored by Senators Bob Casey and Richard Lugar, that for the first time would mandate the U.S. to fund genetic engineering projects in foreign agriculture research. Meanwhile, the Gates Foundation has billions invested in the "Alliance for a Green Revolution in Africa."

2   As an African American farmer from Mississippi who has visited and traveled to Africa many times, I am stunned that the real solutions continue to be ignored. We face multiple crises—financial, climate, energy, and water. Business as usual will not solve our global hunger crisis. More expensive genetically modified seeds, pesticides, and chemical-intensive practices won't help the hungry and will only allow more profits and control for seed companies like Monsanto and Syngenta.

3   While the G8 calls for more "free trade" in agriculture and more biotechnology, groundbreaking scientific reports and actions at the United Nations are actively calling for a different vision of agriculture. This would be based on agroecological methods that respect our planet's resources and provide a decent living for family farmers. In 2008, the International Assessment of Agricultural Knowledge, Science and Technology for Development (IAASTD), backed by United Nations agencies, the World Bank, and over 400 contributing scientists from 80 countries found that the most promising solutions to the world's food crisis include investing in agroecological research, extension, and farming. The Congress and Obama Administration need to take a serious look at the IAASTD report before funneling scarce resources into another Green Revolution in Africa.

4   Past public-private partnerships in Africa have proven to be failures, such as the 14-year project between Monsanto, USAID, and the Kenyan Agricultural Research Institute to engineer a

virus-resistant sweet potato. The GM sweet potato failed to show any resistance to the virus while local varieties actually outperformed the GM variety in field trials. The U.S. approach to helping Africa should not be a top-down process that excludes the voices of African farmers who have the knowledge of their land and what food to grow.

5   The UN is helping to move the discussion towards "food sovereignty" by appointing a Special Rapporteur on the "Right to Food," and convening a Panel on the Right to Food. I was privileged to hear General Coordinator of La Via Campesina Henry Saragih of Indonesia and Professor Olivier De Schutter before the United Nations General Assembly. De Schutter said, "the right to food is not simply about more production, but about distribution and access. While high food prices are bad for consumers, so too are depressed prices for farmers who can't make a living. De Schutter pointed out that 60% of hungry people in the world are small farmers, pastoralists, fisherfolk, and others who make a living off the land. An additional 20% are landless agriculture workers."

6   A "right to food" framework therefore goes deeper than simply the misguided obsession with yields and productivity, and more fundamentally towards questions regarding democracy and access to resources, including land, water and credit. A recent report by Union of Concerned Scientists titled "Failure to Yield: Evaluating the Performance of Genetically Engineered Crops," showed that despite 20 years of research and 13 years of commercialization, genetic engineering has failed to significantly increase U.S. crop yields while only driving up costs for farmers. In comparison, traditional breeding continues to deliver better results. The scientific research and renewed focus on the "right to food" exposes why we must move away from Green Revolution monoculture practices and instead embrace ecologically sound practices, more equitable trade rules and local food distribution systems to empower family farmers. Now the governments of the world and the Gates Foundation need to finally get the message as well.

GREGORY JAFFE

Lessen the Fear of Genetically Engineered Crops

Protesters carrying signs stating "Biocide is Homicide" and shouting concerns about the risks of eating genetically engineered foods recently demonstrated outside the biotechnology industry's annual convention. Inside the convention center, industry extolled the safety of genetically engineered foods and the benefits of future crops like "golden rice."

2   Neither corporate hyperbole nor radical slogans do much to inform the public. What is needed is the shaping of sensible measures to ensure that genetically engineered foods are safe. The first few engineered crops are already providing remarkable benefits. Cotton modified to kill insects has greatly diminished farmers' use of toxic insecticides, thereby reducing costs, increasing yields, and, presumably, reducing harm to nontarget species. Likewise, biotech soybeans facilitate no-till farming, which reduces soil erosion and water pollution.

3   Despite such benefits, agricultural biotechnology is under siege for reasons good and bad. Activists have burned fields and bombed labs. Farmers will not plant genetically engineered sweet corn, sugar beets, and apples, for fear of consumer rejection. And countries in Europe and Asia refuse to import U.S.-grown genetically engineered crops. Some countries now require labeling of foods containing engineered ingredients. Those requirements have spurred food processors, who want to avoid negative-sounding labels, to eliminate bioengineered ingredients.

4   Buffeted by the polarized debate, many Americans oppose biotech foods, in part because farmers and seed companies get the benefits while consumers bear the risk. If anti-genetically engineered sentiment increases, U.S. farmers may be forced to forgo the advantages of engineered crops. And most public and private investment in agricultural biotechnology would dry up.

5   To reap the benefits of agricultural biotechnology, minimize the risks, and boost public confidence, the U.S. must upgrade its flawed regulatory system. Currently, the Food and Drug Administration (FDA) does not formally approve any genetically engineered crops as safe to eat. Instead, it reviews safety data provided voluntarily by seed companies. That consultation process, which the FDA admits is "not a comprehensive scientific review of the data," culminates with the FDA stating only that it has "no further questions . . . at this time." Although no health problems with genetically engineered crops have been detected, that industry-driven process is weak insurance. The recent FDA proposal requiring a formal notification before marketing a biotech food is an improvement.

6   All biotech foods should go through a mandatory approval process with specific testing and data requirements. The National Academy of Sciences should be commissioned to recommend a precise method of assessment.

7   Genetically engineered crops also raise environmental concerns. They could lead to pesticide-resistant insects and weeds and might contaminate plants that are close relatives of the crops. To safeguard our ecosystem, the current laws need fixing. Congress should close regulatory gaps to ensure that all future applications of biotechnology, ranging from fast-growing fish to corn plants that produce industrial chemicals, receive thorough environmental reviews. Also, the Environmental Protection Agency must enforce restrictions it has imposed on bioengineered crops to help prevent emergence of insecticide-resistant pests.

8   Although strong regulations would minimize environmental and safety risks, nothing would boost public confidence more than engineered products that benefit consumers. No beneficial products currently exist.

9   Worldwide acceptance of biotechnology will occur only when other countries reap benefits from this technology. Instead of spending millions of dollars on feel-good advertising campaigns, the biotech industry should train developing-country scientists and fund research in those countries. Companies—and universities—should donate patented crops and processes to developing countries. Agricultural biotechnology is not a panacea for all agricultural problems here or abroad, nor is it free from risk. But, with adequate safeguards, it could provide tremendous benefits for an ever-populous, pesticide-drenched, and water-deficient globe.

FROM READING TO WRITING

1. In this section, you read Bill Joy's written argument for caution in the development of new nanotechnologies, followed by Merkle's reaction to Joy's piece, which takes place in the form of an interview. Conduct a rhetorical analysis of these two forms of argumentation: What are some of the rhetorical differences between arguing through a written essay versus speaking out via a moderated verbal dialogue? Consider questions of audience, the process of argument construction, ethos, rhetorical impact, and so on.

2. In his essay, Bill Gates writes glowingly of the potential for robots to benefit human society. Yet, as you have also seen (in the arguments put forth by Joy and Marks), robots are not without their critics. Exactly what is a robot, anyway? What differentiates robots from other machines? Write an essay that shows your attitude toward robots by defining them in a particular way. (For advice on writing definitions, see Chapter 10.)

3. One of the major methods for convincing people of the need for organ donor compensation or stem cell research is the use of personal examples—narratives—about people who might benefit. Beginning from your own informed beliefs, write a story that illustrates your position on a particular scientific issue—stem cell, organ donation, genetically modified foods, or some other controversial process or technology. If possible, draw from your personal experience with the subject at hand. (For advice on narrative arguments, see Chapter 13.)

4. Construct a short narrative (perhaps after the example of "The Birth-Mark") that makes an argument about science and society.

5. Evaluate—on the basis of practicality, ethics, or esthetics (or all of them)—one of the scientific processes or technologies discussed in this chapter. (See Chapter 12 for information on how evaluation arguments work.)

6. Based on the guidelines in Chapter 15, write a proposal argument that defends or undermines the practice of genetic modification of food crops *from a human rights perspective*. Is genetic engineering the solution to world hunger (or at least a part of that solution)? Or will it only exacerbate the existing polarization between the "haves" and the "have-nots?" Conduct your own research prior to constructing your argument.

26 | Privacy

New Challenges to Personal Privacy

How does a conference room design like this one, with transparent glass and open blinds in the middle of an office building, reflect (or push for) new attitudes about privacy?

The Dog Poop Girl (as she came to be known) was riding the subway in Seoul, South Korea, one day when her dog decided to "take care of business." According to a *Washington Post* story written by Jonathan Krim on July 7, 2005, the woman (a university student) made no move to clean up the mess, so fellow passengers grew agitated. One of them recorded the scene on a cell phone camera and then posted photos on a Web site. Web surfers came upon the photos and began referring to her as Dog Poop Girl. One thing led to another, and soon her privacy was completely gone: people revealed her true name, began asking for and sharing more information about her, launched blogs commenting about her and her relatives, and generally crackled with gossip about her and her behavior. Ultimately she became the subject of sermons and online discussions, and her story made the national news. In humiliation, Dog Poop Girl withdrew from her university.

According to an American Civil Liberties Union (ACLU) Web posting in May 2010, the Department of Justice was seeking to obtain the contents of a Yahoo! e-mail account without the e-mailer's permission and without a search warrant. Government investigators in the process of building a criminal case were maintaining that because the Yahoo! e-mail had been accessed by the user, it no longer qualified as "in electronic storage" (protected as private property under the Stored Communications Act). But Yahoo! asked a federal court judge to block the government attempt, and the company was supported by the ACLU, the Electronic Frontier Foundation (EFF), Google, and many other public interest organizations. "The government is trying to evade federal privacy law and the Constitution," said EFF Senior Staff Attorney Kevin Bankston. "The Fourth Amendment protects these stored e-mails, just like it does our private papers. We all have a reasonable expectation of privacy in the

> "You have zero privacy now—get over it."
>
> —SCOTT MCNEALY, CEO OF SUN MICROSYSTEMS

contents of our e-mail accounts, and the government should have to make a showing of probable cause to a judge before it rifles through our private communications."

A third incident was reported by Felisa Cardona in the *Denver Post* on August 2, 2005. A computer security breach at the University of Colorado left 29,000 students and 7,000 faculty and staff vulnerable to identity theft. It seems that hackers attacked the university computers in order to gain access to the Buff One ID card used by many students and staff. Though no information seems to have been used due to this attack, 6,000 students had to be issued new cards in order to gain access to their dorms. Moreover, after the incident, Colorado officials decided to stop using Social Security number identifications, and many other universities have done the same because they too have been targeted by identity thieves.

A biometric measuring instrument at Busch Gardens helps staff make sure the same person uses the same ticket each day.

These three incidents illustrate some of the new challenges to personal privacy that have been raised in response to technology developments and concerns about security that are one legacy of the September 11, 2001, attacks. There is no doubt that electronic technologies have given people a new degree of personal freedom: hand-held computers, cell phones, e-mail, and Web shopping are now routine time-savers. But there is also no doubt that a price has been paid for that freedom: That price is the surveillance side of the Internet and other technologies. In the wake of September 11, other terrorist attacks, and the increased attention to security that has ensued, privacy issues have been an increasing concern in American life. Law enforcement officials seek access to information about potential conspiracies, parents are placing devices on their children in order to keep tabs on their whereabouts, and businesses increasingly gather information about people to individualize marketing campaigns, keep an eye out for good (and bad) credit risks, and customize customers. (Businesses and police also increasingly spy on their own employees.)

One emerging technology—biometrics—measures physical and behavioral data, such as fingerprints or keystroke patterns, in order to identify individual human beings. Biometric recognition provides a deeply personalized means of identification that enhances security, say its supporters, but a national biometric database also raises questions of privacy, say its detractors. What would it mean in terms of national security and surveillance to store citizens' inherently unique characteristics in a nationwide database?

And when is freedom too much freedom? If bloggers act as a posse, tracking down criminals and turning them over to law enforcement, is that appropriate action or vigilante action? What about efforts to replicate what was done to the Dog Poop Girl? Should laws prevent people from publicizing and branding people who seem undesirable? Is too much sharing going on via Facebook? Should people who wish to share secrets—whether the secrets are true or not—have the anonymity and apparent protection afforded by the Internet? Must e-mail users simply accept as a fact of life that they are bombarded by hundreds of unauthorized, unsolicited spam messages? And what are the limits of what government officials should be able to do to inspect the personal records of citizens?

Contemporary Arguments

Is it possible, in other words, to have both security and freedom in the United States? What is the proper balance of the two?

On the one hand, some people support a national ID card (like those already used, incidentally, in several European nations) or sign up for in-vehicle security systems such as OnStar (always on the watch!) as a safety feature. They root for police to pursue potential terrorists, they use E-ZPass without giving a thought to the fact that they are giving out their whereabouts, they approve when cameras are mounted to watch over high-crime areas, they wink when Internet service providers disclose customer records to government agents if they feel that a crime is being committed, and they appreciate being notified that convicted felons have moved into the neighborhood. On the other hand, they also protest when police use wiretaps without explicit legal permission, worry about the ability of global positioning systems to snoop on people from satellites (especially by zeroing in on cell phones or implanted homing devices), and protest when roving surveillance cameras are mounted in stores and at street corners, in public parks and on school playgrounds.

Everyone these days seems to be monitored or monitoring. On-line data collectors record which Web sites people visit; airlines record data on people's travels; companies routinely perform background checks on potential employees; bus and train companies check passenger lists against

While surveillance cameras may be designed to provide security, they also intrude on individuals' privacy, often without their knowledge.

records of "suspicious" characters; businesses seek to develop systems that can deliver customized marketing information to particular households and commuters; and supermarkets record purchases in order to fine-tune their stocking patterns. In the future, some say, we can look forward to smart cars, smart airports, smart TVs, smart credit cards, and smart homes—all designed to give us certain freedoms, if at the price of losing some of our privacy.

The arguments in this chapter discuss all these questions related to privacy. Adam Penenberg's "The Surveillance Society" overviews the brave new world that is now developing (for better or for worse), and the selections that follow argue about aspects of technology that undermine our privacy. Robert Cringely sounds an alert about Facebook. Jonathan Locker worries about OnStar. Jay Stanley (speaking for the American Civil Liberties Union) contends that body searches of airline passengers are neither effective nor constitutional. And Adam Cohen makes a plea for citizens to be able to walk down the street without being monitored by cameras—to be able to enjoy what he calls "locational privacy." These are just a small sample of the issues that are facing Americans as it becomes easier and easier for us to watch each other.

Because the emerging field of biometrics effectively illustrates the tensions between protection and privacy, we look in detail at this emerging technology in the Issue in Focus. The selections reproduced there describe the technologies (such as signature analysis, keystroke patterns, and vein biometric systems) and dramatize the excitement—and the fears—that accompany them. On one hand, biometric technologies hold out the promise of improved crime fighting and national security. On the other, such technologies inevitably encroach on individuals' privacy and may even open the door to DNA identify theft. What price are we willing to pay for privacy (or security)? At what point does it make sense to forfeit private information for protection and convenience?

ADAM PENENBERG

The Surveillance Society

Adam L. Penenberg's Web site indicates that he is assistant director of the Business and Economic Program at New York University. He is the author of several books, including *Spooked: Espionage in Corporate America* and *Viral Loop: From Facebook to Twitter, How Today's Smartest Businesses Grow Themselves*. Formerly senior editor at *Forbes*, Penenberg is now a contributing writer to *Fast Company* and has also written for *Inc.*, the *New York Times*, *Slate*, *Playboy*, *Mother Jones*, and *Wired*, in which the following article appeared in December 2001, shortly after 9/11.

W ithin hours of the attacks on the World Trade Center and the Pentagon, as federal officials shut down airports and U.S. strategists began plotting a military response, Attorney General John Ashcroft was mobilizing his own forces. In meetings with top aides at the FBI's Strategic Information and Operations Center—during which the

Surveillance cameras have become a part of the urban landscape.

White House as well as the State and Defense departments dialed in via secure video-conference—Ashcroft pulled together a host of antiterrorism measures. Days later, the attorney general sent to Capitol Hill a bill (the Patriot Act) that would make it easier for the government to tap cell phones and pagers, give the Feds broad authority to monitor email and Web browsing, strengthen money-laundering laws, and weaken immigrants' rights. There were whispers of a national identity card and of using face-recognition software and retinal scans at airports and in other public spaces. And high above it all would sit an Office of Homeland Security, run by former Pennsylvania Governor Tom Ridge, who would report directly to the Oval Office.

2   Such talk usually generates fractious debate between privacy hawks and security hounds. By now, most of us can recite the familiar *Nightline* arguments and counterarguments. But this time the acrimony has been muted. The terrorist assault on America shifted the balance between privacy and security. What was considered Orwellian one week seemed perfectly reasonable—even necessary—the next. Politicians who routinely clash were marching in lockstep. "When you're in this type of conflict—when you're at war—civil liberties are treated differently," said Senate Republican Trent Lott. "This event will change the balance between freedom and security," echoed House Democrat Richard Gephardt. "There's a whole range of issues that we're going to be grappling with in the next month that takes us to this basic trade-off."

3   Almost immediately, there were unmistakable signs that new surveillance tools would be a linchpin in the war on terrorism. The FBI met with AOL, EarthLink, and other large ISPs, and there was renewed talk of using DCS 1000 to let the FBI monitor email traffic. Visionics—a maker of face-recognition software used in surveillance cameras in London and Tampa, Florida, and in the databases of close to a dozen state law enforcement agencies—reported that its switchboards were jammed. The stock prices of some companies in the security business spiked as the rest of the market crumbled.

4   But truth be told, the U.S. was embracing the Surveillance Society well before September 11. In the name of safety, we have grown increasingly comfortable with cameras monitoring us whenever we stop to buy a Slurpee, grab cash from an ATM, or park in a downtown lot. And in the name of convenience, we've happily accepted a range of products and services, from cell phones to credit cards to Web browsers, that make our lives easier and have the secondary effect of permitting us to be tracked. They're not spy technologies—but they might as well be.

5   Americans don't seem to be spooked by these incursions. "Apparently, consumers don't feel their privacy is threatened," says Barbara Bellissimo, owner of a now-defunct dotcom that offered anonymous Web browsing. "That's why there are no profitable privacy companies." (It might also be why millions of Americans watch reality-based television shows like *Survivor* that package round-the-clock surveillance as entertainment.)

6   Just how vast is the new surveillance world? Let's start with cameras. More than 60 communities in a dozen states have set up traffic-light cameras that ticket drivers for running red lights or speeding. Casinos in Las Vegas zoom in on the cards we hold at the blackjack table. Cameras are mounted on police cars, they hang from trees in public parks, they're affixed to the walls in sports stadiums and shopping malls. David Brin, author of *The Transparent Society,* postulates a "Moore's law of cameras." He sees them roughly "halving in size, and doubling in acuity and movement capability and sheer numbers, every year or two."

7   The surveillance net also has a digital arm. With computers home to the data entrails of half a billion bank accounts, just as many credit card accounts, and hundreds of millions of medical claims, mortgages, and retirement funds, there exists a significant cache of online data about each of us.

8   Then there's the matter of monitoring our daily travels. Debit cards like New York's E-ZPass deduct a fee as commuters zip through tollbooths *and* track our comings and goings on the road; transit cards chart riders' subway journeys; employee ID cards can show when we arrived at work, when we left, and where we went within the office complex. Phone cards mark who we call and, often, from where. Credit card records etch us in time and space more reliably than any eyewitness. So do airline tickets—even if you pay cash. And as for the cell phone: "If you turn it on, you can be tracked," says Jim Atkinson, a countersurveillance expert who is president of Granite Island Group in Gloucester, Massachusetts.

9   OnStar, GM's onboard communications system, offers a GPS service to its 1.5 million customers. That means that at any given moment, OnStar can locate each of those 1.5 million cars. (OnStar will track a car only at the request of the driver or, in some instances, the police; the company keeps no historical database of car locations, though if it had the inclination—or was pressured—to gather and store reams of data, it could.) Mercedes' TeleAid and Ford's Wingcast provide similar services. As does

AirIQ, which Hertz, Avis, and Budget use for their premium fleets: If a car is abandoned, AirIQ can locate it; if it's stolen, the company can disable its motor.

10   For now, the information about each of us resides in dozens of separate databases owned by the credit card companies and the phone carriers, the rental car agencies and police departments, the ISPs and the IRS. But the aftermath of September 11 could change all that by creating in many of us an appetite for information and a willingness to be monitored. And this raises a disquieting possibility: Will the disparate elements of our surveillance society be assembled into a surveillance web? Will the private companies and the government agencies come together to create a superdatabase accessible to . . . who? Will it strip us not just of personal privacy—we seem resigned, even OK, with that—but of public anonymity?

11   Worrying is a waste of time. Surveillance is here. It was inevitable. But the surveillance state is not.

12   A few days after September 11, Akram Jaber was driving his Chevy Suburban over the pothole-strewn streets of Chicago's south side. With his 15-month-old son in the backseat, he was heading to the liquor store he owns to lock up for the night. A battered Chevy Caprice sped by, then stopped in front of him at a red light. Two men emerged; one pointed a gun at Jaber. "Take it easy," Jaber called out. "I have my son in the car." He left the keys in the ignition, unhitched his son, and turned over the $50,000 vehicle.

13   As the carjackers sped away, Jaber whipped out his cell phone to dial 911. Then he called an operator at OnStar. (He had been paying $16.95 a month for the basic Safety & Security plan: roadside and emergency assistance, remote lock and unlock, and stolen vehicle tracking.) He gave his name, license plate number, and four-digit PIN. The operator called Jaber's vehicle and requested GPS data, then updated the car's position by pinging it every minute. The operator relayed the car's heading to the police officer on the scene, who forwarded it to a dispatcher. Within minutes, officers swooped in on the vehicle and arrested the men. "The police were amazed at how easy it was," say Jaber, who himself was awfully pleased.

14   What's really amazing is just how many similar tools are becoming available to law enforcement. A suspect's alibi can be checked out by looking at the location data trail created by use of his tollbooth pass, transit card, or credit card. Surveillance cameras capture images that authorities can cross-check against a database of criminals through the use of face-recognition software. And cell phones have become the digital equivalent of Hansel and Gretel's bread crumbs.

15   When a cell phone is turned on, it broadcasts an identification number to the closest antennas, which allow the carrier to chart its customers. It's a simple matter—known as triangulation—to track the signal as it arrives at different towers, then calculate the location of the phone based on time differences. The police have taken full advantage of this tracking trick, though—technically, at least—they need a court order to access the information. Earlier this year, Timothy Crosby, 40, was busted for raping and robbing a Brooklyn woman after the police located him by homing in on his cell phone signal. In November 2000, authorities pursued Kofi Apea Orleans-Lindsay for allegedly killing a Maryland state trooper during a buy-and-bust operation. Police used cell data to track Orleans-Lindsay to Brooklyn, where they arrested him.

16   Then there was the case of Christopher Stewart, a New York subway employee whose alibi in the March slaying of his ex-girlfriend crumbled when police subjected his

MetroCard transit pass to detailed analysis (MetroCard use can be traced by a serial number). Stewart had claimed he was boarding a Staten Island ferry at the time she was killed. But data from the MetroCard, still in his possession, had him exiting a subway station near the crime scene just before the murder. He was arrested and indicted by a grand jury. MetroCard records were also used against Marco Valencia, who was charged in the December 1999 assault and robbery of a supermarket manager in Manhattan. Valencia claimed he was in Staten Island, but his MetroCard told a different tale, and when confronted, he pleaded guilty.

17   In light of the way cell phones and transit cards are being used to track criminals, video cameras seem remarkably, well, obvious. But they're a cornerstone of the surveillance society, and they've proved an important weapon in law enforcement's arsenal. Prior to September 11, such cameras stirred up controversy. When the Tampa Police Department installed face-recognition software in its network last June, the public was outraged, and House majority leader Dick Armey joined with civil rights groups to protest. There was similar push-back in Britain in 1996, when authorities installed 300 cameras in the East London neighborhood of Newham in an effort to gather intelligence on suspected IRA bombings. The cameras didn't help much in the fight on terrorism, but overall crime rates fell 30 percent after they were deployed, according to city figures. Crime dropped an additional 34 percent in 1998, after the cameras were equipped with Visionic's face-recognition software. Last year, illegal activities in surrounding areas increased between 10 and 20 percent, but Newham's inched up less than half a percent. The program has been so successful that Visionics has been retained to hook up closed-circuit TV cameras in five more nearby London neighborhoods.

18   Although face-recognition surveillance systems are not foolproof, most Brits now view "spy" cameras as a part of everyday life, and polls indicate a majority of citizens support their use. England already boasts about 1.5 million police surveillance cameras—more than any other country—and the government plans to double that number within three years. With so many cams, the average city denizen can expect to be taped every five minutes, according to *The Times* of London.

19   Even as new surveillance technologies increase the amount of information available about each of us, there's something reassuring in the fact that this data is extremely far-flung. It would, today, take a considerable amount of sleuthing and multiple search warrants for anyone—individuals, private companies, public agencies—to aggregate the fruits of the surveillance web in any useful way.

20   But there are signs that in the future it might be much easier to access disparate data about individuals—where they've been, what they bought, who they were with, what they were wearing, who they called, what Web sites they visited, what they wrote in email. After all, the information exists, and from a technical perspective, it's easy to tap (cell phones, credit cards, ATMs, tollbooth passes—all are part of the same bitstream of 0s and 1s). The legal protections that might have prevented access to this data are eroding. And as the line between the public and private sectors blurs, the data will likely flow in ways it never has before.

21   So what do we get? Think of all these factoids residing not in some static database but in a dynamic environment in which strands of information can be pulled together from a huge variety of sources based on a user's request. It's not Microsoft Outlook, it's Google. In fact, researchers at Applied Systems Intelligence in Roswell,

Georgia, are working on just such software. Called Karnac (Knowledge Aided Retrieval in Activity Context), the program would scan everything from gun registrations and credit card records to newspapers and Web sites. While Karnac or a similar program may be a long way off, more modest developments provide a glimpse into where we could be headed. In the weeks following the attacks, airport authorities hatched plans for security systems that would link biometric techniques like iris scans with a government database of known or suspected terrorists. Such systems could easily migrate to other public spaces, motivated by a concern for community safety and a desire to catch criminals.

22   Eventually, surveillance cameras in every mom-and-pop store could use face-recognition software and network databases to link you to your Social Security number, consumer profile, credit report, home and work addresses, and criminal and driving records. Networked street cams could track your location—and keep the digital footage on file.

23   The gated communities of tomorrow will be monitored by cameras, motion detectors, and sensors of all kinds embedded in the walls, floors—every surface. Such systems, hyped as smart-house technologies, are already in beta at universities and corporate labs across the country. Tools such as Bluetooth and 802.11 will turn every object and street corner into a node of the wireless Web, aware of and communicating with the Net-connected PDA and cell of every passerby. Like transit cards and toll-booth passes, the wireless Web isn't a surveillance technology per se, but it will have that effect.

24   Look out a few more years and nano-cameras as small as grains of sand will create a world in which the wind has eyes. Fingerprint-scanning doorknobs and steering wheels could know their users by touch.

25   There will be limits, of course—legal mechanisms like search warrants that protect individuals from undue surveillance. But those safeguards will change with the times. In an effort to bring wiretapping laws into the cellular age, Attorney General Ashcroft proposed—and Congress approved—"roving wiretaps" to give the government authority to monitor a suspect's calls from any phone and any jurisdiction. As communications technologies continue to multiply and blur, it will be increasingly difficult to say where the telephone network ends and the Web begins. Cell phones send messages to pagers. Cars log on to the Internet. The search warrants of the surveillance era will need to span multiple technologies and will likely be written with increasingly broad language.

26   If all this raises the specter of Big Brother, well, that's understandable. But it's also wrong. Even as we trade privacy for security and convenience, we're hardly headed toward totalitarianism. Orwell's greatest error, says Peter Huber, author of *Orwell's Revenge,* was his view that the government had a monopoly on surveillance technologies. Says Huber: "If the Thought Police use telescreens, so can others—that's just the way telescreens work, if they work at all."

27   Indeed, citizens have already learned to use surveillance tools to keep government accountable. When motorist Rodney King was beaten by Los Angeles police officers in 1991, a bystander caught the incident on video. Though the subsequent trial ended in acquittal of the officers, it proved the potency of videotape as evidence.

"Video cameras create a potential counterbalance—a kind of ombudsman," says Sam Gregory, a program coordinator for Witness, a New York nonprofit that lends video equipment to human rights activists around the world. "They let citizens protect themselves and hold the state accountable." Recent projects sponsored by Witness include *Operation Fine Girl,* which documents rape as a weapon of war in Sierra Leone, and *Behind the Labels,* an exposé of the clothing-industry sweatshops in Saipan.

28   In Orange County, California, the sheriff's department mounted video cameras on its patrol cars with the idea that footage of arrests could be used to protect against false accusations of excessive force. Not surprisingly, those tapes have been used against the police officers themselves. In June, Robert Delgiudice, who was beaten by police for resisting arrest, had his case dismissed when the video showed that the officer had lied in his police report and preliminary hearing testimony. (Delgiudice is now planning a civil suit.) As Don Landis Jr., the Orange County deputy public defender who argued Delgiudice's case, puts it: "The cameras bring accountability."

29   They also bring transparency, which is almost always a good thing. An antidote to corruption, it keeps financial markets strong, governments honest, and corporations accountable. In public institutions and on city streets, the more transparency the better. Sometimes the reverse is true: The darkness of privacy is essential to the conversations between doctor and patient, to the personal information sent by letter, and to the things we do and say within our bedrooms. In those cases, privacy must be staunchly defended.

30   "Just about the only Fourth Amendment concern that the Supreme Court protects, year after year, decision after decision, is a U.S. citizen's privacy in his own home," says Landis. Earlier this year, the court upheld this principle again, deciding that the police in Florence, Oregon, had violated the Fourth Amendment when, without a warrant, they used thermal imaging technology to detect the heat lamps inside the house of a man they suspected of growing marijuana. Any technology that enables law enforcement to see or hear through walls, the court decreed, required a search warrant; without a warrant, the practice amounted to an unreasonable search.

31   The Constitution itself, therefore, stands in the way of Big Brother. OK, privacy is eroding. But liberty, and the safeguards inherent in due process, remain strong. The government can collect megabytes of information about us, but where and when they do and how that information is used is still subject to the laws designed to keep the state from abusing its power. And of course, even as Congress and the judicial system struggle to maintain the balance of privacy and security, citizens will continue to take technology into their own hands.

32   "Look at all the cameras and cell phones, a gazillion of them, that documented everything on September 11," says David Brin. "The powers of vision and information are expanding exponentially in the hands of the people, far faster than they are being acquired by government." In the long run, Brin predicts, it will be people—empowered by the surveillance web—who thwart the thugs, the tyrants, and even the terrorists.

Mike Luckovich's Pulitzer Prize–winning political cartoons appear in the *Atlanta Journal-Constitution* and are frequently reprinted. This one appeared first on May 27, 2010, just after Facebook founder Mark Zuckerberg announced that he was taking steps, in response to criticism, to protect the privacy of Facebook participants.

Robert X. Cringely

Facebook Puts Your Privacy on Parade

From 1987 to 1995 Robert X. Cringely wrote the "Notes from the Field" column in *InfoWorld,* a weekly computer trade newspaper. More recently, his writing has appeared in the *New York Times*, *Newsweek*, *Forbes*, *Upside*, *Success*, and *Worth*, among other publications. The argument printed here originally appeared on InfoWorld's Web site in January 2010. In May 2010, Facebook responded to its critics by altering its privacy controls (see the cartoon above), but the criticism has not stopped.

Once again Facebook is involved in a privacy imbroglio, and once again it's because boy-founder Mark Zuckerberg opened his yap and stuck his Keds-clad foot inside.

2   Last week at The Crunchies, the annual awards party thrown by TechCrunch doyenne Michael Arrington, Zuckerberg got on stage briefly and made the following statement (per Gawker):

When I got started in my dorm room at Harvard, the question a lot of people asked was "why would I want to put any information on the Internet at all? Why would I want to have a website?"

And then in the last 5 or 6 years, blogging has taken off in a huge way and all these different services that have people sharing all this information. People have really gotten comfortable not only sharing more information and different kinds, but more openly and with more people. That social norm is just something that's evolved over time.

We view it as our role in the system to constantly be innovating and be updating what our system is to reflect what the current social norms are.

So now, a lot of companies would be trapped by the conventions and their legacies of what they've built, [and so] doing a privacy change for 350 million users is not the type of thing that a lot of companies would do. But we viewed that as a really important thing, to always keep a beginner's mind and think: what would we do if we were starting the company now, and starting the site now, and we decided that these would be the social norms now and we just went for it.

3   Allow me to translate. By "innovating and updating" his system, Zuckerberg means the modifications to user privacy settings Facebook unveiled a few weeks ago that made Facebookers' information more easily accessible by Google et al. by default. And by "current social norms," Zuckerberg means "stuff we think we can get away with today that we couldn't get away with three or four years ago."

Facebook.com founder Mark Zuckerberg at the company's Palo Alto, California, headquarters.

4   Interestingly, after Facebook's default settings changed, Zuckerberg's personal profile went from being virtually inaccessible (unless you were the CEO's friend) to nearly wide open, allowing any Facebooker to view the 290 photos he'd posted. These included several of Zucky the Party Animal (the worst of which Gawker happily scooped up and republished). A couple of days later those photos were mysteriously inaccessible again.

5   So much for social norms.

6   After those changes, ten privacy groups banded together and filed a protest with the FTC about Facebook's sudden open-book privacy policy. In response, Facebook also made a few small tweaks to restore some (but not all) of its previous privacy settings.

7   Zuckerberg's comments last week just re-ignited the Facebook privacy debate, including the inevitable responses from knuckleheads like Arrington "that privacy is already really, really dead. . . . We don't really care about privacy anymore. And Facebook is just giving us exactly what we want." (There is, however, no truth to the rumor that Zuckerberg is planning to publish nude pix of himself on his profile as part of Facebook's new "bare it and share it" campaign.)

8   It's almost always the case that people who like to say "privacy is dead, get over it," (a) have a financial interest in buying and selling personal information, and (b) guard their own personal information zealously, even if they live otherwise very public lives. For example: I'm still waiting for Arrington to share his Social Security number with the world, like the Lifelock CEO he seems to like so much, or to post pix from his vacation at that nudist colony (I'm making that last bit up—I hope). Even if he did, that doesn't mean other people should.

9   People may not give a damn about some kinds of personal information, but they care a great deal about other information. The stuff they care about just varies from person to person. In fact, it's usually the most public of us that have the greatest need for privacy. Exotic dancers may take their clothes off in public (or on MySpace), but they don't usually use their real names or broadcast their home address. Their bodies may be public, but not their identities.

10   Likewise, just because women shared their bra colors on Facebook to raise awareness of breast cancer doesn't mean they want to share that information with the marketers at Victoria's Secrets. (Facebook is not explicitly doing this, but opening up people's status updates to searches makes that possible.)

11   I think people want the ability to easily control what information is and isn't private. While Facebook offers a lot of control—you

might even say a confusing amount for most people—it's still doing its best to encourage you to share early and often. If you can't easily determine how someone wants a particular piece of information to be treated, you should assume it is private, not that they want to share it with the world. The latter is the assumption Facebook is making and Zuckerberg was defending.

12   What people really want is not what Facebook is giving us. As Read Write Web's Marshall Fitzpatrick points out, Facebook's popularity stems in part from how carefully it protected its members' information—at first limiting access to college students, then just to your networks of friends. Now it seems to have forgotten all of that, to its detriment.

13   Why? In a word, money. You can't easily monetize data that's private. The more data you can share with the world, the more revenue you can generate. Facebook isn't trying to give users what they want or to conform with "social norms." It's trying to make a buck out of each and every one of its 350 million users, over and over again. Nothing wrong with that, except perhaps how you go about it.

Jonathan Locker

OnStar: Big Brother's Eye in the Sky

Jonathan I. Locker contributed the following article to the Web site "The Truth About Cars," which presents automotive news, reviews, and editorials. The article appeared February 14, 2008.

Ever since the Model T hit the silver screen, evading the long arm of the law has been a cinematic theme. From the General Lee locomotive outrunning Boss Hogg, to Smokey being outwitted by Burt Reynolds' mustache, the public imagination has always associated fast cars with police pursuit. While the majority of motorists would never dream of trying to outrun the long arm of the law, soon, they won't have to. It'll be resting on their shoulder.

2   Consider OnStar.

3   OnStar is a telemetry system providing a central data bank with real-time data on virtually every system in your car, including GPS. OnStar's computer knows where you were, when you were there, and how fast you went. It knows if and when you applied the brakes, if and when the air bags deployed, and what speed you were going at the time. It knows if and when your car was

serviced. OnStar operators can determine if you have a passenger in the front seat (airbag detection). All interactions with OnStar's operators are automatically recorded (hence the commercials). By the same token, under certain conditions, OnStar can switch on your GM car's microphone remotely and record any and all sounds within the vehicle (i.e., conversations).

4   But wait, there's more. As of 2009, customers who upgrade to OnStar's "Safe & Sound" plan automatically receive the "Stolen Vehicle Slowdown" service. (Yes, it's an "opt out" deal.) If the OnStar-equipped vehicle is reported stolen and law enforcement has "established a clear line of sight of the stolen vehicle," the police may ask OnStar to slow it down remotely.

5   Many customers find OnStar immensely reassuring; it's their guardian e-angel. No question: OnStar has saved lives and provided its customers with valuable services. Otherwise, they wouldn't be in business.

6   But what if the police are investigating a crime. They ask OnStar where your car was on a certain date and time, to corroborate an alibi. Or what if you're in a crash and the other guy's attorney would like to know how fast you were driving when you ran the red light? Would OnStar surrender the information? GM notes that "OnStar is required to locate the car to comply with legal requirements, including valid court orders showing probable cause in criminal investigations." And OnStar may use gathered information to "protect the rights, property, or safety of you or others."

7   Imagine the following scenario. The FBI shows up at OnStar master command and tells them your car's been stolen by a terrorist, who may be using it to commit a crime at this very moment. Contacting the owner is out of the question; the owner may also be a terrorist. What does OnStar do? They cooperate with the FBI and give them everything they've got on your car. No warrant needed and no notification to you. Hell, you may not even have the service enabled. In other words, you not only have to trust OnStar to protect your privacy, you have to trust the police not to ask the questions in the first place.

8   The Constitution of the United States protects us from the heavy hand of government. However, when it comes to protection from private entities, it does little. Into this void, multiple privacy laws have entered, creating a farrago of local, state, and federal laws which provide limited and haphazard protection to citizens. Whatever privacy protection these laws provide are usually nullified when companies violate them in "good faith" (e.g., while assisting the authorities).

9   So who is going to stop the government from monitoring your car? The Bill of Rights protects you from an unreasonable search and seizure; the government cannot take what belongs to you without a warrant. OnStar owns the information they collect about your car. In short, there is nothing to stop the police or OnStar from using the information you paid for against you.

10   And the next step is even more insidious. Imagine GPS speed limiters which only allow you to go the speed limit based upon a map uploaded into your car's navigation system. Now Sammy Hagar will only be driving 55 no matter how hard he stomps on the go pedal. This is the ultimate assault on pistonheads. The only place where driving will be fun will be on the track—if OnStar and/or the car's manufacturer (e.g., the Japanese GT-R) let you.

11   There's only one sensible response to this trend: boycott vehicles equipped with OnStar, even if you don't sign up for the service. (Remember: it can be remotely enabled.) If customers actively avoid vehicles that spy on them, manufacturers will have to stop installing the monitoring software and hardware. And law enforcement agencies and prosecutors will have to get their information and apprehend criminals the old-fashioned way: through legally-sanctioned police work.

12   In short, I don't buy OnStar, and neither should you.

Jay Stanley

ACLU Opposes Body Cavity Searches for Airline Passengers

Jay Stanley works for the American Civil Liberties Union (ACLU) Technology and Liberty Program, and he especially writes and speaks about privacy issues related to technology. He is the coauthor of *Bigger Monster, Weaker Chains: The Growth of an American Surveillance Society*, an ACLU report examining how the government infringes on people's privacy. The following statement was published on the ACLU site December 31, 2009, in response to calls for increased screenings at U.S. airports.

Okay, so no one is explicitly calling for body cavity searches for all airline travelers—yet. But the logic of those pushing for body scanners for all airline passengers, and criticizing the ACLU for opposing that, leads to the inescapable conclusion that these critics would support such a policy.

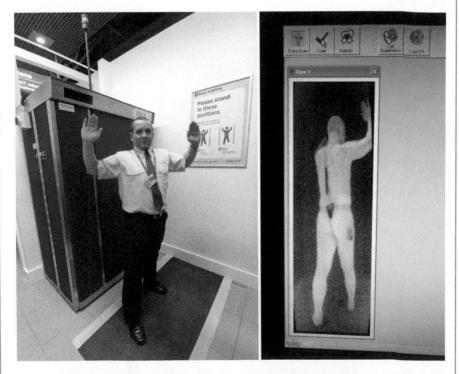

How much should airport scanners be able to reveal? Are full-body scanners ethical?

2   Consider:

1. When Richard Reid brought explosives onto an airliner hidden in his shoes, the authorities began making everyone remove their shoes. When security experts and other critics pointed out that this was "silly security," defenders argued that we must put up with it in order to block that particular kind of plot.

2. Now that a disturbed person has brought explosives onto an airliner in his underwear, panicked voices want the TSA to essentially view naked pictures of every passenger who boards an airline—that's up to 2.5 million people per day on domestic flights alone. When the ACLU and members of Congress object, critics cry that we must abandon our personal dignity and privacy in order to block that particular kind of plot.

3. It is far from clear that body scanners will, as so many people seem to be assuming, detect explosives concealed the way that Umar Farouk Abdulmutallab concealed them. Some experts have said plastic explosives can be concealed against the human body. It's not clear how good scanner operators would have been at detecting the "anatomically congruent" explosives Abdulmutallab hid in his underwear (let alone how consistently effective bored operators would be if these $200,000 machines were placed at every screening station in every airport for 2.5 million people a day).

4. However, if terrorists even *perceive* that scanners will work, they take the next logical step and conceal explosives in their body cavities. Al Qaeda has already used this technique; in September a suicide bomber stowed a full pound of high explosives and a detonator inside his rectum, and attempted to assassinate a Saudi prince by blowing himself up. (The prince survived.)

3   So it seems that when the next terrorist tries to blow up an airliner using this technique, all the usual jittery voices surely will once again say that we must abandon our personal dignity and privacy in order to block that particular kind of plot. So we'd just like to get ahead of the game and state right now that the ACLU will be opposed to that.

4   Of course, even if body cavity searches for all were made policy, terrorists would probably shift their efforts to just hiding explosives in their carryon baggage, and the TSA's level of success in catching contraband has always been, shall we say, mixed. And reliably catching every possible means of hiding 50 grams of explosives is probably impossible given the millions of people who fly each day.

5   Yes, the government must zealously work to make us as safe as possible and must take every reasonable step to make sure security breaches like the ones that led to the Christmas Day attempted attack are not repeated. But we need to act wisely. That means not trading away our privacy for ineffective policies. We should be investing in developing technologies such as trace portal detectors (a.k.a. "puffer machines") that provide a layer of security without invading privacy, and in developing competent law enforcement and intelligence agencies that will stop terrorists *before* they show up at the airport.

6   Ultimately, it is up to the American people to figure out just how much privacy they want to abandon to block a few particular means of carrying out terrorist attacks. The ACLU represents those who value privacy in this debate. But when Americans make that decision, they should do so with their eyes wide open, without any illusions that this will prevent all attacks on airliners, much less attacks on shopping malls or all the infinite number of other plots and targets that terrorists could come up with if they are not stopped by competent law enforcement and intelligence agencies.

ADAM COHEN

A Casualty of the Technology Revolution: "Locational Privacy"

Adam Cohen is a member of the *New York Times* editorial board; before that he was a senior writer at *Time*. Since he holds a law degree, he naturally writes on legal issues, particularly when they involve technology. Among other things, he is the author of *Nothing to Fear: FDR's Inner Circle* and *American Pharaoh: Mayor Richard J. Daley.* The editorial printed below was published by the *New York Times* in September 2009.

When I woke up the other day, I went straight to my computer to catch up on the news and to read e-mail. About 20 minutes later, I walked half a block to the gym, where I exercised for 45 minutes. I took the C train to The New York Times building, and then at the end of the day, I was back on the C train. I had dinner on my friends' (Elisabeth and Dan's) rooftop, then walked home seven blocks.

2   I'm not giving away any secrets here—nothing I did was secret to begin with. Verizon online knows when I logged on, and New York Sports Club knows when I swiped my membership card. The M.T.A. could trace (through the MetroCard I bought with a credit card) when and where I took the subway, and *The Times* knows when I used my ID to enter the building. AT&T could follow me along the way through my iPhone. There

may also be videotape of my travels, given the ubiquity of surveillance cameras in New York City. There are thousands of cameras on buildings and lampposts around Manhattan, according to the New York Civil Liberties Union, many near my home and office. Several may have been in a position to film my dinner on Elisabeth and Dan's roof.

3   A little-appreciated downside of the technology revolution is that, mainly without thinking about it, we have given up "locational privacy." Even in low-tech days, our movements were not entirely private. The desk attendant at my gym might have recalled seeing me, or my colleagues might have remembered when I arrived. Now the information is collected automatically and often stored indefinitely.

4   Privacy advocates are rightly concerned. Corporations and the government can keep track of what political meetings people attend, what bars and clubs they go to, whose homes they visit. It is the fact that people's locations are being recorded "pervasively, silently, and cheaply that we're worried about," the Electronic Frontier Foundation said in a recent report.

5   People's cellphones and E-ZPasses are increasingly being used against them in court. If your phone is on, even if you are not on a call, you may be able to be found (and perhaps picked up) at any hour of the day or night. As disturbing as it is to have your private data breached, it is worse to think that your physical location might fall into the hands of people who mean you harm.

6   This decline in locational privacy, from near-absolute to very little in just a few years, has not generated much outrage, or even discussion. That is partly because so much of it is a side-effect of technology that people like. Drivers love E-ZPasses. G.P.S. enables all sorts of cool smart phone applications, from driving directions and find-a-nearby-restaurant features to the ever-popular "Take Me to My Car."

Location-aware cell phones, iPads, and other mobile devices make it easy for anyone to track your location and movements. Privacy advocates are concerned; are you?
© 2010 Google-Map Data © Google, Sanborn

7   And people usually do not know that they are being monitored. The transit authority does not warn buyers that their MetroCards track their subway use (or that the police have used the cards in criminal investigations). Cameras that follow people on the street are placed in locations that are hard to spot. It is difficult for cellphone users to know precisely what information their devices are sending about their current location, when they are doing it, and where that information is going. Some privacy advocates were upset by recent reports that the Palm Pre, which has built-in G.P.S., has a feature that regularly sends its users' location back to Palm without notifying them at the time.

8   What can be done? As much as possible, location-specific information should not be collected in the first place, or not in personally identifiable form. There are many ways, as the Electronic Frontier Foundation notes, to use cryptography and anonymization to protect locational privacy. To tell you about nearby coffee shops, a cellphone application needs to know where you are. It does not need to know who you are.

9   In addition, when locational information is collected, people should be given advance notice and a chance to opt out. Data should be erased as soon as its main purpose is met. After you pay your E-ZPass bill, there is no reason for the government to keep records of your travel.

10   The idea of constantly monitoring the citizenry's movements used to conjure up images of totalitarian states. Now, technology does the surveillance—generally in the name of being helpful. It's time for a serious conversation about how much of our privacy of movement we want to give up.

ISSUE IN FOCUS

BIOMETRICS: Measuring the Body for Identity

The 1997 film *Gattaca,* starring Ethan Hawke and Uma Thurman, features the supposedly futuristic plot of a "natural" man stealing genetic information to pose as an elite citizen—someone who was genetically engineered before birth. Using stolen biometric identifiers, Hawke's character poses as another person, but the film's final message just may be that the "natural" man still triumphs: spirit trumps technology. Another more recent film, *Minority Report* (2002), starring Tom Cruise, also involves biometric technologies. Cruise's character takes someone else's retinas in order to clear his name of a crime he supposedly commits in the future. Like *Gattaca, Minority Report* employs futuristic biometric technologies that today are not entirely feasible but are no longer beyond the realm of possibility. Indeed, both films characterize the possibilities—fascinating and frightening—of biometrics that no longer belong exclusively to the realm of science fiction.

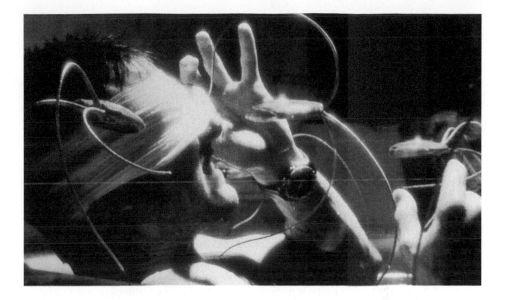

Biometrics encompasses a variety of identification strategies. You've seen them on TV shows like *CSI* and *Person of Interest*. Biometric devices can record physical characteristics such as irises, retinas, fingerprints, hands, knuckles, palms, veins, faces, DNA, sweat, pores, lips, odors, and voices. In addition, biometric technologies can analyze human behavior patterns such as signatures, keyboard keystroke patterns, and gaits. Some of these technologies are more advanced and more feasible than others, but the goal of biometrics is to conclusively determine individual identity and thus remove the element of human error that comes with lost, stolen, hacked, copied, or shared passwords and tokens. Biometrics helps us bypass these pitfalls by securing data that belongs exclusively to one person—since that data is actually part of the person.

There are more everyday problems with biometrics than *CSI* and *Person of Interest, Gattaca,* and *Minority Report* suggest. For one thing, in large-scale uses of biometrics, there are likely to be portions of the population for whom some facets of the technology simply don't work, as well as small percentages of overlap that make identity difficult to determine. In addition to concerns about the cleanliness and safety of the machinery used to collect and measure biometric data, some detractors raise concerns about security and privacy: if biometric data is stolen, individuals can be permanently vulnerable because, unlike passwords and tokens, biometric information is difficult, if not impossible, to change. Furthermore, biometrics incites fears that individuals who protect valuable property with biometrics might be physically harmed or endangered if someone tries to steal the property. These concerns about biometrics extend beyond the cost and logistics to the ways in which we use, store, and manipulate our bodies for security's sake.

The reading selections in this section describe the range of types and uses of biometrics and argue about advantages and disadvantages that accompany this emerging technology. Because biometric recognition technologies effectively illustrate the tensions between protection and privacy, we include images and articles that dramatize the excitement and fear surrounding them.

The section opens with an article by Steven C. Bennett, a partner in a law firm who teaches a course in privacy law at Hunter College. He gives an even-handed discussion of the pros and cons of biometric technologies and goes on to argue that the biometrics industry should set standards that protect the privacy of individuals. Less even-handed is a page from the FBI Web site, which extols the benefits of these technologies. Paul Saffo, Managing Director of Foresight at Discern Analytics and teacher at Stanford, is a writer whose essays have appeared in *Fortune, The Harvard Business Review*, the *Los Angeles Times, Newsweek,* the *New York Times,* the *Washington Post*, and *Wired*. He explains the not-so-science-fiction possibility of DNA identity theft and cautions against blind faith: in biometrics. We conclude with Ben Goldacre lamenting "the biometric blues"; a physician and medical researcher in Britain, Goldacre contributes frequently to the British national newspaper *The Guardian*—especially in a regular column entitled "Bad Science."

As you read and analyze the texts and images, consider the desirability of biometrics—a technology that started as science fiction but has been studied and advanced by the U.S. military in efforts to secure the nation and catch terrorists. What about this technology captivates our imaginations in so many different ways? What balance are we willing to strike between personal privacy and national security, or even personal protection? How does biometrics alter our sense of ourselves as unique individuals—both in terms of what information we would share publicly and in terms of identity theft? These selections introduce you to a complex and significant technological advance, and they can prompt further thinking, reading, research, and writing as you enter this important contemporary debate about security and privacy.

STEVEN C. **BENNETT**

Privacy Implications of Biometrics

B roadly speaking, biometrics is a term for any measurement of individuals used either to identify or authenticate their claimed identity. Fingerprints and wanted posters, for example, are well-established biometric methods used by law enforcement to track down, identify, and authenticate suspects. Modern information technology has added a number of new machine-based identification techniques, such as facial scanning and recognition, and improved the older techniques. These mechanical innovations offer a host of benefits, chiefly speed, efficiency, and vast analytical power. Several nations, including the United States and most of Europe, have begun to take advantage of the security benefits of these advances by issuing passports and other forms of identification encoded with biometric information. With such benefits, however, may come significant risks to the privacy and data security rights of consumers, workers, and citizens at large. The development of "best practices" in managing the use of biometrics is essential to strike an appropriate balance, ensuring proper use of these techniques and safeguards against abuse. If industry does not develop and follow such guidelines, more stringent regulations may be imposed.

2   A prime example of both the potential benefits and the threats of rapidly evolving biometric technology appears in the use of facial scanning technology at several recent NFL Superbowls. Before the 2001 Superbowl in Tampa, over 30 closed-circuit television cameras were installed to monitor the crowd and compare images of spectators to images of known criminals. Approximately 20 matches were made, several during the game. There was a widespread outcry, including dramatic media accounts labeling the game the "Snooper Bowl," disparaging the Orwellian overtones, after this use of biometrics became public knowledge. These complaints were muted at the New Orleans Superbowl in 2002, perhaps as a consequence of the September 11th attacks. Nonetheless, the use of facial recognition technology during the Superbowl has since been abandoned.

WHAT IS BIOMETRICS?

3   Essentially, biometrics is the use of human physical characteristics as identifiers. While any trait can be used, several specific types have proven to be most useful. The three most common genres of biometric identifiers are appearance, physiography, and bio-dynamics. Physical appearance is primarily judged through the use of photographs or other still images, but can also be validated through written descriptions of an individual's height, weight, coloration, hair, and visible markings. Physiography, on the other hand, requires some form of measurement—such as fingerprints, dental measurements, optical scans of the retina or iris, hand geometry, or DNA testing. As opposed to these two static characteristics, bio-dynamics measures patterned active behavior—voice fluctuation, keystroke tendencies, manner of writing a signature, and habituated body signals such as gait.

4   To perform the task of identification or authentication, biometrics relies on the comparison of live data supplied—voluntarily or not—by the subject to a dataset or template containing pre-existing information. The prime difference between the objectives of identification and authentication lies in the scope of pre-existing information required for each task. Identification can assign a name or other value to a previously anonymous person by comparing the live data to a large number of samples, a "1·N search," to determine whether there is a match. Authentication, on the other hand, merely requires confirmation that individuals are who they claim to be. The comparison, then, is between the live data and previously supplied data from a single individual, or a "1:1 search." Both searches can either be positive or negative; they can ensure either that a person is already within the database and permitted access (positive) or, as in the Superbowl example, that a person is not within a database and therefore permitted access (negative).

5   Basic forms of biometrics are all around us. The typical driver's license or state identification card, for example, contains a photograph and some form(s) of physical description (such as height and eye color). The license often also contains a sample

signature from the individual; and the individual's address. All of these, in some ways, are forms of biometrics:

- The photograph may be compared to the individual carrying the license;
- The physical characteristics described on the license may also be compared to those of the individual;
- The individual may be asked for a signature sample, and that sample compared to the license sample;
- The individual may be asked to recall (unaided) his or her address, and that answer compared to the license information.

What Is Different About Machine Biometrics?

6 Biometrics standing alone are just characteristics; they neither protect nor threaten individual privacy. As the license example suggests, the use of biometrics has been accepted and commonplace for over 100 years. It is how biometric technologies are used that determines their effect on privacy. The rise of mechanical biometric technology, especially computers and computerized databases, and the consequent automation of the identification process have radically increased both the ability to identify individuals biometrically and the potential for abuse of biometrics. These changes extend to almost every aspect of biometrics—data capture, analysis, communication, and storage—and must be understood before analyzing their implications for privacy and data security rights of individuals.

Data Capture

7 Technological advances now allow for involuntary or unknowing capture of biometric characteristics. The Superbowl provides an example—if the security firm had chosen to store the captured images rather than merely test and destroy them, it would have created the possibility for biometric identification of all who attended the game. Even when the submission of information is voluntary, many biometrics are very difficult for a human to gather unaided. For example, scanning the retina of the human eye requires light-producing and magnification devices, and meaningful analysis of the results requires imaging and comparison technology. These techniques, however, may offer highly individualized identification when used properly. Even biometric methods that can be performed competently by humans (such as fingerprint or hand shape identification) can be greatly improved through machine operation.

Data Analysis

8 Though Moore's law of increasing computer capacity is only observational, the exponential growth of computing power has allowed for ever more rapid identification searches, even as databases expand. Fingerprinting technology provides the perfect lens through which to view this growth. Originally, fingerprinting could only be used to authenticate the identity of criminals who had left their prints at a crime scene, noting any 1:1 matches. Gradually, a classification system (the Henry system) developed, which allowed for identification searches, but these searches required significant amounts of time to perform. By 1971, the FBI possessed over 200 million paper fingerprint files, including records on 30 million criminals, and J. Edgar Hoover had

unsuccessfully promoted universal fingerprinting. The true technological shift, however, came in the 1990s, when new fingerprint scanners cut the time to identify prints from months to hours.

Data Communication

9 Many forms of biometrics were impossible to communicate until recently. Before the creation of reasonably high quality photographs and copies, accurate re-creation of most biometrics via transmission was impossible. The year 1924 witnessed the first transmission of fingerprints from Australia to Scotland Yard via telegraph. Since then, modern communication has dramatically enhanced the efficiency of biometrics. Just as computational analysis has followed the predictions of Moore's law, so too the field of communications has lived up to the even more aggressive predictions of the "Photon Law"—that bandwidth will more than double every year. As bandwidth increases, more biometrics can be transmitted, and data transfer is faster. This allows for linkage of varied biometric data sets, as well as non-biometric information.

Data Storage

10 Finally, the ability to reduce biometrics to electronic datasets of relatively small size has allowed for construction of large, searchable electronic databases. As a result of the falling costs of electronic data storage and the rising ability to transmit that data rapidly across long distances, technological shifts have allowed for creation of massive interlinked databases of biometric information. The FBI's Integrated Automated Fingerprint Identification System ("IAFIS") is the largest biometric database in the world, containing the fingerprints and related criminal history of over 47 million individuals. Remote electronic submissions for criminal inquiries can receive a response from IAFIS within two hours. The IAFIS data illustrate a final observational law of technology, Metcalfe's law, which states that the power of a network increases (exponentially, though this value is debated) as every node is added. Thus, the ability to integrate and store information from many different databases dramatically increases the value of biometric data.

THE VALUE OF MACHINE BIOMETRICS

11 The efficiency gained from mechanization of biometrics is clear. Fingerprint searches that a decade ago took three months to complete now can be completed in under two hours. Biometrics also has an intrinsic value in its ability to function as (potentially) the most effective security safeguard, restricting access to sensitive information or physical areas. To secure such access, authorization (or identity) must be validated. The rise in identity theft demonstrates the weakness of validating systems based purely on possession of particular information about the individual. These faults have caused many in business to turn to biometrics as a more secure method of identifying or authenticating individuals.

12 In response to digital hackers, many password systems now require frequent changes or the use of special symbols and non-repetitive character strings. These shifts, designed to protect security, tend instead to undermine it as users often write their passwords on a sticky note by their desks. Relying on access cards is equally

problematic—such cards can be lost, stolen, or left right by the computer to which they provide access. A recent survey, moreover, found that 70 percent of Americans, in response to an unsolicited email or phone call, would share information such as an account number, or provide the answer to a security code question. A majority also indicated they would not want their accounts locked after three failed attempts to verify the identity of someone trying to gain access. More than two-thirds of respondents in this survey were open to using biometric technologies—they want technology that is as secure as it is convenient.

13   The weaknesses and security lapses in other validation mechanisms have increasingly caused industry innovators to turn to biometrics. Banco Azteca was created in 2001 by the massive Grupo Elektra, to target the previously untapped 70 percent of Mexico's population that did not use banks at all. One of the problems the new bank confronted in enrolling customers in underserved communities was the lack of any form of secure identification papers, driver's licenses, or the like. In response, the bank turned to biometrics and fingerprint scans. Over seven million Banco Azteca customers have enrolled in the biometric identification program; more than 75 percent of the bank's business comes from customers who have dealt with a bank for the first time due to this program.

HOW CAN MACHINE BIOMETRICS THREATEN PRIVACY?

14   Although biometrics techniques may provide new opportunities for security, these techniques also present the potential for abuse. Biometric information is inherently linked to individuality and functions as a unique identifier in a way that would make its loss irreplaceable. The potentially unrestrained scope of data collecting, sharing, linking, and warehousing also may invite misuse. Finally, the potential for pervasive monitoring of movement and activities may chill discourse and protest.

15   Identity theft in a biometric world may be particularly problematic. When a check is lost or stolen, one immediately requests a stop payment order. When a credit card is taken, one calls the company to freeze the account and order a new card. What does one do when biometric information is stolen? Once biometric information is reduced to electronic data, that data can be captured or altered by hackers. Hackers can then reproduce the data in a way that convinces biometric scanners that they are authorized, and thereby gain access to supposedly secure information or locations. Essentially, biometrics are the equivalent of a PIN that is impossible to change. The theft of biometric information amounts to permanent identity theft, and thus may be extremely difficult to counteract.

16   Use of biometrics also risks the problem of data creep, in which information given voluntarily to one recipient for one purpose may be transferred, without permission or knowledge, to another recipient, linked with other data, or applied to a new purpose. The average American's personal information is now available in approximately 50 different commercial databases. Linkage of such information could permit discrimination based on physical characteristics that might otherwise remain unknown.

17   Followed to its logical extreme, moreover, the linkage of digital images into a single database with facial recognition technology would permit the tracking of everyone's movements. The possibility of such tracking, however remote, epitomizes the threat that widespread use of biometrics poses for personal privacy. If an organization or

government can monitor movement and actions, it could discriminate against individuals based on their associations. As anonymous behavior becomes less possible, dissent may be suppressed.

WHAT FORM OF REGULATION IS APPROPRIATE?

18   Individual autonomy is the cornerstone of the American legal and social structure. The free flow of information, however, is equally essential to a functioning democracy. The challenge of regulating biometrics lies in resolving the tension between the rights to privacy, free speech, and information security.

19   Americans generally disfavor broad government regulation of industry practices regarding personal information. Congress prefers to rely on industry self-regulation when possible. Nevertheless, the government will step in to regulate a market when the market clearly has failed to provide adequate safeguards. Notable examples of such government intervention include the Child Online Protection Act, the Graham-Leach-Bliley Act, and the Health Insurance Portability and Accountability Act. If the biometrics industry wishes to avoid potentially strict sector-specific government regulations, it must self-regulate, to harmonize the tensions between the fundamental benefits of biometrics while limiting the potential for abuse. In establishing such best practices, the industry must proceed from two basic principles: notice and security.

Notice

20   Individuals must know when data collection occurs. A notice requirement recognizes the importance of individual autonomy and enables people to choose whether to participate. Notice, however, means more than simply saying "surveillance cameras are in use," when police apply facial recognition software at the Superbowl. When any biometric system is used, there should ideally be an open statement of its scope, purpose, function, and application, including the system's potential uses. The evaluation of potential uses is beneficial because biometric systems rarely threatens abuse in themselves. The true threat to privacy comes from the mission creep permitted by latent capabilities. Biometric systems should be narrowly tailored to the job they are to perform. Participation, if at all possible, should be optional. Any change in scope once in use should have the same public disclosure, and participants should be given the option to unenroll from the system.

21   While enrolled within a system, participants should be able to access and correct their personal information contained within the system. Failure to provide for access and correction will increase error in the program and may violate privacy principles.

22   The final notice element of a good self-regulatory program is third-party oversight. Some independent oversight should be implemented to ensure conformity with "best practices," and to suggest other improvements. Periodic audits of the scope and operation of the system coupled with public disclosure of the results of the audits may provide particular deterrence against abuse.

Security

23   To ensure adequate security of biometric information requires both limits on construction of system capabilities as well as protections for data use. System operators should

inform participants of the different security measures a biometric identification system will undertake.

24   Data collected should be protected by techniques such as encryption, data hashing, and the use of closed networks and secure facilities. Wireless transmissions of data, even when encrypted, should be avoided. To the extent possible, data should not be stored in a warehouse or database but rather with the individual participant, by means of an encrypted smart card. If storage is necessary, the initial collection of biometric data should be used to generate templates of authorized people and not linked to any one individual.

Government Oversight

25 If the biometrics industry establishes adequate notice and security practices, it may avoid potentially more restrictive governmental regulations. Some system of enforcement of best practice principles may be necessary. The Federal Trade Commission's power to prosecute unfair, deceptive, or fraudulent business activities may help prevent violations of security procedures or unannounced expansions of a biometric system's purview. The FTC already leads in the data protection field, having developed its own set of information practice principles.

WHAT IS THE FUTURE OF BIOMETRICS?

26 A decade ago, Bill Gates forecast that biometrics would be among "the most important IT innovations of the next several years." Technological innovation has dramatically increased the breadth, depth, and speed with which disparate data sets can be connected and analyzed. Recent developments demonstrate the widespread growth and potential power of biometrics. Use of this technology will certainly continue to grow in the next decade. Taken on its own, biometrics is neither a friend nor a foe to privacy rights; their relationship depends on the manner in which the technology is used.

27   If the biometrics industry wishes to maintain its current flexibility and avoid overly stringent regulations, it must respond to the potential threats to privacy by formulating and adopting best practice principles, keeping in mind the essential need for notice and security. Such self-regulation in managing the use of biometrics will allow the market to strike an appropriate balance between the rights to privacy, free speech, and effective use of information technology.

PAUL **SAFFO**

A Trail of DNA and Data

I f you're worried about privacy and identity theft, imagine this:

2   The scene: Somewhere in Washington. The date: April 3, 2020.

3   You sit steaming while the officer hops off his electric cycle and walks up to the car window. "You realize that you ran that red light again, don't you, Mr. Witherspoon?" It's no surprise that he knows your name; the intersection camera scanned your license plate and your guilty face, and matched both in the DMV database. The cop had the full scoop before you rolled to a stop.

4   "I know, I know, but the sun was in my eyes," you plead as you fumble for your driver's license.

5   "Oh, don't bother with that," the officer replies, waving off the license while squinting at his hand-held scanner. Of course. Even though the old state licensing system had been revamped back in 2014 into a "secure" national program, the new licenses had been so compromised that the street price of a phony card in Tijuana had plummeted to five euros. In frustration, law enforcement was turning to pure biometrics.

6   "Could you lick this please?" the officer asks, passing you a nanofiber blotter. You comply and then slide the blotter into the palm-sized gizmo he is holding, which reads your DNA and runs a match against a national genomic database maintained by a consortium of drug companies and credit agencies. It also checks half a dozen metabolic fractions looking for everything from drugs and alcohol to lack of sleep.

7   The officer looks at the screen, and frowns, "Okay. I'll let you off with a warning, but you really need more sleep. I also see that your retinal implants are past warranty, and your car tells me that you are six months overdue on its navigation firmware upgrade. You really need to take care of both or next time it's a ticket."

8   This creepy scenario is all too plausible. The technologies described are already being developed for industrial and medical applications, and the steadily dropping cost and size of such systems will make them affordable and practical police tools well before 2020. The resulting intrusiveness would make today's system of search warrants and wiretaps quaint anachronisms.

9   Some people find this future alluring and believe that it holds out the promise of using sophisticated ID techniques to catch everyone from careless drivers to bomb-toting terrorists in a biometric dragnet. We have already seen places such as Truro, Mass., Baton Rouge, La. and Miami ask hundreds or thousands of citizens to submit to DNA mass-testing to catch killers. Biometric devices sensing for SARS symptoms are omnipresent in Asian airports. And the first prototypes of systems that test in real time for SARS, HIV and bird flu have been deployed abroad.

10   The ubiquitous collection and use of biometric information may be inevitable, but the notion that it can deliver reliable, theft-proof evidence of identity is pure science fiction. Consider that oldest of biometric identifiers—fingerprints. Long the exclusive domain of government databases and FBI agents who dust for prints at crime scenes,

fingerprints are now being used by electronic print readers on everything from ATMs to laptops. Sticking your finger on a sensor beats having to remember a password or toting an easily lost smart card.

11   But be careful what you touch, because you are leaving your identity behind every time you take a drink. A Japanese cryptographer has demonstrated how, with a bit of gummi bear gelatin, some cyanoacrylic glue, a digital camera and a bit of digital fiddling, he can easily capture a print off a glass and confect an artificial finger that foils fingerprint readers with an 80 percent success rate. Frightening as this is, at least the stunt is far less grisly than the tale, perhaps apocryphal, of some South African crooks who snipped the finger off an elderly retiree, rushed her still-warm digit down to a government ATM, stuck it on the print reader and collected the victim's pension payment. (Scanners there now gauge a finger's temperature, too.)

12   Today's biometric advances are the stuff of tomorrow's hackers and clever crooks, and anything that can be detected eventually will be counterfeited. Iris scanners are gaining in popularity in the corporate world, exploiting the fact that human iris patterns are apparently as unique as fingerprints. And unlike prints, iris images aren't left behind every time someone gets a latte at Starbucks. But hide something valuable enough behind a door protected by an iris scanner, and I guarantee that someone will figure out how to capture an iris image and transfer it to a contact lens good enough to fool the readers. And capturing your iris may not even require sticking a digital camera in your face—after all, verification requires that the representation of your iris exist as a cloud of binary bits of data somewhere in cyberspace, open to being hacked, copied, stolen and downloaded. The more complex the system, the greater the likelihood that there are flaws that crooks can exploit.

13   DNA is the gold standard of biometrics, but even DNA starts to look like fool's gold under close inspection. With a bit of discipline, one can keep a card safe or a PIN secret, but if your DNA becomes your identity, you are sharing your secret with the world every time you sneeze or touch something. The novelist Scott Turow has already written about a hapless sap framed for a murder by an angry spouse who spreads his DNA at the scene of a killing.

14   The potential for DNA identity theft is enough to make us all wear a gauze mask and keep our hands in our pockets. DNA can of course be easily copied—after all, its architecture is designed for duplication—but that is the least of its problems. Unlike a credit card number, DNA can't be retired and swapped for a new sequence if it falls into the hands of crooks or snoops. Once your DNA identity is stolen, you live with the consequences forever.

15   This hasn't stopped innovators from using DNA as an indicator of authenticity. The artist Thomas Kinkade signs his most valuable paintings with an ink containing a bit of his DNA. (He calls it a "forgery-proof DNA Matrix signature.") We don't know how much of Tom is really in his paintings, but perhaps it's enough for forgers to duplicate the ink, as well as the distinctive brush strokes.

16   The biggest problem with DNA is that it says so much more about us than an arbitrary serial number does. Give up your Social Security number and a stranger can inspect your credit rating. But surrender your DNA and a snoop can discover your

innermost genetic secrets—your ancestry, genetic defects and predispositions to certain diseases. Of course we will have strong genetic privacy laws, but those laws will allow consumers to "voluntarily" surrender their information in the course of applying for work or pleading for health care. A genetic marketplace not unlike today's consumer information business will emerge, swarming with health insurers attempting to prune out risky individuals, drug companies seeking customers and employers managing potential worker injury liability.

17   Faced with this prospect, any sensible privacy maven would conclude that DNA is too dangerous to collect, much less use for a task as unimportant as turning on a laptop or working a cash machine. But society will not be able to resist its use. The pharmaceutical industry will need our DNA to concoct customized wonder drugs that will fix everything from high cholesterol to halitosis. And crime fighters will make giving DNA information part of our civic duty and national security. Once they start collecting, the temptation to use it for other purposes will be too great.

18   Moreover, snoops won't even need a bit of actual DNA to invade our privacy because it will be so much easier to access its digital representation on any number of databanks off in cyberspace. Our Mr. Witherspoon will get junk mail about obscure medical conditions that he's never heard of because some direct marketing firm "bot" will inspect his digital DNA and discover that he has a latent disease or condition that his doctor didn't notice at his annual checkup.

19   It is tempting to conclude that Americans will rise up in revolt, but experience suggests otherwise. Americans profess a concern for privacy, but they happily reveal their deepest financial and personal secrets for a free magazine subscription or cheesy electronic trinket. So they probably will eagerly surrender their biometric identities as well, trading fingerprint IDs for frequent shopper privileges at the local supermarket and genetic data to find out how to have the cholesterol count of a teenager.

20   Biometric identity systems are inevitable, but they are no silver bullet when it comes to identity protection. The solution to identity protection lies in the hard work of implementing system-wide and nationwide technical and policy changes. Without those changes, the deployment of biometric sensors will merely increase the opportunities for snoops and thieves—and escalate the cost to ordinary citizens.

21   It's time to fix the problems in our current systems and try to anticipate the unique challenges that will accompany the expanded use of biometrics. It's the only way to keep tomorrow's crooks from stealing your fingers and face and, with them, your entire identity.

FBI

Using Technology to Catch Criminals

The FBI's enthusiasm for biometric technologies is reflected on its Web site. The page shown here was posted on December 27, 2005.

Home | Site Map | FAQs

FEDERAL BUREAU OF INVESTIGATION

Celebrating a Century 1908-2008

SEARCH

Contact Us
- Your Local FBI Office
- Overseas Offices
- Submit a Crime Tip
- Report Internet Crime
- More Contacts

Learn About Us
- Quick Facts
- What We Investigate
- Natl. Security Branch
- Information Technology
- Fingerprints & Training
- Laboratory Services
- Reports & Publications
- History
- More About Us

Get Our News
- Press Room
- E-mail Updates
- News Feeds

Be Crime Smart
- Wanted by the FBI
- More Protections

Use Our Resources
- For Law Enforcement
- For Communities
- For Researchers
- More Services

Visit Our Kids' Page

Apply for a Job

Headline Archives

USING TECHNOLOGY TO CATCH CRIMINALS
Fingerprint Database "Hits" Felons at the Border

12/27/05

A CBP officer takes a passenger's fingerprint scan to compare with the IAFIS database.

When U.S. Customs and Border Protection installed technology that can quickly check the fingerprints of illegal immigrants against the FBI's massive biometric database, its chief called the measure "absolutely critical."

"This technology helps...shed light on those with criminal backgrounds we could never have identified before," Commissioner Robert C. Bonner said in a press statement in October, a month after our Integrated Automated Fingerprint Identification System (IAFIS) became fully available in all 136 border patrol stations.

A very bright light, it turns out. Since last September, IAFIS has returned "hits" on 118,557 criminal subjects who were trying to enter this country illegally, according to Customs and Border Protection officials.

Many of the "hits"—a match of an individual's 10 fingerprints—led to arrests of dangerous criminal suspects, including:

- 460 individuals for homicide
- 155 for kidnapping
- 599 for sexual assault
- 970 for robbery
- 5,919 for assault
- 12,077 for drug-related charges

Border Patrol officials began using our biometric tool in the summer of 2001, connecting two of their facilities in San Diego to our Criminal Justice Information Services Division facility in Clarksburg, West Virginia. Congress sought the deployment to supplement the Border Patrol's 10-year-old biometric database called IDENT, which relies on matching an individual's index fingers, rather than the comprehensive 10-finger prints made by IAFIS.

With IAFIS in place, Border Patrol agents can simultaneously check IDENT's specialized databases and IAFIS's 49 million sets of prints.

Voice Verification for Transactions

VoiceVerified's patent-pending Point Service Provider (PSP) platform uses voice verification to help businesses secure remote transactions, protect consumer data, and combat identity fraud. During the verification process, a user is prompted to repeat five random numeric digits to create a voice sample that is compared to a previously enrolled voiceprint to determine a match.

Somerset, Pa.–based Somerset Trust has purchased the PSP to secure wire transfers, and the bank envisions future usage across all banking services requiring multifactor authentication. VoiceVerified is currently in discussions with several other financial institutions as banks seek to comply with the Federal Financial Institutions Examination Council's recent guidelines advocating multifactor user authentication during electronic transactions.

BEN **GOLDACRE**

Now for ID Cards—and the Biometric Blues

Sometimes just throwing a few long words about can make people think you know what you're talking about. Words like "biometric."

2   When Alistair Darling was asked if the government will ditch ID cards in the light of this week's data crack-up, he replied: "The key thing about identity cards is, of course, that information is protected by personal biometric information. The problem at present is that, because we do not have that protection, information is much more vulnerable than it should be."

3   Yes, that's the problem. We need biometric identification. Fingerprints. Iris scans. Gordon Brown says so too: "What we must ensure is that identity fraud is avoided, and the way to avoid identity fraud is to say that for passport information we will have the biometric support that is necessary."

4   Tsutomu Matsumoto is a Japanese mathematician, a cryptographer who works on security, and he decided to see if he could fool the machines which identify you by your fingerprint. This home science project costs about £20. Take a finger and make a cast with the moulding plastic sold in hobby shops. Then pour some liquid gelatin (ordinary food gelatin) into that mould and let it harden. Stick this over your finger pad: it fools fingerprint detectors about 80% of the time. The joy is, once you've fooled the machine, your fake fingerprint is made of the same stuff as fruit pastilles, so you can simply eat the evidence.

5   But what if you can't get the finger? Well, you can chop one off, of course—another risk with biometrics. But there is an easier way. Find a fingerprint on glass. Sorry, I should have pointed out that every time you touch something, if your security systems rely on biometric ID, then you're essentially leaving your pin number on a post-it note.

6   You can make a fingerprint image on glass more visible by painting over it with some cyanoacrylate adhesive. That's a posh word for superglue. Photograph that with a digital camera. Improve the contrast in a picture editing program, print the image on to a transparency sheet, and then use that to etch the fingerprint on to a copper-plated printed circuit boar. (It sounds difficult, but you can buy a beginner's etching set for about for £10.) This gives an image with some three-dimensional relief. You can now make your gelatin fingerpad using this as a mould.

7   Should I have told you all that, or am I very naughty? Yes to both.

8   It's well known that security systems which rely on secret methods are less secure than open systems, because the greater the number of people who know about the system, the more people there are to spot holes in it, and it is important that there are no holes. If someone tells you their system is perfect and secret, that's like quacks who tell you their machine cures cancer but they can't tell you how. Open the box, quack. In fact you might sense that the whole field of biometrics and ID is rather like medical quackery: as usual, on the one hand we have snake oil salesmen promising the earth, and on the other a bunch of humanities graduates who don't understand technology, science, or even human behaviour: buying it; bigging it up; thinking it's a magic wand.

9   But it's not. Leaks occur not because of unauthorized access, and they can't be stopped with biometrics; they happen because of authorized access, often ones which are managed with contemptible, cavalier incompetence. The damaging repercussions will not be ameliorated by biometrics.

10   So will biometrics prevent ID theft? Well, it might make it more difficult for you to prove your innocence. And once your fingerprints are stolen, they are harder to replace than your pin number. But here's the final nail in the coffin. Your fingerprint data will be stored in your passport or ID card as a series of numbers, called the "minutiae template." In the new biometric passport with its wireless chip, remember, all your data can be read and decrypted with a device near you, but not touching you.

11   What good would the data be, if someone lifted it? Not much, insisted Jim Knight, the minister for schools and learners, in July: "It is not possible to recreate a fingerprint using the numbers that are stored. The algorithm generates a unique number, producing no information of any use to identity thieves." Crystal clear, Jim.

12   Unfortunately, a team of mathematicians published a paper in April this year, showing that they could reconstruct a fingerprint from this data alone. In fact, they printed out the images they made, and then—crucially, completing the circle—used them to fool fingerprint readers.

13   Ah biometrics. Such a soothingly technical word. Repeat it to yourself.

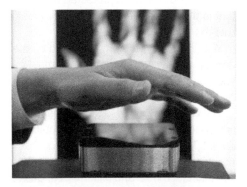

Fujitsu Computer Products of America launched its palm vein authentication device that captures a person's palm vein pattern and checks it against a preregistered palm vein pattern from that individual. The device offers users a high level of accuracy and security. It is in use at some of Asia's leading financial institutions.

FROM READING TO WRITING

1. Examine the outcries of biometrics critics and consider writing a rebuttal of one or more of their arguments. (Consult Chapter 14 on writing a rebuttal.)

2. In a causal argument (see Chapter 11), consider how the technological age in which we live exacerbates issues of privacy.

3. Evaluate any one of the technologies described in this chapter, based on practicality and/or constitutional principles. Has the technology actually helped in the war on terrorism? Has it actually led to significant privacy violations? (See Chapter 12 for advice on evaluation.)

4. Consider popular portrayals of security technologies and biometrics (like those in *CSI*, or *Person of Interest*). Why are these technologies so fascinating within the realm of science fiction? What qualities do these popular versions exaggerate, and why? What effect might these popular images have on viewers' opinions of real-life technologies, and why?

5. Analyze the visual images associated with this issue, building on Chapter 8 of this text. What is the nature of the arguments made in these visuals? How do they work to persuade an audience?

6. Write a narrative argument (such as the ones described in Chapter 13) that contributes to the debates represented in this chapter. How does a single incident—drawn from the news, an interview, or your own experience—contribute to this conversation? Alternatively, write a short story portraying the issue with a science fiction or futuristic slant.

27 | Regulating Substances

Private Bodies, Public Controls

Regulation is often about deciding where lines may be crossed—and where they should not be crossed. How would we decide which burgers (if any) should be regulated?

The U.S. prison population—now at 2.3 million, the Justice Department reported in 2008—has more than quadrupled since the early 1980s, which means that our nation now has the highest rate of incarceration in the world. Although only 4 percent of the world population is in the United States, the United States has a quarter of the entire world's prison population, and 1 in every 31 American adults is now in prison, on probation, or on parole. A great many of those in prison are nonviolent offenders of laws against substance abuse of one kind or another, usually people who need help with their addictions to drugs or alcohol. In the face of other addictions, to things like tobacco and fatty foods, some citizens are proposing laws that would further regulate the things we put into our bodies. If we criminalize harmful substances like illegal drugs, if we take legal steps to discourage smoking (especially by minors and especially in public places), and if we regulate alcohol so that it can be consumed only by adults under controlled circumstances, then why not do the same to discourage other dangerous or unhealthy social practices? Why not do more to discourage smoking, drug use, or the consumption of unhealthy foods?

Then again, maybe we should not be so hard on drug and alcohol abusers, no matter how much we disapprove of them. Is the state and federal governments' "war on drugs" going so poorly that it should be abandoned? Many people think so. Critics call attention not only to the figures on incarceration but also to the other social costs associated with strict drug laws. For example, many addicts resist treatment because they fear punishment; instead, they commit crimes to support their bad habits. Widespread urine

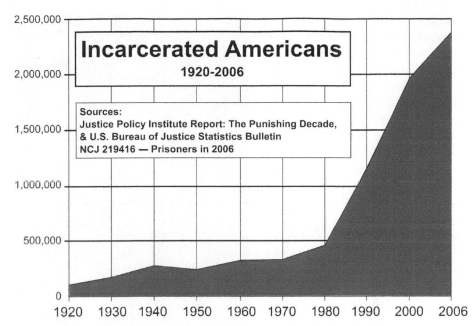

Number of inmates in U.S. prisons, 1920 to 2006. The number of inmates in U.S. prisons has more than quadrupled since the early 1980s.

testing and seizures of drug-related property have threatened basic civil rights and undermined respect for police. Americans' demand for illegal substances and extensions of the drug war have led to conflicts with other nations. Recognizing that illegal drugs often are no worse and no better than alcohol (legal since the disastrous 1920s experiment known as Prohibition), Californians voted to legalize marijuana use for cancer and AIDS patients. The war on drugs might be maintained—but without quite so much prison warehousing.

On the other hand, many people argue for a continuing hard line on drugs and alcohol because of the damage that they do. Those people point to the health risks and social costs—to early deaths, lost work days, and broken lives attributable to substance abuse. In the tradition of Carrie Nation and other temperance warriors who successfully lobbied for prohibition of alcohol in the 1920s, they have evidence that drug use has decreased during the years of the war on drugs, that alcohol and marijuana may be "gateway drugs" to more dangerous substances (because young marijuana smokers and alcohol drinkers are far more likely to try other drugs), and that the war on drugs is worth waging for all sorts of other reasons.

Advocates of a hard line on drugs sometimes take on others—alcohol producers, Big Tobacco, performance-enhancing drug users. For example, they promote stiff taxes on cigarettes and alcohol on the grounds that making harmful substances expensive discourages use and pays for the social costs involved. And they are often proponents of testing athletes for the use of unfair and dangerous performance-enhancing substances, such as steroids (which promote muscle growth but have harmful side effects), synthetic forms of testosterone (for which 2006 Tour de France winner Floyd Landis tested positive, causing him to be stripped of his title), and creatine (a dietary supplement that many athletes feel helps their training). They point to the popularity of such substances among young people. They also work to combat binge drinking on campuses because they see it as a frightening epidemic that encourages date rape, promotes vandalism, and otherwise ruins or undermines the lives of countless college students.

Reformer Carrie Nation holding the weapons of her trade: a hatchet for destroying liquor containers and a copy of the Bible

Contemporary Arguments

Should certain substances be regulated—and, if so, which ones? Is substance abuse a victimless crime that we have to live with in order to preserve a free society? Is education the only proper approach to the problem? If not, what exactly should be done about various drugs, alcohol, tobacco, and other controversial and harmful practices and substances? Just how should we weigh the risks of drug and alcohol use against the social costs of overzealous law enforcement?

The essays in this section provide a number of perspectives on public control over the harmful practices of private citizens. Consider, for instance, Bill James's essay on steroid use in baseball: does his historical perspective convince us to take a more forgiving attitude toward the apparent steroid use of famous stars such as Barry Bonds, Mark McGwire, Roger Clemens, and Alex Rodriguez? A well known baseball analyst, James on his Web site asks whether our collective condemnation of performance-enhancing drugs (PEDs) will soften in the coming years. Where exactly should lines be drawn between personal freedom—what we choose to do with our own bodies—and government intervention on behalf of health and public safety? That question underlies the other arguments that we present for your consideration in this chapter—arguments and images about body weight and image, controlling tobacco, and disability. We conclude the chapter with an Issue in Focus concerning the obesity epidemic: what, if anything, should be done to address the health threats that is being presented by the consumption of too much sugar, too many fatty foods, too many other unhealthy items?

Finally, consider as you read this chapter how visuals can serve to regulate bodies indirectly, both through the ideals that are present and the concepts and values that are omitted. Photos, cartoons, and other visuals available for your inspection throughout this chapter suggest that our identifications with certain body types can influence our behaviors; that argument also applies to advertisements in magazines and on TV.

When Barry Bonds hit his 756th Major League Baseball home run on August 7, 2007, he broke the all-time record held by Henry Aaron. Although Bonds has never failed an official steroid test, he has been implicated frequently in the taking of steroids, and his home run record is embroiled in controversy. Other prominent players, most famously Roger Clemens and Alex Rodriguez, also have been implicated.

Bill James

Cooperstown and the 'Roids

Bill James (born 1949) is one of the most influential people in baseball history—though he never played the game professionally. A statistician who has brought social science methods, an open mind, and excellent writing ability to the study of professional baseball, James since the late 1970s has written many books and articles about baseball history and the performance of baseball players and teams. As a result of his work and the work of like-minded individuals affiliated with the Society for American Baseball Research, people now consider ballpark factors when they evaluate players, newspapers publish "onbase plus slugging percentages" as well as batting averages, and teams look at hard numbers (not just what they see with the naked eye) when they evaluate prospects. Amazingly, *Time* named him one of the one hundred most influential people in the world in 2006. James now serves as an adviser to the Boston Red Sox and maintains a Web site, billjamesonline.com, where the essay below appeared in July 2009.

For the last ten years or so people have been asking me to comment on the issue of steroids and the Hall of Fame. To this point I have resisted addressing these questions, arguing—as I do with the Hall of Fame status of active players—that there is nothing to be gained by trying to guess where objects still in motion will eventually land. With the passage of time the dust will settle, and we will see the issue more clearly.

2   After ten years, however, the dust does not seem to be settling very rapidly. There seem to be as many different and contradictory opinions on the issue now as there were five or eight years ago. We are all tired of arguing about it, but we still don't agree. In any case, I am finally ready to say what I have to say about it. It is my opinion that, in time, the use of steroids or other Performance Enhancing Drugs will mean virtually nothing in the debate about who gets into the Hall of Fame and who does not.

3   The process of arriving at this conclusion began when I was studying aging patterns in the post-steroid era. One of the characteristics of the steroid era was that we had several dozen players who continued to improve beyond the normal aging time frame, so that many of them had their best seasons past the age of 32. This is historically not normal. In the post-steroid era we are returning to the historic norm in which players hit a wall sometime in their early thirties. But what does this mean?

4   It means that *steroids keep you young.* You may not like to hear it stated that way, because steroids are evil, wicked, mean and nasty and youth is a good thing, but ... that's what it means. Steroids help the athlete resist the effects of aging.

5   Well, if steroids help keep you young, what's wrong with that?

6   What's wrong with that is that steroids may help keep players "young" at some risk to their health, and the use of steroids by athletes may lead non-athletes to risk their health as well. But the fact is that, with time, the use of drugs like steroids will not disappear from our culture. It will, in fact, grow, eventually becoming so common that it might almost be said to be ubiquitous. *Everybody wants to stay young.* As we move forward in time, more and more people are *going* to use more and more drugs in an effort to stay young. Many of these drugs are going to be steroids or the descendants of steroids.

7   If we look into the future, then, we can reliably foresee a time in which *everybody is going to be using steroids* or their pharmaceutical descendants. We will learn to control the health risks of these drugs, or we will develop alternatives to them. Once that happens, people will start living to age 200 or 300 or 1,000, and doctors will begin routinely prescribing drugs to help you live to be 200 or 300 or 1,000. If you look into the future 40 or 50 years, I think it is quite likely that every citizen will routinely take anti-aging pills every day.

8   How, then, are those people of the future—who are taking steroids every day—going to look back on base-ball players who used steroids? They're going to look back on them as pioneers. They're going to look back at it and say "So what?"

9   The argument for discriminating against PED users rests upon the assumption of the moral superiority of non-drug users. But in a culture in which *everyone* routinely uses steroids, that argument cannot possibly prevail. You can like it or you can dislike it, but your grandchildren are going to be steroid users. Therefore, they are very likely to be people who do not regard the use of steroids as a moral failing. They are more likely to regard the banning of steroids as a bizarre artifice of the past.

10   Let us suppose that I am entirely wrong about all of that; let us suppose that our grandchildren do *not* wind up regularly ingesting chemicals to extend their youth. I would still argue that, in the long run, the use of steroids will eventually become a non-issue in who gets into the Hall of Fame.

11   My second argument is this:

1. Eventually, *some* players who have been associated with steroids are going to get into the Hall of Fame. This is no longer at issue. One cannot keep Barry Bonds, Roger Clemens, A-Rod, Manny Ramirez, Mark McGwire, Sammy Sosa and all of the others out of the Hall of Fame forever. *Some* of them have to get in. If nothing else, somebody will

eventually get in and *then* acknowledge that he used steroids.

2. Once *some* players who have been associated with steroids are in the Hall of Fame, the argument against the others will become un-sustainable.

12   When the time comes at which two or three or four players are in the Hall of Fame who have acknowledged some steroid use, the barrier to other steroid users rests upon some sort of balancing test. Did this player use *too many* steroids to be considered legitimate? Is his career a creation of the steroids? Would he have been a Hall of Fame player without the steroids?

13   I am not suggesting that it is inappropriate for any one sportswriter or any one Hall of Fame voter to balance these considerations as best he can. But one does not build a house upon a well-balanced rock. The way that each sportswriter looks at these issues is going to be different from the way that each other looks at them. There can only be a consensus on one of two positions:

a. that steroid users should not be in the Hall of Fame,

or

b. that steroid use is not an issue in the debate.

14   Between the two extreme positions, it becomes a fluid discussion. Once we move away from the one extreme, in my view, we will begin to drift inevitably toward the other.

15   I would liken this to attitudes about sexuality and television. At one point there was a firm consensus that there was no place for sex on TV. Married couples, on TV, slept in twin beds. The first departures from this firm position were small and insignificant ... PBS specials on prostitution, chewing gum and soft drink commercials that pushed the boundaries of "taste", and edited-for-TV movies that were not quite as edited as they would have been a few years ago. Once there was no longer a firm consensus at an extreme position, there was a fluid standard that moved inevitably toward more and more openness about sexuality.

16   I will note that this happened without the consent and without the approval of most of the American public. It was never true that *most* people wanted to see more sex on TV. Probably it was generally true that most Americans disliked what they regarded as the erosion of standards of decency. But it was always true that *some* people wanted to see more sex on TV, and that was all that mattered, because that created a market for

shows that pushed the envelope, and thus eroded the barriers. It was like a battle line that disintegrated once the firing started. The importance of holding the battle line, in old-style military conflict, was that once the line was breached, there was no longer an organized point of resistance. Once the consensus against any sexual references on TV was gone, there was no longer any consensus about what the standards should be—thus, a constant moving of the standards.

17   I think the same thing will happen here: Once there is no longer a firm consensus against steroid users in the Hall of Fame, there will be a fluid situation which moves inevitably in the direction of more and more inclusiveness. It is not necessary that people approve of this movement in principle. It is only necessary that there be advocates for those who are still on the outside looking in ... for Sammy Sosa, let's say, and Manny Ramirez. And there is no question that there will be those advocates.

18   Third argument. History is forgiving. Statistics endure.

19   At the time that Dick Allen left the major leagues, virtually no one thought of him as a Hall of Fame player. In his first year of eligibility for the Hall of Fame, he received the support of a little less than 4% of the voters. In his fifteen years of eligibility for BBWAA selection, he never reached 20% in the voting.

20   Dick Allen did not have imaginary sins or imaginary failings as a player. He had very real offenses. But as time passes, the details of these incidents (and eventually the incidents themselves) are forgotten, and it becomes easier for Allen's advocates to re-interpret them as situations in which Allen was the victim, rather than the aggressor or offender. The people who were there die off. A certain number of people want to play the role of Dick Allen's advocate. No one—including me—wants to play the role of persistently denigrating Dick Allen; in fact, I'm pretty sure you can go to hell for that. People who were friends of Dick Allen speak up; the dozens or hundreds of exteammates who despised Dick Allen keep silent, or speak of him as well as they can manage.

21   For very good reasons, we do not nurture hatred. We let things pass. This leads history to be forgiving. Perhaps it is right, perhaps it is wrong, but that is the way it is. Sometime between 2020 and 2030, Dick Allen will be elected to the Hall of Fame.

22   The same thing has happened, more slowly, with the Black Sox. In 1950 no one thought Joe Jackson should be in the Hall of Fame. Now it is a common opinion—perhaps a majority opinion—that he should. People question whether he "really" did the things that he clearly admitted doing. His virtues are

celebrated; his sins are minimized. Perhaps this is right; perhaps it is wrong. It is the way of history.

23   History will rally on the side of the steroid users in the same way that it has rallied on the side of Dick Allen, Joe Jackson, Orlando Cepeda, Hack Wilson and many others. But with the steroid users, we are not talking about a single isolated "offender," but about a large group of them, representing the bulk of the dominant players of their generation. The forces that push for their acceptance will get organized much more quickly and will move with much greater force. This, in my view, will make the use of steroids a non-factor in Hall of Fame discussions within 30 to 40 years.

24   Fourth argument. Old players play a key role in the Hall of Fame debate. It seems unlikely to me that aging ballplayers will divide their ex-teammates neatly into classes of "steroid users" and "non-steroid users."

25   One of the key reasons that Dick Allen will eventually be in the Hall of Fame is that one of his ex-teammates—Goose Gossage— feels strongly that he should be, and is outspoken on this issue. Goose Gossage is now a Hall of Famer. His voice carries weight.

26   Eventually, younger players who were teammates of Mark McGwire, Sammy Sosa, A-Rod and Roger Clemens are going to be in the Hall of Fame. Andy Pettitte is probably going to be in the Hall of Fame. When he is in the Hall of Fame—if he gets there before Roger—he is *going* to speak up for Roger Clemens. Hell, somebody might even speak up for Barry Bonds.

27   Once this happens, it will erode the prejudice against steroid users in the Hall of Fame, to the extent that that prejudice might otherwise exist. *You* might choose to divide the world of baseball players into steroid users and non-steroid users, but this is not a division that makes intuitive sense when you know the people involved. Therefore, this is not the division that will ultimately endure, once the long historical sorting-out process that makes Goose Gossage relevant and Lindy McDaniel irrelevant has run its course.

28   I have a fifth argument here, but before I get to that, let me speak for a moment on the other side of the issue. Let us adopt, as the face of the non-steroid user, Will Clark. Will Clark and Rafael Palmeiro were college teammates, and apparently were not the best of friends. As players they were rivals. Texas had Palmeiro (1989–1993) and then had Clark (1994–1998), while Palmeiro went to Baltimore. After the 1998 season the Orioles— then a strong franchise—signed Clark, while Palmeiro went back to the Rangers. Later on Palmeiro went back to the Orioles, so that both the Rangers and the Orioles had Palmeiro, then Clark,

then Palmeiro. There was always a debate about which was the better player.

29   I've always been a great admirer of Will Clark, who I think was a great player and is a historically under-rated player in part because his numbers are dimmed by comparison to the steroid-inflated numbers that came just after him. Will Clark, in the pre-steroid era, was a much better player than Palmeiro, although Palmeiro was good. Palmeiro, as we entered the steroid era, gradually pulled ahead of Clark. I have no idea whether Will Clark ever used steroids or not, but let us use Will Clark as the face of the player who chose *not* to use steroids in order to stay in the game, the player who chose the natural route and suffered the consequences of that.

30   Is it fair to Will Clark to compare him to players who chose to cheat in order to move beyond that level? No, it is not. Absolutely, it is not. But the critical issue is, Is this cheating? If you choose to regard it as cheating, if you choose not to support the Hall of Fame candidacy of a steroid user because you regard it as cheating, I would not argue with you. I think that Will Clark has a perfect right to feel that he was cheated out of a fair chance to compete for honors in his time, and, if you choose to look at it from the standpoint of Will Clark, I don't think that you are wrong to do so.

31   But at the same time, I do not believe that history will look at this issue from the standpoint of Will Clark. I don't see how it can. What it seems to me that the Will Clark defenders have not come to terms with is the breadth and depth of the PED problem, which began in the 1960s and expanded without resistance for almost 40 years, eventually involving generations of players. It seems to me that the Will Clark defenders are still looking at the issue as one of "some" players gaining an advantage by using Performance Enhancing Drugs. But it wasn't really an issue of *some* players gaining an advantage by the use of performance Enhancing Drugs; it is an issue of *many* players using Performance Enhancing drugs in competition with one another. Nobody knows how many. It would be my estimate that it was somewhere between 40 and 80%.

32   The discrimination against PED users in Hall of Fame voting rests upon the perception that this was *cheating*. But is it cheating if one violates a rule that nobody is enforcing, and which one may legitimately see as being widely ignored by those within the competition?

33   It seems to me that, at some point, this becomes an impossible argument to sustain—that all of these players were "cheating," in a climate in which most everybody was doing the same things, and in which there was either no rule against doing these things

or zero enforcement of those rules. If one player is using a corked bat, like Babe Ruth, clearly, he's cheating. But if 80% of the players are using corked bats and no one is enforcing any rules against it, are they all cheating? One better: if 80% of the players are using corked bats and it is unclear whether there are or are not any rules against it, is that cheating?

34   And ... was there really a rule against the use of Performance Enhancing Drugs? At best, it is a debatable point. The Commissioner issued edicts banning the use of Performance Enhancing Drugs. People who were raised on the image of an all-powerful commissioner whose every word was law are thus inclined to believe that there was a rule against it.

35   But "rules", in civilized society, have certain characteristics. They are agreed to by a process in which all of the interested parties participate. They are included in the rule book. There is a process for enforcing them. Someone is assigned to enforce the rule, and that authority is given the powers necessary to enforce the rule. There are specified and reasonable punishments for violation of the rules.

36   The "rule" against Performance Enhancing Drugs, if there was such a rule before 2002, by-passed all of these gates. It was never agreed to by the players, who clearly and absolutely have a right to participate in the process of changing any and all rules to which they are subject. It was not included in any of the various rule books that define the conduct of the game from various perspectives. There was no process for enforcing such a rule. The punishments were draconian in theory and non-existent in fact.

37   It seems to me that, with the passage of time, more people will come to understand that the commissioner's periodic spasms of self-righteousness do not constitute baseball law. It seems to me that the argument that it is cheating must ultimately collapse under the weight of carrying this great contradiction—that 80% of the players are cheating against the other 20% by violating some "rule" to which they never consented, which was never included in the rule books, and for which there was no enforcement procedure. History is simply *not* going to see it that way.

38   The end of the day here is about the year 2040, perhaps 2050. It will come upon us in a flash. And, at the end of the day, Mark McGwire is going to be in the Hall of Fame, and Roger Clemens, and Sammy Sosa, and Rafael Palmeiro, and probably even Barry Bonds. I am not especially advocating this; I simply think that is the way it is. I only hope that, when all of these players are enshrined, they will extend a hand up to a few players from the Will Clark division of the game.

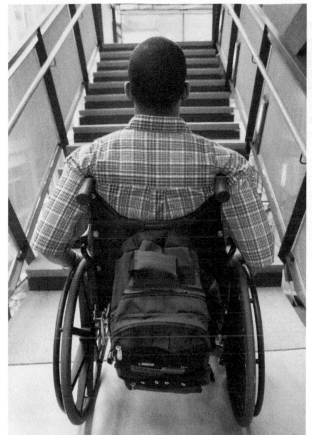

This photo makes an argument about the inaccessibility of many spaces for individuals with physical disabilities. What details in the photo make it an especially powerful argument? Would the argument be even more powerful if the person in the chair were wearing a military uniform, as if he had just returned from military service in Iraq or Afghanistan—or would that make the argument about something else besides accessibility issues for the people with disabilities?

David Edelstein

Up in Smoke: Give Movies with Tobacco an Automatic 'R'

David Edelstein, an occasional playwright, is a film critic for *New York Magazine* and National Public Radio's *Fresh Air*, as well as an occasional commentator on *CBS Sunday Morning*. His work has also appeared in the *Village Voice, Rolling Stone, Slate*, and the *New York Times*. The following blog post appeared on *New York Magazine's* Web site in January 2010 as a response to a January 5 *New York Times* article by A. O. Scott called "Movies and Vice" that concluded, "Tobacco use is part of history—of movie history in particular. And in the course of that history lighting up has acquired connotations of individualism, rebellion, sophistication and sex that will be hard to eradicate even as they become increasingly shrouded in nostalgia."

A. O. Scott's meditation on tobacco in movies is a savvy piece of hipsterism: admit that smoking is bad but argue that anti-vice cultural crusaders are worse, and end with the hope that cigarettes will someday be akin to "time travel, or slapstick, or a mad drive to the airport to stop the one you love from getting on that plane— something that only happens in the movies." Those comparisons are facetious, of course. It's unlikely we'll see time travel in our lifetime; pratfalls in the real world are involuntary; and no one has to race to the airport in an era when anti-terrorist screenings hold passengers up for hours. Smoking, on the other hand, is a choice, and one that's deeply responsive to social cues. That's why tobacco companies pay millions to studios to have glamorous actors light up and strike sultry poses. In Scott's nicotine-fueled brain he knows this, but he doesn't want to sound like a bluestocking.

2   Over the years, I've gotten a lot of e-mails from anti-smoking groups demanding either a ban on cigarettes in movies or an automatic "R" rating when a character uses tobacco. My first response is indignation at the "nanny state." I remember how, more than two decades ago, I was forbidden from mentioning smoking in a profile I did in the late *Mirabella* on Jan Hooks, who chain-smoked through our two interviews. I loved her—but I also could see by how she smoked that she was very, very high-strung. It was an important detail, except that editor Grace Mirabella's husband, Dr. William Cahan, was an anti-tobacco crusader, and no mention of cigarettes was allowed in the magazine, ever. I fought and fought and finally, *finally* Mirabella yielded—but only if I wrote something like, "Her yellow-stained fingers trembling, she nervously inserted another death stick between her brown, misshapen teeth." I was furious. I still am.

3   On the other hand, editors at a well-known music publication that same year told me that no anti-smoking references would ever appear in their magazine: Tobacco companies paid big bucks for ads on the back cover and to sponsor the regular live-performance centerpiece. Against such vast financial resources, anti-smoking crusaders had no leverage. In the end, it was only the dread "nanny state" that could keep tobacco ads away from the young and impressionable.

4   These days, I don't believe that the anti-smoking crusaders are so out of line, at least in their demand that movies with cigarettes get an automatic "R" rating. No, that doesn't mean we expunge smoking from movies already made. We just make it tougher for new films with cigarette use to influence kids. Just as important, when tobacco companies pay to put their wares in a film, that information needs to appear in the credits— *prominently*.

It's one thing when everyone lights up in *Good Night and Good Luck*, in which the ubiquitous tobacco smoke evokes the era better than anything onscreen. (Too bad there was no list at the end of all the characters' real-life counterparts who died of lung cancer or associated heart disease.) It's another when cigarettes are a product placement akin to Cheerios or Apple computers.

5   This isn't an easy call. I treasure the image of William Powell and Myrna Loy attempting to out-drink one another in *The Thin Man*—I think of it often as I order my fourth or fifth whiskey. Somewhere, I still have a poster of Cheech and Chong in *Up in Smoke*, which probably retains the aroma of the bong that sat proudly beneath it in my dorm room. And damn if Bogie and Belmondo aren't still the apogee of cool. Scott is dead right in arguing that vice in movies can be very entertaining. But for our kids' sake, let's treat the addiction to deadly chemicals *as* a vice and not as a normal, healthy part of everyday life.

6   *Update*: Some people have written to accuse me of having a double standard, and to say that, if one follows my logic, kids should no longer be exposed to drinking, overeating, brutally killing people, or anything that might corrupt our little angels. And then, of course, as one correspondent put it, "Our movies would be a little less true." I happen to believe that glamorizing the act of sucking tar and nicotine into one's lungs results in images a lot less true than, say, skeletal lung-cancer patients dissolving from the inside out in an Intensive Care Unit. But let's leave that aside. I'm not arguing that smoking should be banned from movies or *always* associated onscreen with delinquency or death. I enjoy movies about people doing things that might not be good for them, whether it's lighting up or shooting up or crashing cars or screwing sheep. Let's have a cinema for grown-ups that depicts anything and everything, healthy and unhealthy. But let's also keep tobacco companies and the greedheads who take their money from bombarding kids with the message that smoking is what cool people do.

Tony Newman

Criminalizing Smoking Is Not the Answer: Bans on Cloves and Outdoor Smoking Will Backfire!

Tony Newman is the director of media relations at the Drug Policy Alliance Network, which promotes policy alternatives to the War on Drugs. Before joining the organization, he was media director for the human rights organization Global Exchange and cofounded the public relations firm Communication Works. The following article appeared in September 2009 on *Huffington Post*, an Internet newspaper known for a slightly left-of-center political stance.

The war on cigarettes is heating up. This week a new federal ban went into effect making flavored cigarettes and cloves illegal. The new regulation halted the sale of vanilla and chocolate cigarettes that anti-smoking advocates claim lure young people into smoking. This ban is the first major crackdown since Congress passed a law in June giving the Food and Drug Administration the authority to regulate tobacco. There is already talk of banning Menthol cigarettes next.

2   Meanwhile, another major initiative to limit smoking wafted out of New York City last week. A report to Mayor Michael Bloomberg from the city's Health Commissioner called for a smoking ban at city parks and beaches to help protect citizens from the harms of second hand smoke. To his credit, Bloomberg rejected this measure citing concern over stretched city and police resources.

3   While I support many restrictions on public smoking, such as at restaurants and workplaces, and I appreciate public education campaigns and efforts aimed at discouraging young people from smoking, I believe the outdoor smoking ban and prohibition of cloves and possibly Menthols will lead to harmful and unintended consequences. All we have to do is look at the criminalization of other drugs, such as marijuana, to see some of the potential pitfalls and tragedies.

4   Cities across the country—from New York to Santa Cruz, California—are considering or have already banned smoking at parks and beaches. I am afraid that issuing tickets to people for smoking outdoors could easily be abused by overzealous law enforcement.

5   Let's look at how New York handles another "decriminalized" drug in our state, marijuana. Despite decriminalizing marijuana more than 30 years ago, New York is the marijuana arrest capital of the world. If possession of marijuana is supposed to be decriminalized in New York, how does this happen? Often it's because, in the course of interacting with the police, individuals are asked to empty their pockets, which results in the pot being "open to public view"—which is, technically, a crime.

6   More than 40,000 people were arrested in New York City last year for marijuana possession, and 87 percent of those arrested were black or Latino, despite equal rates of marijuana use among whites. The fact is that blacks and Latinos are arrested for pot at

much higher rates in part because officers make stop-and-frisk searches disproportionately in black, Latino and low-income neighborhoods.

7   Unfortunately, when we make laws and place restrictions on both legal and illegal drugs, people of color are usually the ones busted. Drug use may not discriminate, but our drug policies and enforcement do.

8   Now let's look at the prohibition of cloves and other flavored cigarettes. When we prohibit certain drugs, it doesn't mean that the drugs go away and people don't use them; it just means that people get their drugs from the black market instead of a store or deli. We've been waging a war on marijuana and other drugs for decades, but you can still find marijuana and your drug of choice in most neighborhoods and cities in this country.

9   For many people, cloves or Menthols are their smoke of choice. I have no doubt that someone is going to step in to meet this demand. What do we propose doing to the people who are caught selling illegal cigarettes on the street? Are cops going to have to expend limited resources to enforce this ban? Are we going to arrest and lock up people who are selling the illegal cigarettes? Prisons are already bursting at the seams (thanks to the drug laws) in states across the country. Are we going to waste more taxpayer money on incarceration?

10   The prohibition of flavored cigarettes also moves us another step closer to total cigarette prohibition. But with all the good intentions in the world, outlawing cigarettes would be just as disastrous as the prohibition of other drugs. After all, people would still smoke, just as they still use other drugs that are prohibited, from marijuana to cocaine. But now, in addition to the harm of smoking, we would find a whole range of "collateral consequences," such as black market-related violence, that crop up with prohibition.

11   Although we should celebrate our success curbing cigarette smoking and continue to encourage people to cut back or give up cigarettes, let's not get carried away and think that criminalizing smoking is the answer.

12   We need to realize that drugs, from cigarettes to marijuana to alcohol, will always be consumed, whether they are legal or illegal. Although drugs have health consequences and dangers, making them illegal—and keeping them illegal—will only bring additional death and suffering.

New York State Department of Health anti-smoking advertisement (AP Photo/NYS Department of Health).

Garry Trudeau (1948-) won the Pulitzer Prize in 1975 for his comic strip *Doonesbury*. The strip published here appeared in January 2002.

MADD—Mothers Against Drunk Driving—is one of the most respected nonprofit organizations in the United States. For the past 25 years MADD has championed the rights of victims of drunk driving and has promoted public awareness of the consequences of drunk driving. The ad on this page is one of many that were displayed on the MADD Web site (www.madd.org) in the summer of 2005.

ISSUE IN FOCUS

What Should We Do About Obesity?

Is obesity a disease or a condition? Whatever it is, obesity seems to have reached epidemic proportions in the United States. Fifty years ago parents were concerned about the effects on their children of infectious diseases—polio, measles, whooping cough, and so on—but now it is obesity that concerns parents. And it is obesity that is directly affecting parents themselves because their own weight gain is associated with increasing rates of heart disease, diabetes, and other chronic conditions. By most estimates more than a third of all Americans are now obese or seriously overweight, including many preschoolers.

The obesity crisis isn't simply a health crisis; it is also an economic issue. It costs all of us untold amounts in the form of lost lives, lost productivity, lost dollars. Obesity probably accounts for more than 10 percent of our annual health care costs, and an increasing obesity rate may account for the increased health costs that have plagued American society for the past decades. And that doesn't even consider the costs associated with weight-loss programs, fad diets, exercise machines, health club memberships, and slim-fast magazine subscriptions.

How should our society address this phenomenon? You are already aware of many of the proposals offered to ameliorate the obesity problem. Have school administrators in your community been under pressure to extricate refined sugar, unsaturated fats, and salt from foods on school lunch menus? Have candy machines been removed from schools, dorms, or other public places? Should soft drinks be taxed just as if they were sinful indulgences equivalent to beer or liquor or cigarettes? Do television ads, cooking shows, and their celebrity chefs—*Iron Chef* or *Top Chef* or *The Ace of Cakes*—promote the consumption of rich, fatty foods? Should the size of restaurant portions be scaled back?

Michelle Obama and White House horticulturalist Dale Haney break ground for work on a vegetable garden with kids from Washington's Bancroft Elementary School.

Or are we going too far? Is the obesity scare just another food fad? Should we really pass laws, levy fines, and impose taxes to address obesity, or is it all a matter of personal self-discipline, moderate portions, and regular exercise? For everyone who is alarmed at the health issue, it seems that there is someone else who is unconvinced or unmoved.

First Lady Michelle Obama is certainly among those who are concerned. In a July 12, 2010, speech before the NAACP convention that is reproduced here in this Issue in Focus, she announced a national "Let's Move" effort designed to reverse child obesity through increased exercise, better nutrition, and government encouragement. Jordan Rubin, a physician and writer who is just as committed to healthy living as Michelle Obama, argues that there is a causal link between cartoons and obesity. His argument first appeared on blog entry located on a Web site entitled *Raw Vegetables* that is dedicated to the promotion of healthy eating.

Obama's and Rubin's arguments are countered, however, by Kim Brittingham and Jeffrey Friedman. Concerned that our society is overly obsessed with thinness (she has written a book entitled *Read My Hips: How I Learned to Love My Body*), Brittingham directly answers Michelle Obama in an essay published two weeks after Obama's speech. Friedman, meanwhile, in an article that appeared September 9, 2009, in the *Daily Beast*, an online publication associated with *Newsweek*, claims that obesity is mostly the result of genetics, not personal choice or weakness. Finally, we conclude the segment with an academic essay by Patrick Johnson, a clinical exercise physiologist who writes frequently about health, nutrition, and fitness claims. His essay, which offers a balanced interpretation, was published in the Fall of 2005 in the *Skeptical Inquirer*, a journal committed to dispassionate inquiry and investigation.

Which essay makes the most persuasive case?

Jordan Rubin

Beware of Saturday Morning Cartoons

The influence of media is nothing new, and most of us could not imagine life without today's technology. There's a down side, though, and perhaps the greatest negative impact is that the media is used to market unhealthy foods, drinks, and lifestyles to our kids. Case in point: 70 percent of polled six-to-eight-year-olds who watch a lot of television believe that fast foods are more nutritious than healthy, home-cooked foods.

2   It's no wonder kids think that way. Studies show that ads targeted to kids 12 and under lead them to request and consume high-calorie, low-nutrient products such as soft drinks, sweets, salty snacks, and fast food—adding up to more than one-third of their daily calories. Our kids are listening, watching, and believing the ads—and getting fat in the process. According to the Centers for Disease Control (CDC), the proportion of overweight children ages 6–11 has more than doubled, and the rate for adolescents has tripled since 1980. This development often sets them up for a lifetime of being overweight since around 80 percent of overweight adolescents become obese adults.

3   Looking back, it all began in the 1960s when marketers targeted children as a separate demographic category, prompting advertisers to move on this lucrative new market. In the 1970s, children were viewing an average of 20,000 TV commercials a year. By the late 1970s, research indicated that children could not distinguish between television programs and commercials, and they had little to no understanding of ads' persuasive intentions—making them especially vulnerable to ads' claims and appeals. In 1978, the Federal Trade Commission attempted to ban TV commercials aimed at youngsters—to no avail.

4   When cable channels exploded in the 1990s, opportunities to advertise directly to children expanded as well. Estimates now indicate that children spend an average of five and one-half hours a day using media (television, the Internet, radio, etc.) and see or hear an average of over 40,000 TV commercials a year.

5   Marketing junk to kids has worked. In 1997 alone, kids aged 7–12 spent $2.3 billion (and teenagers spent a whopping $58 billion) of discretionary money on snacks and beverages—mostly unhealthy, high-fat, high-sugar ones. The sad truth is that advertising likely has more influence on what kids eat and drink

than parents or schools do. Despite attempts at limiting or disallowing advertisements directly to children, the trend of marketing junk to kids has gained momentum as the modes of marketing have diversified and intensified. One advertising executive summed up their tactics in this manner: "You've got to reach kids throughout the day—in school, as they're shopping in the mall . . . or at the movies. You've got to become part of the fabric of their lives."

6   That's exactly what has happened. Advertising has infiltrated our kids' lives even in supposedly "controlled" environments: at home (through television, the Internet, video games, etc.); at the movies (highlighting unhealthy branded foods in so-called "product placements"); at school (via piped-in advertising through programs such as Channel One, field trips, and others); and even on the way to school (via advertising on the outside and inside of buses, plus listening to BusRadio), directly impacting what our kids eat, drink, do and how much weight they gain.

7   Not surprisingly, there are direct correlations between the amount of time a child spends in front of screen media and the risk and degree of obesity. For every hour a child watches TV or plays video games, the risk of obesity can double. Watching TV and playing video games also slows down metabolism—burning fewer calories than reading does and almost as few as sleeping does.

8   Companies also pay a lot of money to place their products in movies. Branded foods (mostly soda, followed by candy, chips, and pretzels) average about one to two in a typical movie. And this is only in the movie itself; it does not include all the junk food advertisements prior to the start of the featured flick.

9   Additionally, many school districts struggle to make ends meet and some have come up with a creative way to do so—advertising on school buses. While not all ads are for sugary soft drinks, fast food, or unhealthy snacks, some are, and the buses provide a captive audience to influence our kids' eating and lifestyle habits.

10   So what can be done? We need to talk to our kids and tell them (and model for them) what healthy eating and living is—and why. If we don't get to our kids first, the marketers and advertisers sure won't mind telling them what to buy, eat, and do.

Michelle Obama	# Remarks to the NAACP National Convention, July 18, 2010

One hundred and one years ago, the NAACP was established in pursuit of a simple goal, and that was to spur this nation to live up to the founding ideals, to secure those blessings of liberty, to fulfill that promise of equality. And since then, the work of this organization has been guided by a simple belief: that while we might not fully live out that promise or those blessings for ourselves, if we worked hard enough, and fought long enough, and believed strongly enough, that we could secure them for our children and for our grandchildren, and give them opportunities that we never dreamed of for ourselves.

2   So, for more than a century, the men and women of the NAACP have marched and protested. You have lobbied Presidents and fought unjust laws. You've stood up and sat in and risked life and limb so that African Americans could take their rightful places not just at lunch counters and on buses, but at universities and on battlefields and in hospitals and boardrooms; in Congress and the Supreme Court; and, yes, even in the White House. Think about it—even the White House.

3   So I know that I stand here today, and I know that my husband stands where he is today, because of this organization and because of the struggles and the sacrifices of all those who came before us.

4   But I also know that their legacy isn't an entitlement to be taken for granted. And I know it is not simply a gift to be enjoyed. Instead, it is an obligation to be fulfilled. And when so many of our children still attend crumbling schools, and a black child is still far more likely to go to prison than a white child, I think the founders of this organization would agree that our work is not yet done. When African American communities are still hit harder than just about anywhere by this economic downturn, and so many families are just barely scraping by, I think the founders would tell us that now is not the time to rest on our laurels. When stubborn inequalities still persist—in education and health, in income and wealth—I think those founders would urge us to increase our intensity, and to increase our discipline and our focus and keep fighting for a better future for our children and our grandchildren.

5   And that's why I really wanted to come here today—because I wanted to talk with you about an issue that I believe cries out for our attention, one that is of particular concern to me, not just as First Lady, but as a mother who believes that we owe it to our kids to prepare them for the challenges that we know lie ahead.

And that issue is the epidemic of childhood obesity in America today.

6   Now, right now in America, one in three children is overweight or obese, putting them at greater risk of obesity-related conditions like diabetes and cancer, heart disease, asthma. And we're already spending billions of dollars in this country a year to treat these conditions, and that number is only going to go up when these unhealthy children reach adulthood.

7   But it's important to be clear that this issue isn't about how our kids look. It's not about that. It's about how our kids feel. It's about their health and the health of our nation and the health of our economy.

8   And there's no doubt that this is a serious problem. It's one that is affecting every community across this country. But just like with so many other challenges that we face as a nation, the African American community is being hit even harder by this issue. We are living today in a time where we're decades beyond slavery, we are decades beyond Jim Crow, when one of the greatest risks to our children's future is their own health. African American children are significantly more likely to be obese than are white children. Nearly half of African American children will develop diabetes at some point in their lives. People, that's half of our children!

9   And if we don't do something to reverse this trend right now, our kids won't be in any shape to continue the work begun by the founders of this great organization. They won't be in any condition to confront all those challenges that we know still remain. So we need to take this issue seriously, as seriously as improving under-achieving schools, as seriously as eliminating youth violence or stopping the spread of HIV/AIDS, or as seriously as any of the other issues that we know are devastating our communities.

10   But in order to address this challenge, we also need to be honest with ourselves about how we got here, because we know that it wasn't always like this for our kids and our communities. The way we live today is very different from even when I was growing up. (And I like to tell my kids I'm not that old. They don't agree.) Many of you probably grew up like I did—in a community that wasn't rich, not even middle class, but where people knew their neighbors, and they looked out for each other's kids.

11   In these strong African American communities, we went to neighborhood schools around the corner. So many of us had to walk to and from school every day, rain or shine. I know you've told that story. And in Chicago, where I was raised, we did it in the dead of winter. It was hard, but we walked! And in school, we had recess twice a day and gym class twice a week, like it or not.

And then when we got home in the afternoon, after school or in the summer, there was no way we'd be allowed to lie around the house watching TV. (First of all, there weren't that many channels!) Our parents made us get up and play outside. Had to get up, get out, just couldn't be inside. And we would spend hours riding bikes, playing softball, freeze tag, jumping double-dutch. Kids nowadays don't even know how to jump double-dutch! We were constantly on the move, only stopping to eat or whatever—when the streetlights came on, right?

12   And eating was a totally different experience back then. In my house, we rarely ate out—rarely. Even when both parents worked outside of the home, most families in my neighborhood sat down at the table together as a family for a meal. And in my house, Marian Robinson's house, we ate what we were served. My mother never cared whether me or my brother liked what was on our plates. We either ate what was there or we didn't eat. It was as simple as that. We never ate anything fancy, but the portion sizes were reasonable and there were rarely seconds—maybe for your father, but not for you. And there was always a vegetable on the plate.

13   And many of our grandparents tended their own gardens or they relied on, as my father told me, "The Vegetable Man" who brought fresh produce. That was how people got by back then—they had fresh fruits and vegetables in their own backyards, and in jars in their cellar during the winter. And that wasn't just being thrifty—that was healthy too, little did we know. And unless it was Sunday, or somebody's birthday, there was no expectation of dessert after our meals. And we didn't dream of asking for soda or pop. That was for special occasions.

14   Now, if you were lucky, you might get a quarter or two to take to the corner store and get some penny candy. But you did not eat it all at once because you never knew when you'd see another piece of candy. So you saved it in that little brown bag under your bed. That bag would be all worn out and sweaty. You'd hold on to that bag, take out a half a piece of candy every other day. Back then, without any expert advice and without spending too much money, we managed to lead pretty healthy lives.

15   But things are a little different today, and many kids these days aren't so fortunate. So many kids can't attend neighborhood schools or don't, so instead of walking to school, they ride in a car or they're in a bus. And in too many schools, recess and gym class have been slashed because of budget cuts. Fears about safety mean that those afternoons outside have been replaced by afternoons inside with TV, video games, the Internet. In fact, studies have found that African American children spend an average of nearly six hours a day watching TV—and that every extra hour

of TV they watch is associated with the consumption of an additional 167 calories.

16   For many folks, those nutritious family meals are a thing of the past, because a lot of people today are living in communities without a single grocery store, so they have to take two, three buses, a taxi, walk for miles just to buy a head of lettuce for a salad or to get some fresh fruit for their kids. Most folks don't grow their own food the way many of our parents and grandparents did. A lot of folks also just don't have the time to cook at home on a regular basis. So instead, they wind up grabbing fast food or something from the corner store or the mini-mart—places that have few, if any, healthy options.

17   And we've seen how kids in our communities regularly stop by these stores on their way to school—buying themselves sodas and pop and chips for breakfast. And we've seen how they come right back to those same stores after school to buy their afternoon snack of candy and sugary drinks. According to one study, on an average trip to the corner store, a child will walk out of that store with more than 350 calories worth of food and beverage—this is on average. So if they're going two and three times a day, that can really add up.

18   And taken together, all of these things have made for a perfect storm of bad habits and unhealthy choices—a lifestyle that's dooming too many of our children to a lifetime of poor health and undermining our best efforts to build them a better future. See, we can build our kids the best schools on earth, but if they don't have the basic nutrition they need to concentrate, they're still going to have a challenge learning. And we can create the best jobs in the world—we must—but that won't mean that folks will have the energy and the stamina to actually do those jobs. We can offer people the best health care money can buy, but if they're still leading unhealthy lives, then we'll still just be treating those diseases and conditions once they've developed rather than keeping people from getting sick in the first place.

19   See, the thing is that none of us wants that kind of future for our kids or for our country. And surely the men and women of the NAACP haven't spent a century organizing and advocating and working day and night only to raise the first generation in history that might be on track to live shorter lives than their parents.

20   And that's why I've made improving the quality of our children's health one of my top priorities.

21   As many of you may know, my efforts began with the planting of a garden on the South Lawn of the White House. But it's important to understand that this garden symbolizes so much more than just watching beautiful things grow. It's become a way

to spark a broader conversation about the health and well-being not just of our kids but of our communities.

22   And in an effort to elevate that conversation nationally, we launched "Let's Move." It's a nationwide campaign to rally this country around a single, ambitious goal, and that is to solve childhood obesity in a generation so that children born today reach adulthood at a healthy weight. Through this initiative, we are bringing together governors and mayors, businesses and community groups, educators, parents, athletes, health professionals—you name it—because it is going to take all of us, working together, to help our kids lead healthier lives right from the beginning.

23   "Let's Move," the campaign, has four components.

24   First, we're working to give parents the information they need to make healthy decisions for their families. For example, we're working with the FDA and the food industry to provide better labeling, something simple, so folks don't have to spend hours squinting at labels, trying to figure out whether the food they're buying is healthy or not. Our new health care legislation requires chain restaurants to post the calories in the food they serve so that parents have the information they need to make healthy choices for their kids in restaurants.

25   And we're working with doctors and pediatricians to ensure that they routinely screen our children for obesity. And I can personally attest to the value of these screenings based on my own personal experiences, because it wasn't that long ago when the Obamas weren't exactly eating as healthy as we should have been. And it was our daughters' pediatrician who actually pulled us aside and suggested that I think about making some changes to our family's diet. And it made a world of difference.

26   But we also know that giving better information to parents is not enough, because with 31 million American children participating in federal school meal programs, many of our kids are consuming as many as half their daily calories at school. That's why the second part of "Let's Move" is to get healthier food into our schools.

27   We're working to reauthorize our child nutrition legislation that will make significant new investments to revamp our school meals and improve the food that we offer in those school vending machines, so that we're serving our kids less sugar, salt, and fat, and more vegetables, fruits, and whole grains.

28   This is bipartisan legislation and it is critically important for the health and success of our children, and we are hoping that Congress will act swiftly to get this passed.

29   But we also know that healthy eating is only half the battle. Experts recommend at least 60 minutes a day of activity. That's at least the bare minimum, and many of our kids aren't even close. So the third part of "Let's Move" is to help our kids get moving, to find new ways for them to get and stay active and fit. And we're working to get more kids participating in daily physical education classes and to get more schools offering recess for their students. We've set a goal of increasing the number of kids who walk or ride their bikes to school by 50 percent in the next five years. And we've recruited professional athletes—they've been fantastic—from different sports leagues to inspire our kids to get up off that couch and to get moving.

30   But we know that even if we offer the most nutritious school meals, and we give kids every opportunity to be fit, and we give parents the information they need to prepare healthy food for their families, all that won't mean much if our families still live in communities where that healthy food simply isn't available in the first place. And that brings me to the fourth and final component of the campaign, and that is to ensure that all families have access to fresh, affordable food in their communities where they live.

31   And one of the most shocking statistics for me in all of this is that right now, 23.5 million Americans, including 6.5 million children, live in what we call "food deserts"—areas without a single supermarket. This is particularly serious in African American communities where folks wind up buying their groceries at places like gas stations and bodegas and corner stores where they often pay higher prices for lower-quality food.

32   But the good news is that we know that this trend is reversible, because when healthier options are available in our community, we know that folks will actually take advantage of those options. One study found that African Americans ate 32 percent more fruits and vegetables for each additional supermarket in their community.

33   So we know the kind of difference that we can make with some changes. We know that when we provide the right incentives—things like grants and tax credits, and help securing permits and zoning—businesses are willing to invest and lay down roots in our communities. And many grocers are finding that when they set up shop in high-need areas, they can actually make a decent profit. They're learning that they can do well by doing good.

34   So as part of "Let's Move," we've proposed a Healthy Food Financing Initiative—a $400 million a year fund that we'll use to attract hundreds of millions of more dollars from the private and non-profit sectors to bring grocery stores and other healthy food retailers to underserved areas across the country. And our goal is ambitious—we want to eliminate food deserts in this country within

seven years, and create jobs and revitalize neighborhoods along the way.

35   I know these goals are ambitious, and there are many, many more. And as First Lady, I am going to do everything that I can to ensure that we meet them.

36   But I also know that at the end of the day, government can only do so much. I have spoken to so many experts about this issue, and not a single one of them said that the solution is to have government tell people what to do. It's not going to work. Instead, this is about families taking responsibility and making manageable changes that fit with their budgets and their needs and their tastes. That's the only way it's going to work. It's about making those little changes that can really add up—simple things like taking the stairs instead of the elevator, walking instead of riding in a car or bus, even something as simple as turning on the radio and dancing with your children in the middle of your living room for hours. That will work up a sweat.

37   How about replacing all of that soda and those sugary drinks with water? Kids won't like it at first, trust me. But they'll grow to like it. Or deciding that they don't get dessert with every meal: as I tell my kids, dessert is not a right. Or they don't get it every day. Or just being more thoughtful about how we prepare our food— baking instead of frying. (I know. Don't shoot me.) And cutting back on those portion sizes.

38   Look, no one wants to give up Sunday meal. No one wants to say goodbye to mac and cheese and fried chicken and mashed potatoes—oh, I'm getting hungry!—forever. No one wants to do that. Not even the Obamas, trust me. But chefs across the country are showing us that with a few simple changes and substitutions, we can find healthy, creative solutions that work for our families and our communities.

39   And that's why I am excited about our new "Let's Cook" video series, which we're launching on our "Let's Move" website at letsmove.gov. This is a great series featuring Sam Kass, who a lot of people think is cute—I don't know if that helps. But this series features some of the country's top chefs, who will be demonstrating how folks can prepare simple, affordable, nutritious meals for their families. The first guest chef is a guy by the name of Marvin Woods, who's known for his cuisine based in North Africa, the Caribbean, South America, the Low Country. He's demonstrating how to prepare a week of healthy and tasty dinners for a family of four on a tight budget. And he provides recipes, shopping lists, so that folks can do it all themselves at home.

40   And finally, one thing we can think about is working to make sure that our kids get a healthy start from the beginning, by pro-

moting breastfeeding in our communities. One thing we do know is that babies that are breastfed are less likely to be obese as children, but 40 percent of African American babies are never breastfed at all, not even during the first weeks of their lives. We know this isn't possible or practical for some moms, but we've got a program that's providing new support to low-income moms who want to try so that they get the support they need. And under the new health care legislation, businesses will now have to accommodate mothers who want to continue breastfeeding once they get back to work. (Now, the men, you may not understand how important that is. But trust me, it's important to have a place to go.)

41   But let's be clear. This isn't just about changing what our kids are eating and the lifestyles they're leading—it's also about changing our own habits as well. Because believe it or not, if you're obese, there's a 40 percent chance that your kids will be obese as well. And if both you and the child's other parent are obese, that number jumps to 80 percent.

42   And this is more than just genetics at work. The fact is, we all know we are our children's first and best teachers and role models. We teach them healthy habits not just by what we say but by how we live. Shoot, I can't tell Malia and Sasha to eat their vegetables if I'm sitting around eating French fries—trust me, they will not let that happen. And I can't tell them to go run around outside if I'm spending all my free time on the couch watching TV.

43   And this isn't just about the example that we set as individuals and as families, but about the lifestyle we're promoting in our communities as well. It's about the example we set in our schools. It's about schools like the Kelly Edwards Elementary School in Williston, South Carolina. It's a Bronze Award winner in our USDA Healthier U.S. School Challenge. This is a school where students have planted their own garden so that they can taste all kinds of fresh vegetables; they can stay active because they've got their own dance team.

44   And it's about establishing strong community partnerships that involve folks from every sector and every background. There's a Fresh Food Financing Initiative in Pennsylvania—it's a great example. This initiative is a collaboration between business, non-profits, and government that's funded more than 80 supermarket projects, bringing nutritious food to hundreds of thousands of people in underserved communities.

45   These are just a couple of the thousands of programs and projects that are making a difference in communities across the country already.

46   So if there's anybody here, after all this talking I've done, who feels a little overwhelmed by this challenge—because it can be

overwhelming—if there is anyone here who might even already be losing hope thinking about how hard it will be to get going, or giving up, I just want you to take a look around at all the things that are already being accomplished, because I want folks to learn from each other and to be inspired by each other, because that's what we've always done.

47   That is exactly what happened here in this city half a century ago. See, because back in 1958, folks right here in Kansas City saw what folks down in Montgomery had achieved with their bus boycott. So they were inspired by all those men and women who walked miles—walked miles home each day on aching feet because they knew there was a principle at stake. So folks here organized their own boycott of department stores that refused to serve African Americans. Handbills publicizing their meetings stated (and this is a quote): "They stopped riding in Montgomery, so let's stop buying in Kansas City." A local music teacher even composed a song that became the anthem for their efforts. It was entitled "Let's take the walk that counts."

48   And then, as you know, a few years later, in April of 1964, folks turned out in droves to pass a public accommodations law mandating that all residents, regardless of their skin color, be served in restaurants, hotels and other public places. Even folks who were too sick to walk showed up to vote. One organizer recalled that they used wheelchairs to get people to the polls and even brought one man in on a stretcher. So think about that— being carried to the ballot box on a stretcher. Those folks didn't do all that just for themselves. They did it because they wanted something better for their children and for their grandchildren. That's why they did it.

49   And in the end, that's what has driven this organization since its founding. It is why Daisy Bates endured hate mail and death threats to guide those nine young men and women who would walk through those schoolhouse doors in Little Rock. It is why Thurgood Marshall fought so hard to ensure that children like Linda Brown—and children like my daughters and your sons and daughters—would never again know the cruel inequality of separate but equal. It is why so many men and women—legends and icons and ordinary folks—have faced down their doubts, their cynicism and their fears, and they've taken that walk that counts.

50   We owe it to all those who've come before us to ensure that all those who come after us—our children and our grandchildren—that they have the strength and the energy and the enduring good health that they need to continue and complete that journey.

51   So I'm asking you, NAACP, will you move with me? Let's move! I'm going to need you, NAACP. This is not an endeavor that I can do by myself. We cannot change the health of our community alone. I'm going to need each and every single one of you to work together for this campaign for our children's future. If we do this together, we can change the way our children think about their health forever.

52   Thank you.

Kim Brittingham

Michelle Obama: No Friend to Fat Kids

Dear Mrs. Obama,

I'm writing response to your e-mail of July 18, 2010, from which I quote: "help us tackle an issue that is dear to my heart—childhood obesity. As some of you know one of my top priorities as First Lady is the Let's Move! campaign, where we have made it our goal to put a stop to the challenge of childhood obesity within a generation, so children who are born today grow up at a healthy weight."

2   Mrs. Obama, my respect for you has taken a serious hit since you initiated your campaign against childhood obesity. It isn't that I want to force-feed our nation's children and turn them all into lumbering giants; rather, I thought you were smarter and had more vision than to approach the issue as clumsily and insensitively as you have.

3   There's nothing wrong with encouraging children to get more physically active, as your "Let's Move!" campaign does. There's also nothing wrong with educating children about good nutrition. However, your campaign is unintelligent at its core, because instead of simply encouraging all children to eat right and stay active, you have *made the choice* to cast obesity *itself* as the enemy to be destroyed. When we frame our battle for healthier children as a battle against fatness itself, we're merely proclaiming open season on fat people. We're encouraging an already fat-prejudiced society to further demonize those who bear the fat—worst of all, the *children* who bear it.

4   If you promote healthful eating and physical activity, then you're automatically promoting a lifestyle that will reduce the weight of *some* children. Therefore, why bring obesity into the equation at all, Mrs. Obama?

5   See, what happens is that the kids whose bodies *don't* shrink in response to carrot sticks and playing tag will be left feeling stigmatized. "What I am is *wrong*. I'm a *freak*. What I am is something everyone—including the First Lady—wants to wipe out. What I am is *soooo* incredibly wrong, that the First Lady *chose* to use her considerable platform to launch a nationwide *campaign* against what I am."

6   Mrs. Obama, your campaign assumes that all fat children are fat because they don't exercise or eat right. It's the same assumption so many people erroneously make about fat adults. I've known kids who were just plain chubby, *not* because they overate, *not* because they weren't active. They were just chubby. Their bodies weren't finished yet. They were *children*, you see. And when they got older, they slimmed down—naturally. I've also known children who appeared "fat" by our societal standards, who were only reflecting their family's genetic code to be stocky. Not necessarily obese, but short and solid. As children, perhaps they "appeared" fat. They, however, like their siblings and parents, were in perfect health.

7   But what happens when you bring in an entire society, conducted by a misguided First Lady, who wants to *fight* what these kids are? The kid who didn't have an eating disorder before might develop one now, or might develop another harmful way to cope with his or her anxiety. They're guaranteed to develop poor self-esteem because the *entire country* is telling them that what they are is *wrong*, and must be *fought*. And WOW, no worse time to fill somebody's head with negative, unhelpful messages than *childhood* if you really want them to stick.

8   Look at it this way. Let's say you have a choice between: (a) standing up before a room full of children and encouraging them to exercise more; or (b) standing up before a room full of children and encouraging them to exercise more, and then throwing a handful of knives into the audience. Why would you select (b), unless you wanted to hurt someone?

9   You can help children get healthier without doing harm. But by pinning the "fight against childhood obesity" onto messages about your "Let's Move" campaign, you are reminding fat children that they need to be "fixed"—not the kind of positive reinforcement that generally works. (And fat children already know they're fat. BELIEVE ME. We never let them forget it.) As for the thin children, you're merely reinforcing the fact that the fat kids have something "wrong" with them, which for kids often translates into the "different" child becoming a target for cruelty, ostracization, etc.

10   Imagine this. Somewhere, there's an eight-year-old kid who's under five feet tall and already 300 pounds. He takes your messages to heart, Mrs. Obama, and makes some changes, and drops 100 pounds. We can both agree that's a lot of weight, right? But then, his weight stops moving. He's eating moderate food portions, his diet is nutritionally balanced, he gets plenty of exercise. If he eats any less he'll be starving. He's doing everything right, but still, no further weight loss. His parents and teachers applaud him for his significant accomplishment, but to the rest of the world, this now-200-pound child still appears "fat."

11   Meanwhile, your battle against childhood obesity continues to rage. Grown-ups at Little League murmur behind the child's back, "What a shame, to be that big, and so young. His mother should be reported for child abuse." The child wonders, "What more can I do to get these people off my back?" He starts thinking of ways to restart his weight loss. Never mind that he's a growing boy and what's left of his body fat may shift on its own as he gets older. "What more can I do? I'm still not good enough for them yet." Maybe he stops eating altogether. Maybe he starts vomiting. Now, we're in dangerous territory.

12   Maybe, just maybe, if this kid had understood that his goal was simply to change his habits—not necessarily to "not be FAT anymore"—he would've wound up better off in the end. His newfound healthy relationship with food would not have turned unhealthy as he tried to force further weight loss. He'd be feeling good about himself and what he'd already achieved. Maybe he even would've dropped more weight. After all, the release of stress hormones can hinder weight loss. And if he'd not felt like such a failure after only 100 pounds lost, maybe he wouldn't have felt so much stress.

13   We've got an awful lot of people out there who are emphatically "against" fatness because they feel it's unhealthy—including you, Mrs. Obama. It stands to reason, then, that you and concerned others like you would be in favor of anything that permanently (for lack of a better word) "cures" fatness. So, if encouraging healthy habits WITHOUT harping on obesity MIGHT WORK, Mrs. Obama, why aren't you giving it a chance? Does it sound too "easy" on the fat kids? If so, then it sounds to me like you want fat people *punished*, first and foremost. And what's that about? Is that good will for the children's sake, or just plain hatred?

14   Besides, we have a pretty ridiculous idea of what counts as "being fat" in this country. That's why we have so many women with anorexia and bulimia. That's why we have so many little girls who *aren't* fat on *diets*. And that dieting is stunting their growth. It's making them sick.

15   We've got a heck of a lot of un-fat people going on diets in this country, because they're scared stiff to be fat. Because they know fat people get the least love, the least respect. But, irony of all ironies, that dieting is what makes a good number of people fatter in the end. The more we stigmatize "being fat," the more likely we are to have people who can't co-exist healthfully with food.

16   Additionally, there are a lot of short-sighted, angry people in this country who are quick to blame fat people for their fatness. "Buck up and get some willpower!" they seethe. "This is a choice—stop playing the victim!" Isn't it interesting, though, that a lot of people got on board with making the tobacco industry take responsibility for pushing its cancer sticks on the populace, particularly young people. And yet not many people are willing to tell Big Food to stop loading up their edibles with combinations of fat, salt, and sugar that have been proven to be as physically addictive as cocaine, and which is completely unnecessary. Few people are willing to make the parent companies of chain restaurants take responsibility for pushing huge gooey portions of food on prime time TV viewers, or for creating unnecessarily huge portions, for "supersizing" their meals or inventing "Fourth Meal" as Taco Bell has done—all in the name of SELLING MORE. It's classic, corporate greed.

17   Our energy and attention would be much better spent focusing on education, and investigating the possible variety of causes of fatness—particularly those that have received the least attention in order to protect corporate profits. But it's so popular to condemn fat people that few people really want to make Big Food accountable. It would mean we'd have to shift our blame away from fat people, and kicking them is just too much fun to sacrifice. There are so many fat people out there (40% of the population, according to recent stats) that we're bound to run into a few of them each day—and each encounter is a brand new chance for us to unleash our frustration, our guilt for our own gluttony, our self-hate of our own "imperfect" bodies, onto somebody else. Gee, it's not nearly as effective a release as directing your hatred towards some faceless corporation. It's much more satisfying to sneer at a real person, to watch a fat person's swollen face fall as you reject them—for a job, for a date, for friendship.

18   Michelle Obama, you need to take "fighting obesity" out of the equation. Focusing on the positive—eating well and exercising—is *enough*. Children who are perhaps fat because of how they eat will learn to eat better. Period. Mission accomplished, without doing harm.

Jeffrey
Friedman

The Real Cause of Obesity

Despite receiving a MacArthur genius award for her work in Alabama "forging an inspiring model of compassionate and effective medical care in one of the most underserved regions of the United States," Regina Benjamin's qualifications to be surgeon general have been questioned. Why? She is overweight. "It tends to undermine her credibility," Dr. Marcia Angell, former editor of *The New England Journal of Medicine*, said in an interview with ABC News. "I do think at a time when a lot of public-health concern is about the national epidemic of obesity, having a surgeon general who is noticeably overweight raises questions in people's minds."

2   It is not enough, it seems, that the obese must suffer the medical consequences of their weight, consequences that include diabetes, heart disease, and cancer, and that cause nearly 300,000 deaths in the United States each year. They must also suffer the opprobrium heaped on them by people like Angell or Rep. James Sensenbrenner (R-WI), who has advised the obese to "Look in the mirror because you are the one to blame." In our society, perhaps no group is more stigmatized than the obese.

3   The abuse is nothing new, of course. Four hundred years ago, Shakespeare had Prince Hal hurl a barrage of insults at Falstaff, calling him "fat-witted," "horseback-breaker," and a "huge hill of flesh." But Shakespeare had an excuse. In his time essentially nothing was known about the real reasons that people are fat. Today we have no such excuse. Modern medical science has gone a long way toward explaining the causes of obesity, and the bottom line is clear: obesity is not a personal choice. The obese are so primarily as a result of their genes.

4   Genetic studies have shown that the particular set of weight-regulating genes that a person has is by far the most important factor in determining how much that person will weigh. The heritability of obesity—a measure of how much obesity is due to genes versus other factors—is about the same as the heritability of height. It's even greater than that for many conditions that people accept as having a genetic basis, including heart disease, breast cancer, and schizophrenia. As nutrition has improved over the past 200 years, Americans have gotten much taller on average, but it is still the genes that determine who is tall or short today. The same is true for weight. Although our high-calorie, sedentary lifestyle contributes to the approximately 10-pound average weight gain of Americans compared to the recent past, some people are more severely affected by this lifestyle than others. That's because they have inherited genes that increase their

predisposition for accumulating body fat. Our modern lifestyle is thus a necessary, but not a sufficient, condition for the high prevalence of obesity in our population.

5   Over the past decade, scientists have identified many of the genes that regulate body weight and have proved that in some instances, different variants of these genes can lead a person to be fat or thin. These genes underlie a weight-regulating system that is remarkably precise. The average person takes in a million or more calories per year, maintaining within a narrow range over the course of decades. This implies that the body balances calorie consumption with calorie expenditure, and does with a precision greater than 99.5 percent. Even the most vigilant calorie counter couldn't compete, if for no other reason than that the calorie counts on food labels are often off by 10 percent or more.

6   The genes that control food intake and metabolism act to keep weight in a stable range by creating a biological force that resists weight change in either direction. When weight is gained, hunger is reduced. When weight is lost, the unconscious drive to eat is stimulated and acts to return weight to the starting point. Moreover, the greater the amount of weight that is lost, the greater the sense of hunger that develops. Thus, when the obese lose large amounts of weight by conscious effort, their bodies fight back even more strongly by increasing hunger and reducing energy expenditure. If you think it is hard to lose 10 to 20 pounds (and it is), try to imagine what it would feel like to lose many tens or even hundreds of pounds.

7   Anyone who doubts the power of this biologic system should study the case of a young boy in England a few years back. He had a mutation in a critical gene, the one that produces the hormone leptin. Leptin is made by fat tissue and sends a signal informing the brain that there are adequate stores of energy. When leptin drops, appetite increases. Because of a genetic error, this boy could not make this hormone, which left him ravenously hungry all of the time. At age 4 he ate 1,125 calories at a single meal—about half of what a normal adult eats in an entire day. As a result he already weighed 90 pounds and was well on his way to developing diabetes. At the time, his similarly affected cousin was 8 and weighed 200 pounds. After a few leptin injections, the boy's calorie intake dropped to 180 calories per meal, and by the time he was 6 his weight had dropped into the normal range. Nothing changed except the hormone levels: his parents weren't more or less permissive, his snacks did not switch from processed to organic, his willpower was not bolstered. Rather this boy was a victim of a malfunctioning weight-regulating system that led to an uncontrollable drive to eat. This example illustrates that feeding

behavior is a basic drive, similar to thirst and other life-sustaining drives. The key role of leptin and other molecules to control feeding behavior undercuts the common misconception that food intake is largely under voluntary control.

8   While mutations in the leptin gene like the cases described above are rare, nearly 10 percent of morbidly obese individuals carry defects in genes that regulate food intake, metabolism, and body weight. The evidence further indicates that the rest of the obese population carries genetic alterations in other, as yet unidentified, single genes or combinations of genes (polygenes) interacting with environmental factors.

9   So if you are thin, it might be more appropriate for you to thank your own "lean" genes and refrain from stigmatizing the obese. A broad acceptance of the biologic basis of obesity would not only be fair and right, but would also allow us to collectively focus on what is most important—one's health rather than one's weight. There is no evidence that obese individuals need to "normalize" their weight to reap health benefits. In fact, it is not even clear whether there are enduring health benefits to weight loss among obese individuals who do not suffer from diabetes, heart disease, hypertension, or liver disease. What is known is that the obese who do suffer from these conditions receive a disproportionately large benefit from even modest weight loss, which together with exercise and a heart-healthy diet can go a long way toward improving health.

10   While research into the biologic system that controls weight is moving toward the development of effective therapies for obesity, we are not there yet. In the meantime we must change our attitudes toward the obese and focus less on appearance and more on health. In their efforts to lose weight they are fighting against their biology. But they also are fighting against a society that wrongly believes that obesity is a personal failing.

The two visual arguments on this page, produced by an organization called Consumer Freedom, ridicule the idea that American corporations might be responsible for obesity.

Patrick
Johnson

Obesity: Epidemic or Myth?

You have probably heard that we are in the midst of an obesity epidemic. The Centers for Disease Control and Prevention (CDC) have been fervently warning that we are in imminent danger from our expanding waistlines since the beginning of this decade. However, evidence has recently emerged indicating that the CDC's warnings were based on questionable data that resulted in exaggerated risks.

2   This new evidence has led to a hostile backlash of sorts against the CDC. The editors of the *Baltimore Sun* recently called the earlier estimates the "Chicken Little Scare of 2004." The Center for Consumer Freedom, a group that has long been critical of the CDC, declared unequivocally on its Web site and in print ads in several newspapers around the country that the obesity scare was a myth. Even Jay Leno poked fun at the CDC in one of his *Tonight Show* monologues, making the observation that "not only are we fat. . . . We can't do math either." Not everybody believes the new data, however. Cable talk show host Bill Maher commented during an episode of his show *Real Time with Bill Maher* about it being a shame that lobbyists were able to manipulate the CDC into reducing the estimated risk.

3   So which is it? Are we in imminent danger, or is the whole concept a myth? Looking at the scientific evidence makes it clear that the extreme views on either side of the argument are incorrect. There is no doubt that many of our concerns about obesity are alarmist and exaggerated, but it is also apparent that there is a real health risk associated with it.

The Controversy

4   Between 1976 and 1991 the prevalence of overweight and obesity in the United States increased by about 31 percent (Heini and Weinsier 1997); then between 1994 and 2000 it increased by another 24 percent (Flegal et al. 2002). This trend, according to a 2004 analysis, shows little sign of slowing down (Hedley et al. 2004). The fact that more of us are getting fatter all the time raises a significant public health concern. The Centers for Disease Control and Prevention (CDC) began calling the problem an epidemic in the beginning of this decade as the result of research that estimated 280,000 annual deaths as a consequence of obesity (Allison et al. 1999). Since then there has been a strong media campaign devoted to convincing Americans to lose weight. In 2003, Dr. Julie Gerberding, the director of the CDC, made a speech claiming that the health impact of obesity would be worse than the influenza epidemic of the early

twentieth century or the black plague of the Middle Ages. In 2004 the campaign reached a fever pitch when a report was released that increased the estimate of obesity-related deaths to 400,000 (Mokdad et al. 2004). Finally, in March of this year, a report appeared in the *New England Journal of Medicine* that predicted a decline in life expectancy in the United States as a direct result of obesity (Olshansky et al. 2005).

5   Despite the assertions that obesity is causing our society great harm, however, many scientists and activist groups have disputed the level of danger that it actually poses. Indeed, a recent analysis presented in the *Journal of the American Medical Association (JAMA)* by Katherine Flegal of the CDC and her colleagues calls the severity of the dangers of excess body fat into question, indicating that the number of overweight and obesity-related deaths is actually about 26,000—about one fifteenth the earlier estimate of 400,000 (Flegal et al. 2005).

6   There is little argument about the fact that, as a nation, more of us are fatter than ever before; the disagreement lies in the effect that this has on our health. The campaign to convince us to lose weight gained much of its momentum in 2004; not only were there high-profile public health initiatives devoted to stopping the obesity epidemic, but the idea had pervaded popular culture as well. Movies like Morgan Spurlock's *Super Size Me* were the topic of many a discussion, and there were regular news reports about the dangers of too much fat.

7   During this campaign, however, there were some notable dissenters. Paul Ernsberger, a professor of nutrition at Case Western Reserve University, has been doing research since the 1980s that led him to assert that obesity is not the cause of ill health but rather the effect of sedentary living and poor nutrition, which are the actual causes. Another prominent researcher, Steven Blair, director of the Cooper Institute of Aerobics Research in Dallas, Texas, has been an author on several studies indicating that the risks associated with obesity can be significantly reduced if one engages in regular physical activity, even if weight loss is not present. According to Blair, weight loss should not be ignored, but a greater focus should be placed on physical activity and good nutrition. Both Ernsberger and Blair indicated to me that they thought the new research by Flegal and her colleagues provides a more accurate picture of the mortality risk associated with obesity.

8   While scientists like Ernsberger and Blair have been presenting their conclusions in the scientific forum, others have taken a more inflammatory approach. In his 2004 book, *The Obesity Myth*, Paul Campos argues that the public health problem we have associated with obesity is a myth and further claims that our loathing of fat has damaged our culture. The most antagonistic group, however,

is the Center for Consumer Freedom (CCF) (www.consumerfreedom
.com), which implies that the obesity epidemic is a conspiracy
between the pharmaceutical industries and the public health establishment to create a better market for weight-loss drugs.
Numerous articles on the organization's Web site bash several of
the most prominent obesity researchers who have disclosed
financial ties to the pharmaceutical industries. Paul Ernsberger
echoed this sentiment. He told me that the inflated mortality statistics were all based on the work of David Allison, a well-known
pharmacoeconomics expert. "These experts create cost-benefit
analyses which are part of all drug applications to the FDA.
These self-serving analyses start by exaggerating as much as
possible the cost to society of the ailment to be treated (obesity
in the case of weight-loss drugs). The risks associated with the
new drug are severely underestimated, which results in an
extremely favorable risk-benefit analysis, which is almost never
realized once the drug is on the market. Experts who can
produce highly favorable risk-benefit analyses are very much in
demand, however."

9   The claims made by the CCF are given some credence by
Ernsberger's corroboration; however, there is a noteworthy problem with their own objectivity. On their Web site they present
themselves as a consumer-minded libertarian group that exists to
"promote personal responsibility and protect consumer choices."
Upon closer examination, however, it becomes evident that the
CCF is an advocacy group for restaurants and food companies,
who have as much to gain by the threat of obesity being a myth
as the pharmaceutical industry does by the danger being dire.

10   It is clear that there are agenda-determined interests on
both sides of the issue. Therefore, the best way to discern what is
necessary for good health is to shift our focus away from the sensational parts of the controversy and look at the science itself.

Current Science and Obesity Risks

11   In their recent article, Katherine Flegal and her colleagues (2005)
point out that the earlier mortality estimates were based on
analyses that were methodologically flawed because in their cal-
culations the authors used *adjusted* relative risks in an equation
that was developed for *unadjusted* relative risk. This, according to
Flegal's group, meant that the old estimates only partially
accounted for confounding factors. The older estimates, furthermore "did not account for variation by age in the relation of body
weight to mortality, and did not include measures of uncertainty
in the form of [standard errors] or confidence intervals." These authors also point out that the previous estimates relied on studies
that had notable limitations: "Four of six included only older data

(two studies ended follow-up in the 1970s and two in the 1980s), three had only self-reported weight and height, three had data only from small geographic areas, and one study included only women. Only one data set, the National Health and Nutrition Examination Survey I, was nationally representative" (Flegal et al. 2005). In their current investigation, Flegal's group addressed this problem by using data only from nationally representative samples with measured heights and weights. Further, they accounted for confounding variables and included standard errors for the estimates.

12   Obesity was determined in this analysis using each subject's body mass index, which is a simple height-to-weight ratio. A BMI of 18 to 24 is considered to be the normal weight, 25–29 is considered overweight, and 30 and above is considered obese. The data from this study indicated that people who were underweight experienced 33,746 more deaths than normal-weight people, and that people who were overweight or obese experienced 25,814 more deaths than the normal-weight folks. This estimate is being reported in the popular media as being one-fifteenth the earlier estimate of 400,000. However, conflating the categories of overweight and obesity this way is misleading.

13   At first glance, it appears that underweight poses a bigger threat to our health than overweight and obesity, and that the earlier estimates were profoundly exaggerated. However, in this study the people who fit into the *obese* category actually experienced 111,909 excess deaths compared to normal-weight subjects. In contrast, those who were categorized as *overweight* experienced 86,094 fewer deaths than those who were normal weight. The figure of 25,815 is the difference between the obesity deaths and the overweight survivals. In the original study by David Allison and his colleagues (Allison et al. 1999) it is actually estimated that 280,000 deaths result from overweight and obesity and that 80 percent, or 224,000, of these deaths occurred in people who were in the obese category. However, the study by Mokdad and colleagues (2004), using the same methods developed by Allison et al., estimated 400,000 obesity-related deaths, and subsequently fueled much of the recent fervor surrounding the obesity epidemic. In this study, no distinction was made between overweight and obesity and the authors failed to distinguish between obesity, physical inactivity, and poor diet. All of these variables were simply lumped together.

14   A few things become clearer after examining the data. First, it appears that our categories are mislabeled; being classified as overweight appears to give one an advantage (statistically, anyway) over those who are in the ideal weight range. Moreover, it is inappropriate to consider overweight and obese as one group. Despite the current hype, the initial overestimation by Allison and

his group was not as exaggerated as is being publicized; compared to that study, the new estimate is actually about half of the old number. Finally, it is apparent that many at the CDC were simply confirming their own biases when they accepted the estimate by Mokdad et al. The categories in that study—that was, intriguingly, co-authored by CDC director Julie Gerberding, which may provide some insight into why it was so readily accepted— were far too broad to provide useful information. The fact that this flaw was ignored shows how easy it is to accept evidence that supports our preconceived notions or our political agendas.

15   There is another problem inherent in all of the above mortality estimates. They are based on epidemiological data that show correlation but leave us guessing as to causation. Various factors are interrelated with increased mortality—obesity, inactivity, poor nutrition, smoking, etc. Yet, without carefully controlled experiments, it is hard to determine which factors cause—and which are symptoms of—poor health. This is a difficult limitation to overcome, however, because we can't recruit subjects and have them get fat to see if they get sick and/or die sooner. Most institutional review boards would not approve that sort of research, and furthermore I can't imagine that there would be a large pool of subjects willing to participate. There are, however, observational data that were collected with fitness in mind, which help to clarify the picture somewhat.

16   In 1970 researchers at the Cooper Institute for Aerobics Research in Dallas, Texas, began to gather data for a longitudinal study that was called, pragmatically enough, the Aerobics Center Longitudinal Study (ACLS). This study looked at a variety of different variables to estimate the health risks and benefits of certain behaviors and lifestyle choices. What set this study apart from other large-scale observational studies, however, was that instead of relying on self-reporting for variables like exercise habits, they tested fitness levels directly by way of a graded exercise test (GXT). A GXT requires a person to walk on a treadmill as long as he or she can with increases in speed and incline at regular intervals. This is the most reliable way we know of to assess a person's physical fitness.

17   With an accurate measure of the subjects' fitness levels, researchers at the Cooper Institute have been able to include fitness as a covariate with obesity. Analysis of the data obtained in the ACLS shows that there is a risk associated with obesity, but when you control for physical activity, much of that risk disappears (Church et al. 2004; Katzmarzyk et al. 2004; Katzmarzyk et al. 2004; Lee et al. 1999). One study showed that obese men who performed regular exercise had a lower risk of developing cardiovascular disease than lean men who were out of shape (Lee et al. 1999).

18   Steven Blair, who runs the Cooper Institute and was an author on all four of the above-mentioned studies, however, does not think obesity should be ignored. "I do think obesity is a public health problem, although I also think that the primary cause of the obesity epidemic is a declining level of average daily energy expenditure. . . . It will be unfortunate if it is now assumed that we should ignore obesity. I do not think that the [health] risk of obesity is a myth, although it has been overestimated." Blair believes that a focus on good nutrition and increased physical activity rather than on weight loss will better serve us.

19   In spite of the fact that there are virtually no controlled clinical trials examining the effects of obesity in people, we can make some inferences from animal research. Investigations performed by Ernsberger and his colleagues have shown that, over time, weight cycling (temporary weight loss followed by a regain of that weight, otherwise known as yo-yoing) in obese laboratory animals increases blood pressure, enlarges the heart, damages the kidney, increases abdominal fat deposits, and promotes further weight gain (Ernsberger and Koletsky 1993; Ernsberger et al. 1996; Ernsberger and Koletsky 1999). This indicates that the yo-yo effect of crash dieting may be the cause of many of the problems we attribute to simply being fat.

20   Even though there is a health risk from being too fat, you can eliminate much of the potential risk by exercising. Moreover, it is probably a bad idea to jump from diet to diet given the negative consequences the yo-yo effect can have. According to another study published in *JAMA*, the risk of cardiovascular disease has declined across all BMI groups over the past forty years as the result of better drugs (Gregg et al. 2005).

21   None of this means, however, that we should simply abandon our attempts to maintain a healthy weight; obese people had twice the incidence of hypertension compared to lean people and, most significantly, there has been (according to the above study) a 55 percent increase in diabetes that corresponds to the increase in obesity. So while we are better at dealing with the problem once it occurs, it is still better to avoid developing the problem in the first place.

Condemning the CDC

22   Whatever side of the argument you are on, it is apparent that many in the CDC acted irresponsibly. However, despite the fact that the initial, exaggerated estimate came from people at the CDC, we should keep in mind that *so did the corrected number*. While this can be frustrating to the casual observer, it is also a testament to the corrective power of the scientific method.

23   Science is about provisional truths that can be changed when evidence indicates that they should be. The fact that scientific information is available to the public is its greatest strength. Most of us, for whatever reason—whether it's self-interest or self-delusion—don't view our own ideas as critically as we should. The fact that scientific ideas are available for all to see allows those who disagree to disprove them. This is what has happened at the CDC; the most current study has addressed the flaws of the earlier studies. It is true that many of those in power at the CDC uncritically embraced the earlier estimates and overreacted, or worse simply accepted research that was flawed because it bolstered their agendas. But that failure lies with the people involved, not with the CDC as an institution or with the science itself.

24   The evidence still shows that morbid obesity is associated with an increased likelihood of developing disease and suffering from early mortality, but it also shows that those who are a few pounds overweight don't need to panic. What's more, it is clear that everyone, fat or thin, will benefit from regular exercise regardless of whether they lose weight.

25   The lesson to be learned from this controversy is that rational moderation is in order. Disproving one extreme idea does not prove the opposite extreme. As Steven Blair told me, "It is time to focus our attention on the key behaviors of eating a healthful diet (plenty of fruits and veggies, a lot of whole grains, and not too much fat and alcohol) and being physically active every day."

References

Allison, D.B., et al. 1999. Annual deaths attributable to obesity in the United States. *Journal of the American Medical Association* 282: 1530–38.

Blair, Steven, and James Morrow, Jr. 2005. Comments on U.S. dietary guidelines. *Journal of Physical Activity and Health* 2: 137–142.

Campos, Paul. 2004. *The Obesity Myth*. New York, New York: Gotham Books.

Church, T., et al. 2004. Exercise capacity and body composition as predictor of mortality among men with diabetes. *Diabetes Care* 27(1): 83–88.

Ernsberger, Paul, and Richard Koletsky. 1993. Biomedical rationale for a wellness approach to obesity: An alternative to a focus on weight loss. *Journal of Social Issues* 55(2): 221–259.

Ernsberger, Paul, and Richard Koletsky. 1999. Weight cycling and mortality: support from animal studies. *Journal of the American Medical Association* 269: 1116.

Ernsberger P., et al. 1994. Refeeding hypertension in obese spontaneously hypertensive rats. *Hypertension* 24: 699–705.

Frnsberger P., et al. 1996. Consequences of weight cycling in obese spontaneously hypertensive rats. *American Journal of Physiology: Regulatory, Integrative and Comparative Physiology* 270: R864–R872.

Flegal, Katherine M., et al. 2000. *Journal of the American Medical Association* 288(14): 1723–1727.

Flegal, K., et al. 2005. Excess deaths associated with underweight, overweight, and obesity. *Journal of the American Medical Association* 293(15): 1861–67.

Gregg, E., et al. 2005. Secular trends in cardiovascular disease risk factors according to body mass index in U.S. adults. *Journal of the American Medical Association* 293(15): 1868–74.

Hedley, A., et al. 2004. Prevalence of overweight and obesity among US children, adolescents, and adults, 1999–2000. *Journal of the American Medical Association* 291: 2847–2850.

Heini, Adrian F., and Roland L. Weinsier. 1997. Divergent trends in obesity and fat intake patterns: The American paradox. *Journal of the American Medical Association* 102(3): 254–264.

Katzmarzyk, Peter, et al. 2004. Metabolic syndrome, obesity, and mortality. *Diabetes Care* 28(2): 391–97.

Katzmarzyk, Peter, Timothy Church, and Steven Blair. 2004. Cardiorespiratory fitness attenuates the effects of the metabolic syndrome on all-cause and cardiovascular disease mortality in men. *Archives of Internal Medicine* 164: 1092–97.

Lee, Chong Do, Steven Blair, and Andrew Jackson. 1999. Cardiorespiratory fitness, body composition, and all-cause and cardiovascular disease mortality in men. *American Journal of Clinical Nutrition* 69: 373–80.

Mark, David. 2005. Deaths attributable to obesity. *Journal of the American Medical Association* 293(15): 1918–19.

Mokdad, A.H., et al. 2004. Actual causes of death in the United States. *Journal of the American Medical Association* 291: 1238–45.

Olshansky, S, Jay. et al. 2005. A potential decline in life expectancy in the United States in the 21st century. *New England Journal of Medicine* 352(11): 1138–45.

FROM READING TO WRITING

1. Analyze and compare any two arguments made in this chapter. How is each argument a product of its audience and purpose? What sources of argument are used—ethical appeals, logical appeals, emotional appeals—and what string of "good reasons" is proposed in order to make a case? Why do the composers of those arguments make those particular appeals? (For more on rhetorical analysis, see Chapter 7.)

2. Examine and compare the various visual arguments that appear in this chapter—the photos, ads, and cartoons. What argument, exactly, is being made in each case? How is that argument supported? (See Chapter 8 for information on analyzing visuals.)

3. Write an argument that makes its point by defining a key term related to the regulation of substances like tobacco, high-calorie food, alcohol, and so on. You might seek to change people's attitudes by redefining freedom or government regulation or advertising in such a way that your definition supports your views on regulating substances. (See Chapter 10 for more on writing definition arguments.)

4. Propose a particular policy related to the regulation of substances that is important in your community. For example, if binge drinking is an issue in your community, you might propose a single measure that might help to ameliorate the situation. Should your institution permit fans to purchase beer at sporting events? What should be the policy of major league baseball toward performance-enhancing drugs? (See Chapter 15 for advice on proposal arguments.)

5. Write a rebuttal of an argument in this chapter concerning the regulation of alcohol, tobacco, steroids, or other substances. (See Chapter 14.) Consider whether you want to show the weaknesses in the argument, or whether you wish to counterargue, or to do both.

6. Write an essay that recounts a personal experience of yours that makes an argument related to the regulation of a particular substance. What exactly does your personal experience lead you to conclude? See Chapter 13 for advice on narrative arguments. Alternatively, consider making your argument based on your observation of another person's experience.

28 | New Media

Personal Space in Cyberspace

Twenty-five years ago, everything seemed so simple and stable. There were a few cable TV stations, but the major networks—NBC, CBS, ABC—still ruled. Radio was delivering comfortable and predictable news, weather, and music to their listeners: Top 40 on one channel, country on another, oldies on a third; talk radio was a late-night-only phenomenon, and sports on the radio was built around familiar voices who were associated with particular teams over many years. The daily local newspaper arrived in the morning or afternoon or both. Every house and office had a central phone line, usually with a few extensions and usually serviced by AT&T.

Is this the future of media? In this publicity still from *Avatar*, all eyes are on the display. What are the consequences of the shift from old to new media?

Then everything changed. Cable television stations multiplied so that the established networks lost market share as well as their monopoly on evening entertainment and news coverage. Even sports coverage changed fundamentally when ESPN began offering its hour-long *SportsCenter* show, and network news gave up market share to the host of news and quasi-news shows that compete so vigorously for an audience today. When Rush Limbaugh created a large audience for his conservative political commentary, many radio stations created or expanded their talk-radio formats. And all that became jumbled still further with the advent of the Internet, which seems to be causing the slow demise of print journalism even as it encourages new, more participatory forms of media in cyberspace. Finally, social networking media and cell phone technologies in the past decade have put a sophisticated communications tool into the pockets and purses of just about everyone.

With these changes have come many concerns and controversies. The effects of new media on our political processes have been particularly criticized. On October 15, 2004, for example, less than three weeks before the presidential elections, popular Comedy Central comedian Jon Stewart, a guest on CNN's political talk show *Crossfire,* got into a celebrated donnybrook with news commentator Tucker Carlson. Stewart, whose hilarious political satire in the form of a mock TV news show sends many Americans to bed with smiles on their faces, took the opportunity of his appearance on *Crossfire* to challenge Carlson about the abysmal level of political commentary in the nation's media. At one point Stewart charged that *Crossfire* and shows like it—he was no doubt thinking of Bill O'Reilly and Rush Limbaugh and Keith Olbermann—are "bad, very bad," for America because they oversimplify and polarize discussion. "It's hurting America," said Stewart. "Stop, stop, stop, stop, stop hurting America." When Carlson protested that *Crossfire* presents intelligent debate from the political left and right, Stewart was outraged: "[Saying *Crossfire* is a debate show is] like saying pro wrestling is a show about athletic competition. You're doing theater when you should be doing debate. . . . What you do is not honest. What you do is partisan hackery . . . just knee-jerk reactionary talk."

While Stewart and his fans were taking their frustrations out on *Crossfire,* they were surely also thinking of much more. In the past decade many Americans have been increasingly concerned about certain trends in the popular media, especially in new media, including Internet news sites, podcasts, and blogs: the development of partisan (rather than "fair and balanced") news coverage; the concentration of news outlets and newspapers into the hands of a few powerful corporations; the impact of sensationalistic and one-sided talk radio and talk TV shows; the effects of the Internet on the political and cultural process; the dubious morality depicted on "reality TV"; attack coverage of events by bloggers and podcasters; and the effects of persistent advertising, violence, graphic sexuality, and cultural stereotyping that are associated now with films, magazines, and television programs. No wonder so many people cringe when they recall the nonstop, no-holds-barred, months-long tabloidization of Tiger Woods's marital infidelities.

Developments in new media—like Wikipedia, avatars, blogs, and Internet social networking sites—are making information and recreation more widely available, but the simplicity of posting anything on the Internet results in an overwhelming volume of material, a good deal of which is dubious in content. Between the partisanship (both obvious and subtle) of more traditional media and the questionable credibility of new media, many Americans are left wondering where to turn for reliable news and information, and for safe sources of family entertainment. Many, in fact, turn to relentless self-expression via blogs, Twitter, Facebook, and the like—to the personal spaces in cyberspace that may or may not reflect reality. The writers of the selections in this chapter tease out the tensions between freedom and censorship, public and private, in both old and new media; and they ponder the implications of the various new media.

Contemporary Arguments

This chapter opens with four pieces that explore the delicate balance between freedom and restriction on the Internet, as well as the potential consequences of swinging too far in one direction. In "Is Google's Data Grinder Dangerous?" Andrew Keen accuses Google of nefariously plotting for world domination and suggests that the Internet is not (and never will be) the utopian, free intellectual space that John Perry Barlow describes in "A Declaration of the Independence of Cyberspace." Similarly, John Seigenthaler describes a less-than-utopian experience of being the subject of a false Wikipedia biography and the obstacles to finding the identity of the writer. Walt Handelsman's "Information Superhighway" cartoon follows the Internet thread as well; his humorous roadway image shows a strikingly real portrait of priorities on the Internet. All these pieces come together under the broad topic of media and its uses. What is the Internet's purpose? Who should control it? Whose opinions should it publish and validate? And, finally, what are the hidden effects, sacrifices, and benefits when people (and small nonprofit organizations) develop a significant Internet presence?

For many people worldwide, such questions take a backseat to the daily influence of the media in their lives. The balance of the selections in this chapter take up the issue of the Internet, identities, and the burgeoning trend of developing alter egos—and richly detailed alternative worlds—online. In "Where the Avatars Roam," Michael Gerson looks at cyberspace role-playing from a moral perspective: What happens to morality and freedom when we spend so much time in alternative realities where any choice is possible—even criminal or socially undesirable choices? Daniel Okrent follows with a 1999 speech on the future of print media; you will find it highly relevant in the light of what is happening these days to print newspapers, magazine circulation, and e-book technologies such as the Kindle and the iPad. Then David Carr offers an endorsement of Twitter. Together, these articles tackle the tricky terrain of the private and the public in cyberspace. What kinds of personal expression are meant for public consumption? Should we differentiate between amateur and professional participation online, particularly if amateur expression is so common and so popular? Finally, just what is (and what should be) the purpose of new media—dissemination of information, recreation, commerce, or something else? Are we creating new media, or is it creating us?

The chapter concludes with an Issue in Focus: electronic games. As Chris Kohler indicates in his account of a new fitness game, Nintendo's Wii system actually can provide some exercise for participants, and so he counters concerns that rampant child obesity is the result of all video games. Can other new technologies like the Wii and Xbox's Kinect encourage people to be more active? And what about the other charges against video games—that they undermine learning, encourage teen violence, isolate children socially, and reinforce harmful gender stereotypes? The Issue in Focus takes up all these matters and more. More broadly speaking, to what purposes can we put new media, and how will these technological shifts influence our lives and cultures?

ANDREW KEEN

Is Google's Data Grinder Dangerous?

In *The Cult of the Amateur: How Today's Internet Is Killing Our Culture* (2007), Andrew Keen argues that the slew of amateur writing on the Internet—by anyone, about anything—doesn't contribute to knowledge or information, but rather bogs us down with uninformed opinions. Keen's view of the Internet is also evident in the article printed below. First published on July 12, 2007, in the *Los Angeles Times*, "Is Google's Data Grinder Dangerous?" puts a nefarious spin on the most popular Internet search engine—and its seeming quest to know all our private information so it can dominate the world (or at least make billions in advertising).

What does Google want? Having successfully become our personal librarian, Google now wants to be our personal oracle. It wants to learn all about us, know us better than we know ourselves, to transform itself from a search engine into a psychoanalyst's couch or a priest's confessional. Google's search engine is the best place to learn what Google wants. Type "Eric Schmidt London May 22" into Google, and you can read about a May interview the Google chief executive gave to journalists in London. Here is how he described what he hoped the search engine would look like in five years: "The goal is to enable Google users to be able to ask the question such as 'What shall I do tomorrow?' And 'What job shall I take?'"

2   Schmidt's goal is not inconsiderable: By 2012, he wants Google to be able to tell all of us what we want. This technology, what Google co-founder Larry Page calls the "perfect search engine," might not only replace our shrinks but also all those marketing professionals whose livelihoods are based on predicting—or guessing—consumer desires. Schmidt acknowledges that Google is still far from this goal. As he told the

London journalists: "We cannot even answer the most basic questions because we don't know enough about you. That is the most important aspect of Google's expansion."

3   So where is Google expanding? How is it planning to know more about us? Many—if not most—users don't read the user agreement and thus aren't aware that Google already stores every query we type in. The next stage is a personalized Web service called iGoogle. Schmidt, who perhaps not coincidentally sits on the board of Apple, regards its success as the key to knowing us better than we know ourselves.

4   iGoogle is growing into a tightly-knit suite of services—personalized homepage, search engine, blog, e-mail system, mini-program gadgets, Web-browsing history, etc.—that together will create the world's most intimate information database. On iGoogle, we all get to aggregate our lives, consciously or not, so artificially intelligent software can sort out our desires. It will piece together our recent blog posts, where we've been online, our e-commerce history and cultural interests. It will amass so much information about each of us that eventually it will be able to logically determine what we want to do tomorrow and what job we want.

5   The real question, of course, is whether what Google wants is what we want too. Do we really want Google digesting so much intimate data about us? Could iGoogle actually be a remix of "1984's" Room 101—that Orwellian dystopia in which our most secret desires and most repressed fears are revealed? Any comparison with 20th century, top-down totalitarianism is, perhaps, a little fanciful. After all, nobody can force us to use iGoogle. And—in contrast to Yahoo and Microsoft (which have no limits on how long they hang on to our personal data)—Google has committed to retaining data for only 18 months. Still, if iGoogle turns out to be half as wise about each of us as Schmidt predicts, then this artificial intelligence will challenge traditional privacy rights as well as provide us with an excuse to deny responsibility for our own actions. What happens, for example, when the government demands access to our iGoogle records? And will we be able to sue iGoogle if it advises us to make an unwise career decision?

6   Schmidt, I suspect, would like us to imagine Google as a public service, thereby affirming the company's "do no evil" credo. But Google is not our friend. Schmidt's iGoogle vision of the future is not altruistic, and his company is not a nonprofit group dedicated to the realization of human self-understanding. Worth more than $150 billion on the public market, Google is by far the dominant Internet advertising outlet—according to Nielsen ratings, it reaches about 70% of the global Internet audience. Just in the first quarter of 2007, Google's revenue from its online properties was up 76% from the previous year. Personal data are Google's most valuable currency, its crown jewels. The more Google knows our desires, the more targeted advertising it can serve up to us and the more revenue it can extract from these advertisers.

7   What does Google really want? Google wants to dominate. Its proposed $3.1-billion acquisition of DoubleClick threatens to make the company utterly dominant in the online advertising business. The $1.65-billion acquisition of YouTube last year made it by far the dominant player in the online video market. And, with a personalized service like iGoogle, the company is seeking to become the algorithmic monopolist of our online behavior. So when Eric Schmidt says Google wants to know us better than we know ourselves, he is talking to his shareholders rather than us. As a Silicon Valley old-timer, trust me on this one. I know Google better than it knows itself.

John Perry Barlow

A Declaration of the Independence of Cyberspace

After seventeen years as a Wyoming rancher who, on the side, wrote songs for the Grateful Dead, John Perry Barlow (born 1947) in the late 1980s began writing about computer-mediated communications. He served on the board of directors of WELL (the Whole Earth Lectronic Link), posts regularly on the WELL Web site, and is a cofounder of the Electronic Frontier Foundation, which advocates keeping government regulations out of the Internet. Since May 1998, he has been a fellow at Harvard Law School's Berkman Center for Internet and Society.

Governments of the Industrial World, you weary giants of flesh and steel, I come from Cyberspace, the new home of Mind. On behalf of the future, I ask you of the past to leave us alone. You are not welcome among us. You have no sovereignty where we gather.

2   We have no elected government, nor are we likely to have one, so I address you with no greater authority than that with which liberty itself always speaks. I declare the global social space we are building to be naturally independent of the tyrannies you seek to impose on us. You have no moral right to rule us nor do you possess any methods of enforcement we have true reason to fear.

3   Governments derive their just powers from the consent of the governed. You have neither solicited nor received ours. We did not invite you. You do not know us, nor do you know our world. Cyberspace does not lie within your borders. Do not think that you can build it, as though it were a public construction project. You cannot. It is an act of nature and it grows itself through our collective actions.

4   You have not engaged in our great and gathering conversation, nor did you create the wealth of our marketplaces. You do not know our culture, our ethics, or the unwritten codes that already provide our society more order than could be obtained by any of your impositions.

5   You claim there are problems among us that you need to solve. You use this claim as an excuse to invade our precincts. Many of these problems don't exist. Where there are real conflicts, where there are wrongs, we will identify them and address them by our means. We are forming our own Social Contract. This governance will arise according to the conditions of our world, not yours. Our world is different.

6   Cyberspace consists of transactions, relationships, and thought itself, arrayed like a standing wave in the web of our communications. Ours is a world that is both everywhere and nowhere, but it is not where bodies live.

7   We are creating a world that all may enter without privilege or prejudice accorded by race, economic power, military force, or station of birth.

8   We are creating a world where anyone, anywhere may express his or her beliefs, no matter how singular, without fear of being coerced into silence or conformity.

9   Your legal concepts of property, expression, identity, movement, and context do not apply to us. They are based on matter. There is no matter here.

10   Our identities have no bodies, so, unlike you, we cannot obtain order by physical coercion. We believe that, from ethics, enlightened self-interest, and the commonweal, our governance will emerge. Our identities may be distributed across many of your jurisdictions. The only law that all our constituent cultures would generally recognize is the Golden Rule. We hope we will be able to build our particular solutions on that basis. But we cannot accept the solutions you are attempting to impose.

11   In the United States, you have today created a law, the Telecommunications Reform Act, which repudiates your own Constitution and insults the dreams of Jefferson, Washington, Mill, Madison, deToqueville, and Brandeis. These dreams must now be born anew in us.

12   You are terrified of your own children, since they are natives in a world where you will always be immigrants. Because you fear them, you entrust your bureaucracies with the parental responsibilities you are too cowardly to confront yourselves. In our world, all the sentiments and expressions of humanity, from the debasing to the angelic, are parts of a seamless whole, the global conversation of bits. We cannot separate the air that chokes from the air upon which wings beat.

13   In China, Germany, France, Russia, Singapore, Italy, and the United States, you are trying to ward off the virus of liberty by erecting guard posts at the frontiers of Cyberspace. These may keep out the contagion for a small time, but they will not work in a world that will soon be blanketed in bit-bearing media.

14   Your increasingly obsolete information industries would perpetuate themselves by proposing laws, in America and elsewhere, that claim to own speech itself throughout the world. These laws would declare ideas to be another industrial product, no more noble than pig iron. In our world, whatever the human mind may create can be reproduced and distributed infinitely at no cost. The global conveyance of thought no longer requires your factories to accomplish.

15   These increasingly hostile and colonial measures place us in the same position as those previous lovers of freedom and self-determination who had to reject the authorities of distant, uninformed powers. We must declare our virtual selves immune to your sovereignty, even as we continue to consent to your rule over our bodies. We will spread ourselves across the Planet so that no one can arrest our thoughts.

16   We will create a civilization of the Mind in Cyberspace. May it be more humane and fair than the world your governments have made before. ■

JOHN **SEIGENTHALER**

A False Wikipedia "Biography"

John Seigenthaler, now retired, is a distinguished journalist who founded the Freedom Forum First Amendment Center at Vanderbilt University—so he is anything but a censor at heart. Nevertheless, in the following essay (published in November 2005 in *USA Today*, a newspaper he helped launch) he expresses grave reservations about Wikipedia as he recounts a personal experience. The article printed below generated serious discussion about the reliability, credibility, and ethics of Wikipedia, which changed some of its policies subsequently. You can read more about the episode by going to en.wikipedia.org/wiki/ Seigenthaler_controversy. For a writing activity on Wikipedia, see page 681.

> John Seigenthaler Sr. was the assistant to Attorney General Robert Kennedy in the early 1960s. For a brief time, he was thought to have been directly in-volved in the Kennedy assassinations of both John and his brother Bobby. Nothing was ever proven.
>
> —*Wikipedia*

This is a highly personal story about Internet character assassination. It could be your story. I have no idea whose sick mind conceived the false, malicious "biog-raphy" that appeared under my name for 132 days on Wikipedia, the popular, online, free encyclopedia whose authors are unknown and virtually untraceable. There was more:

2   "John Seigenthaler moved to the Soviet Union in 1971, and returned to the United States in 1984," Wikipedia said. "He started one of the country's largest public relations firms shortly thereafter."

3   At age 78, I thought I was beyond surprise or hurt at anything negative said about me. I was wrong. One sentence in the biography was true. I was Robert Kennedy's administrative assistant in the early 1960s. I also was his pallbearer. It was mind-boggling when my son, John Seigenthaler, journalist with NBC News, phoned later to say he found the same scurrilous text on Reference.com and Answers.com.

4   I had heard for weeks from teachers, journalists and historians about "the wonderful world of Wikipedia," where millions of people worldwide visit daily for quick reference "facts," composed and posted by people with no special expertise or knowledge—and sometimes by people with malice.

5   At my request, executives of the three websites now have removed the false content about me. But they don't know, and can't find out, who wrote the toxic sentences.

Anonymous Author

6   I phoned Jimmy Wales, Wikipedia's founder and asked, "Do you . . . have any way to know who wrote that?"

7   "No, we don't," he said. Representatives of the other two websites said their computers are programmed to copy data verbatim from Wikipedia, never checking whether it is false or factual. Naturally, I want to unmask my "biographer." And, I am in-terested in letting many people know that Wikipedia is a flawed and irresponsible research tool.

8   But searching cyberspace for the identity of people who post spurious information can be frustrating. I found on Wikipedia the registered IP (Internet Protocol) number of my "biographer"—65-81-97-208. I traced it to a customer of BellSouth Internet.
That company advertises a phone number to report "Abuse Issues." An electronic voice
said all complaints must be e-mailed. My two e-mails were answered by identical form
letters, advising me that the company would conduct an investigation but might not tell
me the results. It was signed "Abuse Team."

9   Wales, Wikipedia's founder, told me that BellSouth would not be helpful. "We
have trouble with people posting abusive things over and over and over," he said. "We
block their IP numbers, and they sneak in another way. So we contact the service
providers, and they are not very responsive."

10   After three weeks, hearing nothing further about the Abuse Team investigation, I
phoned BellSouth's Atlanta corporate headquarters, which led to conversations between my lawyer and BellSouth's counsel. My only remote chance of getting the name,
I learned, was to file a "John or Jane Doe" lawsuit against my "biographer." Major communications Internet companies are bound by federal privacy laws that protect the
identity of their customers, even those who defame online. Only if a lawsuit resulted in
a court subpoena would BellSouth give up the name.

Little Legal Recourse

11   Federal law also protects online corporations—BellSouth, AOL, MCI, Wikipedia, etc.—
from libel lawsuits. Section 230 of the Communications Decency Act, passed in 1996,
specifically states that "no provider or user of an interactive computer service shall be
treated as the publisher or speaker." That legalese means that, unlike print and broadcast companies, online service providers cannot be sued for disseminating defamatory
attacks on citizens posted by others. Recent low-profile court decisions document that
Congress effectively has barred defamation in cyberspace. Wikipedia's website acknowledges that it is not responsible for inaccurate information, but Wales, in a recent
C-Span interview with Brian Lamb, insisted that his website is accountable and that his
community of thousands of volunteer editors (he said he has only one paid employee)
corrects mistakes within minutes.

12   My experience refutes that. My "biography" was posted May 26. On May 29, one
of Wales' volunteers "edited" it only by correcting the misspelling of the word "early." For
four months, Wikipedia depicted me as a suspected assassin before Wales erased it
from his website's history Oct. 5. The falsehoods remained on Answers.com and
Reference.com for three more weeks. In the C-Span interview, Wales said Wikipedia
has "millions" of daily global visitors and is one of the world's busiest websites. His volunteer community runs the Wikipedia operation, he said. He funds his website through
a non-profit foundation and estimated a 2006 budget of "about a million dollars."

13   And so we live in a universe of new media with phenomenal opportunities for
worldwide communications and research—but populated by volunteer vandals with
poison-pen intellects. Congress has enabled them and protects them.

14   When I was a child, my mother lectured me on the evils of "gossip." She held a
feather pillow and said, "If I tear this open, the feathers will fly to the four winds, and I
could never get them back in the pillow. That's how it is when you spread mean things
about people." For me, that pillow is a metaphor for Wikipedia.

Michael Gerson

Where the Avatars Roam

Michael Gerson, who once worked as a policy analyst and speechwriter under President George W. Bush, is columnist for the *Washington Post* and contributes to *PostPartisan*. His book about the future of conservative politics, *Heroic Conservatism*, was published in 2007. His areas of expertise span democracy and human rights, health and diseases, and religion and politics. Gerson is senior research fellow at the Institute for Global Engagement's Center on Faith and International Affairs. In "Where the Avatars Roam," published in the *Washington Post* July 6, 2007, Gerson asks, what happens to human freedom and human choices in alternative realities constructed online?

I am not usually found at bars during the day, though the state of the Republican Party would justify it. But here I was at a bar talking to this fox—I mean an actual fox, with fluffy tail and whiskers. It turns out that, in the online world of Second Life, many people prefer to take the shape of anthropomorphic animals called "furries," and this one is in a virtual bar talking about her frustrating job at a New York publishing house. But for all I know, she could be a man in outback Montana with a computer, a satellite dish and a vivid imagination.

2　　For a columnist, this is called "research." For millions of Americans, it is an addictive form of entertainment called MMORPGs—massively multiplayer online role-playing games. In this entirely new form of social interaction, people create computer-generated bodies called avatars and mingle with other players in 3-D fantasy worlds.

3　　Some of these worlds parallel a form of literature that J.R.R. Tolkien called "subcreation"—the Godlike construction of a complex, alternative reality, sometimes with its own mythology and languages. I subscribe along with my two sons (an elf and a dwarf) to The Lord of the Rings Online, based on Tolkien's epic novels, which sends its participants on a series of heroic quests. I'm told that World of Warcraft, which has more than 8 million subscribers, takes a similar approach. Some of the appeal of these games is the controlled release of aggression—cheerful orc killing. But they also represent a conservative longing for medieval ideals of chivalry—for a recovery of honor and adventure in an age dominated by choice and consumption.

If you were to create an avatar, would you want it to look like yourself or someone or something else? Why?

4　　Second Life, however, is a different animal. Instead of showing the guiding hand of an author, this universe is created by the choices of its participants, or "residents." They can build, buy, trade and talk in a world entirely without rules or laws; a pure market where choice and consumption are the highest values. Online entrepreneurs make real money selling virtual clothing, cars and "skins"—the photorealistic faces and bodies of avatars. Companies such as Dell, IBM and Toyota market aggressively within Second Life.

5　　The site has gotten some recent attention for its moral lapses. A few of its residents have a disturbing preference for "age play"—fantasy sex with underage avatars—which has attracted the attention of prosecutors in several countries.

6   But Second Life is more consequential than its moral failures. It is, in fact, a large-scale experiment in libertarianism. Its residents can do and be anything they wish. There are no binding forms of community, no responsibilities that aren't freely chosen and no lasting consequences of human actions. In Second Life, there is no human nature at all, just human choices.

7   And what do people choose? Well, there is some good live music, philanthropic fundraising, even a few virtual churches and synagogues. But the main result is the breakdown of inhibition. Second Life, as you'd expect, is highly sexualized in ways that have little to do with respect or romance. There are frequent outbreaks of terrorism, committed by online anarchists who interrupt events, assassinate speakers (who quickly reboot from the dead) and vandalize buildings. There are strip malls everywhere, pushing a relentless consumerism. And there seems to be an inordinate number of vampires, generally not a sign of community health.

8   Libertarians hold to a theory of "spontaneous order"—that society should be the product of uncoordinated human choices instead of human design. Well, Second Life has plenty of spontaneity, and not much genuine order. This experiment suggests that a world that is only a market is not a utopia. It more closely resembles a seedy, derelict carnival—the triumph of amusement and distraction over meaning and purpose.

9   Columnists, like frontier trackers, are expected to determine cultural directions from faint scents in the wind. So maybe there is a reason that *The Lord of the Rings* is ultimately more interesting than Second Life. Only in a created world, filled with moral rules, social obligations and heroic quests, do our free choices seem to matter. And even fictional honor fills a need deeper than consumption.

10   G.K. Chesterton wrote that when people are "really wild with freedom and invention" they create institutions, such as marriages and constitutions; but "when men are weary they fall into anarchy." In that anarchy, life tends to be nasty, brutish, short—and furry. ■

Daniel Okrent

The Death of Print?

Daniel Okrent (born 1948) has spent his career in the publishing industry, as the writer of articles and books (his latest book, published in 2010, is on the Prohibition Era in the United States), as an editor for *Time* and *Life* and the *New York Times*, and in other roles. (He is also credited with inventing fantasy sports games in 1980.) The following was delivered as a lecture at Columbia University's School of Journalism on December 14, 1999, and archived by *The Digital Journalist* in February 2000.

L ooking out at an audience of so many people who would forgo tonight's episode of "Dharma and Greg" or "Rivera Live" to come hear me talk, I feel highly responsible to provide you with entertainment or elucidation sufficient to justify your sacrifice. I also feel the burden to live up to the provocative title that the J-school's lecture producers and I have cooked up to get you out of your apartments and into this hall: "The Death of Print?" has both a nice, millenarian finality to it, and a perfect op-ed page sort of cop-out attached to it, namely that temporizing question mark.

2   "The Death of Print" also makes it pretty clear that I'm not going to be talking about the shrinking news staffs at the major networks, or the increasing tendency of local television news shows to devote their time to either highway mayhem or idiotic, grinning man-or-woman on the street interviews with people whose only qualification for demanding our attention is that they are, in fact, on the street.

3   If you sense a certain antipathy to television journalism in my tone, you're right. This is one way that I hope to establish my credentials with you as a paragon of print, an ink-stained wretch, someone with printer's ink coursing through his veins—pick your print media cliché, and it applies to me. I even spent some time looking through George Will's entire library of quotation dictionaries trying to find some apposite quote about the importance of print journalism, to show how widely read—in Quotation Dictionaries—I am. But all I could find was a sequence of pomposities and self-evidencies uttered decades ago by Walter Lippmann, our profession's most predicable Capital G Capital M Great Man. That's the problem with talking about the future of media or journalism, the tendency to float away on the helium of one's own pretentiousness.

4   So here goes. I am going to take a portion of my time this evening to sing a hymn of praise to print, to its irreplaceable role in our lives.

5   Newspapers, magazines, books—all those other wonderful creatures made possible by Gutenberg five centuries ago are, I'm sure you'll agree, the media that matter. I've spent my entire career engaged by them—going back to working on a daily newspaper when I was in college, then nine years in the book business, several more as a writer of books, and finally, until 1996, 14 years as a magazine editor. Forgive me the three years I spent on the web, navigating a turbulent sea of bits and bytes as Time Inc.'s editor of new media. I touched land several months ago, and now I'm writing and editing again. It's nice to be back.

6   Newspapers, magazines, books: A newspaper gives you timeliness, a magazine perspective, a book lasting value. Each is a firm, palpable entity, a presence in our lives, a companion to our days. I remember what it was like when I was a child, and my father brought home the newspaper after work. My mother would take what we called in those distant, benighted days the women's section—recipes, fashion news, the advice columns. My older brother, who was readying himself for a business career—he took the stock market pages. I reached for sports, the news of the athletic wonders committed daily by my heroes. My father had the general news section, and we'd each disappear into our own engagements with the wider world, regrouping in time for dinner and a shared conversation about what we had encountered in the daily paper. What could possibly replace something so comfortable, so safe, so adaptable as a daily newspaper?

7   As for magazines—well, I work for the world's largest magazine company, so it shouldn't be hard for me to make a case for the magazine. There are nearly 10,000 different magazines available in the U.S. today. Great, giant, mass circulation magazines like those Time Inc. publishes—*Time, Life, People, Fortune*, and so on—and tiny, narrowly focused magazines to cater to the reader's most special interest. I'm a scuba diver. I subscribe to two different scuba diving magazines, and if I wanted to I could subscribe to a dozen more. Interested in orchids? There are magazines for you. Guitars? I have a 19-year-old friend who subscribes to three guitar magazines. Magazines of every stripe and substance are there to build connections among those of us of a particular interest, or to set the terms of the national conversation on subjects of importance to all of us. Through the pages of *Ocean Realm* magazine I share a set of knowledge on our common passion with a scuba diver who lives 3,000 miles away from me. Through the pages of *Time*, I participate in a dialogue with him on matters of national concern—and with all of his neighbors, as well. Magazines bring us together into real communities, coming into our house as regular, periodic welcome visitors, requiring us to do nothing more than make a once-a-year request to the publisher to keep them coming. What could be easier than that?

8   Books? Every one of us in this room could write an anthem to the book. The feel of a fine binding, the smell of newly opened pages, the satisfying heft of a book in your hands—can anything top it? When I get home at night, before dinner I sit with a drink in my hand in a room full of books, each one of them an old friend who has accompanied me on part of my life voyage. The book of poems I loved in college, the biography that first introduced me to a great historical figure twenty years ago, the novel that entertained me on a vacation, or maybe the one that explained a piece of the world to me. As I was thinking about this talk, I happened to notice on my bookshelf a copy of the best novel about journalism ever written, Evelyn Waugh's *Scoop*, a book which I re-read every ten years or so to make certain that, if I stay in this business, I need to remain very, very careful.

9   As you can see, I can get sentimental about these things we call, by inference, the old media. They mean a lot to me, emotionally as well as economically—and I suspect they do to all of you, too. I believe they are, after food, clothing, and shelter, and after our family relations and our friendships, the most important things in our lives.

10   And I believe one more thing: I believe they, and all forms of print, are dead. Finished. Over. Perhaps not in my professional lifetime, but certainly in that of the youngest people in this room. Remove the question mark from the title of this talk. The Death of Print, full stop.

11   Twenty, thirty, at the outside forty years from now, we will look back on the print media the way we look back on travel by horse and carriage, or by wind-powered ship. In fact, that carriage, and that ship, will have their own print counterparts, which I will get to later. But first I would like to tell you why I am so convinced that those media to which I have devoted my 30 years of professional life are as relevant to our future as the carrier pigeon.

12   And please understand: I did not come to this conclusion as a zealot. Until I moved into my job as editor of new media for Time Inc., the Internet was merely a place for me to get late stock market news, or the baseball box scores. I didn't move into my

current job out of passion, or conviction, or technological facility, or even a particular interest in the subject. When I asked Don Logan, Time Inc.'s CEO, why he and Norman Pearlstine, our editor-in-chief, thought I was right for this job, Don said, "Because we need a little gray hair in that organization." In other words, I qualified because I was old.

13   So, to the point: why is print dead? It's a two-part argument, the first part fairly simple but worth some elaboration, the second part as obvious as the morning sun.

14   Part one, in a phrase, is that we have, I believe, finally learned not to underestimate the march of technological progress. A little over thirty years ago, I saw my first electronic calculator. It was about the shape of a laptop computer, maybe three inches deep, it weighed eight or nine pounds, and it cost my father's law firm $500 in 1967 dollars. Today, you can buy calculators the size and heft of a credit card in a convenience store for two dollars. I purchased my first computer, an Apple 2E, in 1980. What a wonder it was! White type—capital letters only—dropped out of a black screen; it processed words at a speed less than 1% as fast as the three-pound laptop that has become the locus, the library, and the lever of my entire professional life. Its built-in memory couldn't accommodate a long magazine article. And my friends and neighbors—sophisticated, educated people—would come over evenings to watch me move blocks of text from HERE to THERE on it. It was that new, that extraordinary. I don't need to tell you what the average computer can do today, nor do I need to tell you similar stories about telephones, or audio equipment, or any other piece of new technology. If we imagine it, they will build it.

15   So imagine this (and if you find it hard to imagine, trust me: I've seen it already, in the development office of a well-established Japanese computer electronics company): Imagine a tablet, maybe half an inch thick, shaped when held one way like an open book or magazine, when turned sideways much like a single page of a newspaper. It weighs six ounces. It's somewhat flexible, which makes it easy to transport. (The truly flexible one, which you'll be able to roll up and put in your pocket, is still a couple of years away, so this one will have to do.) Its screen, utterly glare-free, neither flickers nor fades nor grows dull. To move beyond the first screen in whatever it is that you're reading, you run your finger across the top of the tablet LIKE THIS—a physical metaphor for the turning of the page. You are sitting on a beach on a Saturday afternoon with this little wonder, and you're reading this week's *Time* magazine. Then you decide you'd like something a little more, oh, entertaining. You press a series of buttons HERE, and a cellular hookup to a satellite-connected database instantaneously delivers you—well, Evelyn Waugh's *Scoop*. And when you've had enough of that—click, click—you move on, to the football news, or the office memoranda you didn't finish reading on Friday afternoon, or whatever it is that you want. Click, click again: each download, coming to you at dazzling speeds, and a central rights-clearance computer charges your account, much like a telephone account, for what you've read or listened to. The satellite operator keeps a small portion of the income, and the rest goes to the "publisher"—that is, to the agency that either created the material you are reading, or that represents the interests of those who created it.

16   Or imagine this: another message comes to you, from—let's say Coca Cola. It's an advertising message, and you have been paid to read it. You have been targeted by

Coca Cola, the marketers from that company have found you on the beach, and for the privilege of getting their message in front of you they have paid the satellite operator a carriage fee. The satellite operator, wanting to guarantee the advertising agency that the impression has been made, credits your master account a few cents. For reading the one-minute message from Coca Cola, you get the first five minutes of tomorrow's electronic newspaper for free. Everyone's happy.

17   As I said, this technology already exists. It's far too expensive today, and the critical elements of payment systems and copyright protection and royalty accounting have not yet been created. But, I guarantee you that such systems are either in development today or soon will be.

18   But, you say, who wants to read a good novel on a computer screen, no matter how clear and snappy and portable it is? Who wants to forgo the tactile engagement with a newspaper or magazine, or even moreso the deeper, more gratifying physical connection with a book, and replace it with this potentially alienating form of modern technology?

19   Well, that brings me to part two of my argument, the part I promised was as obvious as the morning sun. And that is this: last year, Time Inc., spent $1 billion dollars on paper and postage.

20   End of argument.

21   Or, if you'd like, let me put it this way: you may prefer to ride across town in horse-and-carriage, or across a lake in a wind-powered yacht, but no one makes that carriage or that yacht for you anymore, at least not at a reasonable price. So too with the book: in the future that I am imagining with you tonight, the book becomes an elite item for the very few, an *objet,* a collectible—valuable not for the words on the page but for the vessel that contains those words. Will it matter to the book-loving *litterateurs* who stalk Morningside Heights? Probably so, though I can't imagine why. Will it matter to the millions who buy a John Grisham paperback and toss it when it's done? Not a chance.

22   Nor should it. For we—we who work today by accident in paper and ink; who demand, however sheepishly, that vast forests be cut down to make our paper, for vast sums to be invested in hypermodern printing presses and bindery machines that consume megawatts of environment-befouling energy—we should be happy. For we know—we *must* know—that the words and pictures and ideas and images and notions and substance that we produce is what matters—and *not* the vessel that they arrive in.

23   I want to step back for a few moments here to elaborate on business models, consumer prejudices, and what I hope is a somewhat sober-sided consideration of a few of the risks this new world will pose.

24   First, business models. To date, we have seen very few media institutions find a way to charge for their digitally-delivered content: the *Wall Street Journal*, which is as close as one gets in American journalism to being both unique and essential, has been the leader to date. I admire the *Journal* hugely, both in print and online, but I do want to share with you the real reason for its success, the thing that makes it essential. This was explained to me by my boss, Norm Pearlstine, several years ago when he was the

Journal's editor: the paper's indispensability, he said, is predicated on the mortal fear, shared by every middle manager in American business, that the boss will say to him or her, "Did you see the piece in the *Journal* this morning about X?"

25   Well, that works online, too, and several hundred thousand people are now paying Dow-Jones for the online paper. But note that they are paying $59 for an annual subscription to the online edition, while the print edition costs $175. That's partly because the physical costs—the nearly $1 billion a year, in our case, that Time Inc. spends on manufacturing and distribution—have evaporated. In other words, savings have been passed on to the reader, and everybody wins. Except, of course, the paper manufacturers, the delivery services, and the US Post Office—so all of you who have been planning careers at International Paper or with the Postal Service, forget it.

26   But the real power of the business model resides in the potential of digital advertising. Except for direct mail, until the Internet came along no advertising medium existed in which the advertiser could be sure his message was received by his targeted audience. We go to the bathroom during commercials, we flip the pages past magazine and newspaper ads, radio and billboards are white noise. But with a truly interactive medium—with say, a question about the advertisement asked next to the button that gives you your thirty cent credit against the cost of reading your *Wall Street Journal*—the effectiveness of media advertising changes radically. And if you don't think advertisers influence the direction of American mass media, you ought to talk to Tom Goldstein about the curriculum here at the J-school.

27   Second digression: consumer prejudices. Inevitably, whenever and wherever I talk about the Death of Print, someone jumps up and says, "But I hate reading on a computer." This is after I have already explained that the technology will change, that economic incentive will create consumer-friendly reading devices, that my father once paid as much for a four-function telephone book-sized calculator as he did for a low-end used car. Or that Oscar Dystel, the former chairman of Bantam Books and one of the founders of the American paperback book industry in the 1940s, once said, "In due course, the word 'paperback' will lose its taint of unpleasantness." And he said that in 1984.

28   No, you won't be reading on a cathode ray tube sitting on your desk. No, the screen won't flicker, and the type won't have visible ragged edges. It won't feel anything like a computer. It won't even feel like those early avatars of the form, the Rocket eBook and the SoftBook Reader, that are already showing up in Christmas catalogs and in consumer electronics stores—not any more than a Model T feels or looks or drives like a 1999 BMW Z3. There's even a guy at MII, an engineering genius named Jacobson, who's devised something called electronic ink, a palette of digitally changeable molecules that sit on a surface very much like a sheet of paper, and rearrange themselves sequentially into actual sentences and paragraphs.

29   Ah, but you say, who will be able to afford such wonderful devices? In fact, nearly everyone. Because we—the big media companies like Time Warner, the eight or ten major copyright oligarchs, as I like to call them, who control so much of the nation's supply of worthwhile content—we will give them away, for all practical purposes, on the

cell phone model. Agree to subscribe to *Time* and *Sports Illustrated* for two years, as well as to listen to a certain amount of, say, Warner Brothers Music, and we'll give you the device. We aren't interested in making money off of hardware; we make money off of what you read and watch and listen to.

30   Last digression: risk. Yes, there are risks. Disaggregated content has already been somewhat socially injurious, and it's only going to get worse, at least insofar as we like to imagine a citizenry that is not only informed, but informed across a range of subjects. The ability to be your own editor—to pick just what news on what topics you wish to read—destroys the potential for serendipity, and the ease with which we achieve balance. I don't know how we'll solve this one, but we must.

31   Similarly, there's a risk in the mutability of digital content. The good news is that if you libel someone at 9 A.M., you can correct it at 9:10 or at noon or whenever it is that you learn of your mistake; it's not like sending out a fleet of trucks with a million copies of the *Times* and then realizing what you did wrong. But by the same token, if the words are never written in stone, or at least in ink, what happens to the notion of historical record?

32   But, of course, that cat is already out of the bag. If great writers are producing their works on computer, as most now do, first drafts no longer exist for the study of future scholars—just as the hurried prose of a daily newspaper, "the first rough draft of history," as it has been called, may disappear to the corrections of lawyers.

33   Yet I think we can live with these things, largely because we must.

34   I will assert once again that The Death of Print is going to happen, far sooner than many of you may think. The word "Internet" was all but unknown in the U.S. six years ago, and Time Inc., which had not yet even imagined its potential impact, had no one working in the Internet arena. Today, the Internet is inescapable; through the advent of email, it is ubiquitous. In the financial markets, it as essential as dollars. Throughout Time Warner, more than 1,000 people are developing copyrighted internet product, or marketing it to consumers. Someday, we may even make money at it.

35   For now, though, all of this is destabilizing, particularly for those of us who are investing substantially in a future so tantalizingly clear in the ultimate goal, but the path to which is so tangled in thickets of doubt, uncertainty, and confusion. Yet I, for one, take a strange kind of solace in this. What I know to be true is that the human species is hungry for information; that the quality, timeliness, and reliability of information is paramount; and that those of us who grew up in print, who look at the technological future through unconfident eyes, will be asked to do tomorrow exactly what we have done in the past, which is to reach people—intellectually, viscerally, any way we can—on matters they care about it. My colleagues and I did not grow up wanting to be in the ink and paper and staples business; we wanted to be in—we *are* in—the business of words and sentences and pictures and ideas. Don't worry about the future of newspapers or magazines or books any more than you would worry about corrugated boxes or shrink-wrap. They are containers; the substance resides elsewhere—for instance, in this room. So thank you for your attention; you may now throw tomatoes at me.

DAVID **CARR**

Why Twitter Will Endure

David Carr is the author of "Media Equation," a column in the business section of the *New York Times* that focuses on media issues. His work analyzes media as it intersects with business, culture, and government. His writing has also appeared in *The Atlantic Monthly* and *New York Magazine.* The following *Times* article was published on January 3, 2010.

I can remember when I first thought seriously about Twitter. Last March, I was at the SXSW conference, a conclave in Austin, Tex., where technology, media, and music are mashed up and re-imagined, and, not so coincidentally, where Twitter first rolled out in 2007. As someone who was oversubscribed on Facebook, overwhelmed by the computer-generated RSS feeds of news that came flying at me, and swamped by incoming e-mail messages, the last thing I wanted was one more Web-borne intrusion into my life.

2   And then there was the name. Twitter. In the pantheon of digital nomenclature— brands within a sector of the economy that grew so fast that all the sensible names were quickly taken—it would be hard to come up with a noun more trite than Twitter. It impugns itself, promising something slight and inconsequential, yet another way to make hours disappear and have nothing to show for it. And just in case the noun is not sufficiently indicting, the verb, "to tweet" is even more embarrassing.

3   Beyond the dippy lingo, the idea that something intelligent, something worthy of mindshare, might occur in the space of 140 characters—Twitter's parameters were set by what would fit in a text message on a phone—seems unlikely.

4   But it was clear that at the conference, the primary news platform was Twitter, with real-time annotation of the panels on stage and critical updates about what was happening elsewhere at a very hectic convention. At 52, I succumbed, partly out of professional necessity.

5   And now, nearly a year later, has Twitter turned my brain to mush? No, I'm in narrative on more things in a given moment than I ever thought possible, and instead of spending a half-hour surfing in search of illumination, I get a sense of the day's news and how people are reacting to it in the time that it takes to wait for coffee at Starbucks. Yes, I worry about my ability to think long thoughts—where was I, anyway?—but the tradeoff has been worth it.

6   Some time soon, the company won't say when, the 100-millionth person will have signed on to Twitter to follow and be followed by friends and strangers. That may sound like a MySpace waiting to happen—remember MySpace?—but I'm convinced Twitter is here to stay.

7   And I'm not alone. "The history of the Internet suggests that there have been cool Web sites that go in and out of fashion and then there have been open standards that become plumbing," said Steven Johnson, the author and technology observer who wrote a seminal piece about Twitter for Time last June. "Twitter is looking more and more like plumbing, and plumbing is eternal."

8   Really? What could anyone possibly find useful in this cacophony of short-burst communication? Well, that depends on whom you ask, but more importantly whom you

follow. On Twitter, anyone may follow anyone, but there is very little expectation of reciprocity. By carefully curating the people you follow, Twitter becomes an always-on data stream from really bright people in their respective fields, whose tweets are often full of links to incredibly vital, timely information.

9 The most frequent objection to Twitter is a predictable one: "I don't need to know someone is eating a donut right now." But if that someone is a serious user of Twitter, she or he might actually be eating the curmudgeon's lunch, racing ahead with a clear, up-to-the-second picture of an increasingly connected, busy world. The service has obvious utility for a journalist, but no matter what business you are in, imagine knowing what the thought leaders in your industry were reading and considering. And beyond following specific individuals, Twitter hash tags allow you to go deep into interests and obsession: #rollerderby, #physics, #puppets and #Avatar, to name just a few of many thousands.

10 The act of publishing on Twitter is so friction-free—a few keystrokes and hit send—that you can forget that others are out there listening. I was on a Virgin America cross-country flight, and used its wireless connection to tweet about the fact that the guy next to me seemed to be the leader of a cult involving Axe body spray. A half-hour later, a steward approached me and said he wondered if I would be more comfortable with a seat in the bulkhead. (He turned out to be a great guy, but I was doing a story involving another part of the company, so I had to decline the offer. @VirginAmerica, its corporate Twitter account, sent me a message afterward saying perhaps it should develop a screening process for Axe. It was creepy and comforting all at once.)

11 Like many newbies on Twitter, I vastly overestimated the importance of broadcasting on Twitter; and after a while, I realized that I was not Moses and neither Twitter nor its users were wondering what I thought. Nearly a year in, I've come to understand that the real value of the service is listening to a wired collective voice.

12 Not that long ago, I was at a conference at Yale and looked at the sea of open laptops in the seats in front of me. So why wasn't my laptop open? Because I follow people on Twitter who serve as my Web-crawling proxies, each of them tweeting links that I could examine and read on a Blackberry. Regardless of where I am, I surf far less than I used to.

13 At first, Twitter can be overwhelming, but think of it as a river of data rushing past that I dip a cup into every once in a while. Much of what I need to know is in that cup: if it looks like Apple is going to demo its new tablet, or Amazon sold more Kindles than actual books at Christmas, or the final vote in the Senate gets locked in on health care, I almost always learn about it first on Twitter.

14 The expressive limits of a kind of narrative developed from text messages, with less space to digress or explain than this sentence, has significant upsides. The best people on Twitter communicate with economy and precision, with each element—links, hash tags and comments—freighted with meaning. Professional acquaintances whom I find insufferable on every other platform suddenly become interesting within the confines of Twitter.

15 Twitter is incredibly customizable, with little of the social expectations that go with Facebook. Depending on whom you follow, Twitter can reveal a nation riveted by the

last episode of "Jersey Shore" or a short-form conclave of brilliance. There is plenty of nonsense—#Tiger had quite a run—but there are rich threads on the day's news and bravura solo performances from learned autodidacts. And the ethos of Twitter, which is based on self-defining groups, is far more well-mannered than many parts of the Web—more Toastmasters than mosh pit. On Twitter, you are your avatar and your avatar is you, so best not to act like a lout and when people want to flame you for something you said, they are responding to their own followers, not yours, so trolls quickly lose interest.

16   "Anything that is useful to both dissidents in Iran and Martha Stewart has a lot going for it; Twitter has more raw capability for users than anything since e-mail," said Clay Shirky, who wrote "Here Comes Everybody," a book about social media. "It will be hard to wait out Twitter because it is lightweight, endlessly useful and gets better as more people use it. Brands are using it, institutions are using it, and it is becoming a place where a lot of important conversations are being held." Twitter helps define what is important by what Mr. Shirky has called "algorithmic authority," meaning that if all kinds of people are pointing at the same thing at the same instant, it must be a pretty big deal.

17   Beyond the throbbing networked intelligence, there is the possibility of practical magic. Twitter can tell you what kind of netbook you should buy for your wife for Christmas—thanks Twitter!—or call you out when you complain about the long lines it took to buy it, as a tweeter on behalf of the electronics store B & H did when I shared the experience on my Blackberry while in line. I have found transcendent tacos at a car wash in San Antonio, rediscovered a brand of reporter's notepad I adore, uncovered sources for stories, all just by typing a query into Twitter.

18   All those riches do not come at zero cost: If you think e-mail and surfing can make time disappear, wait until you get ahold of Twitter, or more likely, it gets ahold of you. There is always something more interesting on Twitter than whatever you happen to be working on.

19   But in the right circumstance, Twitter can flex some big muscles. Think of last weekend, a heavy travel period marked by a terrorist incident on Friday. As news outlets were scrambling to understand the implications for travelers on Saturday morning, Twitter began lighting up with reports of new security initiatives, including one from @CharleneLi, a consultant who tweeted from the Montreal airport at about 7:30 A.M.: "New security rules for int'l flights into US. 1 bag, no electronics the ENTIRE flight, no getting up last hour of flight." It was far from the whole story and getting ahead of the news by some hours would seem like no big deal, but imagine you or someone you loved was flying later that same day: Twitter might seem very useful.

20   Twitter's growing informational hegemony is not assured. There have been serious outages in recent weeks, leading many business and government users to wonder about the stability of the platform. And this being the Web, many smart folks are plotting ways to turn Twitter into so much pixilated mist. But I don't think so. I can go anywhere I want on the Web, but there is no guarantee that my Twitter gang will come with me. I may have quite a few followers, but that doesn't make me Moses.

Are Video Games Good for You?

The video game *Tomb Raider,* featuring Lara Croft as its British-archeologist heroine, was released in 1996 and soon developed into a pop culture phenomenon. In addition to becoming the most popular video game in history, *Tomb Raider* became a movie, and then a second movie (with Angelina Jolie in the starring role)—and then a comic book, a novel, and even a theme park ride. Lara Croft's fans regard her as an ideal female icon—as brave as she is beautiful, strong and daring and smart, resourceful and fiercely independent.

2   But Lara Croft has not been without her critics. Skeptics, noting how Lara Croft's body porportions seemed to increase along with her popularity, have contended that she is simply reinforcing traditional stereotypes, that her popularity derives from her starring role in the fantasies of the predominantly male audience that enjoys "playing with her." Almost all teenage boys play video games, but only about half of girls do so, and so no wonder parents worry about the effect of video games on their consumers' gender attitudes. For *Tomb Raider* is hardly the only game that depicts women and men in traditional roles, the men as active adventurers, the women as passive victims or sex objects.

3   Critics of video games wonder about other issues as well, just as an earlier generation worried about the effects of television. While many video games depend on social interactions, requiring or permitting multiple players to interact via networked systems and thus bringing people together, many other games can be played individually. Do video games lead to social isolation? Is there an addictive element to gaming that makes their consumers socially inept?

4   And what about the stylized violence that lies at the heart of many video games? If games ask players to abuse women and shoot policemen, is it any wonder that those activities persist in real life? When those who carry out school shootings are shown to be devotees of video games, shouldn't we worry about the effects of prolonged exposure to gaming? True, the games are age-rated, like movies are, but it is easy to evade the rules and obtain adult-rated games illegally. And it is worrisome that adult males are especially eager players of violent video games, particularly when the violence in the games is directed at women. Even though juvenile crime rates actually seem to be down, suggesting that people can usually distinguish the difference between game life and real life, it seems natural to expect that video games are affecting people's values—and actions—negatively. Are video games a kind

of propaganda—do the games sensationalize drugs and alcohol and illicit sex, in effect "advertising" a way of life that is socially destructive? Or is it all in good fun?

5   Indeed, people criticize video games irrespective of their content. They contend that video games make people not just socially inept but also sedentary. Is the national obesity epidemic related to the popularity of video gaming? Do games, like television, encourage people to avoid real physical activity in order to perform fantasy deeds in front of a screen? And are children playing video games instead of reading or doing homework? In other words, are video games compromising our educational aspirations? Or do they actually help their users, not only by honing hand-eye coordination and visual perception skills but by improving the analytical and problem-solving abilities of users as well as their creativity and ability to concentrate. It has even been suggested that video games can assist in the treatment of autism and certain other mental health conditions.

6   The selections in this Issue in Focus propose answers to those questions. John Beck and Mitchell Wade blame video games for giving people an unreal

sense of reality, while James Paul Gee defends video games for their educational value. Leigh Alexander ponders (from her personal experience) the effects that gaming might have on young women's identities. Finally, Clay Shirky concludes the segment, and the chapter, with a fascinating defense of new media that is based on their ability to bring us together and shake us into becoming our most creative selves. (You should also consult the essay on this topic by student Armadi Tansal in Chapter 11.)

John C. Beck and Mitchell Wade

How the Gamer Revolution Is Reshaping Business Forever

DEFINITELY NOT IN KANSAS ANYMORE

Games are a technology that has been universally adopted by a large, young cohort and ignored by their elders. That's powerful enough to start with. But when you look at the experience that technology delivers—the content and the nature of the gamers' world—things really get interesting. Universally, and almost subliminally, games deliver a "reality" where the rules are quite different from any found out here in the rest of the world. Take a look at this quick overview of the lessons games teach:

The Individual's Role

2

- *You're the star.* You are the center of attention of every game unlike, say, Little League, where most kids will *never* be the star.
- *You're the boss.* The world is very responsive to you. You can choose things about reality, or switch to different experiences, in a way that is literally impossible in real life.
- *You're the customer, and the customer is always right.* Like shopping, the whole experience is designed for your satisfaction and entertainment; the opponents are tough, but never *too* tough.
- *You're an expert.* You have the experience of getting really, really good—especially compared to others who actually see you perform—early and often.
- *You're a tough guy.* You can experience all sorts of crashes, suffering, and death—and it doesn't hurt.

How the World Works

3
- *There's always an answer.* You might be frustrated for a while, you might even never find it, but you know it's there.
- *Everything is possible.* You see yourself or other players consistently do amazing things: defeat hundreds of bad guys singlehandedly, say, or beat the best N.B.A. team ever.
- *The world is a logical, human-friendly place.* Games are basically fair. Events may be random but not inexplicable, and there is not much mystery.
- *Trial-and-error is almost always the best plan.* It's the only way to advance in most games, even if you ultimately break down and buy a strategy guide or copy others on the really hard parts.
- *Things are (unrealistically) simple.* Games are driven by models. Even complex models are a lot simpler than reality. *You can figure a game out, completely.* Try that with real life.

How People Relate

4
- *It's all about competition.* You're always competing; even if you collaborate with other human players, you are competing against some character or score.
- *Relationships are structured.* To make the game work, there are only a few pigeonholes people (real or virtual) can fit into, such as competitor/ally and boss/subordinate.
- *We are all alone.* The gaming experience is basically solitary, even if played in groups. And you don't experience all of the activity, for any sustained time, as part of a group.
- *Young people rule.* Young people dominate gaming. Paying your dues takes a short time, youth actually helps, and there is no attention paid to elders.
- *People are simple.* Most in games are cartoon characters. Their skills may be complex, multidimensional, and user-configurable, but their personality types and behaviors are simple. There's big and strong, wild and crazy, beautiful and sexy, and a few other caricatures. That's it.

What You Should Do

5
- *Rebel.* Edginess and attitude are dominant elements of the culture.
- *Be a hero.* You always get the star's role; that is the only way to succeed or get satisfaction.
- *Bond with people who share your game experience, not your national or cultural background.* It's a very global world, in design, consumption, and characters, and in the phenomenon of the game generation.
- *Make your own way in the world.* Leaders are irrelevant and often evil; ignore them.
- *Tune out and have fun.* The whole experience of gaming is escapist. When reality is boring, you hop into game world. When a game gets boring, you switch to one that isn't.

6
Not exactly like "real life," is it? And remember, this other-worldly experience has been exclusive to gamers. ■

JAMES PAUL **GEE**

Games, Not Schools, Are Teaching Kids to Think

The US spends almost $50 billion each year on education, so why aren't kids learning? Forty percent of students lack basic reading skills, and their academic performance is dismal compared with that of their foreign counterparts. In response to this crisis, schools are skilling-and-drilling their way "back to basics," moving toward mechanical instruction methods that rely on line-by-line scripting for teachers and endless multiple-choice testing. Consequently, kids aren't learning how to think anymore— they're learning how to memorize. This might be an ideal recipe for the future Babbitts of the world, but it won't produce the kind of agile, analytical minds that will lead the high tech global age. Fortunately, we've got *Grand Theft Auto: Vice City* and *Deus X* for that.

2 After school, kids are devouring new information, concepts, and skills every day, and, like it or not, they're doing it controller in hand, plastered to the TV. The fact is, when kids play videogames they can experience a much more powerful form of learning than when they're in the classroom. Learning isn't about memorizing isolated facts. It's about connecting and manipulating them. Doubt it? Just ask anyone who's beaten *Legend of Zelda* or solved *Morrowind*.

3 The phenomenon of the videogame as an agent of mental training is largely unstudied; more often, games are denigrated for being violent or they're just plain ignored. They shouldn't be. Young gamers today aren't training to be gun-toting carjackers. They're learning how to learn. In *Pikmin*, children manage an army of plantlike aliens and strategize to solve problems. In *Metal Gear Solid 2*, players move stealthily through virtual environments and carry out intricate missions. Even in the notorious *Vice City*, players craft a persona, build a history, and shape a virtual world. In strategy games like *WarCraft III* and *Age of Mythology*, they learn to micromanage an array of elements while simultaneously balancing short- and long-term goals. That sounds like something for their resumes.

4 The secret of a videogame as a teaching machine isn't its immersive 3-D graphics but its underlying architecture. Each level dances around the outer limits of the player's abilities, seeking at every point to be hard enough to be just doable. In cognitive science, this is referred to as the "regime of competence principle," which results in a feeling of simultaneous pleasure and frustration—a sensation as familiar to gamers as sore thumbs. Cognitive scientist Andy diSessa has argued that the best instruction hovers at the boundary of a student's competence. Most schools, however, seek to avoid invoking feelings of both pleasure and frustration, blind to the fact that these emotions can be extremely useful when it comes to teaching kids.

5 Also, good videogames incorporate the principle of expertise. They tend to encourage players to achieve total mastery of one level, only to challenge and undo that mastery in the next, forcing kids to adapt and evolve. This carefully choreographed dialectic has been identified by learning theorists as the best way to achieve expertise in any field. This doesn't happen much in our routine-driven schools, where "good" students are often just good at "doing school."

6 How did videogames become such successful models of effective learning? Game coders aren't trained as cognitive scientists. It's a simple case of free-market economics:

If a title doesn't teach players how to play it well, it won't sell well. Game companies don't rake in $6.9 billion a year by dumbing down the material—aficionados condemn short and easy games like *Half Life: Blue Shift* and *Devil May Cry 2*. Designers respond by making harder and more complex games that require mastery of sophisticated worlds and as many as 50 to 100 hours to complete. Schools, meanwhile, respond with more tests, more drills, and more rigidity. They're in the cognitive-science dark ages.

7   We don't often think about videogames as relevant to education reform, but maybe we should. Game designers don't often think of themselves as learning theorists. Maybe they should. Kids often say it doesn't feel like learning when they're gaming—they're much too focused on playing. If kids were to say that about a science lesson, our country's education problems would be solved.

Leigh Alexander

What I Discovered from Gaming Like a Girl

When I had the opportunity to play a favorite game all over again with Persona 3 Portable, I was happy to do so. I didn't realize a virtual sex change would make the experience anything but the same as before.

2   The PlayStation Portable adaptation of Persona 3 adds an interesting twist: The ability to play as a female. There are plenty of games that let you choose your gender, but few of those that are story-driven. And few of those equate a gender pick with anything other than a graphics swap and a few tweaked story references. Recent games like Mass Effect and its sequel should be lauded for including character customization deep enough for the player to both personalize and gender the experience—but even then how long can people discuss Mass Effect in the public forum without getting down to "Blue Alien Sex Scene"? The most relevant issue in player gender choices becomes romance.

3   I fall for anime-pretty-boy tropes as easily as the rest of the female audience to whom those things tend to be marketed. I admit it: Despite some excellent modifications to the game mechanics to make it more user-friendly and portable-suitable, the primary thing I desired when firing up Persona 3 Portable was getting to date elegant tough-guy Akihiko or chip-on-his-shoulder semi-adversary Shinjiro.

4   I seldom roleplay as myself in a game like this, aside from in-
dulging my inner squee and picking my favorite boys to date. I don't
necessarily make the decisions I would make if that character was
really me. Chalk it up to being a writer. Rather than visualizing myself in a fantasy scenario, I decide on a character concept that I
think would be interesting to try out (in BioShock, I decided to kill
all the Little Sisters not because I have a vicious streak, but
because I thought it would make for a darker, more interesting
story than being a savior).

5   I wasn't expecting the ways the game would feel different
when playing as a girl, even outside of romantic interactions.

6   The latter Persona games—especially the third and fourth install-
ments, which have been largely responsible for the franchise's surge
in Western popularity—
are interesting beasts to
begin with. Persona isn't
just a name; the games'
stories deal with the
way one conceptualizes
the self in one's interactions with others, a
theme that ties directly
into the nitty-gritty of the
battling and leveling
mechanics as players
summon alternate
"selves" to do battle for
them.

7   The players' Personas are strengthened through their social relationships. Persona 3, when it originally launched on PlayStation 2, employed this unique leveling mechanic with a dark twist: The formation
of relationships is directly correlated to a gain in power, so interacting
with your classmates in the game's hip high school setting becomes
less about making friends and "being yourself as it is about telling people what they most wanted to hear in order to gain their confidence.

8   I liked that subtly sinister way of behaving in the game when I
played as a male. But it makes the social interactions of Persona 3
Portable inherently more complicated when I'm a female playing as
a female. Swap the gender and suddenly my ideas of who I'd like
my character to be—aloof, clever and a little dark, as my Persona 3
male character was—collide with my own knee-jerk reflex to conform to the sort of social expectations women are often told they
should fulfill in order to be likeable. I found myself hesitating
between conversation responses that would be consistent with the
character I had visualized, and those that were more closely
aligned with the ideals of "be attractive, sweet and likeable."

9   Early in the game, tension over who should be the group's leader becomes more than the simple power struggle it was in the original—it's an all too familiar situation for women who want to be in charge. Once again I felt the clash between the need to be assertive and the desire to make everyone happy. Isn't that the conflict many women claiming positions of power often face? It also feels far less natural for me to eschew the empathetic or apologetic dialog options when dealing with a character that requires me to respond in a tough or cold way to gain their approval.

10   From the get-go, I noticed that I immediately reacted differently to Yukari Takeba, a main character who is part of the player's core party throughout the game. Takeba—or "Yuka-tan," as your bro-on-board Junpei calls her—is something of an aggressive personality, opinionated and expressive, yet overtly insecure as she compares herself to your elegant Senpai, the mature and beautiful hyper-achiever Mitsuru. I found her dislikeable the first time around—and yet when I played as a female, I found I empathized with her better. That Mitsuru, whom I admired very much through the eyes of a boy, really is irritatingly perfect, isn't she? Where I once felt Yukari's tendency to question all the authority around her annoying, this time I started selecting dialogue options that supported her point of view. We girls have to stick together, after all. It was like being in high school all over again.

11   For another ex-ample: Fuuka Yama-gishi is a character that appears fairly early on in the game as a "support member" for the player's combat party. Fragile and demure (and helped none by famously grating voice acting), I used to find Fuuka hard to like, as she nervously foisted her poor cook-

ing on my male protagonist in an effort to gain confidence. I had little interest in developing my social link with her, even if it meant some of my Personas would be less powerful in battle. But the female story arc adds the option for the player to form a cooking club with Fuuka, supporting her in her shy efforts to improve in the kitchen—a cause to which I've been much, much more sympathetic this time around.

12   Cynical view: Suddenly I like playing in the Home Economics room with Fuuka because society has taught me that baking truffles is an activity in which it is appropriate for chicks to engage?

13   Moderate view: As a female peer, rather than a male paramour, Fuuka's insecurities become sympathetic, rather than repulsive. We're taught that men like independent women, but girls like to share things and help each other. Definitely, my real-world social experiences as a woman were weighing on me as I experienced Persona 3 as a female.

14   The game itself didn't overtly impose any obvious gender expectations on me—I can be as cool, impassive and tough as I was when I was a male character, and my in-game classmates admire me just as much for my sharp study habits and level head as they do for being "cute" (in the male arc, the protagonist attracts admirers in a similar way). But there is one unfortunate major constraint in play: There just aren't as many dating options for the female protagonist.

15   The male protagonist is allowed—or even encouraged, since gameplay rewards it—to be a Lothario, pursuing romance with some seven women (one of them via the Internet) at a time. However, when you play as a female, several of the male character's romantic prospects are replaced with different characters . . . who are simply new female friends for the protagonist. These new storylines are well-considered and interesting, but the result is you can't "play the field" as a female—if I can be a lady-killer, shouldn't I get to be a man-eater, too? Is the game telling me that's unladylike, or that men pursue women and not the other way around?

16   The Persona 3 protagonist's over-arching objective in the game is unstated but evident: Put on whatever face is most appropriate for the situation, both socially and in battle. This created interesting and sometimes challenging moments for me. Sometimes the dialogue option I needed to choose in order to achieve the greatest synergy with a social partner conflicted with instinct that I must conclude comes from being socialized as a woman. I had no problem being ruthless as a male, but as a female, the urge to care-give, to people-please and to back down kicked in.

17   I found myself comparing my female protagonist to my male protagonist, and finding I liked her less because the gameplay choices I was making weren't "feminine." I even realized I had held in mind a series of pre-approved traits for what constitutes an acceptable "tough gal." She's still got to be lively, spirited and "cute," right? I wanted to be able to picture her with the male heroes I admired in the game. It made me anxious.

18   I didn't think I was the kind of woman who bowed to those social expectations. I mean, I'm a female video game journalist, something incomprehensible to most of my gal pals. But the narrow-minded, old-school impulses of mine that surfaced through my "blank slate" female protagonist were more than a little uncomfortable to face. Persona 3 is a game that asks players to consider the importance of their relationships with other people—really, though, I've just been thinking about my relationship with myself.

Clay Shirky

Gin, Television, and Social Surplus: A Speech—April 26, 2008

I was recently reminded of some reading I did in college, way back in the last century, by a British historian arguing that the critical technology, for the early phase of the industrial revolution, was gin. The transformation from rural to urban life was so sudden, and so wrenching, that the only thing society could do to manage was to drink itself into a stupor for a generation. The stories from that era are amazing—there were gin pushcarts working their way through the streets of London.

2   And it wasn't until society woke up from that collective bender that we actually started to get the institutional structures that we associate with the industrial revolution today. Things like public libraries and museums, increasingly broad education for children, elected leaders—a lot of things we like—didn't happen until having all of those people together stopped seeming like a crisis and started seeming like an asset. It wasn't until people started thinking of this as a vast civic surplus, one they could design for rather than just dissipate, that we started to get what we think of now as an industrial society.

3   If I had to pick the critical technology for the 20th century, the bit of social lubricant without which the wheels would've come off the whole enterprise, I'd say it was the sitcom. Starting with the Second World War a whole series of things happened—rising GDP per capita, rising educational attainment, rising life expectancy and, critically, a rising number of people who were working five-day work weeks. For the first time, society forced onto an enormous number of its citizens the requirement to manage something they had never had to manage before—free time.

4   And what did we do with that free time? Well, mostly we spent it watching TV.

5   We did that for decades. We watched "I Love Lucy." We watched "Gilligan's Island." We watch "Malcolm in the Middle." We watch "Desperate Housewives." "Desperate Housewives" essentially functioned as a kind of cognitive heat sink, dissipating thinking that might otherwise have built up and caused society to overheat. And it's only now, as we're waking up from that collective bender, that we're starting to see the cognitive surplus as an asset rather than as a crisis. We're seeing things being designed to take advantage of that surplus, to deploy it in ways more engaging than just having a TV in everybody's basement.

6   This hit me in a conversation I had about two months ago. I've finished a book called *Here Comes Everybody*, which has recently come out, and this recognition came out of a conversation I had about the book. I was being interviewed by a TV producer to see whether I should be on their show, and she asked me, "What are you seeing out there that's interesting?" I started telling her about the Wikipedia article on Pluto. You may remember that Pluto got kicked out of the planet club a couple of years ago, so all of a sudden there was all of this activity on Wikipedia. The talk pages light up, people are editing the article like mad, and the whole community is in

a ruckus—"How should we characterize this change in Pluto's status?" And a little bit at a time they move the article—fighting offstage all the while—from, "Pluto is the ninth planet," to "Pluto is an odd-shaped rock with an odd-shaped orbit at the edge of the solar system."

7   So I tell her all this stuff, and I think, "Okay, we're going to have a conversation about authority or social construction or whatever." That wasn't her question. She heard this story and she shook her head and said, "Where do people find the time?" That was her question. And I just kind of snapped. And I said, "No one who works in TV gets to ask that question. You know where the time comes from. It comes from the cognitive surplus you've been masking for 50 years."

8   So how big is that surplus? If you take Wikipedia as a kind of unit, all of Wikipedia, the whole project—every page, every edit, every talk page, every line of code, in every language that Wikipedia exists in—that represents something like the cumulation of 100 million hours of human thought. I worked this out with Martin Wattenberg at IBM; it's a back-of-the-envelope calculation, but it's the right order of magnitude, about 100 million hours of thought.

9   And television watching? Two hundred billion hours, in the U.S. alone, every year. Put another way, now that we have a unit, that's 2,000 Wikipedia projects a year spent watching television. Or put still another way, in the U.S., we spend 100 million hours every weekend, just watching the ads. This is a pretty big surplus. People asking, "Where do they find the time?" when they're looking at things like Wikipedia don't understand how tiny that entire project is, as a carve-out of this asset that's finally being dragged into what Tim calls an architecture of participation.

10   Now, the interesting thing about a surplus like that is that society doesn't know what to do with it at first—hence the gin, hence the sitcoms. Because if people knew what to do with a surplus with reference to the existing social institutions, then it wouldn't be a surplus, would it? It's precisely when no one has any idea how to deploy something that people have to start experimenting with it, in order for the surplus to get integrated, and the course of that integration can transform society.

11   The early phase for taking advantage of this cognitive surplus, the phase I think we're still in, is all special cases. The physics of participation is much more like the physics of weather than it is like the physics of gravity. We know all the forces that combine to make these kinds of things work: there's an interesting community over here, there's an interesting sharing model over there, those people are collaborating on open source software. But despite knowing the inputs, we can't predict the outputs yet because there's so much complexity. The way you explore complex ecosystems is you just try lots and lots and lots of things, and you hope that everybody who fails fails informatively so that you can at least find a skull on a pikestaff near where you're going. That's the phase we're in now.

12   Just to pick one example, one I'm in love with, but it's tiny. A couple of weeks one of my students forwarded me a project started by a professor in Brazil, in Fortaleza, named Vasco Furtado. It's a Wiki Map for crime in Brazil. If there's an assault, if there's a burglary, if there's a mugging, a robbery, a rape, a murder, you can go and put a push-pin on a Google Map, and you can characterize the assault, and you start to see a map of where these crimes are occurring.

13   Now, this already exists as tacit information. Anybody who knows a town has some sense of, "Don't go there. That street corner is dangerous. Don't go in this neighborhood. Be careful there after dark." But it's something society knows without society really knowing it, which is to say there's no public source where you can take advantage of it. And the cops, if they have that information, they're certainly not sharing. In fact, one of the things Furtado says in starting the Wiki crime map was, "This information may or may not exist some place in society, but it's actually easier for me to try to rebuild it from scratch than to try and get it from the authorities who might have it now."

14   Maybe this will succeed or maybe it will fail. The normal case of social software is still failure; most of these experiments don't pan out. But the ones that do are quite incredible, and I hope that this one succeeds, obviously. But even if it doesn't, it's illustrated the point already, which is that someone working alone, with really cheap tools, has a reasonable hope of carving out enough of the cognitive surplus, enough of the desire to participate, enough of the collective goodwill of the citizens, to create a resource you couldn't have imagined existing even five years ago.

15   So that's the answer to the question, "Where do they find the time?" Or, rather, that's the numerical answer. But beneath that question was another thought, this one not a question but an observation. In this same conversation with the TV producer I was talking about World of Warcraft guilds, and as I was talking, I could sort of see what she was thinking: "Losers. Grown men sitting in their basement pretending to be elves."

16   At least they're doing something.

17   Did you ever see that episode of "Gilligan's Island" where they almost get off the island and then Gilligan messes up and then they don't? I saw that one. I saw that one a lot when I was growing up. And every half-hour that I watched that was a half an hour I wasn't posting at my blog or editing Wikipedia or contributing to a mailing list. Now I had an ironclad excuse for not doing those things, which is that none of those things existed then. I was forced into the channel of media the way it was because it was the only option. Now it's not, and that's the big surprise. However lousy it is to sit in your basement and pretend to be an elf, I can tell you from personal experience it's worse to sit in your basement and try to figure if Ginger or Mary Ann is cuter.

18   And I'm willing to raise that to a general principle. It's better to do something than to do nothing. Even lolcats, even cute pictures of kittens made even cuter with the addition of cute captions, hold out an invitation to participation. When you see a lolcat, one of the things it says to the viewer is, "If you have some sans-serif fonts on your computer, you can play this game, too." And that's message—I can do that, too—is a big change.

19   This is something that people in the media world don't understand. Media in the 20th century was run as a single race—consumption. How much can we produce? How much can you consume? Can we produce more and you'll consume more? And the answer to that question has generally been yes. But media is actually a triathlon, it's three different events. People like to consume, but they also like to produce, and they like to share. And what's astonished people who were committed to the structure of the previous society, prior to trying to take this surplus and do something interesting, is that they're discovering that when you offer people the opportunity to produce and to share, they'll take you up on that offer. It doesn't mean that we'll never sit around mindlessly watching "Scrubs" on the couch. It just means we'll do it less.

20   And this is the other thing about the size of the cognitive surplus we're talking about. It's so large that even a small change could have huge ramifications. Let's say that everything stays 99 percent the same, that people watch 99 percent as much television as they used to, but 1 percent of that is carved out for producing and for sharing. The Internet-connected population watches roughly a *trillion* hours of TV a year. That's about five times the size of the annual U.S. consumption. One per cent of that is 100 Wikipedia projects per year worth of participation.

21   I think that's going to be a big deal. Don't you?

22   Well, the TV producer did not think this was going to be a big deal; she was not digging this line of thought. And her final question to me was essentially, "Isn't this all just a fad?" You know, sort of the flagpole-sitting of the early early 21st century? It's fun to go out and produce and share a little bit, but then people are going to eventually realize, "This isn't as good as doing what I was doing before, and settle down. And I made a spirited argument that no, this wasn't the case, that this was in fact a big one-time shift, more analogous to the industrial revolution than to flagpole-sitting. I was arguing that this isn't the sort of thing society grows out of. It's the sort of thing that society grows into. But I'm not sure she believed me, in part because she didn't want to believe me, but also in part because I didn't have the right story yet. And now I do.

23   I was having dinner with a group of friends about a month ago, and one of them was talking about sitting with his four-year-old daughter watching a DVD. And in the middle of the movie, apropos nothing, she jumps up off the couch and runs around behind the screen. That seems like a cute moment. Maybe she's going back there to see if Dora is really back there or whatever. But that wasn't what she was doing. She started rooting around in the cables. And her dad said, "What you doing?" And she stuck her head out from behind the screen and said, "Looking for the mouse."

24   Here's something four-year-olds know: A screen that ships without a mouse ships broken. Here's something four-year-olds know: Media that's targeted at you but doesn't include you may not be worth sitting still for. Those are things that make me believe that this is a one-way change. Because four-year-olds, the people who are soaking most deeply in the current environment, who won't have to go through the trauma that I have to go through of trying to unlearn a childhood spent watching "Gilligan's Island," they just assume that media includes consuming, producing and sharing.

25   It's also become my motto, when people ask me what we're doing—and when I say "we" I mean the larger society trying to figure out how to deploy this cognitive surplus, but I also mean we, especially, the people who are working hammer and tongs at figuring out the next good idea. From now on, that's what I'm going to tell them: We're looking for the mouse. We're going to look at every place that a reader or a listener or a viewer or a user has been locked out, has been served up passive or a fixed or a canned experience, and ask ourselves, "If we carve out a little bit of the cognitive surplus and deploy it here, could we make a good thing happen?" And I'm betting the answer is yes.

26   Thank you very much.

FROM READING TO WRITING

1. Analyze the arguments by Michael Gerson and Daniel Okrent: How is each argument the product of its audience and purpose? What sources of argument (ethical appeals, emotional appeals, and logical appeals) does each author choose and why? (See Chapter 7 for more on rhetorical analysis.)

2. Write an argument that makes its point by defining a key term related to new media. You might choose to change someone's attitude toward a particular technology or concept in order to defend or challenge it, for instance, by defining it in a certain way. For example, you might start with the claim that "Facebook is just a marketing ploy based on the same principles that define high school yearbooks" or "Second Life is actually a blessing for people who are shy by nature." (See Chapter 10 for strategies for writing definition arguments.)

3. Write a humorous story about your own experience with a particular new media technology—but write your story in order to make a point. (See Chapter 13 for advice on writing narrative arguments.) For example, you could report on your unfortunate experience with a new cell phone or video game in order to convince people to avoid making the same mistake.

4. Propose a change in policy related to a technology issue in your community. Are there regulations that would improve the social impact of video games, for example, or Wikipedia? (See Chapter 15 for help with writing a proposal argument.)

5. Write a rebuttal of an article related to the new media in your local or school newspaper. Are there misperceptions that you want to correct? (See Chapter 14 for advice on rebuttals.) Consider whether you wish to show the weaknesses in the article, whether you wish to counterargue, or both.

6. Write an essay that argues for the existence of a particular social effect that has resulted from a new media technology. For example, you might argue that the success of a particular local charity derives from its ability to connect with people despite a small staff. Or you might write about the effects of new technology on your local library's internal architecture. Or you could argue that new technologies have actually created a range of new jobs at your university. (For more on cause and effect arguments, see Chapter 11.)

7. Many new media technologies permit people to participate anonymously. Wikipedians, for example, are notoriously anonymous, video games networked through the Internet permit people to play with anonymous others, and people are able to make anonymous comments in response to online news sources. Analyze the effects of this anonymity: reflect on the impact of anonymity on your own participation, or your own consumption, of online media.

Glossary

A

abstract A summary of an article or book

aesthetic criteria Evaluative criteria based on perceptions of beauty and good taste

alternating pattern Organizational method that moves back and forth between points and counterpoints of an argument

analyst Role that a reader-writer takes on when responding to a source's argument in a nuanced way, agreeing with some points and disagreeing with others

analogy An extended comparison of one situation or item to another

APA American Psychological Association

APA documentation Documentation style commonly used in social-science and education disciplines

argument A claim supported by at least one reason

assumption An unstated belief or knowledge that connects a claim with evidence

audience Real or assumed individuals or groups to whom a verbal or written communication is directed

B

bandwagon appeal A fallacy of argument based on the assumption that something is true or correct because "everyone" believes it to be so

bar chart Visual depiction of data created by the use of horizontal or vertical bars that comparatively represent rates or frequencies

because clause A statement (often beginning with the word because) that provides a supporting reason for a claim

begging the question A fallacy of argument that uses the claim as evidence for its own validity

bias A personal belief that may skew one's perspective or presentation of information

bibliography List of books and articles about a specific subject

blog A Web-based journal or diary featuring regular entries about a particular subject or daily experiences (also known as a Web log)

brainstorming A method of finding ideas by writing a list of questions or statements about a subject

C

causal argument An argument that seeks to identify the reasons behind a certain event or phenomenon

claim A declaration or assertion made about any given topic

claim of comparison A claim that argues something is like or not like something else

common factor method A method used by scientists to identify a recurring factor present in a given cause–effect relationship

concomitant variation A way to establish causation by observing a shared pattern of variation in a possible cause and a possible effect

consequence The cause–effect result of a given action

context The combination of author, subject, and audience and the broader social, cultural, and economic influences surrounding a text

contextual analysis A type of rhetorical analysis that focuses on the author, the audience, the time, and the circumstances of an argument

contributor Role that a reader-writer takes on when responding by agreeing with the author of a source and adding another point

correlation The relationship between events that happen after or at the same time as another; not necessarily the same as *causation*, it can also be coincidence

counterargument An argument offering an opposing point of view with the goal of demonstrating that it is the stronger of two or more arguments

criteria Standards used to establish a definition or an evaluation

critical reading A process of reading that surpasses an initial understanding or impression of basic content and proceeds with the goal of answering specific questions or examining particular elements

cropping In photography, the process of deleting unwanted parts of an image

cultural assumptions Widely held beliefs that are considered common sense in a particular culture

D

database Large collection of digital information organized for efficient search and retrieval

debate A contest or game in which two or more individuals attempt to use arguments to persuade others to support their opinion

definition argument An argument made by specifying that something does or does not possess certain criteria

definition from example A definition argument built from examples that are typical of the concept, even if the situation is unusual

diction The choice and use of words in writing and speech

E

either-or A fallacy of argument that presents only two choices in a complex situation

emotional appeal An argumentation strategy that attempts to persuade by stirring the emotions of the audience

empirical research Research that collects data from observation or experiment

ethos An appeal to the audience based on the character and trustworthiness of the speaker or writer

evaluation argument An argument that judges something based on ethical, aesthetic, and/or practical criteria

evaluation of sources The assessment of the relevance and reliability of sources used in supporting claims

evidence Data, examples, or statistics used to support a claim

experimental research Research based on obtaining data under controlled conditions, usually by isolating one variable while holding other variables constant

F

fallacy of argument Failure to provide adequate evidence to support a claim. See *bandwagon appeal, begging the question, false analogy, hasty generalization, namecalling, non sequitur, oversimplification, polarization, post hoc fallacy, rationalization, slippery slope, straw man*

false analogy A fallacy of argument that compares two unlike things as if they were similar

feasibility The ability of a proposed solution to be implemented

figurative language The symbolic transference of meaning from one word or phrase to another, such as with the use of metaphor, synecdoche, and metonymy

firsthand evidence Evidence such as interviews, observations, and surveys collected by the writer

font The specific size and weight of a typeface

formal definition Dictionary definition of a word; the categorization of an item into the next-higher classification, providing criteria that distinguish the item from other items within that classification

formal outline Writing plan that helps organize a paper, typically begins with the thesis statement, which anchors the entire outline

freewriting A method of finding ideas by writing as fast as possible about a subject for a set length of time

G

generalization A conclusion drawn from knowledge based on past occurrences of the phenomenon in question

good reason A reason that an audience accepts as valid

H

hasty generalization A fallacy of argument resulting from making broad claims based on a few occurrences

hyperbole Exaggeration, common in oral discourse, can add voice and texture to prose

I

idea map A brainstorming tool that visually depicts connections among different aspects of an issue

image editor Software that allows you to create and manipulate images

intellectual property Any property produced by the intellect, including copyrights for literary, musical, photographic, and cinematic works; patents for inventions and industrial processes; and trademarks

isocolon Parallel structure wherein all members are of the same length

J

journal A general category of publications that includes popular, trade, and scholarly periodicals

K

keyword search A Web-based search that uses a robot and indexer to produce results based on a chosen word or words

L

line graph A visual presentation of data represented by a continuous line or lines plotted at specific intervals

litotes Understatement, often used for a similar (if seemingly opposite) effect as hyperbole, can add voice and texture to prose

logical fallacies Various types of faulty reasoning in logic, emotion, or language

logos An appeal to the audience based on reasoning and evidence

M

metaphor A figure of speech using a word or phrase that commonly designates one thing to represent another, thus making a comparison

metonymy A type of figurative language that uses one object to represent another that embodies its defining quality

MLA Modern Language Association

MLA documentation Documentation style commonly used in humanities and fine-arts disciplines

multimedia The use of multiple content forms including text, voice and music audio, video, still images, animation, and interactivity

N

name calling A fallacy of argument resulting from the use of undefined, and therefore meaningless, names

narrative arguments A form of argument based on telling stories that suggest the writer's position rather than explicitly making claims

non sequitur A fallacy of argument resulting from connecting two or more unrelated ideas

O

operational definition A concept's meaning as constructed and agreed upon by researchers (Many concepts cannot be easily defined by formal definitions)

opposing views Arguments or claims that differ from or directly refute an position; acknowledging and rebutting them is an important part of making a credible argument

oversimplification A fallacy in argument caused by neglecting to account for the complexity of a subject

P

pathos An appeal based on the audience's emotions or deeply held values

periodical A journal, magazine, or newspaper published at standard intervals, usually daily, weekly, monthly, or quarterly

periodical index Paper or electronic resource that catalogs the contents of journals, magazines, and newspapers

pie chart A circular chart resembling a pie that illustrates percentages of the whole through the use of delineated wedge shapes

plagiarism The improper use of the unauthorized and unattributed words or ideas of another author

podcast Digital media files available on the Internet for playback on a portable media player, such as an iPod

polarization A fallacy of argument based on exaggerating the characteristics of opposing groups to highlight division and extremism

popular journal A magazine aimed at the general public; usually includes illustrations, short articles, and advertisements

position argument A general kind of argument in which a claim is made for an idea or way of thinking about a subject

post hoc fallacy A fallacy of argument based on the assumption that events that follow each other have a causal relationship

practical criteria Evaluative criteria based on usefulness or likely results

primary research Information collected directly by the writer through observations, interviews, surveys, and experiments

process of elimination method A means of finding a cause by systematically ruling out all other possible causes

proposal argument An argument that either advocates or opposes a specific course of action

R

rationalization A fallacy of argument based on using weak explanations to avoid dealing with the actual causes

reason In an argument, the justification for a claim

rebuttal argument An argument that challenges or rejects the claims of another argument

reference librarian Library staff member who is familiar with information resources and who can show you how to use them (you can find a reference librarian at the reference desk in your library)

refutation A rebuttal argument that points out the flaws in an opposing argument

relevance The appropriateness of particular evidence to the case at hand

rhetorical analysis Careful study of a written argument or other types of persuasion aimed at understanding how the components work or fail to work

rhetorical situation Factors present at the time of writing or speaking, including the writer or speaker, the audience, the purpose of communicating, and the context

S

sans serif type A style of type recognized by blunt ends and a consistency in thickness

scholarly journals Journals containing articles written by experts in a particular field; also called peer-reviewed or academic journals

secondary research Information obtained from existing knowledge, such as research in the library

secondhand evidence Evidence from the work of others found in the library, on the Web, and elsewhere

sequential pattern Organizational method that organizes an argument by first listing all the main points and then explaining each more fully, providing supporting evidence

serif type A style of type developed to resemble the strokes of an ink pen and recognized by wedge-shaped ends on letter forms

single difference method A method of finding a cause for differing phenomena in very similar situations by identifying the one element that varies

skeptic Role that a reader-writer takes on when disagreeing with a source, persuasively rebutting its claims and providing support for an opposing view

slippery slope A fallacy of argument based on the assumption that if a first step is taken, additional steps will inevitably follow

straw man A fallacy of argument based on the use of the diversionary tactic of setting up the opposing position in such a manner that it can be easily rejected

sufficiency The adequacy of evidence supporting a claim

synecdoche A type of figurative language in which a part is used to represent the whole

synthesis The act of incorporating and integrating ideas from multiple sources into a writer's own work

T

textual analysis A type of rhetorical analysis that focuses exclusively on the text itself

thesis One or more sentences that state the main idea of an argument

typeface A style of type, such as serif, sans serif, or decorative

U

URL (Universal Resource Locator) An address on the Web

V

visual argument A type of persuasion using images, graphics, or objects

voice In writing, the distinctive style of a writer that provides a sense of the writer as a person

W

Web directory A subject guide to Web pages grouped by topic and subtopic

Web editors Programs that allow you to compose Web pages

wiki A Web-based application designed to let multiple authors write, edit, and review content, such as Wikipedia

working outline Sketch of how an argument's major sections will be arranged

working thesis A preliminary statement of the main claim of an argument, subject to revision

Credits

Photo Credits

Text Credits

Index